A Short Course in
Business
Statistics

A Short Course in
Business
Statistics

Richard I. Levin
University of North Carolina

David S. Rubin
University of North Carolina

Prentice-Hall, Inc.
Englewood Cliffs, New Jersey 07632

Library of Congress Cataloging in Publication Data

LEVIN, RICHARD L.
  A short course in business statistics.

  Abridgement of: Statistics for management. 2nd ed.
©1981.
  Includes index.
  1. Social sciences—Statistical methods. 2. Commercial statistics. 3. Management—Statistical
methods. 4. Statistics. I. Rubin, David S. II. Title.
HA29.L38872 1983   519.5   82-18582
ISBN 0-13-809129-3

227413
4

Editorial/production supervision and
  interior design: *Steve Young*
Cover design: *Jayne Conte*
Manufacturing buyer: *Ed O'Dougherty*

Printed in the United States of America

10 9 8 7 6 5 4 3 2 1

ISBN 0-13-809129-3

Prentice-Hall International, Inc., *London*
Prentice-Hall of Australia Pty. Limited, *Sydney*
Editora Prentice-Hall do Brasil, Ltda., *Rio de Janeiro*
Prentice-Hall Canada Inc., *Toronto*
Prentice-Hall of India Private Limited, *New Delhi*
Prentice-Hall of Japan, Inc., *Tokyo*
Prentice-Hall of Southeast Asia Pte. Ltd., *Singapore*
Whitehall Books Limited, *Wellington, New Zealand*

Contents

vi Contents

vii   Contents

Preface

Our basic approach in this book is threefold: (1) to design a business statistics book that is particularly appropriate to a one semester or one quarter course, (2) to insure that critical topics like multiple regression, use of the computer in regression, nonparametric statistics, analysis of variance, and decision theory are included instead of being sacrificed as they are in almost all short books, and (3) to remove the anxiety from studying and learning statistics.

We use commonsense explanations to help folks learn this material and actually have some fun while they are doing it. You will find lots of intuitive explanations—extensions of things students already know—instead of complicated statistical proofs. It's better to know *when* to use a statistical technique and *how* it works and *what* kinds of problems it will really solve, and what *form* the output takes—then leave the proofs to the professional statistician.

The nearly 500 problems in this book cover a broad section of managerial activity, from aptitude tests to utility management. They represent a wide sample of both private and public organizations—and many of the issues in these problems can be read about in the daily newspapers.

We have designed quite a few learning aids into this book to help make studying statistics easier and a word or two about each of them may be in order. Each chapter opens with a photograph describing an opportunity to use statistics in making a decision. This chapter-opening problem is worked out later in the chapter. At the end of each chapter you'll find a glossary of all the terms that were introduced in that chapter. Each chapter ends with a 30 question chapter review quiz (answers provided in the book). All equations introduced in a chapter are reviewed in detail in a separate section at the end of that chapter. Liberal use has been made of marginal notes to enhance studying. And each chapter ends with its own chapter review exercises representing broad coverage of all the statistical techniques presented in the chapter. All of these approaches have been designed into the book to make it a more useful learning aid to the student.

We are in debt to a number of folks who have left a special mark on this book. Our editor, Steve Young, has provided guidance and support during these many months, our families have graciously given up time to this project, and our colleagues both here at the University of North Carolina and elsewhere have made many useful suggestions on content and pedagogy. We are also grateful to the literary executor of the late Sir Ronald A. Fisher, F.R.S., to Dr. Frank Yates, F.R.S., and to Longman Group, London, for permission to reprint Tables from their book, *Statistical Tables for Biological, Agricultural and Medical Research*, 6th edition, 1974.

We hope you like this book and we especially hope you find that it makes studying, teaching, and learning statistics less painful—even fun.

Dick Levin

Dave Rubin

A Short Course in
Business
Statistics

Introduction

1

This book was written for students taking statistics for the first time. A glance at this chapter should convince any concerned citizen and future manager that a working knowledge of basic statistics will be quite useful in coping with the complex problems of our society. Your first look will also convince you that this book is dedicated to helping you acquire that knowledge with virtually no previous formal mathematical training and with no pain at all.

1 DEFINITIONS

Different meanings of statistics depending on use

The word *statistics* means different things to different people. To a football fan, statistics are the information about rushing yardage, passing yardage, and first downs, given at halftime. To the manager of a power generating station, statistics may be information about the quantity of pollutants being released into the atmosphere. To a school principal, statistics are information on absenteeism, test scores, and teacher salaries. To a medical researcher investigating the effects of a new drug, statistics are evidence of the success of research efforts. And to a college student, statistics are the grades made on all the quizzes in a course this semester.

Each of these people is using the word *statistics* correctly, yet each uses it in a slightly different way and for a somewhat different purpose. *Statistics* is a word that can refer to quantitative data (such as wheat yield per acre) or to a field of study (you may, for example, major in statistics).

Today, statistics and statistical analysis are used in nearly every profession. For managers in particular, statistics have become a most valuable tool.

2 HISTORY

Origin of the word

The word *statistik* comes from the Italian word *statista* (meaning "statesman"). It was first used by Gottfried Achenwall (1719–1772), a professor at Marlborough and Göttingen. E. A. W. Zimmerman introduced the word *statistics* into England. Its use was popularized by Sir John Sinclair in his work, *Statistical Account of Scotland 1791–1799.* Long before the eighteenth century, however, people had been recording and using data.

Early government records

Official government statistics are as old as recorded history. The Old Testament contains several accounts of census taking. Governments of ancient Babylonia, Egypt, and Rome gathered detailed records of populations and resources. In the Middle Ages, governments began to register the ownership of land. In A.D. 762, Charlemagne asked for detailed descriptions of church-owned properties. Early in the ninth century, he completed a statistical enumeration of the serfs attached to the land. About 1086, William the Conqueror ordered the writing of the *Domesday Book*, a record of the ownership, extent, and value of the lands of England. This work was England's first statistical abstract.

An early prediction from statistics

Because of Henry VII's fear of the plague, England began to register its dead in 1532. About this same time, French law required the clergy to register baptisms, deaths, and marriages. During an outbreak of the plague in the late 1500s, the English government started publishing weekly death statistics. This practice continued, and by 1632 these *Bills of Mortality* listed births and deaths by sex. In 1662, Captain John Graunt used thirty years of these Bills to make predictions about the number of persons who would die from various diseases and the proportion of male and female births that could be expected. Summarized in his work, *Natural and Political Observations... Made Upon the Bills of Mortality*, Graunt's study was a pioneer effort in statistical analysis. For his achievement using past records to predict future events, Graunt was made a member of the original Royal Society.

The history of the development of statistical theory and practice is a lengthy one. We have only begun to list the people who have made significant contributions to this field. Later we will encounter others whose names are now attached to specific laws and methods. Many people have brought to the study of statistics refinements or innovations that, taken together, form the theoretical basis of what we will study in this book.

3 SUBDIVISIONS WITHIN STATISTICS

Managers apply some statistical technique to virtually every branch of public and private enterprise. These techniques are so diverse that statisticians commonly separate them into two broad categories: *descriptive statistics* and *inferential statistics*. Some examples will help us understand the difference between the two.

Descriptive statistics

Suppose a professor computes an average grade for one history class. Since statistics describe the performance of that one class but do not make a generalization about several classes, we can say that the professor is using *descriptive* statistics. Graphs, tables, and charts that display data so that they are easier to understand are all examples of descriptive statistics.

Inferential statistics

Now suppose that the history professor decides to use the average grade achieved by one history class to estimate the average grade achieved in all ten sections of the same history course. The process of estimating this average grade would be a problem in *inferential* statistics. Statisticians also refer to this category as *statistical inference*. Obviously, any conclusion the professor makes about the ten sections of the course will be based on a generalization that goes far beyond the data for the original history class; and the generalization may not be completely valid, so the professor must state how likely it is to be true. Similarly, statistical inference involves generalizations and statements about the *probability* of their validity.

Decision theory

The methods and techniques of statistical inference can also be used in a branch of statistics called *decision theory*. Knowledge of decision theory is very helpful for managers because it is used to make decisions under conditions of uncertainty—when, for example, a manufacturer of stereo sets cannot specify precisely the demand for its products or when the chairperson of the English department at your school must schedule faculty teaching assignments without knowing precisely the student enrollment for next fall.

4 STRATEGY, ASSUMPTIONS, AND APPROACH

For students, not statisticians

This book is designed to help you get the feel of statistics—what it is, how and when to apply statistical techniques to decision making situations, and how to interpret the results you get. Since we are not writing for professional statisticians, our writing is tailored to the backgrounds and needs of college students who, as future citizens, probably accept the fact that statistics can be of considerable help to them in their future occupations but are, very likely, apprehensive about studying the subject.

We discard mathematical proofs in favor of intuitive ones. You will be guided through the learning process by reminders of what you already know, by examples with which you can identify, and by a step-by-step process instead of statements like "it can be shown" or "it therefore follows."

Symbols are simple and explained

As you thumb through this book and compare it with other basic business statistics textbooks, you will notice a minimum of mathematical notation. In the past, the complexity of the notation has intimidated many students who got lost in the symbols, even though they were motivated and intellectually capable of understanding the ideas. Each symbol and formula that is used is explained in detail, not only at the point at which it is introduced but also in a section at the end of the chapter.

No math beyond simple algebra required

If you felt reasonably comfortable when you finished your high school algebra course, you have enough background to understand *everything* in this book. Nothing beyond basic algebra is either assumed or used. Our goals are for you to be comfortable as you learn and for you to get a good intuitive grasp of statistical concepts and techniques. As a future manager, you will need to know when statistics can help your decision process and which tools to use. If you do need statistical help, you can find a statistical expert to handle the details.

Text problems cover a wide variety of situations

The problems used to introduce material in the chapters and the exercises at the end of each section within the chapter are drawn from a wide variety of situations you are already familiar with or are likely to confront quite soon. You will see problems involving all facets of the private sector of our economy: accounting, finance, individual and group behavior, marketing, and production. In addition, you will encounter managers in the public sphere coping with problems in public education, social services, the environment, consumer advocacy, and health systems.

Goals

In each problem situation, a manager is trying to use statistics creatively and productively. Helping you become comfortable doing exactly that is our goal.

Arranging Data to Convey Meaning: Tables and Graphs

2

The water quality control engineer of Charlotte, North Carolina, is responsible for the chlorination level of the water. It must be close to the level required by the department of health. To watch the chlorine, without checking every gallon of water leaving the plant, the engineer samples several gallons each day, measures chlorine content, and draws a conclusion about the average chlorination level of water treated that day. The table below shows the chlorine levels of the 30 gallons selected as one day's sample. These levels are the raw data from which the engineer can draw conclusions about the entire population of that day's treatment.

Chlorine levels in parts per million (ppm) in 30 gallons of treated water

16.2	15.4	16.0	16.6	15.9	15.8	16.0	16.8	16.9	16.8
15.7	16.4	15.2	15.8	15.9	16.1	15.6	15.9	15.6	16.0
16.4	15.8	15.7	16.2	15.6	15.9	16.3	16.3	16.0	16.3

Using the methods introduced in this chapter, we can help the water quality control engineer draw the proper conclusions.

Chapters 2, 3, and 4 introduce the concepts and techniques of descriptive statistics. Chapter 2 examines two methods for describing a collection of items: tables and graphs. If you have ever heard a long-winded report droning about dues owed by all eighty club members, and you have wished for a quick graphic display to ease the pain, you already have an appreciation of what's to come in Chapter 2.

Some definitions

Data are collections of any number of related observations. We can collect the number of telephones that several workers install on a given day or that one worker installs per day over a period of several days, and we can call the results our data. A collection of data is called a *data set*, and a single observation a *data point*.

1 HOW CAN WE ARRANGE DATA?

For data to be useful, our observations need to be organized so that we can pick out trends and come to logical conclusions. This chapter introduces the techniques of arranging data in tabular and graphical forms. Chapter 3 will show how to use numbers to describe data.

Collecting data

Represents all groups

Statisticians select their observations so that all relevant groups are represented in the data. To determine the potential market for a new product, for example, analysts might study 100 consumers in a certain geographical area. The analysts must be certain that this group contains a variety of people representing variables such as income level, race, education, and neighborhood.

Find data by observations or from records

Data can come from actual observations or from records that are kept for normal purposes. For billing purposes and doctors' reports, a hospital, for example, will record the number of patients using the X-ray facilities. But this information can also be organized to produce data that statisticians can describe and interpret.

Use data about the past to make decisions about the future

Data can assist decision makers in educated guesses about the *causes* and therefore the probable *effects* of certain characteristics in given situations. Also, knowledge of trends from past experience can enable concerned citizens to be aware of potential outcomes and to plan in advance. Our marketing survey may reveal that the product is preferred by black housewives of suburban communities, average incomes, and average educations. The product's advertising copy should address this target audience. And if hospital records show that more patients used the X-ray facilities in June than in January, the hospital Personnel Division should determine if this was accidental to this year or an indication of a trend, and perhaps it should adjust its hiring and vacation practices accordingly.

When data are arranged in compact, usable form, decision makers can take reliable information from the environment and use it to make intelligent decisions. Today, computers allow statisticians to collect enormous volumes of observations and compress them instantly into tables, graphs, and numbers. These are all compact, usable forms—but are they reliable? Remember that the data that come out of a computer are only as accurate as the data that go in. As computer programmers say, "GIGO!" or "Garbage In, Garbage Out!" Managers must be very careful to be sure that the data they are using are based on correct assumptions and interpretations. Before relying on any interpreted data, from a computer or not, test the data by asking these questions:

Tests for data

1. Where did the data come from? Is the source biased; that is, is it likely to have an interest in supplying data points that will lead to one conclusion rather than another?
2. Do the data support or contradict other evidence we have?
3. Is evidence missing that might cause us to come to a different conclusion?
4. How many observations do we have? Do they represent all the groups we wish to study?
5. Is the conclusion logical? Have we made conclusions that the data do not support?

Study your answers to these questions. Are the data worth using? Or should we wait and collect more information before acting? If the hospital was caught short-handed because it hired too few nurses to staff the X-ray room, its administration relied on insufficient data. If the advertising agency targeted its copy only toward black suburban housewives when it could have tripled its sales by appealing to white suburban housewives too, it also relied on insufficient data. In both cases, testing available data would have helped managers make better decisions.

Difference between samples and populations

Sample and population defined

Statisticians gather data from a sample. They use this information to make inferences about the population that the sample represents. Thus, *sample* and *population* are relative terms. A population is a whole, and a sample is a fraction or segment of that whole.

Function of samples

We will study samples in order to be able to describe populations. Our hospital may study a small, not unrepresentative group of X-ray records rather than examine each record for the last fifty years. The Gallup Poll may interview a sample of only 2,500 adult Americans in order to predict the opinion of all adults living in the United States. Studying samples is obviously easier than studying whole populations, and it is reliable if carefully and properly done.

*Function
of populations*

A *population* is a collection of all the elements we are studying and about which we are trying to draw conclusions. We must define this population so that it is clear whether or not an element is a member of the population. The population for our marketing study may be all women within a 15-mile radius of center-city Cincinnati, who have annual family incomes between $10,000 and $25,000, and have completed at least 11 years of school. A woman living in downtown Cincinnati with a family income of $15,000 and a college degree would be a part of this population. A woman living in San Francisco or with a family income of $7,000 or with 5 years of schooling would not qualify as a member of this population.

*Need for a
representative
sample*

A *sample* is a collection of some, but not all, of the elements of the population. The population of our marketing survey is *all* women who meet the qualifications listed above. Any group of women who meet these qualifications can be a sample, as long as the group is only a fraction of the whole population. A large helping of cherry filling with only a few crumbs of crust is a sample of a pie, but it is not a representative sample because the proportions of the ingredients are not the same in the sample as they are in the whole.

A *representative sample* contains the relevant characteristics of the population *in the same proportion* as they are included in that population. If our population of women is $\frac{1}{3}$ black, then a sample of the population that is representative in terms of race will also be $\frac{1}{3}$ black. Specific methods for sampling will be covered in detail in Chapter 7.

Finding a meaningful pattern in the data

*Data come in a
variety of forms*

There are many ways to sort data. We can simply collect and keep them in order. Or if the observations are measured in numbers, we can list the data points from the lowest to the highest in numerical value. But if the data are skilled workers (such as carpenters, masons, and iron workers) required at construction sites, or the different types of automobiles manufactured by all automakers, or the various colors of sweaters manufactured by a given firm, we will need to organize them differently. We will need to present the data points in alphabetical order or by some other organizing principle. One useful way to organize data is to divide them into similar categories or classes and then count the number of observations that fall into each category. This method produces a *frequency distribution* and is discussed later in this chapter.

*Why should we
arrange data?*

Information before it is arranged and analyzed is called *raw data*. It is "raw" because it is unprocessed by statistical methods. The purpose of organizing data is to enable us to see quickly all the possible characteristics in the data we have collected. We look for things such as the range (the largest and smallest values), apparent trends, what values the data may tend to group around, what values appear most often, and so on. The more information of this kind that we can learn from our sample, the better we can understand the population from which it came, and the better we can make decisions.

─────────────────────────── **EXERCISES** ───────────────────────────

2·1 Three out of four doctors recommend aspirin. Is this conclusion drawn from a sample or a population? Explain.

2·2 Sales have declined in the past 5 years at Donaldo's, a fast-food chain serving Italian food. A survey of 30 franchises from 5 states showed a mean decrease of 4.5 percent. Comment on this statement from the viewpoint of populations and samples.

2·3 Discuss the data given in the chapter-opening problem in terms of the 5 tests for data.

2·4 "Dewey Beats Truman," announced the newspaper headlines the morning following the 1948 election. For weeks, the pollsters had been predicting a Dewey landslide. Everyone was so confident Dewey would win that some newspapers had preset the headline type and printed the morning papers without waiting for full returns. Truman, however, was elected. Give some possible reasons for the pollsters' incorrect predictions.

2 ARRANGING DATA USING THE DATA ARRAY AND THE FREQUENCY DISTRIBUTION

Data array defined

The data array is one of the simplest ways to present data. It arranges values in ascending or descending order. Table 2 · 1 takes the chlorine data from our chapter-opening problem and rearranges these numbers in a data array in ascending order.

Advantages of data arrays

Data arrays offer several advantages over raw data:

1. *We can quickly notice the lowest and highest values in the data.* In our chlorination example, the range is from 15.2 to 16.9 ppm.

2. *We can easily divide the data into sections.* In Table 2 · 1, the first 15 values (the lower half of the data) are between 15.2 and 16.0 ppm, and the last 15 values (the upper half) are between 16.0 and 16.9 ppm. Similarly, the lowest third of the values range from 15.2 to 15.8 ppm, the middle third from 15.9 to 16.2 ppm, and the upper third from 16.2 to 16.9 ppm.

3. *We can see whether any values appear more than once in the array.* Equal values appear together. Table 2 · 1 shows that 9 levels occurred more than once when the sample of 30 gallons of water was tested.

TABLE 2·1   Data array of chlorine levels in ppm of 30 gallons of treated water

15.2	15.7	15.9	16.0	16.2	16.4
15.4	15.7	15.9	16.0	16.3	16.6
15.6	15.8	15.9	16.0	16.3	16.8
15.6	15.8	15.9	16.1	16.3	16.8
15.6	15.8	16.0	16.2	16.4	16.9

4. *We can observe the distance between succeeding values in the data.* In Table 2 · 1, 16.6 and 16.8 are succeeding values. The distance between them is .2 ppm, (16.8 − 16.6).

Disadvantages of data arrays

In spite of these advantages, sometimes a data array isn't helpful. Since it lists every observation, it is a cumbersome form for displaying large quantities of data. We need to compress the information and still be able to use it for interpretation and decision making. How can we do this?

A better way to arrange data: the frequency distribution

Frequency distributions handle more data

One way we can compress data is to use a *frequency table* or a *frequency distribution*. To understand the difference between this and an array, take as an example the average inventory (in days) for 20 convenience stores.

They lose some information

In Tables 2 · 2 and 2 · 3, we have taken identical data concerning the average inventory and displayed them first as an array in ascending order and then as a frequency distribution. To obtain Table 2 · 3, we had to divide the data into groups of similar values. Then we recorded the number of data points that fell into each group. Notice that we lose some information in constructing the frequency distribution. We no longer know, for example, that the value 5.5 appears 4 times or that the value 5.1 does not appear at all. Yet we gain information concerning

But they gain other information

the *pattern* of average inventories. We can see from Table 2 · 3 that the average inventory falls most often in the range from 3.8 to 4.3 days. It is unusual to find an average inventory in the range from 2.0 to 2.5 days or from 2.6 to 3.1 days. Inventories in the ranges of 4.4 to 4.9 days and 5.0

TABLE 2·2 Data array of average inventory (in days) for 20 convenience stores

2.0	3.4	3.8	4.1	4.1	4.3	4.7	4.9	5.5	5.5
3.4	3.8	4.0	4.1	4.2	4.7	4.8	4.9	5.5	5.5

TABLE 2·3 Frequency distribution of average inventory (in days) for 20 convenience stores (6 classes)

Class (group of similar values of data points)	Frequency (number of observations in each class)
2.0 to 2.5	1
2.6 to 3.1	0
3.2 to 3.7	2
3.8 to 4.3	8
4.4 to 4.9	5
5.0 to 5.5	4

to 5.5 days are not prevalent but occur more frequently than some others. Thus, frequency distributions sacrifice some detail but offer us new insights into patterns of data.

Function of classes in a frequency distribution

A frequency distribution is a table that organizes data into *classes*; that is, into groups of values describing one characteristic of the data. "The average inventory" is one characteristic of the 20 convenience stores. In Table 2 · 2, this characteristic has 11 different values. But this same data could be divided into any number of classes. Table 2 · 3, for example, uses 6. We could compress the data even further and use only the 2 classes "less than 3.8" and "greater than, or equal to, 3.8." Or we could increase the number of classes by using smaller intervals.

Why it is called a "frequency" distribution

A frequency distribution shows the number of observations from the data set that fall into each of the classes. If you can determine the frequency with which values occur in each class of a data set, you can construct a frequency distribution.

Characteristics of relative frequency distributions

Relative frequency distribution defined

So far, we have expressed the frequency with which values occur in each class as the total number of data points that fall within that class. We can also express the frequency of each value as a *fraction* or a *percentage* of the total number of observations. The frequency of an average inventory of 4.4 to 4.9 days, for example, is 5 in Table 2 · 3 but .25 in Table 2 · 4. To get this value of .25, we divided the frequency for that class (5) by the total number of observations in the data set (20). The answer can be expressed as a fraction ($\frac{5}{20}$), a decimal (.25), or a percentage (25 percent). A *relative frequency distribution* presents frequencies in terms of fractions or percentages.

Classes are all-inclusive

Notice in Table 2 · 4 that the sum of all the relative frequencies equals 1.00, or 100 percent. This is true because a relative frequency distribution pairs each class with its appropriate fraction or percentage of the total data. Therefore, the classes in any relative or simple frequency distribution are *all-inclusive*. All the data fit into one category or another.

TABLE 2·4 Relative frequency distribution of average inventory (in days) for 20 convenience stores

Classes	Frequencies	Relative frequencies: fraction of observations in each class
2.0 to 2.5	1	.05
2.6 to 3.1	0	.00
3.2 to 3.7	2	.10
3.8 to 4.3	8	.40
4.4 to 4.9	5	.25
5.0 to 5.5	4	.20
	$\overline{20}$	$\overline{1.00}$ sum of the relative frequencies of all classes

TABLE 2·5 Mutually exclusive and overlapping classes

Mutually exclusive	1 to 4	5 to 8	9 to 12	13 to 16
Not mutually exclusive	1 to 4	3 to 6	5 to 8	7 to 10

They are mutually exclusive

Also notice that the classes in Table 2 · 4 are *mutually exclusive*; that is, no data point falls into more than one category. Table 2 · 5 illustrates this concept by comparing mutually exclusive classes with ones that overlap. In frequency distributions, there are no overlapping classes.

Classes of qualitative data

To this point, our classes have consisted of numbers and have described some quantitative attribute of the items sampled. We can also classify information according to qualitative characteristics, such as race, religion, and sex, which do not fall naturally into numerical categories. Like classes of quantitative attributes, these classes must be all-inclusive and mutually exclusive. Table 2 · 6 shows how to construct both simple and relative frequency distributions using the qualitative attribute of occupations.

Although Table 2 · 6 does not list every occupation held by the graduates of Central College, it is still all-inclusive. Why? The class "other" covers all the observations that fail to fit one of the enumerated categories. We will use a word like this whenever our list does not specifically list all the possibilities. If, for example, our characteristic can occur in any month of the year, a complete list would include 12 categories. But if we wish to list only the 8 months from January to August, we can use the term "other" to account for our observations

Open-ended classes for lists that are not exhaustive

during the 4 months of September, October, November, and December. Although our list does not specifically list all the possibilities, it is all-inclusive. This "other" is called an *open-ended class* when it allows either the upper or the lower end of a quantitative classification scheme to be limitless. If we were dealing with data on the age of the residents of

TABLE 2·6 Occupations of sample of 100 graduates of Central College

Occupational class	Frequency distribution (1)	Relative frequency distribution (1) ÷ 100
Actor	5	.05
Banker	8	.08
Businessperson	22	.22
Chemist	7	.07
Doctor	10	.10
Insurance representative	6	.06
Journalist	2	.02
Lawyer	14	.14
Teacher	9	.09
Other	17	.17
	100	1.00

a certain town, it would be common to find an *open-ended class* "70 and older" at the top end of our relative frequency distribution.

Discrete classes

     Classification schemes can be either quantitative or qualitative *and* either discrete or continuous. *Discrete* classes are separate entities that do not progress from one class to the next without a break. Such classes as the number of children in each family, the number of trucks owned by moving companies, or the occupations of Central College graduates are discrete. Discrete data are data that can take on only a limited number of values. Central College graduates can be classified as either doctors or chemists but not something in between. The closing price of AT&T stock can be $56\frac{3}{4}$ or your basketball team can have a center who is 7 feet $1\frac{1}{2}$ inches tall.

Continuous classes

     Continuous data do progress from one class to the next without a break. They involve numerical measurement such as the weights of cans of tomatoes, the pounds of pressure on concrete, or the high school GPA's of college seniors. Continuous data can be expressed in either fractions or whole numbers.

EXERCISES

2·5 Arrange the data below in a data array from lowest to highest.

708	541	528	546	631	541	622	592	534	663
546	641	603	650	502	592	618	631	599	637
578	483	578	619	586	567	644	641	622	547
644	689	557	612	644	531	536	695	645	578

  a) What are the highest and lowest data values?
  b) Between what values do the lowest $\frac{1}{4}$ of the data fall? The highest $\frac{1}{4}$ of the data?
  c) How many values appear more than once in the data set, and what are they?

2·6 For the data set in problem 2 · 5, determine how many observations fall between 450.0 and 499.9, between 500.0 and 549.9, between 550.0 and 599.9, between 600.0 and 649.9, between 650.0 and 699.9, and between 700.0 and 749.9.

2·7 Construct a frequency distribution with intervals of 7 days from the following data obtained from shipping records of a mail order firm.

Time from receipt of order to delivery (days)

3	11	7	13	10	5	5	12	14	10
12	22	6	23	9	14	22	8	25	5

2·8 Given the following data set, construct a relative frequency distribution using (a) 7 equal intervals and (b) 13 equal intervals.

80	52	67	59	60	79	62	55	52	90
64	87	65	64	50	71	72	64	71	67
40	56	74	69	97	67	81	77	77	57
35	86	71	99	88	43	54	48	68	77
93	70	84	78	68	63	47	56	66	57

2·9 The Environmental Protection Agency took water samples from 10 different rivers and streams that feed into Lake Erie. These samples were tested in the EPA laboratory and rated as to the amount of solid pollution suspended in each sample. The results of the testing are given in the following table:

Sample	1	2	3	4	5	6	7	8	9	10
Pollution rating (ppm)	27.2	38.7	64.3	52.8	47.6	23.4	33.9	45.0	56.7	41.1

a) Arrange the data into an array from highest to lowest.

b) Determine the number of samples having a pollution content between 20.0 and 29.9, 30.0 and 39.9, 40.0 and 49.9, 50.0 and 59.9, 60.0 and 69.9.

c) If 40.0 is the number used by the EPA to indicate excessive pollution, how many samples would be rated as having excessive pollution?

d) What is the largest distance between any two consecutive samples?

---

3 CONSTRUCTING A FREQUENCY DISTRIBUTION

Now that we have learned how to divide a sample into classes, we can take raw data and actually construct a frequency distribution. To solve the chlorination problem on the first page of the chapter, follow these three steps:

Classify the data

1. *Decide on the type and number of classes for dividing the data.* In this case, we have already chosen to classify the data by the quantitative measure of the number of ppm of chlorine in treated water rather than by a qualitative attribute like the color or odor of the water. Next, we need to decide how many different classes to use and the range (from where to where) each class should cover. The range must be divided by

Divide the range by equal classes

equal classes; that is, the width of the interval from the beginning of one class to the beginning of the next class needs to be the same for every class. If we choose a width of .5 ppm for each class in our water example, the classes will be those shown in Table 2 · 7.

Problems with unequal classes

If the classes were unequal and the width of the intervals differed among the classes, then we would have a distribution that is much more difficult to interpret than one with equal intervals.

TABLE 2·7 Chlorine levels in samples of treated water with .5 ppm class intervals

Class (ppm)	Frequency
15.1–15.5	2
15.6–16.0	16
16.1–16.5	8
16.6–17.0	4
	30

The number of classes depends on the number of data points and the range of the data collected. The more data points or the wider the range of the data, the more classes it takes to divide the data. Of course, if we have only 10 data points, it is senseless to have as many as 10 classes. As a rule, statisticians rarely use fewer than 6 or more than 15 classes.

Because we need to make the class intervals of equal size, the number of classes determines the width of each class. To find the intervals, we can use this equation:

$$\frac{\text{Width of}}{\text{class intervals}} = \frac{\text{Next unit value after largest value in data} - \text{Smallest value in data}}{\text{Total number of class intervals}} \quad (2 \cdot 1)$$

We must use the *next value of the same units* because we are measuring the *interval* between the first value of one class and the first value of the next class. In our water study, the last value is 16.9, so 17.0 is the next value. Since we are using 6 classes in this example, the width of each class will be:

$$\frac{\text{Next unit value after largest value in data} - \text{Smallest value in data}}{\text{Total number of class intervals}}$$

$$= \frac{17.0 - 15.2}{6} \quad (2 \cdot 1)$$

$$= .3 \text{ ounce} \leftarrow \text{width of class intervals}$$

Step 1 is now complete. We have decided to classify the data by the quantitative measure of how many ppm of chlorine are in the treated water. We have chosen 6 classes to cover the range of 15.2 to 16.9 and, as a result, will use .3 ppm as the width of our class intervals.

2. *Sort the data points into classes and count the number of points in each class.* This we have done in Table 2 · 8. Every data point fits into at least one class, and no data point fits into more than one class. Therefore, our classes are all-inclusive and mutually exclusive. Notice that the lower boundary of the first class corresponds with the smallest data point

TABLE 2·8 Chlorine levels in samples of treated water with .3 ppm class intervals

Class	Frequency
15.2–15.4	2
15.5–15.7	5
15.8–16.0	11
16.1–16.3	6
16.4–16.6	3
16.7–16.9	3
	30

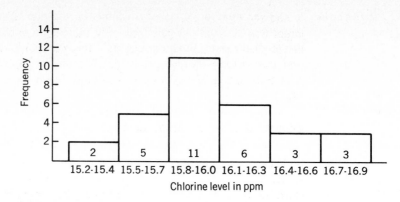

Figure 2·1 Frequency distribution of chlorine levels in samples of treated water using .3 ppm class intervals

in our sample, and the upper boundary of the last class corresponds with the largest data point.

      3. *Illustrate the data in a chart.* (See Fig. 2 · 1.)

      These three steps enable us to arrange the data in both tabular and graphic form. In this case, our information is displayed in Table 2 · 8 and in Fig. 2 · 1. These two frequency distributions omit some of the detail contained in the data of Table 2 · 1, but they make it easier for us to notice trends in the data. One obvious characteristic, for example, is that the class 15.8–16.0 contains the most elements; class 15.2–15.4, the fewest.

Notice any trends   Notice in Fig. 2 · 1 that the frequencies in the classes of .3 ppm widths follow a regular progression: the number of data points begins with 2 for the first class, builds to 5, reaches 11 in the third class, falls to

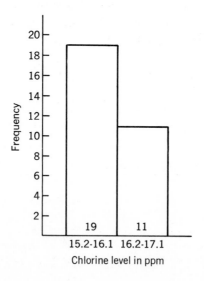

Figure 2·2 Frequency distribution of chlorine levels in samples of treated water using 1 ppm class intervals

6, and tumbles to 3 in the fifth and sixth classes. We will find that the larger the width of the class intervals, the smoother this progression will be. However, if the classes are too wide, we lose so much information that the chart is almost meaningless. If, for example, we collapse Fig. 2 · 1 into only two categories, we obscure the trend. This is evident in Fig. 2 · 2.

Class limits and class marks

Statisticians use the term *class limits* to refer to the smallest and largest values that go into any given class. But two different kinds of class limits exist. In Table 2 · 8 the lower and upper class limits for the first class are 15.2 and 15.4, respectively. These are the *stated* limits. The *real* limits, however, are 15.15 and 15.45. This it true because we round the values 15.15, 15.16, 15.17, 15.18, and 15.19 *up* to 15.2. As a result, *all* these values fall into the class with the lower limit equal to 15.2.

The real limits of the next class are 15.45 and 15.75. Notice that the upper limit of one class is the lower limit of the succeeding class. Therefore, 15.45 is the upper limit of the class with stated limits of 15.2 and 15.4 *and* the lower limit of the class with stated limits of 15.5 and 15.7.

The distinction between real limits and stated limits is made only with continuous variables; we make this distinction because continuous variables are rounded. However, for discrete variables, which are usually counted (rather than measured), we do not make any distinction between the two kinds of limits. For instance, if we have a frequency distribution of weekly car sales by salespeople, and if one of the frequency classes is 0–5, then zero is *both* the real and the stated lower limit, and 5 is *both* the real and the stated upper limit.

Statisticians use another term, *class marks*, to describe the midpoints of the classes. To calculate the class mark, we simply average the lower and upper limits by applying Equation 2 · 2:

$$\text{Class mark} = \frac{\text{Stated lower limit} + \text{Stated upper limit}}{2} \qquad (2 \cdot 2)$$

Suppose that we are classifying a hi-fi store's accounts receivable, and our first two classes are \$0–\$49.99 and \$50–\$99.99. Then the class mark for the first class would be:

$$\frac{\text{Stated lower limit} + \text{Stated upper limit}}{2} = \frac{\$0 + \$49.99}{2} \qquad (2 \cdot 2)$$
$$= \$24.995 \leftarrow \text{class mark}$$

In this case, we would round up so that \$25.00 would be the class mark. This rounding enables us to work with much more convenient values, and is usually done whenever we deal with discrete variables (cents, in this case) and with wide intervals (5,000 cents, in this case). In such situations we use a modified version of Equation 2 · 2:

$$\text{Class mark} = \frac{\text{Stated lower limit} + \text{Stated lower limit of the next class}}{2}$$

$$(2 \cdot 3)$$

So, in our accounts-receivable problem, we would find the class mark like this:

$$\frac{\text{Stated lower limit} + \text{Stated lower limit of the next class}}{2} = \frac{\$0 + \$50}{2}$$

$$= \$25 \leftarrow \text{class mark}$$

$$(2 \cdot 3)$$

A word of advice

A hint
when constructing
class intervals

If possible, try to construct class intervals so that values *cluster* around the values of class marks. To do this, examine the raw data and look for values around which data points are concentrated. Look at Table 2 · 9, which illustrates the raw data from a sample of 20 weeks of penny production at the Philadelphia mint. The director of the mint wants to know how many pennies are stamped each week.

Notice that in Table 2 · 9 the values cluster around 4, 7, and 9. In constructing class intervals for the frequency distribution, then, we should attempt to have these three values as class marks. We have done this in Table 2 · 10. Of course, values do not always cluster so neatly. The important thing is to choose intervals so that as many values as possible are close to the values of the class marks.

TABLE 2 · 9   Philadelphia mint weekly penny production (millions)

4	4	4	5	6	7	7	7	7	7	7	7	7	8	9	9	9	9	9	10	10

TABLE 2 · 10   Frequency distribution of Philadelphia mint weekly penny production

Class (millions)	Frequency	Class mark
3 to 5	4	4
6 to 8	10	7
9 to 11	6	10

EXERCISES

2·10 Given the following class marks for the intervals of a frequency distribution, determine the real and stated class limits of the intervals.

	Class mark		
8.50	14.50	20.50	26.50
11.50	17.50	23.50	29.50

2·11 For the following data, construct
a) a 6-category closed classification
b) a 5-category open-ended classification
c) relative frequency distributions to go with the frequency distributions above

34.1	39.0	38.3	41.6	36.4	43.9	33.2	56.4	33.9	34.5
46.4	42.1	41.8	49.4	42.2	51.7	42.4	44.5	46.7	40.6
45.7	50.7	37.6	36.0	34.9	38.9	44.6	49.0	51.4	48.3

2·12 Construct a discrete, closed classification for the possible responses to the "marital status" portion of an employment application. Also, construct a three-category, discrete, open-ended classification for the same responses.

2·13 Listings for a stock exchange usually contain the company name, high and low bids, closing price, and the change from the previous day's closing price. For example:

Name	High bid	Low bid	Closing	Change
Jefferson Pilot	$28\frac{1}{2}$	$27\frac{3}{4}$	$28\frac{1}{4}$	$+1\frac{1}{4}$

Is a distribution of all
a) stocks on the New York Stock Exchange by industry
b) closing prices on a given day
c) changes in prices on a given day
1) quantitative or qualitative? **2)** continuous or discrete? **3)** open-ended or closed?
Would your answer to part c be different if the change were expressed simply as "higher," "lower," or "unchanged"?

2·14 The noise level in decibels of aircraft taking off from JFK Airport in New York City was rounded to the nearest tenth of a decibel and grouped in a table having the following class marks: 102.45, 107.45, 112.45, 117.45, 122.45, 127.45, 132.45, and 137.45. What are the stated and real class limits?

2·15 The president of Ocean Airlines is trying to estimate when the Civil Aeronautics Board (CAB) is most likely to rule on the company's application for a new route between Charlotte and Nashville. Assistants to the president have assembled the following waiting times for applications filed during the past year. The data are given in days from the date of application until a CAB ruling.

32	38	26	29	32	41	28	31	45	36
45	35	40	30	31	40	27	33	28	30
30	41	39	38	33	35	31	36	37	32
23	45	39	37	38	36	33	35	42	38
34	22	37	43	52	32	35	30	46	36

a) Construct a frequency distribution using 10 closed intervals, equally spaced. Which interval occurs most often?

b) Construct a frequency distribution using 5 closed intervals, equally spaced. Which interval occurs most often?

---

4 GRAPHING FREQUENCY DISTRIBUTIONS

Identifying the horizontal and vertical axes

Figures 2 · 1 and 2 · 2 (both on page 16) are previews of what we are going to discuss now: how to present frequency distributions graphically. Graphs give data in a two-dimensional picture. On the *horizontal* axis, we can show the values of the variable (the characteristic we are measuring), such as the chlorine level in ppm. On the *vertical* axis, we mark the frequencies of the classes shown on the horizontal axis. Thus, the height of the boxes in Fig. 2 · 1 measures the number of observations in each of the classes marked on the horizontal axis.

Function of graphs

Graphs of frequency distributions and relative frequency distributions are useful because they emphasize and clarify trends that are not so readily discernible in tables. They attract a reader's attention to trends in the data. Graphs can also help us do problems concerning frequency distributions. They will enable us to estimate some values at a glance and will provide us with a pictorial check on the accuracy of our solutions.

Histograms

Histograms described

Figures 2 · 1 and 2 · 2 on page 16 are two examples of histograms. A *histogram* is a series of rectangles, each proportional in width to the range of values within a class and proportional in height to the number of items falling in the class. If the classes we use in the frequency distribution are of equal width, then the vertical bars in the histogram are also of equal width. The height of the bar for each class corresponds to the number of items in the class. As a result, the area contained in each rectangle (width times height) is the same percentage of the area of all the rectangles as the relative frequency of that class is to all the observations made.

Function of a relative frequency histogram

A histogram that uses the relative frequency of data points in each of the classes rather than the actual number of points is called a *relative frequency histogram*. The relative frequency histogram has the same shape as an absolute frequency histogram made from the same data set. This is true because in both the relative size of each rectangle is the frequency of that class compared to the total number of observations.

Recall that the relative frequency of any class is the number of observations in that class divided by the total number of observations made. The sum of all the relative frequencies for any data set is equal to

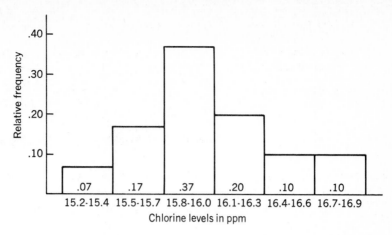

Figure 2·3 Relative frequency distribution of chlorine levels in samples of treated water using .3 ppm class intervals

1.0. With this in mind, we can convert the histogram of Fig. 2 · 1 into a relative frequency histogram such as we find in Fig. 2 · 3. Notice that the only difference between these two is the left-hand vertical scale. Whereas the scale in Fig. 2 · 1 is the *absolute* number of observations in each class, the scale in Fig. 2 · 3 is the number of observations in each class as a *fraction* of the total number of observations.

Advantage of the relative frequency

Being able to present data in terms of the relative rather than the absolute frequency of observations in each class is useful because, while the absolute numbers may change (as we test more gallons of water for example), the relationship among the classes may remain stable. Twenty percent of all the gallons of water may fall in the class "16.1–16.3 ppm" whether we test 30 gallons or 300 gallons. It is easy to compare data from different sizes of samples when we use relative frequency histograms.

Frequency polygons

Use class marks on the horizontal axis

Although less widely used, frequency polygons are another way to portray graphically both simple and relative frequency distributions. To construct a frequency polygon, we mark the frequencies on the vertical axis and the values of the variable we are measuring on the horizontal axis, as we did with histograms. Next, we plot each class frequency by drawing a dot above its class mark, or midpoint, and connect the successive dots with a straight line to form a polygon (a many-sided figure).

Add two classes

Figure 2 · 4 is a frequency polygon constructed from the data in Table 2 · 8. If you compare this figure with Fig. 2 · 1, you will notice that classes have been added at *each end* of the scale of observed values.

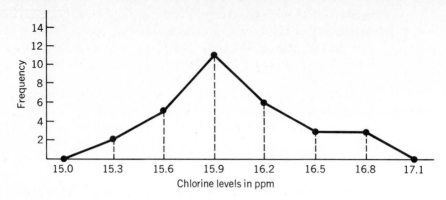

Figure 2·4 Frequency polygon of chlorine levels in samples of treated water using .3 ppm class intervals

These two new classes contain zero observations but allow the polygon to reach the horizontal axis at both ends of the distribution.

Converting a frequency polygon to a histogram

How can we turn a frequency polygon into a histogram? A frequency polygon is simply a line graph that connects the midpoints of all the bars in a histogram. Therefore, we can reproduce the histogram by drawing vertical lines from the bounds of the classes (as marked on the horizontal axis) and connecting them with horizontal lines at the heights of the polygon at each class mark. We have done this with dashed lines in Fig. 2 · 5.

Constructing a relative frequency polygon

A frequency polygon that uses the relative frequency of data points in each of the classes rather than the actual number of points is called a *relative frequency polygon*. The relative frequency polygon has the same shape as the frequency polygon made from the same data set but a different scale of values on the vertical axis. Rather than the absolute

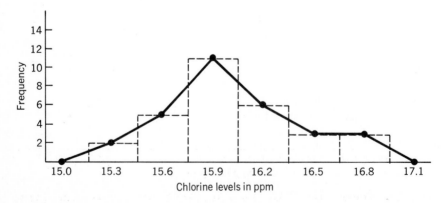

Figure 2·5 Histogram drawn from the points of the frequency polygon in Fig. 2 · 4

number of observations, the scale is the number of observations in each class as a fraction of the total number of observations.

Advantages of histograms

Histograms and frequency polygons are similar. Why do we need both? The advantages of histograms are:

1. The rectangle clearly shows each separate class in the distribution.
2. The area of each rectangle, relative to all the other rectangles, shows the proportion of the total number of observations that occur in that class.

Advantages of polygons

Frequency polygons, however, have certain advantages too.

1. The frequency polygon is simpler than its histogram counterpart.
2. It sketches an outline of the data pattern more clearly.
3. The polygon becomes increasingly smooth and curvelike as we increase the number of classes and the number of observations.

Creating a frequency curve

A polygon such as the one we have just described, smoothed by added classes and data points, is called a *frequency curve*. In Fig. 2 · 6, we have used our water example, but we have increased the number of observations to 300 and the number of classes to 10 (the first and last dots do not represent class marks). Notice that we have connected the points with curved lines to approximate the way the polygon would look if we had an infinite number of data points and very small class intervals.

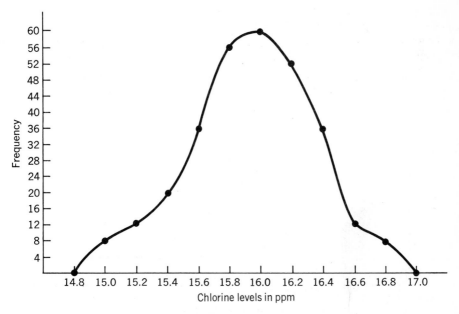

Figure 2·6 Frequency curve of the chlorine levels in 300 gallons of water using .2 ppm intervals

Ogives

Cumulative frequency distribution defined

A cumulative frequency distribution enables us to see how many observations lie above or below certain values, rather than merely recording the numbers of items within intervals. If, for example, we wish to know how many of our original 30 gallons of water contain less than 17.0 ppm we can use a table recording the cumulative "less than" frequencies in our sample, such as Table 2 · 11.

A "more than" ogive

A graph of a cumulative frequency distribution is called an *ogive* (pronounced "**oh**-jive"). The ogive for the cumulative distribution in Table 2 · 11 is shown in Fig. 2 · 7. The plotted points represent the number of gallons having less chlorine than the ppm shown on the

TABLE 2·11 Cumulative "less than" frequency distribution of chlorine levels in ppm

Class	Cumulative frequency
Less than 15.2	0
Less than 15.5	2
Less than 15.8	7
Less than 16.1	18
Less than 16.4	24
Less than 16.7	27
Less than 17.0	30

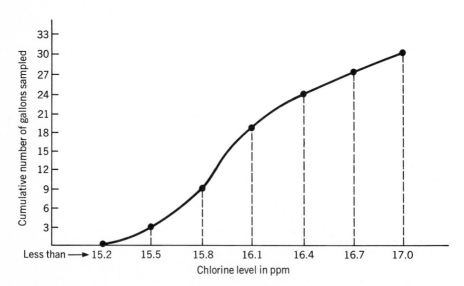

Figure 2·7 "Less than" ogive of the distribution of chlorine levels in ppm for 30 gallons of treated water

TABLE 2·12 Relative cumulative frequency distribution of chlorine levels in ppm

Class	Cumulative frequency	Cumulative relative frequency
Less than 15.2	0	.00
Less than 15.5	2	.07
Less than 15.8	7	.23
Less than 16.1	18	.60
Less than 16.4	24	.80
Less than 16.7	27	.90
Less than 17.0	30	1.00

horizontal axis.

The S-shaped curve shown in Fig. 2·7 is typical of ogives. This "less than" curve slopes upward and to the right. If we had drawn a "more than" ogive, it would have sloped downward and to the right.

We could construct an ogive of a relative frequency distribution in the same manner in which we drew the ogive of the absolute frequency distribution in Fig. 2·7. There would be one change—the vertical scale would use relative frequencies, and would thus mark the *fraction* of the total number of observations that fall at or below each level.

To construct a cumulative "less than" ogive in terms of relative frequencies, we can refer to a relative frequency distribution (like Fig. 2·3) and set up a table using the data (like Table 2·12). Then, we can convert the figures there to an ogive (as in Fig. 2·8). Notice that Figs. 2·7 and 2·8 are equivalent except for the left-hand vertical axis.

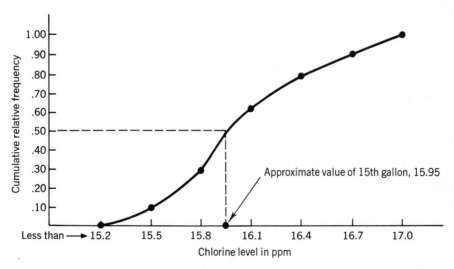

Figure 2·8 "Less than" ogive of the distribution of chlorine levels in ppm for 30 gallons of treated water indicating approximate middle value in original data array

Suppose we now draw a line perpendicular to the vertical axis at the .50 mark to intersect our ogive. (We have done this in Fig. 2 · 8.) In this way, we can read an approximate value for the chlorine level in the 15th gallon of an array of the 30 gallons. Thus, we are back to the first data arrangement discussed in this chapter. From the data array, we can construct frequency distributions. From frequency distributions, we can construct cumulative frequency distributions. From these, we can graph an ogive. And from this ogive, we can approximate the values we had in the data array. However, we normally cannot recover the *exact* original data from any of the graphic representations we have discussed.

EXERCISES

2·16 Construct a histogram for the data in the following frequency distribution:

Class	Frequency	Class	Frequency
75–89	9	150–164	24
90–104	12	165–179	10
105–119	24	180–194	8
120–134	25	195–209	6
135–149	30	210–224	2

2·17 For the following frequency distribution,
  a) Construct a cumulative relative frequency ogive using frequencies of values "less than" the interval limits.
  b) Estimate the value of the middle observation in the original data set.

Class	Frequency	Class	Frequency
0.5–0.9	13	2.5–2.9	30
1.0–1.4	20	3.0–3.4	35
1.5–1.9	22	3.5–3.9	41
2.0–2.4	24	4.0–4.4	15

2·18 For the following frequency distribution, construct
  a) a cumulative frequency distribution for frequencies of values "less than" the interval limits
  b) an ogive based on part a
  c) a cumulative frequency distribution for frequencies of values "more than" the interval limits
  d) an ogive for part c

Class	Frequency	Class	Frequency
3.00–3.19	1	4.00–4.19	11
3.20–3.39	4	4.20–4.39	8
3.40–3.59	11	4.40–4.59	7
3.60–3.79	15	4.60–4.79	6
3.80–3.99	12		

2·19 At a newspaper office, the time required to set the entire front page in type was recorded for 50 days. The data, to the nearest tenth of a minute, are given below.

20.8	22.8	21.9	22.0	20.7	20.9	25.0	22.2	22.8	20.1
25.3	20.7	22.5	21.2	23.8	23.3	20.9	22.9	23.5	19.5
23.7	20.3	23.6	19.0	25.1	25.0	19.5	24.1	24.2	21.8
21.3	21.5	23.1	19.9	24.2	24.1	19.8	23.9	22.8	23.9
19.7	24.2	23.8	20.7	23.8	24.3	21.1	20.9	21.6	22.7

a) Arrange the data in an array from lowest to highest.
b) Construct a frequency distribution and a "less than" cumulative frequency distribution from the data using intervals of .8 minute.
c) Construct a frequency polygon from the data.
d) Construct a "less than" frequency ogive from the data.

---

5 TERMS INTRODUCED IN CHAPTER 2

class limits The smallest and largest values that go into any given class.

class mark The midpoint of a class in a frequency distribution; the average of the lower and upper limits.

continuous data Data that may progress from one class to the next without a break and may be expressed by either whole numbers or fractions.

cumulative frequency distribution A tabular display of data showing how many observations lie above, or below, certain values.

data A collection of any number of related observations on one or more variables.

data array The arrangement of raw data by observations in either ascending or descending order.

data point A single observation from a data set.

data set A collection of data.

discrete data Data that do not progress from one class to the next without a break; i.e., where classes represent distinct categories or counts and may be represented by whole numbers.

frequency curve A frequency polygon smoothed by adding classes and data points to a data set.

frequency distribution An organized display of data that shows the number of observations from the data set that fall into each of a set of mutually exclusive classes.

frequency polygon A line graph connecting the midpoints of each class in a data set, plotted at a height corresponding to the frequency of the class.

histogram A graph of a data set, composed of a series of rectangles, each proportional in width to the range of values in a class and proportional in height to the number of items falling in the class, or the fraction of items in the class.

ogive A graph of a cumulative frequency distribution.

open-ended class A class that allows either the upper or lower end of a quantitative classification scheme to be limitless.

population A collection of all the elements we are studying and about which we are trying to draw conclusions.

raw data Information before it is arranged or analyzed by statistical methods.

relative frequency distribution The display of a data set that shows the fraction or percentage of the total data set that falls into each of a set of mutually exclusive classes.

representative sample A sample which contains the relevant characteristics of the population in the same proportion as they are included in that population.

sample A collection of some, but not all, of the elements of the population under study, used to describe the population.

p. 15

$$\frac{\text{Width of}}{\text{class intervals}} = \frac{\begin{array}{c}\text{Next unit value after}\\\text{largest value in data}\end{array} - \text{Smallest value in data}}{\text{Total number of class intervals}} \qquad 2 \cdot 1$$

To arrange raw data, decide the number of classes in which you will divide the data (normally, between 6 and 15), and then use Equation 2 · 1 to determine the *width of class intervals of equal size*. This formula uses the next value of the same units because it measures the interval between the first value of one class and the first value of the next class.

p. 17

$$\text{Class mark} = \frac{\text{Stated lower limit} + \text{Stated upper limit}}{2} \qquad 2 \cdot 2$$

The midpoint of a class, that is, its *class mark*, is calculated by averaging the lower and upper limits of that class.

p. 18

$$\text{Class mark} = \frac{\text{Stated lower limit} + \text{Stated lower limit of the next class}}{2} \qquad 2 \cdot 3$$

When we are dealing with discrete variables and wide intervals, the midpoint of a class (its class mark) is calculated by using a slight modification of Equation 2 · 2. This enables us to work with more convenient values.

7 CHAPTER REVIEW EXERCISES

2·20 City engineers made a study of the average time (in hours) cars remained parked at a new city parking lot. The data were rounded to the nearest tenth of an hour and grouped in a table whose classes have the following real limits: .05, .35, .65, .95, 1.25, 1.55, 1.85, 2.15, 2.45, 2.75, 3.05, and no limit for the last interval. Determine the stated limits and class marks for each interval.

2·21 If the following age groups are included in the proportions indicated, how many of each age group should be included in a sample of 3,000 individuals to make the sample representative?

Age group	Relative proportion in population
12–17	.15
18–23	.33
24–29	.25
30–35	.17
36 +	.10
	1.00

2·22 The National Safety Council randomly sampled the tread depth of 60 right front tires on passenger vehicles stopped at a rest area on an interstate highway. From their data, they constructed the following frequency distribution:

Tread depth (inches)	Frequency	Tread depth (inches)	Frequency
16/32 (new tire)	5	4/32–6/32	7
13/32–15/32	10	1/32–3/32	4
10/32–12/32	20	0/32 (bald)	2
7/32–9/32	12		

Approximately what was the tread depth of the 30th tire in the data array?

2·23 A questionnaire on attitudes about sex education in the schools is sent out to a random sample of 2,000 people; 880 are completed and returned to the researcher. Comment on the data available from these questionnaires in terms of the five tests for data.

2·24 With each appliance that Central Electric produces, the company includes a warranty card for the purchaser. In addition to validating the warranty and furnishing the company with the purchaser's name and address, the card asks for the following information that is used for marketing studies: (1) age, (2) yearly income, (3) marital status, (4) where appliance was purchased, and (5) why appliance was purchased.

Determine the most likely characteristics of these categories that would be used by the company to record the information. In particular, would they be: (1) quantitative or qualitative? (2) continuous or discrete? (3) open-ended or closed? Briefly state the reasoning behind your answers.

2·25 The High Point Fastener Company produces 15 basic items. The company keeps records on the number of each item produced per month in order to examine the relative production levels. Records show the following numbers of each item were produced by the company for the last month of 20 operating days.

9,897	10,052	10,028	9,722	9,908
10,098	10,587	9,872	9,956	9,928
10,123	10,507	9,910	9,992	10,237

Construct both a frequency distribution and a relative frequency distribution of items produced per day, using intervals of 5 units per day.

2·26 All 50 states send the following information to the Department of Labor: the average number of workers absent daily during each of the 13 weeks of a financial quarter and the percentage of absentees for each state. Is this an example of raw data? Explain.

2·27 The vice-president of finance for Home Plastics needed to invest a large amount of surplus cash generated from unexpectedly high sales. Various investment opportunities were classified according to potential risk and anticipated rate of return. The data regarding rate of return was recorded in a distribution with 14.65, 15.25, 15.85, 16.45, 17.05, 17.65, 18.25, and 18.85 as the real class limits (data recorded as a percentage and measured to the nearest tenth of a percentage point). Determine the stated class limits and class marks for each interval of the distribution.

2·28 Below are the measurements on an entire population of 100 elements.
a) Select two samples: one sample of the first 10 elements and another sample of the largest 10 elements.
b) Are the two samples equally representative of the population? If not, which sample is more representative and why?

226	198	210	233	222	175	215	191	201	175
264	204	193	244	180	185	190	216	178	190
174	183	201	238	232	257	236	222	213	207
233	205	180	267	236	186	192	245	218	193
189	180	175	184	234	234	180	252	201	187
155	175	196	172	248	198	226	185	180	175
217	190	212	198	212	228	184	219	196	212
220	213	191	170	258	192	194	180	243	230
180	135	243	180	209	202	242	259	238	227
207	218	230	224	228	188	210	205	197	169

2·29 In the population under study, there are 2,000 women and 8,000 men. If we are to select a sample of 250 individuals from this population, how many should be women to make our sample considered strictly representative?

2·30 The Kawahondi Computer Company compiled data regarding the number of interviews required for each of its 20 salespeople to make a sale. Following are a frequency distribution and a relative frequency distribution of the number of interviews required per salesperson per sale. Fill in the missing data.

Number of interviews (classes)	Frequency	Relative frequency
0–10	?	.05
11–20	0	?
21–30	1	?
31–40	?	?
41–50	?	.15
51–60	?	.20
61–70	2	?
71–80	?	.00
81–90	3	?
91–100	?	.00
Total	?	?

2·31 The production manager of the Browner Typewriter Company posted final worker performance ratings based on total units produced, percentage of rejects, and total hours worked. Is this an example of raw data? Why or why not? If not, what would it be in this situation?

2·32 The Ferebee Ergonomic Toy Company hired consultant Robin Clark to design a new management investment program. In order to estimate the various amounts managers would be willing to invest from their respective paychecks, Clark researched the second incomes of managers' families. His data reveal that no family has a second income over $20,000, and several families appear to have no second income. In a preliminary analysis, he decides to construct both a frequency and relative frequency distribution for second income. He wants to use $2,000 intervals.

a) Develop a continuous, closed distribution that meets his requirements.

b) Develop a continuous distribution with 9 categories that meets his requirements and that is open at both ends. You may relax the requirement for $2,000 intervals for the open-ended category.

---

8 CHAPTER CONCEPTS TEST

Answers are in the back of the book.

T F   1. In comparison to a data array, the frequency distribution has the advantage of representing data in compressed form.

T F   2. The smallest and largest values that go into any given class of a frequency distribution are referred to as the class limits.

T F   3. A histogram is a series of rectangles, each proportional in width to the number of items falling within a specific class of data.

T F 4. A single observation is called a data point, whereas a collection of data is known as a tabular.

T F 5. The classes in any relative frequency distribution are all-inclusive and mutually exclusive.

T F 6. When a sample contains the relevant characteristics of a certain population in the same proportion as they are included in that population, the sample is said to be a representative sample.

T F 7. The distinction between real class limits and stated class limits is made only when we are dealing with continuous variables.

T F 8. If we were to connect the midpoints of the consecutive bars of a frequency histogram with a series of lines, we would be graphing a frequency polygon.

T F 9. Before information is arranged and analyzed, using statistical methods, it is known as preprocessed data.

T F 10. One disadvantage of the data array is that it does not allow us easily to find the highest and lowest values in the data set.

T F 11. Discrete data can be expressed only in whole numbers.

T F 12. As a general rule, statisticians regard a frequency distribution as incomplete if it has fewer than 20 classes.

T F 13. It is always possible to construct a histogram from a frequency polygon.

T F 14. The vertical scale of an ogive for a relative frequency distribution marks the fraction of the total number of observations that fall into each class.

T F 15. A data array is formed by arranging raw data in order of time of observation.

16. Which of the following represents the most accurate scheme of classifying data?
    a) quantitative methods
    b) qualitative methods
    c) a combination of quantitative and qualitative methods
    d) A scheme can only be determined with specific information about the situation.

17. Which of the following is NOT an example of compressed data?
    a) frequency distribution   c) histogram
    b) data array   d) ogive

18. Which of the following statements about histogram rectangles is correct?
    a) The rectangles are proportional in height to the number of items falling in the classes.
    b) The rectangles are proportional in width to the size of the class marks.
    c) The area in a rectangle depends only on the number of items in the class as compared to the number of items in all other classes.
    d) All of the above.
    e) a and c but not b.

19. Why is it true that classes in frequency distributions are all-inclusive?
    a) No data point falls into more than one class.
    b) Every class has a class mark.
    c) All data fit into one class or another.
    d) All of the above.
    e) a and c but not b.

20. When constructing a frequency distribution, the first step is:
    a) Calculate the class marks for the data.
    b) Sort the data points into classes and count the number of points in each class.

c) Decide on the type and number of classes for dividing the data.

d) None of the above.

21. As the numbers of observations and classes increase, the shape of a frequency polygon:

a) tends to become increasingly smooth

b) tends to become jagged

c) stays the same

d) varies only if data become more reliable

22. Which of the following statements is true of cumulative frequency ogives for a particular set of data?

a) Both "more than" and "less than" curves have the same slope.

b) "More than" curves slope up and to the right.

c) "Less than" curves slope down and to the right.

d) "Less than" curves slope up and to the right.

23. From an ogive constructed for a particular set of data:

a) The original data can always be reconstructed exactly.

b) The original data can always be approximated.

c) The original data can never be approximated or reconstructed, but valid conclusions regarding the data can be drawn.

d) None of the above.

e) a and b but not c.

24. When constructing a frequency distribution, the number of classes used depends upon:

a) number of data points

b) range of the data collected

c) size of the population

d) all of the above

e) a and b but not c

25. Which of the following statements is true?

a) The size of a sample can never be as large as the size of the population from which it is taken.

b) Classes describe only one characteristic of the data being organized.

c) A class mark is calculated by averaging the lower and upper limits of a class.

d) All of the above.

e) b and c but not a.

26. A _____ is a collection of all the elements in a group. A collection of some, but not all, of these elements is a _____ .

27. Dividing data points into similar classes and counting the number of observations in each class will give a _____ distribution.

28. If data can take on only a limited number of values, the classes of this data are called _____ . Otherwise, the classes are called _____ .

29. The midpoint of a class is called the class _____ .

30. A graph of cumulative frequency distributions is called a _____ .

Summary Measures of Frequency Distributions

3

The manager of the Lake Ico hydroelectric power plant has 10 generators in her system. She needs some measure of the time her 10 generators are out of service. With this information, she can plan manpower requirements, schedule maintenance, and arrange backup service. This table represents data from last year for each generator.

Generator	1	2	3	4	5	6	7	8	9	10
Days out of service	7	23	4	8	2	12	6	13	9	4

The manager would like some single measure of days out of service for all generators, to use in planning. This chapter introduces several measures useful to her and to others who must make similar plans.

Chapter 3 focuses on special ways to describe a collection of items, particularly the way observations tend to cluster or bunch up. Here, we shall encounter some familiar terms, such as the concept of an average. If the basketball coach at your university says the average height of the members of his team is 6 feet 11 inches, he is really saying that there is a tendency for the heights of the players to bunch up around 6 feet 11 inches. For a basketball team with this much height, you intuitively know that the chances of a winning season are quite good — even before you formally study statistics. In Chapter 3, we also study the mean, the median, and the mode — all ways of measuring and locating data.

1 BEYOND TABLES AND GRAPHS: DESCRIPTIVE MEASURES OF FREQUENCY DISTRIBUTIONS

Summary statistics describe the characteristics of a data set

In Chapter 2, we learned to construct tables and graphs using raw data. The resulting "pictures" of frequency distributions enabled us to discern trends and patterns in the data. But what if we need more exact measures of a data set? In that case, we can use single numbers, called *summary statistics*, to describe certain characteristics of a data set. From these, we can gain a more precise understanding of the data than we can from our tables and graphs. And these numbers will enable us to make quicker and better decisions because we will not need to consult our original observations.

Four of these characteristics are particularly important:

Middle of a data set

1. *Measures of central tendency.* Like averages, measures of central tendency tell us what we can expect a typical or middle data point to be. They are also called *measures of location.* In Fig. 3 · 1, the central location of curve B lies to the right of those of curve A and curve C. Notice that the central location of curve A is equal to that of curve C.

Range of a data set

2. *Measures of dispersion.* Dispersion refers to the spread of the data, that is, the extent to which the observations are scattered. In Chapter 4, we shall study a measure of dispersion called the range. The range indicates how far it is from the lowest data point to the highest. Notice that curve C in Fig. 3 · 1 has a wider spread, or dispersion, than curve A.

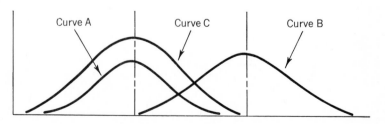

Figure 3 · 1 Comparison of central location of three curves

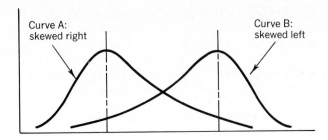

Figure 3·2 Comparison of two skewed curves

Symmetry of a data set

3. *Measures of skewness*. Curves representing the data points in the data set may be either symmetrical or skewed. *Symmetrical* curves, like the ones in Fig. 3 · 1, are such that a vertical line drawn from the peak of the curve to the horizontal axis will divide the area of the curve into two equal parts. Each part is the mirror image of the other.

Skewness of a data set

Curves A and B in Fig. 3 · 2 are *skewed* curves. They are skewed because values in their frequency distributions are concentrated at either the low end or the high end of the measuring scale on the horizontal axis. The values are not equally distributed. Curve A is skewed to the right (or *positively* skewed), because it tails off toward the high end of the scale. Curve B is just the opposite. It is skewed to the left (*negatively* skewed), because it tails off toward the low end of the scale.

Curve A might represent the frequency distribution of the number of days' supply on hand in the wholesale fruit business. The curve would be skewed to the right with many values at the low end and few at the high because the inventory must turn over rapidly. Similarly, curve B could represent the frequency of the number of days a real-estate broker requires to sell a house. It would be skewed to the left with many values at the high end and few at the low because the inventory of houses turns over very slowly.

Peakedness of a data set

4. *Measures of kurtosis*. When we measure the *kurtosis* of a distribution, we are measuring its peakedness. In Fig. 3 · 3, for example, curves A and B differ only by the fact that one is more peaked than the other. They have the same central location and dispersion, and both are symmetrical. Statisticians say that the two curves have different degrees of kurtosis.

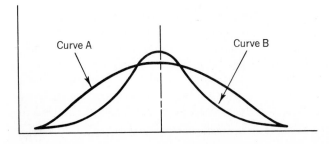

Figure 3·3 Two curves with the same central location but different kurtosis

Now that we have briefly described these characteristics of frequency distributions, we can discuss in greater detail three common *measures of central tendency:* the *mean*, the *median*, and the *mode*.

--- **EXERCISES** ---

3·1 If the following two curves represent the distribution of scores for a group of students on two tests, which test appears to be more difficult for the students, A or B? Explain.

3·2 Draw three curves, all symmetrical and with the same dispersion, but with the following central locations:
a) 0.0   **b)** 1.0   **c)** −1.0

3·3 For the following distributions, indicate which distribution
a) has the larger average value
b) is more likely to produce a small value than a large value
For the next two distributions, indicate which distribution, if any,

c) has values most evenly distributed across the range of possible values
d) is more likely to produce a value near 0
e) has a greater likelihood of producing large values than small values

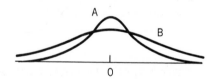

2 A MEASURE OF CENTRAL TENDENCY: THE ARITHMETIC MEAN

Most of the time when we refer to the "average" of something, we are talking about the arithmetic mean. This is true in cases such as the average winter temperature of New York City, the average life of a flashlight battery, and the average corn yield from an acre of land.

The arithmetic mean is an average

Table 3 · 1 repeats the data from our chapter opening example. Data in the table represent the number of days the generators are out of service owing to regular maintenance or some malfunction. To find the arithmetic mean, we sum the values and divide by the number of

TABLE 3·1 Downtime of generators at Lake Ico station

Generator	1	2	3	4	5	6	7	8	9	10
Days out of service	7	23	4	8	2	12	6	13	9	4

observations:

$$\text{Arithmetic mean} = \frac{7 + 23 + 4 + 8 + 2 + 12 + 6 + 13 + 9 + 4}{10}$$

$$= 8.8 \text{ days}$$

In this one-year period the generators were out of service for an average of 8.8 days. With this figure, the power plant manager has a reasonable single measure of the behavior of *all* of the generators.

Conventional symbols

Characteristics of a sample are called statistics

To write equations for these measures of frequency distributions, we need to learn the mathematical notations used by statisticians. A *sample* of a population consists of n observations (a lowercase n) with a mean of $\bar{x}$ (read *x*-bar). Remember that the measures we compute for a sample are called *statistics*.

Characteristics of a population are called parameters

The notation is different when we are computing measures for the entire *population;* that is, for the group containing every element we are describing. The mean of a population is symbolized by μ, which is the Greek letter *mu*. The number of elements in a population is denoted by the capital italic letter N. Generally in statistics, we use Roman letters to symbolize sample information and Greek letters to symbolize population information.

Calculating the mean from ungrouped data

Finding the population and sample means

In the example, the average of 8.8 days would be μ (the population mean) if the population of generators is exactly 10. It would be $\bar{x}$ (the sample mean) if the 10 generators are a sample drawn from a larger population of generators. To write the formulas for these two means, we combine our mathematical symbols and the steps we used to determine the arithmetic mean. If we add the values of the observations and divide this sum by the number of observations, we will get:

population mean   sum of values of all observations

$$\mu = \frac{\Sigma x}{N}$$

number of elements in the population

(3 · 1)

TABLE 3·2 Percentile increase in S.A.T. verbal scores

Student	1	2	3	4	5	6	7
Increase	9	7	7	6	4	4	2

and:

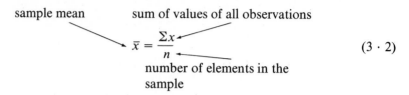

sample mean

sum of values of all observations

$$\bar{x} = \frac{\Sigma x}{n} \qquad\qquad (3 \cdot 2)$$

number of elements in the
sample

Since μ is the *population arithmetic mean*, we use N to indicate that we divide by the number of observations or elements in the population. Similarly, $\bar{x}$ is the *sample arithmetic mean*, and n is the number of observations in the sample. The Greek letter *sigma*, Σ, indicates that all the values of x are summed together.

Another example: Table 3 · 2 lists the percentile increase in S.A.T. verbal scores shown by 7 different students taking an S.A.T. preparatory course.

The data are arrayed in descending order. We assume there are too many students in the course to survey each one. Therefore, we use our sample and compute the mean as follows:

$$\bar{x} = \frac{\Sigma x}{n}$$

$$\left(= \frac{9 + 7 + 7 + 6 + 4 + 4 + 2}{7} \right) \qquad\qquad (3 \cdot 2)$$

$= 5.6$ points per student ← sample mean

*Dealing with
ungrouped data*

Notice that to calculate this mean, we added every observation separately, in no special order. Statisticians call this *ungrouped* data. The computations were not difficult because our sample size was small. But suppose we are dealing with the weight of 5,000 head of cattle and prefer not to add each of our data points separately. Or suppose we have access to only the frequency distribution of the data, not to every individual observation. In these cases, we will need a different way to calculate the arithmetic mean.

Calculating the mean from grouped data

*Dealing with
grouped data*

A frequency distribution consists of data that are grouped by classes. Each value of an observation falls somewhere in one of the classes. Unlike the S.A.T. example, we do not know the separate values of every

TABLE 3·3 Average monthly balances of 600 customers

Class (dollars)	Frequency
0–49.99	78
50.00–99.99	123
100.00–149.99	187
150.00–199.99	82
200.00–249.99	51
250.00–299.99	47
300.00–349.99	13
350.00–399.99	9
400.00–449.99	6
450.00–499.99	4
	600

observation. Suppose we have a frequency distribution (illustrated in Table 3 · 3) of average monthly checking account balances of 600 customers at a branch bank. From the information in this table, we can easily compute an *estimate* of the value of the mean of this grouped data. It is an estimate because we do not use all 600 data points in the sample. Had we used the original, ungrouped data, we could have calculated the actual value of the mean—but only after we had averaged the 600 separate values. For ease of calculation we must give up accuracy.

Estimating the mean

To find the arithmetic mean of grouped data, we first calculate the midpoint of each class (the class mark) using the modified form of Equation 2 · 2. Then we multiply each class mark by the frequency of observations in that class, sum all these results, and divide the sum by the total number of observations in the sample. The formula looks like this:

Calculating the mean

$$\bar{x} = \frac{\Sigma(f \times x)}{n} \qquad (3 \cdot 3)$$

where:

$\bar{x}$ = the sample mean

Σ = the symbol meaning "the sum of"

f = the frequency (number of observations) in each class

x = the class mark for each class in the sample

n = the number of observations in the sample

Table 3 · 4 illustrates how to calculate the arithmetic mean from our grouped data, using Equation 3 · 3.

In our sample of 600 customers, the average monthly checking account balance is $142.25. This is our approximation from the frequency distribution. Notice that since we did not know every data point in the sample, we assumed that every value in a class was equal to its class mark. Our results, then, can only approximate the actual average monthly balance.

TABLE 3·4 Calculation of arithmetic sample mean from grouped data in Table 3 · 3

Class (dollars) (1)	Class marks (x) (2)		Frequency (f) (3)		$f \times x$ $(3) \times (2)$
0– 49.99	25.00	×	78	=	1,950
50.00– 99.99	75.00	×	123	=	9,225
100.00–149.99	125.00	×	187	=	23,375
150.00–199.99	175.00	×	82	=	14,350
200.00–249.99	225.00	×	51	=	11,475
250.00–299.99	275.00	×	47	=	12,925
300.00–349.99	325.00	×	13	=	4,225
350.00–399.99	375.00	×	9	=	3,375
400.00–449.99	425.00	×	6	=	2,550
450.00–499.99	475.00	×	4	=	1,900
		$\Sigma f = n =$	600		$85,350 \leftarrow \Sigma(f \times x)$

$$\bar{x} = \frac{\Sigma(f \times x)}{n} = \frac{85,350}{600} = 142.25 \leftarrow \text{sample mean (dollars)} \qquad (3 \cdot 3)$$

Comparing the estimated mean with the actual mean

Let's compare an approximate mean calculated from grouped data with an actual mean compiled from ungrouped data. Consider the example presented in Tables 3 · 5 and 3 · 6 recording the annual snowfall (in inches) over 20 years in Harlan, Kentucky. If we use ungrouped data, the average annual snowfall can be verified to be 21.65 inches. If we use grouped data, the estimated average is 21.5. The difference is small. And when the number of observations is large, you will appreciate the convenience offered by using grouped data.

TABLE 3·5 Annual snowfall in Harlan, Kentucky

Year	1962	63	64	65	66	67	68	69	70	71
Snowfall (inches)	23	8	14	31	5	26	11	27	32	46

Year	1972	73	74	75	76	77	78	79	80	81
Snowfall (inches)	12	28	8	36	16	9	42	30	7	22

TABLE 3·6 Annual snowfall in Harlan, Kentucky

Class (grouped data) (1)	Class mark (x) (2)		Frequency (f) (3)		$f \times x$ $(3) \times (2)$
0– 7	3.5	×	2	=	7.0
8–15	11.5	×	6	=	69.0
16–23	19.5	×	3	=	58.5
24–31	27.5	×	5	=	137.5
32–39	35.5	×	2	=	71.0
40–47	43.5	×	2	=	87.0
					$430.0 \leftarrow \Sigma(f \times x)$

$$\bar{x} = \frac{\Sigma(f \times x)}{n} = \frac{430}{20} = 21.5 \leftarrow \text{average annual snowfall} \qquad (3 \cdot 3)$$

Coding

We can further simplify our calculation of the mean from grouped data. Using a technique called *coding*, we eliminate the problem of large or inconvenient class marks. Instead of using the actual class marks to perform our calculations, we can assign small-value consecutive integers (whole numbers) called *codes* to each of the class marks. The integer zero can be assigned anywhere, but to keep the integers small, we will assign zero to the class mark in the *middle* (or the one nearest to the middle) of the frequency distribution. Then we can assign negative integers to values smaller than that class mark and positive integers to those larger, as follows:

Class	1–5	6–10	11–15	16–20	21–25	26–30	31–35	36–40	41–45
Code (u)	-4	-3	-2	-1	0	1	2	3	4

$$\uparrow$$
$$x_0$$

Symbolically, statisticians use x_0 to represent the class mark that is assigned the code 0 and u for the coded class marks. The following formula is used to determine the sample mean using codes:

$$\bar{x} = x_0 + w\frac{\Sigma(u \times f)}{n} \qquad (3 \cdot 4)$$

where:

$\bar{x}$ = mean of sample

x_0 = value of the class mark assigned the code 0

w = numerical width of the class interval

u = code assigned to each class

f = frequency or number of observations in each class

n = total number of observations in the sample

Keep in mind that $\Sigma(u \times f)$ simply means that we (1) multiply u by f for every class in the frequency distribution and (2) sum all of these products. Table $3 \cdot 7$ illustrates how to code the class marks and find the sample mean. The result is the same as it was when we calculated the mean from grouped data without coding (illustrated in Table $3 \cdot 6$).

Advantages and disadvantages of the arithmetic mean

The arithmetic mean, as a single number representing a whole data set, has important advantages. First, its concept is familiar to most people

TABLE 3·7 Annual snowfall in Harlan, Kentucky

Class (1)	Class mark (x) (2)	Code (u) (3)		Frequency (f) (4)		u × f (3) × (4)
0–7	3.5	−2	×	2	=	−4
8–15	11.5	−1	×	6	=	−6
16–23	19.5 ← x_0	0	×	3	=	0
24–31	27.5	1	×	5	=	5
32–39	35.5	2	×	2	=	4
40–47	43.5	3	×	2	=	6
				$\Sigma f = n = 20$		$5 \leftarrow \Sigma(u \times f)$

$$\bar{x} = x_0 + w\frac{\Sigma(u \times f)}{n} = 19.5 + (8)\left(\frac{5}{20}\right) = 21.5 \leftarrow \text{average annual snowfall} \qquad (3 \cdot 4)$$

and intuitively clear. Second, every data set has a mean. It is a measure that can be calculated, and it is unique because every data set has one and only one mean. Finally, the mean is useful for performing statistical procedures such as comparing the means from several data sets (a procedure we will carry out in Chapter 9).

Disadvantages of the mean

Yet, like any statistical measure, the arithmetic mean has disadvantages of which we must be aware. First, while the mean is reliable in that it reflects all the values in the data set, it may also be affected by extreme values that are not representative of the rest of the data.

A second problem with the mean is the same one we encountered with our 600 checking account balances: it is tedious to compute the mean because we *do* use every data point in our calculation (unless, of course, we take the shortcut method of using grouped data to approximate the mean).

The third disadvantage is that we are unable to compute the mean for a data set that has open-ended classes at either the high or low end of the scale.

━━━━━━━━━━━━━━━━━━━ **EXERCISES** ━━━━━━━━━━━━━━━━━━━

3·4 Using the following set of data:
  a) Construct a frequency distribution using intervals 35–44, etc.
  b) Compute the sample mean from the raw data.
  c) Compute the sample mean from the frequency distribution.
  d) Compare parts b and c.

95	76	72	67	69	48	37	76	74	60
78	80	48	86	59	68	73	77	51	82
94	95	48	58	75	69	55	51	89	91
89	93	69	81	68	49	86	74	79	100

3·5 From the frequency distribution below:
a) Compute the sample mean, using the class mark method.
b) Compute the sample mean, using the coding method and assigning 0 to the fourth class.
c) Compute the sample mean, using the coding method and assigning 0 to the sixth class.
d) Verify that the answers to parts a, b, and c are equal.

Class	Frequency	Class	Frequency
10.0–10.9	2	15.0–15.9	10
11.0–11.9	3	16.0–16.9	9
12.0–12.9	5	17.0–17.9	6
13.0–13.9	7	18.0–18.9	8
14.0–14.9	12	19.0–19.9	2

3·6 Davis Furniture Company has a revolving credit agreement with the First National Bank. The loan showed the following ending monthly balances last year:

Jan.	$75,800	Apr.	$45,500	July	$36,700	Oct.	$33,000
Feb.	$70,100	May	$45,500	Aug.	$38,200	Nov.	$30,750
Mar.	$45,500	June	$35,800	Sept.	$31,500	Dec.	$28,800

What was the mean monthly balance for the loan last year?

3·7 National Tire Company holds reserve funds in short-term marketable securities. The ending daily balance (in millions) of the marketable securities account for 2 weeks is shown below:

Week 1	$1.973	$1.970	$1.972	$1.975	$1.976
Week 2	1.969	1.892	1.893	1.887	1.895

What was the average (mean) amount invested in marketable securities during (a) the first week? (b) the second week? (c) the 2-week period?

---

3 A SECOND MEASURE OF CENTRAL TENDENCY: THE WEIGHTED MEAN

A weighted mean

The weighted mean enables us to calculate an average that takes into account the importance of each value to the overall total. Consider, for example, the company in Table 3 · 8, which uses three grades of labor—unskilled, semiskilled, and skilled—to produce two end products. Using Equation 3 · 2, we would calculate the arithmetic mean of the hourly wage rates to be ($4 + $6 + $8)/3 = $6 per hour.

TABLE 3·8 Labor input in manufacturing process

		Labor hours per unit of output	
Grade of labor	Hourly wage (x)	Product 1	Product 2
Unskilled	$4.00	1	4
Semiskilled	6.00	2	3
Skilled	8.00	5	3

Using this average rate, we would compute the labor cost of one unit of product 1 to be $6(1 + 2 + 5) = 48, and of one unit of product 2 to be $6(4 + 3 + 3) = 60. But these answers are incorrect because we did not take into account the fact that different amounts of each grade of labor are used. To calculate the correct average cost per hour for the two products, we must take a *weighted average* of the cost of the three grades of labor, by weighting the hourly wage for each grade by its proportion of the total labor required to produce the product.

Symbolically, the formula for calculating the weighted mean is:

$$\bar{x}_w = \frac{\Sigma(w \times x)}{\Sigma w} \qquad (3 \cdot 5)$$

where:

$\bar{x}_w$ = symbol for the weighted mean*

w = weight assigned to each observation $\left(\frac{1}{8}, \frac{2}{8}, \text{ and } \frac{5}{8}\right.$

for product 1 in our example).

$\Sigma(w \times x)$ = sum of the weight of each element times that element

Σw = sum of all the weights

If we apply Equation $3 \cdot 5$ to product 1 in our labor cost example, we find:

$$\bar{x}_w = \frac{\Sigma(w \times x)}{\Sigma w}$$

$$= \frac{\left(\frac{1}{8} \times \$4\right) + \left(\frac{2}{8} \times \$6\right) + \left(\frac{5}{8} \times \$8\right)}{\frac{1}{8} + \frac{2}{8} + \frac{5}{8}} \qquad (3 \cdot 5)$$

$$= \$7.00/\text{hour}$$

Notice that Equation $3 \cdot 5$ states more formally something we have done previously. When we calculated the arithmetic mean from grouped data (page 38), we actually found a weighted mean, using the class marks for the x values and the frequencies of each class as the weights. We divided this product by the sum of all the frequencies, which is the same as dividing by the sum of all the weights.

In like manner, *any* mean computed from all the values in a data set according to Equation $3 \cdot 1$ or $3 \cdot 2$ is really a weighted average of the components of the data set. What those components are, of course, determines what the mean measures. In a factory, for example, we could determine the weighted mean of all the wages (skilled, semiskilled, and unskilled), or of the wages of men workers, women workers, or union and nonunion members.

*The symbol $\bar{x}_w$ is read *x-bar sub w*. The lowercase w is called a subscript and is a reminder that this is not an ordinary mean but one that is weighted according to the relative importance of the values of x.

3·8 A professor has decided to use a weighted average in figuring final grades for his seminar students. The homework average will count for 30 percent of a student's grade; the midterm, 20 percent; the final, 25 percent; the term paper, 15 percent; and quizzes, 10 percent. From the data below, compute the final average for the five students in the seminar.

Student	Homework	Quizes	Paper	Midterm	Final
1	85	89	94	87	90
2	78	84	88	91	92
3	94	88	93	86	89
4	82	79	88	84	93
5	95	90	92	82	88

3·9 Given the following prices and the number of each item sold, find the average price of the items sold.

Price	$1.29	$2.95	$3.49	$5.00	$7.50	$10.95
Number sold	7	9	12	8	6	3

3·10 Keyes Home Furnishings ran six local newspaper advertisements during December. The following frequency distribution resulted:

Number of times subscriber saw ad during December	0	1	2	3	4	5	6
Frequency	998	983	1,417	727	294	236	210

What is the average number of times a subscriber saw a Keyes advertisement during December?

---

4 A THIRD MEASURE OF CENTRAL TENDENCY: THE MEDIAN

Median defined

The median is a measure of central tendency different from either of the means we have discussed so far. The median is a single value from the data set that measures the central item in the data. This single item is the *middlemost* or *most central* item in the set of numbers. Half of the items lie above this point, and the other half lie below it.

Calculating the median from ungrouped data

Finding the median of ungrouped data

To find the median of a data set, first array the data in ascending or descending order. If the data set contains an *odd* number of items, the middle item of the array is the median. If there is an *even* number of items, the median is the average of the two middle items. In formal language, the median is:

number of items in the array

$$\text{Median} = \left(\frac{n+1}{2}\right)\text{th item in a data array}$$ (3 · 6)

An odd number of items

Suppose we wish to find the median of 7 items in a data array. According to Equation 3 · 6, the median is the $(7 + 1)/2 = 4$th item in the array. If we apply this to the times for 7 members of a track team given in Table 3 · 9, we discover that the fourth element in the array is 4.8 minutes. This is the median time for the track team. Notice that the median is *not* distorted by the presence of the last value (9.0). This value could have been 16.0 or even 45.4 minutes, and the median would have been the same! However, the mean behaves very differently. The mean of the times in Table 3 · 9 is 5.3 minutes. If the last value were 16.0, the mean would be 6.3 minutes; and if the last value were 45.4, the mean would be 10.5 minutes. Although the median is not affected by extreme values that are not representative of the rest of the data, the mean *is* distorted by such values.

Median not distorted by extreme values

Now let's calculate the median for an array with an even number of items. Consider the data shown in Table 3 · 10 concerning the number of patients treated daily in the emergency room of a hospital. The data are arrayed in descending order. The median of this data set would be:

An even number of items

$$\text{Median} = \left(\frac{n+1}{2}\right)\text{th item in a data array}$$

$$= \frac{8+1}{2}$$ (3 · 6)

$$= 4.5\text{th item}$$

Finding the median

Since the median is the 4.5th element in the array, we need to average the fourth and fifth elements. The fourth element in Table 3 · 10 is 43, and

TABLE 3 · 9 Times for track team members

Item in data array	1	2	3	4	5	6	7
Time (minutes)	4.2	4.3	4.7	4.8	5.0	5.1	9.0
				↑			
				median			

TABLE 3 · 10 Patients treated in emergency room on 8 consecutive days

Item in data array	1	2	3	4	5	6	7	8
Number of patients	86	52	49	43	35	31	30	11
				↑				
			median of 39					

the fifth is 35. The average of these two elements is equal to (43 + 35)/2, or 39. Therefore, 39 is the median number of patients treated in the emergency room per day during the 8-day period.

Calculating the median from grouped data

Finding the median of grouped data

Often, we have access to data only after it has been grouped in a frequency distribution. We do not, for example, know every observation that led to the construction of Table 3 · 11, the data on 600 bank customers originally introduced earlier. Instead, we have 10 class intervals and a record of the frequency with which the observations appear in each of the intervals.

Locate the median class

Nevertheless, we can compute the median checking account balance of these 600 customers by determining which of the 10 class intervals *contains* the median. We now assume that the observations in this median class are evenly spaced. This gives us the following formula to compute the median.

$$\text{sample median} \rightarrow \tilde{m} = \left(\frac{(n + 1)/2 - (F + 1)}{f_m} \right) w + L_m \quad (3 \cdot 7)$$

where:

$\tilde{m}$ = sample median

n = total number of items in the distribution

F = sum of all the class frequencies *up to*, but *not including*, the median class

f_m = frequency of the median class

w = class interval width

L_m = lower limit of the median class interval

TABLE 3 · 11   Average monthly balances for 600 customers

Class in dollars	Frequency
0– 49.99	78
50.00– 99.99	123
100.00–149.99	187 ← median class
150.00–199.99	82
200.00–249.99	51
250.00–299.99	47
300.00–349.99	13
350.00–399.99	9
400.00–449.99	6
450.00–499.99	4
	600

If we use Equation 3 · 7 to compute the median of our sample of checking account balances, then $n = 600$, $F = 201$, $f_m = 187$, $w = \$50$, and $L_m = \$100$.

$$\tilde{m} = \left(\frac{(n+1)/2 - (F+1)}{f_m} \right) w + L_m$$

$$= \left(\frac{601/2 - 202}{187} \right) \$50 + \$100 \qquad (3 \cdot 7)$$

$$= \$126.35 \leftarrow \text{estimated sample median}$$

Advantages and disadvantages of the median

Advantages of the median

The median has several advantages over the mean. The most important, demonstrated in our track team example in Table 3 · 9, is that extreme values do not affect the median as strongly as they do the mean. The median is easy to understand and can be calculated from any kind of data *unless* the median falls into an open-ended class.

We can find the median even when our data are qualitative descriptions like color or sharpness, rather than numbers. Suppose, for example, we have 5 runs of a printing press, the results from which must be rated according to sharpness of the image. We can array the results from best to worst: extremely sharp, very sharp, sharp, slightly blurred, and very blurred. The median of the 5 ratings is the $(5 + 1)/2$, or third rating (sharp).

Disadvantages of the median

The median has some disadvantages as well. Certain statistical procedures that use the median are more complex than those that use the mean. Also, because the median is an average of position, we must array the data before we can perform any calculations. This is time consuming for any data set with a large number of elements. Therefore, if we want to use a sample statistic as an estimate of a population location parameter, the mean is easier to use than the median. In Chapter 8 we will discuss estimation in detail.

EXERCISES

3·11 Find the median of the following set of data:

1.08	.98	.97	1.10	1.03	1.13	1.07	1.24	.99	1.13
.99	1.43	1.18	1.02	1.12	1.17	.98	1.28	.98	1.09

3·12 For the frequency distribution below, determine
    a) which is the median class
    b) which number item represents the median item
    c) the width of the equal steps in the median class

d) the estimated value of the median for these data

Class	Frequency	Class	Frequency
100–149.5	12	300–349.5	72
150–199.5	14	350–399.5	63
200–249.5	27	400–449.5	36
250–299.5	58	450–499.5	18

3·13 For the following data, calculate an estimate of the median using Equation 3 · 7:

Class	0–24.9	25–49.9	50–74.9	75–99.9	100–124.9	125–149.9
Frequency	6	11	14	16	13	10

3·14 Calculate the median for the data given in the following table.

Minutes for bus ride from O'Hare Airport to John Hancock Center

15	15	16	16	17	17	17	18	18	18
18	18	18	18	19	20	20	21	22	25
26	27	27	27	27	27	28	28	29	29
30	30	31	31	33	33	33	34	34	34
34	34	34	34	35	35	35	35	35	36
37	38	40	43	49	50	51	53	58	64

---

5 A FINAL MEASURE OF CENTRAL TENDENCY: THE MODE

Mode defined

The mode is a measure of central tendency that is different from the mean but somewhat like the median because it is not actually calculated by the ordinary processes of arithmetic. The mode is *that value that is repeated most often in the data set.*

Limited use of mode of ungrouped data

As in every other aspect of life, chance can play a role in the arrangement of data. Sometimes chance causes a single unrepresentative item to be repeated often enough to be the most frequent value in the data set. For this reason, we rarely use the mode of ungrouped data as a measure of central tendency. Table 3 · 12, for example, shows the number of delivery trips per day made by a redi-mix concrete plant. The modal value is 15 because it occurs more often than any other value (three times). A mode of 15 implies that the plant activity is higher than

TABLE 3 · 12   Delivery trips per day in one 20-day period

Trips arrayed in ascending order					
0	2	5	7	15	
0	2	5	7	15	← mode
1	4	6	8	15	
1	4	6	12	19	

TABLE 3·13   Frequency distribution of delivery trips

Class in number of trips	0–3	4–7	8–11	12 and more
Frequency	6	8	1	5
		↑		
		modal class		

6.7 (6.7 is the answer we'd get if we calculated the mean). The mode tells us that 15 is the most frequent number of trips, but it fails to let us know that most of the values are under 10.

Now let's group these data into a frequency distribution, as we have done in Table 3 · 13. If we select the class with the most observations, which we can call the *modal class*, we would choose "4–7" trips. This class is more representative of the activity of the plant than is the mode of 15 trips per day. For this reason, whenever we use the mode as a measure of the central tendency of a data set, we should calculate the mode from grouped data.

The mode in symmetrical and skewed distributions

Let's study Figs. 3 · 4 through 3 · 6, each of which shows a frequency distribution. Figure 3 · 4 is symmetrical, Fig. 3 · 5 is skewed to the right, and Fig. 3 · 6 is skewed to the left.

In Fig. 3 · 4, where the distribution is symmetrical and there is only one mode, the three measures of central tendency—the mode, median, and mean—coincide with the highest point on the graph. In Fig. 3 · 5, the data set is skewed to the right. Here, the mode is still at the highest

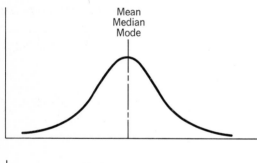

Figure 3·4   Symmetrical distribution, showing that the mean, median, and mode coincide

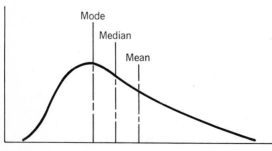

Figure 3·5   Distribution is skewed to the right

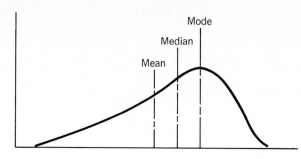

Figure 3·6 Distribution is skewed to the left

point on the graph, but the median lies to the right of this point and the mean falls to the right of the median. When the distribution is skewed to the left as in Fig. 3 · 6, the mode is at the highest point on the graph, the median lies to the left of the mode, and the mean falls to the left of the median. No matter what the shape of the curve, the mode is always located at the highest point.

Calculating the mode from grouped data

Finding the mode in the modal class

When our data are already grouped in a frequency distribution, we must assume that the mode is located in the class with the most items; that is, with the highest frequency. To determine a single value for the mode from this modal class, we use Equation 3 · 8:

$$\text{mode} \searrow \quad Mo = L_{Mo} + \frac{d_1}{d_1 + d_2} w \qquad (3 \cdot 8)$$

where:

L_{Mo} = lower limit of the modal class

d_1 = frequency of the modal class minus the frequency of the class *directly below it*

d_2 = frequency of the modal class minus the frequency of the class *directly above it*

w = width of the modal class interval

If we use Equation 3 · 8 to compute the mode of our checking account balances given in Table 3 · 11 on page 47, then L_{Mo} = $100, d_1 = 187 − 123 = 64, d_2 = 187 − 82 = 105, and w = $50.

$$Mo = L_{Mo} + \frac{d_1}{d_1 + d_2} w$$

$$= \$100 + \frac{64}{64 + 105} \$50 \qquad (3 \cdot 8)$$

$$= \$119.0 \leftarrow \text{Mode}$$

Multimodal distributions

When we have two different values that each appear more than any other values in the data set, the distribution has two modes and is called a

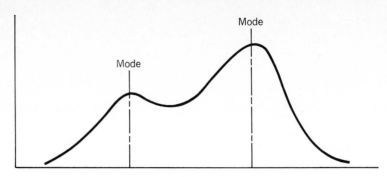

Figure 3·7 Bimodal distribution with two unequal modes

bimodal distribution. Figure 3 · 7 illustrates a bimodal distribution with two unequal modes.

Advantages and disadvantages of the mode

Advantages of the mode

The mode, like the median, can be used as a central location for qualitative as well as quantitative data. If a printing press turns out 5 impressions, which we rate "very sharp," "sharp," "sharp," "sharp," and "blurred," then the modal value is "sharp."

Also like the median the mode is not unduly affected by extreme values. Even if the high values are very high and the low values very low, we choose the most frequent value of the data set to be the modal value. We can use the mode no matter how large, how small, or how spread out the values in the data set happen to be.

A third advantage of the mode is that we can use it even when one or more of the classes are open-ended.

Disadvantages of the mode

Despite these advantages, the mode is not used as often to measure central tendency as are the mean and median. Too often, there is no modal value because the data set contains no values that are repeated more than once. Other times, every value is the mode because every value occurs the same number of times. Clearly, the mode is a useless measure in these cases. Another disadvantage is that when data sets contain two, three, or many modes, they are difficult to interpret and compare.

EXERCISES

3·15 Find:

a) the modal class for the following data set:

Class	20–23	24–27	28–31	32–35	36–39	40–43	44–47
Frequency	3	4	7	15	12	6	2

b) the mode of the following sample: 5, 8, 11, 9, 8, 6, 8, 7, 12, 8, 7, 7, 11, 8, 6, 10, 13, 7, 8

3·16 Estimate the modal value of the following distribution by using Equation 3 · 8.

Class	48–51.9	52–55.9	56–59.9	60–63.9	64–67.9	68–71.9	72–75.9
Frequency	2	8	20	32	56	28	4

3·17 For the following data:
a) Find the mode of the data.
b) Construct a frequency distribution with intervals 10–14.9, 15–19.9, etc.
c) Estimate the modal value using Equation 3 · 8.
d) Compare parts a and c.

19	15	14	11	20	13	17	24	12	20
13	19	25	15	19	20	15	12	13	16
18	16	15	26	21	11	19	20	11	24
16	16	17	18	16	11	10	27	18	13

---

6 COMPARING THE MEAN, MEDIAN, AND MODE

Mean, median, and mode are identical in symmetrical distribution

When we work statistical problems, we must decide whether to use the mean, the median, or the mode as the measure of central tendency. Symmetrical distributions that contain only one mode always have the same value for the mean, the median, and the mode, as we illustrated in Fig. 3 · 4. In these cases, we need not choose the measure of central tendency because the choice has been made for us.

In a positively skewed distribution (one skewed to the right, such as the one in Fig. 3 · 5), the values are concentrated at the left end of the horizontal axis. Here, the mode is at the highest point of the distribution; the median is to the right of that; and the mean is to the right of both the mode and the median. In a negatively skewed distribution, such as in Fig. 3 · 6, the values are concentrated at the right end of the horizontal axis. The mode is at the highest point of the distribution, and the median is to the left of that. The mean is to the left of both the mode and the median.

The median may be best in skewed distributions

When the population is skewed negatively or positively, the median is often the best measure of location because it is always between the mean and the mode. The median is not as highly influenced by the frequency of occurrence of a single value as is the mode, nor is it pulled by the extreme values as is the mean.

Otherwise, there are no universal guidelines for applying the mean, median, or mode as the measure of central tendency for different populations. Each case must be judged independently, according to the guidelines we have discussed.

EXERCISES

3·18 For which type of distribution (positively skewed, negatively skewed, or symmetric) is
    a) the mean less than the median?
    b) the mode less than the mean?
    c) the median less than the mode?

3·19 When the distribution of data is symmetrical and bell-shaped, selection of a measure of location is considerably simplified. Why?

7 TERMS INTRODUCED IN CHAPTER 3

bimodal distribution A distribution of data points in which two values occur more frequently than the rest of the values in the data set.

coding A method of calculating the mean for grouped data by recoding values of class marks to more simple values.

kurtosis The degree of peakedness of a distribution of points.

mean A central tendency measure representing the arithmetic average of a set of observations.

measure of central tendency A measure indicating the value to be expected of a typical or middle data point.

measure of dispersion A measure describing how scattered or spread out the observations in a data set are.

median The middle point of a data set, a measure of location that divides the data set into halves.

median class The class in a frequency distribution that contains the median value for a data set.

mode The value most often repeated in the data set. It is represented by the highest point in the distribution curve of a data set.

parameters Numerical values that describe the characteristics of a whole populations, commonly represented by Greek letters.

skewness The extent to which a distribution of data points is concentrated at one end or the other; the lack of symmetry.

statistics Numerical measures describing the characteristics of a sample.

summary statistics Single numbers that describe certain characteristics of a data set.

symmetrical A characteristic of a distribution in which each half is the mirror image of the other half.

weighted mean An average calculated to take into account the importance of each value to the overall total; i.e., an average in which each observation value is weighted by some index of its importance.

8 EQUATIONS INTRODUCED IN CHAPTER 3

p. 37
$$\mu = \frac{\Sigma x}{N}$$
3·1

The *population arithmetic mean* is equal to the sum of the values of all the elements in the population (Σx) divided by the number of elements in the population (N).

p. 38
$$\bar{x} = \frac{\Sigma x}{n}$$
3·2

To derive the *sample arithmetic mean*, sum the values of all the elements in the sample (Σx) and divide by the number of elements in the sample (n).

p. 39
$$\bar{x} = \frac{\Sigma(f \times x)}{n}$$
3·3

To find the *sample arithmetic mean of grouped data*, calculate the class marks (x) for each class in the sample. Then multiply each class mark by the frequency (f) of observations in that class, sum (Σ) all these results, and divide by the total number of observations in the sample (n).

p. 41
$$\bar{x} = x_0 + w\frac{\Sigma(u \times f)}{n}$$
3·4

This formula enables us to calculate the *sample arithmetic mean of grouped data* using codes to eliminate dealing with large or inconvenient class marks. Assign these codes (u) as follows: give the value of zero to the middle class mark (called x_0), positive consecutive integers to class marks larger than x_0, and negative consecutive integers to smaller class marks. Then, multiply the code assigned to each class (u) by the frequency (f) of observations in each class and sum (Σ) all of these products. Divide this result by the total number of observations in the sample (n), multiply by the numerical width of the class interval (w), and add the value of the class mark assigned the code zero (x_0).

p. 44
$$\bar{x}_w = \frac{\Sigma(w \times x)}{\Sigma w}$$
3·5

The *weighted mean*, $\bar{x}_w$, is an average that takes into account how important each value is to the overall total. We can calculate this average by multiplying the weight, or proportion, of each element (w) times that element (x), summing the results (Σ), and dividing this amount by the sum of all the weights (Σw).

p. 46
$$\text{Median} = \left(\frac{n+1}{2}\right)\text{th item in a data array}$$
3·6
$$\text{where: } n = \text{number of items in the data array}$$

The *median* is a single value that measures the central item in the data set. Half the items lie above the median, half below it. If the data set contains an odd number of items, the middle item of the array is the median. For an even number of items, the median is the average of the two middle items. Use this formula when the data are ungrouped.

p. 47
$$\tilde{m} = \left(\frac{(n+1)/2 - (F+1)}{f_m}\right)w + L_m$$
3·7

This formula enables us to find the *sample median of grouped data*. In it, n equals the total number of items in the distribution; F equals the sum of all the class frequencies up to, but not including, the median class; f_m is the frequency of observations in the median class; w is the class interval width; and L_m is the lower limit of the median class interval.

p. 51
$$Mo = L_{Mo} + \frac{d_1}{d_1 + d_2}w$$
3·8

The *mode* is that value most often repeated in the data set. To find the *mode of grouped data* (symbolized Mo), use this formula and let L_{Mo} = the lower limit of the modal class; d_1 = the frequency of the modal class minus the frequency of the class directly below it; d_2 = the frequency of the modal class minus the frequency of the class directly above it; and w = the width of the modal class interval.

3·20 The gross displacement of each ship utilizing the Panama Canal during a one-week period was compiled into the frequency distribution below.

Gross displacement (thousands of tons)	0–2.99	3–5.99	6–8.99	9–11.99	12–14.99	15–17.99	18–20.99
Frequency	30	47	69	32	18	3	1

a) Compute the sample mean of this data, using Equation 3 · 3.
b) Verify that you get the same result using the coding method.

3·21 From the data below, find the average age of the participants at a state sports meet:

Age	13	14	15	16	17	18	19	20	21	22	23	24	25
Frequency	25	48	62	81	105	75	54	40	63	32	24	22	19

3·22 The following table gives the distribution of miles per gallon (mpg) ratings for the engines produced by one Detroit automobile manufacturer:

MPG	10–12.99	13–15.99	16–18.99	19–21.99	22–24.99	25–27.99	28–30.99
Relative frequency	.05	.10	.20	.30	.25	.05	.05

What is the mean value for the engines tested?

3·23 Which measure of central tendency would you recommend to represent the following distributions?

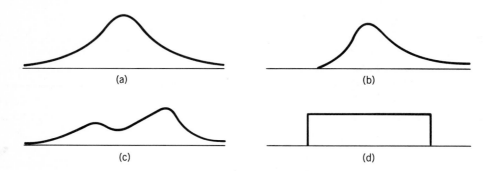

(a)   (b)

(c)   (d)

3·24 United Food Services operates four cafeterias within area manufacturing plants. The cafeterias are similar in terms of layout, equipment, and menu. During the past year, the average customer capacity per cafeteria was 420 people. This year, by adding employees and tables, two of the cafeterias increased their capacity by 10 percent, which made all four cafeterias equal in customer capacity. What capacities did the four cafeterias have before the increase?

3·25 The table below gives the relative distribution of sales calls made on Bancroft Pharmaceuticals' active accounts in the past month.

Number of sales calls	0	1	2	3	4	5 or more
Relative frequency	.21	.18	.38	.19	.03	.01

What is the mode of the distribution?

3·26 The weights of a sample of packages shipped by air freight are given in the following distribution:

Weight (lbs)	0–9.99	10.0–19.99	20.0–29.99	30.0–39.99	40.0–49.99	50.0 and above
Frequency	28	25	14	8	4	1

What is the median?

3·27 A survey of 20 households concerning the quality of a particular TV program yielded the following distribution of ratings, with positive numbers indicating a favorable rating and negative numbers (denoted in parentheses) indicating an unfavorable one:

Quality rating	(30.0)–(20.1)	(20.0)–(10.1)	(10.0)–(0.1)	0.0–9.9	10.0–19.9	20.0–29.9
Frequency	3	7	5	2	2	1

Use the coding method to find the average rating given to the TV program.

3·28 The operations manager of a digital watch manufacturer is considering switching from a batch production process to a continuous assembly line. To help him make a decision, he conducts a stopwatch study of the batch process. From the data he gathered, the following frequency distribution of total production time for one watch resulted:

Production time (min)	Frequency	Production time (min)	Frequency
5.00 and below	15	7.51–8.00	58
5.01–5.50	21	8.01–8.50	63
5.51–6.00	38	8.51–9.00	27
6.01–6.50	39	9.01–9.50	21
6.51–7.00	45	9.51–10.00	19
7.01–7.50	51	Above 10.00	14

Determine the median.

3·29 Suppose that the distributions illustrated in Fig. 3 · 1 represent the heat output distributions from 3 types of solar furnaces.
a) On average, which furnace produces the most heat?
b) Is it possible for all three types to have the same heat output?
c) Is it possible for type A to have a greater output than type B?

─────────────── *10 CHAPTER CONCEPTS TEST* ───────────────

Answers are in the back of the book.

T F 1. The value of every observation in the data set is taken into account when we calculate its median.

T F 2. When the population is either negatively or positively skewed, it is often preferable to use the median as the best measure of location because it always lies between the mean and the mode.

T F 3. Measures of central tendency in a data set refer to the extent to which the observations are scattered.

T F 4. A measure of the peakedness of a distribution curve is its skewness.

T F 5. With ungrouped data, the mode is most frequently used as the measure of central tendency.

T F 6. If we arrange the observations in a data set from highest to lowest, the data point lying in the middle is the median of the data set.

T F 7. When working with grouped data, we may compute an approximate mean by assuming each value in a given class is equal to its class mark.

T F 8. The value most often repeated in a data set is called the arithmetic mean.

T F 9. If the curve of a certain distribution tails off toward the left end of the measuring scale on the horizontal axis, the distribution is said to be negatively skewed.

T F 10. After grouping a set of data into a number of classes, we may identify the median class as being the one that has the largest number of observations.

T F 11. A mean calculated from grouped data always gives a good estimate of the true value, although it is seldom exact.

T F 12. We can compute a mean for any data set, once we are given its frequency distribution.

T F 13. The mode is always found at the highest point of a graph of a data distribution.

T F 14. The number of elements in a population is denoted by n.

T F 15. For a data array with 50 observations, the median will be the value of the 25th observation in the array.

16. If a group of data has only one mode and its value is less than that of the mean, it can be concluded that the graph of the distribution is:
a) symmetrical   c) skewed to the right
b) skewed to the left   d) bimodal

17. For a skewed distribution, the best measure of central tendency to report is (choose one):
a) the mean   c) depends on the direction of skewness
b) the median   d) the mode

18. What is the major assumption we make when computing a mean from grouped data?
a) All values are discrete.
b) Every value in a class is equal to the class mark.
c) No value occurs more than once.
d) Each class contains exactly the same number of values.

19. Which of the following statements is NOT correct?
a) Some data sets do not have means.
b) Calculation of a mean is affected by extreme data values.
c) A weighted mean should be used when it is necessary to take the importance of each value into account.
d) All of the above statements are correct.

20. Which of the following is the first step in calculating the median of a data set?
a) Average the middle two values of the data set.
b) Array the data.
c) Determine the relative weights of the data values in terms of importance.
d) None of the above.

21. Which of the following is NOT an advantage of using a median?
a) Extreme values affect the median less strongly than they do the mean.
b) A median can be calculated for qualitative descriptions.

c) The median can be calculated for every set of data, even for all sets containing open-ended classes.

d) The median is easy to understand.

e) All of the above are advantages of using a median.

22. Why is it usually better to calculate a mode from grouped, rather than ungrouped, data?

a) The ungrouped data tend to be bimodal.

b) The mode for the grouped data will be the same, regardless of the skewness of the distribution.

c) Extreme values have less effect on grouped data.

d) The chance of an unrepresentative value being chosen as the mode is reduced.

23. In which of these cases would the mode be most useful as an indicator of central tendency?

a) Every value in a data set occurs exactly once.

b) All but three values in a data set occur once; three values occur 100 times each.

c) All values in a data set occur 100 times each.

d) Every observation in a data set has the same value.

24. Which of the following is an example of a parameter?

a) $\bar{x}$

b) n

c) μ

d) all of the above

e) b and c but not a

25. Which of the following is NOT a measure of central tendency?

a) weighted mean

b) median

c) mode

d) arithmetic mean

e) All of the above are measures of central tendency.

26. If a curve can be divided into two equal parts which are mirror images, it is _____ _____ . If it cannot be divided in this way, it is _____ .

27. The symbol $\bar{x}$ denotes the mean of a _____ . μ denotes the mean of a _____ .

28. Assigning small-value consecutive integers to class marks during calculation of the mean is called _____ .

29. One _____ of using the mean as a measure of central tendency is that it is distorted by _____ values which are not representative of the rest of the data.

30. If two values in a group of data occur more often than any others, the distribution of the data is said to be _____ .

Measuring Variability

4

The vice-president of marketing of a fast-food chain is studying the sales performance of the 100 stores in his eastern district and has compiled this frequency distribution of annual sales.

Sales (000's)	Frequency	Sales (000's)	Frequency
700 – 799	4	1300 – 1399	13
800 – 899	7	1400 – 1499	10
900 – 999	8	1500 – 1599	9
1000 – 1099	10	1600 – 1699	7
1100 – 1199	12	1700 – 1799	2
1200 – 1299	17	1800 – 1899	1

The vice-president would like to compare the eastern district with the other 3 districts in the country. To do so, he will summarize the distribution, but with an eye toward getting more information than just a measure of central tendency. This chapter discusses how he can measure the variability in a distribution and thus get a much better feel for the data.

Chapter 4 finishes our study of descriptive statistics by looking at methods that enable us to measure the tendency of a group of data to spread out, or disperse. Suppose an airline requires that its pilots be, on the average, 6 feet tall, and you recruit a 4-foot person and an 8-foot person to apply for jobs. You would not get much praise for your efforts, even though these two unusual persons do average 6 feet. Instead, the airline is likely to reject both of your candidates because their heights are too far from the desired average. In this situation, the 6-foot average is an inadequate summary description of your two candidates. Chapter 4 provides better descriptions of variability.

1 MEASURES OF DISPERSION

Need to measure dispersion or variability

In Chapter 3, we learned that two sets of data can have the same central location and yet be very different if one is more spread out than the other. This is true of the three distributions in Fig. 4 · 1. The mean of all three curves is the same, but curve A has less spread (or *variability*) than curve B, and curve B has less variability than curve C. If we measure only the mean of these three distributions, we will miss an important difference among the three curves. Likewise for any data, the mean, the median, and the mode tell us only part of what we need to know about the characteristics of the data. To increase our understanding of the pattern of the data, we must also measure its *dispersion*—its spread, or variability.

Uses of dispersion measures

Why is the dispersion of the distribution such an important characteristic to understand and measure? First, it gives us additional information that enables us to judge the reliability of our measure of the central tendency. If data are widely dispersed, such as those in curve C in Fig. 4 · 1, the central location is less representative of the data as a whole than it would be for data more closely centered around the mean, as in curve A. Second, because there are problems peculiar to widely

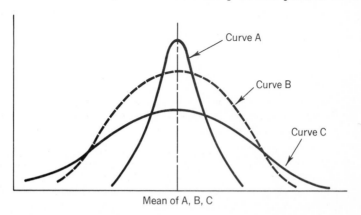

Mean of A, B, C

Figure 4 · 1 Three curves with the same mean but different variabilities

dispersed data, we must be able to recognize that data are widely dispersed before we can tackle those problems. And, third, we may wish to compare dispersions of various samples. If a wide spread of values away from the center is undesirable or presents an unacceptable risk, we need to be able to recognize and avoid choosing those distributions with the greatest dispersion.

Financial use

Financial analysts are concerned about the dispersion of a firm's earnings. Widely dispersed earnings—those varying from extremely high to low or even negative levels—indicate a higher risk to stockholders and creditors than do earnings remaining relatively stable. Similarly, quality control experts analyze the dispersion of a product's quality levels. A drug that is average in purity but ranges from very pure to highly impure may endanger lives.

Quality control use

EXERCISES

4·1 A firm using two different methods to ship orders to its customers found the following distributions of delivery time for the two methods, based on past records. From available evidence, which shipment method would you recommend?

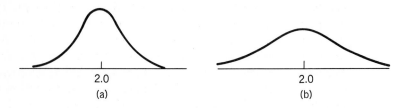

2.0
(a)

2.0
(b)

4·2 For which of the following distributions is the mean more representative of the data as a whole? Why?

(a)

(b)

4·3 Of the three curves shown in Fig. 4 · 1, choose one that would best describe the distribution of values for the ages of the following groups: members of Congress, newly elected members of the House of Representatives, the chairmen of major congressional committees. In making your choices, disregard the common mean of the curves in Fig. 4 · 1 and consider only the variability of the distributions. Briefly state your reasons for your choices.

4·4 How do you think the concept of variability might apply to an investigation by the Federal Trade Commission (FTC) into possible price fixing by a group of manufacturers?

---

2 DISPERSION: DISTANCE MEASURES

Two distance measures

Dispersion may be measured in terms of the difference between two values selected from the data set. In this section, we shall study two of these so-called *distance measures*: range and interfractile range.

Range

Defining and computing the range

As we said in Chapter 2, *the range is the difference between the highest and lowest observed values.* In equation form, we can say:

$$\text{Range} = \frac{\text{Value of highest}}{\text{observation}} - \frac{\text{Value of lowest}}{\text{observation}} \qquad (4 \cdot 1)$$

Using this equation, we compare the ranges of annual payments from Blue Cross–Blue Shield received by the two hospitals illustrated in Table 4 · 1.

The range of annual payments to Cumberland is $1,883,000 − $863,000 = $1,020,000. For Valley Falls, the range is $690,000 − $490,000 = $200,000.

Characteristics of the range

The range is easy to understand and to find, but its usefulness as a measure of dispersion is limited. The range considers only the highest and lowest values of a distribution and fails to take account of any other observation in the data set. As a result, it ignores the nature of the variation among all the other observations, and it is heavily influenced by extreme values. Because it measures only two values, the range is likely to change drastically from one sample to the next in a given population, even though the values that fall between the highest and lowest value may be quite similar. Keep in mind, too, that open-ended distributions have no range because no "highest" or "lowest" value exists in the open-ended class.

Interfractile range

Fractiles

In a frequency distribution, a given fraction or proportion of the data lie at or below a *fractile*. The median, for example, is the .5 fractile because half of the data set are less than or equal to this value. You will notice

TABLE 4 · 1 Annual payments from Blue Cross–Blue Shield (000's omitted)

Cumberland	863	903	957	1,041	1,138	1,204
Valley Falls	490	540	560	570	590	600
Cumberland	1,354	1,624	1,698	1,745	1,802	1,883
Valley Falls	610	620	630	660	670	690

that fractiles are similar to percentages. In any distribution, 25 percent of the data lie at or below the .25 fractile; likewise, 25 percent of the data lie at or below the 25th percentile. The *interfractile range* is a measure of the spread between two fractiles in a frequency distribution; that is, the difference between the values of two fractiles.

Meaning of the interfractile range

Calculating the interfractile range

Suppose we wish to find the interfractile range between the first and second *thirds* of Cumberland's receipts from Blue Cross–Blue Shield. We begin by dividing the observations into thirds, as we have done in Table 4 · 2. Each third contains 4 items ($\frac{1}{3}$ of the total of 12 items). Therefore, $33\frac{1}{3}$ percent of the items lie at $1,041,000 or below it, and $66\frac{2}{3}$ percent are equal to or less than $1,624,000. Now we can calculate the interfractile range between the $\frac{1}{3}$ and $\frac{2}{3}$ fractiles by subtracting the value $1,041,000 from the value $1,624,000. This difference of $583,000 is the spread between the top of the first third of the payments and the top of the second third.

Special fractiles: deciles, quartiles and percentiles

Fractiles may have special names, depending on the number of equal parts into which they divide the data. Fractiles that divide the data into 10 equal parts are called *deciles*. *Quartiles* divide the data into 4 equal parts. *Percentiles* divide the data into 100 equal parts. You've probably encountered percentiles in reported test scores. You know that if you scored in the 75th percentile, $\frac{3}{4}$ or 75 percent of all the people who took the test did no better than you did.

The interquartile range

One commonly used measure of dispersion is the interquartile range. This is defined as the third quartile minus the first quartile. It measures approximately how far from the median we must go on either side before we can include one-half of the values of the data set. Using Equation 4 · 2 and the data from Table 4 · 1, we find that the interquartile range for payments to Cumberland Hospital is $741,000.

$$\text{Interquartile range} = Q_3 - Q_1$$

$$= 1,698 - 957 \qquad (4 \cdot 2)$$

$$= 741 \text{ thousand dollars}$$

Figure 4 · 2 shows the interquartile range graphically. Notice in that

TABLE 4 · 2 Blue Cross–Blue Shield annual payments to Cumberland Hospital (000's omitted)

First third	Second third	Last third
863	1,138	1,698
903	1,204	1,745
957	1,354	1,802
1,041 ← $\frac{1}{3}$ fractile	1,624 ← $\frac{2}{3}$ fractile	1,883

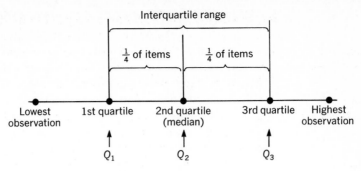

Figure 4·2   Interquartile range

figure that the width of the 4 sections that the quartiles divide the data into need not be the same.

EXERCISES

4·5 For the data below, calculate the
  a) range
  b) interfractile range between the third and seventh deciles
  c) interfractile range between the fourth and sixth deciles

98	69	58	87	73	89	83	65	82	63
88	91	77	68	94	86	96	89	98	85
55	59	87	84	59	82	73	95	68	81

4·6 For the sample below, compute the
  a) range
  b) interfractile range between the 20th and 80th percentiles
  c) interquartile range
  d) interfractile range between the first and second quartiles

2,696	2,880	2,575	2,748	2,762	2,572	3,233	2,733	2,890	2,878
3,100	3,321	2,693	2,865	2,784	3,296	2,977	2,090	2,905	3,350

4·7 For the following data, compute the interquartile range.

97	72	87	57	39	81	70	84	93	79
84	81	65	97	75	72	84	46	94	77

4·8 The New Mexico State Highway Department is charged with maintaining all state roads in good condition. One measure of condition is the number of cracks present in each 100 feet of roadway. From the department's yearly survey, the following distribution was constructed.

Cracks per 100 feet

2	5	6	7	7	8	9	10	10	11
12	12	12	13	13	13	14	14	15	15
15	15	16	16	17	17	18	19	19	20

Calculate interfractile range between the 20th, 40th, 60th, and 80th percentiles.

---

3 DISPERSION: AVERAGE DEVIATION MEASURES

*Two measures
of average
deviation*

The most comprehensive descriptions of dispersion are those that deal with the average deviation from some measure of central tendency. Two of these measures are important to our study of statistics: the *variance* and the *standard deviation*. Both of these tell us an average distance of any observation in the data set from the mean of the distribution.

Average absolute deviation

*Meaning
of average
absolute deviation*

We will have a better understanding of the variance and the standard deviation if we focus first on what statisticians call the *average absolute deviation*. To compute this, we begin by finding the mean of our sample. Then we determine the absolute value of the difference between each item in the data set and the mean. In other words, we subtract the mean from every value in the data set and ignore the sign (positive or negative), thereby taking each to be positive. Finally, we add all these differences together and divide by the total number of items in our sample.

Symbolically, the formula for finding the average absolute deviation looks like this:

$$\text{Average absolute deviation} = \frac{\Sigma|x - \mu|}{N} \text{ for a population} \quad (4 \cdot 3)$$

and like this:

$$\text{Average absolute deviation} = \frac{\Sigma|x - \bar{x}|}{n} \text{ for a sample} \quad (4 \cdot 4)$$

where:

x = item or observation
μ = population mean
N = number of items in the population
$\bar{x}$ = sample mean
n = number of items in the sample

Remember that Σ means "the sum of all the values." In this case, they are $|x - \mu|$ or $|x - \bar{x}|$. Also notice the straight lines surrounding $|x - \mu|$ and $|x - \bar{x}|$, which indicate that we want the *absolute value* of that distance (expressed in positive, not negative, numbers). This means that if the distance $x - \bar{x}$ is -10, then the absolute value is 10. Similarly, the absolute value of -25 is 25.

*Calculating
the average
absolute deviation*

Let's compute the average absolute deviation of the annual Blue Cross–Blue Shield payments to Cumberland in Table 4 · 1. First we note that the mean is 1,351 thousand dollars. Using the step-by-step process outlined in Table 4 · 3, we find the absolute deviation of every observation from this mean of $1,351,000. Now we can divide the sum of these

TABLE 4·3 Determination of the average absolute deviation of annual Blue Cross–Blue Shield payments to Cumberland Hospital (000's omitted)

Observation (x) (1)		Mean ($\bar{x}$) (2)		Deviation $(x - \bar{x})$ (1) − (2)	Absolute deviation $(\lvert x - \bar{x}\rvert)$ $\lvert(1) - (2)\rvert$
863	−	1,351	=	−488	488
903	−	1,351	=	−448	448
957	−	1,351	=	−394	394
1,041	−	1,351	=	−310	310
1,138	−	1,351	=	−213	213
1,204	−	1,351	=	−147	147
1,354	−	1,351	=	3	3
1,624	−	1,351	=	273	273
1,698	−	1,351	=	347	347
1,745	−	1,351	=	394	394
1,802	−	1,351	=	451	451
1,883	−	1,351	=	532	532
$\overline{16,212} \leftarrow \Sigma x$					$\overline{4,000} \leftarrow \Sigma\lvert x - \bar{x}\rvert$

absolute deviations by the number of items in the sample to learn the value of the average absolute deviation:

$$\text{Average absolute deviation} = \frac{\Sigma\lvert x - \bar{x}\rvert}{n}$$

$$= \frac{4,000}{12} \qquad (4 \cdot 4)$$

$$= 333.3 \text{ thousand dollars}$$

Characteristics of the average absolute deviation

This average absolute deviation is a better measure of dispersion than the ranges we have already calculated because it takes *every* observation into account. It weights each item equally and indicates how far, on average, each observation lies from the mean. In spite of this advantage, however, for technical reasons beyond the scope of this text, this average deviation method is rarely used.

Population variance

Variance

In the next two sections, we are going to focus on populations rather than samples. We shall begin with the fact that each population has a variance, which is symbolized by σ^2 (*sigma squared*).

Relationship of variance to average absolute deviation

The population variance is similar to an average absolute deviation computed for an entire population. But in this case, we are using the sum of the *squared* distances between the mean and each item divided by the total number of elements in the population. By squaring each distance, we automatically make every number positive and therefore have no need to take the absolute value of each deviation.

Formula for
the variance

The formula for calculating the variance is similar to Equation 4 · 3. But this time, because we are finding the average squared distance between the mean and each item in the population, we will square each difference of $x - \mu$:

$$\sigma^2 = \frac{\Sigma(x - \mu)^2}{N} = \frac{\Sigma x^2}{N} - \mu^2 \qquad (4 \cdot 5)$$

where:

σ^2 = population variance

x = item or observation

μ = population mean

N = total number of items in the population

Σ = sum of all the values $(x - \mu)^2$, or all the values x^2

In Equation 4 · 5, the middle expression $\frac{\Sigma(x - \mu)^2}{N}$ is the definition of σ^2. The last expression $\frac{\Sigma x^2}{N} - \mu^2$ is *mathematically* equivalent to the definition but is often much more convenient to use if we actually must compute the value of σ^2, since it frees us from calculating the deviations from the mean. However, when the x values are large and the $x - \mu$ values are small, it may be more convenient to use the middle expression $\frac{\Sigma(x - \mu)^2}{N}$ to compute σ^2. Before we can use this formula in an example, we need to discuss an important problem concerning the variance. In solving that problem, we will learn what the standard deviation is and how to calculate it. Then we can return to the variance itself.

Units in which
the variance
is expressed
cause a problem

Earlier, when we calculated the range, the interquartile deviation, and the average absolute deviation, the answers were expressed in the same units as the data itself. (In our examples, the units were "thousands of dollars of payments.") For the variance, however, the units are the *squares of the units* of the data, for example, "squared dollars" or "dollars squared." Squared dollars or dollars squared are not intuitively clear or easily interpreted. For this reason, we have to make a significant change in the variance to compute a useful measure of deviation, one that does not give us a problem with units of measure and thus is less confusing. This measure is called the standard deviation, and it is the square root of the variance. The square root of $100 squared is $10 because we take the square root of both the value and the units in which it is measured. The standard deviation, then, is in units that are the same as the original data.

Population standard deviation

Relationship of standard deviation to the variance

The population standard deviation, or σ, is simply the square root of the population variance. Since the variance is the average of the squared distances of the observations from the mean, the standard deviation is the square root of the average of the squared distances of the observations from the mean. While the variance is expressed in the square of the units used in the data, the standard deviation is in the same units as those used in the data. The formula for the standard deviation is:

$$\sigma = \sqrt{\sigma^2} = \sqrt{\frac{\Sigma(x - \mu)^2}{N}} = \sqrt{\frac{\Sigma x^2}{N} - \mu^2} \qquad (4 \cdot 6)$$

where:

x = observation

μ = population mean

N = total number of elements in the population

Σ = symbol for the sum of all the $(x - \mu)^2$, or all the values x^2

σ = population standard deviation

σ^2 = population variance

Use the positive square root

The square root of a positive number may be either positive or negative since $a^2 = (-a)^2$. When taking the square root of the variance to calculate the standard deviation, however, statisticians consider only the positive square root.

Computing the standard deviation

To calculate either the variance or the standard deviation, we construct a table, using every element of the population. If we have a population of 15 vials of compound produced in one day and we test each vial to determine its purity, our data might look like Table 4 · 4. In Table 4 · 5 we show how to use this data to compute the mean (column 1 divided by N = 2.49/15), the deviation of each value from the mean (column 3), the square of the deviation of each value from the mean (column 4), and the sum of the squared deviations. From this, we can compute the variance, which is .0034 percent squared. (Table 4 · 5 also computes σ^2 using the second half of Equation 4 · 5, $\frac{\Sigma x^2}{N} - \mu^2$. Note

TABLE 4·4 Results of purity test on compounds

Observed percent of impurity				
.04	.14	.17	.19	.22
.06	.14	.17	.21	.24
.12	.15	.18	.21	.25

TABLE 4·5 Determination of the variance and standard deviation of percent impurity of compounds

Observation (x) (1)	Mean $(\mu) = 2.49\,/\,15$ (2)	Deviation $(x - \mu)$ (3) = (1) − (2)	Deviation squared $(x - \mu)^2$ (4) = $[(1) - (2)]^2$	Observation squared (x^2) (5) = $(1)^2$
.04	− .166 =	− .126	.016	.0016
.06	− .166 =	− .106	.011	.0036
.12	− .166 =	− .046	.002	.0144
.14	− .166 =	− .026	.001	.0196
.14	− .166 =	− .026	.001	.0196
.15	− .166 =	− .016	.000	.0225
.17	− .166 =	.004	.000	.0289
.17	− .166 =	.004	.000	.0289
.18	− .166 =	.014	.000	.0324
.19	− .166 =	.024	.001	.0361
.21	− .166 =	.044	.002	.0441
.21	− .166 =	.044	.002	.0441
.22	− .166 =	.054	.003	.0484
.24	− .166 =	.074	.005	.0576
.25	− .166 =	.084	.007	.0625
$\overline{2.49} \leftarrow \Sigma x$			$\overline{.051} \leftarrow \Sigma(x - \mu)^2$	$\overline{.4643} \leftarrow \Sigma x^2$

$$\sigma^2 = \frac{\Sigma(x - \mu)^2}{N}$$

$$= \frac{.051}{15} \quad (4 \cdot 5)$$

$$= .0034 \text{ percent squared}$$

← OR →

$$\sigma^2 = \frac{\Sigma x^2}{N} - \mu^2$$

$$= \frac{.4643}{15} - (.166)^2 \quad (4 \cdot 5)$$

$$= .0034 \text{ percent squared}$$

$$\sigma = \sqrt{\sigma^2}$$

$$= \sqrt{.0034} \quad (4 \cdot 6)$$

$$= .058 \text{ percent}$$

that we get the same result but do a bit less work, since we do not have to compute the deviations from the mean.) Taking the square root of σ^2, we can compute the standard deviation, .058 percent.

Uses of the standard deviation

Chebyshev's theorem

The standard deviation enables us to determine, with a great deal of accuracy, where the values of a frequency distribution are located in relation to the mean. We can do this according to a theorem devised by the Russian mathematician P. L. Chebyshev (1821–1894). Chebyshev's theorem says that no matter what the shape of the distribution, at least 75 percent of the values will fall within plus-and-minus 2 standard deviations from the mean of the distribution, and at least 89 percent of the values will lie within plus-and-minus 3 standard deviations from the mean.

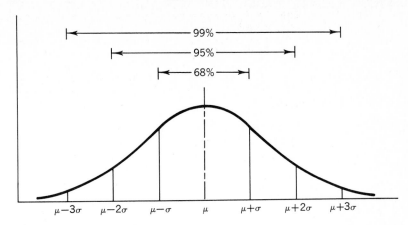

Figure 4·3 Location of observations around the mean of a bell-shaped frequency distribution

We can measure with even more precision the percentage of items that fall within specific ranges under a symmetrical, bell-shaped curve like the one in Fig. 4 · 3. In these cases, we can say that:

1. About 68 percent of the values in the population will fall within plus-or-minus 1 standard deviation from the mean.
2. About 95 percent of the values will lie within plus-or-minus 2 standard deviations from the mean.
3. About 99 percent of the values will be in an interval ranging from 3 standard deviations below the mean to 3 standard deviations above the mean.

Using Chebyshev's theorem

In light of Chebyshev's theorem, let's analyze the data in Table 4 · 5. There, the mean impurity of the 15 vials of compound is .166 percent, and the standard deviation is .058 percent. Chebyshev's theorem tells us that at least 75 percent of the values (at least 11 of our 15 items) are between .166 − 2(.058) = .050 and .166 + 2(.058) = .282. In fact, 93 percent of the values (14 of the 15 values) are actually in that interval. Notice that the distribution is reasonably symmetrical and that 93 percent is close to the theoretical 95 percent for an interval of plus-or-minus 2 standard deviations from the mean of a bell-shaped curve.

Concept of the standard score

The standard deviation is also useful in describing how far individual items in a distribution depart from the mean of the distribution. A measure called the standard score gives us the number of standard deviations a particular observation lies below or above the mean. If we let x symbolize the observation, the standard score computed from population data is:

$$\text{Population standard score} = \frac{x - \mu}{\sigma} \qquad (4 \cdot 7)$$

71   Sec. 3   Dispersion: average deviation measures

where:

x = observation from the population

μ = population mean

σ = population standard deviation

Suppose we observe a vial of compound that is .108 percent impure. Since our population has a mean of .166 and a standard deviation of .058, an observation of .108 would have a standard score of −1;

$$\text{Standard score} = \frac{x - \mu}{\sigma}$$

$$= \frac{.108 - .166}{.058} = -1 \qquad (4 \cdot 7)$$

Calculating the standard score

An observed impurity of .282 percent would have a standard score of +2:

$$\text{Standard score} = \frac{x - \mu}{\sigma}$$

$$= \frac{.282 - .166}{.058} = 2 \qquad (4 \cdot 7)$$

Interpreting the standard score

The standard score indicates that an impurity of .282 percent deviates from the mean by 2(.058) = .116 unit, which is equal to +2 in terms of units of standard deviations away from the mean.

Calculation of variance and standard deviation using grouped data

Calculating the variance and standard deviation for grouped data

In our chapter-opening example, data on sales of 100 fast-food restaurants were already grouped in a frequency distribution. With such data we can use the following formulas to calculate the variance and the standard deviation:

$$\sigma^2 = \frac{\Sigma f(x - \mu)^2}{N} = \frac{\Sigma fx^2}{N} - \mu^2 \qquad (4 \cdot 8)$$

and:

$$\sigma = \sqrt{\sigma^2} = \sqrt{\frac{\Sigma f(x - \mu)^2}{N}} = \sqrt{\frac{\Sigma fx^2}{N} - \mu^2} \qquad (4 \cdot 9)$$

where:

σ^2 = population variance x = class mark for each class

σ = population standard deviation μ = population mean

f = frequency of each of the classes N = size of the population

TABLE 4·6 Determination of the variance and standard deviation of sales of 100 fast-food restaurants in the eastern district (000's omitted)

Class	Class mark (x) (1)	Frequency (f) (2)	f × x (3) = (2) × (1)	Mean (μ) (4)	x − μ (1) − (4)	(x − μ)² [(1) − (4)]²	f(x − μ)² (2) × [(1) − (4)]²
700– 799	750	4	3,000	1,250	− 500	250,000	1,000,000
800– 899	850	7	5,950	1,250	− 400	160,000	1,120,000
900– 999	950	8	7,600	1,250	− 300	90,000	720,000
1,000–1,099	1,050	10	10,500	1,250	− 200	40,000	400,000
1,100–1,199	1,150	12	13,800	1,250	− 100	10,000	120,000
1,200–1,299	1,250	17	21,250	1,250	0	0	0
1,300–1,399	1,350	13	17,550	1,250	100	10,000	130,000
1,400–1,499	1,450	10	14,500	1,250	200	40,000	400,000
1,500–1,599	1,550	9	13,950	1,250	300	90,000	810,000
1,600–1,699	1,650	7	11,550	1,250	400	160,000	1,120,000
1,700–1,799	1,750	2	3,500	1,250	500	250,000	500,000
1,800–1,899	1,850	1	1,850	1,250	600	360,000	360,000
		100	125,000				6,680,000

$$\bar{x} = \frac{\Sigma(f \times x)}{n} = \frac{125,000}{100} = 1,250 \text{ dollars} \leftarrow \text{mean} \qquad (3 \cdot 3)$$

$$\sigma^2 = \frac{\Sigma f(x - \mu)^2}{N} = \frac{6,680,000}{100} = 66,800 \text{ (or 66,800 dollars squared)} \leftarrow \text{variance} \qquad (4 \cdot 8)$$

$$\sigma = \sqrt{\sigma^2} = \sqrt{66,800} = 258.5 \leftarrow \text{standard deviation} = \$258,500 \qquad (4 \cdot 9)$$

Table 4 · 6 shows how to apply these equations to find the variance and standard deviation of the sales of 100 fast-food restaurants.

We leave it as an exercise for the curious reader to verify that the second half of Equation 4 · 8, $\frac{\Sigma f x^2}{N} - \mu^2$, will yield the same value of σ^2.

Switching to sample variance and sample standard deviation

Now we are ready to compute the sample statistics that are analogous to the population variance σ^2 and the population standard deviation σ. These are the sample variance s^2 and the sample standard deviation s. In the next section, you'll notice we are changing from Greek latters (which denote population parameters) to the Latin letters of sample statistics.

Sample standard deviation

To compute the sample variance and the sample standard deviation, we use the same formulas as Equations 4 · 5 and 4 · 6, replacing μ with $\bar{x}$ and N with $n - 1$. The formulas look like this:

$$s^2 = \frac{\Sigma(x - \bar{x})^2}{n - 1} = \frac{\Sigma x^2}{n - 1} - \frac{n \bar{x}^2}{n - 1} \qquad (4 \cdot 10)$$

and

$$s = \sqrt{s^2} = \sqrt{\frac{\Sigma(x - \bar{x})^2}{n - 1}} = \sqrt{\frac{\Sigma x^2}{n - 1} - \frac{n\bar{x}^2}{n - 1}} \qquad (4 \cdot 11)$$

where:

s^2 = sample variance

s = sample standard deviation

x = value of each of the n observations

$\bar{x}$ = mean of the sample

$n - 1$ = number of observations in the sample minus one

*Use of n − 1 as
the denominator*

Why do we use $n - 1$ as the denominator instead of n? Statisticians can prove that if we take many samples from a given population, find the sample variance (s^2) for each sample, and average each of these together, then this average tends not to equal the population variance, σ^2, unless we use $n - 1$ as the denominator. In Chapter 8, we shall learn the statistical explanation of why this is true.

*Calculating
sample variance
and standard
deviation for
Cumberland
Hospital data*

Equations 4 · 10 and 4 · 11 enable us to find the sample variance and the sample standard deviation of the annual Blue Cross–Blue Shield payments to Cumberland Hospital discussed in Table 4 · 3. We do this in Table 4 · 7, noting that both halves of Equation 4 · 10 yield the same result.

*Computing sample
standard scores*

Just as we used the population standard deviation to derive population standard scores, we may also use the sample standard deviation to compute sample standard scores. These sample standard scores tell us how many standard deviations a particular sample observation lies below or above the sample mean. The appropriate formula is:

$$\text{Sample standard score} = \frac{x - \bar{x}}{s} \qquad (4 \cdot 12)$$

where

x = observation from the sample

$\bar{x}$ = sample mean

s = sample standard deviation

In the example we just did, we see that the observation 863 corresponds to a standard score of -1.28:

$$\text{Sample standard score} = \frac{x - \bar{x}}{s} = \frac{863 - 1351}{380.64} = -1.28 \quad (4 \cdot 12)$$

TABLE 4·7 Determination of the sample variance and standard deviation of annual Blue Cross–Blue Shield payments to Cumberland Hospital (000's omitted)

Observation (x) (1)	Mean $(\bar{x})$ (2)	$x - \bar{x}$ (1) – (2)	$(x - \bar{x})^2$ $[(1) - (2)]^2$	x^2 $(1)^2$
863	1,351	−488	238,144	744,769
903	1,351	−448	200,704	815,409
957	1,351	−394	155,236	915,849
1,041	1,351	−310	96,100	1,083,681
1,138	1,351	−213	45,369	1,295,044
1,204	1,351	−147	21,609	1,449,616
1,354	1,351	3	9	1,833,316
1,624	1,351	273	74,529	2,637,376
1,698	1,351	347	120,409	2,883,204
1,745	1,351	394	155,236	3,045,025
1,802	1,351	451	203,401	3,247,204
1,883	1,351	532	283,024	3,545,689

$$\Sigma(x - \bar{x})^2 \rightarrow \overline{1,593,770} \qquad \overline{23,496,182} \leftarrow \Sigma x^2$$

$$\left\{ s^2 = \frac{\Sigma(x - \bar{x})^2}{n - 1} = \frac{1,593,770}{11} \right. \tag{4·10}$$

$$= 144,888 \text{ (or \$144,888 million squared)} \leftarrow \text{sample variance}$$

$$s = \sqrt{s^2} = \sqrt{144,888}$$

$$= 380.64 \text{ (that is, \$380,640)} \leftarrow \text{sample standard deviation} \tag{4·11}$$

OR

$$\left\{ s^2 = \frac{\Sigma x^2}{n - 1} - \frac{n\bar{x}^2}{n - 1} = \frac{23,496,182}{11} - \frac{12(1351)^2}{11} \right. \tag{4·10}$$

$$= \frac{1,593,770}{11} = 144,888$$

Characteristics of the standard deviation

This section has demonstrated why the standard deviation is the measure of dispersion used most often. We can use it to compare distributions and to compute standard scores, an important element of statistical inference to be discussed later. Like the average absolute deviation, it takes into account every observation in the data set. But the standard deviation has some disadvantages too. It is not as easy to calculate as the range, and it cannot be computed from open-ended distributions. In addition, extreme values in the data set distort the value of the standard deviation, although to a lesser extent than they do the range.

75 Sec. 3 Dispersion: average deviation measures

4·9 For the following measurements, compute the
a) average absolute deviation
b) population variance
c) population standard deviation

50	53	52	51	43	52	51	50	56	54
45	48	54	52	49	48	47	58	51	56

4·10 The following values represent a sample from a large population. Compute the
a) average absolute deviation for the sample
b) sample variance
c) sample standard deviation

26	17	24	29	26	21	33	31	29	27

4·11 The Federal Reserve Board has given permission to all member banks to raise interest rates $\frac{1}{2}$ percent for all depositors. Old rates for passbook savings were $5\frac{1}{4}\%$; for certificates of deposit (CD's): 1-year CD, $7\frac{1}{2}\%$; 18-month CD, $8\frac{3}{4}\%$; 2-year CD, 9%; 3-year CD, $10\frac{1}{2}\%$; 5-year CD, 11%. The president of The First State Bank wants to know what the characteristics of the new distribution of rates will be if the full $\frac{1}{2}$ percent is added to all rates. How are the new characteristics related to the old ones?

4·12 The administrator of a Georgia hospital conducted a survey of the number of days patients stayed in the hospital following an operation. The data are given below:

Hospital stay (days)	1–3	4–6	7–9	10–12	13–15	16–18	19–21	22–24
Frequency	32	108	67	28	14	7	3	1

a) Calculate the mean and standard deviation.
b) According to Chebyshev's theorem, how many stays should be between 0 and 15 days? How many are actually in that interval?
c) Since this distribution is roughly bell-shaped, how many of the stays can we expect to fall between 0 and 15 days?

4·13 The Creative Illusion Advertising Company has three offices in three different cities. Wage rates differ from state to state. In the Washington, D.C., office, the average wage increase for the past year was $1,250, with a standard deviation of $355. In the New York office the average raise was $2,580 with a standard deviation of $578. In Durham, N.C., the average increase was $533 with a standard deviation of $42. Three employees were interviewed. The Washington employee received a raise of $1,000; the New York employee a raise of $2,300; and the Durham employee a raise of $500. Which of the three had the smallest raise in relation to the mean and standard deviation of this office?

4 RELATIVE DISPERSION: THE COEFFICIENT OF VARIATION

The standard deviation is an *absolute* measure of dispersion that expresses variation in the same units as the original data. The annual Blue Cross–Blue Shield payments to Cumberland Hospital (Table 4 · 7) have a standard deviation of $380,640. The annual Blue Cross–Blue Shield payments to Valley Falls Hospital (Table 4 · 1) have a standard deviation (which you can compute) of $57,390. Can we compare the values of these two standard deviations? Unfortunately, no.

Shortcomings of the standard deviation

The standard deviation cannot be the sole basis for comparing two distributions. If we have a standard deviation of 10 and a mean of 5, the values vary by an amount twice as large as the mean itself. If, on the other hand, we have a standard deviation of 10 and a mean of 5,000, the variation relative to the mean is insignificant. Therefore, we cannot know the dispersion of a set of data until we know the standard deviation, the mean, *and* how the standard deviation compares with the mean.

The coefficient of variation, a relative measure

What we need is a *relative* measure that will give us a feel for the magnitude of the deviation relative to the magnitude of the mean. The *coefficient of variation* is one such relative measure of dispersion. It relates the standard deviation and the mean by expressing the standard deviation as a percentage of the mean. The unit of measure, then, is "percent" rather than the same units as the original data. For a population, the formula for the coefficient of variation is:

standard deviation of the population

$$\text{Population coefficient of variation} = \frac{\sigma}{\mu}(100) \qquad (4 \cdot 13)$$

mean of the population

Using this formula in an example, we may suppose that each day, laboratory technician A completes 40 analyses with a standard deviation of 5. Technician B completes 160 analyses per day with a standard deviation of 15. Which employee shows less variability?

At first glance, it appears that technician B has three times more variation in the output rate than technician A. But B completes analyses at a rate four times faster than A. To take all this information into account, compute the coefficient of variation for both technicians:

$$\text{Coefficient of variation} = \frac{\sigma}{\mu}(100) = \frac{5}{40}(100)$$
$$= 12.5\% \leftarrow \text{ for technician A} \qquad (4 \cdot 13)$$

Computing the coefficient of variation

and

$$\text{Coefficient of variation} = \frac{15}{160}(100) = 9.4\% \leftarrow \text{ for technician B}$$

So we find that technician B, who has more *absolute* variation in output than technician A, has less *relative* variation because the mean output for B is much greater than for A.

4·14 A drug company that supplies hospitals with premeasured doses of certain medications uses different machines for medications requiring different dosage amounts. One machine designed to produce doses of 100 cc has as its mean dose 100 cc with a standard deviation of 2.6 cc. Another machine produces premeasured amounts of 180 cc of medication and it has a standard deviation of 5.3 cc. Which machine is the less accurate from the standpoint of relative dispersion?

4·15 In two samples of size 50 each, the mean value for the first sample was 1.16 with a standard deviation of .21; the second sample had a mean of 1.75 and a standard deviation of .35. Which sample exhibits greater relative dispersion?

4·16 Bassart Electronics is considering employing one of two training programs. Two groups were trained for the same task. Group 1 was trained by program A; group 2, by program B. For the first group it took an average of 28.74 hours to train each employee, with a variance of 79.39. For the second group it took an average of 20.5 hours to train each employee, with a variance of 54.76. Which training program has less relative variability in its performance?

4·17 The following two samples are believed to represent the same population but were collected separately. Determine the relative dispersion of scores for the two samples and indicate which sample shows greater relative variability.

Sample 1	20	19	27	20	18	26	30	24	25	26
Sample 2	24	25	27	16	22	20	35	28	18	32

5 TERMS INTRODUCED IN CHAPTER 4

average absolute deviation In a data set, the average distance of the observations from the mean.

Chebyshev's theorem No matter what the shape of a distribution, at least 75 percent of the values in the population will fall within 2 standard deviations of the mean, and at least 89 percent will fall within 3 standard deviations.

coefficient of variation A relative measure of dispersion, comparable across distributions, which expresses the standard deviation as a percentage of the mean.

deciles Fractiles that divide the data into 10 equal parts.

dispersion The scatter or variability in a set of data.

distance measure A measure of dispersion in terms of the difference between two values in the data set.

fractile In a frequency distribution, the location of a value at, or above, a given fraction of the data.

interfractile range A measure of the spread between two fractiles in a distribution; i.e., the difference between the values of two fractiles.

interquartile range The difference between the values of the first and third quartiles, indicating the range of the middle half of the data set.

percentiles Fractiles that divide the data into 100 equal parts.

quartiles Fractiles that divide the data into 4 equal parts.

range The distance between the highest and lowest values in a data set.

standard deviation The positive square root of the variance; a measure of dispersion in the same units as the original data, rather than in the squared units of the variance.

standard score Expressing an observation in terms of standard deviation units above or below the mean; i.e., the transformation of an observation by subtracting the mean and dividing by the standard deviation.

variance A measure of the average squared distance between the mean and each item in the population.

6 EQUATIONS INTRODUCED IN CHAPTER 4

p. 63
$$\text{Range} = \frac{\text{Value of highest}}{\text{observation}} - \frac{\text{Value of lowest}}{\text{observation}}$$
4·1

The *range* is the difference between the highest and lowest observed values in a frequency distribution.

p. 64
$$\text{Interquartile range} = Q_3 - Q_1$$
4·2

The *interquartile range* measures approximately how far from the median we must go on either side before we can include one-half of the values of the data set. To compute this range, divide the data into four equal parts. The *quartiles* (Q) are the highest values in each of these four parts. The *interquartile range* is the difference between the values of the first and third quartiles (Q_1 and Q_3).

p. 66
$$\text{Average absolute deviation} = \frac{\Sigma|x - \mu|}{N} \text{ for a population}$$
4·3

This formula enables us to calculate the *average absolute deviation for a population*. Because this measure of variability deals with the absolute value of the difference between each item in the data set and the mean, it is not as useful for further calculation as is the variance, which squares each distance.

p. 66
$$\text{Average absolute deviation} = \frac{\Sigma|x - \bar{x}|}{n} \text{ for a sample}$$
4·4

For a *sample*, use this formula to determine the average absolute deviation. Unlike Equation 4 · 3, this formula uses the sample mean $\bar{x}$ and the number of items in the sample n.

p. 68
$$\sigma^2 = \frac{\Sigma(x - \mu)^2}{N} = \frac{\Sigma x^2}{N} - \mu^2$$
4·5

This formula enables us to calculate the *population variance*, a measure of the average *squared* distance between the mean and each item in the population. The middle expression, $\frac{\Sigma(x - \mu)^2}{N}$ is the definition of σ^2. The last expression $\frac{\Sigma x^2}{N} - \mu^2$ is mathematically equivalent to the definition but is often much more convenient to use, since it frees us from calculating the deviations from the mean.

p. 69
$$\sigma = \sqrt{\sigma^2} = \sqrt{\frac{\Sigma(x - \mu)^2}{N}} = \sqrt{\frac{\Sigma x^2}{N} - \mu^2}$$
4·6

The population standard deviation, σ, is the square root of the population variance. It is a more useful parameter than the variance because it is expressed in the same units as the data itself (whereas the units of the variance are the squares of the units of the data). Notice that the standard deviation is always the *positive* square root of the variance.

p. 71
$$\text{Population standard score} = \frac{x - \mu}{\sigma}$$
4·7

The *standard score* of an observation is the number of standard deviations the observation lies below or above the mean of the distribution. The standard score enables us to make comparisons between distribution items that differ in order of magnitude or in the units employed. Use Equation 4 · 7 to find the standard score of an item in a *population*.

p. 72
$$\sigma^2 = \frac{\Sigma f(x - \mu)^2}{N} = \frac{\Sigma fx^2}{N} - \mu^2$$
4·8

This formula in either form enables us to calculate the *variance* of data already *grouped* in a frequency distribution.

p. 72
$$\sigma = \sqrt{\sigma^2} = \sqrt{\frac{\Sigma f(x - \mu)^2}{N}} = \sqrt{\frac{\Sigma fx^2}{N} - \mu^2}$$
4·9

Take the square root of the variance, and you have the *standard deviation using grouped data*.

p. 73
$$s^2 = \frac{\Sigma(x - \bar{x})^2}{n - 1} = \frac{\Sigma x^2}{n - 1} - \frac{n\bar{x}^2}{n - 1}$$
4·10

To compute the *sample variance*, use the same formula as Equation 4 · 5, replacing μ with $\bar{x}$ and N with $n - 1$. Chapter 8 contains an explanation of why we use $n - 1$ rather than n to calculate the sample variance.

p. 74
$$s = \sqrt{s^2} = \sqrt{\frac{\Sigma(x - \bar{x})^2}{n - 1}} = \sqrt{\frac{\Sigma x^2}{n - 1} - \frac{n\bar{x}^2}{n - 1}}$$
4·11

The *sample standard deviation* is the square root of the sample variance. It is similar to Equation 4 · 6, except that μ is replaced by the sample mean $\bar{x}$ and N is changed to $n - 1$.

p. 74
$$\text{Sample standard score} = \frac{x - \bar{x}}{s}$$
4·12

Use this equation to find the standard score of an item in a *sample*.

p. 77
$$\text{Population coefficient of variation} = \frac{\sigma}{\mu}(100)$$
4·13

The *coefficient of variation* is a relative measure of dispersion that enables us to compare two distributions. It relates the standard deviation and the mean by expressing the standard deviation as a percentage of the mean.

---
7 CHAPTER REVIEW EXERCISES

4·18 The Martin Rubber Company has a plant in Ohio and one in North Carolina. Both companies employ many high school students in the summer. In the North Carolina plant, the students average $98.20 a week, with a standard deviation of $15.40. In Ohio, students average $120.80, with a standard deviation of $21.40. Which plant has the greatest relative dispersion?

4·19 Two economists are studying fluctuations in the price of gold. One is examining the period of 1968–1972. The other is examining the period of 1975–1979. What differences would you expect to find in the variability of their data?

4·20 On two successive days, a sample was taken of the lengths of missions flown by pilots at an overseas air force base. The data are shown below:

Length of mission (hours)				
Day 1	1.1	1.3	1.4	1.5	3.0
Day 2	1.2	1.4	1.6	1.9	2.2

a) Calculate the range of the two distributions.

b) Comment on using the range as a measure of dispersion for these data.

4·21 As part of a control program, samples are taken of welfare payments issued at each regional welfare office each week. The following data were collected during the final week in July at one such office:

Individual welfare payments (dollars)

89.70	112.35	113.90	114.90	116.75
90.25	112.40	114.05	115.00	117.60
102.75	113.00	114.55	115.50	119.00

Calculate the range and the interfractile range between the $\frac{1}{3}$ and $\frac{2}{3}$ fractiles.

4·22 The owner of Records Anonymous, a large record retailer, employs two different formulas for predicting monthly sales. The first formula has an average miss of 700 records, with a standard deviation of 35 records. The second formula has an average miss of 300 records, with a standard deviation of 16. Which formula is relatively less accurate?

4·23 Using the following population data, calculate the average absolute deviation, variance, and standard deviation:

Average heating fuel cost per gallon for eight states

$1.03	$1.08	$1.04	$1.13	$1.12	$1.05	$1.09	$1.06

4·24 Below is the average number of New York City policemen and policewomen on duty each day between 8 and 12 P.M. in the borough of Manhattan.

Mon. 2,950 Tues. 2,900 Wed. 2,900 Thurs. 2,980 Fri. 3,285 Sat. 3,430 Sun. 2,975

Calculate the variance and standard deviation of the distribution.

4·25 The financial controller for the Bacchus Wine Company has the company's short-term cash in a variety of savings accounts and short-term notes with the following interest rates:

5.25%, 5.5%, 5.75%, 6%, 6.5%, 7%

Calculate the mean, variance, and standard deviation for these rates.

4·26 How would you reply to the following statement? "Variability is not an important factor, because even though the outcome is more uncertain, you still have an equal chance of falling either above or below the median. Therefore, on average, the outcome will be the same."

---

8 CHAPTER CONCEPTS TEST

Answers are in the back of the book.

T F 1. The dispersion of a data set gives insight into the reliability of the measure of central tendency.

T F 2. The standard deviation is equal to the square root of the variance.

T F 3. The difference between the highest and lowest observations in a data set is called the quartile range.

T F 4. The interquartile range is based upon only two values taken from the data set.

T F 5. The standard deviation is measured in the same units as the observations in the data set.

T F 6. A fractile is a location in a frequency distribution where a given proportion (or fraction) of the data lies at or above.

T F 7. The average absolute deviation, like the standard deviation, takes into account every observation in the data set.

T F 8. The coefficient of variation is an absolute measure of dispersion.

T F 9. The measure of dispersion most often used by statisticians is the standard deviation.

T F 10. One of the advantages of dispersion measures is that any statistic that measures absolute variation also measures relative variation.

T F 11. One disadvantage of using the range to measure dispersion is that it ignores the nature of the variations among most of the observations.

T F 12. The variance indicates the average distance of any observation in the data set from the mean.

T F 13. Every population has a variance, which is signified by s^2.

T F 14. According to Chebyshev's theorem, no more than 11 percent of the observations in a population can have population standard scores greater than 3 or less than -3.

T F 15. The interquartile range is a specific example of an interfractile range.

16. Which of the following is an example of a distance measure?
a) range
b) interfractile range
c) a and b
d) none of the above

17. Which pair of phrases best completes this sentence? Fractiles that divide data into _____ equal parts are called _____.
a) 100... deciles   c) 10... percentiles
b) 4... quartiles   d) 16... octiles

18. How does one calculate the interquartile range?
a) Subtract the third quartile from the first quartile.
b) Subtract the second quartile from the third quartile.
c) Multiply the third quartile times 2.
d) Subtract the first quartile from the third quartile.

19. Why is it necessary to square the differences from the mean when computing the population variance?
a) So that extreme values will not affect the calculation.
b) Because it is possible that N could be very small.
c) Some of the differences will be positive and some will be negative.
d) None of the above.

20. Assume that a population has $\mu = 100$, $\sigma = 10$. If a particular observation has a standard score of 1, it can be concluded that:
a) Its value is 110.
b) It lies between 90 and 110, but its exact value cannot be determined.
c) Its value is greater than 110.
d) Nothing can be determined without knowing N.

21. Assume that a population has $\mu = 100$, $\sigma = 10$, and $N = 1,000$. According to Chebyshev's theorem, which of the following situations is NOT possible?
a) 150 values are greater than 130.

b) 930 values lie between 100 and 108.

c) 22 values lie between 120 and 125.

d) 90 values are less than 70.

e) All of the above situations are possible.

22. Which of the following is an example of a relative measure of dispersion?

    a) standard deviation

    b) variance

    c) coefficient of variation

    d) all of the above

    e) a and b but not c

23. Which of the following is true?

    a) The variance can be calculated for grouped or ungrouped data.

    b) The standard deviation can be calculated for grouped or ungrouped data.

    c) The standard deviation can be calculated for grouped or ungrouped data, but the variance can only be calculated for ungrouped data.

    d) a and b but not c.

24. If one were to divide the standard deviation of a population by the mean of the same population and multiply this value by 100, one would have calculated the

    a) population standard score

    b) population variance

    c) average absolute deviation

    d) population coefficient of variation

    e) none of the above

25. How does the computation of a sample variance differ from the computation of a population variance?

    a) μ is replaced by $\bar{x}$.

    b) N is replaced by $n - 1$.

    c) N is replaced by n.

    d) a and c but not b.

    e) a and b but not c.

26. In a frequency distribution, the median is the .5 _____ because half of the data set are less than or equal to this value.

27. The difference between the values of the first and third quartiles is the _____ range.

28. The measure of the average squared distance between the mean and each item in the population is the _____. The positive square root of this value is the _____.

29. The expression of the standard deviation as a percentage of the mean is the _____.

30. The number of standard deviation units that an observation lies above or below the mean is called the _____.

Probability I: Introductory Ideas

Gamblers have used odds to make bets during most of recorded history. But it wasn't until the seventeenth century that a French nobleman named Antoine Gombauld (1607 – 1684) questioned the mathematical basis for success and failure at the dice tables. He asked the French mathematician Blaise Pascal (1623 – 1662), "What are the odds of rolling two sixes at least once in twenty-four rolls of a pair of dice?" Pascal solved the problem, having become as interested in the idea of probabilities as was Gombauld. They shared their ideas with the famous mathematician Pierre de Fermat (1601 – 1665), and the letters written by these three constitute the first academic journals in probability theory. We have no record of the degree of success enjoyed by these gentlemen at the dice tables, but we do know that their curiosity and research introduced many of the concepts we shall study in this chapter and the next.

Chapter 5 introduces the basic concepts of probability (or chance). With Chapter 6, it is a foundation for our study of statistical inference in later chapters. Here, we examine methods of calculating and using probabilities under various conditions. If you are one of 200 students in a class and it seems that the professor calls on you each time the class meets, you might accuse that professor of not calling on students at random. If, on the other hand, you are one student in a class of 8 and you never prepare for class, assuming that the professor will not get around to you, then you may be the one who needs to examine probability ideas a bit more.

1 RELEVANCE OF PROBABILITY THEORY

Need for probability theory

Probability theory has been successfully applied at the gambling tables and, more relevant to our study, to other more consequential social and economic problems. The insurance industry, which emerged in the nineteenth century, required precise knowledge about the risk of loss in order to calculate premiums. Within fifty years, many learning centers were studying probability as a tool for understanding social phenomena. Today, the mathematical theory of probability is the basis for statistical applications in both social and decision-making research.

Examples of the use of probability theory

Probability is a part of our everyday lives. In personal and managerial decisions, we face uncertainty and use probability theory whether or not we admit the use of something so sophisticated. When we hear a weather forecast of a 70 percent chance of rain, we change our plans from a picnic to a pool game. Playing bridge, we make some probability estimate before attempting a finesse. Managers who deal with inventories of highly styled women's clothing must wonder about the chances that sales will reach or exceed a certain level, and the buyer who stocks up on skateboards considers the probability of the life of this particular fad. Before Muhammad Ali's highly publicized fight with Leon Spinks, Ali was reputed to have said, "I'll give you odds I'm still the greatest when it's over." And when you begin to study for the inevitable quiz attached to the use of this book, you may ask yourself, "What are the chances the professor will ask us to recall something about the history of probability theory?"

We live in a world in which we are unable to forecast the future with complete certainty. Our need to cope with uncertainty leads us to the study and use of probability theory. In many instances we, as concerned citizens, will have some knowledge about the possible outcomes of a decision. By organizing this information and considering it systematically, we will be able to recognize our assumptions, communicate our reasoning to others, and make a sounder decision than we could by using a shot-in-the-dark approach.

5·1 The insurance industry uses probability theory to calculate premium rates; but life insurers know for *certain* that every policyholder is going to die. Does this mean that probability theory does not apply to the life insurance business? Explain.

5·2 "Warning: The Surgeon General has determined that cigarette smoking is dangerous to your health." How might probability theory have played a part in that statement?

5·3 Is there really any such thing as an "uncalculated risk"? Explain.

5·4 A well-known manufacturer of children's clothing decides to expand its product line by adding preteen clothing. In what ways do you think the decision involves probability theory?

---

2 SOME BASIC CONCEPTS IN PROBABILITY

In general, probability is the chance something will happen. Probabilities are expressed as fractions $\left(\frac{1}{6}, \frac{1}{2}, \frac{8}{9}\right)$ or as decimals (.167, .500, .889) between zero and one. Assigning a probability of zero means that something can never happen; a probability of one indicates that something will always happen.

Events

In probability theory, an *event* is one or more of the possible outcomes of doing something. If we toss a coin, getting a tail would be an *event*, and getting a head would be another event. Similarly, if we are drawing from a deck of cards, selecting the ace of spades would be an event. An example of an event closer to your life, perhaps, is being picked from a class of 100 students to answer a question. When we hear the frightening predictions of highway traffic deaths, we hope not to be one of those events.

The activity that produces such an event is referred to in probability theory as an *experiment*. Using this formal language, we could ask the question, "In a coin toss *experiment*, what is the probability of the event *head*?" And, of course, if it is a fair coin with an equal chance of coming down on either side (and no chance of landing on its edge), we would answer, "$\frac{1}{2}$" or ".5." The set of all possible outcomes of an experiment is called the *sample space* for the experiment. In the coin toss experiment,

Sample space

the sample space is:

$$S = \{\text{head, tail}\}$$

In the card drawing experiment, the sample space has 52 members: ace of hearts, deuce of hearts, and so on.

Most of us are less excited about coins or cards than we are interested in questions like, "What are the chances of making that plane connection?" or "What are my chances of getting a second job interview?" In short, we are concerned with the chances that certain events will happen.

Mutually exclusive events

Events are said to be *mutually exclusive* if one and only one of them can take place at a time. Consider again our example of the coin. We have two possible outcomes, heads and tails. On any toss, either heads or tails may turn up but not both. As a result, the events heads and tails on a single toss are said to be mutually exclusive. Similarly, you will either pass or fail this course or, before the course is over, you may drop it without a grade. Only one of those three outcomes can happen: they are said to be mutually exclusive events. The crucial question to ask in deciding whether events are really mutually exclusive is: "Can two or more of these events occur at one time?" If the answer is yes, the events are *not* mutually exclusive.

A collectively exhaustive list

When a list of the possible events that can result from an experiment includes every possible outcome, the list is said to be *collectively exhaustive*. In our coin example, the list "head and tail" is collectively exhaustive (unless, of course, the coin stands on its edge when we toss it). In a presidential campaign, the list of outcomes "Democratic candidate and Republican candidate" is *not* a collectively exhaustive list of outcomes, since an independent candidate or the candidate of another party could conceivably win.

─────────────────────── **EXERCISES** ───────────────────────

5·5 Give a collectively exhaustive list of the possible outcomes of tossing two dice.

5·6 Give the probability for each of the following totals in the rolling of two dice: 1, 2, 5, 6, 7, 10, 11.

5·7 Give the sample space of outcomes for the following "experiments" in terms of their sex makeup: the birth of (a) twins, (b) triplets.

5·8 In a recent meeting of union members supporting Joe Royal for union president, Royal's leading supporter said "chances are good" that Royal will defeat the single opponent facing him in the election.

a) What are the "events" that could take place with regard to the election?

b) Is your list collectively exhaustive? Are the events in your list mutually exclusive?

c) Disregarding the supporter's comments and knowing no other additional information, what probabilities would you assign to each of your events?

───

3 THREE TYPES OF PROBABILITY

There are three basic ways of classifying probability. These three represent rather different conceptual approaches to the study of probability theory; in fact, experts disagree about which approach is the proper one to use. Let us begin by defining the

1. classical approach
2. relative frequency approach
3. subjective approach

Classical probability

Classical probability defines the probability that an event will occur as:

$$\text{Probability of an event} = \frac{\begin{array}{c}\text{Number of outcomes where}\\\text{the event occurs}\end{array}}{\text{Total number of possible outcomes}} \qquad (5 \cdot 1)$$

It must be emphasized that in order for Equation 5 · 1 to be valid, each of the possible outcomes must be equally likely. This is a rather complex way of defining something that may seem intuitively obvious to us, but we can use it to write our coin toss and dice rolling examples in symbolic form. First, we would state the question, "What is the probability of getting a head on one toss?" as:

$$P(\text{head})$$

Then, using formal terms, we get:

$$P(\text{head}) = \frac{1}{1 + 1}$$

number of outcomes of one toss where the event occurs (in this case, the number that will produce a head)

total number of possible outcomes of one toss (a head or a tail)

$$= .5, \text{ or } \tfrac{1}{2}$$

And for the dice rolling example:

$$P(5) = \frac{1}{1 + 1 + 1 + 1 + 1 + 1}$$

number of outcomes of one roll of the die which will produce a 5

$$= \frac{1}{6}$$

total number of possible outcomes of one roll of the die (getting a 1, a 2, a 3, a 4, a 5, or a 6)

Classical probability is often called *a priori* probability because if we keep using orderly examples like fair coins, unbiased dice, and standard decks of cards, we can state the answer in advance (a priori) *without* tossing a coin, rolling a die, or drawing a card. We do not have to perform experiments to make our probability statements about fair coins, standard card decks, and unbiased dice. Instead, we can make statements based on logical reasoning before any experiments take place.

This approach to probability is useful when we deal with card games, dice games, coin tosses, and the like but has serious problems when we try to apply it to the less orderly decision problems we encounter in management. The classical approach to probability assumes a world that does not exist. It assumes away situations that are very unlikely but that could conceivably happen. Such occurrences as a coin landing on its edge, your classroom burning down during a discussion of probabilities, or your eating pizza while on a business trip at the North Pole are all extremely unlikely but not impossible. Nevertheless, the classical approach assumes them all away. Classical probability also assumes a kind of symmetry about the world, and that assumption can get us into trouble. Real-life situations, disorderly and unlikely as they often are, make it useful to define probabilities in other ways.

Relative frequency of occurrence

Suppose we begin asking ourselves complex questions such as, "What is the probability that I will live to be 85?" or "What are the chances that I will blow one of my stereo speakers if I turn my 200-watt amplifier up to wide open?" or "What is the probability that the location of a new paper plant on the river near our town will cause a substantial fish kill?" We quickly see that we may not be able to state in advance, without experimentation, what these probabilities are. Other approaches may be more useful.

Probability redefined

In the 1800s, British statisticians, interested in a theoretical foundation for calculating risk of losses in life insurance and commercial insurance, began defining probabilities from statistical data collected on births and deaths. Today this approach is called *relative frequency of occurrence*. It defines probability as either:

1. the observed relative frequency of an event in a very large number of trials or
2. the proportion of times that an event occurs in the long run when conditions are stable

Using the relative frequency of occurrence approach

This method uses the relative frequencies of past occurrences as probabilities. We determine how often something has happened in the past and use that figure to predict the probability that it will happen again in the future. Let us look at an example. Suppose an insurance company knows from past actuarial data that of all males 40 years old, about 60 out of every 100,000 will die within a one-year period. Using this method, the company estimates the probability of death for that age group as:

$$\frac{60}{100,000} \text{ or } .0006$$

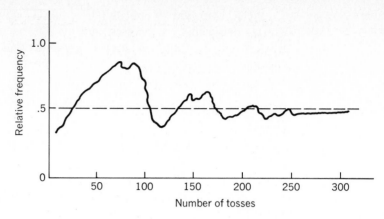

Figure 5·1 Relative frequency of occurrence of heads in 300 tosses of a fair coin

More trials,
greater accuracy

A second characteristic of probabilities established by the relative frequency of occurrence method can be shown by tossing one of our fair coins 300 times. Figure 5 · 1 illustrates the outcomes of these 300 tosses. Here we can see that although the proportion of heads was far from .5 in the first hundred tosses, it seemed to stabilize and approach .5 as the number of tosses increased. In statistical language, we would say that the relative frequency becomes stable as the number of tosses becomes large (if we are tossing the coin under uniform conditions). Thus, when we use the relative frequency approach to establish probabilities, our probability figure will gain accuracy as we increase the number of observations. Of course, this improved accuracy is not free; although more tosses of our coin will produce a more accurate probability of heads occurring, we must bear both the time and the cost of additional observations.

One difficulty with the relative frequency approach is that people often use it without evaluating a sufficient number of outcomes. If you heard someone say, "My aunt and uncle got the flu this year, and are both over 65, so everyone in that age bracket will probably get the flu," you would know that your friend did not base his assumptions on enough evidence. He has insufficient data for establishing a relative frequency of occurrence probability.

Subjective probabilities

Subjective
probability
defined

Subjective probabilities are based on the beliefs of the person making the probability assessment. In fact, subjective probability can be defined as the probability assigned to an event by an individual, based on whatever evidence is available. This evidence may be in the form of relative frequencies of past occurrences, or it may be just an educated guess. Probably the earliest subjective probability estimate of the likelihood of rain occurred when someone's Aunt Bess said, "My corns hurt; I think we're in for a downpour." Subjective assessments of probability permit the widest flexibility of the three concepts we have discussed. The decision maker can use whatever evidence is available and temper this with personal feelings about the situation.

Using the subjective approach

Subjective probability assignments are frequently found when events occur only once or at most a very few times. Consider the judge who is deciding whether to allow the construction of a nuclear power plant on a site where there is some evidence of a geological fault. He must ask himself the question, "What is the probability of a major nuclear accident at this location?" The fact that there is no relative frequency of occurrence evidence of previous accidents at this location does not excuse him from making a decision. He must use his best judgment in trying to determine the subjective probabilities of a nuclear accident.

Since most higher level social and managerial decisions are concerned with specific, unique situations, rather than with a long series of identical situations, decision makers at this level make considerable use of subjective probabilities.

The subjective approach to assigning probabilities was introduced in 1926 by Frank Ramsey in his book, *The Foundation of Mathematics and Other Logical Essays*. The concept was further developed by Bernard Koopman, Richard Good, and Leonard Savage, names that appear regularly in advanced work in this field. Savage pointed out that two reasonable people faced with the same evidence could easily come up with quite different subjective probabilities for the same event. Two people who make opposing bets on the outcome of an Indiana basketball game would understand quite well what he meant.

─────────────── **EXERCISES** ───────────────

5·9 Below is a frequency distribution of annual sales commission from a survey of 255 media salespersons. Based on this information, what is the probability that a media salesperson makes a commission
a) between $8,000 and $12,000   **c)** more than $24,000
b) less than $8,000   **d)** between $12,000 and $16,000

Annual commissions (dollars)	Frequency
0–3,999	5
4,000–7,999	15
8,000–11,999	40
12,000–15,999	90
16,000–19,999	30
20,000–23,999	25
24,000 +	20

5·10 Determine the probabilities of the following events in drawing a card from a standard deck of 52 cards:

a) A queen **d)** A red card
b) A club **e)** A face card (king, queen, or jack)
c) An ace in a red suit **f)** What type of probability estimates are these?

5·11 The office manager of an insurance company has the following data on the functioning of the copiers in the office:

Copier number	Days functioning	Days out of service
1	244	16
2	252	8
3	237	23
4	208	52
5	254	6

What is the probability of a copier being out of service on a given day?

5·12 Classify the following probability estimates as to their type (classical, relative frequency, or subjective):

a) The probability that you will make a B in this course is .75. *Fr*
b) The probability that a randomly selected family from a particular community has two children is .25. *C*
c) The probability that my candidate will win the election is .60.
d) The probability that a student from this high school will go on to college is .90. *F*
e) The probability of my ticket winning a raffle drawing for which 1,000 tickets were sold is .001. *C*

---

4 PROBABILITY RULES

Most managers who use probabilities are concerned with two conditions:

1. the case where one event *or* another will occur
2. the situation where two or more events will both occur

We are interested in the first case when we ask, "What is the probability that today's demand will exceed our inventory?" To illustrate the second situation, we could ask, "What is the probability that today's demand will exceed our inventory *and* that more than 10 percent of our sales force will not report for work?" In the sections to follow, we shall illustrate methods of determining answers to questions like these under a variety of conditions.

Some commonly used symbols, definitions, and rules

Symbol for a marginal probability. In probability theory, we use symbols to simplify the presentation of ideas. As we discussed earlier in this chapter, the probability of the event A would be expressed as:

$$P(A) \quad \textbf{probability of event } A \text{ happening}$$

Marginal or
unconditional
probability

A *single* probability means that only one event can take place. It is called a *marginal*, or *unconditional probability*. To illustrate, let us suppose that 50 members of a school class drew tickets to see which student would get a free trip to the National Rock Festival. Any one of the students could calculate his or her chances of winning by the formulation:

$$P(\text{winning}) = \frac{1}{50}$$

$$= .02$$

In this case, a student's chance is 1 in 50 because we are certain that the possible events are mutually exclusive; that is, only one student can win at a time.

There is a nice diagrammatic way to illustrate this example and other probability concepts. We use a pictorial representation called a *Venn diagram*, after the nineteenth-century English mathematician, John Venn. In these diagrams, the entire sample space is represented by a rectangle, and events are represented by parts of the rectangle. If two events *are* mutually exclusive, their parts of the rectangle will not overlap each other, as shown in Fig. 5 · 2(a). If two events are *not* mutually exclusive, their parts of the rectangle *will* overlap, as in Fig. 5 · 2(b).

Venn diagrams

Since probabilities behave a lot like areas, we shall let the rectangle have an area of one (because the probability of *something* happening is one). Then the probability of an event is the area of *its* part of the rectangle. Figure 5 · 2(c) illustrates this for the National Rock Festival example. There the rectangle is divided into 50 equal, nonoverlapping parts.

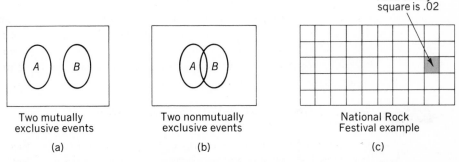

Two mutually exclusive events	Two nonmutually exclusive events	National Rock Festival example
(a)	(b)	(c)

Figure 5 · 2 Some Venn diagrams

Addition rule for mutually exclusive events.   Often, however, we are interested in the probability that one thing *or* another will occur. If these two events are mutually exclusive, we can express this probability using the addition rule for mutually exclusive events. This rule is expressed symbolically as:

$$P(A \text{ or } B) \qquad \textbf{probability} \text{ of either } A \text{ or } B \text{ happening}$$

and is calculated as follows:

$$P(A \text{ or } B) = P(A) + P(B) \qquad\qquad (5 \cdot 2)$$

This addition rule is illustrated by the Venn diagram in Fig. 5 · 3, where we note that the area in the two circles together (denoting the event *A* or *B*) is the sum of the areas of the two circles.

Now to use this formula in an example. Five equally capable students are waiting for a summer job interview with a company that has announced that it will hire only one of five by random drawing. The group consists of Bill, Helen, John, Sally, and Walter. If our question is, "What is the probability that John will be the candidate?" we can use Equation 5 · 1 and give the answer:

$$P(\text{John}) = \frac{1}{5} = .2$$

If, however, we ask, "What is the probability that either John *or* Sally will be the candidate?" we would use Equation 5 · 2:

$$P(\text{John or Sally}) = P(\text{John}) + P(\text{Sally})$$
$$= \frac{1}{5} + \frac{1}{5} = \frac{2}{5} = .4$$

Let's calculate the probability of two or more events happening once more. Table 5 · 1 contains data on the size of families in a certain town. We are interested in the question, "What is the probability that a family chosen at random from this town will have 4 or more children

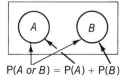

$$P(A \text{ or } B) = P(A) + P(B)$$

Figure 5·3 Venn diagram for the addition rule for mutually exclusive events

TABLE 5·1 Family size data

Number of children	0	1	2	3	4	5	6 or more
Proportion of families having this many children	.05	.10	.30	.25	.15	.10	.05

(that is, 4, 5, or 6 or more children)?" Using Equation 5 · 2, we can calculate the answer as:

$$P(4, 5, 6 \text{ or more}) = P(4) + P(5) + P(6 \text{ or more})$$
$$= .15 + .10 + .05 = .30$$

A special case of Equation 5 · 2

There is an important special case of Equation 5 · 2. For any event A, either A happens or it doesn't. So the events A and *not A* are exclusive and exhaustive. Equation 5 · 2 yields the result:

$$P(A) + P(not\ A) = 1$$

or equivalently:

$$P(A) = 1 - P(not\ A)$$

For example, referring back to Table 5 · 1, the probability of a family having 5 or fewer children is most easily obtained by subtracting from 1 the probability of the family having 6 or more children, and thus is seen to be .95.

Probability of one or more events not *mutually exclusive*

Addition rule for events that are not mutually exclusive. If two events are not mutually exclusive, it is possible for both events to occur. In these cases, our addition rule must be modified. For example, what is the probability of drawing either an ace *or* a heart from a deck of cards? Obviously, the events ace and heart can occur together because we could draw the ace of hearts. Thus, ace and heart are not mutually exclusive events. We must adjust our Equation 5 · 2 to avoid double counting; that is, we have to *reduce* the probability of drawing either an ace or a heart *by the chance* that we could draw both of them together. As a result, the correct equation for the probability of one or more of two events that are not mutually exclusive is:

probability of A happening   probability of A and B happening
                                                   together

$$P(A \text{ or } B) = P(A) + P(B) - P(A \text{ and } B) \qquad (5 \cdot 3)$$

probability of A *or* B happening   probability of B happening
when A and B are *not* mutually
exclusive

A Venn diagram illustrating Equation 5 · 3 is given in Fig. 5 · 4. There, the event A or B is outlined with a heavy line. The event A *and* B is the crosshatched wedge in the middle. If we add the areas of circles A and B, we *double count* the wedge, and so we must subtract it, to make sure it is counted only once.

Using Equation 5 · 3 to determine the probability of drawing either an ace *or* a heart, we can calculate:

$$P(\text{ace or heart}) = P(\text{ace}) + P(\text{heart}) - P(\text{ace and heart})$$
$$= \frac{4}{52} + \frac{13}{52} - \frac{1}{52} = \frac{16}{52} = \frac{4}{13}$$

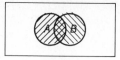

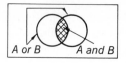

Figure 5·4 Venn diagram for the addition rule for two events not mutually exclusive

Let's do a second example. The employees of a certain company have elected five of their number to represent them on the employee-management productivity council. Profiles of the five are as follows:

Sex	Male	Male	Female	Female	Male
Age	30	32	45	20	40

This group decides to elect a spokesperson by drawing a name from a hat. Our question is, "What is the probability the spokesperson will be *either* female *or* over 35?" Using Equation 5 · 3, we can set up the solution to our question like this:

$$P(\text{female or over 35}) = P(\text{female}) + P(\text{over 35}) - P(\text{female and over 35})$$

$$= \frac{2}{5} + \frac{2}{5} - \frac{1}{5} = \frac{3}{5}$$

We can check our work by inspection and see that, of the five persons in the group, three would fit the requirements of being either female or over 35.

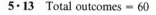 **EXERCISES**

From the Venn diagrams below, which indicate the number of outcomes of an experiment corresponding to each event and the number of outcomes that do not correspond to either event, give the probabilities indicated:

5·13 Total outcomes = 60

P(*A*) =
P(*B*) =
P(*A* or *B*) =

5·14 Total outcomes = 50

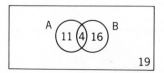

P(*A*) =
P(*B*) =
P(*A* or *B*) =

5·15 As the safety officer of an airline, Debbie Best has been asked to give a talk to the press concerning engine safety. As part of her talk, she has decided to include the probability of a two-engine jet having engine failure on a flight. After consulting her records, she finds the following information about last year's operating record for two-engine aircraft:

> Twenty-nine reported failure of the right engine alone.
> Thirty-three reported failure of the left engine alone.
> There was one crash attributed to double engine failure.
> There were 345,000 flights during the year.

What probability should she report to the press?

5·16 The manager of a chemical plant located on the Mississippi River knows that in an upcoming court case the company may be found guilty of polluting the river. Further, he knows that if found guilty, the company will be required to install a water purification system, pay a fine, or both. Thus far, only 10 percent of the companies involved in similar cases have been both fined and required to install the purification system. In addition, when the court's ruling has not involved both penalties, a company has been three times more likely to be fined than to be required to install the purification system. If 28 percent of the companies have been found guilty thus far, what is the probability that this company will be required to install a purification system?

---

5 PROBABILITIES UNDER CONDITIONS OF STATISTICAL INDEPENDENCE

Independence defined

When two events happen, the outcome of the first event may or may not have an effect on the outcome of the second event. That is, the events may be either dependent or independent. In this section, we examine events that are *statistically independent*: the occurrence of one event *has no effect* on the probability of the occurrence of any other event. There are three types of probabilities under statistical independence:

1. marginal
2. joint
3. conditional

Marginal probabilities under statistical independence

Marginal probability of independent events

As we explained previously, a marginal or unconditional probability is the simple probability of the occurrence of an event. In a fair coin toss, $P(H) = .5$ and $P(T) = .5$; that is, the probability of heads equals .5, and the probability of tails equals .5. This is true for every toss, no matter how many tosses have been made or what their outcomes have been. Every toss stands alone and is in no way connected with any other toss. Thus the outcome of *each* toss of a fair coin is a statistically independent event.

Imagine that we have a biased or unfair coin that has been altered in such a way that heads occurs .90 of the times and tails .10 of the time. On each individual toss, $P(H) = .90$ and $P(T) = .10$. The outcome of any particular toss is completely unrelated to the outcomes of the tosses that may precede or follow it. The outcome of each toss of *this* coin is a statistically independent event, too, even though the coin is biased.

Joint probabilities under statistical independence

Multiplication rule
for joint,
independent
events

The probability of two or more independent events occurring together or in succession is the product of their marginal probabilities. Mathematically, this is stated:

$$P(AB) = P(A) \times P(B) \qquad (5 \cdot 4)$$

where:

$P(AB)$ = probability of events A and B occurring together or in succession; this is known as a *joint probability*
$P(A)$ = marginal probability of event A occurring
$P(B)$ = marginal probability of event B occurring

In terms of the fair coin example, the probability of heads on two successive tosses is the probability of heads on the first toss (which we shall call H_1) times the probability of heads on the second toss (H_2). That is $P(H_1 H_2) = P(H_1) \times P(H_2)$. We have shown that the events are statistically independent because the probability of any outcome is not affected by any preceding outcome. Therefore, the probability of heads on any toss is .5, and $P(H_1 H_2) = .5 \times .5 = .25$. Thus the probability of heads on two successive tosses is .25.

Likewise, the probability of getting 3 heads on three successive tosses is $P(H_1 H_2 H_3) = .5 \times .5 \times .5 = .125$.

Assume next that we are going to toss an unfair coin that has $P(H) = .8$ and $P(T) = .2$. The events (outcomes) are independent because the probabilities of all tosses are exactly the same—the individual tosses are completely separate and in no way affected by any other toss or outcome. Suppose our question is, "What is the probability of getting 3 heads on three successive tosses?" We use Equation 5 · 4 and discover that:

$$P(H_1 H_2 H_3) = P(H_1) \times P(H_2) \times P(H_3) = .8 \times .8 \times .8 = .512$$

Now let us ask the probability of getting 3 tails on three successive tosses:

$$P(T_1 T_2 T_3) = P(T_1) \times P(T_2) \times P(T_3) = .2 \times .2 \times .2 = .008$$

Note that these two probabilities do not add up to 1 because the events $H_1 H_2 H_3$ and $T_1 T_2 T_3$ do not constitute a collectively exhaustive list. They *are* mutually exclusive, because if one occurs, the other cannot.

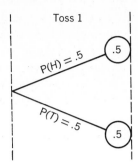

Toss 1

P(H) = .5 → .5

P(T) = .5 → .5

Figure 5·5 Probability tree of one toss

We can make the probabilities of events even more explicit using a *probability tree*. Figure 5 · 5 is a probability tree showing the possible outcomes and their respective probabilities for one toss of a fair coin.

For toss 1 we have two possible outcomes, heads and tails, each with a probability of .5. Assume that the outcome of toss 1 is heads. We toss again. The second toss has two possible outcomes, heads and tails, each with a probability of .5. In Fig. 5 · 6 we add these two branches of the tree. Had the outcome of toss 1 been tails, the second toss would have stemmed from the lower branch in Fig. 5 · 5. Notice that on two

tosses we have four possible outcomes: H_1H_2, H_1T_2, T_1H_2, and T_1T_2 (remember that the subscripts indicate the toss number and that T_2, for example, means tails on toss 2). Thus, after two tosses we may arrive at any one of four possible points. Since we are going to toss three times, we must add more branches to the tree.

Assuming that we have had heads on the first two tosses, we are now ready to begin adding branches for the third toss. As before, the two possible outcomes are heads and tails, each with a probability of .5. The additional branches are added in exactly the same manner. The completed probability tree is shown in Fig. 5 · 7. Notice that both heads and tails have a probability of .5 of occurring no matter how far from the origin (first toss) any particular toss may be. This follows from our

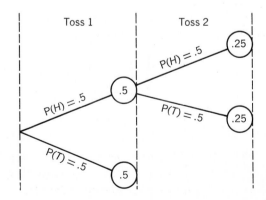

Toss 1   Toss 2

P(H) = .5 → .5
P(H) = .5 → .25
P(T) = .5 → .25
P(T) = .5 → .5

Figure 5·6 Probability tree of partial second toss

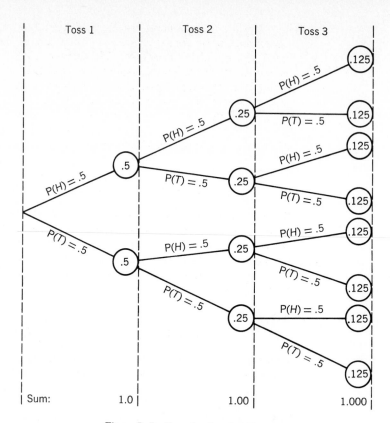

Figure 5·7 Completed probability tree

*All tosses
are independent*

definition of independence: no event is affected by the events preceding or following it.

Suppose we are going to toss a fair coin and want to know the probability that all three tosses will result in heads. Expressing the problem symbolically, we want to know $P(H_1 H_2 H_3)$. From the mathematical definition of the joint probability of independent events, we know that

$$P(H_1 H_2 H_3) = P(H_1) \times P(H_2) \times P(H_3) = .5 \times .5 \times .5 = .125$$

We could have read this answer from the probability tree in Fig. 5 · 7 by following the branches giving $H_1 H_2 H_3$. Try solving these problems using the probability tree in Fig. 5 · 7:

Example 1

What is the probability of getting tails, tails, heads *in that order* on three successive tosses of a fair coin?

Solution. If we follow the branches giving tails on the first toss, tails on the second toss, and heads on the third toss, we arrive at the probability of .125. Thus $P(T_1 T_2 H_3) = .125$.

It is important to notice that the probability of arriving at a given point by a given route is *not* the same as the probability of, say, heads on the third toss. $P(H_1 T_2 H_3) = .125$, but $P(H_3) = .5$. The first is a case of *joint probability*, that is, the probability of getting heads on the first toss, tails on the second, and heads on the third. The latter, by contrast, is simply the *marginal probability* of getting heads on a particular toss, in this instance toss 3.

Notice that the sum of the probabilities of all the possible outcomes for each toss is 1. This results from the fact that we have mutually exclusive and collectively exhaustive lists of outcomes.

Example 2

What is the probability of *at least* two heads on three tosses?

Solution. Recalling that the probabilities of mutually exclusive events are additive, we can note the possible ways that at least two heads on three tosses can occur, and we can sum their individual probabilities. The outcomes satisfying the requirement are $H_1 H_2 H_3$, $H_1 H_2 T_3$, $H_1 T_2 H_3$, and $T_1 H_2 H_3$. Since each of these has an individual probability of .125, the sum is .5. Thus the probability of at least two heads on three tosses is .5.

Example 3

What is the probability of *at least* 1 tail on three tosses?

Solution. There is only one case in which no tails occur, namely, $H_1 H_2 H_3$. Therefore, we can simply subtract for the answer:

$$1 - P(H_1 H_2 H_3) = 1 - .125 = .875$$

The probability of at least 1 tail occurring in three successive tosses is .875.

Conditional probabilities under statistical independence

Conditional probability

Thus far we have considered two types of probabilities, marginal (or unconditional) probability and joint probability. Symbolically, marginal probability is $P(A)$ and joint probability is $P(AB)$. Besides these two, there is one other type of probability, known as *conditional* probability. Symbolically, conditional probability is written:

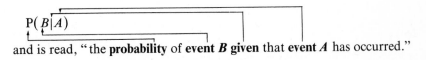

and is read, "the **probability** of **event** B **given** that **event** A has occurred."

Conditional probability of independent events

Conditional probability is the probability that a second event (B) will occur *if* a first event (A) has already happened.

For statistically independent events, the conditional probability of event B given that event A has occurred is simply the probability of event B:

$$P(B|A) = P(B) \qquad (5 \cdot 5)$$

At first glance, this may seem contradictory. Remember, however, that by definition, independent events are those whose probabilities are in no way affected by the occurrence of each other. In fact, statistical independence is defined symbolically as the condition in which $P(B|A) = P(B)$.

We can understand conditional probability better by solving an illustrative problem. Our question is, "What is the probability that the second toss of a fair coin will result in heads, given that heads resulted on the first toss? Symbolically, this is written as $P(H_2|H_1)$. Remember that for two independent events, the results of the first toss have absolutely no effect on the results of the second toss. Since the probabilities of heads and tails are identical for every toss, the probability of heads on the second toss is .5. Thus, we must say that $P(H_2|H_1) = .5$.

Table $5 \cdot 2$ summarizes the three types of probabilities and their mathematical formulas under conditions of statistical independence.

TABLE $5 \cdot 2$ Probabilities under statistical independence

Type of probability	Symbol	Formula
Marginal	$P(A)$	$P(A)$
Joint	$P(AB)$	$P(A) \times P(B)$
Conditional	$P(B|A)$	$P(B)$

─────────────── **EXERCISES** ───────────────

5·17 Use a probability tree to answer the following questions. Assuming that A, B, and C are independent events with marginal probabilities: $P(A) = .2$, $P(B) = .5$, $P(C) = .3$; and that the subscripts represent trial numbers, find
    a) $P(A_1 B_2 C_3)$ **b)** $P(C_1 C_2 C_3)$ **c)** $P(A_1 C_2 B_3 C_4)$ **d)** $P(A_1 B_2)$ **e)** $P(B_1 B_2)$

5·18 What is the probability that, in selecting two cards, one at a time, from a deck with replacement, the second card is
    a) a spade, given that the first card was a heart?
    b) black, given that the first card was red?
    c) a queen, given that the first card was a queen?

5·19 A social psychologist plans to use two current topics of interest—abortion and support for nuclear power plants— in a proposed study of attitude changes. He knows from a questionnaire completed at the beginning of the experiment that 35 percent of the subjects favor the construction of nuclear power plants and 50 percent are in favor of federally subsidized abortions. He also knows that individual support for one issue is independent of support for the other issue.
    a) What is the probability that a subject supports both federally funded abortions and the construction of nuclear power plants?
    b) What is the probability that a person supports federally funded abortions or nuclear power plants, but not both?

5·20 What is the probability that a couple's second child will be

    a) a boy, given that their first child was a girl?

    b) a girl, given that their first child was a girl?

---

6 PROBABILITIES UNDER CONDITIONS
OF STATISTICAL DEPENDENCE

Dependence defined

Statistical dependence exists when the probability of some event is dependent upon or affected by the occurrence of some other event. Just as with independent events, the types of probabilities under statistical dependence are

1. conditional
2. joint
3. marginal

Conditional probabilities under statistical dependence

Conditional and joint probabilities under statistical dependence are more involved than marginal probabilities are. We shall discuss conditional probabilities first, because the concept of joint probabilities is best illustrated by using conditional probabilities as a basis.

Examples of conditional probability of dependent events

    Assume that we have one box containing 10 balls distributed as follows:

        3 are white and dotted
        1 is white and striped
        2 are gray and dotted
        4 are gray and striped

The probability of drawing any one ball from this box is .1, since there are 10 balls, each with equal probability of being drawn. The discussion of the following examples will be facilitated by reference to Table 5 · 3 and to Fig. 5 · 8 which shows the contents of the box in diagram form.

Question 1

Suppose that someone draws a white ball from the box. What is the probability that it is dotted? What is the probability it is striped?

Solution. This question can be expressed symbolically as $P(D|W)$, or "What is the conditional probability that this ball is dotted, *given* that it is white?"

    We have been told that the ball that was drawn is white. Therefore, to calculate the probability that the ball is dotted, we will ignore *all* gray balls and concern ourselves with white only. In diagram form, we consider only what is shown in Fig. 5 · 9.

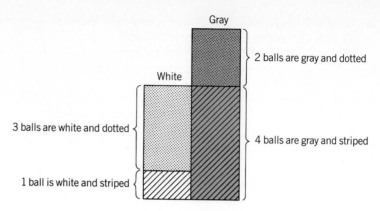

Figure 5·8 Contents of the box

TABLE 5·3 Color and configuration of 10 balls

Event	Probability of event	
1	.1 ⎫	
2	.1 ⎬	white and dotted
3	.1 ⎭	
4	.1 ⎬	white and striped
5	.1 ⎫	gray and dotted
6	.1 ⎭	
7	.1 ⎫	
8	.1 ⎬	gray and striped
9	.1 ⎪	
10	.1 ⎭	

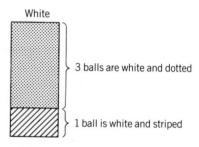

Figure 5·9 Probability of dotted and striped, given white

From the statement of the problem, we know that there are 4 white balls, 3 of which are dotted and 1 of which is striped. Our problem is now to find the simple probabilities of dotted and striped. To do so we divide the number of balls in each category by the total number of white balls:

$$P(D|W) = \frac{3}{4} = .75$$

$$P(S|W) = \frac{1}{4} = \frac{.25}{1.00}$$

In other words, three-fourths of the white balls are dotted, and one-fourth of the white balls are striped. Thus, the probability of dotted, given that the ball is white, is .75. Likewise, the probability of striped, given that the ball is white is .25.

Now we can see how our reasoning will enable us to develop the formula for conditional probability under statistical dependence. We can first assure ourselves that these events *are* statistically dependent by observing that the color of the balls (white or gray) determines the probabilities that they are either striped or dotted. For example, a gray ball is more likely to be striped than a white ball. Since color affects the probability of striped or dotted, these two events are dependent.

To calculate the probability of dotted given white, $P(D|W)$, we divided the probability of white and dotted balls (3 out of 10, or .3) by the probability of white balls (4 out of 10, or .4):

$$P(D|W) = \frac{P(DW)}{P(W)}$$

Expressed as a general formula using the letters A and B to represent the two events, the equation is:

Formula for conditional probability of dependent events

$$P(B|A) = \frac{P(BA)}{P(A)} \qquad\qquad (5 \cdot 6)$$

This is the formula for *conditional probability under statistical dependence*.

Question 2

Continuing with our example of the white and gray balls, let's answer the questions, "What is $P(D|G)$?" and "What is $P(S|G)$?"

Solution.

$$P(D|G) = \frac{P(DG)}{P(G)} = \frac{.2}{.6} = \frac{1}{3}$$

$$P(S|G) = \frac{P(SG)}{P(G)} = \frac{.4}{.6} = \frac{\frac{2}{3}}{1.0}$$

The total probability of gray is .6 (6 out of 10 balls). To determine the probability that the ball (which we know is gray) will be dotted, we divide the probability of gray and dotted (.2) by the probability of gray (.6), or .2/.6 = 1/3. Similarly, to determine the probability that the ball will be striped, we divide the probability of gray and striped (.4) by the probability of gray (.6), or .4/.6 = 2/3.

Question 3

Calculate $P(G|D)$ and $P(W|D)$.

Solution. Since we have been told that the ball that was drawn is dotted, we can disregard striped and consider only dotted. Now see Fig. 5 · 10 showing the probabilities of gray and white given dotted. Notice that the relative proportions

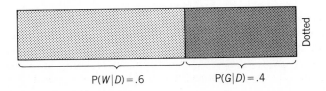

$P(W|D) = .6$ $P(G|D) = .4$

Figure 5 · 10 Probability of white and gray, given dotted

of the two are as .4 is to .6. The calculations used to arrive at these proportions were:

$$P(G|D) = \frac{P(GD)}{P(D)} = \frac{.2}{.5} = .4$$

$$P(W|D) = \frac{P(WD)}{P(D)} = \frac{.3}{.5} = \frac{.6}{\overline{1.0}}$$

Question 4

Calculate $P(W|S)$ and $P(G|S)$

Solution.

$$P(W|S) = \frac{P(WS)}{P(S)} = \frac{.1}{.5} = .2$$

$$P(G|S) = \frac{P(GS)}{P(S)} = \frac{.4}{.5} = \frac{.8}{\overline{1.0}}$$

Joint probabilities under statistical dependence

We have shown that the formula for conditional probability under conditions of statistical dependence is:

$$P(B|A) = \frac{P(BA)}{P(A)} \qquad (5 \cdot 6)$$

If we solve this for $P(BA)$ by cross multiplication, we have the formula for *joint probability under conditions of statistical dependence*:

Multiplication rule for joint, dependent events

joint probability of events B and A happening together or in succession

probability of event B given that event A has happened

$$P(BA) = P(B|A) \times P(A)* \qquad (5 \cdot 7)$$

probability that event A will happen

Notice that this formula is *not* $P(BA) = P(B) \times P(A)$, as it would be under conditions of statistical independence.

Converting the general formula $P(BA) = P(B|A) \times P(A)$ to our example and to the terms of white, gray, dotted, and striped, we have $P(WD) = P(W|D) \times P(D)$, or $P(WD) = .6 \times .5 = .3$. Here .6 is the probability of white given dotted (computed in example 3 above), and .5 is the probability of dotted.

*To find the joint probability of events A and B, you could also use the formula $P(BA) = P(AB) = P(A|B) \times P(B)$. This is because $BA = AB$.

$P(WD) = .3$ can be verified in Table 5 · 3, where we originally arrived at the probability by inspection: 3 balls out of 10 are white and dotted.

Several examples The following joint probabilities are computed in the same manner and can also be substantiated by reference to Table 5 · 3.

$$P(WS) = P(W|S) \times P(S) = .2 \times .5 = .1$$
$$P(GD) = P(G|D) \times P(D) = .4 \times .5 = .2$$
$$P(GS) = P(G|S) \times P(S) = .8 \times .5 = .4$$

Marginal probabilities under statistical dependence

Marginal probabilities under statistical dependence are computed by summing up the probabilities of all the joint events in which the simple event occurs. In the example above, we can compute the marginal probability of the event white by summing the probabilities of the joint events in which white occurred:

$$P(W) = P(WD) + P(WS) = .3 + .1 = .4$$

Similarly, the marginal probability of the event gray can be computed by summing the probabilities of the joint events in which gray occurred:

$$P(G) = P(GD) + P(GS) = .2 + .4 = .6$$

In like manner, we can compute the marginal probability of the event dotted by summing the probabilities of the joint events in which dotted occurred:

$$P(D) = P(WD) + P(GD) = .3 + .2 = .5$$

And finally, the marginal probability of the event striped can be computed by summing the probabilities of the joint events in which striped occurred:

$$P(S) = P(WS) + P(GS) = .1 + .4 = .5$$

TABLE 5 · 4 Probabilities under statistical independence and dependence

Type of probability	Symbol	Formula under statistical independence	Formula under statistical dependence
Marginal	$P(A)$	$P(A)$	Sum of the probabilities of the joint events in which A occurs
Joint	$P(AB)$ or $P(BA)$	$P(A) \times P(B)$ $P(B) \times P(A)$	$P(A|B) \times P(B)$ $P(B|A) \times P(A)$
Conditional	$P(B|A)$	$P(B)$	$\dfrac{P(BA)}{P(A)}$
	or $P(A|B)$	$P(A)$	$\dfrac{P(AB)}{P(B)}$

These four marginal probabilities $P(W) = .4$, $P(G) = .6$, $P(D) = .5$, and $P(S) = .5$ can be verified by inspection of Table 5 · 3.

We have now considered the three types of probability (conditional, joint, and marginal) under conditions of statistical dependence. Table 5 · 4 provides a résumé of our development of probabilities under both statistical independence and statistical dependence.

--- **EXERCISES** ---

5·21 Myers Clothiers knows that 1 out of 10 families in its trading area qualifies for their charge accounts and that 1 out of 15 families in this area has applied for the accounts. From past records, 90 percent of credit applications are accepted. What is the probability that an area family will apply for a Myers charge card and be accepted?

5·22 Two events, A and B, are statistically dependent. $P(A) = .25$, $P(B) = .33$, and $P(A$ or $B) = .43$. Find the probability that
a) Neither A nor B will occur.　c) B will occur, given that A has occurred.
b) Both A and B will occur.　d) A will occur, given that B has occurred.

5·23 Given that $P(A) = \frac{1}{6}$, $P(B) = \frac{1}{3}$, $P(C) = \frac{4}{9}$, $P(A$ and $C) = \frac{1}{12}$, and $P(B|C) = \frac{1}{4}$, find the following probabilities:
a) $P(A|C)$　b) $P(C|A)$　c) $P(B$ and $C)$　d) $P(C|B)$

5·24 The Virginia National Bank estimates that 10 percent of adults in Charlottesville have checking accounts with Virginia National, and 5 percent of adults there have passbook savings accounts at that bank. In addition, 3 percent of adults in Charlottesville have both checking and passbook savings accounts with the Virginia National Bank.
a) What is the probability that an adult in Charlottesville will have a checking account with the bank, if that depositor has a savings account with them?
b) What is the probability that an adult in Charlottesville will have a savings account with the bank, if he or she has a Virginia National Bank checking account?

5·25 In a study of the number of men and women employed at a plant, data show that 65 percent of the employees are males, 40 percent of the employees are production workers, and that the probability that an employee is a male production worker is .30. If a randomly selected employee turns to be a production worker, what is the probability that the employee is a male?

7 REVISING PRIOR ESTIMATES OF PROBABILITIES: BAYES' THEOREM

At the beginning of the baseball season, the fans of last year's pennant winner thought that their team had a good chance of winning again. As the season progressed, however, injuries sidelined their shortstop and their chief rivals drafted a terrific homerun hitter. The team began to lose. Late in the season, the fans realized that they must alter their prior probabilities of winning.

A similar situation often occurs in business. If a manager of a boutique finds that most of the purple and chartreuse ski jackets that she thought would sell so well are hanging on the rack, she must revise her prior probabilities and order a different color combination.

In both these cases, certain probabilities were altered after the people involved got additional information. The new probabilities are known as revised, or *posterior* probabilities. Because probabilities can be revised as more information is gained, probability theory is of great value in managerial decision making.

The origin of the concept of obtaining posterior probabilities with limited information is attributable to the Reverend Thomas Bayes (1702–1761), and the basic formula for conditional probability under dependence,

$$P(B|A) = \frac{P(BA)}{P(A)} \qquad (5 \cdot 6)$$

is called *Bayes' theorem.*

Bayes, an Englishman, was a Presbyterian minister and a competent mathematician. He pondered how he might prove the existence of God by examining whatever evidence the world about him provided. Attempting to show "that the Principal End of the Divine Providence... is the Happiness of His Creatures," Reverend Bayes used mathematics to study God. Unfortunately, the theological implications of his findings so alarmed the good Reverend Bayes that he refused to permit publication of his work during his lifetime. Nevertheless, his work outlived him, and modern decision theory is often called Bayesian decision theory in his honor.

Bayes' theorem offers a powerful statistical method of evaluating new information and revising our prior estimates (based on limited information only) of the probability that things are in one state or another. If correctly used, it avoids the necessity of gathering masses of data over long periods of time in order to make decisions based upon probabilities.

Calculating posterior probabilities

Consider the problem of a Little League baseball team that has been using an automatic pitching machine. If the machine is correctly set up—that is, properly adjusted—it will pitch strikes 85 percent of the time. If it is incorrectly set up, it will pitch strikes only 35 percent of the time. Past experience indicates that 75 percent of the setups of the machine are correctly done. After the machine has been set up at batting practice one day, it throws a strike on the first pitch. What is the revised probability that the setup has been done correctly? Table 5 · 5 illustrates how we can answer this question. We can interpret the table column

TABLE 5·5 Posterior probabilities with joint events

Event	P(event)	P(1 strike|event)	P(event, 1 strike)
Correct	.75	.85	.85 × .75 = .6375
Incorrect	.25	.35	.35 × .25 = .0875
	1.00		P(1 strike) = .7250

headings in Table 5 · 5 as follows:

1. P(*event*) describes the individual probabilities of correct and incorrect. P(correct) = .75 is given in the problem. Thus we can compute:

$$P(\text{incorrect}) = 1.00 - P(\text{correct}) = 1.00 - .75 = .25$$

2. P(*1 strike*|*event*) represents the probability of a strike given that the setup is correct or incorrect. These probabilities are given in the problem.

3. P(*event*, 1 strike) is the probability of the joint occurrence of the event (correct or incorrect) and 1 strike. We can compute the probabilities in this problem as follows:

$$P(\text{correct, 1 strike}) = .85 \times .75 = .6375$$

$$P(\text{incorrect, 1 strike}) = .35 \times .25 = .0875$$

Notice that if A = event and B = strike, these last two probabilities conform to the general mathematical formula for joint probabilities under conditions of dependence: $P(AB) = P(BA) = P(B|A) \times P(A)$, Equation 5 · 7.

After finishing the computations in Table 5 · 5, we are ready to determine the revised probability that the machine is correctly set up. We use the general formula.

$$P(A|B) = \frac{P(AB)}{P(B)} \qquad (5 \cdot 6)$$

and convert it to the terms and numbers in this problem:

$$P(\text{correct}| 1 \text{ strike}) = \frac{P(\text{correct, 1 strike})}{P(1 \text{ strike})}$$

$$= \frac{.6375}{.7250} = .8793$$

The *posterior probability* that the machine is correctly set up is .8793 or 87.93 percent. We have thus revised our original probability of a correct setup from 75 to 87.93 percent, based on 1 strike being thrown.

Two more strikes are thrown

Posterior probabilities with more data. Now suppose that we observe two more pitches, and that both of them are strikes too. This is even stronger evidence that the machine has been correctly set up. But

TABLE 5·6 Posterior probabilities after 3 strikes

Event	P(event)	P(3 strikes|event)	P(event, 3 strikes)
Correct	.75	.85 × .85 × .85 = .6141	.6141 × .75 = .4606
Incorrect	.25	.35 × .35 × .35 = .0429	.0429 × .25 = .0107
			P(3 strikes) = .4713

$$P(\text{correct setup} \mid 3 \text{ strikes}) = \frac{P(\text{correct setup}, 3 \text{ strikes})}{P(3 \text{ strikes})}$$

$$= \frac{.4606}{.4713} = .9773$$

how strong is this evidence? In Table 5 · 6, we solve this problem and see that P(correct|3 strikes) = .9773 or 97.73 percent.

Posterior probabilities with inconsistent outcomes

An example with inconsistent outcomes

But little league pitchers don't throw just strikes and neither do pitching machines throw strikes consistently. In the case of the pitching machine for example, we might find the first five pitches to be: strike, ball, strike, strike, strike. Calculating our posterior probability that the machine is correctly set up in this case is really no more difficult than it would be with a set of perfectly consistent outcomes. Using the notation S = strike and B = ball, we have solved this example in Table 5 · 7.

TABLE 5 · 7 Posterior probabilities with inconsistent outcomes

Event	P(event)	P(S|event)	P(SBSSS|event)	P(event, SBSSS)
Correct	.75	.85	.85 × .15 × .85 × .85 × .85 = .07830	.07830 × .75 = .05873
Incorrect	.25	.35	.35 × .65 × .35 × .35.×.35 = .00975	.00975 × .25 = .00244
	1.00			P(SBSSS) = .06117

$$P(\text{correct setup} \mid SBSSS) = \frac{P(\text{correct setup}, SBSSS)}{P(SBSSS)}$$

$$= \frac{.05873}{.06117} = .9601$$

EXERCISES

5·26 Given: the probabilities of three events, A, B, and C, occurring are: P(A) = .5, P(B) = .3, and P(C) = .2. Assuming that A, B, or C has occurred, the probabilities of another event, X, occurring are: P($X|A$) = .6, P($X|B$) = .8 and P($X|C$) = .4. Find P($A|X$); P($B|X$); P($C|X$).

5·27 Martin Coleman, credit manager for Beck's, knows that the company uses 3 methods to encourage collection of delinquent accounts. From past collection records, he knows that 60 percent of the accounts are called on personally to collect, 25 percent are phoned, and 15 percent are sent a letter. The probability of collecting an overdue amount from an account with the 3 methods is .80, .50, and .40, respectively. Mr. Coleman has just received payment from a past due account.

a) Given this information, what is the probability that the account was called on personally?

b) What is the probability that the account remitted payment after receiving a phone call?

c) What is the probability that the account received a letter and sent payment?

5·28 A public interest group was planning to make a court challenge to auto insurance rates at one of three cities: Atlanta, Denver, or Indianapolis. The probability that it would choose Atlanta was .40; Denver, .30; Indianapolis, .30. The group also knew that it had a 50 percent chance of a favorable court ruling if it chose Atlanta, 60 percent if it chose Denver, and 75 percent if it chose Indianapolis. If the group did receive a favorable ruling, which city did it most likely choose?

5·29 In a particular town there are two Sunday newspapers, the *Times* and the *Herald*, each of which has a classified ad section. Twenty percent of the employers in the city place a want ad only in the *Times*, 10 percent place an ad only in the *Herald*, and 70 percent place an ad in both newspapers. In the past, 75 percent of the ads appearing only in the *Times* have received more than one reply, 65 percent of the ads appearing only in the *Herald* have received more than one reply, and 90 percent of the ads appearing in both newspapers have received more than one reply. If an employer places an ad and receives only one reply, what is the probability that the ad appeared in both papers?

---

8 TERMS INTRODUCED IN CHAPTER 5

a priori probability Probability estimate made prior to receiving new information.

Bayes' theorem The formula for conditional probability under statistical dependence.

classical probability The number of outcomes favorable to the occurrence of an event divided by the total number of possible outcomes.

collectively exhaustive events The list of events that represents all the possible outcomes of an experiment.

conditional probability The probability of one event occurring, given that another event has occurred.

event One or more of the possible outcomes of doing something, or one of the possible outcomes of an experiment.

experiment The activity that results in, or produces, an event.

joint probability The probability of two events occurring together or in succession.

marginal probability The unconditional probability of one event occurring; the probability of a single event.

mutually exclusive events Events that cannot happen together.

posterior probability A probability that has been revised after additional information was obtained.

probability The chance that something will happen.

probability tree A graphical representation showing the possible outcomes of a series of experiments and their respective probabilities.

relative frequency of occurrence The proportion of times that an event occurs in the long run when conditions are stable, or the observed relative frequency of an event in a very large number of trials.

sample space The set of all possible outcomes of an experiment.

statistical dependence The condition when the probability of some event is dependent upon, or affected by, the occurrence of some other event.

statistical independence The condition when the occurrence of one event has no effect upon the probability of occurrence of any other event.

subjective probability Probabilities based on the personal beliefs of the person making the probability estimate.

Venn diagram A pictorial representation of probability concepts, in which the sample space is represented as a rectangle and the events in the sample space as portions of that rectangle.

9 EQUATIONS INTRODUCED IN CHAPTER 5

p. 88
$$\text{Probability of an event} = \frac{\text{Number of outcomes where the event occurs}}{\text{Total number of possible outcomes}} \qquad \textbf{5·1}$$

This is the definition of the *classical* probability that an event will occur.

p. 93
$$P(A) = \text{Probability of event } A \text{ happening}$$

A single probability refers to the probability of one particular event occurring, and it is called *marginal* probability.

p. 94
$$P(A \text{ or } B) = P(A) + P(B) \qquad \textbf{5·2}$$

The probability of either A or B happening when A and B are mutually exclusive equals the sum of the probability of event A happening and of the probability of event B happening. This is the *addition rule for mutually exclusive events*.

p. 95
$$P(A \text{ or } B) = P(A) + P(B) - P(A \text{ and } B) \qquad \textbf{5·3}$$

The addition rule for events that are not mutually exclusive shows that the probability of A or B happening when A and B are not mutually exclusive is equal to the probability of event A happening plus the probability of event B happening minus the probability of A and B happening together, symbolized P(AB).

p. 98
$$P(AB) = P(A) \times P(B) \qquad \textbf{5·4}$$

where:

$P(AB) = $ joint probability of events A and B occurring together or in succession

$P(A) = $ marginal probability of event A occurring

$P(B) = $ marginal probability of event B occurring

The *joint* probability of two or more *independent* events occurring together or in succession is the product of their marginal probabilities.

p. 101
$$P(B|A) = \text{probability of event } B \text{, given that event } A \text{ has occurred}$$

This notation shows *conditional* probability, the probability that a second event (B) will occur if a first event (A) has already happened.

p. 101
$$P(B|A) = P(B) \qquad \textbf{5·5}$$

For *statistically independent* events, the *conditional* probability of event B, given that event A has occurred, is simply the probability of event B. Independent events are those whose probabilities are in no way affected by the occurrence of each other.

$$P(B|A) = \frac{P(BA)}{P(A)}$$

and

$$P(A|B) = \frac{P(AB)}{P(B)}$$

For statistically *dependent* events, the *conditional* probability of event B, given that event A has occurred, is equal to the joint probability of events A and B divided by the marginal probability of event A.

$$P(AB) = P(A|B) \times P(B)$$

and

$$P(BA) = P(B|A) \times P(A)$$

Under conditions of statistical *dependence*, the *joint* probability of events A and B happening together or in succession is equal to the probability of event A, given that event B has already happened, multiplied by the probability that event B will happen.

──────────── *10 CHAPTER REVIEW EXERCISES* ────────────

5·30 A real estate agent estimates that your house will go up in market value by 15 percent or more in the next 6 months, with probability .60. He estimates that the probability that my house will increase in market value by 15 percent or more in the next 6 months is .8. He also estimates that the probability of a certain client taking his advice and buying your house is .7. If at the end of 6 months, the client's new home has indeed increased in value by 15 percent or more, what is the probability that the client bought (a) my house, (b) your house?

5·31 Life insurance premiums are higher for older persons, but auto insurance premiums are generally higher for younger individuals. What does this suggest about the risks and probabilities associated with these two areas of the insurance business?

5·32 "The chance of rain today is 80 percent." Which of the following best explains this statement?
a) It will rain 80 percent of the day today.
b) It will rain in 80 percent of the area for which this forecast applies today.
c) In the past, weather conditions of this sort have produced rain in this area 80 percent of the time.

5·33 "There is a .25 probability that a restaurant in the United States will go out of business this year." When researchers make such statements, how have they arrived at their conclusions?

5·34 As an aid in diagnosing the cause of automobile malfunctions, small computers are currently being used in dealerships of a German car. The company that supplies the dealerships with the computers claims that they make errors in pinpointing the cause of malfunctions only .1 percent of the time.
a) Suppose that in a nationwide screening of 10,000 cars, 6,000 are diagnosed by Model 101 computers and 4,000 are diagnosed by Model 102 computers. If the cause of one car's malfunctioning is found to be misdiagnosed, what is the probability that the diagnosis was made by Model 101?
b) Suppose that after three years, records indicate that .2 percent of the diagnoses made by Model 101 were incorrect and .3 percent of the diagnoses made by Model 102 were incorrect. In another screening of 10,000 cars, 6,000 are diagnosed on Model 101 and 4,000 on Model 102. If an automobile is found to be misdiagnosed in this group, what is the probability that the diagnosis was done by Model 102?

5·35 As the administrator of a hospital, Cindy Turner wants to know what the probability is that a person checking into the hospital will require X-ray treatment and will also have hospital insurance that will cover the X-ray treatment. She knows that during the past 5 years, 12 percent of the people entering the hospital required X-rays and that during the same period, 58 percent of the people checking into the hospital had insurance that covered X-ray treatments. What is the correct probability?

5·36 Determine the probability that
a) a person is a heroin addict and smokes marijuana, given that 62 percent of all heroin addicts smoke marijuana and that the probability of a person being a heroin addict is .005
b) a child in a certain school district comes from an intact family with an income over $20,000, given that 50 percent of the intact families in the district have incomes over $20,000 and 95 percent of the families in the district are intact

5·37 A company faced with a problem of distribution of its new product at the retail level studied the relationship between personal sales calls to outlets and the number of outlets that carry the product. It found that 72 percent of the stores called upon by a company salesperson now carried the brand. If 20 percent of total retail outlets have had a visit from a sales representative, what is the probability that a retail outlet has both received a sales call and carries the product? What information would you need in order to determine the probability of a given store carrying their brand?

5·38 Which of the following pairs of events are statistically independent?
a) the number of union members in a unionized aluminum can factory and the number of men working in the plant
b) the number of women in the United States who have annual incomes over $20,000 and the number of women who have college degrees
c) the number of seconds it takes worker A to assemble a switch and the number of seconds it takes worker B to assemble the switch

5·39 Betty Barnes has worked with the U.S. Postal Service for 12 years. During this time, she has inspected many letters and has made a list of the most common mistakes that people make when addressing letters. Here is her list:

No zip code	Too much postage
No return address	Not enough postage
No street address	

a) In probability theory, would each item on the list be classified as an "event"?
b) Are all the items on the list mutually exclusive? Are any of them mutually exclusive?
c) Is Betty's list collectively exhaustive? (Remember, if you answer no, then you should be able to add at least one more item to the list. Can you?)

5·40 A contractor knows that in the past year his revenue declined by 10 percent, revenues from government contracts declined by 12 percent, and revenues from private contracts increased by 2 percent. Is the probability of an increase in next year's sales revenue for the contractor greater with private or government contracts?

5·41 The scheduling officer for a local police department is trying to decide whether to schedule additional patrol units in each of two neighborhoods. She knows that on any given day during the past year the probabilities of major crimes and minor crimes being committed in the northern neighborhood were .589 and .342, respectively, and that the corresponding probabilities in the southern neighborhood were .507 and .863.
a) What is the probability that a crime of either type will be committed in the northern neighborhood on a given day?

b) What is the probability that a crime of either type will be committed in the southern neighborhood on a given day?

c) What is the probability that *no* crime will be committed in either neighborhood on a given day?

---

11 CHAPTER CONCEPTS TEST

Answers are in the back of the book.

T F 1. In probability theory, the outcome from some experiment is known as an activity.

T F 2. The probability of two or more statistically independent events occurring together or in succession is equal to the sum of their marginal probabilities.

T F 3. Using Bayes' theorem, we may develop revised probabilities based upon new information; these revised probabilities are also known as posterior probabilities.

T F 4. In classical probability, we can determine a priori probabilities based upon logical reasoning before any experiments take place.

T F 5. The set of all possible outcomes of an experiment is called the sample space for the experiment.

T F 6. Under statistical dependence, a marginal probability may be computed for some simple event by taking the product of the probabilities of all joint events in which the simple event occurs.

T F 7. When a list of events resulting from some experiment includes all possible outcomes, the list is said to be collectively exclusive.

T F 8. An unconditional probability is also known as a marginal probability.

T F 9. A subjective probability may be nothing more than an educated guess.

T F 10. When the occurrence of some event has no effect upon the probability of occurrence of some other event, the two events are said to be statistically independent.

T F 11. When using the relative frequency approach, probability figures become less accurate for large numbers of observations.

T F 12. Symbolically, a marginal probability is denoted P(AB).

T F 13. If A and B are statistically dependent events, the probability of A and B occurring is P(A) × P(B).

T F 14. Classical probability assumes that each of the possible outcomes of an experiment is equally likely.

T F 15. One reason that decision makers at high levels often use subjective probabilities is that they are concerned with unique situations.

16. Why are the events of a coin toss mutually exclusive?
   a) The outcome of any toss is not affected by the outcomes of those preceding it.
   b) Both a head and a tail cannot turn up on any one toss.
   c) The probability of getting a head and the probability of getting a tail are the same.
   d) All of the above.
   e) a and b but not c.

17. If a Venn diagram were drawn for events A and B, which are mutually exclusive, which of the following would always be true of A and B?

a) Their parts of the rectangle will overlap.
b) Their parts of the rectangle will be equal in area.
c) Their parts of the rectangle will not overlap.
d) None of the above.
e) b and c but not a.

18. What is the probability that a value chosen at random from a particular population is larger than the median of the population?
a) .25   b) .5   c) 1.0   d) .67

19. Assume that a single, fair die is rolled once. Which of the following is true?
a) The probability of rolling a number higher than one is $1 - P(\text{one is rolled})$.
b) The probability of rolling a three is $1 - P(1, 2, 4, 5, \text{ or } 6 \text{ is rolled})$.
c) The probability of rolling a 5 or 6 is higher than the probability of rolling a 3 or 4.
d) All of the above.
e) a and b but not c.

20. If A and B are mutually exclusive events, then $P(A \text{ or } B) = P(A) + P(B)$. How does the calculation of $P(A \text{ or } B)$ change if A and B are not mutually exclusive?
a) $P(A \text{ and } B)$ must be subtracted from $P(A) + P(B)$.
b) $P(A \text{ and } B)$ must be added to $P(A) + P(B)$.
c) $[P(A) + P(B)]$ must be multiplied by $P(A \text{ and } B)$.
d) $[P(A) + P(B)]$ must be divided by $P(A \text{ and } B)$.
e) None of the above.

21. Leo C. Swartz, a taxi driver in Chicago, has found that the weather affects his customers' tipping. If it is raining, his customers usually tip poorly. When it is not raining, however, they usually tip well. Which of the following is true?
a) Tips and weather are statistically independent.
b) The weather conditions Leo cited are not mutually exclusive.
c) P(good tip|rain) is larger than P(bad tip|rain).
d) None of the above.
e) a and c but not b.

22. Assume that a die is rolled twice in succession and that you are asked to draw the probability tree showing all possible outcomes of the two rolls. How many branches will your tree have?
a) 6   b) 12   c) 36   d) 42   e) 48

Questions 23 – 25 refer to the following situation. Ten numbered balls are placed in an urn. Numbers 1 – 4 are red and numbers 5 – 10 are blue.

23. What is the probability that a ball drawn at random from the urn is blue?
a) .1   b) .4   c) .6   d) 1.0
e) Cannot be determined from the information given.

24. The probability of drawing the ball numbered 3, of course, is .1. A ball is drawn, and it is red. Which of the following is true?
a) P(ball drawn is #3|ball drawn is red) = .1
b) P(ball drawn is #3|ball drawn is red) < .1
c) P(ball drawn is #3|ball drawn is red) > .1
d) P(ball drawn is red|ball drawn is #3) = .25
e) c and d only

25. In question 24, the probability of drawing the #3 ball was reconsidered after it was found that the ball drawn was red. The new probabilities we considered are called:
    a) exhaustive   b) a priori   c) marginal   d) subjective   e) none of these

26. One of the possible outcomes of doing something is a _____ . The activity that produces this outcome is a _____ .

27. The set of all possible outcomes of an activity is the _____ .

28. A pictorial representation of probability concepts, using symbols to represent outcomes, is a _____ .

29. Events that cannot happen together are called _____ .

30. The probability of one event occurring, given that another event has occurred, is called _____ probability.

Probability II: Distributions and Decision Theory

Modern filling machines are designed to work efficiently and with high reliability. Machines like the one pictured can fill soft-drink bottles to within .1 ounce of the desired level 80 percent of the time. A visitor to the bottling plant, watching filled bottles being placed into six-pack cartons, asked, "What's the chance that exactly half the bottles in a six-pack selected at random will be filled to within .1 ounce of the desired level?" Although we cannot make an exact forecast, the ideas about probability distributions discussed in this chapter enable us to give a pretty good answer to the question.

In Chapter 6, we are concerned with probability distributions; that is, the various ways data array themselves when we graph them. Here again we are laying the foundation for later work in statistical inference. You may have a notion about probability distributions if you have dealt with the bell-shaped curve in psychology or mathematics. Or if you are a male who wears a 16EE shoe or a female who wears size 3AAAA, you may have an intuitive idea about probability distributions. When you cannot be fitted, you probably wish the shoe store manager would order a larger distribution of sizes; but a manager who thinks in terms of correct probability distributions will probably not order such unusual sizes and won't be able to accommodate people with very large or very small feet.

Most consequential managerial decisions are made under conditions of uncertainty because decision makers seldom have complete information about what the future will bring. Also introduced in Chapter 6 is statistical decision theory, those methods that are useful when we must decide among alternatives despite uncertain conditions.

1 INTRODUCTION TO PROBABILITY DISTRIBUTIONS

Probability distributions and frequency distributions

In Chapters 2, 3, and 4, we described frequency distributions as a useful way of summarizing variations in observed data. We prepared frequency distributions by listing all the possible outcomes of an experiment and then indicating the observed frequency of each possible outcome. *Probability distributions* are related to frequency distributions. In fact, we can think of a probability distribution as a theoretical frequency distribution. Now, what does that mean? A theoretical frequency distribution is a probability distribution that describes how outcomes are *expected* to vary. Since these distributions deal with expectations, they are useful models in making inferences and decisions under conditions of uncertainty. In later chapters, we will discuss the methods we use under these conditions.

Voting example

To begin our study of probability distributions, consider this example. A political candidate for local office is considering the votes she can get in a coming election. Assume that votes can take on only four possible values. If the candidate's assessment is like this:

Number of votes	1,000	2,000	3,000	4,000	
Probability this will happen	.1	.3	.4	.2	Total 1.0

then the graph of the probability distribution representing her expectations will be like the one shown in Fig. 6·1.

Difference between frequency distributions and probability distributions

Before we move on to other aspects of probability distributions, we should point out that a frequency distribution is a listing of the observed frequencies of all the outcomes of an experiment that actually occurred when the experiment was done, whereas a probability distribution is a listing of the probabilities of all the possible outcomes that *could* result if the experiment were done. Probability distributions can be based on

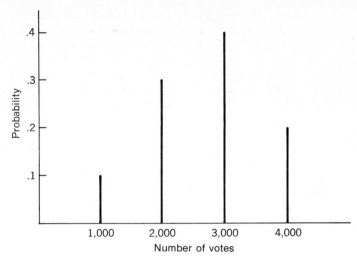

Figure 6·1 Probability distribution of number of votes

theoretical considerations (the tosses of a coin) or on a subjective assessment of the likelihood of certain outcomes (the candidate's estimate). Probability distributions can also be based on experience. Insurance company actuaries determine insurance premiums, for example, by using long years of experience with death rates to establish probabilities of dying among various age groups.

Types of probability distributions

Discrete probability distributions

Probability distributions are classified as either *discrete* or *continuous*. A discrete probability is allowed to take on only a limited number of values. An example of a discrete probability distribution is shown in Fig. 6 · 1, where we expressed the candidate's ideas about the coming election. There, votes were allowed to take on only four possible values (1,000, 2,000, 3,000, or 4,000). Similarly, the probability that you were born in a given month is also discrete, since there are only twelve possible values (the twelve months of the year).

Continuous probability distributions

In a continuous probability distribution, on the other hand, the variable under consideration is allowed to take on any value within a given range. Suppose we were examining the level of effluent in a variety of streams and we measured the level of effluent by parts of effluent per million parts of water. We would expect quite a continuous range of ppm (parts per million), all the way from very low levels in clear mountain streams to extremely high levels in polluted streams. In fact, it would be quite normal for the variable "parts per million" to take on an enormous number of values. We would call the distribution of this

121   Sec. 1   Introduction to probability distributions

variable (ppm) a continuous distribution. Continuous distributions are convenient ways to represent discrete distributions that have many possible outcomes, all very close to each other.

--------------------------------------- **EXERCISES** ---------------------------------------

6·1 The manager of Nickels Department Store is attempting to estimate how many people he will have to hire over the next year. Historical information regarding the turnover rate resulted in the following data concerning the probabilities of hiring various numbers of employees. Draw a graph illustrating this probability distribution.

Number of employees hired	0	5	10	15	25
Probability	.08	.18	.30	.24	.20

6·2 In Chapter 5 we looked at the possible outcomes of tossing two dice, and we calculated some probabilities associated with various outcomes. Construct a table and a graph of the probability distribution representing the outcomes (in terms of total number of dots showing on both dice) for this experiment.

6·3 Southport Autos offers a variety of luxury options on its cars. Because of the six to eight months' waiting period for custom orders, Larry Toppman, the dealer, stocks his cars with a variety of options. Currently, Mr. Toppman, who prides himself on being able to meet his customers' needs immediately, is worried because of an industrywide shortage of cars with sun roofs. Toppman offers the following luxury combinations.

  1. power windows, vinyl roof, electric sun roof
  2. electric sun roof, FM stereo, power windows
  3. vinyl roof, FM stereo, leather interior
  4. FM stereo, electric sun roof, vinyl roof

Toppman assigns an equal chance that any of the combinations will be ordered.
a) What is the probability that any one customer ordering a luxury car will order one including a sun roof?
b) Assume that two customers order luxury cars. Construct a table showing the probability distribution of the number of sun roofs ordered.

6·4 Erika Rosenberg, the product manager for a new support hose recently designed by Knees, is on the verge of releasing her product in a test market. Before releasing the product, Rosenberg must clearly tell her superiors how she expects the product to perform. In this test market she feels that she can sell 16,000 pairs, with a 60 percent probability. Her marketing assistants feel, however, that 4,000 of these sales are tenuous. They feel that there is half as much chance of getting 12,000 sales as there is of getting all 16,000. The assistants and Rosenberg also agree that with a slight change in the product's positioning, the product could, with some probability, pick up an additional 2,000 sales; but they feel this is the maximum the product could obtain. Looking at the blocks of sales as Rosenberg and her assistants see it, construct a table and draw a graph of the probability distribution of sales.

Random variable defined

A random variable is a variable that takes on different values as a result of the outcomes of a random experiment. A random variable can be either discrete or continuous. If a random variable is allowed to take on only a limited number of values, it is a *discrete random variable*. On the other hand, if it is allowed to assume any value within a given range, it is a *continuous random variable*.

Example of discrete random variables

You can think of a random variable as a value or magnitude that changes from occurrence to occurrence in no predictable sequence. A breast cancer screening clinic for example, has no way of knowing exactly how many women will be screened on any one day. So tomorrow's number of patients is a random variable. The values of a random variable are the numerical values corresponding to each possible outcome of the random experiment. If past daily records of the clinic indicate that the values of the random variable range from 100 to 115 patients daily, the random variable is a discrete random variable.

Table 6 · 1 illustrates the number of times each level has been reached during the last 100 days. Note that Table 6 · 1 gives a frequency distribution.

To the extent that we believe that the experience of the past 100 days has been typical, we can use this historical record to assign a probability to each possible number of patients and find a probability distribution. We have accomplished this in Table 6 · 1, by normalizing

TABLE 6 · 1 Number of women screened daily during 100 days

Number screened	Number of days this level was observed	Probability that the random variable will take on this value
100	1	.01
101	2	.02
102	3	.03
103	5	.05
104	6	.06
105	7	.07
106	9	.09
107	10	.10
108	12	.12
109	11	.11
110	9	.09
111	8	.08
112	6	.06
113	5	.05
114	4	.04
115	2	.02
	100	1.00

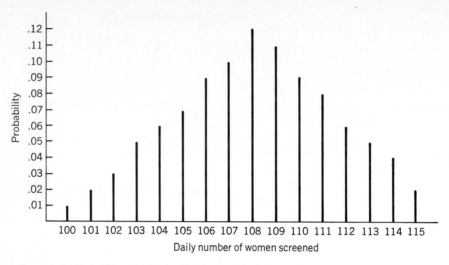

Figure 6·2 Probability distribution for the discrete random variable "daily number screened"

the observed frequency distribution (in this case, dividing each value in the middle column by 100, the total number of days for which the record has been kept). The probability distribution for the random variable "daily number screened" is illustrated graphically in Fig. 6 · 2. Notice that the probability distribution for a random variable provides a probability for each possible value and that these probabilities must sum to one. Table 6 · 1 shows that both of these requirements have been met. Furthermore, both Table 6 · 1 and Fig. 6 · 2 give us information about the long-run frequency of occurrence of daily patient screenings we would expect to observe if this random "experiment" is repeated.

The expected value of a random variable

Suppose you toss a coin 10 times and get 7 heads like this:

Heads	Tails	Total
7	3	10

Hmm, strange, you say. You then ask a friend to try tossing the coin 20 times; she gets 15 heads and 5 tails. So now you have, in all, 22 heads and 8 tails out of 30 tosses.

What did you expect? Was it something closer to 15 heads and 15 tails (half and half)? Now suppose you turn the tossing over to a machine and get 792 heads and 208 tails out of 1,000 tosses of the same coin. You might now be suspicious of the coin because it didn't live up to what you expected.

Expected value is a fundamental idea in the study of probability distributions. For many years, the concept has been put to considerable practical use in the insurance industry, and in the last twenty years, it has been widely used by many others who must make decisions under conditions of uncertainty.

Expected value defined

To obtain the expected value of a discrete random variable we multiply each value that the random variable can assume by the probability of occurrence of that value and then sum these products. Table 6 · 2 illustrates this procedure for our clinic problem. The total in Table 6 · 2 tells us that the expected value of the discrete random variable "number screened" is 108.02 women. What does this mean? It means that over a long period of time, the number of daily screenings should average about 108.02. Remember that an expected value of 108.02 does *not* mean that tomorrow exactly 108.02 women will visit the clinic.

The clinic director would base her decisions on the expected value of daily screenings because the expected value is a *weighted average of the outcomes she expects in the future*. Expected value weights each possible outcome by the frequency with which it is expected to occur. Thus, more common occurrences are given more weight than are less common ones. As conditions change over time, the director would recompute the expected value of daily screenings and use this new figure as a basis for decision making.

Deriving expected value

In our clinic example, the director used past patients' records as the basis for calculating the expected value of daily screenings. The expected

TABLE 6 · 2   Calculating the expected value of the discrete random variable "daily number screened"

Possible values of the random variable (1)	Probability that the random variable will take on these values (2)	(1) × (2)
100	.01	1.00
101	.02	2.02
102	.03	3.06
103	.05	5.15
104	.06	6.24
105	.07	7.35
106	.09	9.54
107	.10	10.70
108	.12	12.96
109	.11	11.99
110	.09	9.90
111	.08	8.88
112	.06	6.72
113	.05	5.65
114	.04	4.56
115	.02	2.30

Expected value of the random variable "daily number screened" → 108.02

value can also be derived from the director's subjective assessments of the probability that the random variable will take on certain values. In that case, the expected value represents nothing more than her personal convictions about the possible outcome.

In this section, we have worked with the probability distribution of a random variable in tabular form (Table 6 · 1) and in graphic form (Fig. 6 · 2). In many situations, however, we will find it more convenient, in terms of the computations that must be done, to represent the probability distribution of a random variable in *algebraic* form. By doing this, we can make probability calculations by substituting numerical values directly into an algebraic equation. In the following sections, we illustrate situations in which this is appropriate and methods for accomplishing it.

Thong th

─────────────────────── **EXERCISES** ───────────────────────

6·5 Construct a table for a possible probability distribution based on the frequency distribution given below.

Outcome	10	12	14	16	18	20
Frequency	15	20	45	42	18	10

a) Draw a graph of the hypothetical probability distribution.
b) Compute the expected value of the outcome.

6·6 The only information available to you regarding the probability distribution of a set of outcomes is the following list of frequencies:

X	0	1	2	3	4	5
Frequency	18	48	180	252	72	30

a) Construct a possible probability distribution for the set of outcomes.
b) Find the expected value of an outcome.

6·7 Bob Walters, who frequently invests in the stock market, carefully studies any potential investment. He is currently examining the possibility of investing in the Trinity Power Company. Through studying past performance, Walters has broken the potential results of an investment into 5 possible outcomes with accompanying probabilities. The outcomes are annual rates of return on a single share of stock which currently costs $100. Find the expected value of the return on investing in a single share of Trinity Power.

Return on investment ($)	0.00	5.00	10.00	25.00	50.00
Probability	.25	.40	.20	.10	.05

If Walters purchases stock only if the expected rate of return exceeds 10 percent, will he purchase this stock, according to this data?

6·8 Production levels for Giles Fashion vary greatly according to consumer acceptance of the latest styles. Therefore, the company's weekly orders of wool cloth are difficult to predict in advance.

On the basis of 5 years of data, the following probability distribution for the company's weekly demand for wool has been computed.

Amount of wool (lb)	3,000	4,000	4,500	5,000
Probability	.2	.4	.2	.2

From this data, the raw materials purchaser computed the expected number of pounds required. Recently he noticed that the company's sales were lower in the last year than in years before. Extrapolating, he observed that the company will be lucky if its weekly demand averages 2,500 this year.

a) What was the expected weekly demand for wool based on the distribution from past data?

b) If each pound of wool generates $5 in revenue and costs $4 to purchase, ship, and handle, how much would Giles Fashion stand to gain or lose each week if it orders wool based on past data and the company's demand is only 2,500?

---

3 THE BINOMIAL DISTRIBUTION

The binomial distribution, a Bernoulli process

One widely used probability distribution of a discrete random variable is the binomial distribution. It describes a variety of processes of interest to managers. The binomial distribution describes discrete, not continuous, data, resulting from an experiment known as a *Bernoulli process* after the seventeenth-century Swiss mathematician Jacob Bernoulli. The tossing of a fair coin a fixed number of times is a Bernoulli process, and the outcomes of such tosses can be represented by the binomial probability distribution. The success or failure of interviewees on an aptitude test may also be described by a Bernoulli process. On the other hand, the lives of the fluorescent lights in a factory would be measured on a continuous scale of hours, and so their distribution would not qualify as a binomial distribution.

Use of the Bernoulli process

Bernoulli process defined

We can use the outcomes of a fixed number of tosses of a fair coin as an example of a Bernoulli process. We can describe this process as follows:

1. Each trial (each toss, in this case) has only *two* possible outcomes: heads or tails, yes or no, success or failure.
2. The probability of the outcome of any trial (toss) remains *fixed* over time. With a fair coin, the probability of heads remains .5 for each toss regardless of the number of times the coin is tossed.
3. The trials are *statistically independent*; that is to say, the outcome of one toss does not affect the outcome of any other toss.

Characteristic probability defined

Each Bernoulli process has its own characteristic probability. Take the situation in which historically seven-tenths of all persons who applied for a certain type of job passed the job test. We would say that the characteristic probability here is .7, but we could describe our testing results as Bernoulli only if we felt certain that the proportion of those passing the test (.7) remained constant over time. The other characteristics of the Bernoulli process would also have to be met, of course. Each test would have to have only two outcomes (success or failure), and the results of each test would have to be statistically independent.

The symbols p, q, r, and n
In more formal language the symbol p represents the probability of a success (in our example .7), and the symbol q, $(q = 1 - p)$, the probability of a failure (.3). To represent a certain number of successes, we will use the symbol r, and to symbolize the total number of trials, we use the symbol n. In the situations we will be discussing, the number of trials is fixed before the experiment is begun.

Using this language in a simple problem, we can calculate the chances of getting exactly two heads (in any order) on three tosses of a fair coin. Symbolically, we express the values as follows:

p = characteristic probability or probability of success = .5

$q = 1 - p$ = probability of failure = .5

r = number of successes desired = 2

n = number of trials undertaken = 3

Binomial formula
We can solve the problem by using the *binomial formula*:

$$\text{Probability of } r \text{ successes in } n \text{ trials} = \frac{n!}{r!(n-r)!}p^r q^{n-r} \quad (6 \cdot 1)$$

Although this formula may look somewhat complicated, it can be used quite easily. The symbol $!$ means *factorial*, which is computed as follows: 3! means $3 \times 2 \times 1$, or 6. To calculate 5!, we multiply $5 \times 4 \times 3 \times 2 \times 1 = 120$. Mathematicians define 0! as equal to 1. Using the binomial formula to solve our problem, we discover:

$$\text{Probability of 2 successes in 3 trials} = \frac{3 \times 2 \times 1}{(2 \times 1)(1 \times 1)}(.5^2)(.5^1)$$

$$= .375$$

Thus there is a .375 probability of getting two heads on three tosses of a fair coin.

By now you've probably recognized that we can use the binomial distribution to determine the probabilities for the soft drink bottling problem we introduced at the beginning of this chapter. Recall that historically eight-tenths of the bottles were correctly filled (successes). If we want to compute the probability of getting exactly 3 of 6 bottles (half a six-pack) correctly filled, we can define our symbols this way:

$$p = .8 \quad q = .2 \quad r = 3 \quad n = 6$$

and then use the binomial formula as follows:

$$\text{Probability of } r \text{ successes in } n \text{ trials} = \frac{n!}{r!(n-r)!}p^r q^{n-r} \qquad (6 \cdot 1)$$

$$\begin{array}{l}\text{Probability of 3 out of 6} \\ \text{bottles correctly filled}\end{array} = \frac{6 \times 5 \times 4 \times 3 \times 2 \times 1}{(3 \times 2 \times 1)(3 \times 2 \times 1)}(.8^3)(.2^3)$$

$$= .08192$$

Of course, we *could* have solved these two problems using the probability trees we developed in Chapter 5; but for larger problems, trees become quite cumbersome. In fact, using the binomial formula (Equation 6 · 1) is no easy task when we have to compute the value of something like 46 factorial. For this reason, binomial probability tables have been developed, and we shall use them shortly.

Some graphic illustrations of the binomial distribution

To this point, we have dealt with the binomial distribution only in terms of the binomial formula, but the binomial, like any other distribution, can be expressed graphically as well.

To illustrate several of these distributions, consider a situation at Kerr Elementary School where students are often late. Five students are in kindergarten. The principal has studied the situation over a period of time and has determined that there is a .4 chance of any one student being late and that students arrive independently of one another. How would we draw a binomial probability distribution illustrating the probabilities of 0, 1, 2, 3, 4, or 5 students being late simultaneously? To do this we would need to use the binomial formula where:

$$p = .4 \qquad q = .6 \qquad n = 5*$$

and to make a separate computation for each r, from 0 through 5. Remember that mathematically any number to the zero power is defined as being equal to one. Beginning with our binomial formula,

Using the formula to derive the binomial probability distribution

$$\begin{array}{l}\text{Probability of } r \text{ late arrivals} \\ \text{out of } n \text{ students}\end{array} = \frac{n!}{r!(n-r)!}p^r q^{n-r} \qquad (6 \cdot 1)$$

For $r = 0$, we get:

$$P(0) = \frac{5 \times 4 \times 3 \times 2 \times 1}{(1)(5 \times 4 \times 3 \times 2 \times 1)}(.4^0)(.6^5) = .07776$$

*When we define n, we look at the number of students. The fact that there is a possibility that none will be late does not alter our choice of $n = 5$.

For $r = 1$, we get:

$$P(1) = \frac{5 \times 4 \times 3 \times 2 \times 1}{(1)(4 \times 3 \times 2 \times 1)}(.4^1)(.6^4) = .2592$$

For $r = 2$, we get:

$$P(2) = \frac{5 \times 4 \times 3 \times 2 \times 1}{(2 \times 1)(3 \times 2 \times 1)}(.4^2)(.6^3) = .3456$$

For $r = 3$, we get:

$$P(3) = \frac{5 \times 4 \times 3 \times 2 \times 1}{(3 \times 2 \times 1)(2 \times 1)}(.4^3)(.6^2) = .2304$$

For $r = 4$, we get:

$$P(4) = \frac{5 \times 4 \times 3 \times 2 \times 1}{(4 \times 3 \times 2 \times 1)(1)}(.4^4)(.6^1) = .0768$$

Finally, for $r = 5$, we get:

$$P(5) = \frac{5 \times 4 \times 3 \times 2 \times 1}{(5 \times 4 \times 3 \times 2 \times 1)(1)}(.4^5)(.6^0) = .01024$$

The binomial distribution for this example is shown graphically in Fig. 6 · 3.

General appearance of binomial distributions

Without doing all the calculations involved, we can illustrate the general appearance of a family of binomial probability distributions. In Fig. 6 · 4, for example, each distribution represents $n = 5$. In each case, the p and q have been changed and are noted beside each distribution. From Fig. 6 · 4, we can make the following generalizations:

1. When p is small (.1), the binomial distribution is skewed to the right.
2. As p increases (to .3, for example), the skewness is less noticeable.

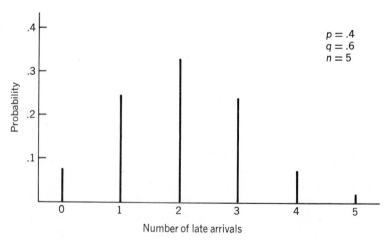

Figure 6 · 3   Binomial probability distribution of late arrivals

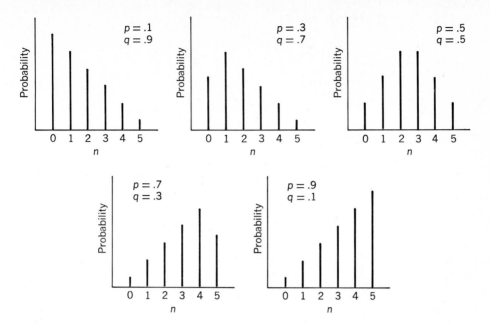

Figure 6·4 Family of binomial probability distributions with constant *n* = 5 and various *p* and *q* values

3. When *p* = .5, the binomial distribution is symmetrical.
4. When *p* is larger than .5, the distribution is skewed to the left.
5. The probabilities for .3, for example, are the same as those for .7 except that the values of *p* and *q* are *reversed*. This is true for any pair of complementary *p* and *q* values (.3 and .7), (.4 and .6), and (.2 and .8).

Let us examine graphically what happens to the binomial distribution when *p* stays constant but *n* is increased. Figure 6 · 5 illustrates the general shape of a family of binomial distributions with a constant *p* of .4 and *n*'s from 5 to 30. As *n* increases, the vertical lines not only become more numerous but also tend to bunch up together to form a *bell shape*. We shall have more to say about this bell shape shortly.

Using the binomial tables

Solving problems using the binomial tables

Earlier we recognized that it is tedious to calculate probabilities using the binomial formula when *n* is a large number. Fortunately, we can use Appendix Table 3 to determine binomial probabilities quickly.

To illustrate the use of the binomial tables, consider this problem. What is the probability that 8 or more of the 15 registered Democrats on Prince Street will fail to vote in the coming primary if the probability of an individual's not voting is .30, and if people decide independently of each other whether or not to vote? First we represent the elements in this

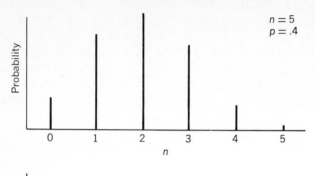

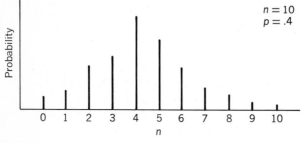

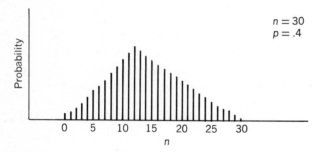

Figure 6·5 Family of binomial probability distributions with constant $p = .4$ and $n = 5$, 10, and 30

problem in binomial distribution notation:

$n = 15$ number of registered Democrats

$p = .30$ probability that any one individual won't vote

$r = 8$ number of individuals who will fail to vote

Then, since the problem involves 15 trials, we must find the table corresponding to $n = 15$. Since the probability of an individual's not voting is .30, we must look through the $n = 15$ table until we find the column where $p = .30$. (This is denoted as 30.) We then move down that column until we are opposite the $r = 8$ row. The answer there is 0500, which can be interpreted as being a probability value of .0500. This represents the probability of 8 or more nonvoters, since the tables are so constructed.

Our problem asked for the probability of 8 or more nonvoters. If it had asked for the probability of more than 8 nonvoters we would have looked up the probability of 9 or more nonvoters. Had the problem asked for the probability of exactly 8 nonvoters we would have sub-tracted .0152 (the probability of 9 or more nonvoters) from .0500 (the probability of 8 or more nonvoters). The answer would be .0348 = the probability of exactly 8 nonvoters. Finally, if the problem had asked for the probability of fewer than 8 nonvoters we would have subtracted .0500 (the probability of 8 or more nonvoters) from 1.0 for an answer of .9500. (Note that Appendix Table 3 only goes up to $p = .50$. Instructions for using the table when p is larger than .50 are found on the first page of Appendix Table 3.)

Measures of central tendency and dispersion for the binomial distribution

Computing the mean and the standard deviation

Earlier in this chapter we encountered the concept of the expected value or mean of a probability distribution. The binomial distribution has an expected value or mean (μ) and a standard deviation (σ), and we should be able to compute both of these statistical measures. Intuitively, we can reason that if a certain machine produces good parts with a $p = .5$, then, over time, the mean of the distribution of the good parts in the output would be .5 times the total output. If there is a .5 chance of tossing a head with a fair coin, over a large number of tosses the mean of the binomial distribution of the number of heads would be .5 times the total number of tosses.

Symbolically, we can represent the mean and the standard deviation of a binomial distribution as:

$$\mu = np \qquad (6 \cdot 2)$$

and

$$\sigma = \sqrt{npq} \qquad (6 \cdot 3)$$

where:

$$n = \text{number of trials}$$

$$p = \text{probability of success}$$

$$q = \text{probability of failure} = 1 - p$$

To see how to use Equations $6 \cdot 2$ and $6 \cdot 3$, take the case of a packaging machine that produces 20 percent defective packages. If we take a random sample of 10 packages, we can compute the mean and the standard deviation of the binomial distribution of that process like this:

$$\mu = np = (10)(.2) = 2 \leftarrow \text{mean} \qquad (6 \cdot 2)$$

$$\sigma = \sqrt{npq} = \sqrt{(10)(.2)(.8)} = 1.265 \leftarrow \begin{array}{l}\text{standard} \\ \text{deviation}\end{array} \qquad (6 \cdot 3)$$

Meeting the conditions for using the Bernoulli process

Applying the binomial distribution to real-life situations

We need to be careful in the use of the binomial probability distribution to make certain that the three conditions necessary for a Bernoulli process introduced on page 127 are met, particularly conditions 2 and 3. Condition 2 requires the probability of the outcome of any trial to remain fixed over time. In many industrial processes, however, it is extremely difficult to guarantee that this is indeed the case. Each time an industrial machine produces a part, for instance, there is some infinitesimal wear on the machine. If this wear accumulates beyond a reasonable point, the proportion of acceptable parts produced by the machine will be altered, and condition 2 for the use of the binomial distribution may be violated. This problem is not present in a coin toss experiment, but it is an integral consideration of all real applications of the binomial probability distribution.

Condition 3 requires that the trials of a Bernoulli process be statistically independent; that is, the outcome of one trial cannot affect in any way the outcome of any other trial. Here, too, we can encounter some problems in real applications. Consider an interviewing process in which high-potential candidates are being screened for top political positions. If the interviewer has talked with five unacceptable candidates in a row, he may not view the sixth with complete impartiality. The trials, therefore, would not be statistically independent.

--- EXERCISES ---

6·9 The Hart Ketchup Company offers a semi-annual national consumer discount through the use of coupons. Historical data supplied by Hart's marketing department shows that 80 percent of the consumers buying ketchup during the discount period do not take advantage of the coupon. Find the following probabilities (to 4 decimal places) without the use of the tables.
  a) One day during the discount period, 8 customers at Ken's Quik-Mart bought Hart's ketchup. What is the probability that exactly 6 did not use the coupons?
  b) Exactly 7?

6·10 For a binomial distribution with $n = 6$ and $p = .3$, find
  a) $P(r = 5)$ **b)** $P(r > 4)$ **c)** $P(r < 2)$ **d)** $P(r \geqslant 3)$

6·11 For a binomial distribution with $n = 15$ and $p = .2$, use Appendix Table 3 to find
  a) $P(r = 6)$ **b)** $P(r > 9)$ **c)** $P(r \leqslant 12)$

6·12 Find the mean and standard deviation of the following binomial distributions:
  a) $n = 12, p = .25$ **b)** $n = 25, q = .4$ **c)** $n = 500, p = .10$

6·13 The financial manager for the Aycock Sheetrock Company will randomly sample 4 customers' accounts. Aycock offers a 2 percent trade discount for payments received within 10 days of the order. The manager knows from previous research that 60 percent of Aycock's customers capitalize on this discount.
  a) What is the probability that the manager's sample will contain exactly two accounts that utilize the discount? Do not use the tables. Use the binomial formula.
  b) What is the probability that there will be 4 accounts in the sample that utilize the discount? Solve this without using the tables.

4 THE POISSON DISTRIBUTION

There are many discrete probability distributions, but our discussion will focus on only two: the *binomial*, which we have just concluded, and the *Poisson*, which is the subject of this section. The Poisson distribution is named for Siméon Denis Poisson (1781–1840), a Frenchman who developed the distribution from studies during the latter part of his lifetime.

Examples of Poisson distributions

The Poisson distribution is used to describe a number of processes, including the distribution of telephone calls going through a switchboard system, the demand (needs) of patients for service at a health institution, the arrivals of trucks and cars at a toll booth, and the number of accidents at an intersection. These examples all have a common element: they can be described by a discrete random variable that takes on integer (whole) values (0, 1, 2, 3, 4, 5, and so on). The number of patients who arrive at a physician's office in a given interval of time will be 0, 1, 2, 3, 4, 5, or some other whole number. Similarly, if you count the number of cars arriving at a toll booth on the New Jersey Turnpike during some 10-minute period, the number will be 0, 1, 2, 3, 4, 5, and so on.

Characteristics of processes that produce a Poisson probability distribution

Conditions leading to a Poisson probability distribution

The number of vehicles passing through a single turnpike toll booth at rush hour serves as an illustration of Poisson probability distribution characteristics:

1. The average (mean) arrivals of vehicles per rush hour can be estimated from past traffic data.
2. If we divide the rush hour into periods (intervals) of 1 second each, we will find these statements to be true:
   a) The probability that exactly one vehicle will arrive at the single booth per second is a very small number and is constant for every 1-second interval.
   b) The probability that two or more vehicles will arrive within a 1-second interval is so small that we can assign it a zero value.
   c) The number of vehicles that arrive in a given 1-second interval is independent of the time at which that 1-second interval occurs during the rush hour.
   d) The number of arrivals in any 1-second interval is not dependent on the number of arrivals in any other 1-second interval.

Now, we can generalize from these 4 conditions described for our toll booth example and apply them to other processes. If these new processes meet the same four conditions, then we can use a Poisson probability distribution to describe them.

Calculating probabilities using the Poisson distribution

The Poisson probability distribution, as we have shown, is concerned with certain processes that can be described by a discrete random variable. The letter X usually represents that discrete random variable, and X can take on integer values (0, 1, 2, 3, 4, 5, and so on). We use capital X to represent the random variable and lowercase x to represent a specific value that capital X can take. The probability of *exactly* x occurrences in a Poisson distribution is calculated with the formula

$$P(x) = \frac{\lambda^x \times e^{-\lambda}}{x!} \qquad (6 \cdot 4)$$

Look more closely at each part of this formula:

lambda (the mean number of occurrences per interval of time) raised to the x power

e, or 2.71828 (the base of the Naperian or natural logarithm system), raised to the negative lambda power

$$\left(P(x)\right) = \frac{\left(\lambda^x\right)\left(e^{-\lambda}\right)}{\left(x!\right)} \qquad x \text{ factorial}$$

probability of *exactly* x occurrences

Suppose that we are investigating the safety of a dangerous intersection. Past police records indicate a mean of 5 accidents per month at this intersection. The number of accidents is distributed according to a Poisson distribution and the Highway Safety Division wants us to calculate the probability in any month of exactly 0, 1, 2, 3, and 4 accidents. We can use Appendix Table 4 to avoid having to calculate e's to negative powers. Applying the formula:

An example using the Poisson formula

$$P(x) = \frac{\lambda^x \times e^{-\lambda}}{x!} \qquad (6 \cdot 4)$$

we can calculate the probability of exactly 0 accidents:

$$P(0) = \frac{(5^0)(e^{-5})}{0!} = \frac{(1)(.00674)}{1} = .00674$$

For exactly 1 accident:

$$P(1) = \frac{(5^1)(e^{-5})}{1!} = \frac{(5)(.00674)}{1} = .03370$$

For exactly 2 accidents:

$$P(2) = \frac{(5^2)(e^{-5})}{2!} = \frac{(25)(.00674)}{2 \times 1} = .08425$$

For exactly 3 accidents:

$$P(3) = \frac{(5^3)(e^{-5})}{3!} = \frac{(125)(.00674)}{3 \times 2 \times 1} = .14042$$

Finally, for exactly 4 accidents:

$$P(4) = \frac{(5^4)(e^{-5})}{4!} = \frac{(625)(.00674)}{4 \times 3 \times 2 \times 1} = .17552$$

*What
our calculations
mean*

Our calculations will answer several questions. Perhaps we want to know the probability of there being 0, 1, or 2 accidents in any month. We find this by adding together the probabilities of exactly 0, 1, and 2 accidents like this:

$$P(0) = .00674$$
$$P(1) = .03370$$
$$P(2) = .08425$$
$$P(0, 1, 2) = \overline{.12469}$$

We will take action to improve the intersection if the probability of more than 3 accidents per month exceeds .65. Should we act? To solve this problem, we need to calculate the probability of having 0, 1, 2, or 3 accidents and then subtract the sum from 1.0 to get the probability for more than 3 accidents. We begin like this:

$$P(0) = .00674$$
$$P(1) = .03370$$
$$P(2) = .08425$$
$$P(3) = .14042$$
$$P(3 \text{ or fewer}) = \overline{.26511}$$

Because the Poisson probability of 3 or fewer accidents is .26511, the probability of more than 3 must be .73489, (1.00000 − .26511). Since .73489 exceeds .65, steps should be taken to improve the intersection.

*Constructing
a Poisson
probability
distribution*

We could continue calculating the probabilities for more than 4 accidents and eventually produce a Poisson probability distribution of the number of accidents per month at this intersection. Table 6 · 3 illustrates such a distribution. To produce this table, we have used Formula 6 · 4. Try doing the calculations yourself for the probabilities beyond exactly 4 accidents. Figure 6 · 6 illustrates graphically the Poisson probability distribution of the number of accidents.

Poisson distribution as an approximation of the binomial distribution

Sometimes, if we wish to avoid the tedious job of calculating binomial probability distributions, we can use the Poisson instead. The Poisson distribution can be a reasonable approximation of the binomial, but only

TABLE 6·3 Poisson probability distribution of accidents per month

x = Number of accidents	P(x) = Probability of exactly that number
0	.00674
1	.03370
2	.08425
3	.14042
4	.17552
5	.17552
6	.14627
7	.10448
8	.06530
9	.03628
10	.01814
11	.00824
	.99486 ← probability for 0 through 11 accidents
12 or more	+ .00514 ← probability for 12 or more (1.0 − .99486)
	1.00000

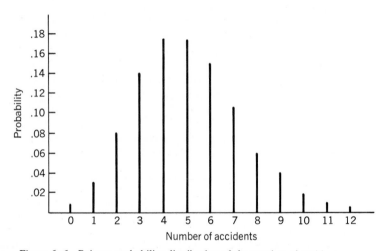

Figure 6·6 Poisson probability distribution of the number of accidents

Using a modification of the Poisson formula to approximate binomial probabilities

under certain conditions. These conditions are when n is large and p is small; that is, when the number of trials is large and the binomial probability of success is small. The rule most often used by statisticians is that the Poisson is a good approximation of the binomial when n is equal to, or greater than, 20 and p is equal to or less than .05. In cases that meet these conditions, we can substitute the mean of the binomial distribution (np) in place of the mean of the Poisson distribution (λ), so that the formula becomes:

$$P(x) = \frac{(np)^x \times e^{-np}}{x!} \qquad (6 \cdot 5)$$

TABLE 6·4 Comparison of Poisson and binomial probability approaches to the kidney dialysis situation

Poisson approach	Binomial approach
$$P(x) = \frac{(np)^x \times e^{-np}}{x!} \quad (6 \cdot 5)$$	$$P(r) = \frac{n!}{r!(n-r)!} p^r q^{n-r} \quad (6 \cdot 1)$$
$$P(3) = \frac{(20 \times .02)^3 e^{-(20 \times .02)}}{3!}$$	$$P(3) = \frac{20!}{3!(20-3)!}(.02^3)(.98^{17})$$
$$= \frac{(.4^3)(e)^{-.4*}}{(3 \times 2 \times 1)}$$	$$= .0065$$
$$= \frac{(.064)(.67032)}{6}$$	
$$= .00715$$	

*Use Appendix Table 4 to find the value of $(e)^{-.4}$.

Comparing the Poisson and binomial formulas

Let us use both the binomial probability formula (6 · 1) and the Poisson approximation formula (6 · 5) on the same problem to determine the extent to which the Poisson is a good approximation of the binomial. Say that we have a hospital with 20 kidney dialysis machines and that the chance of any one of them malfunctioning during any day is .02. What is the probability that exactly 3 machines will be out of service on the same day? Table 6 · 4 shows the answers to this question. As we can see, the difference between the answers using the two probability distributions is slight (only about 10 percent in this example).

─────────────────── **EXERCISES** ───────────────────

6·14 Guy Ford, production supervisor for the Winstead Company's Charlottesville plant, is worried about an elderly employee's ability to keep up the minimum work pace. In addition to the normal daily breaks, this employee stops for short rest periods an average of 4.1 times per hour. The rest period is a fairly consistent 3 minutes each time. Ford has decided that if the probability of the employee resting for 12 minutes (not including normal breaks) or more per hour is greater than .5, he will move the employee to a different job. Should he do so?

6·15 Owing to both a sugar shortage and an increasing tendency for consumers to hoard commodities, the demand for sugar has skyrocketed. During this current rush, Peggy Sackett, inventory manager for an Atlanta Squiggly Piggly food store, has determined that the shelves empty an average of 5.4 times a day.
a) What is the probability that the shelves will be emptied exactly 5 times?
b) If the probability that the shelves will be emptied 4 or fewer times is .3733, what is the probability that the shelves will be emptied more than 5 times?

6·16 Given a binomial distribution with $n = 20$ trials and $p = .04$, use the Poisson approximation to the binomial to find
a) $P(r \geqslant 2)$ **b)** $P(r < 5)$ **c)** $P(r = 0)$

6·17 Southcentral Telephone Company employs the Boynton Delivery Service to deliver its telephone books. Southcentral has been pleased with the service because over the years Boynton has delivered telephone books to 97 percent of the names that were supplied to it by the phone company. Nevertheless, Southcentral continues to make spot checks, randomly calling numbers that should be supplied with new telephone books.

a) What is the probability that out of 100 calls made, exactly 3 people will not have received telephone books?

b) Exactly one person?

6·18 Given $\lambda = 3.5$, for a Poisson distribution, find

a) $P(X \leqslant 2)$ **b)** $P(X \geqslant 4)$ **c)** $P(X = 6)$

---

5 THE NORMAL DISTRIBUTION: A DISTRIBUTION OF A CONTINUOUS RANDOM VARIABLE

Continuous distribution defined

So far in this chapter, we have been concerned with discrete probability distributions. In this section, we shall turn to cases in which the variable can take on *any* value within a given range and in which the probability distribution is continuous.

A very important continuous probability distribution is the *normal* distribution. Several mathematicians were instrumental in its development, among them the eighteenth-century mathematician-astronomer Karl Gauss. In honor of his work, the normal probability distribution is often called the Gaussian distribution.

Importance of the normal distribution

There are two basic reasons why the normal distribution occupies such a prominent place in statistics. First, it has some properties that make it applicable to a great many situations in which it is necessary to make inferences by taking samples. In Chapter 7, we will find that the normal distribution is a useful sampling distribution. Second, the normal distribution comes close to fitting the actual observed frequency distributions of many phenomena, including human characteristics (weights, heights, and I.Q.'s), outputs from physical processes (dimensions and yields), and other measures of interest to managers both in the public and private sectors.

Characteristics of the normal probability distribution

The normal curve described

Look for a moment at Fig. 6 · 7. This diagram suggests several important features of a normal probability distribution:

1. The curve has a single peak; thus, it is unimodal. It has the bell shape that we described earlier.

2. The mean of a normally distributed population lies at the center of its normal curve.

3. Because of the symmetry of the normal probability distribution, the median and the mode of the distribution are also at the center; thus for a normal curve, the mean, median, and mode are the same value.

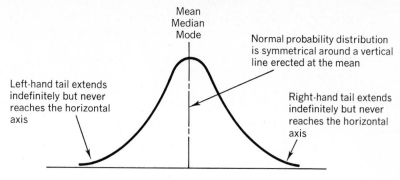

Mean
Median
Mode

Normal probability distribution is symmetrical around a vertical line erected at the mean

Left-hand tail extends indefinitely but never reaches the horizontal axis

Right-hand tail extends indefinitely but never reaches the horizontal axis

Figure 6·7 Frequency curve for the normal probability distribution

4. The two tails of the normal probability distribution extend indefinitely and never touch the horizontal axis (graphically, of course, this is impossible to show).

Significance of the two parameters

Most real-life populations do not extend forever in both directions; but for such populations, the normal distribution is a convenient approximation. There is no single normal curve but rather a family of normal curves. To define a particular normal probability distribution, we need only two parameters: the mean (μ) and the standard deviation (σ). In Table 6 · 5 each of the populations is described only by the mean and the standard deviation, and each has a particular normal curve.

Figure 6 · 8 shows three normal probability distributions, each of which has the same mean but a different standard deviation. Although these curves differ in appearance, all three are "normal curves."

Figure 6 · 9 illustrates a "family" of normal curves, all with the same standard deviation but each with a different mean. The normal probability distributions illustrated in Figs. 6 · 8, and 6 · 9 demonstrate that the normal curve can describe a large number of populations, differentiated only by the mean and/or the standard deviation.

TABLE 6·5 Different normal probability distributions

Nature of the population	*Its mean*	*Its standard deviation*
Annual earnings of employees at one plant	$10,000/year	$1,000
Length of standard 8-foot building lumber	8 feet	.5 inch
Air pollution in one community	2,500 particles per million	750 particles per million
Per capita income in a single developing country	$1,400	$300
Violent crimes per year in a given city	8,000	900

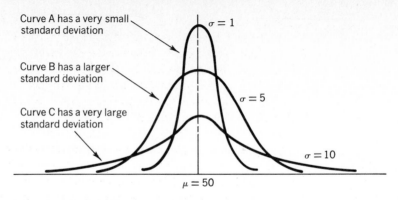

Figure **6·8** Normal probability distributions with identical means but different standard deviations

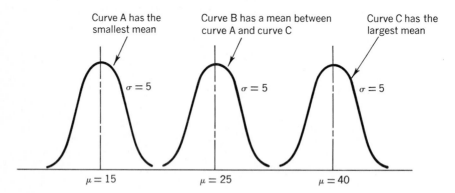

Figure **6·9** Normal probability distributions with different means but the same standard deviations

Areas under the normal curve

Measuring the area under a normal curve

No matter what the values of μ and σ are for a normal probability distribution, the total area under the normal curve is 1.00, so that we may think of areas under the curve as probabilities. Mathematically, it is true that:

1. Approximately 68 percent of all the values in a normally distributed population lie within 1 standard deviation (plus and minus) from the mean.

2. Approximately 95.5 percent of all the values in a normally distributed population lie within 2 standard deviations (plus and minus) from the mean.

3. Approximately 99.7 percent of all the values in a normally distributed population lie within 3 standard deviations (plus and minus) from the mean.

These three statements are shown graphically in Fig. 6 · 10.

Figure 6 · 10 shows three different ways of measuring the area under the normal curve. However, very few of the applications we shall make of the normal probability distribution involve intervals of *exactly* 1, 2, or 3 standard deviations (plus and minus) from the mean. What should we do about all these other cases? Fortunately, we can refer to statistical tables constructed for precisely these situations. They indicate portions of the area under the normal curve that are contained within any number of standard deviations (plus and minus) from the mean.

Standard normal probability distribution

It is not possible or necessary to have a different table for every possible normal curve. Instead, we can use a table of a *standard normal probability distribution* to find area under any normal curve. With this table, we can determine the area, or probability, that any normally distributed random variable will lie within certain distances from the mean. These distances are defined in terms of standard deviations.

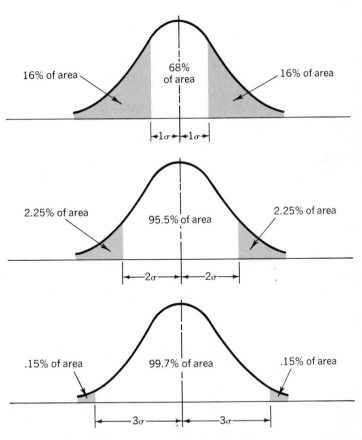

Figure 6 · 10   Relationship between the area under the curve for a normal probability distribution and the distance from the mean measured in standard deviations

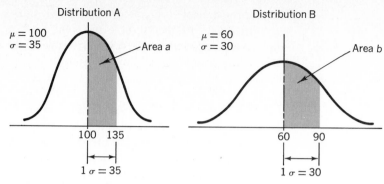

Figure 6·11 Two intervals, each one standard deviation to the right of the mean

We can better understand the concept of the standard normal probability distribution by examining the special relationship of the standard deviation to the normal curve. Look at Fig. 6 · 11. Here we have illustrated two normal probability distributions, each with a different mean and a different standard deviation. Both area *a* and area *b*, the shaded areas under the curves, contain the same proportion of the total area under the normal curve. Why? Because both of these areas are defined as being the area between the mean and one standard deviation to the right of the mean. *All* intervals containing the same number of standard deviations from the mean will contain the same proportion of the total area under the curve for any normal probability distribution. This makes possible the use of only one standard normal probability distribution table.

Deriving the percentage of the total area under the curve

Let's find out what proportion of the total area under the curve is represented by shaded areas in Fig. 6 · 11. In Fig. 6 · 10, we saw that an interval of one standard deviation (plus *and* minus) from the mean contained about 68 percent of the total area under the curve. In Fig. 6 · 11, however, we are interested only in the area between the mean and one standard deviation to the *right* of the mean (plus, *not* plus and minus). This area must be half of 68 percent, or 34 percent, for both distributions.

Using the standard normal probability distribution table

Appendix Table 1 shows the area under the normal curve between the mean and any value of the normally distributed random variable. Notice in this table the location of the column labeled z. The value for z is derived from the formula:

Formula for measuring distances under the normal curve

$$z = \frac{x - \mu}{\sigma} \qquad (6 \cdot 6)$$

144 Chap. 6 Probability II: Distributions and decision theory

where:

x = value of the random variable with which we are concerned

μ = mean of the distribution of this random variable

σ = standard deviation of this distribution

z = number of standard deviations from x to the mean
   of this distribution

Why do we use z rather than "the number of standard deviations"? Normally distributed random variables take on many *different units* of measure: dollars, inches, parts per million, pounds, time. Since we shall use one table, Table 1 in the Appendix, we talk in terms of *standard units* (which really means standard deviations) and we give them a symbol of z.

Using z values

We can illustrate this graphically. In Fig. 6 · 12 we see that the use of z is just a change of the scale of measurement on the horizontal axis.

Standard Normal Probability Distribution Table

The Standard Normal Probability Distribution Table, Appendix Table 1, is organized in terms of standard units, or z values. It gives the values for only *half* the area under the normal curve, beginning with 0.0 at the mean. Since the normal probability distribution is symmetrical (return to Fig. 6 · 7 to review this point), the values true for one half of the curve are true for the other. We can use this one table for problems involving both sides of the normal curve. Working a few examples will help us to feel comfortable with the table.

Using the table to find probabilities (an example)

We have a training program designed to upgrade the supervisory skills of production-line supervisors. Because the program is self-administered, supervisors require different numbers of hours to complete the program. A study of past participants indicates that the mean length of time spent on the program is 500 hours and that this normally distributed random variable has a standard deviation of 100 hours.

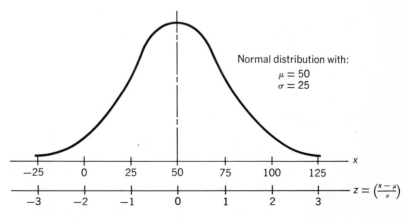

Normal distribution with:
$\mu = 50$
$\sigma = 25$

$z = \left(\frac{x - \mu}{\sigma}\right)$

Figure 6 · 12 Normal distribution illustrating comparability of z values and standard deviations

Question 1

What is the probability that a participant selected at random will require more than 500 hours to complete the program?

Solution. In Fig. 6 · 13 we see that half of the area under the curve is located on either side of the mean of 500 hours. Thus, we can deduce that the probability that the random variable will take on a value higher than 500 is one half, or .5.

Question 2

What is the probability that a candidate selected at random will take between 500 and 650 hours to complete the training program?

Solution. We have shown this situation graphically in Fig. 6 · 14. The probability that will answer this question is represented by the shaded area between the mean (500 hours) and the x value in which we are interested (650 hours). Using Equation 6 · 6, we get a z value of:

$$z = \frac{x - \mu}{\sigma} = \frac{650 - 500}{100} = 1.5 \text{ standard deviations} \qquad (6 \cdot 6)$$

If we look up $z = 1.5$ in Appendix Table 1, we find a probability of .4332. Thus,

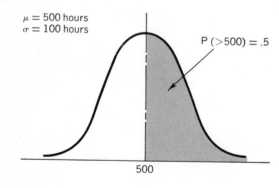

$\mu = 500$ hours
$\sigma = 100$ hours

P (>500) = .5

500

Figure 6·13 Distribution of time required to complete the training program, with interval more than 500 hours shaded

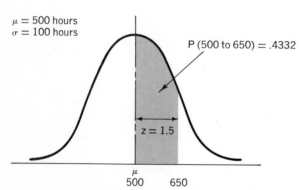

$\mu = 500$ hours
$\sigma = 100$ hours

P (500 to 650) = .4332

$z = 1.5$

μ
500   650

Figure 6·14 Distribution of time required to complete the training program, with interval 500 to 650 hours shaded

the chance that a candidate selected at random would require between 500 and 650 hours to complete the training program is slightly higher than .4.

Question 3

What is the probability that a candidate selected at random will take more than 700 hours to complete the program?

Solution. This situation is different from our previous examples. Look at Fig. 6 · 15. We are interested in the shaded area to the right of the value "700 hours." How can we solve this problem? We can begin by using Equation 6 · 6:

$$z = \frac{x - \mu}{\sigma} = \frac{700 - 500}{100} = 2 \text{ standard deviations} \qquad (6 \cdot 6)$$

Looking in Appendix Table 1 for a z value of 2.0, we find a probability of .4772. That represents the probability the program will require *between* 500 and 700 hours. However, we want the probability it will take *more than* 700 hours (the shaded area in Fig. 6 · 15). Since the right half of the curve (between the mean and the right-hand tail), represents a probability of .5, we can get our answer (the area to the right of the 700-hour point) if we subtract .4772 from .5; (.5000 − .4772 = .0228). Therefore, the are just over 2 chances in 100 that a participant chosen at random would take more than 700 hours to complete the course.

Question 4

Suppose the training program director wants to know the probability that a participant chosen at random would require between 550 and 650 hours to complete the required work.

Solution. This probability is represented by the shaded area in Fig. 6 · 16. This time, our answer will require two steps. First, we calculate a z value for the 650-hour point as follows:

$$z = \frac{x - \mu}{\sigma} = \frac{650 - 500}{100} = 1.5 \text{ standard deviations} \qquad (6 \cdot 6)$$

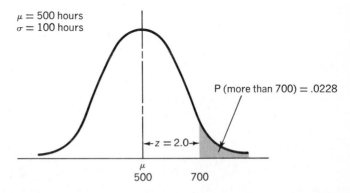

Figure 6 · 15 in the figure:

$\mu = 500$ hours
$\sigma = 100$ hours

P (more than 700) = .0228

←$z = 2.0$→

μ
500   700

Figure 6 · 15 Distribution of time required to complete the training program, with interval above 700 hours shaded

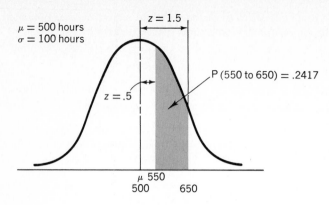

$\mu = 500$ hours
$\sigma = 100$ hours

$z = 1.5$

P (550 to 650) = .2417

$z = .5$

μ 550
500   650

Figure 6·16 Distribution of time required to complete the training program, with interval between 550 and 650 hours shaded

When we look up a z of 1.5 in Appendix Table 1, we see a probability value of .4332 (the probability that the random variable will fall between the mean and 650 hours). Now for step two. We calculate a z value for our 550-hour point like this:

$$z = \frac{x - \mu}{\sigma} = \frac{550 - 500}{100} = .5 \text{ standard deviations} \qquad (6 \cdot 6)$$

In Appendix Table 1, the z value of .5 has a probability of .1915 (the chance that the random variable will fall between the mean and 550 hours). To answer our question we must subtract as follows:

.4332 probability that the random variable
    will lie between the mean and 650 hours

$-$.1915 probability that the random variable
    will lie between the mean and 550 hours

.2417 ← probability that the random variable
    will lie between 550 and 650 hours

Thus, the chance of a candidate selected at random taking between 550 and 650 hours to complete the program is a bit less than one in four.

Question 5

What is the probability that a candidate selected at random will require fewer than 580 hours to complete the program?

Solution. This situation is illustrated in Fig. 6 · 17. Using Equation 6 · 6 to get the appropriate z value for 580 hours we have:

$$z = \frac{x - \mu}{\sigma} = \frac{580 - 500}{100} = .8 \text{ standard deviations} \qquad (6 \cdot 6)$$

Looking in Appendix Table 1 for a z value of .8, we find a probability of .2881—the probability that the random variable will lie between the mean and 580 hours. We must add to this the probability that the random variable will be between the left-hand tail and the mean. Since the distribution is symmetrical with half the area on each side of the mean, we know this value must be .5. As a

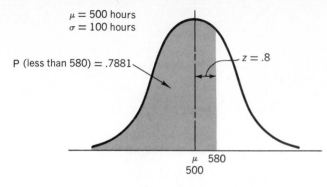

μ = 500 hours
σ = 100 hours

P (less than 580) = .7881

z = .8

μ 580
500

Figure 6·17 Distribution of time required to complete the training program, with interval less than 580 hours shaded

final step, then, we add the two probabilities:

.2881   Probability that the random variable
         will lie between the mean and 580 hours

+.5000   Probability that the random variable
         will lie between the left-hand tail and the mean

.7881 ← Probability that the random variable
        will lie between the left-hand tail and 580 hours

Thus, the chances of a candidate requiring fewer than 580 hours to complete the program are slightly higher than 75 percent.

Question 6

What is the probability that a candidate chosen at random will take between 420 and 570 hours to complete the program?

Solution. Figure 6 · 18 illustrates the interval in question, from 420 to 570 hours. Again the solution requires two steps. First, we calculate a z value for the 570-hour point:

$$z = \frac{x - \mu}{\sigma} = \frac{570 - 500}{100} = .7 \text{ standard deviations} \qquad (6 \cdot 6)$$

We look up the z value of .7 in Appendix Table 1 and find a probability value of .2580. Second, we calculate the z value for the 420-hour point:

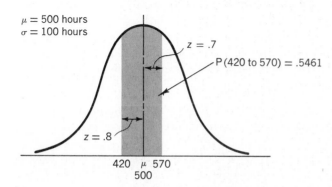

μ = 500 hours
σ = 100 hours

z = .7

P(420 to 570) = .5461

z = .8

420 μ 570
     500

Figure 6·18 Distribution of time required to complete the training program, with interval between 420 and 570 hours shaded

$$z = \frac{x - \mu}{\sigma} = \frac{420 - 500}{100} = -.8 \text{ standard deviations} \qquad (6 \cdot 6)$$

Since the distribution is symmetrical, we can disregard the sign and look for a z value of .8. The probability associated with this z value is .2881. We find our answer by adding these two values as follows:

.2580 Probability that the random variable
will lie between the mean and 570 hours

+.2881 Probability that the random variable
will lie between the mean and 420 hours

.5461 ← Probability that the random variable
will lie between 420 and 570 hours

Thus, there is slightly better than a 50 percent chance that a participant chosen at random will take between 420 and 570 hours to complete the training program.

Shortcomings of the normal probability distribution

Theory and practice

Earlier in this section we noted that the tails of the normal distribution approach but never touch the horizontal axis. This implies that there is some probability (although it may be very small) that the random variable can take on enormous values. It is possible for the right-hand tail of a normal curve to assign a minute probability of a person weighing 2,000 pounds. Of course, no one would believe that such a person exists. (A weight of one ton or more would lie about 50 standard deviations to the right of the mean and would have a probability that began with 250 zeros to the right of the decimal point!) We do not lose much accuracy by ignoring values far out in the tails. But in exchange for the convenience of using this theoretical model, we must accept the fact that it can assign impossible empirical values.

The normal distribution as an approximation of the binomial distribution

Sometimes the normal is used to approximate the binomial

Although the normal distribution is continuous, it is interesting to note that it sometimes can be used to approximate discrete distributions. To see how we can use it to approximate the binomial distribution, suppose we would like to know the probability of getting 5, 6, 7, or 8 heads in 10 tosses of a fair coin. We could use Appendix Table 3 to find this probability as follows:

$$\begin{array}{lll} \text{Probability of 5, 6,} & \text{Probability of} & \text{Probability of} \\ \text{7, or 8 heads} = & \text{5 or more heads} - & \text{9 or more heads} \end{array}$$

$$= \qquad .6230 \quad - \quad .0107$$

$$= \qquad .6123$$

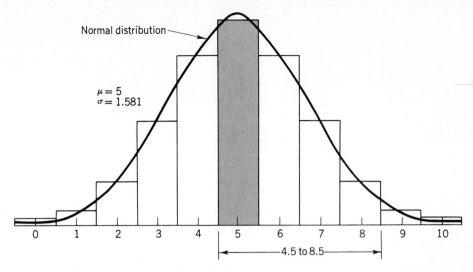

$\mu = 5$
$\sigma = 1.581$

Normal distribution

0 1 2 3 4 5 6 7 8 9 10

|←————4.5 to 8.5————→|

Figure 6·19 Binomial distribution with $n = 10$ and $p = 1/2$ with superimposed normal distribution with $\mu = 5$ and $\sigma = 1.581$

Two distributions with the same means and standard deviations

Figure 6 · 19 shows the binomial distribution for $n = 10$ and $p = \frac{1}{2}$ with a normal distribution superimposed on it with the *same* mean ($\mu = np = 10(\frac{1}{2}) = 5$) and the *same* standard deviation $\left(\sigma = \sqrt{npq} = \sqrt{10(\frac{1}{2})(\frac{1}{2})} = \sqrt{2.5} = 1.581\right)$.

Look at the area under the normal curve between $5 + \frac{1}{2}$ and $5 - \frac{1}{2}$. We see that this area is *approximately* the same size as the area of the shaded bar representing the binomial probability of getting 5 heads. The two $\frac{1}{2}$'s that we add to, and subtract from, 5 are called *continuity*

Continuity correction factors

correction factors and are used to improve the accuracy of the approximation.

Using the continuity correction factors, we see that the binomial probability of 5, 6, 7, or 8 heads can be approximated by the area under the normal curve between 4.5 and 8.5. Compute that probability by finding the z values corresponding to 4.5 and 8.5.

$$\text{At } x = 4.5, z = \frac{x - \mu}{\sigma} = \frac{4.5 - 5}{1.581} = -0.32 \qquad (6 \cdot 6)$$

$$\text{At } x = 8.5, z = \frac{x - \mu}{\sigma} = \frac{8.5 - 5}{1.581} = 2.21 \qquad (6 \cdot 6)$$

Now, from Appendix Table 1, we find

.1255	Probability that z will be between -0.32 and 0 (and correspondingly, that x will be between 4.5 and 5)
+ .4864	Probability that z will be between 0 and 2.21 (and correspondingly, that x will be between 5 and 8.5
= .6119	Probability that x will be between 4.5 and 8.5

Comparing the binomial probability of .6123 (which we got from Appendix Table 3) with this normal approximation of .6119, we can see that the error in the approximation is less than $\frac{1}{10}$ of 1 percent.

The normal approximation to the binomial distribution is very convenient, since it enables us to solve the problem without extensive tables of the binomial distribution. (You might note that Appendix Table 3, which gives binomial probabilities for values of n up to 15, already is 13 pages long.) We should note that some care needs to be taken in using this approximation, but it is quite good whenever both np and nq are at least 5.

Care must be taken

EXERCISES

6·19 The Gilbert Machinery Company has received a big order to produce electric motors for a manufacturing company. The drive shaft of the motor must fit in a groove with a diameter of 4.2 ± .05 (inches). The company's inventory manager realized that there was a large stock of steel rods in inventory with a mean diameter of 4.18″ with a standard deviation of .06″. What is the probability of a steel rod from inventory fitting the groove?

6·20 A new restaurant manager for Speedies, a national chain, wanted to compare his restaurant's performance with that of the rest of the chain. He took his revenue figures to an accountant and explained, "I know the mean monthly gross revenue of a Speedies restaurant is $200,000, but I don't know the standard deviation. I do know that my predecessor's final month resulted in a gross of $68,000, and his supervisors told him the probability of that low a gross was .1210." The accountant quickly computed the standard deviation. What was it?

6·21 Given that a random variable has a binomial distribution with $n = 80$ trials and $p = .40$, use the normal approximation to the binomial to find
a) $P(x > 25)$ **b)** $P(x > 40)$ **c)** $P(x < 35)$ **d)** $P(30 < x < 36)$

6·22 In a normal distribution with a standard deviation of 4.0, the probability that an observation selected at random exceeds 30 is .06.
a) Find the mean of the distribution.
b) Find the value below which 10 percent of the values in the distribution lie.

6·23 Given that a random variable, X, has a normal distribution with mean 5.6 and standard deviation 1.4, find
a) $P(5.0 < x < 6.0)$ **b)** $P(x > 7.0)$ **c)** $P(x < 4.4)$ **d)** $P((x < 3.4)$ or $(x > 6.4))$

6·24 On the basis of past experience, automobile inspectors in New Jersey have noticed that 7 percent of all cars coming in for their annual inspection fail to pass. Using the normal approximation to the binomial distribution, find the probability that between 10 and 20 of the next 200 cars to enter the Eatontown, New Jersey, inspection station will fail the inspection.

6·25 Ron Ledwith is the service manager of Johnson Car Refinishing, Inc., a firm that paints cars. His records indicate an average incoming level of 24 cars daily, with a standard deviation of 4.6, and he believes the distribution to be normal. On any day when more than 30 cars arrive to be painted, Ron must call in 2 extra shop helpers. What proportion of the time should he plan on employing these helpers?

6·26 Maurine Lewis, an editor for a large publishing company, calculates that it requires 11 months on average to complete the publication process from manuscript to finished book, with a standard deviation of 2.4 months. She believes that the normal distribution well describes the distribution of publication times. Out of 19 books she will handle this year, approximately how many will complete the process in less than a year?

---

6 DECISION THEORY

What is decision theory?

In the last 20 years, managers have used newly developed statistical techniques to solve problems for which information was incomplete, uncertain, or in some cases almost completely lacking. This new area of statistics has a variety of names: *statistical decision theory*, *Bayesian decision theory* (after the Reverend Thomas Bayes, whom we introduced in Chapter 5), or simply *decision theory*. These names can be used interchangeably.

In decision theory, we must decide among alternatives by taking into account the *monetary* repercussions of our actions. A manager who must select from among a number of available investments should consider the profit or loss that might result from each alternative. Applying decision theory involves selecting an alternative and having a reasonable idea of the economic consequences of choosing that action.

Expected profit under uncertainty

A decision theory problem

As our first example, consider the case of a fruit and vegetable wholesaler who buys strawberries at $20 a case and resells them at $50 a case. We shall assume that the product has no value if not sold on the first day. If buyers call for more cases tomorrow than the wholesaler has in stock, profits suffer by $30 (selling price minus cost) for each case he cannot sell. On the other hand, costs also result from stocking *too many* units on a given day. If the wholesaler has 13 cases in stock but sells only 10, he makes a profit of $300 ($30 a case on 10 cases). But this profit must be reduced by $60, the cost of the 3 cases not sold and of no value.

A 100-day observation of past sales gives the information shown in Table 6 · 6. The probability values there are obtained just as they were in Table 6 · 1.

TABLE 6·6 Cases sold during 100 days

Daily sales	Number of days sold	Probability of each number being sold
10	15	.15
11	20	.20
12	40	.40
13	25	.25
	100	1.00

Notice that there are only 4 discrete values for sales volume, and as far as we know there is no discernible pattern in the sequence in which these 4 values occur. We assume that the retailer has no reason to believe sales volume will behave differently in the future.

Calculating conditional profits. To illustrate this retailer's problem, we can construct a table showing the results in dollars of all possible combinations of purchases and sales. The only values for purchases and for sales that have meaning to us are 10, 11, 12, and 13 cases, because the retailer has no reason to consider buying fewer than 10 or more than 13 cases.

Conditional profit table

Table 6 · 7, called a *conditional profit table*, shows the profit resulting from any possible combination of supply and demand. The profits could be either positive or negative (although they are all positive in this example) and are conditional in that a certain profit results from taking a specific stocking action (ordering 10, 11, 12, or 13 cases) and having sales of a specific number of cases (10, 11, 12, or 13 cases).

Notice that the stocking of 10 cases each day will always result in a profit of $300. Even on those days when buyers want 13 cases, the retailer can sell only 10. When the retailer stocks 11 cases, his profit will be $330 on days when buyers request 11, 12, or 13 cases. But on days when he has 11 cases in stock and buyers buy only 10 cases, profit drops to $280. The $300 profit on the 10 cases sold must be reduced by $20, the cost of the unsold case. Conditional profits resulting from stock actions of 12 or 13 cases are calculated in the same manner.

Function of the conditional profit table

Such a conditional profit table does *not* show the retailer how many cases he should stock each day in order to maximize profits. It reveals the outcome only if a specific number of cases is stocked and a specific number of cases is sold. Under conditions of uncertainty, the retailer does not know in advance the size of any day's market. However, he must still decide which number of cases, stocked consistently, will maximize profits over a long period of time.

TABLE 6 · 7 Conditional profit table

Possible demand (sales) in cases	Probability of market size	Possible stock action			
		10 cases	11 cases	12 cases	13 cases
10	.15	$300	$280	$260	$240
11	.20	300	330	310	290
12	.40	300	330	360	340
13	.25	300	330	360	390

TABLE 6·8   Expected profit from stocking 10 cases

Market size in cases	Conditional profit		Probability of market size		Expected profit
10	$300	×	.15	=	$ 45.00
11	300	×	.20	=	60.00
12	300	×	.40	=	120.00
13	300	×	.25	=	75.00
			1.00		$300.00

Calculating expected profits.   As we saw on pp. 124–26, we compute the expected value of a random variable by weighting each possible value the variable can take by the probability of its taking on that value. Using this procedure, we can compute the expected daily profit from stocking 10 cases each day. See Table 6 · 8. The figures in column 4 of Table 6 · 8 are obtained by weighting the conditional profit of each possible sales volume (column 2) by the probability of that conditional profit occurring (column 3). The sum in the last column is the expected daily profit resulting from stocking 10 cases each day. It is not surprising that this expected profit is $300, since we saw in Table 6 · 7 that stocking 10 cases each day would always result in a daily profit of $300, regardless of whether buyers wanted 10, 11, 12, or 13 cases.

Table 6 · 9 illustrates the calculation of expected profit for stock actions 11, 12, and 13 cases; it uses the same approach first used in Table 6 · 8.

The *optimum stock action* is the one that results in the greatest expected profit—the largest daily average profits and thus the maximum total profits over a period of time. In this illustration, the proper number to stock each day is 12 cases, since that quantity will give the highest possible average daily profits under the conditions given.

TABLE 6·9   Expected profit from stocking 11, 12, and 13 cases

Market size in cases	Probability of market size	Possible stock actions					
		11 cases		12 cases		13 cases	
		Conditional profit	Expected profit	Conditional profit	Expected profit	Conditional profit	Expected profit
10	.15	$280	$ 42.00	$260	$ 39.00	$240	$ 36.00
11	.20	330	66.00	310	62.00	290	58.00
12	.40	330	132.00	360	144.00	340	136.00
13	.25	330	82.50	360	90.00	390	97.50
	1.00		$322.50	Optimum →	$335.00		$327.50

We have *not* reduced uncertainty in the problem facing the retailer. Rather, we have used his past experience to determine the best stock action open to him. He still does not know how many cases will be requested on any given day. There is no guarantee that he will make a profit of $335.00 tomorrow. However, if he stocks 12 cases each day under the conditions given, he will have *average* profits of $335.00 per day. This is the best he can do, because the choice of any one of the other three possible stock actions will result in a lower expected daily profit.

Expected profit with perfect information. Now suppose that the retailer in our illustration could remove all uncertainty from his problem by obtaining complete and accurate information in advance on how many cases were going to be called for each day. Under these circumstances, the retailer would stock today the exact number of cases buyers will want tomorrow. The expected profit under certainty is shown

in Table 6 · 10. The procedure is the same as that already used, but you will notice that the conditional profit figures in column 2 of Table 6 · 10 are the maximum profits possible for each sales volume. When buyers buy 12 cases, the retailer will always make a profit of $360 under certainty because he will have stocked exactly 12 cases. With perfect information, then, our retailer could count on making an average profit of $352.50 a day. This is a significant figure because it is the *maximum expected profit* possible.

Expected value of perfect information. The retailer in our example can earn average daily profits of $352.50 if he has perfect information about the future (see Table 6 · 10). His best expected daily profit without the predictor is only $335.00 (see Tables 6 · 8 and 6 · 9). The difference of $17.50 is the maximum amount the retailer would be willing to pay, per day, for a perfect predictor, because that is the maximum amount by which he can increase his expected daily profit.

TABLE 6 · 10   Expected profit under certainty

Market size in cases	Conditional profit under certainty		Probability of market size		Expected profit under certainty
10	$300	×	.15	=	$ 45.00
11	330	×	.20	=	66.00
12	360	×	.40	=	144.00
13	390	×	.25	=	97.50
			1.00		$352.50

This difference is the *expected value of perfect information* and is referred to as EVPI. There is no sense in paying more than $17.50 for the predictor; to do so would cost more than the knowledge is worth.

EXERCISES

6·27 Center City Motor Sales has recently incorporated. Its chief asset is a franchise to sell automobiles of a major American manufacturer. CCMS's general manager is planning the staffing of the dealership's garage facilities. From information provided by the manufacturer and from other nearby dealerships, he has estimated the number of annual mechanic hours that the garage will be likely to need.

Hours	10,000	12,000	14,000	16,000
Probability	.2	.3	.4	.1

The manager plans to pay each mechanic $9.00 per hour and to charge his customers $16.00. Mechanics will work a 40-hour week and get an annual 2-week vacation.
a) Determine how many mechanics Center City should hire.
b) How much should Center City pay to get perfect information about the number of mechanics they need?

6·28 Cynthia Baum, merchandise manager for the Grant Shoe Company, was planning production decisions for the coming year's summer line of shoes. Her chief concern was with estimating the summer sales of a new design of fashion sandals. Fashion sandals had posed problems for two reasons: (1) the limited selling season did not provide enough time for the company to produce a second run of a popular item, and (2) the styles changed dramatically from year to year, and unsold sandals became worthless. Cynthia had discussed the new shoe with salespeople and had formulated the following estimate of how the item would sell.

Sandal sales

Pairs (in thousands)	30	35	40	45	50
Probability	.10	.15	.20	.30	.25

Information from the production department revealed that the shoe would cost $7.50 per pair to manufacture. Marketing had informed Cynthia that the wholesale price would be $14.00 a pair. Using the expected value decision criterion, calculate the number of pairs that Cynthia should recommend the company produce.

---

7 DECISION TREE ANALYSIS

Decision tree fundamentals

A decision tree is a graphic model of a decision process. With it, we can introduce probabilities into the analysis of complex decisions involving (1) many alternatives and (2) future conditions that are not known but that can be specified in terms of a set of discrete probabilities or a continuous probability distribution. Decision tree analysis is a useful tool in making decisions concerning investments, the acquisition or disposal of physical property, project management, personnel, and new product strategies.

The term *decision tree* is derived from the physical appearance of the usual graphic representation of this technique. We will use a branch for each alternative and subbranches for each possible outcome or chance event that can occur from that alternative. Because each subbranch can branch again, we eventually build a treelike structure representing all possible outcomes.

A decision tree is like the probability tree we introduced in Chapter 5. But a decision tree contains *both* the probabilities of outcomes *and* the conditional monetary values attached to those outcomes, so that expected values can be computed. Decision trees have standard symbols: squares symbolize decision points, and circles represent chance events. From each square and circle, branches are drawn. These represent each possible outcome or state of nature that could result.

Decision tree illustrating plant expansion problem

With a decision tree, we can analyze whether the Lakeshore Manufacturing Company should build a large or a small plant to process a new product with an expected market life of 10 years.

If Lakeshore builds a large processing plant, it must keep it for 10 years. If it builds a small one, it can either expand in 2 years if demand is high or stay in the small plant making smaller benefits on a small volume of sales. Expanding a small plant after 2 years would cost $2,200,000.

Demand may be high during the first 2 years but low for the remaining 8 if many users find the product unsatisfactory. On the other hand, high demand during the first 2 years may indicate high demand for the next 8 years. If within the first 2 years demand is high and the company does not expand, competitive products will be introduced and the benefits lowered. Table 6 · 11 lists the manager's estimates of demand for the next 10 years.

The manager estimates the financial costs and benefits of the different options available to the company to be:

1. A large plant with high demand would yield $1,000,000 annually in benefits.

TABLE 6 · 11 Estimate of 10-year demand for Lakeshore's new product

Probability	Demand for the first 2 years	Demand for the next 8 years
.6	high	high
.1	high	low
$\overline{.7}$ ← Probability of high demand during first two years		
.3	low	low
0	low	high
$\overline{.3}$ ← Probability of low demand during first two years		

2. A large plant with low demand would yield $100,000 annually because of production inefficiencies.
3. A small plant, not expanded, with a low demand would yield annual benefits of $200,000 for 10 years.
4. A small plant during a 2-year period of high demand would yield $450,000 annually. If high demand continued and the plant were not expanded, the yield would drop (due to competition) to $300,000 annually for the next 8 years.
5. A small plant that is expanded after 2 years to meet high demand would yield $700,000 annually for the next 8 years.
6. A small plant that is expanded after 2 years would yield $50,000 annually for 8 years if demand were low during that period.
7. A large plant would cost $3,000,000 to build and put into operation.
8. A small plant would cost $1,300,000 to build and put into operation.

Figure 6 · 20 illustrates the Lakeshore size-of-plant problem as a decision tree. The decision horizon is divided into two parts: (1) the first 2 years and (2) the remaining 8 years. The first decision point, $\boxed{1}$, is whether to build a large or a small plant; the second decision point comes at the end of year two, $\boxed{2}$, and concerns whether to expand the small plant.

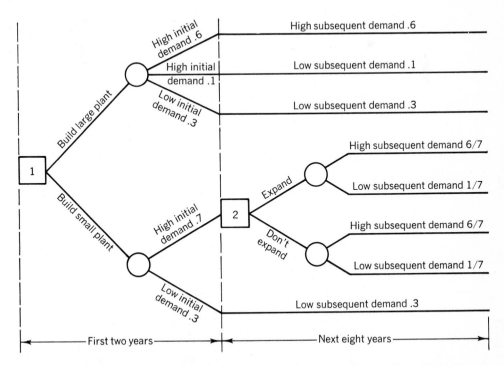

Figure 6 · 20 Decision tree of Lakeshore Manufacturing Company problem, with probabilities of various demand combinations

The upper branch of the decision tree and the three branches that emanate from it in Fig. 6 · 20 illustrate the three outcomes possible if the company elects to build a large plant:

1. high initial demand followed by high subsequent demand
2. high initial demand followed by low subsequent demand
3. low initial demand followed by low subsequent demand

The lower branch of the decision tree and the branches emanating from it illustrate the five outcomes possible if the company decides to build a small plant. These are:

1. high initial demand followed by plant expansion and high subsequent demand
2. high initial demand, plant expansion, and low subsequent demand
3. high initial demand, no plant expansion, and high subsequent demand
4. high initial demand followed by no expansion and low subsequent demand
5. low initial demand followed by low subsequent demand with no expansion

We can begin to combine probability values with conditional monetary values on the upper branch of the decision tree. This has been done in Fig. 6 · 21. Thus, if the Lakeshore Company builds a *large* plant,

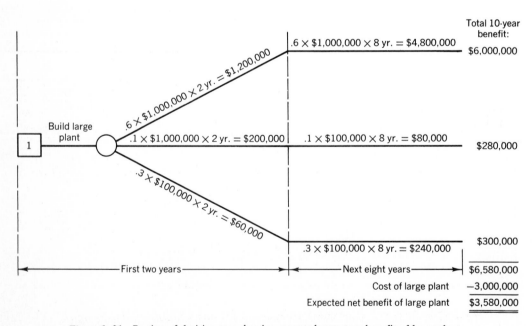

Figure 6·21 Portion of decision tree showing expected monetary benefit of large plant

the total expected benefit (net of plant costs) would be $3,580,000 (the sum of the expected values of all three branches in Fig. 6 · 21).

Rollback process

Next, consider the financial benefits on the lower branch of the original tree, illustrated in Fig. 6 · 22. We begin by concerning ourselves *only* with the portion of the tree that comes after the second decision point, [2]. The second decision about the small plant (to expand or not to expand) affects our original decision. Since we cannot wait 2 years to make the original decision, we must make the second decision now, base it on the best market information available, and incorporate it into the original decision on plant size. The process now moves from right to left. We make future decisions first and then roll them back to become part of earlier decisions. We have 2 rules concerning *rollback* in decision theory analysis:

1. If the branches emanate from a *circle*, we calculate the total expected benefits by summing all the expected values of the branches.
2. If the branches emanate from a *square*, we calculate the expected benefit for each branch emanating from that square and let the total expected benefit be equal to the value of the branch with the highest expected benefit.

Decision criterion: total expected monetary benefits

Figure 6 · 22 shows that after deducting expansion costs, the expected financial benefits of an expanded small plant over an 8-year period are $2,657,143. Over the same 8-year period, the expected finan-

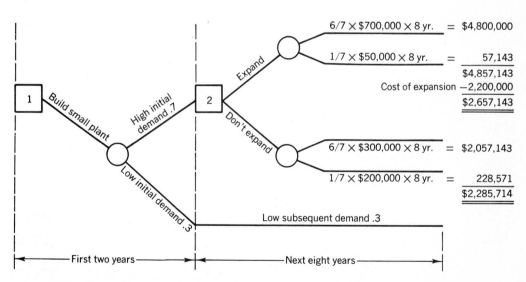

Figure 6 · 22 Portion of decision tree showing expected monetary benefits from expanding or not expanding small plant in two years

cial benefits of an unexpanded small plant are $2,285,714. We can conclude that given the cost and the market information we have now, it would be financially more advantageous (almost $400,000 more expected benefit over 8 years) to expand a small plant after 2 years *if* it is decided now to build a small plant in the first place and *if* demand is high in the first 2 years.

Figure 6 · 23 repeats Fig. 6 · 22 but indicates that decision 2 would result in expansion of a small plant with an expected 8-year benefit of $2,657,143. Thus if demand is high in the first 2 years, our gain from this alternative is $900,000 (in the first 2 years) + $2,657,143 (in the next 8 years). But the chances that demand will be high are only .7. Therefore, we multiply both of these figures by .7 and add the results to get $2,490,000.

If demand in the first 2 years is low, we would not expand the plant. Our gain for the first 2 years would be $400,000 ($200,000 × 2 years), and for the last 8 years it would be $1,600,000 ($200,000 × 8 years). But the chances that demand would be low are only .3. Therefore, we multiply both of these figures by .3 and add the results to get $600,000.

Adding $2,490,000 and $600,000, we get a total expected benefit for the small plant of $3,090,000. Subtracting the cost of the small plant from this figure leaves a net benefit of $1,790,000. This figure is substantially smaller than $3,580,000, the net benefit of a large plant. In *this* case and under *these* assumptions, it would be financially wiser for the Lakeshore Manufacturing Company to build a large plant.

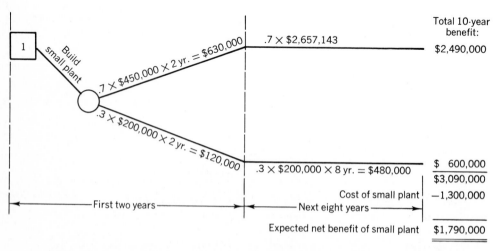

Figure 6 · 23   Portion of decision tree showing expected benefit if small plant is built

EXERCISES

6·29 Refer to the Lakeshore Manufacturing problem, which we have just discussed. The management of Lakeshore has been advised that in addition to the options currently available to them (building a large plant, building a small plant and expanding it 2 years later, and building a small plant and not expanding it), another option exists. This option would allow them to construct a plant of a size between the large and small plant they are currently considering. The cost of building this medium-sized plant is estimated to be $2,100,000, but it would not be expandable. The economic benefits estimated by Lakeshore management to accrue from such a plant under differing conditions are these:

Demand	Benefits / year
High	$750,000
Low	$150,000

a) Will the existence of this third option cause Lakeshore to take an action different from the one they took in the original problem?

b) If your answer to part a is no, then state what the cost of a medium-sized plant would have to be for Lakeshore to consider this new option.

c) In the original problem, are there any nonfinancial considerations that would cause Lakeshore management to prefer the smaller plant to the larger one, even though the expected benefit from the larger plant is considerably higher?

6·30 Jiffy-Burger, a fast-food organization, is considering bringing out a new product for one of its restaurants. In this particular location, there is one competing restaurant. The fixed cost of developing the new food item is estimated to be $25,000. The profit this one restaurant will earn on the new product depends on (a) what kind of a promotional campaign Jiffy-Burger uses to introduce its new product, (b) whether the competitor responds with a similar product of his own, and (c) what kind of promotional campaign the competitor uses if he brings out a competing product. Jiffy-Burger thinks that there is a .7 probability the competitor will bring out a competing product if Jiffy introduces one. Jiffy-Burger can choose 4 different promotion schemes, which can be described as (1) minimal, (2) low, (3) moderate, and (4) comprehensive. If the competitor introduces a competing product, the competitor's promotional response to these campaigns is estimated by Jiffy to be represented by this table:

Competitor's response

Jiffy-Burger campaign	Minimal	Low	Moderate	Comprehensive
Minimal	.8	.1	.05	.05
Low	.2	.6	.1	.1
Moderate	.1	.1	.5	.3
Comprehensive	.1	.1	.1	.7

If the competitor responds, the conditional profits that Jiffy will earn for each of the possible combinations of Jiffy-Burger promotional actions and competitor responses have been estimated by Jiffy's accounting department to be (net of promotional expense):

Competitor's response

Jiffy-Burger campaign	Minimal	Low	Moderate	Comprehensive
Minimal	$ 60,000	$40,000	$20,000	$10,000
Low	70,000	60,000	40,000	20,000
Moderate	90,000	80,000	60,000	30,000
Comprehensive	100,000	90,000	70,000	50,000

If there is no response from the competitor to Jiffy's introduction of a new food product, the conditional profits associated with each possible Jiffy promotional strategy are: minimal ($80,000), low ($95,000), moderate ($120,000), and comprehensive ($150,000). In this particular situation, what should Jiffy's new product decision be? Draw a decision tree for this problem.

8 TERMS INTRODUCED IN CHAPTER 6

Bernoulli process A process in which each trial has only two possible outcomes, the probability of the outcome of any trial remains fixed over time, and the trials are statistically independent.

binomial distribution A discrete distribution describing the results of an experiment known as a Bernoulli process.

certainty The decision environment in which only one state of nature exists.

conditional profit The profit that would result from a given combination of decision alternative and state of nature.

continuous probability distribution A probability distribution in which the variable is allowed to take on any value within a given range.

continuous random variable A random variable allowed to take on any value within a given range.

decision point Branching point that requires a decision.

decision tree Graphic display of the decision environment, indicating decision alternatives, states of nature, probabilities attached to those states of nature and conditional benefits and losses.

discrete probability distribution A probability distribution in which the variable is allowed to take on only a limited number of values.

discrete random variable A random variable that is allowed to take on only a limited number of values.

expected profit The summation of the conditional profits for a given decision alternative, each weighted by the probability that it will happen.

expected profit with perfect information The expected value of profit with perfect certainty about the occurrence of the states of nature.

expected value A weighted average of the outcomes of an experiment.

expected value criterion A criterion requiring the decision maker to calculate the expected value for each decision alternative (the sum of the weighted payoffs for that alternative in which the weights are the probability values assigned by the decision maker to the states of nature that can happen).

expected value of a random variable The sum of the products of each value of the random variable with that value's probability of occurrence.

expected value of perfect information The difference between expected profit (under conditions of risk) and expected profit with perfect information.

node Point at which a chance event takes place on a decision tree.

normal distribution A distribution of a continuous random variable with a single-peaked, bell-shaped curve. The mean lies at the center of the distribution, and the curve is symmetrical around a vertical line erected at the mean. The two tails extend indefinitely, never touching the horizontal axis.

Poisson distribution A discrete distribution in which the probability of the occurrence of an event within a very small time period is a very small number, the probability that two or more such events will occur within the same small time interval is effectively 0, and the probability of the occurrence of the event within one time period is independent of where that time period is.

probability distribution A list of the outcomes of an experiment with the probabilities we would expect to see associated with these outcomes.

random variable A variable that takes on different values as a result of the outcomes of a random experiment.

rollback Also called foldback; method of using decision trees to find optimum alternatives. Involves working from right to left in the tree.

standard normal probability distribution A normal probability distribution, with mean $\mu = 0$ and standard deviation $\sigma = 1$.

9 EQUATIONS INTRODUCED IN CHAPTER 6

p. 128
$$\text{Probability of } r \text{ successes in } \atop n \text{ Bernoulli or binomial trials} = \frac{n!}{r!(n-r)!} p^r q^{n-r}$$
6·1

where

r = number of successes desired

n = number of trials undertaken

p = probability of success (characteristic probability)

q = probability of failure $(q = 1 - p)$

This *binomial formula* enables us to calculate algebraically the probability of success. We can apply it to any Bernoulli process, where (1) each trial has only two possible outcomes—a success or a failure; (2) the probability of success remains the same trial after trial; and (3) the trials are statistically independent.

p. 133
$$\mu = np$$
6·2

The *mean* of a *binomial distribution* is equal to the number of trials multiplied by the probability of success.

p. 133
$$\sigma = \sqrt{npq}$$
6·3

The *standard deviation* of a *binomial distribution* is equal to the square root of the product of (1) the number of trials, (2) the probability of a success, and (3) the probability of a failure (found by taking $q = 1 - p$).

p. 136
$$P(x) = \frac{\lambda^x \times e^{-\lambda}}{x!}$$
6·4

This formula enables us to calculate the probability of a discrete random variable occurring in a *Poisson distribution*. The formula states that the probability of *exactly* x occurrences is equal to λ, or lambda (the mean number of occurrences per interval of time in a Poisson distribution), raised to the x power and multiplied by e, or 2.71828 (the base of the natural logarithm system), raised to the negative lambda power, and the product divided by x factorial. The table of values for $e^{-\lambda}$ is Appendix Table 4.

p. 138
$$P(x) = \frac{(np)^x \times e^{-np}}{x!}$$
6·5

If we substitute in Equation 6·4 the mean of the binomial distribution (np) in place of the mean of the Poisson distribution (λ), we can use the Poisson probability distribution as a reasonable approximation of the binomial. The approximation is good when n is equal to or greater than 20 and p is equal to or less than .05.

p. 144
$$z = \frac{x - \mu}{\sigma}$$
6·6

where:

x = value of the random variable with which we are concerned

μ = mean of the distribution of this random variable

σ = standard deviation of this distribution

z = number of standard deviations from x to the mean of this distribution

Once we have derived z using this formula, we can use the Standard Normal Probability Distribution Table (which gives the value for half the area under the normal curve, beginning with 0.0 at the mean) and determine the probability that the random variable with which we are concerned is within that distance from the mean of this distribution.

---

10 CHAPTER REVIEW EXERCISES

6·31 Capital City Coach maintains a fleet of buses and operates as a commercial carrier with scheduled buses and charters. Over the last several years, Capital City Coach has maintained an excellent safety record and has averaged only one accident for every 250,000 bus miles (including fender-benders and bus station mishaps). For the week of June 17, Capital City Coach has buses scheduled (including charters) for 50,000 bus miles.
  a) What is the probability that in the 7-day period, Capital City Coach will experience only one accident?
  b) No accidents?

6·32 The Sureflight Golf Company recently purchased a patent on a small portable device designed to measure the loft of a golf club. The president of Sureflight believes that the device is as accurate as the large mounted machines used for this. He had 100 of these produced for testing. On each one produced, a reading was taken on a club that had also been measured by a large mounted machine. As long as the reading on the portable was within .0004 inch of the reading on the larger machine, he considered it acceptable. Otherwise, the portable was rejected. He had heard of the Bernoulli process and thought it might be applicable if he could establish the probability of a defect. As described, do you think the production of the portable machines is a Bernoulli process?

6·33 Explain in your own words the difference between discrete and continuous random variables. What difference does such classification make in determining the probabilities of future events?

6·34 Last year, Herb Williams invested his life savings in an antique store. Williams figured that during the first year he took in an average of $400 dollars a week, with a standard deviation of $100.
  a) According to this data what is the probability that on any given week he took in between $350 and $420?
  b) What is the probability that on any given week he took in between $380 and $500?

6·35 Which probability distribution is most likely to appropriate one to use for the following variables: binomial, Poisson, or normal?
  a) distribution of customers arriving at a complaint office
  b) distribution of scores on an intelligence test
  c) number of sales made in 10 house calls by a sales representative
  d) amount of daily rainfall

6·36 United States Customs agents check the documents of incoming foreigners to see if each person entering the country has been vaccinated for smallpox. Departmental records show that 50

percent of all foreigners entering the United States have been vaccinated.

a) From a sample of 15, what is the probability that 6 or more will not have been vaccinated?

b) 8 or more?

c) Fewer than 5?

6·37 A farmer on the Delmarva Peninsula recently planted 15 hills of Half-Runner green beans. Both the seed producer and the local seed store guarantee an 80 percent fertility rate based on years of past experience with that particular brand of seed.

a) What is the probability that more than 12 hills will come up?

b) 12 or more fertile hills?

c) Fewer than 12 fertile hills?

d) 8 or fewer fertile hills?

6·38 Surveys by the Federal Deposit Insurance Corporation have shown that the life of a regular savings account maintained in one of its member banks averages 18 months, with a standard deviation of 6.45 months.

a) If a depositor opened an account at a bank that was a member of the FDIC, what is the probability that there will still be money in that account in 22 months?

b) What is the probability that the account will have been closed before 2 years?

6·39 A textile mill must decide whether to extend $100,000 credit to a new customer who manufactures dresses. The mill's prior experience with a number of dress manufacturers has led it to classify such customers as follows: 30 percent are poor risks; 50 percent are average risks; and 20 percent are good risks. Expected profits on this order (if credit is extended to the dress manufacturer) are − $15,000 if they turn out to be a poor risk, $10,000 if they turn out to be an average risk, and $20,000 if they turn out to be a good risk. Draw a decision tree to determine whether the mill should extend credit to this manufacturer.

6·40 The textile mill in problem 6 · 39 can purchase a comprehensive credit analysis and rating (poor, average, or good) on the manufacturer for a cost of $2,000. The credit agency's past reliability is summed up in the following table, whose entries are the probabilities (from past experience) that the agency will correctly rate the dress manufacturer, given the true credit category in which the manufacturer belongs. Draw a decision tree to determine whether the mill should purchase the credit rating.

	True category		
Agency rating	*Poor*	*Average*	*Good*
Poor	.6	.3	.2
Average	.3	.6	.4
Good	.1	.1	.4

6·41 For the price of $17.50, La Maison du Langouste offers, as an entree, 2 spiny-shelled lobster tails imported from the waters off the Yucatan Peninsula. Because of federal health regulations, the lobsters cannot enter the United States if they are still alive. Accordingly, only refrigerated tails are sent to the United States. At La Maison du Langouste, the chef has found that the texture of the lobster is impaired if it is refrigerated for more than 24 hours. To maintain its image as the quintessence of haute cuisine, La Maison employs an agent to place refrigerated lobster tails on a plane leaving from the peninsula each day. The chef is trying to choose the optimum number of tails for the agent to purchase and send. He wants to satisfy the customers, yet he realizes that always carrying enough to satisfy the customers might be too costly. He has calculated the cost of the lobster tail at $4.65, including transportation. Past experience has shown the following distribution of sales of spiny-shelled lobster tail entrees per day.

Number	22	23	24	25	26	27	28	29
Probability	.08	.09	.10	.15	.18	.16	.13	.11

a) Using expected profit as the decision criterion, how many lobster tails should the chef order?
b) If La Maison du Langouste adopted a policy that required customers to order spiny-shelled lobster a day in advance, how much could they expect to save?

6·42 The Silent Running Boat Company distributes a sailboat made by Tall Ships. On August 1, Carter Fletcher, the company's owner, learned that Tall Ships was halting production for a few weeks. Fletcher found that he had 2 dozen boats left. Fletcher knows how many boats he has sold in the last 2 years, and he consults his records for these figures:

	J	F	M	A	M	J	J	A	S	O	N	D
1979	31	30	28	29	30	29	30	32	30	27	33	32
1980	31	26	31	28	27	29	30	34	28	33	30	32

a) From Fletcher's data, compute the probability of each value indicated for the number of boats sold in a given month.
b) Compute the expected number of boats sold per month.
c) What is Fletcher's expected sales loss for August in total boats?

6·43 The Executive Camera Company provides full expenses for their sales force. When attempting to budget automobile expenses for its employees, the financial department uses mileage figures to estimate gas, tire, and repair expenses. Salespeople average 6,250 miles a month, with a standard deviation of 178. In the interest of conservatism, the financial department wants its expense estimate and subsequent budget to be adequately high and therefore does not want to use the data from drivers who drove less than 6,000 miles. What percentage of drivers drove 6,000 miles or more?

6·44 Rework problem 6 · 36, using the normal approximation. Compare the approximate and the exact answer.

6·45 Try to use the normal approximation for problem 6 · 37. Notice that nq is only 3. Comment on the accuracy of the approximation.

6·46 During a meeting to discuss scheduling plant capacity, production managers for Keystone Foundry and Metalworks were concentrating on planning for the manufacture of castings used by small diesel engine manufacturers. Because of a recent recession, demand by the engine manufactureres had been sluggish, but there were signs that it might increase in the coming year. The managers had made these estimates on the expected sales of castings:

	Pounds	Probability
Weak sales	45,000	.40
Average sales	50,000	.35
Strong sales	55,000	.25

To produce the castings, Keystone had a fixed startup cost of $30,000 and a variable manufacturing cost of $.50 per pound. On the average, sales prices were $1.50 per pound.
a) What is the total cost of producing to meet average sales?
b) Using expected profit as the decision criterion, at what level should Keystone produce?
c) How much should Keystone pay to find out exactly what sales will be?

Answers are in the back of the book.

T F   1. A conditional profits table shows the losses resulting from any possible combination of supply and demand.

T F   2. The value of z for some point x lying in a normal distribution is the area between x and the mean of the distribution.

T F   3. The right and left tails of the normal distribution extend indefinitely, never touching the horizontal axis.

T F   4. For a normal distribution, the mean always lies in between the mode and the median.

T F   5. All but about three-tenths of 1 percent of the area in a normal distribution lies within plus-and-minus three standard deviations from the mean.

T F   6. The area under the curve of a normal distribution between the mean and a point 1.8 standard deviations above the mean is greater for a distribution having a mean of 100 than it is for a distribution having a mean of 0.

T F   7. With perfect information, a retailer would consistently make the maximum profit possible.

T F   8. One advantage of using decision trees is that every outcome, desirable or undesirable, must be investigated.

T F   9. When the probability of success in a Bernoulli process is 50 percent ($p = .5$), its binomial distribution is symmetrical.

T F 10. On the graph of a normal distribution of sales, the area to the right of a vertical line represents the probability of selling that quantity or less.

T F 11. The value of a random variable can usually be predicted in advance of a particular occurrence.

T F 12. Once the value of p has been decided for a Bernoulli process, the value of q is calculated as $(1 - p)$.

T F 13. If the expected number of arrivals in an office is calculated as 5 per hour, one can be reasonably confident that 5 people will arrive with the next hour.

T F 14. The binomial distribution is not really necessary, since its values can always be approximated by another distribution.

15. Which of the following is a characteristic of a probability distribution for a random variable?
    a) A probability is provided for every possible value.
    b) The sum of all probabilities is 1.
    c) No given probability occurs more than once.
    d) All of the above.
    e) a and b but not c.

16. Which of the following could never be described by a binomial distribution?
    a) The number of defective widgets produced by an assembly process.
    b) The amount of water used daily by a single household.
    c) The number of people in your class who can answer this question correctly.
    d) All of the above could always be described by a binomial distribution.

17. If $p = .4$ for a particular Bernoulli process, the calculation $\dfrac{7!}{3! \times 4!}(.4)^3(.6)^4$ gives the probability of getting:
a) exactly 3 successes in 7 trials
b) exactly 4 successes in 7 trials
c) 3 or more successes in 7 trials
d) 4 or more successes in 7 trials
e) none of the above

18. For binomial distributions with $p = .2$:
a) A distribution for $n = 2,000$ would more closely approximate the normal distribution than one for $n = 50$.
b) No matter what the value of n, the distribution is skewed to the right.
c) The graph of this distribution with $p = .2$ and $n = 100$ would be the exact reverse of the graph for the binomial distribution with $n = 100$ and $p = .8$.
d) All of the above.
e) a and b but not c.

19. A manager is deciding whether to buy a new building or to rent it. If he buys, the cost for the next year will be $5,500, which will include mortgage payments, insurance, and other usual expenses. If he rents, the comparable expense for the next year will be either $6,000, $5,300, or $4,200 depending on market fluctuations. The manager wishes to make his choice based upon expected monetary values for the next year. The decision tree for this situation would have:
a) one decision point and no chance events
b) one chance event and one decision point
c) two decision points and three chance events
d) one decision point and three chance events

20. For a normal curve with $\mu = 55$ and $\sigma = 10$, how much area will be found under the curve to the right of the value 55?
a) 1.0   d) .32
b) .68   e) cannot be determined from the information given
c) .5

21. Suppose you are using a normal distribution to approximate a binomial distribution with $\mu = 5$, $\sigma = 2$ and wish to determine the probability of getting more than 7 successes. From the normal table, you would determine the probability that z is greater than:
a) 0   b) .5   c) .75   d) 1.0   e) 1.25

22. Which of the following normal curves looks most like the curve for $\mu = 10$, $\sigma = 5$?
a) curve for $\mu = 10$, $\sigma = 10$ c) curve for $\mu = 20$, $\sigma = 5$
b) curve for $\mu = 20$, $\sigma = 10$ d) curve for $\mu = 12$, $\sigma = 3$

23. The distribution that deals only in successes and failures is the _____ distribution. It is usually used to describe a _____ process.

24. When approximating a binomial distribution by a normal distribution, a _____ correction factor should be used. n and p are known. The standard deviation, σ, is calculated as _____ .

25. For a Poisson distribution, the symbol that represents the mean number of occurrences per interval of time is _____ .

26. Events beyond the control of the decision maker are called _____ or _____ of nature.

27. The maximum amount that a retailer will be willing to pay for a perfect predictor is called the _____ .
28. Rollback is always accomplished from _____ to _____ .   .
29. In decision trees, squares denote _____ and circles _____ .
30. A decision tree is a model of _____ .

Sampling and Sampling Distributions

7

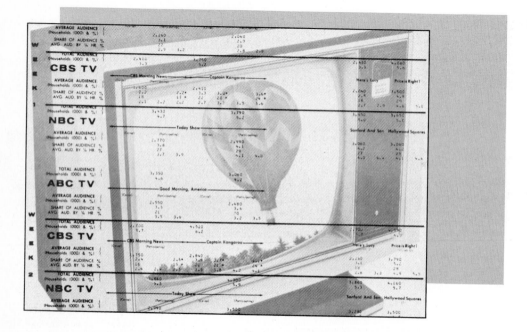

Although there are over a 150 million TV viewers in the United States and somewhat over half that many TV sets, only about a thousand of those sets are sampled to determine what programs Americans watch. Why select only about a thousand sets out of 75 million? Because time and the average cost of an interview prohibit the rating companies from trying to reach millions of people. And since polls are reasonably accurate, interviewing everybody is unnecessary. In this chapter, we examine questions such as these: How many people should be interviewed? How should they be selected? How do we know when our sample accurately reflects the entire population?

Statistical sampling, the subject of Chapter 7, is a systematic approach to selecting a few elements (a sample) from an entire collection of data (a population) in order to make some inferences about the total collection. We shall learn methods that help to ensure that samples represent the entire collection. If you have ever examined a peach on the top of a basket, bought the whole basket on the basis of that peach, and then found the bottom of the basket filled with overripe fruit, you have a good (if somewhat expensive) understanding of statistical sampling and the need for better sampling methods.

1 INTRODUCTION TO SAMPLING

Reasons for sampling

Shoppers often sample a small piece of cheese before purchasing any. They decide from one piece what the larger chunk will taste like. A chemist does the same thing when he takes a sample of whiskey from a vat, determines that it is 90 proof, and infers that all whiskey in the vat is 90 proof. If the chemist tests all the whiskey or the shoppers taste all the cheese, there will be none to sell. Testing all of the product destroys it and is unnecessary. To determine the characteristics of the whole, we have to sample only a portion.

Suppose, as the personnel director of a large bank you need to write a report describing all the employees who have voluntarily left the company in the last ten years. You would have a difficult task locating all these thousands of people. They are not easily accessible as a group—many have died, moved from the community, left the country, or acquired a new name by marriage. How do you write the report? The best idea is to locate a representative sample and interview them, in order to generalize about the entire group.

Time is also a factor when managers need information quickly in order to adjust an operation or change a policy. Take an automatic machine that sorts thousands of pieces of mail daily. Why wait for an entire day's output to check whether the machine is working accurately (whether the *population characteristics* are those required by the postal service)? Instead, samples can be taken at specific intervals, and if necessary, the machine can be adjusted right away.

Census or sample

Sometimes it is possible and practical to examine every person or item in the population we wish to describe. We call this a *complete enumeration*, or *census*. We use sampling when it is not possible to count or measure every item in the population.

Statisticians use the word *population* to refer not only to people but to all items that have been chosen for study. In the cases we have just mentioned, the populations are all the cheese in the chunk, all the whiskey in the vat, all the employees of the large bank who voluntarily left in the last 10 years, and all mail sorted by the automatic machine since the previous sample check. Statisticians use the word *sample* to describe a portion chosen from the population.

Statistics and parameters

Function of statistics and parameters

Mathematically, we can describe samples and populations by using measures such as the mean, median, mode, and standard deviation, which we introduced in Chapters 3 and 4. When these terms describe the characteristics of a sample, they are called *statistics*. When they describe the characteristics of a population, they are called *parameters*. A statistic is a characteristic of a sample, and a parameter is a characteristic of a population.

Suppose that the mean height in inches of all tenth graders in the United States is 60 inches. In this case, 60 inches is a characteristic of the population "all tenth graders" and can be called a *population parameter*. On the other hand, if we say that the mean height in Ms. Jones's tenth-grade class in Bennetsville is 60 inches, we are using 60 inches to describe a characteristic of the sample "Ms. Jones's tenth graders." In that case, 60 inches would be a *sample statistic*. If we are convinced that the mean height of Ms. Jones's tenth graders is an accurate estimate of the mean height of all tenth graders in the United States, we could use the sample statistic "mean height of Ms. Jones's tenth graders" to estimate the population parameter "mean height of all U.S. tenth graders" without having to count all the millions of tenth graders in the United States.

Using statistics to estimate parameters

To be consistent, statisticians use lower-case Roman letters to denote sample statistics and Greek or capital letters for population parameters. Table 7·1 lists these symbols and summarizes the definitions we have studied so far in this chapter.

N, μ, σ, and n, $\bar{x}$, s: standard symbols

TABLE 7·1 Differences between populations and samples

	Population	*Sample*
Definition	Collection of items being considered	Part or portion of the population chosen for study
Characteristics	"parameters"	"statistics"
Symbols	population size $= N$	sample size $= n$
	population mean $= \mu$ (pronounced *mew*)	sample mean $= \bar{x}$ (called "x bar")
	population standard deviation $= \sigma$ (pronounced **sig**-*ma*)	sample standard deviation $= s$

Types of sampling

There are two methods of selecting samples from populations: *nonrandom*, or *judgment*, sampling and *random*, or *probability*, sampling. In probability sampling, all the items in the population have a chance of being chosen in the sample. In judgment sampling, personal knowledge and opinion are used to identify those items from the population that are to be included in the sample. A sample selected by judgment sampling is based on someone's expertise about the population. A forest ranger, for example, would have a judgment sample if he decided ahead of time which parts of a large forested area he would walk through to estimate the total board feet of lumber that could be cut. Sometimes a judgment sample is used as a pilot or trial sample to decide how to take a random sample later. Judgment samples avoid the statistical analysis that is necessary to make probability samples. They are more convenient and can be used successfully even though we are unable to measure their validity. But if a study uses judgment sampling and loses a significant degree of "representativeness," it will have purchased convenience at too high a price.

--- **EXERCISES** ---

7·1 What is the major drawback of judgment sampling?

7·2 Depending on the extent of conclusions drawn from a statistical analysis, a given set of observations may be thought of as a sample or as a population. Explain.

7·3 List the advantages of sampling over complete enumeration, or census.

7·4 What are some of the disadvantages of probability sampling versus judgment sampling?

7·5 Jean Mason, who was hired by Former Industries to determine employee attitudes toward the upcoming union vote, met with some difficulty after reporting her findings to management. Mason's study was based on statistical sampling, and from the beginning data it was clear (or so Jean thought) that the employees were favoring a unionized shop. Jean's report was shrugged off with the comment, "This is no good. Nobody can make statements about employee sentiments when she talks to only a little over 15 percent of our employees. Everyone knows you have to check 50 percent to have any idea of what the outcome of the union vote will be. We didn't hire you to make guesses." Is there any defense for Jean's position?

2 RANDOM SAMPLING

In a random or probability sample, we know what the chances are that an element of the population will or will not be included in the sample. As a result, we can assess objectively the estimates of the population characteristics that result from our sample; that is, we can describe mathematically how objective our estimates are. Let us begin our explanation of this process by introducing 4 methods of random sampling:

1. simple random sampling
2. systematic sampling
3. stratified sampling
4. cluster sampling

Simple random sampling

An example of simple random sampling

Simple random sampling selects samples by methods that allow *each possible sample to have an equal probability of being picked* and *each item in the entire population to have an equal chance of being included in the sample*. We can illustrate these requirements with an example. Suppose we have a population of 4 students in a seminar and we want samples of 2 students at a time for interviewing purposes. Table 7 · 2 illustrates the possible combinations of samples of 2 students in a population size of 4, the probability of each sample being picked, and the probability that each student will be in the sample.

Defining finite *and* replacement

Our example illustrated in Table 7 · 2 uses a *finite* population of 4 students. By *finite*, we mean that the population has a stated or limited size; that is to say, there is a whole number (N) that tells us how many items there are in the population. Certainly, if we sample without "replacing" the student we shall soon exhaust our small population group. Notice, too, that if we sample *with replacement* (that is, if we

TABLE 7 · 2 Chances of selecting samples of 2 students from a population of 4 students

Students A, B, C, and D

Possible samples of two persons: AB, AC, AD, BC, CD, BD
Probability of drawing this sample of two persons must be:

$$AB = \tfrac{1}{6} \quad AC = \tfrac{1}{6} \quad AD = \tfrac{1}{6} \quad BC = \tfrac{1}{6} \quad CD = \tfrac{1}{6} \quad BD = \tfrac{1}{6}$$

(There are only six possible samples of two persons)

Probability of this student being in the sample must be:

$$A = \tfrac{1}{2} \quad B = \tfrac{1}{2} \quad C = \tfrac{1}{2} \quad D = \tfrac{1}{2}$$

[In Chapter 5 we saw that the marginal probability is equal to the *sum* of the joint probabilities of the events within which the event is contained:

$$P(A) = P(AB \text{ or } AC \text{ or } AD) = \tfrac{1}{2}]$$

replace the sampled student immediately after he or she is picked and before the second student is chosen), the same person could appear twice in the sample.

An infinite population

We have used this example only to help us think about sampling from an infinite population. An *infinite* population is a population in which it is theoretically impossible to observe all the elements. Although many populations appear to be exceedingly large, no truly infinite population of physical objects actually exists. After all, given unlimited resources and time, we could enumerate any finite population, even the grains of sand on the beaches of North America. As a practical matter, then, we will use the term *infinite population* when we are talking about a population that could not be enumerated in a reasonable period of time. In this way, we will use the theoretical concept of infinite population as an approximation of a large finite population, just as we earlier used the theoretical concept of continuous random variable as an approximation of a discrete random variable that could take on many closely-spaced values.

How to do random sampling

The easiest way to select a sample randomly is to use random numbers. These numbers can be generated either by a computer programmed to scramble numbers or by a table of random numbers, which should properly be called a *table of random digits*.

Table 7 · 3 illustrates a portion of such a table. Here we have 1,250 random digits in sets of 10 digits. These numbers have been generated by a completely random process. The probability that any one digit from 0 through 9 will appear is the same as that for any other digit, and the probability of one sequence of digits occurring is the same as that for any other sequence of the same length.

Using a table of random digits

To see how to use this table, suppose that we have 100 employees in a company and wish to interview a randomly chosen sample of 10. We could get such a random sample by assigning every employee a number from 00 to 99, consulting Table 7 · 3, and picking a systematic method of selecting two-digit numbers. In this case, let's do the following:

1. Go from the top to the bottom of the columns beginning with the left-hand column, and read only the first two digits in each row. Notice that our first number using this method would be 15, the second 09, the third 41, and so on.
2. If we reach the bottom of the last column on the right and are still short of our desired 10 two-digit numbers of 99 and under, we can go back to the beginning (the top of the left-hand column) and start reading the third and fourth digits of each number. These would begin 81, 28, and 12.

TABLE 7·3   1,250 random digits

1581922396	2068577984	8262130892	8374856049	4637567488
0928105582	7295088579	9586111652	7055508767	6472382934
4112077556	3440672486	1882412963	0684012006	0933147914
7457477468	5435810788	9670852913	1291265730	4890031305
0099520858	3090908872	2039593181	5973470495	9776135501
7245174840	2275698645	8416549348	4676463101	2229367983
6749420382	4832630032	5670984959	5432114610	2966095680
5503161011	7413686599	1198757695	0414294470	0140121598
7164238934	7666127259	5263097712	5133648980	4011966963
3593969525	0272759769	0385998136	9999089966	7544056852
4192054466	0700014629	5169439659	8408705169	1074373131
9697426117	6488888550	4031652526	8123543276	0927534537
2007950579	9564268448	3457416988	1531027886	7016633739
4584768758	2389278610	3859431781	3643768456	4141314518
3840145867	9120831830	7228567652	1267173884	4020651657
0190453442	4800088084	1165628559	5407921254	3768932478
6766554338	5585265145	5089052204	9780623691	2195448096
6315116284	9172824179	5544814339	0016943666	3828538786
3908771938	4035554324	0840126299	4942059208	1475623997
5570024586	9324732596	1186563397	4425143189	3216653251
2999997185	0135968938	7678931194	1351031403	6002561840
7864375912	8383232768	1892857070	2323673751	3188881718
7065492027	6349104233	3382569662	4579426926	1513082455
0654683246	4765104877	8149224168	5468631609	6474393896
7830555058	5255147182	3519287786	2481675649	8907598697

Source: Dudley J. Cowden and Mercedes S. Cowden, *Practical Problems in Business Statistics*, 2d ed. Englewood Cliffs, N.J.: Prentice-Hall, Inc., 1960.

Using slips of paper

Another way to select our employees would be to write the name of each one on a slip of paper and deposit the slips in a box. After mixing them thoroughly, we could draw 10 slips at random. This method works well with a small group of people but presents problems if the people in the population number in the thousands.

Systematic sampling

In systematic sampling, elements are selected from the population at a uniform interval that is measured in time, order, or space. If we wanted to interview every twentieth student on a college campus, we would choose a random starting point in the first twenty names in the student directory and then pick every twentieth name thereafter.

Characteristics of systematic sampling

Systematic sampling differs from simple random sampling in that each *element* has an equal chance of being selected but each *sample* does *not* have an equal chance of being selected. This would have been the case if, in our earlier example, we had assigned numbers between 00 and 99 to our employees and then had begun to choose a sample of ten by picking every tenth number beginning 01, 11, 21, 31, and so forth.

Employees numbered 2, 3, 4, and 5 would have had no chance of being selected.

In systematic sampling, there is the problem of introducing an error into the sampling process. Suppose we were sampling paper waste produced by households, and we decided to sample a hundred households every Monday. Chances are high that our sample would not be representative because Monday's trash would very likely include the Sunday newspaper. Thus, the amount of waste would be biased upward by our choice of this sampling procedure.

Systematic sampling has advantages too, however. Even though systematic sampling may be inappropriate when the elements lie in a sequential pattern, this method may require less time and sometimes results in lower costs than the simple random sampling method.

Stratified sampling

Two ways to take stratified samples

To use stratified sampling, we divide the population into relatively homogeneous groups, called *strata*. Then we use one of two approaches. Either we select at random from each stratum a specified number of elements corresponding to the proportion of that stratum in the population as a whole, or we draw an equal number of elements from each stratum and give weight to the results according to the stratum's proportion of total population. With either approach, stratified sampling guarantees that every element in the population has a chance of being selected.

Stratified sampling is appropriate when the population is already divided into groups of different sizes and we wish to acknowledge this fact. Suppose that the patients of a physician are divided into four groups according to age, as shown in Table 7 · 4. The physician wants to find out how many hours his patients sleep. To obtain an estimate of this characteristic of the population, he could take a random sample from each of the four age groups and give weight to the samples according to the percentage of patients in that group. This would be an example of a stratified sample.

The advantage of stratified samples is that when they are properly designed, they more accurately reflect characteristics of the population from which they were chosen than do other kinds of samples.

TABLE 7·4 Composition of patients by age

Age group	Percentage of total
Birth–19 years	30
20–39 years	40
40–59 years	20
60 years and older	10

Cluster sampling

In cluster sampling, we divide the population into groups, or *clusters*, and then select a random sample of these clusters. We assume that these individual clusters are representative of the population as a whole. If a market research team is attempting to determine by sampling the average number of television sets per household in a large city, they could use a city map to divide the territory into blocks and then choose a certain number of blocks (clusters) for interviewing. Every household in each of these blocks would be interviewed. A well-designed cluster sampling procedure can produce a more precise sample at considerably less cost than that of simple random sampling.

Comparison of stratified and cluster sampling

With both stratified and cluster sampling, the population is divided into well-defined groups. We use *stratified* sampling when each group has small variation within itself, but there is wide variation between the groups. We use *cluster* sampling in the opposite case—when there is considerable variation within each group, but the groups are essentially similar to each other.

Basis of statistical inference: simple random sampling

Systematic sampling, stratified sampling, and cluster sampling attempt to approximate simple random sampling. All are methods that have been developed for their precision, economy, or physical ease. Even so, assume for the rest of the examples and problems in this book that we obtain our material by simple random sampling. This is necessary because the principles of simple random sampling are the foundation for *statistical inference*, the process of making inferences about populations from information contained in samples. Once these principles have been developed for simple random sampling, their extension to the other sampling methods is conceptually quite simple but somewhat involved mathematically. If you understand the basic ideas involved in simple random sampling, you will have a good grasp of what is going on in the other cases, even if you must leave the technical details to the professional statistician.

──────────────────────────── **EXERCISES** ────────────────────────────

7·6 In the following example, probability distributions for 3 natural subgroups of a larger population are shown. For which situation would you recommend stratified sampling?

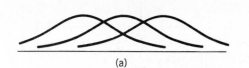 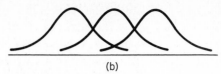

(a)   (b)

7·7   If we have a population of 1,000 individuals and we wish to sample 25 randomly, use the random number table (Table 7 · 3) to select 25 individuals from the 1,000. List the numbers of those elements selected, based on the random number table.

7·8   Morrisville Tobacco Company has recently implemented a wage incentive program to help increase productivity and worker motivation. Management wishes to find out overall employee response to the program. The study will include all of Morrisville's plants, which are under the wage incentive plan, and will sample a large number of employees throughout the company. The management is drawing the sample from a list of all employees who have worked at the company at least one year. Is it a random sample?

7·9   In a study of changing consumer attitudes, an assistant for a marketing research firm is required to listen to taped consumer interviews and to program the responses on computer cards. He usually does approximately 10 tape programmings per day before changing to another type of work, since there are certain fatigue effects involved in listening and coding the data. His supervisor wishes to do a reliability check on his work with this study and is considering a statistical method of sampling to check his accuracy. Would systematic sampling be appropriate?

7·10   The state occupational safety board has decided to do a study of work-related accidents within the state, to examine some of the variables involved in the accidents; e.g., the type of job, the cause of the accident, the extent of the injury, the time of day, and whether the employer was negligent. It has been decided that 250 of the 2,500 work-related accidents reported last year in the state will be sampled. The accident reports are filed by date in a filing cabinet. Marsha Gulley, a department employee, has proposed that the study use a systematic sampling technique and select every tenth report in the file for the sample. Would her plan of systematic sampling be appropriate here? Explain.

7·11   A population is made up of groups that have wide variation within each group but little variation from group to group. The appropriate type of sampling for this population is:
a) stratified   **b)** systematic   **c)** cluster   **d)** judgment

---

3 INTRODUCTION TO SAMPLING
DISTRIBUTIONS

Statistics differ among samples from the same population

In Chapters 3 and 4, we introduced methods by which we can use sample data to calculate statistics such as the mean and the standard deviation. So far in this chapter, we have examined how samples can be taken from populations. If we apply what we have learned and take several samples from a population, the statistics we would compute for each sample need not be the same and most probably would vary from sample to sample.

Suppose our samples each consist of ten 25-year-old women from a city with a population of 100,000 (an infinite population, according to our usage). By computing the mean height and standard deviation of that height for each of these samples, we would quickly see that the mean of each sample and the standard deviation of each sample would be different. A probability distribution of all the possible means of the samples is a distribution of the sample means. Statisticians call this a sampling distribution of the mean.

We could also have a sampling distribution of a proportion. As-sume that we have determined the proportion of beetle infested pine trees in samples of 100 trees taken from a very large forest. We have taken a large number of those 100-item samples. If we plot a probability distri-bution of the possible proportions of infested trees in all these samples, we would see a distribution of the sample proportions. In statistics, this is called a *sampling distribution of the proportion*. (Notice that the term *proportion* refers to the proportion that is infested.)

Describing sampling distributions

Any probability distribution (and, therefore, any sampling distribution) can be partially described by its mean and standard deviation. Table 7 · 5 illustrates several populations. Beside each, we have indicated the sample taken from that population, the sample statistic we have mea-sured, and the sampling distribution that would be associated with that statistic.

Now, how would we describe each of the sampling distributions in Table 7 · 5? In the first example, the sampling distribution of the mean can be partially described by its mean and standard deviation. The sampling distribution of the median in the second example can be

TABLE 7 · 5 Examples of populations, samples, sample statistics, and sampling distributions

Population	Sample	Sample statistic	Sampling distribution
Water in a river	10-gallon containers of water	Mean number of parts of mercury per million parts of water	Sampling distribution of the mean
All professional basketball teams	Groups of 5 players	Median height	Sampling distribution of the median
All parts produced by a manufacturing process	50 parts	Proportion defective	Sampling distribution of the proportion

partially described by the mean and standard deviation of the distribution of the medians. And in the third, the sampling distribution of the proportion can be partially described by the mean and standard deviation of the distribution of the proportions.

Concept of standard error

Derivation of the term standard error

Rather than say "standard deviation of the distribution of sample means" to describe a distribution of sample means, statisticians refer to the *standard error of the mean*. Similarly, the "standard deviation of the distribution of sample proportions" is shortened to the *standard error of the proportion*. The term *standard error* is used because it conveys a specific meaning. An example will help explain the reason for the name. Suppose we wish to learn something about the height of freshmen at a large state university. We could take a series of samples and calculate the mean height for each sample. It is highly unlikely that all of these sample means would be the same; we expect to see some variability in our observed means. This variability in the sample statistic results from *sampling error* due to chance; that is, there are differences between each sample and the population, and among the several samples, owing solely to the elements we happened to choose for the samples.

The standard deviation of the distribution of sample means measures the extent to which we expect the means from the different samples to vary because of this chance error in the sampling process. Thus the standard deviation of the distribution of a sample statistic is known as the standard error of the statistic.

Size of the standard error

The standard error indicates not only the size of the chance error that has been made but also the accuracy we are likely to get if we use a sample statistic to estimate a population parameter. A distribution of sample means that is less spread out (that has a small standard error) is a better estimator of the population mean than a distribution of sample means that is widely dispersed and has a larger standard error.

Table 7 · 6 indicates the proper use of the term *standard error*. In Chapter 8, we shall discuss how to estimate population parameters using sample statistics.

TABLE 7·6 Conventional terminology used to refer to sample statistics

When we wish to refer to the:	We use the conventional term:
Standard deviation of the distribution of sample means	Standard error of the mean
Standard deviation of the distribution of sample proportions	Standard error of the proportion
Standard deviation of the distribution of sample medians	Standard error of the median
Standard deviation of the distribution of sample ranges	Standard error of the range

7·12 A restaurant with a limited number of seats serving businesspeople in a downtown office building is known to have a mean of 120 persons served per day and a standard deviation of 12. Two potential buyers of the restaurant were discussing the probability that in the next 30 days, the average number of persons served per day would be 120. One buyer, who had been in the restaurant business of years, said that it was entirely chance that the average number of persons served in the 30-day period would equal the mean of the population. The younger buyer thought there was a great probability that the sample would average 120, since that was the expected number of daily customers. Which of the buyers is right? Explain.

7·13 The term *error*, in standard error of the mean, refers to what type of error?

7·14 A machine that fills bottles is known to have a mean filling amount of 100 grams and a standard deviation of 15 grams. A quality control manager took a random sample of filled bottles and found the sample mean to be 105. The quality control manager assumed the sample must not have been representative. Is his conclusion correct?

7·15 An electric company has determined that the mean cost per 100 sq ft for the residential population electrical service is $0.242 with a standard error of $0.05. Two different samples are selected at random, and the means are $0.20 and $0.27, respectively. The assistant in charge of data collection concludes that the second sample is the better one because it is better to overestimate than underestimate the true mean. Comment. Is one of the sample means "better" in some way, given the true population mean?

7·16 A survey researcher has mailed out questionnaires to a large sample of people in cities across the nation. Different numbers of questionnaires are sent to different geographic regions, based on the population density of the area. Not all the questionnaires sent out are returned. Upon receiving the ones that were completed, he sorts them according to region and computes the mean response for each region. He then plots the frequency distribution of these means. Does this represent a sampling distribution of the mean for the population? Why or why not?

4 SAMPLING DISTRIBUTIONS IN MORE DETAIL

In the last section of this chapter, we introduced the idea of a sampling distribution. We examined the reasons why sampling from a population and developing a distribution of these sample statistics would produce a sampling distribution, and we introduced the concept of standard error. Now we will study these concepts further, so that we will not only be able to understand them conceptually but also be able to handle them computationally.

Conceptual basis for sampling distributions

Deriving the sampling distribution of the mean

Figure 7 · 1 will help us examine sampling distributions without delving too deeply into statistical theory. We have divided this illustration into three parts. Figure 7 · 1(a) illustrates a *population distribution*. Assume that this population is all the filter screens in a large industrial pollution

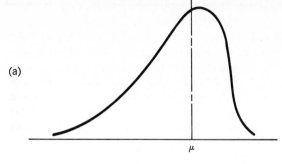

(a)

The population distribution:
This distribution is the distribution of the operating hours of *all* the filter screens. It has:

μ = the mean of this distribution

σ = the standard deviation of this distribution

If somehow we were able to take all the possible samples of a given size from this *population distribution,* they would be represented graphically by these four samples below. Although we have shown only four such samples, there would actually be an enormous number of them.

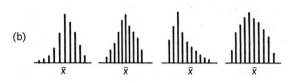

(b)

The sample frequency distributions:
These only *represent* the enormous number of sample distributions possible. *Each* sample distribution is a discrete distribution and has:

$\bar{x}$ = its own mean called "*x* bar"

s = its own standard deviation

Now, if we were able to take the means from all the *sample distributions* and produce a distribution of these sample means, it would look like this:

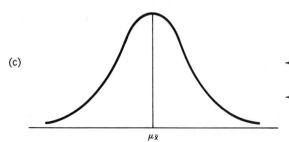

(c)

The sampling distribution of the mean:
This distribution is the distribution of all the sample means and has:

$\mu_{\bar{x}}$ = mean of the sampling distribution of the means called "mu sub *x* bar"

$\sigma_{\bar{x}}$ = standard error of the mean (standard deviation of the sampling distribution of the mean) called "*sigma* sub *x* bar"

Figure 7·1 Conceptual population distribution, sample distributions, and sampling distribution

control system and that this distribution is the operating hours before a screen becomes clogged. The distribution of operating hours has a mean μ (*mu*) and a standard deviation σ (*sigma*).

Suppose that somehow we are able to take all the possible samples of 10 screens from the population distribution (actually, there would be far too many for us to consider). Next we would calculate the mean and the standard deviation for each one of these *samples* as represented in Fig. 7 · 1(b). As a result, *each* sample would have its own mean $\bar{x}$ (*x* bar)

185 Sec. 4 Sampling distributions in more detail

and its own standard deviation *s*. All the individual sample means would *not* be the same as the population mean. They would tend to be near the population mean, but only rarely would they be exactly that value.

As a last step, we would produce a distribution of all the means from every sample that could be taken. This distribution, called the *sampling distribution of the mean*, is illustrated in Fig. $7 \cdot 1$(c). This distribution of the sample means (the sampling distribution) would have its own mean $\mu_{\bar{x}}$ (*mu* sub *x* bar) and its own standard deviation, or standard error, $\sigma_{\bar{x}}$ (*sigma* sub *x* bar).

Function of theoretical sampling distributions

In statistical terminology, the sampling distribution we would obtain by taking all the samples of a given size is a *theoretical sampling distribution*. Figure $7 \cdot 1$(c) describes such an example. In practice, the size and character of most populations prohibit decision makers from taking all the possible samples from a population distribution. Fortunately, statisticians have developed formulas for estimating the characteristics of these theoretical sampling distributions, making it unnecessary for us to collect large numbers of samples. In most cases, decision makers take only one sample from the population, calculate statistics for that sample, and from those statistics infer something about the parameters of the entire population. We shall illustrate this shortly.

Why we use the sampling distribution of the mean

In each example of sampling distributions in the remainder of this chapter, we shall use the sampling distribution of the mean. We could study the sampling distribution of the median, range, or proportion, but we will stay with the mean for the continuity it will add to the explanation. Once you develop an understanding of how to deal computationally with the sampling distribution of the mean, you will be able to apply it to the distribution of any other sample statistic.

Sampling from normal populations

Sampling distribution of the mean from normally distributed populations

Suppose we draw samples from a normally distributed population with a mean of 100 and a standard deviation of 25, and that we start by drawing samples of 5 items each and by calculating their means. The first mean might be 95, the second 106, the third 101, and so on. Obviously, there is just as much chance for the sample mean to be above the population mean of 100 as there is for it to be below 100. Since we are *averaging* 5 items to get each sample mean, very large values in the sample would be averaged down and very small values up. We would reason that we would get less spread among the sample means than we would among the individual items in the original population. That is the same as saying that the standard error of the mean, or standard deviation of the sampling distribution of the mean, would be less than the standard deviation of the *individual* items in the population. Figure $7 \cdot 2$ illustrates this point graphically.

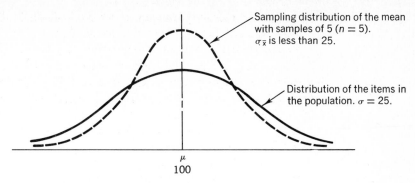

Figure 7·2 Relationship between the population distribution and the sampling distribution of the mean for a normal population

Now suppose we increase our sample size from 5 to 20. This would not change the standard deviation of the items in the original population. But with samples of 20, we have increased the effect of averaging in each sample and would expect even *less* dispersion among the sample means. Figure 7 · 3 illustrates this point.

Properties of the sampling distribution of the mean

The sampling distribution of a mean of a normally distributed population demonstrates the important properties summarized in Table 7 · 7. An example will further illustrate these properties. A bank calculates that its individual savings accounts are normally distributed with a mean of $2,000 and a standard deviation of $600. If the bank takes a random sample of 100 accounts, what is the probability that the sample mean will lie between $1,900 and $2,050? This is a question about the sampling distribution of the mean; therefore, we must first calculate the standard error of the mean. In this case, we shall use the equation for the standard error of the mean designed for situations in which the

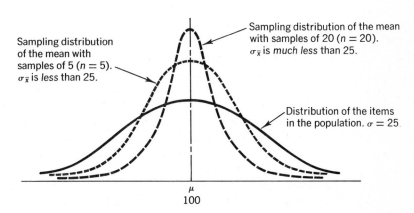

Figure 7·3 Relationship between the population distribution and sampling distribution of the mean with increasing *n*'s

TABLE 7·7 Properties of the sampling distribution of the mean when the population is normally distributed

Property	*Illustrated symbolically*
The sampling distribution has a mean equal to the population mean	$\mu_{\bar{x}} = \mu$
The sampling distribution has a standard deviation (a standard error) equal to the population standard deviation divided by the square root of the sample size	$\sigma_{\bar{x}} = \dfrac{\sigma}{\sqrt{n}}$
The sampling distribution is normally distributed	

population is infinite (later, we shall introduce an equation for finite populations):

$$\text{standard error} \searrow \sigma_{\bar{x}} = \frac{\sigma}{\sqrt{n}} \qquad (7 \cdot 1)$$
$$\text{of the mean}$$

Finding the standard error of the mean for infinite populations

where:

σ = population standard deviation

n = sample size

Applying this to our example, we get:

$$\sigma_{\bar{x}} = \frac{\$600}{\sqrt{100}}$$

$$= \frac{\$600}{10}$$

$$= \$60 \leftarrow \text{standard error of the mean}$$

Next, we need to use the table of z values (Appendix Table 1) and Equation 6 · 6, which enables us to use the Standard Normal Probability Distribution Table. With these we can determine the probability that the sample mean will lie between $1,900 and $2,050.

$$z = \frac{x - \mu}{\sigma} \qquad (6 \cdot 6)$$

Equation 6 · 6 tells us that to convert any normal random variable to a standard normal random variable, we must subtract the mean of the variable being standardized and divide by the standard error (the standard deviation of that variable). Thus, in this particular case, Equation 6 · 6 becomes:

Converting the sample mean to a z value

$$\text{sample mean} \rightarrow z = \frac{\bar{x} - \mu}{\sigma_{\bar{x}}} \swarrow \text{population mean}$$

$$\searrow \text{standard error of the mean} = \frac{\sigma}{\sqrt{n}} \qquad (7 \cdot 2)$$

Now we are ready to compute the two z values as follows:

For $\bar{x} = \$1,900$

$$z = \frac{\bar{x} - \mu}{\sigma_{\bar{x}}}$$

$$= \frac{\$1,900 - \$2,000}{\$60} \qquad (7 \cdot 2)$$

$= -1.67 \leftarrow$ standard deviations from the mean of a standard normal probability distribution

For $\bar{x} = \$2,050$

$$z = \frac{\bar{x} - \mu}{\sigma_{\bar{x}}}$$

$$= \frac{\$2,050 - \$2,000}{\$60} \qquad (7 \cdot 2)$$

$= .83 \leftarrow$ standard deviations from the mean of a standard normal probability distribution

Appendix Table 1 gives us an area of .4525 corresponding to a z value of -1.67, and it gives an area of .2967 for a z value of .83. If we add these two together, we get .7492 as the total probability that the sample mean will lie between $1,900 and $2,050. We have shown this problem graphically in Fig. 7 · 4.

Sampling from non-normal populations

In the preceding section, we concluded that when the population is normally distributed, the sampling distribution of the mean is also normal. Yet decision makers must deal with many populations that are

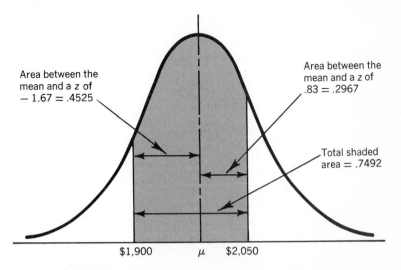

Figure 7·4 Probability of sample mean lying between $1,900 and $2,050

TABLE 7·8 Experience of five motorcycle owners with life of tires

Owner	Carl	Debbie	Elizabeth	Frank	George	
Tire life (months)	3	3	7	9	14	Total: 36 months

$$\text{Mean} = \frac{36}{5} = 7.2 \text{ months}$$

not normally distributed. How does the sampling distribution of the mean react when the population from which the samples are drawn is *not* normal? An illustration will help us answer this question.

The mean of the sampling distribution of the mean equals population mean

Consider the data in Table 7 · 8, concerning five motorcycle owners and the lives of their tires. Since only five people are involved, the population is too small to be approximated by a normal distribution. We'll take all of the possible samples of the owners in groups of three, compute the sample means ($\bar{x}$), list them, and compute the mean of the sampling distribution ($\mu_{\bar{x}}$). We have done this in Table 7 · 9. These calculations show that even in a case in which the population is not normally distributed, $\mu_{\bar{x}}$, the mean of the sampling distribution, is still equal to the population mean μ.

Increase in number of samples leads to a more normal sampling distribution

Now look at Fig. 7 · 5. Part (a) is the population distribution of tire lives for the five motorcycle owners, a distribution that is anything but normal in shape. In Fig. 7 · 5(b), we have shown the sampling distribution of the mean for a sample size of three, taking the information from Table 7 · 9. Notice the difference between the probability distributions in Fig. 7 · 5(a) and (b). In part (b), the distribution looks a little more like the bell shape of the normal distribution.

TABLE 7·9 Calculation of sample mean tire life with $n = 3$

Samples of three	Sample data (tire lives)	Sample mean
EFG*	7 + 9 + 14	10
DFG	3 + 9 + 14	$8\frac{2}{3}$
DEG	3 + 7 + 14	8
DEF	3 + 7 + 9	$6\frac{1}{3}$
CFG	3 + 9 + 14	$8\frac{2}{3}$
CEG	3 + 7 + 14	8
CEF	3 + 7 + 9	$6\frac{1}{3}$
CDF	3 + 3 + 9	5
CDE	3 + 3 + 7	$4\frac{1}{3}$
CDG	3 + 3 + 14	$6\frac{2}{3}$

$$\mu_{\bar{x}} = \frac{72}{10} = 7.2 \text{ months} \qquad 72 \text{ months}$$

*Names abbreviated by first initial.

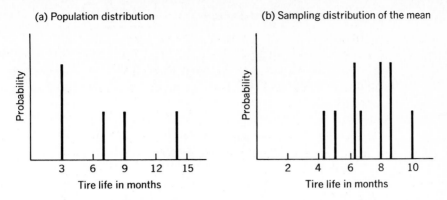

Figure 7·5 Population distribution and sampling distribution of the mean tire life

If we had a long time and much space, we could repeat this example and enlarge the population size to 20. Then we could take samples of *every* size. Next we would plot the sampling distribution of the mean that would occur in *each* case. Doing this would show quite dramatically how quickly the sampling distribution of the mean approaches normality, regardless of the shape of the population distribution. Figure 7 · 6 simulates this process graphically without all the calculations.

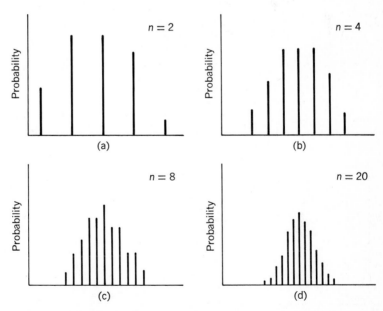

Figure 7·6 Simulated effect of increases in the sample size on appearance of sampling distribution

The central limit theorem

The example in Table 7 · 9 and the two probability distributions in Fig. 7 · 5 should suggest several things to you. First, the mean of the sampling distribution of the mean will equal the population mean regardless of the sample size, even if the population is not normal. Second, as the sample size increases, the sampling distribution of the mean will approach normality, regardless of the shape of the population distribution.

*Significance of
the central limit
theorem*

This relationship between the shape of the population distribution and the shape of the sampling distribution of the mean is called the *central limit theorem*. The central limit theorem is perhaps the most important theorem in all of statistical inference. It assures us that the sampling distribution of the mean approaches normal as the sample size increases. There are theoretical situations in which the central limit theorem fails to hold, but they are almost never encountered in practical decision making. Actually, a sample does not have to be very large for the sampling distribution of the mean to approach normal. Statisticians use the normal distribution as an approximation to the sampling distribution whenever the sample size is at least 30, but the sampling distribution of the mean can be nearly normal with samples of even half that size. The significance of the central limit theorem is that it permits us to use sample statistics to make inferences about population parameters without knowing anything about the shape of the frequency distribution of that population other than what we can get from the sample. Putting this ability to work is the subject of much of the material in the subsequent chapters of this book.

*Using the
central limit
theorem*

Let's illustrate the use of the central limit theorem. The distribution of annual earnings of all bank tellers with 5 years' experience is skewed negatively, as shown in Fig. 7 · 7(a). This distribution has a mean of $15,000 and a standard deviation of $2,000. If we draw a random sample of 30 tellers what is the probability that their earnings will average more than $15,750 annually? In Fig 7 · 7(b), we show the sampling distribu-

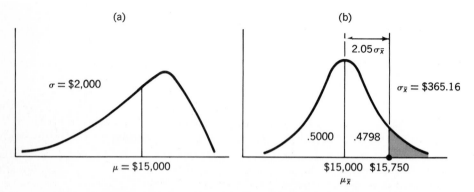

Figure 7·7 Population distribution and sampling distribution for bank tellers' earnings

tion of the mean that would result, and we have shaded the area representing "earnings over $15,750."

Our first task is to calculate the standard error of the mean from the population standard deviation as follows:

$$\sigma_{\bar{x}} = \frac{\sigma}{\sqrt{n}}$$

$$= \frac{\$2,000}{\sqrt{30}} \qquad (7 \cdot 1)$$

$$= \$365.16 \leftarrow \text{standard error of the mean}$$

Since we are dealing with a sampling distribution, we must now use Equation $7 \cdot 2$ and the table of z values (Appendix Table 1):

For $\bar{x} = \$15,750$

$$z = \frac{\bar{x} - \mu}{\sigma_{\bar{x}}}$$

$$= \frac{\$15,750 - \$15,000}{\$365.16} \qquad (7 \cdot 2)$$

$$= 2.05 \leftarrow \begin{array}{l}\text{standard deviations from the mean of a standard} \\ \text{normal probability distribution}\end{array}$$

This gives us an area of .4798 for a z value of 2.05. We show this area in Fig. $7 \cdot 7$ as the area between the mean and $15,750. Since half, or .5000, of the area under the curve lies between the mean and the right-hand tail, the shaded area must be:

.5000   area between the mean and the right-hand tail

− .4798   area between the mean and $15,750

.0202 ← area between the right-hand tail and $15,750

Thus, we have determined that there is slightly more than a 2 percent chance of average earnings being more than $15,750 annually in a group of 30 tellers.

─────────────── **EXERCISES** ───────────────

7·17 Robertson Employment Service customarily gives standard intelligence and aptitude tests to all persons who seek employment through the firm. The firm has collected data for several years and has found that the distribution of scores is not normal, but is skewed to the left with a mean of 83 and a standard deviation of 18. What is the probability that in a sample of 75 applicants taking the test, the mean score will be less than 82.5 or greater than 84?

7·18 Matthews Toy Company, manufacturer of metal toy trucks, estimates that the average direct labor cost per unit is 50.2 cents with a standard deviation of 1.2 cents. If a sample of 20 trucks is taken and the direct labor cost for each determined, can you say with a 98 percent probability that the average direct labor cost per unit of output will be between 49.5 and 50.7 cents?

7·19 Modern Buick sells an average of 10 cars a day, with a variance of 35.5 cars squared. If a sample of 7 days is studied, what is the probability that the sample mean will be
a) more than 16 or fewer than 12 cars sold?
b) fewer than 16 and more than 5 cars sold?

7·20 In a sample of 9 observations from a normal distribution with mean 76.8 and standard deviation 4.8, what is
a) $P(75 < \bar{x} < 80)$
b) Find the corresponding probability, given a sample of 25.

7·21 In a normal distribution with mean 72 and standard deviation of 10, how large a sample must be taken so that there will be a 90 percent chance that its mean is greater than 70?

7·22 In a normal distribution with mean of 250 and standard deviation of 20, how large a sample must be taken so that the probability will be .95 that the sample mean falls between 240 and 260?

---

5 AN OPERATIONAL CONSIDERATION IN SAMPLING: THE RELATIONSHIP BETWEEN SAMPLE SIZE AND STANDARD ERROR

Precision of the sample mean

We saw earlier in this chapter that the standard error, $\sigma_{\bar{x}}$, is a measure of dispersion of the sample means around the population mean. If the dispersion decreases (if $\sigma_{\bar{x}}$ becomes smaller), then the values taken by the sample mean tend to cluster *more* closely around μ. Conversely, if the dispersion increases (if $\sigma_{\bar{x}}$ becomes larger), the values taken by the sample mean tend to cluster *less* closely around μ. We can think of this relationship this way: as the standard error decreases, the value of any sample mean will probably be closer to the value of the population mean. Statisticians describe this phenomenon in another way: as the standard error decreases, the *precision* with which the sample mean can be used to estimate the population mean increases.

If we refer to Equation 7 · 1, we can see that as n increases, $\sigma_{\bar{x}}$ decreases. This happens because in Equation 7 · 1 a larger denominator on the right side would produce a smaller $\sigma_{\bar{x}}$ on the left side. Two examples will show this relationship; both assume the same population standard deviation σ of 100.

$$\sigma_{\bar{x}} = \frac{\sigma}{\sqrt{n}} \qquad (7 \cdot 1)$$

When $n = 10$,

$$\sigma_{\bar{x}} = \frac{100}{\sqrt{10}} = 31.63 \leftarrow \text{standard error of the mean}$$

And when $n = 100$,

$$\sigma_{\bar{x}} = \frac{100}{\sqrt{100}} = 10 \leftarrow \text{standard error of the mean}$$

What have we shown? As we increased our sample size from 10 to 100 (a tenfold increase), the standard error dropped from 31.63 to 10, which is only about one-third of its former value. Our examples suggest that, due to the fact that $\sigma_{\bar{x}}$ varies inversely with the square root of n, there is a diminishing return in sampling.

It is true that sampling more items will decrease the standard error, but this benefit may not be worth the cost. A statistician would say, "The increased precision is not worth the additional sampling cost." In a statistical sense, it seldom pays to take excessively large samples. Managers should always assess *both* the worth and the cost of the additional precision they will obtain from a larger sample before they commit resources to take it.

The finite population multiplier

To this point in our discussions of sampling distributions, we have used Equation 7 · 1 to calculate the standard error of the mean:

$$\sigma_{\bar{x}} = \frac{\sigma}{\sqrt{n}} \qquad (7 \cdot 1)$$

This equation is designed for situations in which the population is infinite, or in which we sample from a finite population with replacement (that is to say, after each item is sampled it is put back into the population before the next item is chosen, so that the same item can possibly be chosen more than once). If you will refer back to page 188 where we introduced Equation 7 · 1, you will recall our parenthesized note, which said, "Later we shall introduce an equation for finite populations." Introducing this new equation is the purpose of this section.

Many of the populations that decision makers examine are finite; that is, of stated or limited size. Examples of these include the employees in a given company, the clients of a city social services agency, the students in a specific class, and a day's production in a given manufacturing plant. Not one of these populations is infinite, so we need to modify Equation 7 · 1 to deal with them. The formula designed to find the standard error of the mean when the population is *finite* is:

$$\sigma_{\bar{x}} = \frac{\sigma}{\sqrt{n}} \times \sqrt{\frac{N-n}{N-1}} \qquad (7 \cdot 3)$$

where:

N = size of the population
n = size of the sample

This new term on the right-hand side, which we multiply by our original standard error, is called the *finite population multiplier*:

$$\text{Finite population multiplier} = \sqrt{\frac{N-n}{N-1}} \qquad (7 \cdot 4)$$

A few examples will help us become familiar with interpreting and using Equation 7 · 3. Suppose we are interested in a population of 20 textile companies of the same size, all of which are experiencing excessive labor turnover. Our study indicates that the standard deviation of the distribution of annual turnover is 75 employees. If we sample 5 of these textile companies and wish to compute the standard error of the mean, we would use Equation 7 · 3 as follows:

$$\sigma_{\bar{x}} = \frac{\sigma}{\sqrt{n}} \times \sqrt{\frac{N-n}{N-1}} \qquad (7 \cdot 3)$$

$$= \frac{75}{\sqrt{5}} \times \sqrt{\frac{20-5}{20-1}} = 29.8 \leftarrow \begin{array}{l} \text{standard error of the mean} \\ \text{of a finite population} \end{array}$$

In this example, a finite population multiplier of .888 reduced the standard error from 33.54 to 29.8.

Sometimes the finite population multiplier is close to 1

In cases in which the population is very large in relation to the size of the sample, this finite population multiplier is close to 1 and has little effect on the calculation of the standard error. Say that we have a population of 1,000 items and that we have taken a sample of 20 items. If we use Equation 7 · 4 to calculate the finite population multiplier, the result would be:

$$\text{Finite population multiplier} = \sqrt{\frac{N-n}{N-1}}$$

$$\qquad (7 \cdot 4)$$

$$= \sqrt{\frac{1,000-20}{1,000-1}} = .99$$

Using this multiplier of .99 would produce little effect on the calculation of the standard error of the mean.

Sampling fraction defined

This last example shows that when we sample a small fraction of the entire population (that is, when the population size N is very large relative to the sample size n), the finite population multiplier takes on a value close to 1.0. Statisticians refer to the fraction n/N as the *sampling fraction* because it *is* the fraction of the population N that is contained in the sample.

When the sampling fraction is small, the standard error of the mean for finite populations is so close to the standard error of the mean for infinite populations that we might as well use the same formula for both, namely Equation 7 · 1: $\sigma_{\bar{x}} = \frac{\sigma}{\sqrt{n}}$. The generally accepted rule is: When the sampling fraction is less than .05, the finite population multiplier need not be used.

Sample size determines sampling precision

When we use Equation 7 · 1, σ is constant, and so the measure of sampling precision $\sigma_{\bar{x}}$ depends only on the sample size n and not on the proportion of the population sampled. That is, to make $\sigma_{\bar{x}}$ smaller, it is necessary to make only n larger. Thus it turns out that it is the absolute size of the sample that determines sampling precision, not the fraction of the population sampled.

EXERCISES

7·23 Every unit in the sample for a certain study costs $2. The information value of various sample sizes may be figured according to the formula $6,400/\sigma_{\bar{x}}$. If a researcher wants to increase the sample until cost equals information value, how many individuals should she sample if the population standard deviation is 200?

7·24 Given a population of size $N = 65$ with a mean of 12 and a standard deviation of 2.1, what is the probability that a sample of size 16 will have a mean between 11.5 and 12.5?

7·25 A stockbroker has named 100 stocks that he predicts will rise in market value an average of 12 percent during the next quarter, with a standard deviation of 4 percent. He is challenging his colleagues to choose 10 stocks at random from the list, to see if his prediction comes true. If his expectations are correct, what is the probability that a colleague following his instructions will see an average market value increase of 10 to 15 percent for the quarter?

7·26 For a population of size $N = 120$ with a mean of 7.5 and a standard deviation of 1.5, find the estimated standard error of the mean for the following sample sizes:
a) $n = 9$ **b)** $n = 25$ **c)** $n = 49$

7·27 George Bransford is the owner of a chain of 25 clothing stores. He has been considering retiring because his health is bad and also because he feels the business is not as profitable as it once was. Over the past several years, the mean net income for each of the 25 stores has been $21,000 with a standard deviation of $3,400. George has said that if the first 5 stores audited at year end do not show total profits of at least $100,000, he will sell the business. What is the probability that George will sell out?

---

6 DESIGN OF EXPERIMENTS

Events and experiments revisited

We have encountered the term *experiment* in Chapter 5, "Probability I." There we defined an *event* as one or more of the possible outcomes of doing something, and an *experiment* as an activity that would produce such events. In a coin toss experiment, the possible events would be heads and tails.

Planning experiments

Sampling is only one part

If we are to conduct experiments that produce meaningful results in the form of useable conclusions, the way in which these experiments are designed is of the utmost importance. A good part of this chapter was taken up with ways of ensuring that random sampling was indeed being done. The way in which sampling is conducted is only a *part* of the total design of an experiment. In fact, the design of experiments is, itself, the subject of quite a number of books, some of them rather formidable, both in scope and volume.

Phases of experimental design

A claim
is made

To get a better feel for the complexity of experimental design without actually getting involved with the complex details, take an example from the many that confront us every day, and follow that example through from beginning to end.

The statement is made that a Crankmaster Battery will start your car's engine better than Battery X. Crankmaster might design its experiment this way:

Objectives
are set

Objective. This is our beginning point. Crankmaster wants to test its battery against the leading competitor. Although it is possible to design an experiment that would test the two batteries on several characteristics (life, size, cranking power, weight, and cost, to name but a few), Crankmaster has decided to limit this experiment to cranking power.

The response
variable
is selected

What is to be measured. This is often referred to as the response variable. If Crankmaster is to design an experiment that measures cranking power of its battery against that of another, it must define how cranking power is to be measured. Again, there are quite a few ways in which this can be done. For example, Crankmaster could measure (1) the time it took for the batteries to run down completely while cranking engines, (2) the total number of engine starts it took to run down the batteries, or (3) the number of months in use that the two batteries could be expected to last.

How many
to test

How large a sample size. Crankmaster wants to be sure that it chooses a sample size large enough to support claims it makes for its battery, without fear of being challenged; however, it knows that the more batteries it tests, the higher the cost of conducting the experiment. As we pointed out in Section 5 of this chapter, there is a diminishing return in sampling; and although sampling more items does, in fact, decrease the standard error, the benefit may not be worth the cost.

Experimental
conditions

Conducting the experiment. Crankmaster must be careful to conduct its experiment under controlled conditions; that is, it has to be sure that it is measuring *cranking power*, and that the other variables (such as temperature, age of engine, and condition of battery cables, to name only a few) are held as nearly constant as practicable. In an effort to accomplish just this, Crankmaster's statistical group uses new cars of the same make and model, conducts the test at the same outside air temperature, and is careful to be quite precise in measuring the time variable.

Data are analyzed

Analyzing the data.   Data on the battery tests are subjected to hypothesis testing in the same way that we shall see in Chapter 9, "Testing Hypotheses." Crankmaster is interested in whether there is a significant difference between the cranking power of its battery and that of its competitor. It turns out that the difference between the mean cranking life of Crankmaster's battery and that of its competitor *is* significant. Crankmaster incorporates the result of this experiment into its advertising campaign.

Reacting to experimental claims

How should the consumer react?

How should we, as consumers, react to Crankmaster's new battery life claims in its latest advertising? Should we conclude from the tests it has run that the Crankmaster batter *is* superior to the competitive battery? If we stop for a moment to consider the nature of the experiment, we may not be too quick to come to such a conclusion.

Are we sure?

How do we know that the ages and conditions of the cars' engines in the experiments *were* identical? And are we absolutely sure that the battery cables were identical in size and resistance to current? And what about the air temperature during the tests: was it the same? These are the normal kinds of questions that we should ask.

How should we react to the statement, if it is made, that "we subjected the experimental results to extensive statistical testing"? The answer to that will have to wait until Chapter 9, "Testing Hypotheses," where we can determine if such a difference in battery lives is too large to be attributed to chance. At this point we, as consumers, need to be "appropriately skeptical."

7 TERMS INTRODUCED IN CHAPTER 7

census   The measurement or examination of every element in the population.

central limit theorem   A rule assuring that the sampling distribution of the mean approaches normal as the sample size increases, regardless of the shape of the population distribution from which the sample is selected.

clusters   Within a population, groups that are essentially similar to each other, although the groups themselves have wide internal variation.

cluster sampling   A method of random sampling in which the population is divided into groups, or clusters of elements, and then a random sample of these clusters is selected.

finite population   A population having a stated or limited size.

finite population multiplier   A factor used to correct an estimate of the standard error of the mean for studying a population of finite size that is small in relation to the size of the sample.

infinite population A population in which it is theoretically impossible to observe all the elements.

judgment sampling A method of selecting a sample from a population in which personal knowledge or expertise are used to identify those items from the population that are to be included in the sample.

parameters Values that describe the characteristics of a population.

precision The degree of accuracy with which the sample mean can estimate the population mean, as revealed by the standard error of the mean.

random or probability sampling A method of selecting a sample from a population in which all the items in the population have an equal chance of being chosen in the sample.

sample A portion of the elements in a population chosen for direct examination or measurement.

sampling distribution of a statistic For a given population, a probability distribution of all the possible values a statistic may take on for a given sample size.

sampling distribution of the mean A probability distribution of all the possible means of samples of a given size, n, from a population.

sampling error Error or variation among sample statistics due to chance: i.e., differences between each sample and the population, and among several samples, which are due solely to the elements we happened to choose for the sample.

sampling fraction The fraction or proportion of the population contained in a sample.

simple random sampling Methods of selecting samples that allow each possible sample an equal probability of being picked *and* each item in the entire population an equal chance of being included in the sample.

standard error The standard deviation of the sampling distribution of a statistic.

standard error of the mean The standard deviation of the sampling distribution of the mean; a measure of the extent to which we expect the means from different samples to vary from the population mean, owing to the chance error in the sampling process.

statistical inference The process of making inferences about populations from information contained in samples.

statistics Measures describing the characteristics of a sample.

strata Groups within a population formed in such a way that each group is relatively homogeneous, but wider variability exists among the separate groups.

stratified sampling A method of random sampling in which the population is divided into homogeneous groups, or strata, and elements within each stratum are selected at random according to one of two rules: (1) a specified number of elements is drawn from each stratum corresponding to the proportion of that stratum in the population, or (2) an equal number of elements is drawn from each stratum, and the results are weighted according to the stratum's proportion of the total population.

systematic sampling A method of random sampling in which elements are selected from the population at a uniform interval that is measured in time, order, or space.

8 EQUATIONS INTRODUCED IN CHAPTER 7

p. 188

$$\sigma_{\bar{x}} = \frac{\sigma}{\sqrt{n}}$$

7·1

Use this formula to derive the *standard error of the mean* when the population is *infinite*, that is, when the elements of the population cannot be enumerated in a reasonable period of time or when we sample with replacement. This equation explains that the sampling distribution has a standard deviation, which we also call a standard error, equal to the population standard deviation divided by the square root of the sample size.

p. 188

$$z = \frac{\bar{x} - \mu}{\sigma_{\bar{x}}}$$

7·2

A modified version of Equation 6 · 6, this formula allows us to determine the distance of the *sample mean* $\bar{x}$ from the population mean μ when we divide the difference by the standard error of the mean $\sigma_{\bar{x}}$. Once we have derived a z value, we can use the Standard Normal Probability Distribution Table and compute the probability that the sample mean will be that distance from the population mean. Because of the central limit theorem, we can use this formula for nonnormal distributions if the sample size is at least 30.

p. 195
$$\sigma_{\bar{x}} = \frac{\sigma}{\sqrt{n}} \times \sqrt{\frac{N-n}{N-1}}$$
7·3

where:

$$N = \text{size of the population}$$
$$n = \text{size of the sample}$$

This is the formula for finding the *standard error of the mean* when the population is *finite*, that is, of stated or limited size.

p. 195
$$\text{Finite population multiplier} = \sqrt{\frac{N-n}{N-1}}$$
7·4

In Equation 7 · 3, the term $\sqrt{(N-n)/(N-1)}$, which we multiply times the standard error from Equation 7 · 1, is called the *finite population multiplier*. When the population is small in relation to the size of the sample, the finite population multiplier reduces the size of the standard error. Any decrease in the standard error increases the precision with which the sample mean can be used to estimate the population mean.

9 CHAPTER REVIEW EXERCISES

7·28 A camera manufacturer is attempting to find out what employees feel are the major problems with the company and what improvements are needed. To assess the opinions of the 37 departments, the management is considering a sampling plan. It has been recommended to the personnel director that the management adopt a cluster sampling plan. The management would choose 6 departments and interview all the employees. Upon collecting and assessing the data gathered from these employees, the company could then make changes and plan for areas of job improvement. Is a cluster sampling plan appropriate in this situation?

7·29 By reviewing sales since the business opened 6 months ago, a restaurant owner found that the average bill for a couple was $16, with a standard deviation of $4. How large would a sample of customers have to be for the probability to be 95.44 percent that the mean cost per meal for the sample would fall between $15.20 and $16.80?

7·30 Hartford Products has recently sent a direct mail advertising piece to area contractors. The literature sent out explains the advantages of using Hartford's insulated windows for both residential and commercial construction. The company now wants to see how many contractors read the information, and it is considering telephoning the contractors who should have received the information. The company has all their phone numbers, and management feels that the task could be accomplished by the receptionists in the office during their spare time. Since the company apparently has both the time and manpower, are there any reasons for it to poll a sample of the contractors rather than the entire population?

7·31 Low-Cal Foods Company uses estimates of the level of activity for various market segments to determine the nutritional composition of its diet food products. Low-Cal is considering the introduction of a liquid diet food for older women, since this segment has special weight problems not met by the competitor's diet foods. To determine the desired calorie content of this new product, Dr. Nell Watson, researcher for the company, conducted tests on a sample of women, to determine calorie consumption per day. Her results showed that the average number of calories expended per day for older women is 1,424 with a standard deviation of 240. Dr. Watson estimates that the benefits she obtains with a sample size of 25 are worth $1,440. She expects that to reduce the standard error by half of its current value will double the benefit. If it costs $20 for every woman in the sample, should Watson reduce her standard error?

7·32 The U.S. Customs Service routinely checks all passengers arriving from foreign countries as they enter the United States. The department reports that on the average 35 people per day, with a standard deviation of 6, are found to be carrying contraband material as they enter the United States through the John F. Kennedy Airport in New York. What is the probability that in 4 days at that airport, the average number of passengers found carrying contraband will exceed 40?

7·33 Donna Ayscue is in charge of training consumer interviewers for a marketing research firm. Since she has other responsibilities, she is not able to observe all of the practice interviews. She arbitrarily observes the trainees interviewing consumers and sometimes watches from an adjoining room, without forewarning the trainees that they will be observed. She feels that this makes her testing and evaluations objective. Is she using random sampling or judgment sampling?

7·34 Members of the Organization for Consumer Action send more than 100 volunteers a day all over the state to increase support for a consumer protection bill that is currently before the state legislature. Usually, each volunteer will visit a household and talk briefly with the resident, in the hope that the resident will sign a petition to be given to the state legislature. On the average, a volunteer will obtain 4.2 signatures for the petition each day, with a standard deviation of .6. What is the probability that a sample of 70 volunteers will result in an average between 4.05 and 4.1 signatures per day?

---

10 CHAPTER CONCEPTS TEST

Answers are in the back of the book.

T F 1. When the items included in a sample are based upon the judgment of the individual conducting the sample, the sample is said to be nonrandom.

T F 2. A statistic is a characteristic of a population.

T F 3. A sampling plan that selects members from a population at uniform intervals in time, order, or space is called stratified sampling.

T F 4. As a general rule, it is not necessary to include a finite population multiplier in a computation for standard error of the mean when the size of the sample is greater than 50.

T F 5. The probability distribution of all the possible means of samples is known as the sampling distribution of the mean.

T F 6. The theoretical foundation for statistical inference is based upon the principles of simple random sampling.

T F 7. The standard error of the mean is the standard deviation of the distribution of sample means.

T F 8. A sampling plan that divides the population into well-defined groups from which random samples are drawn is known as cluster sampling.

T F 9. With increasing sample size, the sampling distribution of the mean approaches normality, regardless of the distribution of the population.

T F 10. The standard error of the mean decreases in direct proportion to sample size.

T F 11. To perform a complete enumeration, one would examine every item in a population.

T F 12. In everyday life, we see many examples of infinite populations of physical objects.

T F 13. To obtain a theoretical sampling distribution, we would have to consider all the samples of a given size.

T F 14. Large samples are always a good idea, since they decrease the standard error.

T F 15. If the mean for a certain population were 15, it is likely that most of the samples we could take from that population would have means of 15.

16. Which of the following is a method of selecting samples from a population?
   a) judgment sampling
   b) random sampling
   c) probability sampling
   d) all of the preceding
   e) a and b but not c

17. Choose the pair of symbols which best completes this sentence:
   _____ is a parameter while _____ is a statistic.
   a) $N \ldots \mu$
   b) $\sigma \ldots s$
   c) $N \ldots n$
   d) all of the preceding
   e) b and c but not a

18. In random sampling, we can describe mathematically how objective our estimates are. Why is this?
   a) We always know the chance that an element of the population will or will not be included in the sample.
   b) Every sample always has an equal chance of being selected.
   c) All of the samples are of exactly the same size and can be counted.
   d) None of the above.
   e) a and b but not c.

19. Suppose you are performing stratified sampling on a particular population and have divided the population into strata of different sizes. How can you now make your sample selection?
   a) Select at random an equal number of elements from each stratum.
   b) Draw an equal number of elements from each stratum and give weights to the results.
   c) Select a specified number of elements from each stratum corresponding to proportions of the population.
   d) a and b only.
   e) b and c only.

20. In which of the following situations would $\sigma_{\bar{x}} = \dfrac{\sigma}{\sqrt{n}}$ be the correct formula to use for computing $\sigma_{\bar{x}}$?

a) Sampling is from an infinite population.
b) Sampling is from a finite population with replacement.
c) Sampling is from a finite population without replacement.
d) a and b only.
e) b and c only.

21. The dispersion among sample means is less than the dispersion among the sampled items themselves because:
a) Each sample is smaller than the population from which it is drawn.
b) Very large values are averaged down, and very small values are averaged up.
c) The sampled items are all drawn from the same population.
d) None of the above.
e) b and c but not a.

22. Suppose that a population with $N = 144$ has $\mu = 24$. What is the mean of the sampling distribution of the mean for samples of size 25?
a) 24
b) 2
c) 4.8
d) cannot be determined from the information given

23. The central limit theorem assures that the sampling distribution of the mean
a) is always normal
b) is always normal for large sample sizes
c) approaches normality as sample size increases
d) appears normal only when N is greater than 1,000

24. Suppose that, for a certain population, $\sigma_{\bar{x}}$ is calculated as 20 when samples of size 25 are taken and as 10 when samples of size 100 are taken. A quadrupling of sample size, then, only halved $\sigma_{\bar{x}}$. We can conclude that increasing sample sizes is:
a) always cost-effective
b) sometimes cost-effective
c) never cost-effective

25. Refer again to the data of question 24. What must be the value of σ for this infinite population?
a) 1,000
b) 500
c) 377.5
d) 100
e) cannot be determined from the information given

26. A portion of the elements in a population chosen for direct examination or measurement is a _____ .

27. The proportion of the population contained in a sample is the _____ .

28. A method of random sampling in which elements are selected from the population at a uniform interval called _____ sampling.

29. _____ is the degree of accuracy with which the sample mean can estimate the population mean.

30. Within a population, groups that are similar to each other (although the groups themselves have wide internal variation) are called _____ .

Estimation

As part of the budgeting process for next year, the manager of the Far Point electric generating plant must estimate the coal he will require for this year. Last year, the plant almost ran out, so he is reluctant to budget for that same amount again. The plant manager, however, does feel that past usage data will help him *estimate* the number of tons of coal to order. A random sample of 10 plant operating weeks chosen over the last 5 years yielded a mean usage of 11,400 tons a week, with a sample standard deviation of 700 tons a week. With the data he has and the methods we shall discuss in this chapter, the plant manager can make a sensible estimate of the amount to order this year, including some idea of the accuracy of the estimate he has made.

Chapters 8 and 9 deal with statistical inference. In Chapter 8, we learn to estimate the characteristics of a population by observing the characteristics of a sample. Two characteristics of special interest will be how a population tends to "bunch up" and how it spreads out.

1 INTRODUCTION

Reasons for estimates

All managers must make estimates. The outcome of these estimates can affect their organizations as seriously as the outcome of your decision as to whether to cross the street. Department heads make estimates of next fall's enrollment in statistics. Credit managers estimate whether a purchaser will eventually pay his bills. Prospective home buyers make estimates concerning the behavior of interest rates in the mortgage market. All these people make estimates without worry about whether they are scientific but with the hope that the estimates bear a reasonable resemblance to the outcome.

Making statistical inferences

The material on probability theory covered in Chapters 5, 6, and 7 forms the foundation for *statistical inference*, the branch of statistics concerned with using probability concepts to deal with uncertainty in decision making. Statistical inference is based on *estimation*, which we shall introduce in this chapter, and *hypothesis testing*, which is the subject of Chapters 9 and 10. In both estimation and hypothesis testing, we shall be making inferences about characteristics of populations from information contained in samples.

How do managers use sample statistics to estimate population parameters? The department head attempts to estimate enrollments next fall from current enrollments in prerequisite courses and preregistration data. The credit manager attempts to estimate the creditworthiness of prospective customers from a sample of their past payment habits. The home buyer attempts to estimate the future course of interest rates by observing the current behavior of those rates. In each case, somebody is trying to infer something about a population from information taken from a sample.

Estimating population parameters

This chapter introduces methods that enable us to estimate with reasonable accuracy the *population proportion* (the proportion of the population that possesses a given characteristic) and the *population mean*. To calculate the exact proportion or the exact mean would be an impossible goal. Even so, we will be able to make an estimate, make a statement about the error that will probably accompany this estimate, and implement some controls to avoid as much of the error as possible.

Types of estimates

Point estimate defined

We can make two types of estimates about a population: a *point* estimate and an *interval* estimate. A point estimate is a single number that is used to estimate an unknown population parameter. If, while watching the first members of a football team come onto the field, you say, "Why, I bet their line must weigh 250 pounds," you have made a point estimate. A department chairwoman would make a point estimate if she said, "Our current data indicate that this course will have 350 students in the fall."

Shortcomings of point estimates

A point estimate is often insufficient because it is either right or wrong. If you are told only that the chairwoman's point estimate of enrollment is wrong, you do not know *how* wrong it is, and you cannot be certain of the estimate's reliability. If you learn that it is off by only 10 students you would accept 350 students as a good estimate of future enrollment. But if the estimate is off by 90 students, you would reject it as an estimate of future enrollment. Therefore a point estimate is much more useful if it is accompanied by an estimate of the error that might be involved.

Interval estimate defined

An interval estimate is a range of values used to estimate a population parameter. It indicates the error in two ways: by the extent of its range and by the probability of the true population parameter lying within that range. In this case, the department chairwoman would say something like, "I estimate that the true enrollment in this course in the fall will be between 330 and 380 and that it is very likely that the exact enrollment will fall within this interval." The chairwoman has a better idea of the reliability of her estimate. If the course is taught in sections of about 100 students each, and if the chairwoman had tentatively scheduled 5 sections, on the basis of her estimate, she can now cancel one of those sections and offer an elective instead.

Estimator and estimates

Estimator defined

Any sample statistic that is used to estimate a population parameter is called an estimator; that is, an estimator is a sample statistic used to estimate a population parameter. The sample mean $\bar{x}$ can be an estimator of the population mean μ, and the sample proportion can be used as an estimator of the population proportion. We can also use the sample range as an estimator of the population range.

Estimate defined

When we observe a specific numerical value of our estimator, we call that value an estimate. In other words, an estimate is a specific observed value of a statistic. We form an estimate by taking a sample and computing the value taken by our estimator in that sample. Suppose that we calculate the mean odometer reading (mileage) from a sample of used taxis and find it to be 98,000 miles. If we use this specific value to estimate the mileage for a whole fleet of used taxis, the value 98,000 miles would be an estimate. Table 8 · 1 illustrates several populations, population parameters, estimators, and estimates.

TABLE 8·1 Populations, population parameters, estimators, and estimates

Population in which we are interested	Population parameter we wish to estimate	Sample statistic we will use as an estimator	Estimate we make
Employees in a furniture factory	Mean turnover per year	Mean turnover for a period of 1 month	8.9% turnover per year
Applicants for town manager of Chapel Hill	Mean formal education (years)	Mean formal education of every 5th applicant	17.9 years of formal education
Teenagers in a given community	Proportion who have a criminal record	Proportion of a sample of 50 teenagers who have a criminal record	.02, or 2%, have a criminal record

Criteria of a good estimator

Qualities of a good estimator

Some statistics are better estimators than are others. Fortunately, we can evaluate the quality of a statistic as an estimator by using three criteria:

1. *Unbiasedness*. This is a desirable property for a good estimator to have. The term *unbiasedness* refers to the fact that a sample mean is an unbiased estimator of a population mean because the mean of the sampling distribution of sample means taken from the same population is equal to the population mean itself. We can say that a statistic is an unbiased estimator if, on the average, it tends to assume values that are above the population parameter being estimated as frequently and to the same extent as it tends to assume values that are below the population parameter being estimated.

2. *Efficiency*. Another desirable property of a good estimator is that it be efficient. Efficiency refers to the size of the standard error of the statistic. If we compare two statistics from a sample of the same size and try to decide which one is the more efficient estimator, we would pick the statistic that has the smaller standard error, or standard deviation of the sampling distribution.

3. *Consistency*. A statistic is a consistent estimator of a population parameter if *as the sample size increases, it becomes almost certain that the value of the statistic comes very close to the value of the population parameter*. If an estimator is consistent, it becomes more reliable with large samples. Thus, if you are wondering whether to increase the sample size to get more information about a population parameter, find out first whether your statistic is a consistent estimator. If it is not, you will waste time and money by taking larger samples.

A given sample statistic is not always the best estimator of its analogous population parameter. Consider a symmetrically distributed population in which the values of the median and the mean coincide. In this instance, the sample mean would be an *unbiased* estimator of the population median because it would assume values that on the average would equal the population median. Also, the sample mean would be a *consistent* estimator of the population median because, as the sample size increases, the value of the sample mean would tend to come very close to the population median. And the sample mean would be a more *efficient* estimator of the population median than the sample median itself because in large samples the sample mean has a smaller standard error than the sample median. At the same time, the sample median in a symmetrically distributed population would be an unbiased and consistent estimator of the population mean but *not the most efficient* estimator because in large samples its standard error is larger than that of the sample mean.

EXERCISES

8·1 What two basic tools are used in making statistical inferences?

8·2 Why do decision makers often measure samples rather than entire populations? What is the disadvantage?

8·3 Explain a shortcoming that occurs in a point estimate but not in an interval estimate. What measure is included with a point estimate to compensate for this problem?

8·4 What is an estimator? How does an estimate differ from an estimator?

8·5 List and describe briefly the criteria of a good estimator.

8·6 What role does consistency play in determining sample size?

---

2 POINT ESTIMATES

The sample mean $\bar{x}$ is the best estimator of the population mean μ. It is unbiased, consistent, the most efficient estimator, and, as long as the sample is sufficiently large, its sampling distribution can be approximated by the normal distribution.

If we know the sampling distribution of $\bar{x}$, we can make statements about any estimate we may make from sampling information. Let's look at a medical supplies company that produces disposable hypodermic syringes. Each syringe is wrapped in a sterile package and then jumble-packed in a large corrugated carton. Jumble packing causes the cartons to contain differing numbers of syringes. Since the syringes are sold on a per unit basis, the company needs an estimate of the number of syringes per carton for billing purposes. We have taken a sample of 35 cartons at random and recorded the number of syringes in each carton. Table 8 · 2 illustrates our results. Using the results of Chapter 3, we can obtain the

TABLE 8·2 Results of sample of 35 cartons of hypodermic syringes (syringes per carton)

101	103	112	102	98	97	93
105	100	97	107	93	94	97
97	100	110	106	110	103	99
93	98	106	100	112	105	100
114	97	110	102	98	112	99

Finding the sample mean

sample mean $\bar{x}$ by finding the sum of all our results, Σx, and dividing this total by n, the number of samples we have taken:

$$\bar{x} = \frac{\Sigma x}{n} \qquad (3 \cdot 2)$$

Using this equation to solve our problem, we get:

$$\bar{x} = \frac{3,570}{35} = 102 \text{ syringes}$$

Thus, using the sample mean $\bar{x}$ as our estimator, the point estimate of the population mean μ is 102 syringes per carton. Since the manufactured price of a disposable hypodermic syringe is quite small (about 25 cents), both the buyer and seller would accept the use of this point estimate as the basis for billing, and the manufacturer can save the time and expense of counting each syringe that goes into a carton.

Point estimate of the population variance and standard deviation

Using the sample standard deviation to estimate the population standard deviation

Suppose the management of the medical supplies company wants to estimate the variance and/or standard deviation of the distribution of the number of packaged syringes per carton. The most frequently used estimator of the population standard deviation σ is the sample standard deviation s. We can calculate the sample standard deviation by using the methods illustrated in Chapter 4 (page 74). When we do this, we discover that the sample standard deviation is 6.01 syringes.

If instead of considering

Why is n –1 the divisor?

$$s^2 = \frac{\Sigma(x - \bar{x})^2}{n - 1} \qquad (4 \cdot 10)$$

as our sample variance, we had considered

$$s^2 = \frac{\Sigma(x - \bar{x})^2}{n}$$

the result would have some *bias* as an estimator of the population variance; specifically, it would tend to be too low. Using a divisor of $n - 1$ gives us an unbiased estimator of σ^2. Thus, we will use s^2 (as defined in Equation 4 · 10) and s (as defined in Equation 4 · 11) to estimate σ^2 and σ.

Point estimate of the population proportion

The proportion of units that have a particular characteristic in a given population is symbolized p. If we know the proportion of units in a sample that has that same characteristic (symbolized $\bar{p}$), we can use this $\bar{p}$ as an estimator of p. It can be shown that $\bar{p}$ has all the desirable properties we discussed earlier; it is unbiased, consistent, and efficient.

Continuing our example of the manufacturer of medical supplies, we shall try to estimate the population proportion from the sample proportion. Suppose the management wishes to estimate the number of cartons that will arrive damaged, owing to poor handling in shipment after the cartons leave the factory. We can check a sample of 50 cartons from their shipping point to the arrival at their destination and then record the presence or absence of damage. If, in this case, we find that the proportion of damaged cartons in the sample is .08, we would say that:

$$\bar{p} = .08 \leftarrow \text{sample proportion damaged}$$

And since the sample proportion $\bar{p}$ is a convenient estimator of the population proportion p, we can estimate that the proportion of damaged cartons in the population will also be .08.

EXERCISES

8·7 Sensing a potential downturn in the demand for cyclamates, Sweetners' principal product, the financial VP was considering shifting his company's resources to a new product area. He selected a sample of 10 firms in the pharmaceutical industry and discovered that they were earning the following percent returns on investment. Find point estimates of the mean and the variance of the population from which the following sample came.

| 17.0 | 25.0 | 13.0 | 8.5 | 27.5 | 20.0 | 18.5 | 17.0 | 16.0 | 12.0 |

8·8 In a sample of 500 textile workers, 284 expressed extreme dissatisfaction regarding a prospective plan to modify working conditions. This dissatisfaction was vehement enough to allow management to interpret plan reaction as being highly undesirable, and they were curious about the proportion of total workers harboring this sentiment. Give a point estimate of this proportion.

---

3 INTERVAL ESTIMATES: BASIC CONCEPTS

The purpose of gathering samples is to learn more about a population. We can compute this information from the samples as either *point* estimates, which we have just discussed, or as *interval* estimates, the subject of the rest of this chapter. *An interval estimate describes a range of values within which a population parameter is likely to lie.*

Suppose the marketing research director needs an estimate in months of the average life of car batteries his company manufactures. We select a random sample of 200 batteries, record the car owner's names and addresses as listed in store records, and interview these owners about the battery life they have experienced. Our sample of 200 users had a mean battery life of 36 months. If we use the point estimate of the sample mean $\bar{x}$ as the best estimator of the population mean μ, we would report that the mean life of the company's batteries is 36 months.

But the director also asks for a statement about the uncertainty that will be likely to accompany this estimate; that is, a statement about the range within which the unknown population mean is likely to lie. To provide such a statement, we need to find *the standard error of the mean*.

We learned from Chapter 7 that if we select and plot a large number of sample means from a population, the distribution of these means will approximate a normal curve. Furthermore, the mean of the sample means will be the same as the population mean. Our sample size of 200 is large enough so that we can apply the central limit theorem, as we have done graphically in Fig. 8 · 1. To measure the spread, or dispersion, in our distribution of sample means, we can use the following formula* and calculate the standard error of the mean:

standard error of the mean for   standard deviation of the
an infinite population   population

$$\sigma_{\bar{x}} = \frac{\sigma}{\sqrt{n}} \qquad (7 \cdot 1)$$

In this case, we have already estimated the standard deviation of the population of the batteries and reported that it is 10 months. Using this standard deviation and the first equation from Chapter 7, we can calculate the standard error of the mean:

$$\sigma_{\bar{x}} = \frac{\sigma}{\sqrt{n}} = \frac{10}{\sqrt{200}} = .707 \text{ months} \leftarrow \begin{array}{l}\text{one standard} \\ \text{error of the mean}\end{array} \qquad (7 \cdot 1)$$

$\mu = 36$ months
$n = 200$

$\mu = 36$

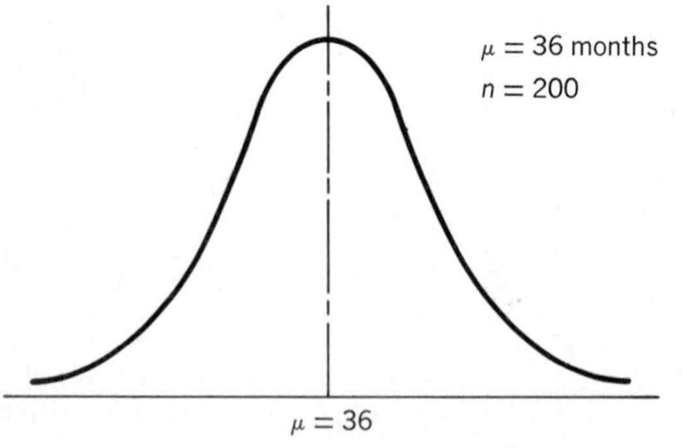

Figure 8 · 1 Sampling distribution of the mean for samples of 200 batteries

*We have not used the finite population multiplier to calculate the standard error of the mean because the population of batteries is large enough to be considered infinite.

We could now report to the director our estimate of the life of the store's batteries is 36 months, and the standard error that accompanies this estimate is .707. In other words, the actual mean life for all the batteries *may* lie somewhere in the interval estimate of from 35.293 to 36.707 months. This is helpful but insufficient information for the director. Next we need to calculate the chance that the actual life will lie in this interval *or* in other intervals of different widths that we might choose, $\pm 2\sigma$, $(2 \times .707)$, $\pm 3\sigma$, $(3 \times .707)$, etc.

Probability of the true population parameter falling within the interval estimate

To begin to solve this problem, we should review relevant parts of Chapter 6. There we worked with the normal probability distribution and learned that specific portions of the area under the normal curve are located between plus and minus any given number of standard deviations from the mean. In Fig. $6 \cdot 10$, we saw how to relate these portions to specific probabilities.

Finding the chance the mean will fall in this interval estimate

Fortunately, we can apply these properties to the standard error of the mean and make the following statement about the range of values in an interval estimate for our battery problem.

The probability is .955 that the mean of a sample size of 200 will be within plus and minus 2 standard errors of the population mean. Stated differently, 95.5 percent of all the sample means are within plus and minus 2 standard errors from μ, and hence μ is within plus and minus 2 standard errors of 95.5 percent of all the sample means. Theoretically, if we select 1,000 samples at random from a given population and then construct an interval of plus and minus 2 standard errors around the mean of each of these samples, about 955 of these intervals will include the population mean. Similarly, the probability is .683 that the mean of the sample will be within plus or minus one standard error of the population mean, and so forth. This theoretical concept is basic to our study of interval construction and of statistical inference. In Fig. $8 \cdot 2$, we have illustrated the concept graphically, showing five such intervals. Only the interval constructed around the sample mean $\bar{x}_4$ does not contain the population mean. In words, statisticians would describe the interval estimate represented in Fig. $8 \cdot 2$ by saying, "The population mean μ will be located within plus or minus 2 standard errors from the sample mean 95.5 percent of the time."

As far as any particular interval in Fig. $8 \cdot 2$ is concerned, it either contains the population mean or it does not, because the population mean is a fixed parameter and does not vary. Since we know that in 95.5 percent of all samples the interval will contain the population mean, we say that we are 95.5 percent confident that the interval contains the population mean.

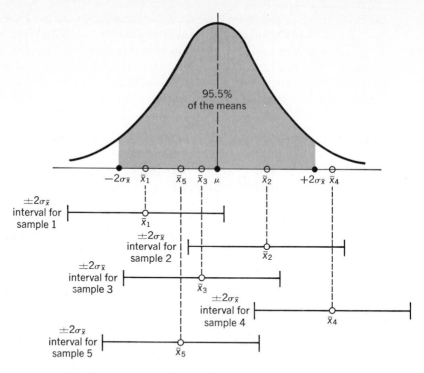

Figure 8·2 A number of intervals constructed around sample means; all except one include the population mean 8-2

Applying this to the battery example, we can now report to the director. Our best estimate of the life of the company's batteries is 36 months, *and* we are 68.3 percent confident that the life lies in the interval from 35.293 to 36.707 months ($36 \pm 1\sigma_{\bar{x}}$). Similarly, we are 95.5 percent confident that the life falls within the interval of 34.586 to 37.414 months ($36 \pm 2\sigma_{\bar{x}}$), and we are 99.7 percent confident that battery life falls within the interval of 33.879 to 38.121 months ($36 \pm 3\sigma_{\bar{x}}$).

EXERCISES

8·9 For a population with a known variance of 196, a sample of 49 leads to 210 as an estimate of the mean.
a) Find the standard error of the mean.
b) Establish an interval estimate that should include the population mean 68.3 percent of the time.

8·10 The manager of the Neuse River Bridge is concerned about the number of cars "running" the toll gates and is considering altering the toll collection procedure if such alteration would be cost effective. She randomly sampled 100 hours to determine the rate of violation. The resulting average violations per hour was 6. If the population standard deviation is known to be .8, estimate an interval that has a 95.5 percent chance of containing the true mean.

8·11 Doug Thompson, an entrepreneur seeking new investment opportunities, studied the dating habits of young metropolitan adults in 36 randomly sampled cities and determined that an average of 36,000 per location frequented discotheques. He knows the standard deviation of this type of data to be 12,000.

   a) Establish an interval estimate for the average number of disco goers, so that we are 68.3 percent certain that the population mean lies within this interval.

   b) Establish an interval estimate for the average number of disco goers, so that we are 95.5 percent certain that the population mean lies within this interval.

---

4 INTERVAL ESTIMATES AND CONFIDENCE INTERVALS

In using interval estimates, we are not confined to plus and minus 1, 2, and 3 standard errors. According to Appendix Table 1, for example, plus and minus 1.64 standard errors includes about 90 percent of the area under the curve; it includes .4495 of the area on either side of the mean in a normal distribution. Similarly, plus and minus 2.58 standard errors includes about 99 percent of the area, or 49.51 percent on each side of the mean.

Confidence level defined

In statistics, the probability that we associate with an interval estimate is called the confidence level. This probability, then, indicates how confident we are that the interval estimate will include the population parameter. A higher probability means more confidence. In estimation, the most commonly used confidence levels are 90 percent, 95 percent, and 99 precent, but we are free to apply *any* confidence level. In Fig. 8 · 2, for example, we used a 95.5 percent confidence level.

Confidence intervals and confidence limits

The confidence interval is the range of the estimate we are making. If we report that we are 90 percent confident that the mean of the population of incomes of persons in a certain community will lie between $8,000 and $24,000, then the range $8,000–$24,000 is our confidence interval. Often, however, we will express the confidence interval in standard errors rather than in numerical values. Thus, we will frequently express confidence intervals like this: $\bar{x} \pm 1.64\sigma_{\bar{x}}$, where:

$$\bar{x} + 1.64\sigma_{\bar{x}} = \text{upper limit of the confidence interval}$$

$$\bar{x} - 1.64\sigma_{\bar{x}} = \text{lower limit of the confidence interval}$$

Thus, confidence limits are the upper and lower limits of the confidence interval. In this case, $\bar{x} + 1.64\sigma_{\bar{x}}$ is called the *upper confidence limit*, and $\bar{x} - 1.64\sigma_{\bar{x}}$ is the *lower confidence limit*.

Relationship between confidence level and confidence interval

The shortcoming of high confidence levels

You may think that we should use a high confidence level, such as 99 percent, in all estimation problems. After all, a high confidence level seems to signify a high degree of accuracy in the estimate. In practice, however, high confidence levels will produce large confidence intervals, and such large intervals are not precise; they give very fuzzy estimates.

Consider an appliance store customer who inquires about the delivery of a new washing machine. In Table 8 · 3 are several of the questions the customer might ask and the likely responses. This table indicates the direct relationship that exists between the confidence level and the confidence interval for any estimate. As the customer sets a tighter and tighter confidence interval, the store manager admits a lower and lower confidence level. Notice, too, that when the confidence interval is too wide, as is the case with a one-year delivery, the estimate may have little real value, even though the store manager attaches a 99 percent confidence level to that estimate. Similarly, if the confidence interval is too narrow ("Will my washing machine get home before I do?"), the estimate is associated with such a low confidence level (1 percent) that we question its value.

TABLE 8 · 3 Illustration of the relationship between confidence level and confidence interval

Customer's question	Store manager's response	Implied confidence level	Implied confidence interval
Will I get my washing machine within 1 year?	I am absolutely certain of that.	Better than 99%	1 yr
Will you deliver the washing machine within 1 month?	I am almost positive it will be delivered this month.	At least 95%	1 mo
Will you deliver the washing machine within a week?	I am pretty certain it will go out within this week.	About 80%	1 wk
Will I get my washing machine tomorrow?	I am not certain we can get it to you then.	About 40%	1 day
Will my washing machine get home before I do?	There is little chance it will beat you home.	Near 1%	1 hr

Using sampling and confidence interval estimation

Estimating from only one sample

In our discussion of the basic concepts of interval estimation, particularly in Fig. 8 · 2, we described samples being drawn repeatedly from a given population in order to estimate a population parameter. We also mentioned selecting a large number of sample means from a population. In practice, however, it is often difficult to take more than one sample from a population. Based on just one sample, we estimate the population parameter. We must be careful, then, about interpreting the results of such a process.

If we calculate from one sample in our battery example the following confidence interval and confidence level: "We are 95 percent confident that the mean battery life of the population lies within 30 and 42 months," this statement does not mean that the chance is .95 that the mean life of all our batteries falls within the interval established from this one sample. Instead, it means that if we select many random samples of this sample size and if we calculate a confidence interval for each of these samples, then in about 95 percent of these cases the population mean will lie within that interval.

EXERCISES

---

8 · 12 Define the confidence interval.

8 · 13 Suppose you wish to use a confidence level of 80 percent. Give the upper limit of the confidence interval in terms of sample mean, $\bar{x}$, and the standard error, $\sigma_{\bar{x}}$.

8 · 14 In what way may an estimate be less meaningful because of:
a) a high confidence level?   **b)** a narrow confidence interval?

8 · 15 Is the confidence level for an estimate based on the interval constructed from one sample?

---

5 CALCULATING INTERVAL ESTIMATES OF THE MEAN FROM LARGE SAMPLES

Finding a 95 percent confidence interval

A large automotive parts wholesaler needs an estimate of the mean life it can expect from windshield wiper blades under typical driving conditions. Already, management has determined that the standard deviation of the population life is 6 months. When we select a simple random sample of 100 wiper blades and collect data on their useful lives we obtain these results:

$n = 100 \leftarrow$ sample size
$\bar{x} = 21$ months $\leftarrow$ sample mean
$\sigma = 6$ months $\leftarrow$ population standard deviation

Since the wholesaler uses tens of thousands of these wiper blades annually, it requests that we find an interval estimate with a confidence level of 95 percent. Since the sample size is greater than 30, we can use the normal distribution as our sampling distribution and calculate the standard error of the mean by using Equation 7 · 1:

$$\sigma_{\bar{x}} = \frac{\sigma}{\sqrt{n}} = \frac{6 \text{ months}}{\sqrt{100}} = .6 \text{ months}$$

$\nwarrow$ standard error of the mean
for an infinite population $\qquad (7 \cdot 1)$

Next, we consider the confidence level with which we are working. Since a 95 percent confidence level will include 47.5 percent of the area on either side of the mean of the sampling distribution, we can search in the body of Appendix Table 1 for the .475 value. We discover that .475 of the area under the normal curve is contained between the mean and a point 1.96 standard errors to the right of the mean. Therefore, we know that (2)(.475) = .95 of the area is located between plus and minus 1.96 standard errors from the mean and that our confidence limits are:

$$\bar{x} + 1.96\sigma_{\bar{x}} \leftarrow \text{upper confidence limit}$$
$$\bar{x} - 1.96\sigma_{\bar{x}} \leftarrow \text{lower confidence limit}$$

Then we substitute numerical values into these two expressions:

$$\bar{x} \pm 1.96\sigma_{\bar{x}} = 21\text{months} \pm 1.96(.6 \text{ months})$$
$$= 22.18 \text{ months} \leftarrow \text{upper confidence limit}$$
$$\text{and} \quad 19.82 \text{ months} \leftarrow \text{lower confidence limit}$$

We can now report that we estimate the mean life of the population of wiper blades to be between 19.82 and 22.18 months with 95 percent confidence.

When the population standard deviation is unknown

Finding a 90 percent confidence interval

A more complex interval estimate problem comes from a social service agency in a local government. It is interested in estimating the mean annual income of 700 families living in a four-square-block section of a community. We take a simple random sample and find these results:

$n = 50 \leftarrow$ sample size
$\bar{x} = \$4,800 \leftarrow$ sample mean
$s = \$950 \leftarrow$ sample standard deviation

The agency asks us to calculate an interval estimate of the mean annual income of all 700 families so that it can be 90 percent confident that the population mean falls within that interval. Since the sample size is over 30, we can use the normal distribution as the sampling distribution.

Notice that one part of this problem differs from our previous examples: we do *not* know the population standard deviation, and so we will use the sample standard deviation to estimate the *population standard deviation*:

$$\text{estimate of the population} \atop \text{standard deviation} \rightarrow \hat{\sigma} = s = \sqrt{\frac{\Sigma(x - \bar{x})^2}{n - 1}} \qquad (8 \cdot 1)$$

The value \$950 is our estimate of the standard deviation of the population. We can also symbolize this *estimated value by $\hat{\sigma}$, which is called sigma hat.*

Now we can estimate the standard error of the mean. Since we have a finite population size of 700, we will use the formula for deriving the standard error of the mean of finite populations:

$$\sigma_{\bar{x}} = \frac{\sigma}{\sqrt{n}} \times \sqrt{\frac{N - n}{N - 1}} \qquad (7 \cdot 3)$$

*Estimating
the standard error
of the mean*

But since we are calculating the standard error of the mean using an *estimate* of the standard deviation of the population, we rewrite this equation so that it is correct symbolically:

symbol that indicates an   estimate of the population
estimated value   standard deviation

$$\hat{\sigma}_{\bar{x}} = \frac{\hat{\sigma}}{\sqrt{n}} \times \sqrt{\frac{N - n}{N - 1}} = \frac{\$950}{\sqrt{50}} \times \sqrt{\frac{700 - 50}{700 - 1}} \qquad (8 \cdot 2)$$

$$= \$129.57 \leftarrow \text{estimate of the standard error of the}$$
mean of a finite population (derived from an estimate of the population standard deviation)

Next we consider the 90 percent confidence level, which would include 45 percent of the area on either side of the mean of the sampling distribution. Looking in the body of Appendix Table 1 for the .45 value, we find that about .45 of the area under the normal curve is located between the mean and a point 1.64 standard errors from the mean. Therefore, 90 percent of the area is located between plus *and* minus 1.64 standard errors from the mean, and our confidence limits are:

$$\bar{x} \pm 1.64\sigma_{\bar{x}} = \$4,800 \pm 1.64(\$129.57)$$
$$= \$5,012.50 \leftarrow \text{upper confidence limit}$$
$$\text{and} \quad \$4,587.50 \leftarrow \text{lower confidence limit}$$

Our report to the social service agency would be: with 90 percent confidence, we estimate that the average annual income of all 700 families living in this four-square-block section falls between \$4,587.50 and \$5,012.50.

8·16 In an automotive safety test conducted by the North Carolina Highway Safety Research Center, the average tire pressure in a sample of 81 tires was found to be 26 pounds per square inch, and the standard deviation was 1.8 pounds per square inch.
  a) Calculate the estimated population standard deviation for this population. (There are about a million cars registered in North Carolina.)
  b) Calculate the estimated standard error of the mean.
  c) Construct a 90 percent confidence interval for the population mean.

8·17 The financial controller for Home Electronics is concerned about rising personnel costs. Recruiting expenses appear to be too high, and the controller suspects that an undue number of applicants are being examined for each new position. From the recently filled positions he sampled 36 and learned that the mean number of applicants interviewed for each position was 38, with a standard deviation of 4.5. Construct a 95 percent confidence interval for the mean number of applicants screened for each new job at Home Electronics.

8·18 Upon collecting a sample of size 100 from a population with known standard deviation of 4.96, the sample mean is found to be 68.4.
  a) Find a 95 percent confidence interval for the population mean.
  b) Find a 99 percent confidence interval for the population mean.

8·19 From a population of size 240, a sample of 49 individuals is taken. From this sample, the mean is found to be 15.8 and the standard deviation 4.2.
  a) Find the estimated standard error of the mean.
  b) Construct a 98 percent confidence interval for the population mean.

6 CALCULATING INTERVAL ESTIMATES OF THE PROPORTION—LARGE SAMPLES

Statisticians often use a sample to estimate a *proportion* of occurrences in a population. For example, the government estimates by a sampling procedure the unemployment rate, or the proportion of unemployed persons, in the U.S. work force.

Review of the binomial distribution

In Chapter 6, we introduced the binomial distribution, a distribution of discrete, not continuous, data. Also, we presented the two formulas for deriving the mean and the standard deviation of the binomial distribution:

$$\mu = np \qquad\qquad (6 \cdot 2)$$

$$\sigma = \sqrt{npq} \qquad\qquad (6 \cdot 3)$$

where:

  n = number of trials
  p = probability of a success
  q = probability of a failure found by taking $1 - p$

Theoretically, the binomial distribution is the correct distribution to use in constructing confidence intervals to estimate a population proportion.

*Shortcomings
of the binomial
distribution*

Because the computation of binomial probabilities is so tedious (the probability of *r* successes in *n* trials is $[n!/r!(n-r)!][p^r q^{n-r}]$), using the binomial distribution to form interval estimates of a population proportion is a complex proposition. Fortunately, as the sample size increases, the binomial can be approximated by an appropriate normal distribution, which we can use to approximate the sampling distribution. Statisticians recommend that in estimation, *n* be more than 30 and *np* and *nq each* be at least 5 when you use the normal distribution as a substitute for the binomial.

*Finding
the mean and
variance of
the sample
proportion*

Symbolically, let's express the proportion of successes in a sample by $\bar{p}$ (pronounced *p-bar*). Then modify Equation 6 · 2, so that we can use it to derive the *mean of the sampling distribution of the proportion of successes*. In words, $\mu = np$ shows that the mean of the binomial distribution is equal to the product of the number of trials, *n*, and the probability of success *p*; that is, *np* equals the mean number of successes. To change this *number* of successes to the *proportion* of successes, we divide *np* by *n* and get *p* alone. The mean in the left-hand side of the equation becomes $\mu_{\bar{p}}$, or the mean of the sampling distribution of the proportion of successes:

$$\mu_{\bar{p}} = p \qquad (8 \cdot 3)$$

Similarly, we can modify the formula for the standard deviation of the binomial distribution $\sqrt{npq}$, which measures the standard deviation in the number of successes. To change number of successes to proportion of successes, we divide $\sqrt{npq}$ by *n* and get $\sqrt{pq/n}$. In statistical terms, the standard deviation for the proportion of successes in a sample is symbolized:

$$\text{standard error of} \searrow \sigma_{\bar{p}} = \sqrt{\frac{pq}{n}} \qquad (8 \cdot 4)$$
$$\text{the proportion}$$

and is called the *standard error of the proportion*.

When the population proportion is unknown

We can illustrate how to use these formulas if we estimate for a very large organization what proportion of the employees prefer to provide their own retirement benefits in lieu of a company sponsored plan. First, we conduct a simple random sample of 75 employees and find that .4 of them are interested in providing their own retirement plan. Our results are:

$n = 75 \leftarrow$ sample size
$\bar{p} = .4 \leftarrow$ sample proportion in favor
$\bar{q} = .6 \leftarrow$ sample proportion not in favor

221   Sec. 6   Interval estimates of the proportion—large samples

Next, management requests that we use this sample to find an interval about which they can be 99 percent confident that it contains the true population proportion.

Estimating a population proportion

But what are p and q for the population? We can estimate the population parameters by substituting the corresponding sample statistics $\bar{p}$ and $\bar{q}$ (*p-bar* and *q-bar*) in the formula for the standard error of the proportion.* Doing this, we get:

symbol indicates that the standard error of the population is estimated

sample statistics

$$\hat{\sigma}_{\bar{p}} = \sqrt{\frac{\bar{p}\bar{q}}{n}} \qquad\qquad (8 \cdot 5)$$

$$= \sqrt{\frac{(.4)(.6)}{75}} = .057 \leftarrow \text{estimated standard error of the proportion}$$

Computing the confidence limits

Now we can provide the estimate management needs by using the same procedure we have used previously. A 99 percent confidence level would include 49.5 percent of the area on either side of the mean in the sampling distribution. The body of Appendix Table 1 tells us that .495 of the area under the normal curve is located between the mean and a point 2.58 standard errors from the mean. Thus, 99 percent of the area is contained between plus *and* minus 2.58 standard errors from the mean. Our confidence limits then become:

$$\bar{p} \pm 2.58\hat{\sigma}_{\bar{p}} = .4 \pm 2.58(.057)$$
$$= .547 \leftarrow \text{upper confidence limit}$$
$$\text{and} \quad .253 \leftarrow \text{lower confidence limit}$$

Thus, we estimate from our sample of 75 employees that with 99 percent confidence we believe that the proportion of the total population of employees who wish to establish their own retirement plans lies between .253 and .547.

EXERCISES

8·20 The vice-president of production for McCormick Tires determined that the production costs for the company's new radials were running over budget. In an effort to target the reasons, he sampled 500 workers and learned that 36 percent were lower on the learning curve than he had expected.

a) Estimate the standard error of the proportion.

b) Construct a 90 percent confidence interval for the true proportion.

*Notice that we do not use the finite population multiplier, because our population size is so large compared with the sample size.

8·21 For a year and a half, now, sales have been falling considerably in all 1,200 franchises of a fast-food chain. A consulting firm has determined that 45 percent of a sample of 64 indicate clear signs of mismanagement. Construct a 95 percent confidence interval for this proportion.

8·22 By randomly surveying 49 of *Fortune* magazine's list of the 500 largest companies, consultant Milton S. Hulme discovered that 80 percent displayed basic management policies roughly equivalent to those taught in most reputable MBA programs. Give the upper and lower limits for a 96 percent confidence interval for the proportion of *Fortune's* 500 companies employing MBA management techniques.

8·23 Jack B. Craven, chief executive officer for the brokerage firm Craven, Craven, and Craven, surveyed 100 of his clients and learned that 60 percent were extremely satisfied with the firm's service.

a) Estimate the standard error of the proportion of clients extremely satisfied.

b) Construct a 98 percent confidence interval for the proportion of clients extremely satisfied with Craven's service.

---

7 INTERVAL ESTIMATES USING THE t DISTRIBUTION

In our three examples so far, the sample sizes were all larger than 30. We sampled 100 windshield wiper blades, 50 families living in a four-square-block section of a community, and 75 employees of a very large organization. Each time, the normal distribution was the appropriate sampling distribution to use to determine confidence intervals.

However, this is not always the case. How can we handle estimates where the normal distribution is *not* the appropriate sampling distribution; that is, when we are estimating the population standard deviation and the sample size is 30 or less? For example, in our chapter-opening problem of coal usage, we had data from only 10 weeks. Fortunately, another distribution exists that is appropriate in these cases. It is called the *t distribution*.

Background of the t distribution

Early theoretical work on *t* distributions was done by a man named W. S. Gossett in the early 1900s. Gossett was employed by the Guinness Brewery in Dublin, Ireland, which did not permit employees to publish research findings under their own names. So Gossett adopted the pen name "Student" and published under that name. Consequently, the *t* distribution is commonly called *Student's t distribution*, or simply *Student's distribution*.

Conditions for using the t distribution

Since it is used when the sample size is 30 or less, statisticians often associate the *t* distribution with small sample statistics. This is misleading because the size of the sample is only *one* of the conditions that leads us to use the *t* distribution. The second condition is that the population standard deviation must be unknown. Use of the *t* distribution for estimating is required whenever the sample size is 30 or less and the population standard deviation is not known. Furthermore, in using the t distribution, we assume that the population is normal or approximately normal.

Characteristics of the t distribution

t distribution compared to normal distribution

Without deriving the t distribution mathematically, we can gain an intuitive understanding of the relationship between the t distribution and the *normal* distribution. Both are symmetrical. In general, the t distribution is flatter than the normal distribution, and there is a different t distribution for every possible sample size. Even so, as the sample size gets larger, the shape of the t distribution loses its flatness and becomes approximately equal to the normal distribution. In fact, for sample sizes of more than 30, the t distribution is so close to the normal distribution that we will use the normal to approximate the t.

Figure 8·3 compares one normal distribution with two t distributions of different sample sizes. This figure shows two characteristics of t distributions: a t distribution is lower at the mean and higher at the tails than a normal distribution. The figure also demonstrates how the t distribution has proportionally more area in its tails than the normal does. This is the reason why it will be necessary to go farther out from the mean of a t distribution to include the same area under the curve. Interval widths from t distributions are, therefore, wider than those based on the normal distribution.

Degrees of freedom

Degrees of freedom defined

We said earlier that there is a separate t distribution for each sample size. In proper statistical language, we would say, "There is a different t distribution for each of the possible *degrees of freedom*." What are

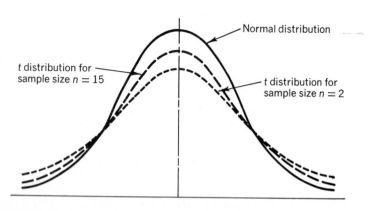

Figure 8·3 Normal distribution, t distribution for sample size $n = 15$, and t distribution for sample size $n = 2$

degrees of freedom? We can define them as the number of values we can choose freely.

Assume that we are dealing with two sample values, a and b, and we know that they have a mean of 18. Symbolically, the situation is:

$$\frac{a + b}{2} = 18$$

How can we find what values a and b can take on in this situation? The answer is that a and b can be any two values whose sum is 36, because $36 \div 2 = 18$.

Suppose we learn that a has a value of 10. Now b is no longer free to take on any value but must have the value of 26. This example shows that when there are two elements in a sample and we know the sample mean of these two elements, we are free to specify only one of the elements because the other element will be determined by the fact that the two elements sum to twice the sample mean. Statisticians say, "We have one degree of freedom."

Look at another example. There are 7 elements in our sample, and we learn that the mean of these elements is 16. Symbolically, we have this situation:

$$\frac{a + b + c + d + e + f + g}{7} = 16$$

In this case, the degrees of freedom, or the number of variables we can specify freely, are $7 - 1 = 6$. We are free to give values to 6 variables, and then we are no longer free to specify the seventh variable. It is determined automatically.

With 2 sample values we had 1 degree of freedom ($2 - 1 = 1$), and with 7 sample values we had 6 degrees of freedom. In each of these two examples, then, we had $n - 1$ degrees of freedom, assuming n is the sample size. Similarly, a sample of 23 would give us 22 degrees of freedom.

Function of degrees of freedom

We will use degrees of freedom when we select a t distribution to estimate a population mean, and we will use $n - 1$ degrees of freedom, letting n equal the sample size. If, for example, we use a sample of 20 to estimate a population mean, we will use 19 degrees of freedom in order to select the appropriate t distribution.

Using the t distribution table

t table compared to z table: 3 differences

The table of t distribution values (Appendix Table 2) differs in construction from the z table we have used previously. The t table is more compact and shows areas and t values for only a few percentages (10, 5,

2, and 1 percent). Since there is a different t distribution for each number of degrees of freedom, a more complete table would be quite lengthy. Although we can conceive of the need for a more complete table, in fact Appendix Table 2 contains all the commonly used values of the t distribution.

A second difference in the t table is that it does *not* focus on the chance that the population parameter being estimated will fall within our confidence interval. Instead, it measures the chance that the population parameter we are estimating will *not* be within our confidence interval (that is, that it will lie *outside* it). If we are making an estimate at the 90 percent confidence level, we would look in the t table under the .10 column (100 percent − 90 percent = 10 percent). This .10 chance of error is symbolized by α, which is the Greek letter *alpha*. We would find the appropriate t values for confidence intervals of 95 percent, 98 percent, and 99 percent under the α columns headed .05, .02, and .01, respectively.

A third difference in using the t table is that we must specify the degrees of freedom with which we are dealing. Suppose we make an estimate at the 90 percent confidence level with a sample size of 14, which is 13 degrees of freedom. Look in Appendix Table 2 under the .10 column until you encounter the row labeled 13 *df* (degrees of freedom). Like a z value, the t value there of 1.771 shows that if we mark off plus and minus $1.771\hat{\sigma}_{\bar{x}}$'s (estimated standard errors of $\bar{x}$) on either side of the mean, the area under the curve between these two limits will be 90 percent, and the area outside these limits (the chance of error) will be 10 percent (see Fig. 8 · 4).

Recall that in our chapter-opening problem, the generating plant manager wanted to estimate the coal needed for this year, and he took a

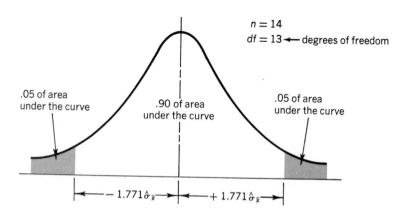

Figure 8·4 A t distribution for 13 degrees of freedom, showing a 90 percent confidence interval

sample by measuring coal usage for 10 weeks. The sample data are summarized below:

$$n = 10 \text{ weeks} \leftarrow \text{sample size}$$
$$df = 9 \leftarrow \text{degrees of freedom}$$
$$\bar{x} = 11,400 \text{ tons} \leftarrow \text{sample mean}$$
$$s = 700 \text{ tons} \leftarrow \text{sample standard deviation}$$

Using the t table to compute confidence limits

The plant manager wants an interval estimate of the mean coal consumption, and he wants to be 95 percent confident that the mean consumption falls within that interval. This problem requires the use of a t distribution because the sample size is less than 30 and the population standard deviation is unknown.

As a first step in solving this problem, recall that we *estimate* the population standard deviation with the sample standard deviation; thus:

$$\hat{\sigma} = s$$
$$= 700 \text{ tons}$$

$(8 \cdot 1)$

Using this estimate of the population standard deviation, we can estimate the standard error of the mean by modifying Equation $8 \cdot 2$ to omit the finite population multiplier (because the population of days is infinite):

$$\hat{\sigma}_{\bar{x}} = \frac{\hat{\sigma}}{\sqrt{n}} = \frac{700}{\sqrt{10}}$$

$(8 \cdot 6)$

$$= 221.38 \text{ tons} \leftarrow \text{estimated standard error of}$$
$$\text{the mean of an infinite population}$$

Now we look in Appendix Table 2 down the .05 column (100 percent − 95 percent = 5 percent) until we encounter the row of 9 degrees of freedom ($10 − 1 = 9$). There we see the t value 2.262 and can set our confidence limits accordingly:

$$\bar{x} \pm 2.262 \hat{\sigma}_{\bar{x}} = 11,400 \text{ tons} \pm 2.262(221.38 \text{ tons})$$
$$= 11,901 \text{ tons} \leftarrow \text{upper confidence limit}$$
$$\text{and} \qquad 10,899 \text{ tons} \leftarrow \text{lower confidence limit}$$

We can report to the plant manager with 95 percent confidence that the mean weekly usage of coal lies between 10,899 and 11,901 tons (Fig. $8 \cdot 5$), and we can use the 11,901 ton figure to estimate how much coal to order.

The only difference between the process we used to make this coal usage estimate and the previous estimating problems is the use of the t distribution as the appropriate distribution. Remember that in any estimation problem in which the sample size is 30 or less *and* the standard deviation of the population is unknown *and* the population is normal (or approximately normal), we use the t distribution.

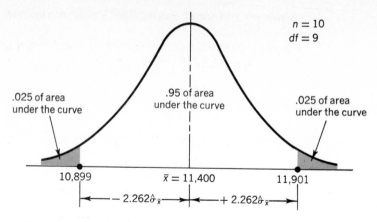

$n = 10$
$df = 9$

.025 of area
under the curve

.95 of area
under the curve

.025 of area
under the curve

10,899 $\bar{x} = 11,400$ 11,901

$\longleftarrow -2.262\hat{\sigma}_{\bar{x}} \longrightarrow |\longleftarrow +2.262\hat{\sigma}_{\bar{x}} \longrightarrow$

Figure 8·5 Coal problem: a t distribution with 9 degrees of freedom and a confidence interval of 95 percent

TABLE 8·4 Summary of formulas for confidence limits estimating mean and proportion

	When the population is finite	When the population is infinite
Estimating μ (the population mean)		
When σ (the population standard deviation) is known	upper limit: $\bar{x} + z\dfrac{\sigma}{\sqrt{n}} \times \sqrt{\dfrac{N-n}{N-1}}$	$\bar{x} + z\dfrac{\sigma}{\sqrt{n}}$
	lower limit: $\bar{x} - z\dfrac{\sigma}{\sqrt{n}} \times \sqrt{\dfrac{N-n}{N-1}}$	$\bar{x} - z\dfrac{\sigma}{\sqrt{n}}$
When σ (the population standard deviation) is not known [$\hat{\sigma} = s$] When n (the sample size) is larger than 30	upper limit: $\bar{x} + z\dfrac{\hat{\sigma}}{\sqrt{n}} \times \sqrt{\dfrac{N-n}{N-1}}$ lower limit: $\bar{x} - z\dfrac{\hat{\sigma}}{\sqrt{n}} \times \sqrt{\dfrac{N-n}{N-1}}$	$\bar{x} + z\dfrac{\hat{\sigma}}{\sqrt{n}}$ $\bar{x} - z\dfrac{\hat{\sigma}}{\sqrt{n}}$
When n (the sample size) is 30 or less	upper limit: $\bar{x} + t\dfrac{\hat{\sigma}}{\sqrt{n}} \times \sqrt{\dfrac{N-n}{N-1}}$ lower limit: $\bar{x} - t\dfrac{\hat{\sigma}}{\sqrt{n}} \times \sqrt{\dfrac{N-n}{N-1}}$	$\bar{x} + t\dfrac{\hat{\sigma}}{\sqrt{n}}$ * $\bar{x} - t\dfrac{\hat{\sigma}}{\sqrt{n}}$
Estimating p (the population proportion) When n (the sample size) is larger than 30	lower limit: $\bar{p} - z\hat{\sigma}_{\bar{p}} \times \sqrt{\dfrac{N-n}{N-1}}$ upper limit: $\bar{p} + z\hat{\sigma}_{\bar{p}} \times \sqrt{\dfrac{N-n}{N-1}}$	$\bar{p} - z\hat{\sigma}_{\bar{p}}$ $\bar{p} + z\hat{\sigma}_{\bar{p}}$

$\left[\hat{\sigma}_{\bar{p}} = \sqrt{\dfrac{\bar{p}\bar{q}}{n}} \right]$

*Remember that the appropriate t distribution to use is the one with $n - 1$ degrees of freedom.

Summary of confidence limits under various conditions

Table 8 · 4 summarizes the various approaches to estimation introduced in this chapter and the confidence limits appropriate for each.

EXERCISES
---

8 · 24 Six housewives were randomly sampled, and it was determined that they walked an average of 34.6 miles per week in their housework, with a sample standard deviation of 2.8 miles per week. Construct a 95 percent confidence interval for the population mean.

8 · 25 For the following sample sizes and confidence levels, find the appropriate t values for constructing confidence intervals.
a) $n = 5$; 99%   **c)** $n = 27$; 95%   **e)** $n = 18$; 95%
b) $n = 18$; 99%   **d)** $n = 16$; 95%   **f)** $n = 14$; 90%

8 · 26 Given the following sample sizes and t values used to construct confidence intervals, find the corresponding confidence levels:
a) $n = 20$; $t = \pm 1.729$ **b)** $n = 12$; $t = \pm 2.201$ **c)** $n = 7$; $t = \pm 3.707$

8 · 27 A sample of size 15 had a mean of 56 and a standard deviation of 12. Construct a 95 percent confidence interval for the population mean.

---

8 DETERMINING THE SAMPLE SIZE IN ESTIMATION

In all our discussions so far, we have used for sample size the symbol n instead of a specific number. Now we need to know how to determine what number to use. How large should the sample be? If it is too small, we may fail to achieve the objectives of our analysis. But if it is too large, we waste resources when we gather the sample.

What sample size is adequate?

Some sampling error will arise because we have not studied the whole population. Whenever we sample, we always miss *some* helpful information about the population. If we want a high level of precision (that is, if we want to be quite sure of our estimate), we have to sample enough of the population to provide the required information. Sampling error is controlled by selecting a sample that is adequate in size. In general, the more precision you want, the larger the sample you will need to take. Let us examine some methods that are useful in determining what sample size is necessary for any specified level of precision.

Sample size for estimating a mean

Suppose a university is performing a survey of the annual earnings of last year's graduates from its business school. It knows from past experience

that the standard deviation of the annual earnings of the entire population (1,000) of these graduates is about $1,500. How large a sample size
should the university take in order to estimate the mean annual earnings
of last year's class within plus and minus $500 and at a 95 percent
confidence level?

*Two ways to
express a
confidence limit*

Exactly what is this problem asking? The university is going to take
a sample of some size, determine the mean of the sample $\bar{x}$, and use it as
a point estimate of the population mean. It wants to be 95 percent
certain that the true mean annual earnings of last year's class are not
more than $500 above or below the point estimate. Row a in Table 8 · 5
summarizes in symbolic terms how the university is defining its confidence limits for us. Row b shows symbolically how we normally express
confidence limits for an infinite population. When we compare these two
sets of confidence limits, we can see that:

$$z\sigma_{\bar{x}} = \$500$$

Thus, the university is actually saying that it wants $z\sigma_{\bar{x}}$ to be equal
to $500. If we look in Appendix Table 1, we find that the necessary z
value for a 95 percent confidence level is 1.96. Step by step:

$$\text{If } z\sigma_{\bar{x}} = \$500 \quad \text{and} \quad z = 1.96$$

$$\text{then } 1.96\sigma_{\bar{x}} = \$500$$

$$\text{and } \sigma_{\bar{x}} = \frac{\$500}{1.96} = \$255 \leftarrow \text{standard error of the mean}$$

Remember that the formula for the standard error is Equation 7 · 1:

$$\sigma_{\bar{x}} = \frac{\sigma}{\sqrt{n}} \leftarrow \text{population standard deviation} \qquad (7 \cdot 1)$$

*Finding
an adequate
sample size*

Using Equation 7 · 1, we can substitute our known population standard
deviation value of $1,500 and our calculated standard error value of $255
and solve for n:

$$\sigma_{\bar{x}} = \frac{\sigma}{\sqrt{n}}$$

$$\$255 = \frac{\$1,500}{\sqrt{n}} \qquad (7 \cdot 1)$$

$$\sqrt{n} = \frac{\$1,500}{\$255} = 5.882$$

$$n = 34.6 \leftarrow \text{sample size for precision specified}$$

TABLE 8 · 5 Comparison of two ways of expressing the same confidence limits

Lower confidence limit	*Upper confidence limit*
a. $\bar{x} - \$500$	a. $\bar{x} + \$500$
b. $\bar{x} - z\sigma_{\bar{x}}$	b. $\bar{x} + z\sigma_{\bar{x}}$

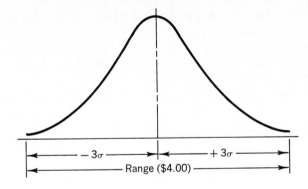

Figure 8·6 Approximate relationship between the range and population standard deviation

Therefore, since n must be greater than, or equal to, 34.6, the university should take a sample of 35 business school graduates to get the precision it wants in estimating the class's mean annual earnings.

Estimating the standard deviation from the range

In this example, we knew the standard deviation of the population, but in many cases the standard deviation of the population is not available. Remember, too, that we have not yet taken the sample, and we are trying to decide how large to make it. We cannot estimate the population standard deviation using methods from the first part of this chapter. If we have a notion about the range of the population, we can use that to get a crude but workable estimate.

Suppose we are estimating hourly manufacturing wage rates in a city and are fairly confident that there is a $4.00 difference between the highest and lowest wage rates. We know that plus and minus 3 standard deviations include 99.7 percent of all the area under the normal curve; that is, plus 3 standard deviations and minus 3 standard deviations include almost all of the distribution. To symbolize this relationship, we have constructed Fig. 8 · 6, in which $4.00 (the range) equals 6 standard deviations (plus 3 and minus 3). Thus, a rough estimate of the population standard deviation would be:

$$6\hat{\sigma} = \$4.00$$
$$\hat{\sigma} = \frac{\$4.00}{6} = \$0.667$$

estimate of the population standard deviation

Our estimate of the population standard deviation using this rough method is not precise, but it may mean the difference between getting a working idea of the required sample size and knowing nothing about that sample size.

Sample size for estimating a proportion

The procedures for determining sample sizes for estimating a population proportion are similar to those for estimating a population mean. Suppose we wish to poll students at a large state university. We want to determine what proportion of them are in favor of a new grading system. We would like a sample size that will enable us to be 90 percent certain of estimating the true proportion that are in favor of the new system within plus or minus .02.

We begin to solve this problem by looking in Appendix Table 1 to find the z value for a 90 percent confidence level. That value is plus and minus 1.64 standard errors from the mean. Since we want our estimate to be within .02, we can symbolize the step-by-step process like this:

Finding an adequate sample size

$$\text{If } z\sigma_{\bar{p}} = .02 \quad \text{and} \quad z = 1.64$$

$$\text{then } 1.64\sigma_{\bar{p}} = .02$$

If we now substitute the right side of Equation 8 · 4 for $\sigma_{\bar{p}}$, we get:

$$1.64\left(\sqrt{\frac{pq}{n}}\right) = .02$$

$$\sqrt{\frac{pq}{n}} = .0122 \leftarrow \text{now square both sides}$$

$$\frac{pq}{n} = .0001488$$

$$n = \frac{pq}{.0001488}$$

To find n, we still need an estimate of the population parameters p and q. If we have strong feelings about the actual proportion in favor of the new system we can use that as our best guess to calculate n. But if we have no idea what p is, then our best strategy is to guess at p in such a way that we choose n in a conservative manner (that is, so that the sample size *is* large enough to supply at least the precision we require no matter what p actually is). At this point in our problem, n is equal to the product of p and q divided by .0001488. The way to get the largest n is to generate the largest possible numerator of that expression, or to pick $p = .5$ and $q = .5$. Then n becomes:

$$n = \frac{pq}{.0001488} = \frac{(.5)(.5)}{.0001488} = 1680 \leftarrow \text{sample size for precision specified}$$

As a result, to be 90 percent certain of estimating the true proportion within .02, we should pick a simple random sample of 1,680 students to interview.

Picking the most conservative proportion

In the problem we have just solved, we picked a value for p that represented the most conservative strategy. The value .5 generated the largest possible sample. We would have used another value of p if we had been able to estimate one *or* if we had a strong feeling about one. Whenever all of these solutions are absent, assume the most conservative possible value for p, or .5.

TABLE 8·6 Sample size *n* associated with different values of *p* and *q*

Choose this value for p	Value of q or 1 − p	$\left(\dfrac{pq}{.0001488}\right)$	Indicated sample size n
.2	.8	$\dfrac{(.2)(.8)}{.0001488}$ =	1,075
.3	.7	$\dfrac{(.3)(.7)}{.0001488}$ =	1,411
.4	.6	$\dfrac{(.4)(.6)}{.0001488}$ =	1,612
.5	.5	$\dfrac{(.5)(.5)}{.0001488}$ =	1,680 ← most conservative
.6	.4	$\dfrac{(.6)(.4)}{.0001488}$ =	1,612
.7	.3	$\dfrac{(.7)(.3)}{.0001488}$ =	1,411
.8	.2	$\dfrac{(.8)(.2)}{.0001488}$ =	1,075

To illustrate that .5 yields the largest possible sample, Table 8 · 6 solves the grading system problem using several different values of *p*. You can see from the sample sizes associated with these different values that for the range of *p*'s from .3 to .7, the change in the appropriate sample size is relatively small. Therefore, even if you knew that the true population proportion was .3 and you used a value of .5 for *p* anyway, you would have sampled only 269 more people (1,680 − 1,411) than was actually necessary for the desired degree of precision. Obviously, guessing values of *p* in cases like this is not as critical as it seems at first glance.

──────────────── **EXERCISES** ────────────────

8·28 The manager of an industrial chemical plant needs to determine the average life span of the vats extensively employed in the manufacturing process. From prior studies, he knows that the population standard deviation is 9 years. How large a sample should be chosen to be 95 percent confident that the sample average is within 2 years of the true average?

8·29 A speed reading course guarantees a certain reading rate increase within 2 days. The teacher knows a few people will not be able to achieve this increase; so before stating the guaranteed reading rate increase, he wants to be 95 percent confident that the percentage has been estimated to within ±3 percent of the true value. What is the most conservative sample size needed for this problem?

8·30 For a test market, find the sample size needed to estimate the true proportion of consumers satisfied with a certain new product within ± .03 at the 95 percent confidence interval. Assume you have no strong feeling about what the proportion is.

8·31 If the population standard deviation is 200, find the sample size necessary to estimate the true mean within 100 points for a confidence level of 90 percent.

9 TERMS INTRODUCED IN CHAPTER 8

confidence interval A range of values that has some designated probability of including the true population parameter value.

confidence level The probability that we associate with an interval estimate of a population parameter indicating how confident we are that the interval estimate will include the population parameter.

confidence limits The upper and lower boundaries of a confidence interval.

consistent estimator An estimator that yields values more closely approaching the population parameter as the sample size increases.

degrees of freedom The number of values in a sample we can specify freely, once we know something about that sample.

efficient estimator An estimator with a smaller standard error than some other estimator of the population parameter; i.e., the smaller the standard error of an estimator, the more efficient that estimator is.

estimate A specific observed value of an estimator.

estimator A sample statistic used to estimate a population parameter.

interval estimate A range of values used to estimate an unknown population parameter.

point estimate A single number that is used to estimate an unknown population parameter.

Student's *t* distribution A family of probability distributions distinguished by their individual degrees of freedom, similar in form to the normal distribution, and used when the population standard deviation is unknown and the sample size is relatively small ($n \leqslant 30$).

unbiased estimator An estimator of a population parameter that, on the average, assumes values above the population parameter as often, and to the same extent, as it tends to assume values below the population parameter.

10 EQUATIONS INTRODUCED IN CHAPTER 8

p. 219 Estimator of the population standard deviation
$$\hat{\sigma} = s = \sqrt{\frac{\Sigma(x - \bar{x})^2}{n - 1}}$$
8·1

This formula indicates that the sample standard deviation can be used as an estimator of the population standard deviation.

p. 219
$$\hat{\sigma}_{\bar{x}} = \frac{\hat{\sigma}}{\sqrt{n}} \times \sqrt{\frac{N - n}{N - 1}}$$
8·2

This formula enables us to derive an *estimated* standard error of the mean of a *finite* population from an *estimate* of the population standard deviation. The symbol ^ called a hat, indicates that the value is estimated. Equation 8 · 6 is the same formula for an infinite population.

$$\mu_{\bar{p}} = p$$

Use this formula to derive the *mean* of the sampling distribution *of the proportion* of successes. The right-hand side, p, is equal to $(n \times p)/n$, where the numerator is the product of the number of trials and the probability of successes and the denominator is the number of trials. Symbolically, the proportion of successes *in a sample* is written $\bar{p}$ and is pronounced *p-bar*.

$$\sigma_{\bar{p}} = \sqrt{\frac{pq}{n}}$$

To get the *standard error of the proportion*, take the square root of the product of the probabilities of success and failure divided by the number of trials.

$$\hat{\sigma}_{\bar{p}} = \sqrt{\frac{\bar{p}\bar{q}}{n}}$$

This is the formula to use to derive an *estimated* standard error of the proportion when the population proportion is unknown and you are forced to use $\bar{p}$ and $\bar{q}$, the sample proportions of successes and failures.

$$\hat{\sigma}_{\bar{x}} = \frac{\hat{\sigma}}{\sqrt{n}}$$

This formula enables us to derive an *estimated* standard error of the mean of an *infinite* population from an *estimate* of the population standard deviation. It is exactly like Equation $8 \cdot 2$ except that it lacks the multiplier.

11 CHAPTER REVIEW EXERCISES

8·32 From previous studies, the population standard deviation for the performance ratings of the sales for The Dutch Food Company has been determined to be 12.4; the ratings fall within a scale of 0 through 100. Ann Clark, vice-president of sales, wants to be 98 percent certain that the average performance rating of a sample falls within ± 3 points of the population's average rating. How large a sample should she select?

8·33 The Taylor Glass Company's production manager, Bill Bohannon, has been concerned about the high percentage of defectives coming off the line. He recently obtained the trial use of a machine reportedly capable of removing the flaws in most defectives. The advertised "cure" rate of this machine is 75 percent. How large a sample should Bohannon run in order to be 98 percent certain that the sample proportion of repaired defectives is within $\pm .04$ of the proportion of all defectives the machine would repair if purchased?

8·34 The executive vice-president of Zayes, a large national retail chain, is contemplating adjusting his store managers' salary mix of base pay and commission. He sampled 100 store managers and found their mean base pay to be \$28,640. The population standard deviation was known to be \$850. For the mean base salary of Zayes' store managers, construct a confidence interval with confidence level (a) 95 percent, (b) 98 percent.

8·35 Given the following expressions for the limits of a confidence interval, find the confidence level associated with the interval:

   a) $\bar{x} - 1.5\sigma_{\bar{x}}$ to $\bar{x} + 1.5\sigma_{\bar{x}}$ **b)** $\bar{x} - 1.7\sigma_{\bar{x}}$ to $\bar{x} + 1.7\sigma_{\bar{x}}$ **c)** $\bar{x} - 2.3\sigma_{\bar{x}}$ to $\bar{x} + 2.3\sigma_{\bar{x}}$

8·36 Mark Semmes, owner of the Aurora Restaurant, is considering purchasing new furniture. To assist him in deciding on the amount he can afford to invest in tables and chairs, he wishes to determine the average revenue per customer. He randomly sampled 8 customers, whose average check turned out to be $10.50, with a standard deviation of $2.50. Construct a 95 percent confidence interval for the size of the average check per customer.

8·37 What are the advantages of using an interval estimate over a point estimate?

8·38 Why is the size of a statistic's standard error important in its use as an estimator? To which characteristic of estimators does this relate?

8·39 Scott Eames, president of a local bank in Lexington, North Carolina, has determined that the average level of deposit in savings accounts must be $85, in order to cover minimum costs. Conservatively, how many accounts should be sampled to be 95 percent certain that he has estimated (within ±.04) the proportion of accounts with savings levels below $85.

8·40 Given a sample mean of 96, a population standard deviation of 4.8, and a sample of size 36, find the confidence level associated with each of the following intervals:
a) (94.4; 97.6)   **b)** (94; 98)   **c)** (95.328; 96.672)

8·41 Based on knowledge about the desirable qualities of estimators, for what reasons might $\bar{x}$ be considered the "best" estimator of the true population mean?

8·42 Ellen Harris, a time-methods engineer, was accumulating normal times for various tasks on a labor-intensive assembly process. This process included 200 separate job stations, each performing the same assembly task. She sampled 5 stations and obtained the following assembly times for each station: 1.8; 2.4; 2.2; 2.6; and 1.6 minutes.
a) Calculate the mean assembly time and the corresponding standard deviation for the sample.
b) Estimate the population standard deviation.
c) Construct a 98 percent confidence interval for the mean assembly time.

8·43 Larry Culler, the federal grain inspector at a seaport, found spoilage in 35 of 100 randomly selected lots of wheat shipped from the port. Construct a 95 percent confidence interval for him for the actual proportion of lots with spoilage in shipments from that port.

8·44 The credit manager for Prangles, a clothing retailer, sampled 300 accounts and found 120 to be a minimum of 30 days delinquent. Given a confidence level equal to .98, construct a confidence interval for the proportion of accounts at least 30 days delinquent.

8·45 From a random sample of 64 buses, Montreal's mass transit office has calculated the mean number of passengers per kilometer to be 3.5. From previous studies, the population standard deviation is known to be 1.6 passengers per kilometer.
a) Find the standard error of the mean. (Assume that the bus fleet is very large.)
b) Construct a 95 percent confidence interval for the mean number of passengers per kilometer for the population.

---

12 CHAPTER CONCEPTS TEST

Answers are in the back of the book.

T F 1. A statistic is said to be an efficient estimator of a population parameter if, with increasing sample size, it becomes almost certain that the value of the statistic comes very close to that of the population parameter.

T F 2. An interval estimate is a range of values used to estimate the shape of a population's distribution.

T F 3. If a statistic tends to assume values higher than the population parameter as frequently as it tends to assume values that are lower, we say that the statistic is an unbiased estimate of the parameter.

T F 4. The probability that a population parameter will lie within a given interval estimate is known as the confidence level.

T F 5. With increasing sample size, the t distribution tends to become flatter in shape.

T F 6. We must always use the t distribution, rather than the normal, whenever the standard deviation of the population is not known.

T F 7. We may obtain a crude estimate of the standard deviation of some population if we have some information about its range.

T F 8. When using the t distribution in estimation, we must assume that the population is approximately normal.

T F 9. Using high confidence levels is not always desirable, because high confidence levels produce large confidence intervals.

T F 10. There is a different t distribution for each possible sample size.

T F 11. A point estimate is often insufficient because it is either right or wrong.

T F 12. A sample mean is said to be an unbiased estimator of a population mean because no other estimator could extract from the sample additional information about the population mean.

T F 13. The most frequently used estimator of σ is s.

T F 14. The standard error of the proportion is calculated as $\sqrt{\dfrac{p(1-p)}{n}}$.

T F 15. The degrees of freedom used in a t-distribution estimation are equal to the sample size.

16. When choosing an estimator of a population parameter, one should consider:
   a) consistency
   b) clarity
   c) efficiency
   d) all of the preceding
   e) a and c but not b

17. Suppose that 200 members of a group were asked whether or not they liked a particular product. Fifty said yes; 150 said no. Assuming "yes" means a success, which of the following is correct?
   a) $\bar{p} = .33$ b) $\bar{p} = .25$ c) $p = .33$ d) $p = .25$ e) b and d only

18. Assume that you take a sample and calculate $\bar{x}$ as 100. You then calculate the upper limit of a 90 percent confidence interval for μ; its value is 112. What is the lower limit of this confidence interval?
   a) 88
   b) 92
   c) 100
   d) cannot be determined from the information given

19. After taking a sample and computing $\bar{x}$, a statistician says, "I am 88 percent confident that the population mean is between 106 and 122." What does she really mean?
   a) The probability is .88 that μ is between 106 and 122.
   b) The probability is .88 that $\mu = 114$, the midpoint of the interval.
   c) 88 percent of the intervals calculated from samples of this size will contain the population mean.
   d) All of the above.
   e) a and c but not b.

20. Which of the following is a necessary condition for using a t-distribution table?
    a) n is small.
    b) s is known but σ is not.
    c) The population is infinite.
    d) All of the preceding.
    e) a and b but not c.

21. Which of the following t distributions would be expected to have the most area in its tails?
    a) $\bar{x} = 8.3$, degrees of freedom = 12
    b) $\bar{x} = 15$, degrees of freedom = 19
    c) $\bar{x} = 15$, $n = 19$
    d) $\bar{x} = 8.3$, $n = 12$

22. Which of the following is a difference between z tables and t tables?
    a) The t table has values for only a few percentages.
    b) The t table measures the chance that the population parameter we are estimating will be in our confidence interval.
    c) We must specify the degrees of freedom with which we are dealing when using a z table.
    d) All of the above.
    e) a and b but not c.

23. Suppose we are attempting to estimate a population variance by using s^2. It is incorrect to calculate s^2 as $\dfrac{\Sigma(x - \bar{x})^2}{n}$ because the value would be
    a) biased   c) inconsistent
    b) inefficient   d) none of the above

24. When considering samples with size greater than 30, we use the normal table, even if the population standard deviation is unknown, Why is this?
    a) Calculation of degrees of freedom becomes difficult for large sample sizes.
    b) The number of percentages we need for calculation of confidence intervals exceeds the number contained in the t tables.
    c) It is difficult to calculate $\bar{x}$ (and hence s^2) for large samples.
    d) None of the above.
    e) a and c but not b.

25. Assume that, from a population with $N = 50$, a sample of size 15 is drawn; σ^2 is known to be 36, and s^2 for the sample is 49; $\bar{x}$ for the sample is calculated as 104. Which of the following should be used for calculating a 95 percent confidence interval for μ?
    a) Student's t distribution
    b) normal distribution
    c) finite population multiplier
    d) a and c but not b
    e) b and c but not a

26. A single number used to estimate an unknown population parameter is a _____ estimate.

27. A range of values used to estimate an unknown population parameter is a _____ estimate.

28. Once we know something about a sample, the number of values in the sample we

can specify freely is called _____ .

29. The family of probability distributions used when population standard deviation is unknown, sample size is small, and values approximate the normal, is the _____ .

30. When we give an interval estimate of a population parameter, we show how sure we are that the interval contains the actual population parameter by setting a _____ level.

Testing Hypotheses

9

The roofing contract for a new sports complex in San Francisco has been awarded to Parkhill Associates, a large architectural firm. Building specifications call for a moveable roof covered by approximately 10,000 sheets of .04-inch-thick aluminum. The aluminum sheets cannot be appreciably thicker than .04 inch because the structure could not support the additional weight. Nor can the sheets be appreciably thinner than .04 inch because the strength of the roof would be inadequate. Because of this restriction on thickness, Parkhill carefully checks the aluminum sheets from its supplier. Of course, Parkhill does not want to measure each sheet, so it randomly samples 100. The sheets in the sample have a mean thickness of .0408 inch. From past experience with this supplier, Parkhill believes that these sheets come from a thickness population with a standard deviation of .004 inch. On the basis of this data, Parkhill must decide whether the 10,000 sheets meet specifications. In Chapter 8, we used sample statistics to estimate population parameters. Now, to solve problems like Parkhill's, we shall learn how to use characteristics of samples to test an assumption we have about the population from which that sample came. Our test for Parkhill, later in the chapter, may lead Parkhill to accept the shipment, or it may indicate that Parkhill should reject the aluminum sheets sent by the supplier.

The subject of Chapter 9 is hypothesis testing. Here we are trying to determine when it is reasonable to conclude, from analysis of a sample, that the entire population possesses a certain property, and when it is not reasonable to reach such a conclusion. Suppose a student purchases a $500 second-hand car from a dealer who advertises "Our cars are the finest, most dependable in town." If the car's repair bills during the first month are $600, that one-car sample may cause the student to conclude that the dealer's population of used cars is probably not as advertised. Chapter 9 will allow us to test and evaluate larger samples than those available to the buyer of the used car.

1 INTRODUCTION

Function of hypothesis testing

Hypothesis testing begins with an assumption, called a *hypothesis*, that we make about a population parameter. Then we collect sample data, produce sample statistics, and use this information to decide how likely it is that our hypothesized population parameter is correct. Say that we assume a certain value for a population mean. To test the validity of our assumption, we gather sample data and determine the difference between the hypothesized value and the actual value of the sample mean. Then we judge whether the difference is significant. The smaller the difference, the greater the likelihood that our hypothesized value for the mean is correct. The larger the difference, the smaller the likelihood.

Unfortunately, the difference between the hypothesized population parameter and the actual sample statistic is more often neither so large that we automatically reject our hypothesis nor so small that we just as quickly accept it. So in hypothesis testing as in most significant real life decisions, clear-cut solutions are the exception, not the rule.

When to accept or reject the hypothesis

Suppose a manager of a large shopping mall tells us that the average work efficiency of her employees is 90 percent. How can we test the validity of her hypothesis? Using the sampling methods we learned in Chapter 7, we could calculate the efficiency of a *sample* of her employees. If we did this and the sample statistic came out to be 93 percent, we would readily accept the manager's statement. However, if the sample statistic were 46 percent, we would reject her assumption as untrue. We can interpret both of these outcomes, 93 percent and 46 percent, using our common sense.

The basic problem will be dealing with uncertainty

Now suppose that our sample statistic reveals an efficiency of 81 percent. This value is relatively close to 90 percent. But is it close enough for us to accept the manager's hypothesis? Whether we accept or reject the manager's hypothesis, we cannot be absolutely certain that our decision is correct; therefore we will have to learn to deal with uncertainty in our decision making. We cannot accept or reject a hypothesis about a population parameter simply by intuition. Instead, we need to learn how to decide objectively, on the basis of sample information, whether to accept or reject a hunch.

EXERCISES

9·1 Why must we be required to deal with uncertainty in our decisions, even when using statistical techniques?

9·2 Theoretically speaking, how might one go about testing the hypothesis that a coin is fair? That a die is fair?

9·3 Is it possible that a false hypothesis will be accepted? How would you explain this?

9·4 Describe the hypothesis testing process.

9·5 How would you explain a large difference between a hypothesized population parameter and a sample statistic if, in fact, the hypothesis is true?

---

2 CONCEPTS BASIC TO THE HYPOTHESIS TESTING PROCEDURE

Sports complex problem

Before we introduce the formal statistical terms and procedures, we'll work our chapter opening sports complex problem all the way through. Recall that the aluminum roofing sheets have a claimed average thickness of .04 inch and that they will be unsatisfactory if they are too thick *or* too thin. The contractor takes a sample of 100 sheets and determines that the sample mean thickness is .0408 inch. On the basis of past experience, he knows that the population standard deviation is .004 inch. Does this sample evidence indicate that the batch of 10,000 sheets of aluminum is suitable for constructing the roof of the new sports complex?

Formulating the hypothesis

If we assume that the true mean thickness is .04 inch, and we know that the population standard deviation is .004 inch, how likely is it that we would get a sample mean of .0408 or more from that population? In other words, if the true mean is .04 inch, and the standard deviation is .004 inch, what are the chances of getting a sample mean that differs from .04 inch by .0008 inch or more?

These questions show that to determine whether the population mean is actually .04 inch, we must calculate the probability that a random sample with a mean of .0408 inch will be selected from a population with a μ of .04 inch and a σ of .004 inch. This probability will indicate whether it is *reasonable* to observe a sample like this if the population mean is actually .04 inch. If this probability is far too low, we must conclude that the aluminum company's statement is false and that the mean thickness of the aluminum sheets is not .04 inch.

To answer the question illustrated in Fig. 9 · 1: if the hypothesized population mean is .04 inch and the population standard deviation is

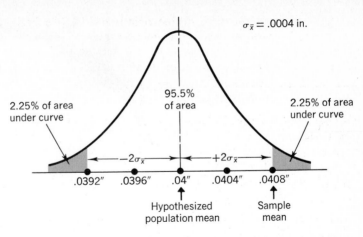

$\sigma_{\bar{x}} = .0004$ in.

2.25% of area under curve

95.5% of area

2.25% of area under curve

$-2\sigma_{\bar{x}}$ $+2\sigma_{\bar{x}}$

.0392"   .0396"   .04"   .0404"   .0408"

Hypothesized population mean   Sample mean

Figure 9 · 1   Probability that $\bar{x}$ will differ from hypothesized μ by 2 standard errors or more

.004 inch, what are the chances of getting a sample mean (.0408 inch) that differs from .04 inch by .0008 inch? First we calculate the standard error of the mean from the population standard deviation:

Calculating the standard error of the mean

$$\sigma_{\bar{x}} = \frac{\sigma}{\sqrt{n}} = \frac{.004 \text{ in.}}{\sqrt{100}} = .0004 \text{ in.} \qquad (7 \cdot 1)$$

Next we use Equation 7 · 2 to discover that the mean of our sample (.0408 inch) lies 2 standard errors to the right of the hypothesized population mean:

$$z = \frac{\bar{x} - \mu}{\sigma_{\bar{x}}} = \frac{.0408 - .04}{.0004} = 2 \leftarrow \begin{array}{l}\text{standard errors}\\ \text{of the mean}\end{array} \qquad (7 \cdot 2)$$

Interpreting the probability associated with this difference

Using Appendix Table 1, we learn that 4.5 percent is the *total chance* of our sample mean differing from the population mean by 2 or more standard errors; that is, the chances that the sample mean would be .0408 inch or larger or .0392 inch or smaller are only 4.5 percent. With this low a chance, Parkhill could conclude that a population with a true mean of .04 inches would not be likely to produce a sample like this. The project supervisor would reject the aluminum company's statement about the mean thickness of the sheets.

The decision maker's role in formulating hypotheses

    In this case, the difference between the sample mean and the hypothesized population mean is too large, and the chance that the population would produce such a random sample is far too low. Why this probability of 4.5 percent is too low, or wrong, is a judgment for decision makers to make. Certain situations demand that decision makers be very sure about the characteristics of the items being tested, and then 4.5 percent is too high to be attributable to chance. Other processes allow for a wider latitude or variation, and a decision maker might accept a hypothesis with a 20 percent probability of chance variation. In each situation, we must try to determine the costs resulting from an incorrect decision and the precise level of risk we are willing to assume.

Risk of rejection   In our example, we rejected the aluminum company's contention that the population mean is .04 inch. But suppose for a moment that the population mean is *actually* .04 inch. If we then stuck to our rejection rule of 2 standard errors or more (the 4.5 percent probability or less in the tails of Fig. 9 · 1), we would reject a perfectly good lot of aluminum sheets 4.5 percent of the time. Therefore, our minimum standard for an acceptable probability, 4.5 percent, is *also* the *risk* we take of *rejecting a hypothesis that is true.* In this or any decision making, there can be no risk-free trade-off.

--------------------------------- **EXERCISES** ---------------------------------

9·6 What do we mean when we reject a hypothesis on the basis of a sample?

9·7 Explain why there is no single level of probability used to reject or accept in hypothesis testing.

9·8 If we reject a hypothesized value because it differs from a sample statistic by more than one standard error, what is the probability that we have rejected a hypothesis that is in fact true?

9·9 How many standard deviations around the hypothesized value should we use to be 95.5 percent certain that we accept the hypothesis when it is correct?

9·10 An automobile manufacturer claims that a particular model gets 24 miles to the gallon. The Environmental Protection Agency, using a sample of 36 automobiles of this model, finds the sample mean to be 23.1 miles per gallon. From previous studies, the population standard deviation is known to be 3 miles per gallon. Could we reasonably expect (within 2 standard deviations) that we could select such a sample if indeed the population mean is actually 24 miles per gallon?

3 TESTING HYPOTHESES

Making a formal statement of the null hypothesis   In hypothesis testing, we must state the assumed or hypothesized value of the population parameter *before* we begin sampling. The assumption we wish to test is called the *null hypothesis* and is symbolized H_0, or "H sub-zero."

Suppose we want to test the hypothesis that the population mean is equal to 500. We would symbolize it as follows and read it, "the null hypothesis is that the population mean is equal to 500":

$$H_0: \mu = 500$$

The term *null* hypothesis arises from earlier agricultural and medical applications of statistics. In order to test the effectiveness of a new fertilizer or drug, the tested hypothesis (the null hypothesis) was that it had *no effect*; that is, there was no difference between treated and untreated samples.

If we use a hypothesized value of a population mean in a problem, we would represent it symbolically as:

$$\mu_{H_0}$$

This is read "the hypothesized value of the population mean."

If our sample results fail to support the null hypothesis, we must conclude that something else is true. Whenever we reject the null hypothesis, the conclusion we do accept is called the *alternative hypothesis* and is symbolized H_1 ("H sub-one"). For the null hypothesis:

$$H_0: \mu = 200 \quad \text{(read: "the null hypothesis is that the population mean is equal to 200.")}$$

Making a formal statement of the alternative hypothesis

we will consider three possible alternative hypotheses:

$H_1: \mu \neq 200 \leftarrow$ "the alternative hypothesis is that the population mean is *not equal* to 200"

$H_1: \mu > 200 \leftarrow$ "the alternative hypothesis is that the population mean is *greater than* 200"

$H_1: \mu < 200 \leftarrow$ "the alternative hypothesis is that the population mean is *less than* 200"

Interpreting the significance level

Selecting the level of risk prior to the test

The purpose of hypothesis testing is not to question the computed value of the sample statistic but to make a judgment about the *difference* between that sample statistic and a hypothesized population parameter. The next step after stating the null and alternative hypotheses, then, is to decide what criterion to use for deciding whether to accept or reject the null hypothesis.

In our sports complex example, we decided that a difference observed between the sample mean $\bar{x}$ and the hypothesized population mean μ_{H_0} had only a 4.5 percent, or .045, chance of occurring. Therefore, we *rejected* the null hypothesis that the population mean was .04 inches ($H_0: \mu = .04$ inches). In statistical terms, the value .045 is called the *significance level*.

Function of the significance level

What if we test a hypothesis at the 5 percent level of significance? This means that we will reject the null hypothesis if the difference between the sample statistic and the hypothesized population parameter is so large that it or a larger difference would occur, on the average, only 5 times or fewer in every 100 samples when the hypothesized population parameter is correct. Assuming the hypothesis is correct, then, the significance level indicates the percentage of sample means that is outside of certain limits. (In estimation, you remember, the confidence level indicated the percentage of sample means that fell *within* the defined confidence limits.)

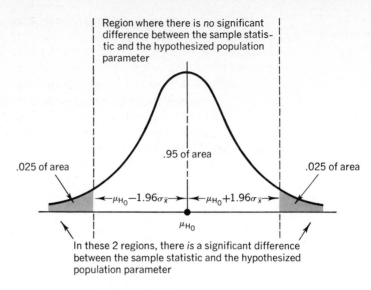

Region where there is *no* significant difference between the sample statistic and the hypothesized population parameter

.95 of area

.025 of area

.025 of area

$\leftarrow \mu_{H_0}-1.96\sigma_{\bar{x}}\rightarrow$ $\leftarrow \mu_{H_0}+1.96\sigma_{\bar{x}}\rightarrow$

μ_{H_0}

In these 2 regions, there *is* a significant difference between the sample statistic and the hypothesized population parameter

Figure 9·2 Regions of significant difference and of no significant difference at a 5 percent level of significance

Area where no significant difference exists

Figure 9 · 2 illustrates how to interpret a 5 percent level of significance. Notice that 2.5 percent of the area under the curve is located in each tail. From Appendix Table 1, we can determine that 95 percent of all the area under the curve is included in an interval extending $1.96\sigma_{\bar{x}}$ on either side of the hypothesized mean. In 95 percent of the area, then, there is no significant difference between the sample statistic and the hypothesized population parameter. In the remaining 5 percent (the shaded regions in Fig. 9 · 2) a significant difference does exist.

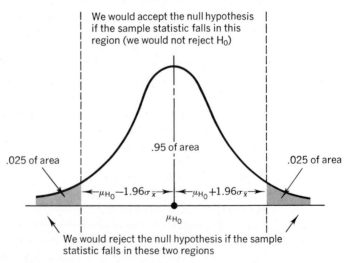

We would accept the null hypothesis if the sample statistic falls in this region (we would not reject H_0)

.95 of area

.025 of area

.025 of area

$\leftarrow \mu_{H_0}-1.96\sigma_{\bar{x}}\rightarrow$ $\leftarrow \mu_{H_0}+1.96\sigma_{\bar{x}}\rightarrow$

μ_{H_0}

We would reject the null hypothesis if the sample statistic falls in these two regions

Figure 9·3 A 5 percent level of significance, with acceptance and rejection regions designated

*Also called
the area where
we accept the
null hypothesis*

Figure $9 \cdot 3$ examines this same example in a different way. Here, the .95 of the area under the curve is where we would accept the null hypothesis. The two shaded parts under the curve, representing a total of 5 percent of the area, are where we would reject the null hypothesis.

A word of caution is appropriate here. Even if our sample statistic in Fig. $9 \cdot 3$ does fall in the nonshaded region (that region comprising 95 percent of the area under the curve), this *does not prove* that our null hypothesis (H_0) is true; it simply does not provide statistical evidence to reject it. Why? Because the only way in which the hypothesis can be accepted with certainty is for us to know the population parameter, and unfortunately this is not possible. Therefore, whenever we say that we accept the null hypothesis, we actually mean that there is not sufficient statistical evidence to reject it. Use of the term *accept*, instead of *do not reject*, has become standard. It means simply that when sample data do not cause us to reject a null hypothesis, we behave as though that hypothesis is true.

Selecting a significance level

There is no single standard or universal level of significance for testing hypotheses. In some instances, a 5 percent level of significance is used. Published research results often test hypotheses at the 1 percent level of significance. It is possible to test a hypothesis at *any* level of significance. But remember that our choice of the minimum standard for an acceptable probability, or the significance level, is also the risk we assume of rejecting a null hypothesis when it is true. The higher the significance level we use for testing a hypothesis, the higher the probability of rejecting a null hypothesis when it is true.

Examining this concept, we refer to Fig. $9 \cdot 4$. Here we have illustrated a hypothesis test at three different significance levels; .01, .10, and .50. Also, we have indicated the location of the same sample mean $\bar{x}$ on each distribution. In parts (a) and (b), we would accept the null hypothesis that the population mean is equal to the hypothesized value. But notice that in part (c) we would reject this same null hypothesis. Why? Our significance level there of .50 is so high that we would rarely accept a null hypothesis when it is *not* true but, at the same time, frequently reject one when it *is* true.

Type I and Type II errors

Statisticians give specific definitions and symbols to the concept illustrated in Fig. $9 \cdot 4$. Rejecting a null hypothesis when it is true is called a Type I error, and its probability (which, as we have seen, is also the significance level of the test) is symbolized α (alpha). Alternately, accepting a null hypothesis when it is false is called a Type II error, and its probability is symbolized β (beta). There is a trade-off between these two

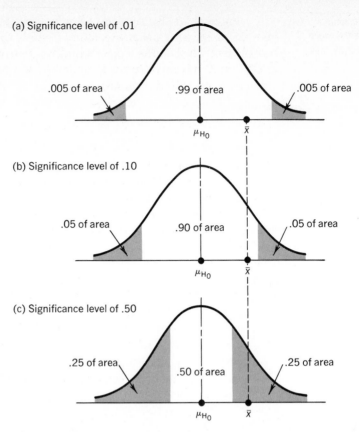

(a) Significance level of .01

.005 of area   .99 of area   .005 of area

μ_{H_0} $\bar{x}$

(b) Significance level of .10

.05 of area   .90 of area   .05 of area

μ_{H_0} $\bar{x}$

(c) Significance level of .50

.25 of area   .50 of area   .25 of area

μ_{H_0} $\bar{x}$

Figure 9·4   Three different levels of significance

types of errors: the probability of making one type of error can only be reduced if we are willing to increase the probability of making the other type of error. Notice in Fig. 9 · 4(c) that our acceptance region is quite small (.50 of the area under the curve). With an acceptance region this small, we will rarely accept a null hypothesis when it is not true, but as a cost of being this sure, we will frequently reject a null hypothesis when it is true. Put another way, in order to get a low β, we will have to put up with a high α. To deal with this trade-off in personal and professional situations, decision makers decide the appropriate level of significance by examining the costs or penalties attached to both types of errors.

Preference for
a Type I error

Suppose that making a Type I error (rejecting a null hypothesis when it is true) involves the time and trouble of reworking a batch of chemicals that should have been accepted. At the same time, making a Type II error (accepting a null hypothesis when it is false) means taking a chance that an entire group of users of this chemical compound will be poisoned. Obviously, the management of this company will prefer a Type I error to a Type II error and, as a result, will set very high levels of significance in its testing to get low β's.

Suppose, on the other hand, that making a Type I error involves disassembling an entire engine at the factory, but making a Type II error involves relatively inexpensive warranty repairs by the dealers. Then the manufacturer is more likely to prefer a Type II error and will set low significance levels in its testing.

Deciding which distribution to use in hypothesis testing

After deciding what level of significance to use, our next task in hypothesis testing is to determine the appropriate probability distribution. We have a choice between the normal distribution, Appendix Table 1, and the t distribution, Appendix Table 2. The rules for choosing the appropriate distribution are similar to those we encountered in Chapter 8. Table 9 · 1 summarizes when to use the normal and t distributions in making tests of means. Later in this chapter, we shall examine the distributions appropriate for testing hypotheses about proportions.

Remember one more rule when testing the hypothesized value of a mean. As in estimation, use the *finite population multiplier* whenever the population is finite in size, sampling is done without replacement, and the sample is more than 5 percent of the population.

Two-tailed and one-tailed tests of hypotheses

In the tests of hypothesized population means that follow, we shall illustrate two-tailed tests and one-tailed tests. These new terms need a word of explanation. A *two-tailed test* of a hypothesis will reject the null hypothesis if the sample mean is significantly higher than *or* lower than the hypothesized population mean. Thus, in a two-tailed test, there are *two* rejection regions. This is illustrated in Fig. 9 · 5.

A two-tailed test is appropriate when the null hypothesis is $\mu = \mu_{H_0}$ (μ_{H_0} being some specified value) and the alternative hypothesis is $\mu \neq \mu_{H_0}$. Assume that a manufacturer of light bulbs wants to produce bulbs with a

TABLE 9 · 1 Conditions for using the normal and t distributions in testing hypotheses about means

	When the population standard deviation is known	*When the population standard deviation is not known*
Sample size n is larger than 30	Normal distribution, z table	Normal distribution, z table
Sample size n is 30 or less and we assume the population is normal or approximately so	Normal distribution, z table	t distribution, t table

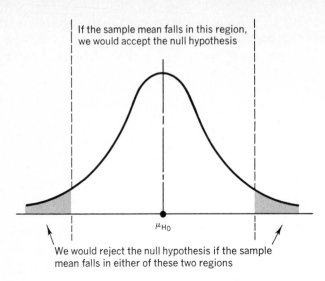

If the sample mean falls in this region,
we would accept the null hypothesis

μ_{H_0}

We would reject the null hypothesis if the sample
mean falls in either of these two regions

Figure 9·5 Two-tailed test of a hypothesis, showing the two rejection regions

mean life of $\mu = \mu_{H_0} = 1,000$ hours. If the lifetime is shorter, he will lose customers to his competition; if the lifetime is longer, he will have a very high production cost because the filaments will be excessively thick. In order to see if his production process is working properly, he takes a sample of the output to test the hypothesis H_0: $\mu = 1,000$. Since he does not want to deviate significantly from 1,000 hours *in either direction*, the appropriate alternative hypothesis is H_1: $\mu \neq 1,000$, and he uses a two-tailed test. That is, he rejects the null hypothesis if the mean life of bulbs in the sample is *either too far above* 1,000 hours *or too far below* 1,000 hours.

Conditions when a two-tailed test may not be appropriate and we must use a one-tailed test

However, there are situations in which a two-tailed test is not appropriate, and we must use a one-tailed test. Consider the case of a wholesaler that buys light bulbs from the manufacturer discussed above. The wholesaler buys bulbs in large lots and does not want to accept a lot of bulbs unless their mean life is 1,000 hours. As each shipment arrives, the wholesaler tests a sample to decide whether it should accept the shipment. The company will reject the shipment only if it feels that the mean life is below 1,000 hours. If it feels that the bulbs are better than expected (with a mean life above 1,000 hours), it certainly will not reject the shipment, because the longer life comes at no extra cost. So the wholesaler's hypotheses are: H_0: $\mu = 1,000$ hours and H_1: $\mu < 1,000$ hours. It rejects H_0 only if the mean life of the sampled bulbs is significantly *below* 1,000 hours. This situation is illustrated in Fig. 9 · 6. From this figure we can see why this test called a *left-tailed test* (or a *lower-tailed test*).

In general, a left-tailed (lower-tailed) test is used if the hypotheses are H_0: $\mu = \mu_{H_0}$ and H_1: $\mu < \mu_{H_0}$. In such a situation, it is sample evidence with the sample mean significantly below the hypothesized

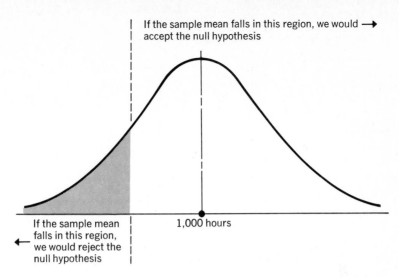

If the sample mean falls in this region, we would → accept the null hypothesis

1,000 hours

If the sample mean falls in this region, we would reject the null hypothesis ←

Figure 9·6 Left-tailed test (a lower-tailed test) with the rejection region on the left side (lower side)

population mean that leads us to reject the null hypothesis in favor of the alternative hypothesis. Stated differently, the rejection region is in the lower tail (left tail) of the distribution of the sample mean, and that is why we call this a lower-tailed test.

Left-tailed tests and right-tailed tests

A left-tailed test is one of the two kinds of one-tailed tests. As you have probably guessed by now, the other kind of one-tailed test is a *right-tailed test* (or an *upper-tailed test*). An upper-tailed test is used when the hypotheses are H_0: $\mu = \mu_{H_0}$ and H_1: $\mu > \mu_{H_0}$. Only values of the sample mean that are *significantly above* the hypothesized population mean will cause us to reject the null hypothesis in favor of the alternative hypothesis. This is called an upper-tailed test because the rejection region is in the upper tail of the distribution of the sample mean.

The following situation is illustrated in Fig. 9 · 7; it calls for the use of an upper-tailed test. A sales manager has asked her salespersons to observe a limit on traveling expenses. The manager hopes to keep expenses to an average of $100 per salesperson per day. One month after the limit is imposed, a sample of submitted daily expenses is taken to see if the limit is being observed. The null hypothesis is H_0: $\mu = \$100.00$, but the manager is concerned only with excessively high expenses. Thus, the appropriate alternative hypothesis is H_1: $\mu > \$100.00$, and an upper-tailed test is used. The null hypothesis is rejected (and corrective measures taken) only if the sample mean is significantly higher than $100.00.

Finally, we should remind you again that in each example of hypothesis testing, when we accept a null hypothesis on the basis of sample information, we are really saying that there is no statistical

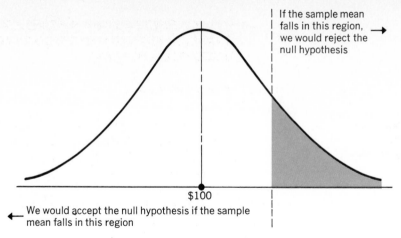

Figure 9·7 Right-tailed (upper-tailed) test

evidence to reject it. We are not saying that the null hypothesis is true. The only way to prove a null hypothesis is to know what the population parameter is, and that is not possible with sampling. Thus, we accept the null hypothesis and behave as though it is true simply because we can find no evidence to reject it.

───────────── **EXERCISES** ─────────────

9·11 Formulate the null and alternative hypotheses to test whether the mean lifetime for men is 68 years.

9·12 Describe what the null and alternative hypotheses typically represent in the hypothesis testing process.

9·13 Define the term *significance level*.

9·14 Define Type I and Type II errors.

9·15 In a trial, the null hypothesis is that an individual is innocent of a certain crime. Would the legal system prefer to commit a Type I or a Type II error with this hypothesis?

9·16 For the following cases, specify which probability distribution to use in a hypothesis test:
a) $H_0: \mu = 1024$ $H_1: \mu \neq 1024$, $\bar{x} = 976$, $\sigma = 60$, $n = 30$
b) $H_0: \mu = 100$ $H_1: \mu > 100$, $\bar{x} = 107$, $s = 3.2$, $n = 16$
c) $H_0: \mu = 500$ $H_1: \mu > 500$, $\bar{x} = 508$, $s = 4$, $n = 40$

9·17 If you have decided that a one-tailed test is the appropriate test to use, how do you decide whether it should be a lower-tailed test or an upper-tailed test?

9·18 Martha Inman, a highway safety engineer, decides to test the load-bearing capacity of a bridge that is 20 years old. Considerable data are available from similar tests on the same type of bridge. Which is appropriate, a one-tailed or a two-tailed test? If the minimum load-bearing capacity of this bridge must be 10 tons, what are the null and alternative hypotheses?

4 HYPOTHESIS TESTING OF MEANS— SAMPLES WITH POPULATION STANDARD DEVIATIONS KNOWN

Two-tailed tests of means

Setting up the problem symbolically

A manufacturer supplies the rear axles for U.S. Postal Service mail trucks. These axles must be able to withstand 80,000 pounds per square inch in stress tests, but an excessively strong axle raises production costs significantly. Long experience indicates that the standard deviation of the strength of its axles is 4,000 pounds per square inch. The manufacturer selects a sample of 100 axles from the latest production run, tests them, and finds that the mean stress capacity of the sample is 79,600 pounds per square inch. Written symbolically, the data in this case are:

μ_{H_0} = 80,000 ← hypothesized value of the population mean
σ = 4,000 ← population standard deviation
n = 100 ← sample size
$\bar{x}$ = 79,600 ← sample mean

If the axle manufacturer uses a significance level (α) of .05 in testing, will the axles meet his stress requirements? Symbolically, we can state the problem:

$H_0: \mu = 80,000$ ← null hypothesis: the true mean is 80,000 pounds per square inch
$H_1: \mu \neq 80,000$ ← alternative hypothesis: the true mean is not 80,000 pounds per square inch
$\alpha = .05$ ← level of significance for testing this hypothesis

Calculating the standard error of the mean

Since we know the population standard deviation, and since the size of the population is large enough to be treated as infinite, we can use the normal distribution in our testing. First, we calculate the standard error of the mean using Equation 7 · 1:

$$\sigma_{\bar{x}} = \frac{\sigma}{\sqrt{n}} = \frac{4,000}{\sqrt{100}}$$

= 400 pounds per square inch ← standard error of the mean

$$(7 \cdot 1)$$

Illustrating the problem

Figure 9 · 8 illustrates this problem, showing the significance level of .05 as the two shaded regions that each contain .025 of the area. The .95 acceptance region contains two equal areas of .475 each. From the normal distribution table (Appendix Table 1), we can see that the appropriate *z* value for .475 of the area under the curve is 1.96. Now we

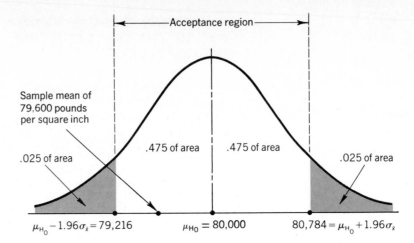

Figure 9·8 Two-tailed hypothesis test at .05 significance level, showing acceptance region and sample mean

Determining the limits of the acceptance region

can determine the limits of the acceptance region:

$$\mu_{H_0} \pm 1.96\sigma_{\bar{x}} = 80{,}000 \pm 1.96(400)$$

$$= 80{,}784 \text{ pounds per square inch} \leftarrow \text{upper limit}$$

$$\text{and} \quad 79{,}216 \text{ pounds per square inch} \leftarrow \text{lower limit}$$

Interpreting the results

These two limits of the acceptance region (80,784 and 79,216) are shown in Fig. 9 · 8. Also, we have indicated the sample mean (79,600 pounds per square inch). Obviously, the sample mean lies within the acceptance region; the manufacturer should accept the null hypothesis, because there is no significant difference between the hypothesized mean of 80,000 and the observed mean of the sample axles. On the basis of this sample, the manufacturer should accept the production run as meeting the stress requirements.

One-tailed tests of means

For a one-tailed test of a mean, suppose a hospital uses large quantities of packaged doses of a particular drug. The individual dose of this drug is 100 cubic centimeters (100 cc). The action of the drug is such that the body will harmlessly pass off excessive doses. On the other hand, insufficient doses do not produce the desired medical effect, and they interfere with patient treatment. The hospital has purchased its requirements of this drug from the same manufacturer for a number of years and knows that the population standard deviation is 2 cc. The hospital inspects 50 doses of this drug at random from a very large shipment and finds the mean of these doses to be 99.75 cc.

$$\mu_{H_0} = 100 \leftarrow \text{hypothesized value of the population mean}$$
$$\sigma = 2 \leftarrow \text{population standard deviation}$$
$$n = 50 \leftarrow \text{sample size}$$
$$\bar{x} = 99.75 \leftarrow \text{sample mean}$$

*Setting up
the problem
symbolically*

If the hospital sets a .10 significance level and asks us whether the dosages in this shipment are too small, how can we find the answer? To begin, we can state the problem symbolically:

$H_0: \mu = 100 \leftarrow$ null hypothesis: the mean of the shipments' dosages is 100 cc.
$H_1: \mu < 100 \leftarrow$ alternative hypothesis: the mean is less than 100 cc.
$\alpha = .10 \leftarrow$ level of significance for testing this hypothesis

*Calculating
the standard error
of the mean*

Then we can calculate the standard error of the mean, using the known population standard deviation and Equation 7 · 1 (because the population size is large enough to be considered infinite):

$$\sigma_{\bar{x}} = \frac{\sigma}{\sqrt{n}} = \frac{2}{\sqrt{50}} = .2829 \text{ cc} \leftarrow \text{standard error of the mean} \quad (7 \cdot 1)$$

*Illustrating
the problem*

The hospital wishes to know whether the actual dosages are 100 cc or whether, in fact, the dosages are too small. The hospital must determine that the dosages are *more* than a certain amount, or it must reject the shipment. This is a *left-tailed* test, which we have shown graphically in Fig. 9 · 9. Notice that the shaded region corresponds to the .10 significance level. Also notice that the acceptance region consists of 40 percent on the left side of the distribution *plus* the entire right side (50 percent), for a total area of 90 percent. Since we know the population standard deviation, and *n* is larger than 30, we can use the normal distribution. From the Appendix Table 1, we can determine that the

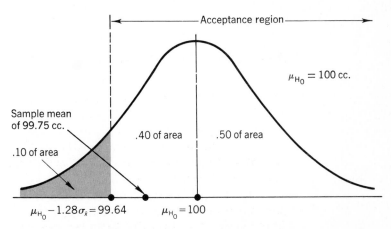

Figure 9 · 9 Left-tailed hypothesis test at .10 significance level, showing acceptance region and the sample mean

Determining the limit of the acceptance region

appropriate z value for 40 percent of the area under the curve is 1.28. Using this information, we can calculate the acceptance region's *lower* limit:

$$\mu_{H_0} - 1.28\sigma_{\bar{x}} = 100 - 1.28(.2829) = 99.64 \text{ cc} \leftarrow \text{lower limit}$$

Interpreting the results

This lower limit of the acceptance region, 99.64 cc, and the sample mean, 99.75, are both shown in Fig. 9 · 9. In this figure, we can see that the sample mean lies within the acceptance region. Therefore, the hospital should accept the null hypothesis because there is no significant difference between our hypothesized mean of 100 cc and the observed mean of the sample. On the basis of this sample of 50 doses, the hospital should accept the doses in the shipment as being sufficient.

--- **EXERCISES** ---

9 · 19 Atlas Sporting Goods has implemented a special trade promotion for its propane stove, and it suspects that the promotion may have resulted in a price change for the consumer. Atlas knows that before the promotion began, the average retail price of the stove was $34, with a standard deviation of $4.20. Atlas sampled 25 of its retail distributors after the promotion began and found the mean price for the stoves was $32.40. At a .05 significance level, using a two-tailed test, does Atlas have reason to believe that the average retail price to the consumer has changed?

9 · 20 Hinton Press hypothesizes that the life of its largest web press is 13,000 hours, with a known standard deviation of 2,000 hours. From a sample of 16 presses, the company finds the sample mean to be 12,000 hours. At a .01 level of significance, should the company conclude that the average life of the presses is less than the hypothesized 13,000 hours?

9 · 21 A computer leasing firm has stated that the average monthly cost for a certain model is $4,800, with a population standard deviation of $900. The firm has sampled 40 of its customers who lease this model and found that the average monthly cost is $4,500. At a 5 percent significance level, is the firm overestimating the cost for this model?

9 · 22 Marshall Bank and Trust Company offers a telephone bill paying service for its customers. Originally, the bank charged $0.05 per bill, and found that customers using the service paid an average of 9.5 bills per month through the bank, with a standard deviation of 4 bills. Last month the bank withdrew the service charge and offered the service free. This month, the bank sampled 36 accounts and found that the average number of bills paid through the service was 10.5. Using a significance level of .02, should the bank conclude that the change to free service has led to an increase in the number of bills per account paid through the service?

5 MEASURING THE POWER OF A HYPOTHESIS TEST

Now that we have considered two examples of hypothesis testing, a step back is appropriate, to discuss what a good hypothesis test *should* do. Ideally, α and β (the probabilities of Type I and Type II errors) should both be small. Recall that a Type I error occurs when we reject a null hypothesis that is true, and that α (the significance level of the test) *is* the probability of making a Type I error. In other words, once we decide upon the significance level, there is nothing else we can do about α. A Type II error occurs when we accept a null hypothesis that is false; the probability of a Type II error is β. What can we say about β?

*Meaning of β
and $1 - \beta$*

Suppose the null hypothesis *is* false. Then managers would like the hypothesis test to reject it all the time. Unfortunately, hypothesis tests cannot be foolproof; sometimes when the null hypothesis is false, a test does not reject it, and thus a Type II error is made. When the null hypothesis is false, μ (the *true* population mean) does not equal μ_{H_0} (the *hypothesized* population mean); instead, μ equals some other value. For each possible value of μ for which the alternative hypothesis is true, there is a different probability (β) of incorrectly accepting the null hypothesis. Of course, we would like this β (the probability of accepting a null hypothesis when it is false) to be as small as possible, or equivalently, we would like $1 - \beta$ (the probability of rejecting a null hypothesis when it is false) to be as large as possible.

*Interpreting
the values of $1 - \beta$*

Since rejecting a null hypothesis when it is false is exactly what a good test ought to do, a high value of $1 - \beta$ (something near 1.0) means the test is working quite well (it is rejecting the null hypothesis when it is false); a low value of $1 - \beta$ (something near 0.0) means that the test is working very poorly (it's not rejecting the null hypothesis when it is false). Since the value $1 - \beta$ is the measure of how well the test is working, it is known as the *power of the test*. If we plot the values of $1 - \beta$ for each value of μ for which the alternative hypothesis is true, the resulting curve is known as a *power curve*.

*Computing
the values
of $1 - \beta$*

In Fig. 9 · 10(a), we have reproduced the left-tailed test first introduced in Fig. 9 · 9. In Fig. 9 · 10(b), we show the power curve that is associated with this test. Computing the values of $1 - \beta$ to plot the power curve is not difficult; three such points are shown in Fig. 9 · 10(b). Recall that with this test we were deciding whether or not to accept a drug shipment. Our test dictated that we should reject the null hypothesis if the sample mean dosage is less than 99.64 cc.

Consider point C on the power curve in Fig. 9 · 10(b). The population mean dosage is 99.42 cc. Given that the population mean is 99.42 cc, we must compute the probability that the mean of a random sample of 50 doses from this population will be less than 99.64 cc (the point below which we decided to reject the null hypothesis). Now look at Fig. 9 · 10(c). On page 255 we computed the standard error of the mean to be .2829 cc, so 99.64 cc is (99.64 − 99.42)/.2829, or .78 standard error above 99.42 cc. Using Appendix Table 1, we can see that the probability of observing a sample mean less than 99.64 cc and thus rejecting the null hypothesis is .7823, the shaded area in Fig. 9 · 10(c). Thus the power of the test ($1 - \beta$) at $\mu = 99.42$ is .7823. This simply means that at $\mu =$

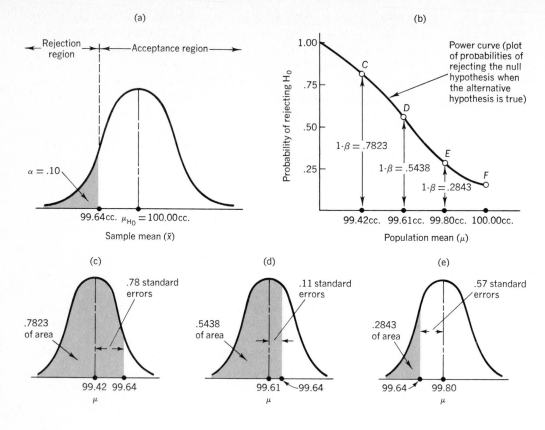

Figure 9·10 Left-tailed hypothesis test, associated power curve, and three values of μ

99.42, the probability that this test will reject the null hypothesis when it is false is .7823.

Now look at point D in Fig. 9 · 10(b). For this population mean dosage of 99.61 cc, what is the probability that the mean of a random sample of 50 doses from this population will be less than 99.64 cc and thus cause the test to reject the null hypothesis? Look at Fig. 9 · 10(d). Here we see that 99.64 is (99.64 − 99.61)/.2829, or .11 standard errors above 99.61 cc. Using Appendix Table 1 again, we can see that the probability of observing a sample mean less than 99.64 cc and thus rejecting the null hypothesis is .5438, the colored area in Fig. 9 · 10(d). Thus the power of the test (1 − β) at μ = 99.61 cc is .5438.

Termination point of the power curve

Using the same procedure at point E, we find the power of the test at μ = 99.80 cc is .2843; this is illustrated as the colored area in Fig. 9 · 10(e). The values of 1 − β continue to decrease to the right of point E. How low do they get? As the population mean gets closer and closer to 100.00 cc, the power of the test (1 − β) must get closer and closer to the probability of rejecting the null hypothesis when the population mean is exactly 100.00 cc. And we know *that* probability is nothing but the significance level of the test, in this case .10. Thus the curve terminates at point *F*, which lies at a height of .10 directly over the population mean.

Interpreting the power curve

What does our power curve in Fig. 9 · 10(b) tell us? Just that as the shipment becomes less satisfactory (as the doses in the shipment become smaller), our test is more powerful (it has a greater probability of recognizing that the shipment is unsatisfactory). It also shows us, however, that because of sampling error, when the dosage is only slightly less than 100.00 cc the power of the test to recognize this situation is quite low. Thus if having *any* dosage below 100.00 cc is completely unsatisfactory, the test we have been discussing is not appropriate.

EXERCISES

---

9 · 23 See problem 9 · 22, p. 256. Compute the power of the test for $\mu = 9.5$, 10.0, and 10.5 bills.

9 · 24 In problem 9 · 22, what happens to the power of the test for $\mu = 9.5$, 10.0, and 10.5 bills if the significance level is changed to .01?

---

6 HYPOTHESIS TESTING OF PROPORTIONS— LARGE SAMPLES

Two-tailed tests of proportions

Dealing with proportions

In this section, we'll apply what we have learned about tests concerning means to tests for *proportions* (that is, the proportion of occurrences in a population). But before we apply it, we'll review the important conclusions we made about proportions in Chapter 8. First, remember that the binomial is the theoretically correct distribution to use in dealing with proportions, since the data are discrete, not continuous. As the sample size increases, the binomial distribution approaches the normal in its characteristics, and we can use the normal distribution to approximate the sampling distribution. Specifically, recall that *np and nq each need to be at least 5* before we can use the normal distribution as a substitute for the binomial.

Setting up the problem symbolically

Consider, as an example, a company that is evaluating the promotability of its employees; that is, the proportion of them whose ability, training, and supervisory experience qualify them for promotion to the next higher level of management. The human resources director tells the president that 80 percent, or .8, of the employees in the company are "promotable." The president assembles a special committee to assess the promotability of all the employees. This committee conducts in-depth interviews with 150 employees and finds that in their judgment, only 70 percent of the sample are qualified for promotion.

$p_{H_0} = .8 \leftarrow$ hypothesized value of the population proportion of successes
(judged promotable, in this case)

$q_{H_0} = .2 \leftarrow$ hypothesized value of the population proportion of failures
(judged not promotable)

$n = 150 \leftarrow$ sample size

$\bar{p} = .7 \leftarrow$ sample proportion of promotables

$\bar{q} = .3 \leftarrow$ sample proportion judged not promotable

The president wants to test at the .05 significance level the hypothesis that .8 of the employees are promotable:

$H_0: p = .8 \leftarrow$ null hypothesis: 80 percent of the employees are promotable

$H_1: p \neq .8 \leftarrow$ alternative hypothesis: the proportion of promotable employees is
not 80 percent

$\alpha = .05 \leftarrow$ level of significance for testing the hypothesis

Calculating the standard error of the proportion

To begin, we can calculate the standard error of the proportion, using the hypothesized value of p_{H_0} and q_{H_0} in Equation 8 · 4:

$$\sigma_{\bar{p}} = \sqrt{\frac{p_{H_0} q_{H_0}}{n}} = \sqrt{\frac{(.8)(.2)}{150}} = .0327 \leftarrow \text{standard error of the proportion} \qquad (8 \cdot 4)$$

Illustrating the problem

In this instance, the company wants to know whether the true proportion is larger *or* smaller than the hypothesized proportion. Thus, a two-tailed test of a proportion is appropriate, and we have shown it graphically in Fig. 9 · 11. The significance level corresponds to the two shaded regions, each containing .025 of the area. The acceptance region of .95 is illustrated as two areas of .475 each. Since *np* and *nq* are each larger than 5, we meet the conditions for using the normal approxima-

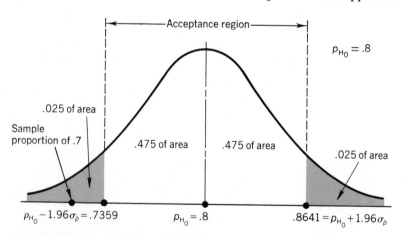

Figure 9 · 11 Two-tailed hypothesis test of a proportion at .05 significance level, showing acceptance region and sample proportion

tion to the binomial distribution. From Appendix Table 1, we can determine that the appropriate z value for .475 of the area under the curve is 1.96. Thus, the limits of the acceptance region are:

$$p_{H_0} \pm 1.96\sigma_{\bar{p}} = .8 \pm 1.96(.0327)$$
$$= .8641 \leftarrow \text{upper limit}$$
$$\text{and} \quad .7359 \leftarrow \text{lower limit}$$

Figure 9 · 11 illustrates these two limits of the acceptance region, .8641 and .7359, as well as our sample proportion, .7. We can see that our sample proportion does *not* lie within the acceptance region. Therefore, in this case the president should reject the null hypothesis and conclude that there *is* a significant difference between the director of human resources' hypothesized proportion of promotable employees (.8) and the observed proportion of promotable employees in the sample. From this, he should infer that the true proportion of promotable employees in the entire company is not 80 percent.

One-tailed tests of proportions

A one-tailed test of a proportion is conceptually equivalent to a one-tailed test of a mean, as can be illustrated with this example. A member of a public interest group concerned with environmental pollution asserts at a public hearing that "fewer than 60 percent of the industrial plants in this area are complying with air pollution standards." Attending this meeting is an official of the Environmental Protection Agency who believes that 60 percent of the plants are complying with the standards; she decides to test that hypothesis at the .02 significance level.

$H_0: p = .6 \leftarrow$ null hypothesis: the proportion of plants complying with air pollution
         standards is .6
$H_1: p < .6 \leftarrow$ alternative hypothesis: the proportion complying with the standards
         is less than .6
   $\alpha = .02 \leftarrow$ level of significance for testing the hypothesis

---

The official makes a thorough search of the records in her office. She samples 60 plants from a population of over 10,000 plants and finds that 33 are complying with air pollution standards. Is the assertion by the member of the public interest group a valid one?

$p_{H_0} = .6 \leftarrow$ hypothesized value of the population proportion that are complying
         with air pollution standards
$q_{H_0} = .4 \leftarrow$ hypothesized value of the population proportion that are not
         complying and thus polluting
   $n = 60 \leftarrow$ sample size
   $\bar{p} = 33/60$ or .55 $\leftarrow$ sample proportion complying
   $\bar{q} = 27/60$ or .45 $\leftarrow$ sample proportion polluting

---

Calculating
the standard error
of the proportion

Next, we can calculate the standard error of the proportion using the hypothesized population proportion as follows:

$$\sigma_{\bar{p}} = \sqrt{\frac{p_{H_0} q_{H_0}}{n}} = \sqrt{\frac{(.6)(.4)}{60}} = .0632 \leftarrow \begin{array}{l}\text{standard error}\\ \text{of the proportion}\end{array} \quad (8 \cdot 4)$$

This is a one-tailed test: the EPA official wonders only whether the actual proportion is less than .6. Specifically, this is a left-tailed test. In order to reject the null hypothesis that the true proportion of plants in compliance is 60 percent, the EPA representative must accept the alternative hypothesis that fewer than .6 have complied. In Fig. 9 · 12 we have shown this hypothesis test graphically.

Since np and nq are each more over 5, we satisfy the conditions for using the normal approximation to the binomial distribution. The appropriate z value from Appendix Table 1 for .48 of the area under the curve is 2.05. Thus, we can calculate the limit of the acceptance region as follows:

$$p_{H_0} - 2.05\sigma_{\bar{p}} = .6 - 2.05(.0632)$$

$$= .47 \leftarrow \text{lower limit}$$

Figure 9 · 12 illustrates the limit of the acceptance region, .47, and the sample proportion, .55, (33/60). Looking at this figure, we can see that the sample proportion lies within the acceptance region. Therefore, the EPA official should accept the null hypothesis that the true proportion of complying plants is .6. Although the observed sample proportion is below .6, *it is not significantly below* .6; that is, it is not far enough below .6 to make us accept the assertion by the member of the public interest

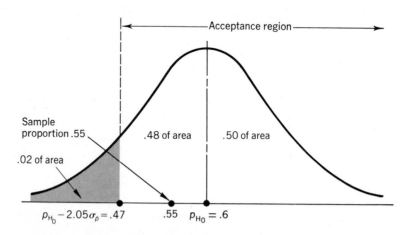

Figure 9 · 12 One-tailed (left-tailed) hypothesis test at .02 significance level, showing acceptance region and sample proportion

9·25 From a total of 8,000 loans made by a state's employees' credit union in the most recent 5-year period, 300 were sampled to determine what proportion were made to women. This sample showed 37 percent of the loans made by the credit union were made to women employees. A similar study made 5 years ago showed that 32 percent of the borrowers were women. At a significance level of .10, has there been a significant change in the proportion of women receiving loans?

9·26 Grant, Inc., a manufacturer of men's dress shirts, knows that its brand is carried in 15 percent of the men's clothing stores in the U.S. Grant recently sampled 75 men's clothing stores on the West Coast and found that 18.7 percent of the stores sampled carried the brand. At the .05 level of significance, is there evidence that Grant has better distribution on the West Coast than nationally?

9·27 Marvin Hendrix, brand manager of a fluoride toothpaste, knows that his brand has consistently been favored by 58 percent of the population. However, a competitor has increased its advertising budget in the past year; and from a recent sample of 500 consumers, the proportion preferring Hendrix's brand was 54 percent.
a) At the .10 level of significance, should Hendrix conclude that his brand's share has declined?
b) Reconsider the question in part a at the .05 level of significance.

7 HYPOTHESIS TESTING OF MEANS UNDER DIFFERENT CONDITIONS

When to use the t distribution

When we estimated confidence intervals in Chapter 8, we learned that the difference in size between large and small samples is important when the population standard deviation σ is unknown and must be estimated from the sample standard deviation. If the sample size n is 30 or less and σ is not known, we should use the t distribution. The appropriate t distribution has $n - 1$ degrees of freedom. These rules apply to hypothesis testing, too.

Two-tailed tests of means using the t distribution

Setting up the problem symbolically

A personnel specialist of a major corporation is recruiting a large number of employees for an overseas assignment. During the testing process, management asks how things are going, and she replies, "Fine. I think the average score on the aptitude test will be 90." When management reviews 20 of the test results compiled, it finds that the mean score is 84, and the standard deviation of this score is 11.

$\mu_{H_0} = 90 \leftarrow$ hypothesized value of the population mean
$n = 20 \leftarrow$ sample size
$\bar{x} = 84 \leftarrow$ sample mean
$s = 11 \leftarrow$ sample standard deviation

If management wants to test her hypothesis at the .10 level of significance, what is the procedure?

H_0: $\mu = 90 \leftarrow$ null hypothesis: the true population mean score is 90
H_1: $\mu \neq 90 \leftarrow$ alternative hypothesis: the mean score is not 90
$\alpha = .10 \leftarrow$ level of significance for testing this hypothesis

---

Since the population standard deviation is not known, we must eliminate it using the sample standard deviation and Equation 8 · 1:

$$\hat{\sigma} = s = 11 \qquad\qquad (8 \cdot 1)$$

Now we can compute the standard error of the mean. Since we are using $\hat{\sigma}$, an estimate of the population standard deviation, the standard error of the mean will also be an estimate. We can use Equation 8 · 6 as follows:

$$\hat{\sigma}_{\bar{x}} = \frac{\hat{\sigma}}{\sqrt{n}} = \frac{11}{\sqrt{20}} = 2.46 \leftarrow \text{estimated standard error of the mean}$$

$$(8 \cdot 6)$$

*Illustrating
the problem*

Figure 9 · 13 illustrates this problem graphically. Since management is interested in knowing whether the true mean score is *larger or smaller* than the hypothesized score, a *two-tailed* test is the appropriate one to use. The significance level of .10 is shown in Fig. 9 · 13 as the two shaded areas, each containing .05 of the area under the t distribution. Since the sample size is 20, the appropriate number of degrees of freedom is 19; that is, $20 - 1$. Therefore, we look in the t-distribution table, Appendix Table 2, under the .10 column until we reach the 19 degrees of freedom row. There we find the t value 1.729.

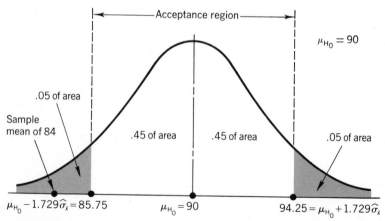

Figure 9 · 13 Two-tailed hypothesis test at .10 level of significance, showing acceptance region and the sample mean

This value is the appropriate one to use in calculating the limits of the acceptance region:

Determining
the limits of the
acceptance region

$$\mu_{H_0} \pm 1.729\hat{\sigma}_{\bar{x}} = 90 \pm 1.729(2.46)$$

$$= 94.25 \leftarrow \text{upper limit}$$

$$\text{and} \quad 85.75 \leftarrow \text{lower limit}$$

*Interpreting
the results*

Figure 9 · 13 illustrates these two limits of the acceptance region, 94.25 and 85.75, and sample mean, 84. We can see that the sample mean lies outside the acceptance region. Therefore, management should reject the null hypothesis (the personnel specialist's assertion that the true mean score of the employees being tested is 90).

One-tailed tests of means using the t distribution

*One difference
from the z tables*

The procedure for a one-tailed hypothesis test using the *t* distribution is the same conceptually as for a one-tailed test using the normal distribution and the *z* table. Performing such one-tailed tests may cause some difficulty, however. Notice that the column headings in Appendix Table 2 represent the *area in both tails combined*. Thus, they are appropriate to use in a two-tailed test with *two* rejection regions.

*Using the t tables
for one-tailed
tests*

If we use the *t* distribution for a one-tailed test, we need to determine the area located in only one tail. So to find the appropriate *t* value for a one-tailed test at a significance level of .05 with 12 degrees of freedom, we would look in Appendix Table 2 under the .10 column opposite the 12 degrees of freedom row. The answer in this case is 1.782. This is true because the .10 column represents .10 of the area under the curve contained in *both tails combined*, and so it also represents .05 of the area under the curve contained in each of the tails separately.

─────────────────── **EXERCISES** ───────────────────

9·28 For a sample of 50 taken from a population of 2,000, the sample mean is 105.1 and the sample standard deviation is 21.5. Using the .05 level of significance, test the hypothesis that the true population mean is 102, against the alternative that it is some other value.

9·29 Given a sample mean of 19.1, a sample standard deviation of 4, and a sample of size 25, test the hypothesis that the value of the population mean is 17, against the alternative that it is greater than 17. Use the .01 significance level.

9·30 If a sample of 10 observations reveals a sample mean of 12 and a sample variance of 1.96, test the hypothesis that the population mean is 13, against the alternative that it is some other value. Use the .05 level of significance.

9·31 The present best-selling remedy for headaches is reported to bring relief in 15 minutes. In a pilot study of 9 individuals, scientists at a pharmaceutical company found that their new formula brought relief in an average of 13.5 minutes, with a standard deviation of 1.2 minutes. At the .025 level of significance, is there reason to believe that the average relief time for the new medication is shorter than that for the old?

---

8 HYPOTHESIS TESTING FOR DIFFERENCES BETWEEN MEANS AND PROPORTIONS

Comparing two populations

In many decision-making situations, people need to determine whether the parameters of two populations are alike or different. A company may want to test, for example, whether its female employees receive lower salaries than its male employees for the same work. A training director may wish to determine whether the proportion of promotable employees at one government installation is different from that at another. A drug manufacturer may need to know whether a new drug causes one reaction in one group of experimental animals but a different reaction in another group.

In each of these examples, decision makers are concerned with the parameters of two populations. In these situations, they are not as interested in the actual value of the parameters as they are in the *relation between* the values of the two parameters, that is, how these parameters differ. *Do* female employees earn less than male employees for the same work? *Is* the proportion of promotable employees at one installation different from that at another? *Did* one group of experimental animals react differently from the other? In this section, we shall introduce methods by which these questions can be answered, using hypothesis testing procedures.

Sampling distribution for the difference between two population parameters — basic concepts

A new way to generate a sampling distribution

In Chapter 7, we introduced the concept of the sampling distribution of the mean as the foundation for the work we would do in estimation and hypothesis testing. For a quick review of the sampling distribution of the mean, you may refer to Fig. $7 \cdot 1$ on page 185.

Since we now wish to study two populations, not just one, the sampling distribution of interest is the *sampling distribution of the difference between sample means*. Figure $9 \cdot 14$ may help us conceptualize this particular sampling distribution. At the top of this figure, we have drawn two populations, identified as population 1 and population 2. These two have means of μ_1 and μ_2 and standard deviations of σ_1 and σ_2, respectively. Beneath each population, we show the sampling distribution of the mean for that population. At the bottom of the figure is the sampling distribution of the difference between the sample means.

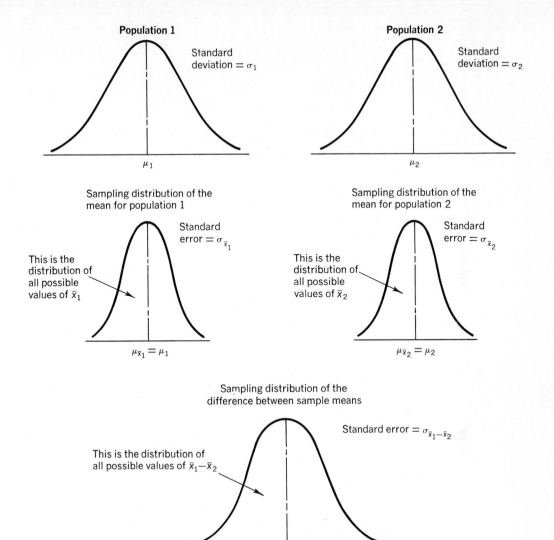

Figure 9 · 14 Basic concepts of population distributions, sampling distributions of the mean, and the sampling distribution of the difference between sample means

Deriving the sampling distribution of the difference between sample means

The two theoretical sampling distributions of the mean in Fig. 9 · 14 are each made up of all the possible samples of a given size that can be drawn from the corresponding population distribution. Now, suppose we take a random sample from the distribution of population 1 and another random sample from the distribution of population 2. If we then subtract the two sample means, we get:

$$\bar{x}_1 - \bar{x}_2 \leftarrow \text{difference between sample means}$$

This difference will be positive if $\bar{x}_1$ is larger than $\bar{x}_2$, and negative if $\bar{x}_2$ is greater than $\bar{x}_1$. By constructing a distribution of *all* the possible sample differences of $\bar{x}_1 - \bar{x}_2$, we end up with the sampling distribution of the difference between sample means, which is shown at the bottom of Fig. 9 · 14.

The mean of the sampling distribution of the difference between sample means is symbolized $\mu_{\bar{x}_1 - \bar{x}_2}$ and is equal to $\mu_{\bar{x}_1} - \mu_{\bar{x}_2}$, which, as we saw in Chapter 7, is the same as $\mu_1 - \mu_2$. If $\mu_1 = \mu_2$, then $\mu_{\bar{x}_1} - \mu_{\bar{x}_2} = 0$.

The standard deviation of the distribution of the difference between the sample means is called the *standard error of the difference between two means* and is calculated using this formula:

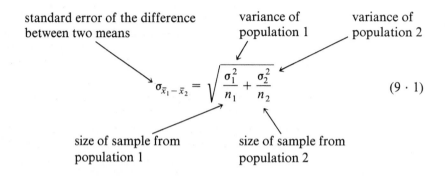

standard error of the difference between two means   variance of population 1   variance of population 2

$$\sigma_{\bar{x}_1 - \bar{x}_2} = \sqrt{\frac{\sigma_1^2}{n_1} + \frac{\sigma_2^2}{n_2}} \qquad (9 \cdot 1)$$

size of sample from population 1   size of sample from population 2

*How to estimate
the standard error
of this sampling
distribution*

If the two population standard deviations are *not* known, we can *estimate* the standard error of the difference between two means. We can use the same method of estimating the standard error that we have used before by letting sample standard deviations estimate the population standard deviations as follows:

$$\hat{\sigma} = s \leftarrow \text{sample standard deviations} \qquad (8 \cdot 1)$$

Therefore, the formula for the estimated standard error of the difference between two means becomes:

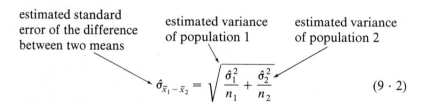

estimated standard error of the difference between two means   estimated variance of population 1   estimated variance of population 2

$$\hat{\sigma}_{\bar{x}_1 - \bar{x}_2} = \sqrt{\frac{\hat{\sigma}_1^2}{n_1} + \frac{\hat{\sigma}_2^2}{n_2}} \qquad (9 \cdot 2)$$

As the following examples show, depending on the sample sizes, we shall use different estimates for $\hat{\sigma}_1$ and $\hat{\sigma}_2$ in Equation 9 · 2.

Two-tailed tests for difference between means (large sample sizes)

*Setting up
the problem
symbolically*

When both sample sizes are greater than 30, this example illustrates how to do a two-tailed test of a hypothesis of the difference between two means. A manpower development statistician is asked to determine whether the hourly wages of semiskilled workers are the same in two cities. The statistician takes simple random samples of hourly earnings in both cities. The results of this survey are presented in Table 9 · 2. Suppose that the company wants to test the hypothesis at the .05 level that there is no difference between hourly wages for semiskilled workers in the two cities:

H_0: $\mu_1 = \mu_2$ ← null hypothesis: there is no difference
H_1: $\mu_1 \neq \mu_2$ ← alternative hypothesis: a difference exists
$\qquad \alpha = .05$ ← level of significance for testing this hypothesis

Since the company is interested only in whether the means are *or* are not equal, this is a two-tailed test.

The standard deviations of the two populations are not known. Therefore, our first step is to estimate them as follows:

$$\hat{\sigma}_1 = s_1 = \$0.40 \qquad \hat{\sigma}_2 = s_2 = \$0.60 \qquad (8 \cdot 1)$$

*Calculating
the standard error
of the difference
between two
means*

Now the estimated standard error of the difference between two means can be determined by:

$$\hat{\sigma}_{\bar{x}_1 - \bar{x}_2} = \sqrt{\frac{\hat{\sigma}_1^2}{n_1} + \frac{\hat{\sigma}_2^2}{n_2}} = \sqrt{\frac{(0.40)^2}{200} + \frac{(0.60)^2}{175}} \qquad (9 \cdot 2)$$

$$= \$0.053 \text{ ← estimated standard error}$$

*Illustrating
the problem*

We can illustrate this hypothesis test graphically. In Figure 9 · 15 the significance level of .05 corresponds to the two shaded areas, each of which contains .025 of the area. The acceptance region contains two equal areas of .475 each. Since both samples are large, we can use the

TABLE 9 · 2 Data from sample survey of hourly wages

City	Mean hourly earnings from sample	Standard deviation of sample	Size of sample
Apex	$6.95	$0.40	200
Eden	7.10	0.60	175

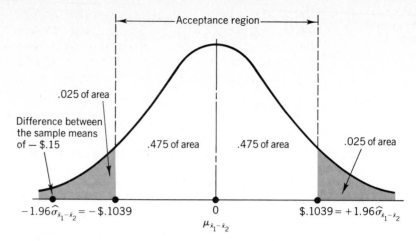

Figure 9·15 Two-tailed hypothesis test of the difference between two means at .05 level of significance, showing acceptance region and difference between sample means

Determining the limits of the acceptance region

normal distribution. From Appendix Table 1, we can determine the appropriate z value for .475 of the area under the curve to be 1.96. Now we can calculate the limits of the acceptance region:

The hypothesized difference between the two population means is zero $\longrightarrow$ $0 \pm 1.96\hat{\sigma}_{\bar{x}_1 - \bar{x}_2} = 0 \pm 1.96(\$0.053)$
$= \$0.1039 \leftarrow$ upper limit
and $-\$0.1039 \leftarrow$ lower limit

Figure 9·15 illustrates these two limits of the acceptance region ($0.1039 and −$0.1039) and indicates the difference between the sample means. It is calculated:

Difference $= \bar{x}_1 - \bar{x}_2$ (from Table 9·2) $= \$6.95 - \$7.10 = -\$0.15$

Figure 9·15 demonstrates that the difference between the two sample means lies outside the acceptance region. Thus, we reject the null hypothesis of no difference and conclude that the population means (the average semi-skilled wages in these two cities) differ.

One-tailed tests for difference between means (small sample sizes)

The procedure for a one-tailed test of the difference between means is conceptually like that for the one-tailed tests of means we have already discussed. The only major difference will be in how we compute the estimated standard error of the difference between the two means. Suppose that a company has been investigating two education programs for increasing the sensitivity of its managers to the needs of its Spanish-speaking employees. The original program consisted of several informal question-and-answer sessions with leaders of the Spanish-speaking community. Over the past few years, a program involving formal classroom contact with professional psychologists and sociologists has been developed. The new program is considerably more expensive and the president wants to know at the .05 level of significance whether this expenditure has resulted in greater sensitivity. Let's test the following:

$H_0: \mu_1 = \mu_2 \leftarrow$ null hypothesis: there is no difference in sensitivity levels achieved by the two programs

$H_1: \mu_1 > \mu_2 \leftarrow$ alternative hypothesis: the new program results in higher sensitivity levels

$\alpha = .05 \leftarrow$ level of significance for testing the hypothesis

---

Table 9·3 contains the data resulting from a sample of the managers trained in both programs. Because only limited data are available for the two programs, the population standard deviations are estimated from the data. The sensitivity level is measured as a percentage on a standard psychometric scale.

The company wishes to test whether the sensitivity achieved by the new program is *significantly higher* than that achieved under the older, more informal program. To reject the null hypothesis (a result that the company desires), the observed difference of sample means would need to fall sufficiently high in the *right* tail of the distribution. Then we would accept the alternative hypothesis that the new program leads to higher sensitivity levels and that the extra expenditures on this program are justified.

Our first task in performing the test is to calculate the standard error of the difference between the two means. Since the population standard deviations are not known, we must use Equation 9·2:

$$\hat{\sigma}_{\bar{x}_1 - \bar{x}_2} = \sqrt{\frac{\hat{\sigma}_1^2}{n_1} + \frac{\hat{\sigma}_2^2}{n_2}} \qquad (9 \cdot 2)$$

In the previous example, where the sample sizes were large (both greater than 30) we used Equation 8·1 and estimated $\hat{\sigma}_1^2$ by s_1^2, and $\hat{\sigma}_2^2$ by s_2^2.

TABLE 9·3   Data from sample of two sensitivity programs

Program sampled	*Mean sensitivity after this program*	*Number of managers observed*	*Estimated standard deviation of sensitivity after this program*
Formal	92%	12	15%
Informal	84%	15	19%

Now, with small sample sizes, that procedure is not appropriate. If we can assume that the unknown population variances are equal we can continue. If we cannot assume that $\sigma_1^2 = \sigma_2^2$, then the problem is beyond the scope of this text.

Estimating
σ^2 with small
sample sizes

Assuming for the moment that $\sigma_1^2 = \sigma_2^2$, how can we estimate the common variance σ^2? If we use either s_1^2 or s_2^2, we get an unbiased estimator of σ^2, but we don't use all of the information available to us since we ignore one of the samples. Instead we use a weighted average of s_1^2 and s_2^2, and the weights are the numbers of degrees of freedom in each sample. This weighted average is called a "pooled estimate" of σ^2. It is given by

$$\text{pooled estimate of } \sigma^2 \rightarrow s_p^2 = \frac{(n_1 - 1)s_1^2 + (n_2 - 1)s_2^2}{n_1 + n_2 - 2} \qquad (9 \cdot 3)$$

Plugging this into Equation 9 · 2 and simplifying gives us

$$\hat{\sigma}_{\bar{x}_1 - \bar{x}_2} = s_p \sqrt{\frac{1}{n_1} + \frac{1}{n_2}} \qquad (9 \cdot 4)$$

When we want to test hypotheses about differences of population means, and we have small samples but equal population variances, we use Equation 9 · 4 to estimate the standard error of the difference between the two means. Then as you might have guessed, the test is based on the t distribution. The appropriate number of degrees of freedom is $(n_1 - 1) + (n_2 - 1)$, or $n_1 + n_2 - 2$, which is the denominator in Equation 9 · 3.

Applying these results to our sensitivity example,

$$s_p^2 = \frac{(n_1 - 1)s_1^2 + (n_2 - 1)s_2^2}{n_1 + n_2 - 2}$$

$$= \frac{(12 - 1)(15)^2 + (15 - 1)(19)^2}{12 + 15 - 2} = 301.160 \qquad (9 \cdot 3)$$

Taking square roots on both sides, we get $s_p = \sqrt{301.160}$ or 17.354, and so

$$\hat{\sigma}_{\bar{x}_1 - \bar{x}_2} = s_p \sqrt{\frac{1}{n_1} + \frac{1}{n_2}}$$

$$= 17.354 \sqrt{\frac{1}{12} + \frac{1}{15}} = 6.721 \qquad (9 \cdot 4)$$

Illustrating
the problem

In Fig. 9 · 16, a graphic illustration of this hypothesis test, the significance level of .05 is represented by the shaded region at the right of the distribution. Sample sizes are less than 30, so the t distribution with $12 + 15 - 2 = 25$ degrees of freedom is the appropriate sampling distribution. The t value for .05 of the area under the curve is 1.708 according

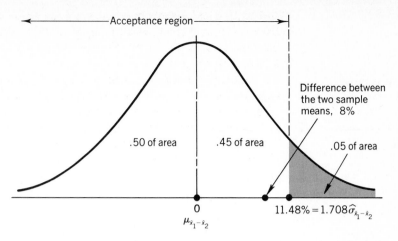

Figure 9·16   One-tailed test of the difference between two means at the .05 level of significance, showing acceptance region and the difference between the sample means

to Appendix Table 2. The value of $\mu_{\bar{x}_1 - \bar{x}_2}$, the mean of the sampling distribution of the hypothesized difference between the two sensitivity means, is equal to zero. Thus, the calculation for determining the limit of the acceptance region is:

$$0 + 1.708\hat{\sigma}_{\bar{x}_1 - \bar{x}_2} = 0 + 1.708(6.721)$$

$$= 0 + 11.48 = 11.48\% \leftarrow \text{upper limit}$$

*Interpreting
the results*

In Fig. 9 · 16 we have illustrated this limit of the acceptance region and the difference between the two sample sensitivities (92% − 84% = 8%). We can see in Fig. 9 · 16 that the difference between the two sample means lies within the acceptance region. Thus, we accept the null hypothesis that there is no difference between the sensitivities achieved by the two programs. The company's expenditures on the formal instructional program have not produced significantly higher sensitivities among its managers.

Testing differences between means with dependent samples

*Conditions
under which
paired samples
aid analysis*

In the last two examples our samples were chosen *independently* of each other. In the wage example, the samples were taken in two different cities. In the sensitivity example, samples were taken of managers who had gone through two different training programs. Sometimes, however, it will make sense to take samples that are not independent of each other. Often the use of such *dependent* (or *paired*) samples will enable us to perform a more precise analysis, because they will allow us to control for extraneous factors. With dependent samples, we still follow the same basic procedure we have followed in all our hypothesis testing. The only differences are that we will use a different formula for the estimated standard error of the sample differences and that we will require that both samples be of the same size.

A health spa has advertised a weight reducing program and has claimed that the average participant in the program loses at least 17 pounds. A somewhat overweight executive is interested in the program but is skeptical about the claims and asks for some hard evidence. The spa allows him to select randomly the records of 10 participants and record their weights before and after the program. These data are recorded in Table 9 · 4. Here we have two samples (a *before* sample and an *after* sample) which are clearly dependent on each other, since the same ten people have been observed twice.

The overweight executive wants to test at the 5 percent significance level the claimed average weight loss of at least 17 pounds. Formally, we may state this problem:

$H_0: \mu_1 - \mu_2 = 17 \leftarrow$ null hypothesis: average weight loss is only 17 pounds
$H_1: \mu_1 - \mu_2 > 17 \leftarrow$ alternative hypothesis: average weight loss exceeds 17 pounds
$\alpha = .05 \leftarrow$ level of significance

Conceptual understanding of differences

What we are really interested in is not the weights before and after but only their *differences*. Conceptually, what we have is *not two samples* of before and after weights, but rather *one sample* of weight losses. If the population of weight losses has a mean μ_l, we can restate our hypotheses as:

$H_0: \mu_l = 17$
$H_1: \mu_l > 17$

Now we compute the individual losses, their mean and standard deviations as usual.

The computations are done in Table 9 · 5.

TABLE 9 · 4 Weights before and after a reducing program

Before	189	202	220	207	194	177	193	202	208	233
After	170	179	203	192	172	161	174	187	186	204

TABLE 9·5 Finding the mean weight loss and its standard deviation

Before	After	Loss (x)	Loss squared (x²)
189	170	19	361
202	179	23	529
220	203	17	289
207	192	15	225
194	172	22	484
177	161	16	256
193	174	19	361
202	187	15	225
208	186	22	484
233	204	29	841
		$\Sigma x = \overline{197}$	$\Sigma x^2 = \overline{4,055}$

$$\bar{x} = \frac{\Sigma x}{n} = \frac{197}{10} = 19.7 \quad (3 \cdot 2) \qquad s = \sqrt{\frac{\Sigma x^2}{n-1} - \frac{n\bar{x}^2}{n-1}} \qquad (4 \cdot 11)$$

$$= \sqrt{\frac{4,055}{9} - \frac{10(19.7)^2}{9}} = 4.40$$

We use Equation 8 · 1 to estimate the unknown population standard deviation:

$$\hat{\sigma} = s = 4.40 \qquad\qquad (8 \cdot 1)$$

and now we can estimate the standard error of the mean:

$$\hat{\sigma}_{\bar{x}} = \frac{\hat{\sigma}}{\sqrt{n}} = \frac{4.40}{\sqrt{10}} = 1.39 \leftarrow \text{estimated standard error of the mean}$$

$$(8 \cdot 6)$$

Figure 9 · 17 illustrates this problem graphically. Since we want to know if the mean weight loss *exceeds* 17 pounds, an upper-tailed test is appropriate. The .05 significance level is shown in Fig. 9 · 17 as the shaded area under the *t* distribution. We use the *t* distribution because the sample size is only 10; the appropriate number of degrees of freedom is 9, (10 − 1). Appendix Table 2 gives the *t* value of 1.833.

We use this *t* value to calculate the upper limit of the acceptance region

$$\mu_{H_0} + 1.833\hat{\sigma}_{\bar{x}} = 17 + 1.833(1.39)$$

$$= 19.55 \text{ pounds} \leftarrow \text{upper limit}$$

Interpreting the results

Figure 9 · 17 also shows the acceptance region and the sample mean 19.7. We see that the sample mean lies outside the acceptance region, so the

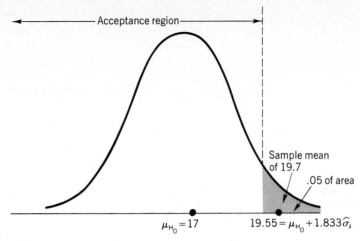

Figure 9·17 One-tailed hypothesis test at .05 level of significance, showing acceptance region and sample mean

executive can reject the null hypothesis and conclude that the claimed weight loss in the program is legitimate.

How does the paired difference test differ?

Let's see how this *paired difference* test differs from a test of the difference of means of *two independent* samples. Suppose that the data in Table 9 · 4 represent two independent samples of 10 individuals *entering* the program and *another* 10 randomly selected individuals *leaving* the program. The means and variances of the two samples are given in Table 9 · 6.

Since the sample sizes are small, we use Equation 9 · 3 to get a pooled estimate of σ^2 and Equation 9 · 4 to estimate $\hat{\sigma}_{\bar{x}_1 - \bar{x}_2}$:

$$s_p^2 = \frac{(n_1 - 1)s_1^2 + (n_2 - 1)s_2^2}{n_1 + n_2 - 2} \qquad (9 \cdot 3)$$

$$= \frac{(10 - 1)(201.96) + (10 - 1)(253.61)}{10 + 10 - 2}$$

$$= 227.79 \leftarrow \text{estimate of common population variance}$$

$$\hat{\sigma}_{\bar{x}_1 - \bar{x}_2} = s_p \sqrt{\frac{1}{n_1} + \frac{1}{n_2}} = \sqrt{227.79} \sqrt{\frac{1}{10} + \frac{1}{10}}$$

$$= 6.79 \leftarrow \text{estimate of } \hat{\sigma}_{\bar{x}_1 - \bar{x}_2} \qquad (9 \cdot 4)$$

TABLE 9·6 Before and after means and variances

Sample	Size	Mean	Variance
Before	10	202.5	253.61
After	10	182.8	201.96

The appropriate test is now based on the t distribution with 18 degrees of freedom $(10 + 10 - 2)$. With a significance level of .05, the appropriate t value from Appendix Table 2 is 1.734, so the upper limit of the acceptance region is

$$17 + 1.734\hat{\sigma}_{\bar{x}_1 - \bar{x}_2} = 17 + 1.734(6.79) = 28.77 \text{ pounds}$$

The observed difference of the sample means is

$$\bar{x}_1 - \bar{x}_2 = 202.5 - 182.8 = 19.7 \text{ pounds}$$

so this test will *not* reject H_0.

Explaining differing results

Why did these two tests give such different results? In the paired sample test, the sample standard deviation of the individual differences was relatively small so 19.7 pounds was significantly larger than the hypothesized weight loss of 17 pounds. With independent samples, however, the estimated standard deviation of the difference between the means depended on the standard deviations of the before weights and the after weights. Since both of these were relatively large, $\hat{\sigma}_{\bar{x}_1 - \bar{x}_2}$ was also large, and thus 19.7 was not significantly larger than 17. The paired sample test controlled this initial and final variability in weights by looking only at the individual changes in weights. Because of this it was better able to detect the significance of the weight loss.

We conclude this section with two examples showing when to treat 2 samples of equal size as dependent or independent.

Should we treat samples as dependent or independent?

1. An agricultural extension service wishes to determine whether a new hybrid seed corn has a greater yield than an old standard variety. If the service asks 10 farmers to record the yield of an acre planted with the new variety and asks another 10 farmers to record the yield of an acre planted with the old variety, the two samples are independent. If, however, it asks 10 farmers to plant one acre with each variety and record the results, then the samples are dependent, and the paired difference test is appropriate. In the latter case, differences due to fertilizer, insecticide, rainfall, etc., are controlled, because each farmer treats his two acres identically. Thus any differences in yield can be attributed solely to the variety planted.

2. The director of the secretarial pool at a large legal office wants to determine whether typing speed depends upon the kind of typewriter used by a secretary. If she tests 7 secretaries using electric typewriters and 7 using manual typewriters, she should treat her samples as independent. If she tests the same 7 secretaries twice (once on each type of machine), then the two samples are dependent. In the paired difference test, differences among the secretaries are eliminated as a contributing factor, and the differences in typing speeds can be attributed to the different types of machines.

Two-tailed tests for difference between proportions

Consider the case of a pharmaceutical manufacturing company testing two new compounds intended to reduce blood pressure levels. The compounds are administered to two different sets of laboratory animals. In group one, 71 of 100 animals tested respond to drug 1 with lower blood pressure levels. In group two, 58 of 90 animals tested respond to drug 2 with lower blood pressure levels. The company wants to test at the .05 level whether there is a difference between the efficacies of these two drugs. How should we proceed with this problem?

As in our previous examples, we can begin by calculating the standard deviation of the sampling distribution we are using in our hypothesis test. In this example, the binomial distribution is the correct sampling distribution.

$\bar{p}_1 = .71 \leftarrow$ sample proportion of successes with drug 1
$\bar{q}_1 = .29 \leftarrow$ sample proportion of failures with drug 1
$n_1 = 100 \leftarrow$ sample size for testing drug 1
$\bar{p}_2 = .644 \leftarrow$ sample proportion of successes with drug 2
$\bar{q}_2 = .356 \leftarrow$ sample proportion of failures with drug 2
$n_2 = 90 \leftarrow$ sample size for testing drug 2

$H_0: p_1 = p_2 \leftarrow$ null hypothesis: there is no difference between these two drugs
$H_1: p_1 \neq p_2 \leftarrow$ alternative hypothesis: there is a difference between them
$\qquad \alpha = .05 \leftarrow$ level of significance for testing this hypothesis

---

Calculating the standard error of the difference between two proportions

We want to find the *standard error of the difference between two proportions*; therefore, we should recall the formula for the *standard error of the proportion*:

$$\sigma_{\bar{p}} = \sqrt{\frac{pq}{n}} \qquad (8 \cdot 4)$$

Using this formula and the same form we previously used in Equation $9 \cdot 1$ for the standard error of the difference between two *means*, we get:

$$\sigma_{\bar{p}_1 - \bar{p}_2} = \sqrt{\frac{p_1 q_1}{n_1} + \frac{p_2 q_2}{n_2}} \qquad (9 \cdot 5)$$

How to estimate this standard error

To test the two compounds, we do not know the population parameters p_1, p_2, q_1 and q_2, and thus we need to estimate them from the sample statistics $\bar{p}_1$, $\bar{p}_2$, $\bar{q}_1$, and $\bar{q}_2$. In this case, we might suppose that the practical formula to use would be:

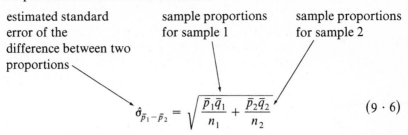

estimated standard error of the difference between two proportions

sample proportions for sample 1

sample proportions for sample 2

$$\hat{\sigma}_{\bar{p}_1-\bar{p}_2} = \sqrt{\frac{\bar{p}_1\bar{q}_1}{n_1} + \frac{\bar{p}_2\bar{q}_2}{n_2}} \qquad (9 \cdot 6)$$

But think about this a bit more. After all, if we hypothesize that there is *no difference* between the two population proportions, then our best estimate of the overall population proportion of successes is probably the *combined* proportion of successes in both samples, that is:

Best estimate of the overall proportion of successes in the population if the 2 proportions are hypothesized to be equal

$$= \frac{\text{Number of successes in sample 1} + \text{Number of successes in sample 2}}{\text{Total size of both samples}}$$

And in the case of the two compounds, we use this equation with symbols rather than words:

$$\hat{p} = \frac{(n_1)(\bar{p}_1) + (n_2)(\bar{p}_2)}{n_1 + n_2} = \frac{(100)(.71) + (90)(.644)}{100 + 90} \qquad (9 \cdot 7)$$

$= .6789 \leftarrow$ estimate of the overall proportion of successes in the combined populations using combined proportions from both samples ($\hat{q}$ would be $1 - .6789 = .3211$)

Now we can appropriately modify Equation 9 · 6 using the values $\hat{p}$ and $\hat{q}$ from Equation 9 · 7.

estimated standard error of the difference between two proportions using combined estimates

estimates of the population proportions using combined proportions from both samples

$$\hat{\sigma}_{\bar{p}_1-\bar{p}_2} = \sqrt{\frac{\hat{p}\hat{q}}{n_1} + \frac{\hat{p}\hat{q}}{n_2}} \qquad (9 \cdot 8)$$

$$= \sqrt{\frac{(.6789)(.3211)}{100} + \frac{(.6789)(.3211)}{90}}$$

$= .0678 \leftarrow$ estimated standard error of the difference between two proportions

What did we save by using Equation 9 · 8 instead of Equation 9 · 6? In Equation 9 · 8 we needed only *one* value for $\hat{p}$ and *one* value for $\hat{q}$; thus we avoided some of the calculations involved in the use of Equation 9 · 6.

Illustrating
the problem

Figure 9 · 18 illustrates this hypothesis test graphically. Since the management of the pharmaceutical company wants to know whether there is a difference between the two compounds, this is a two-tailed test. The significance level of .05 corresponds to the shaded regions in the figure. Both samples are large enough to justify using the normal distribution to approximate the binomial. From Appendix Table 1, we can determine that the appropriate z value for .475 of the area under the curve is 1.96. We can calculate the two limits of the acceptance region as follows:

Determining
the limits of the
acceptance region

$$0 \pm 1.96 \hat{\sigma}_{\bar{p}_1 - \bar{p}_2} = 0 \pm 1.96(.0678)$$
$$= .1329 \leftarrow \text{upper limit}$$

The hypothesized difference
between the 2 proportions is   and $-.1329 \leftarrow$ lower limit
zero

Figure 9 · 18 illustrates these two limits of the acceptance region, .1329 and $-.1329$. It also indicates the difference between the sample proportions, calculated as

$$\text{Difference} = \bar{p}_1 - \bar{p}_2 = .71 - .644 = .066$$

Interpreting
the results

We can see in Fig. 9 · 18 that the difference between the two sample proportions lies within the acceptance region. Thus, we accept the null hypothesis and conclude that the two compounds produce effects on blood pressure that are *not* different.

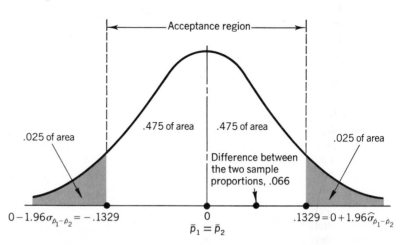

Figure 9 · 18 Two-tailed hypothesis test of the difference between two proportions at the .05 level of significance, showing acceptance region and the difference between sample proportions

How about a one-tailed test of the difference between proportions? You still use Equation 9 · 8 to compute the estimated standard error of the difference between two proportions. Then you use it to compute either the upper limit or lower limit of the acceptance region, whichever is appropriate for the problem at hand. If you understand all the examples of the hypothesis tests we have done so far, you'll have no problem at all with one-tailed tests of differences between proportions.

EXERCISES
---

9 · 32 Elizabeth Kerr, supervisor of a typing pool, is interested in knowing whether typists required to correct their own errors have the same error rate as typists not required to correct their own errors. Of the 40 typists required to correct their own errors, the average number of errors per day is 20.2 with a standard deviation of 2.5. Of the 56 typists not required to correct their own errors, the average number of errors per day is 21.0 with a standard deviation of 3.1. At a significance level of 10 percent, is there a significant difference in the number of errors made by the two kinds of typists?

9 · 33 Two research laboratories have independently produced drugs that provide relief to arthritis sufferers. The first drug was tested on a group of 100 arthritis victims and produced an average of 8.5 hours of relief with a standard deviation of 2 hours. The second drug was tested on 75 arthritis victims, producing an average of 7.8 hours of relief with a standard deviation of 1.5 hours. At the .02 level of significance, does the first drug provide a significantly longer period of relief?

9 · 34 Two different areas of a city are being considered as sites for day-care centers. Of 150 households surveyed in one section, the proportion in which the mother worked full-time was .44. In the other section, 38 percent of the 100 households surveyed had mothers working at full-time jobs. At the .05 level of significance, is there a significant difference in the proportion of working mothers in the two areas of the city?

9 · 35 In order to compare the performance of two training methods, samples of individuals from each of the methods were checked. For the six individuals from training method 1, the mean efficiency score was 35, with a variance of 40. For the eight individuals in training method 2, the mean efficiency score was 27, with a variance of 45.
   a) Compute the standard error of the difference between the two means.
   b) Test whether the efficiency scores by individuals from the two training methods may be concluded to be equal at the .01 level of significance.

9 · 36 The quality control manager of Taylor Sportswear suggested that the piece-rate wage system should be changed so that employees are not paid for defective goods they produce. The company made this change on 10 workers and recorded their daily number of defectives before and after the change. The data is shown below. Test the hypothesis that the change in the wage system reduces defective merchandise. Use the .05 level of significance.

Worker	1	2	3	4	5	6	7	8	9	10
Before	12	14	12	13	15	13	14	13.5	12	12.5
After	9	13	14	10	12	11	13	10	11	13

9 · 37 A mouthwash brand implemented two different trade promotions last year in the U.S. The company divided the country into 9 sales regions; and during the month of each promotion, sales to distributors were recorded (in thousands of cases). The data are given below. Test the hypothesis that the average sales per region (in thousands of cases) during the two promotions were different. Use the .10 level of significance.

Region	1	2	3	4	5	6	7	8	9
Promotion 1	46	54	49	39	42	48	51	55	44
Promotion 2	53	52	49	42	51	50	49	60	43

9 · 38 A coal-fired power plant is comparing two different systems for pollution abatement. The first system has reduced the emission of pollutants to acceptable levels 63 percent of the time, as determined from 200 air samples. The second (and more expensive) system has reduced the emission of pollutants to acceptable levels 79 percent of the time, as determined from 300 air samples. At the .10 level of significance, can management conclude that the more expensive system is not significantly better than the inexpensive system?

9 · 39 A consumer research organization routinely selects several car models a year and tests their claims regarding safety, mileage, and comfort. In one study of two similar subcompact models manufactured by two different automakers, the average gas mileage for 7 cars of make A was 21 miles per gallon with a standard deviation of 5.8. For 9 cars of make B, the average gas mileage was 26 miles per gallon with a standard deviation of 5.3 miles per gallon. Test the hypothesis that the average gas mileage for cars of make B is greater than the average gas mileage for cars of make A at the .05 level of significance.

---

9 TERMS INTRODUCED IN CHAPTER 9

alpha (α) The probability of a Type I error.

alternative hypothesis The conclusion we accept when the data fail to support the null hypothesis.

beta (β) The probability of a Type II error.

dependent samples Samples drawn from two populations in such a way that the elements were not chosen independently of one another, in order to allow a more precise analysis or to control for some extraneous factors.

hypothesis An assumption or speculation we make about a population parameter.

lower-tailed test A one-tailed hypothesis test in which a sample value significantly below the hypothesized population value will lead us to reject the null hypothesis.

null hypothesis The hypothesis, or assumption, about a population parameter we wish to test, usually an assumption of the status quo.

one-tailed test A hypothesis test in which there is only one rejection region; i.e., we are concerned only with whether the observed value deviates from the hypothesized value in one direction.

paired difference test A hypothesis test of the difference between the sample means of two dependent samples.

power curve A graph of the values of the power of a test for each value of μ, or other population parameter, for which the alternative hypothesis is true.

power of the hypothesis test The probability of rejecting the null hypothesis when it is false; i.e., a measure of how well the hypothesis test is working.

significance level A value indicating the percentage of sample values that is outside certain limits, assuming the null hypothesis is correct; i.e., the probability of rejecting the null hypothesis when it is true.

two-tailed test A hypothesis test in which the null hypothesis is rejected if the sample value is significantly higher or lower than the hypothesized value of the population parameter; a test involving two rejection regions.

type I error rejecting a null hypothesis when it is true.

type II error Accepting a null hypothesis when it is false.

upper-tailed test A one-tailed hypothesis test in which a sample value significantly above the hypothesized population value will lead us to reject the null hypothesis.

10 EQUATIONS INTRODUCED IN CHAPTER 9

p. 268

$$\sigma_{\bar{x}_1 - \bar{x}_2} = \sqrt{\frac{\sigma_1^2}{n_1} + \frac{\sigma_2^2}{n_2}}$$

9·1

This formula enables us to derive the standard deviation of the distribution of the difference between the sample means, that is, *the standard error of the difference between two means*. To do this, we take the square root of the value equal to the sum of population 1's variance divided by its sample size and of population 2's variance divided by its sample size.

p. 268

$$\hat{\sigma}_{\bar{x}_1 - \bar{x}_2} = \sqrt{\frac{\hat{\sigma}_1^2}{n_1} + \frac{\hat{\sigma}_2^2}{n_2}}$$

9·2

If the two population standard deviations are unknown, we can use this formula to derive the *estimated* standard error of the difference between two means. We can use this equation after we have used the two sample standard deviations and Equation 8 · 1 to determine the estimated standard deviations of population 1 and population 2. ($\hat{\sigma} = s$)

p. 272

$$s_p^2 = \frac{(n_1 - 1)s_1^2 + (n_2 - 1)s_2^2}{n_1 + n_2 - 2}$$

9·3

With this formula we can get a "pooled estimate" of σ^2. It uses a weighted average of s_1^2 and s_2^2, where the weights are the numbers of degrees of freedom in each sample. Use of this formula assumes that $\sigma_1^2 = \sigma_2^2$ (that the unknown population variances are equal). We use this formula when testing for the differences between means in situations with small sample sizes (less than 30).

p. 272

$$\hat{\sigma}_{\bar{x}_1 - \bar{x}_2} = s_p \sqrt{\frac{1}{n_1} + \frac{1}{n_2}}$$

9·4

With the "pooled estimate" of σ^2 we obtained from Equation 9 · 3, we put this value into Equation 9 · 2 and simplify the expression. This gives us a formula to estimate the standard error of the difference between sample means when we have small samples (less than 30) but equal population variances.

p. 278

$$\sigma_{\bar{p}_1 - \bar{p}_2} = \sqrt{\frac{p_1 q_1}{n_1} + \frac{p_2 q_2}{n_2}}$$

9·5

This is the formula to use to derive the standard error of the difference between two *proportions*. The symbols p_1 and p_2 represent the proportion of successes in population 1 and population 2, respectively, and q_1 and q_2 are the proportion of failures in populations 1 and 2, respectively.

p. 278
$$\hat{\sigma}_{\bar{p}_1 - \bar{p}_2} = \sqrt{\frac{\bar{p}_1 \bar{q}_1}{n_1} + \frac{\bar{p}_2 \bar{q}_2}{n_2}}$$
9 · 6

If the population parameters p and q are unknown, we can use the sample statistics $\bar{p}$ and $\bar{q}$ and this formula to *estimate* the standard error of the difference between two proportions.

p. 279
$$\hat{p} = \frac{(n_1)(\bar{p}_1) + (n_2)(\bar{p}_2)}{n_1 + n_2}$$
9 · 7

Because the null hypothesis assumes that there is *no difference* between the two population proportions, it would be more appropriate to modify Equation 9 · 6 and to use the combined proportions from both samples to estimate the overall proportion of successes in the combined populations. Equation 9 · 7 combines the proportions from both samples. Notice that the value of $\hat{q}$ is equal to $1 - \hat{p}$.

p. 279
$$\hat{\sigma}_{\bar{p}_1 - \bar{p}_2} = \sqrt{\frac{\hat{p}\hat{q}}{n_1} + \frac{\hat{p}\hat{q}}{n_2}}$$
9 · 8

Now we can substitute the results of Equation 9 · 7, both $\hat{p}$ and $\hat{q}$, into Equation 9 · 6 and get a more correct version of Equation 9 · 6. This new equation, 9 · 8, gives us the *estimated* standard error of the difference between the two proportions using combined estimates from both samples.

--------------------------- *11 CHAPTER REVIEW EXERCISES* ---------------------------

9 · 40   A firm has tested two types of point-of-purchase displays for its new erasable pen. A shelf display was placed in a random sample of 36 stores in the test market, and a floor display was placed in 36 other stores in the area. The mean number of pens sold per store in one month with the shelf display was 40 with a standard deviation of 3. With the floor display, the mean number of pens sold per store in the same month was 42 with a standard deviation of 5. At the .05 significance level, was there a significant difference between sales with the two types of displays?

9 · 41   A university librarian suspects that the average number of books checked out to each student per visit has changed recently. In the past, an average of 3.5 books were checked out. However, a sample of 20 students averaged 4.2 books per visit, with a standard deviation of 1.8 books. At the .05 level of significance, has the average checkout changed?

9 · 42   An upholstery center has just received a shipment of 200 bolts of fabric. Each bolt is supposed to have 64 yards, with a standard deviation of 4 yards. A sample of 36 of the bolts is checked and shows an average of 64.8 yards. The upholstery center wants to know if, at the .02 level of significance, they can assume that the bolts contain at least 64 yards.

9 · 43   Given that 55 of 1,000 failed a test in which the proportion that was hypothesized to fail was .04, test at the .01 level of significance the hypothesis that the true proportion is .04 versus the alternative that it is greater than .04.

9 · 44   State inspectors, investigating charges that a Louisiana soft-drink bottling company underfills its product, have sampled 100 bottles and found the average contents to be 31.8 fluid ounces. The bottles are advertised to contain 32 fluid ounces. If the population standard deviation is 2 fluid ounces, should we conclude at the 5 percent significance level that the bottles are being underfilled?

9 · 45   For the following situations, state the null and alternative hypotheses.
   a) A researcher wishes to test whether a certain enrichment class leads to test scores greater than the population average of 85 points.

b) An airlines employee wishes to determine if the average height of stewardesses is at least 66 inches.

c) A university official wishes to determine if average enrollment for the past 10 years is significantly different from a hypothesized value of 12,500.

9·46 Health Electronics, Inc., a manufacturer of pacemaker batteries, specifies that the life of each battery is equal to or greater than 28 months. If scheduling for replacement surgery for the batteries is to be based on this claim, explain to the management of this company the consequences of Type I and Type II errors.

9·47 A personnel manager hypothesized that 15 percent of the company employees work overtime every week. If the observed proportion is .17 for a sample of 200 of the 2,000 employees, test whether we can accept his hypothesis as correct at the .10 level of significance or if we must conclude that some other value is more appropriate.

9·48 In Problem 9 · 20, what would be the power of the test for $\mu = 12,500$; 12,000; and 11,500 if the significance level were changed to .05?

9·49 A stockbroker claims that she can predict with 80 percent accuracy whether a stock's market value will rise or fall during the coming month. As a test, she predicts the outcome of 40 stocks and is correct in 28 of the predictions. Does this evidence support the stockbroker's claim, or may we conclude that her percentage accuracy is less than 80 percent? Use the .05 level of significance.

9·50 A stereo manufacturer, deciding on the appropriate market for a lower priced stereo system, has estimated that no more than 14 percent of college students purchase stereo systems costing over $800. To test this claim, the company surveyed 150 of a college's 1,200 students. The study showed that 17 of the 150 students had purchased stereos that cost over $800. If the company is willing to run a 10 percent risk of rejecting the original estimate when it is true, what should the company conclude?

9·51 Allen Distribution Company hypothesizes that a phone call is more effective than a letter in speeding up collection of a slow account. Two groups of slow accounts were contacted by these two methods and the length of time between receipt of the call or the letter and the time the payment was received was recorded. Below are the collection times (in days) for the two groups.

Method used			Days to collection			
Letter	6	8	9	10	12	9
Phone call	4	5	4	8	6	9

At the .05 level of significance, is there a difference between the average collection time for the two collection methods?

9·52 A landscaping firm has contracted to landscape 120 homes in a new development. In order not to exceed their budget, a landscaping team can spend no more than 8 days, on average, per house. After the completion of 15 houses, the average number of days spent per house is found to be 10, with a sample standard deviation of 3 days. At the .10 level of significance, is there significant reason to believe that the number of days spent per house will exceed an average of 8 for the contract?

9·53 A chemist developing insect repellents wishes to know whether a new formula leads to greater protection from insect bites than given by the most popular product on the market. Sixteen volunteers were used in the experiment, and each had one arm sprayed with the old product and one arm sprayed with the new formula. Then each subject placed his arms in two insect chambers filled with equal numbers of mosquitoes, gnats, and other biting insects. The number of bites received on each arm was recorded and is given below. Test the hypothesis that there is a difference in the amount of protection provided by the two insect repellents. Use the .05 level of significance.

Subject	1	2	3	4	5	6	7	8	9	10	11	12	13	14	15	16
Formulas:																
Old	5	2	5	4	3	6	2	4	2	6	5	7	1	3	4	1
New	3	1	5	1	1	3	4	2	5	2	1	2	1	2	1	4

9·54 A company was recently criticized for not paying women as much as men working in the same positions. It claims that its average salary paid to all employees is $12,500. From a random sample of 36 women in the company, the average salary was calculated to be $11,900. If the population standard deviation is known to be $900 for these jobs, determine whether or not we could reasonably (within 2 standard deviations) expect to find $11,900 as the sample mean if, in fact, the company's claim is true.

9·55 If we wish to accept the null hypothesis 80 percent of the time when it is correct, how many standard errors around the hypothesized value should be used in determining whether to reject it, based on sample information? How many for 90 percent certainty of accepting the null hypothesis when it is true?

---

12 CHAPTER CONCEPTS TEST

Answers are in the back of the book.

T F 1. In hypothesis testing, we assume that some population parameter takes on a particular value before we sample. This assumption to be tested is called an alternative hypothesis.

T F 2. Assuming a given hypothesis about a population mean is correct, then the percentage of a sample means that could fall outside certain limits from this hypothesized mean is called the significance level.

T F 3. In hypothesis testing, the appropriate probability distribution to use is always the normal distribution.

T F 4. If we were to make a Type I error, we would be rejecting a null hypothesis when it is really true.

T F 5. A paired difference test is appropriate when the two samples being tested are dependent samples.

T F 6. A one-tailed test for the difference between means may be undertaken when the sample sizes are either large or small and the procedures are similar. The only difference is that when sample sizes are large, we employ a normal distribution, whereas the t distribution is used when sample sizes are small.

T F 7. If our null and alternative hypotheses are H_0: $\mu = 80$, and H_1: $\mu < 80$, it is appropriate to use a left-tailed test.

T F 8. Suppose a hypothesis test is to be made regarding the difference in means between two populations, and our sample sizes are large. If we do not know the actual standard deviations of the two populations, we can use the sample standard deviations as estimates.

T F 9. The value $1 - \beta$ is known as the power of the test.

T F 10. If we took two independent samples and performed a hypothesis test to evaluate significant differences in their means, we would find the results very similar to a paired difference test performed on the same two samples.

T F 11. It is often, but not always, possible to set the value of α so that we obtain a risk-free trade-off in hypothesis testing.

T F 12. You are performing a two-tailed hypothesis test on a population mean and have set $\alpha = .05$. If the sample statistic falls within the .95 of area around μ_{H_0}, you have proved that the null hypothesis is true.

T F 13. If hypothesis tests were done with a significance level of .60, the null hypothesis would usually be accepted when it was not true.

T F 14. If $\mu_{H_0} = 50$ and $\alpha = .05$, then $1 - \beta$ must be equal to .95 when $\mu = 50$.

T F 15. When performing a two-tailed test for the difference between means, with a null hypothesis of $\mu_1 = \mu_2$, the hypothesized difference between the two population means is zero.

16. If we say that $\alpha = .10$ for a particular hypothesis test, then we are saying that:
    a) 10 percent is our minimum standard for acceptable probability.
    b) 10 percent is the risk we take of rejecting a hypothesis that is true.
    c) 10 percent is the risk we take of accepting a hypothesis that is false.
    d) a and b only.
    e) a and c only.

17. Suppose we wish to test whether a population mean is significantly larger or smaller than 10. We take a sample and find $\bar{x}$ to be 8. What should our alternative hypothesis be?
    a) $\mu < 10$ c) $\mu > 10$
    b) $\mu \neq 10$ d) cannot be determined from information given

18. Suppose that a hypothesis test is being performed for a process in which a Type I error will be very costly, but a Type II error will be relatively inexpensive and unimportant. Which of the following would be the best choice for α in this test?
    a) .01   b) .10   c) .25   d) .50

19. You are performing a right-tailed test of a population mean and σ is not known. A sample of size 26 is taken, and $\bar{x}$ and s are computed. At a significance level of .01, where would you look for a value from a distribution?
    a) z table where .99 of the area is to the left of the z value
    b) z table where .98 of the area is to the left of the z value
    c) t table where, with 25 degrees of freedom, the column heading is .02
    d) t table where, with 25 degrees of freedom, the column heading is .01

20. Suppose you are going to test the difference between two sample means, which you have calculated as $\bar{x}_1 = 22$ and $\bar{x}_2 = 27$. You wish to test whether the difference is significant. What is the value of $\mu_{\bar{x}_1 - \bar{x}_2}$ which you will use?
    a) 5   c) 0
    b) -5 d) cannot be determined from information given

21. Why do we sometimes use paired, as opposed to independent, samples?
    a) The cost of taking paired samples is always less than the cost of independent sampling.
    b) Paired samples allow us to control for extraneous factors.

c) The sample sizes must be the same for paired samples.

d) All of the above.

e) b and c but not a.

22. A set of two dependent samples of size 15 was taken and a hypothesis test was performed. A t value with 14 degrees of freedom was used. If the two sets of samples had been treated as independent, how many degrees of freedom would have been used?

a) 14   b) 28   c) 29   d) 30

23. A farmer has 12 fields of corn in different parts of a certain county. Testing for significantly different yields from year to year, he checks his records for the past 2 years and is able to gather information about production in 11 of the fields for the first year and second years. Should he treat these samples as

a) dependent?   c) cannot be determined from information given

b) independent?

24. In a test of difference between proportions, two samples are under consideration. In the first, a sample of size 100 shows 20 successes; in the second, a sample of size 50 shows 13 successes. What is the value of $\hat{p}$ for this situation?

a) $\dfrac{20 + 13}{150}$ b) $\dfrac{20}{100} + \dfrac{13}{50}$ c) $\dfrac{33}{150} \times \dfrac{117}{150}$ d) none of these

25. What is the major assumption we made when performing one-tailed tests for differences between means with small samples?

a) Unknown population variances were equal.

b) Sampling fractions were quite small.

c) The samples were chosen using judgmental sampling techniques.

d) None of the above.

26. An assumption or speculation made about a population parameter is a _____ .

27. Accepting a null hypothesis when it is false is a Type _____ error. Its probability is denoted by _____ .

28. The assumption about a population parameter that we wish to test is the _____ hypothesis. The conclusion we accept when the data fail to support this assumption is the _____ hypothesis.

29. A hypothesis test of the difference between the sample means of two dependent samples is a _____ difference test.

30. A hypothesis test involving two rejection regions is called a two- _____ test.

Chi-Square and Analysis of Variance

The training director of a company is trying to evaluate three different methods of training new employees. The first method assigns them to an experienced employee for individual help in the factory. The second method puts all new employees in a training room separate from the factory, and the third method uses training firms and programmed learning materials. The training director chooses 16 new employees assigned at random to the three training methods and records their daily production after they complete the programs:

Method 1	15	18	19	22	11	
Method 2	22	27	18	21	17	
Method 3	18	24	19	16	22	15

The director questions the difference in effectiveness among the methods. Using techniques learned in this chapter, we can help answer that question.

Chapter 10 discusses two statistical techniques: chi-square tests and analysis of variance. Chi-square tests are useful in analyzing more than two populations. They can be helpful in marketing data; for example, to test whether preference for a certain product differs from state to state or region to region. Chi-square tests also enable us to determine whether a group of data that we think could be described by the normal distribution actually does conform to that pattern. Analysis of variance, the second subject of Chapter 10, is used to test the difference between several sample means. It is a method an automobile manufacturer might use to evaluate 5 series of tests on the same model. This method can help in answering the question, "Are the miles per gallon results really the same, or do they only appear to be?"

1 INTRODUCTION

In Chapter 9, we learned how to test hypotheses using data from either one or two samples. We used one-sample tests to determine whether a mean or a proportion was significantly different from a hypothesized value. In the two-sample tests, we examined the difference between either two means or two proportions, and we tried to learn whether this difference was significant.

Uses of the chi-square test

Suppose we have proportions from five populations instead of only two. In this case, the methods for comparing proportions described in Chapter 9 do not apply; we must use the *chi-square test*, the subject of the first portion of this chapter. Chi-square tests enable us to test whether more than two population proportions can be considered equal.

Actually, chi-square tests allow us to do a lot more than just test for the equality of several proportions. If we classify a population into several categories with respect to two attributes (for example, age and job performance) we can then use a chi-square test to determine if the two attributes are independent of each other.

Function of analysis of variance

Managers also encounter situations in which it is useful to test for the equality of more than two population means. Again, we cannot apply the methods introduced in Chapter 9 because they are limited to testing for the equality of only two means. The *analysis of variance*, discussed in the fourth section of this chapter, will enable us to test whether more than two population means can be considered equal.

--------- EXERCISES ---------

10·1 Why do we use a chi-square test?

10·2 Why do we use analysis of variance?

10·3 What type of statistical test could be used in the following situations?

    a) We wish to know whether the average sales per outlet of a product is significantly affected by 3 different in-store promotions.

    b) A research group is interested in determining whether there is a significant difference between the purchasing habits of men and women.

    c) We need to compare the differences in the proportions of consumers favoring each of 4 brands.

---

2 CHI-SQUARE AS A TEST OF INDEPENDENCE

Sample differences among proportions: significant or not?

Many times, managers need to know whether the differences they observe among several sample proportions are significant or only due to chance. Suppose the campaign manager for a presidential candidate studies three geographically different regions and finds that 35 percent, 42 percent, and 51 percent of those voters surveyed in the three regions, respectively, recognize the candidate's name. If this difference is significant, the manager may conclude that location will affect the way the candidate should act. But if the difference is not significant (that is, if the manager concludes that the difference is solely due to chance), then he may decide that the place they choose to make a particular policymaking speech will have no effect on its reception. To run the campaign successfully, then, the manager needs to determine whether location and acceptance are dependent or independent.

Contingency tables

Describing a contingency table

Suppose that in four regions the National Health Care Company samples its hospital employees' attitudes toward job performance reviews. Respondents are given a choice between the present method (two reviews a year) and a proposed new method (quarterly reviews). Table 10 · 1, which illustrates the response to this question from the sample polled, is called a *contingency table*. A table such as this is made up of rows and columns, that is:

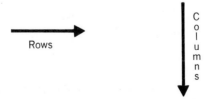

    Notice that the 4 columns in Table 10 · 1 provide one basis of classification—geographical regions—and that the 2 rows classify the

TABLE 10·1 Sample response concerning review schedules for National Health Care hospital employees

	Northeast	Southeast	Central	West Coast		Total
Number who prefer present method	68	75	57	79	=	279
Number who prefer new method	32	45	33	31	=	141
Total employees sampled in each region	100	120	90	110	=	420

information another way: preference for review methods. Table $10 \cdot 1$ is called a "2×4 contingency table," because it consists of 2 rows and 4 columns. We describe the dimensions of a contingency table by first stating the number of rows and then the number of columns. The "total" column and the "total" row are not counted as part of the dimensions.

Observed and expected frequencies

Stating the hypothesis

Suppose we now symbolize the true proportions of the total population of employees who prefer the present plan as:

$p_N \leftarrow$ proportion in Northeast who prefer present plan

$p_S \leftarrow$ proportion in Southeast who prefer present plan

$p_C \leftarrow$ proportion in Central region who prefer present plan

$p_W \leftarrow$ proportion in West Coast region who prefer present plan

Using these symbols, we can state the null and alternative hypotheses as follows:

$H_0: p_N = p_S = p_C = p_W \leftarrow$ null hypothesis
$H_1: p_N, p_S, p_C,$ and p_W are not all equal $\leftarrow$ alternative hypothesis

If the null hypothesis is true, we can combine the data from the four samples and then estimate the proportion of the total work force (the total population) that prefers the present review method:

Combined proportion who prefer present method assuming the null hypothesis of no difference is true

$$= \frac{68 + 75 + 57 + 79}{100 + 120 + 90 + 110}$$

$$= \frac{279}{420}$$

$$= .664$$

Obviously, if the value .664 estimates the population proportion expected to prefer the present compensation method, then .336 (= 1 − .664) is the estimate of the population proportion expected to prefer the proposed new method. Using .664 as the *estimate* of the population proportion who prefer the present review method, and .336 as the *estimate* of the population proportion who prefer the new method, we can estimate the number of sampled employees in each region whom we would expect to prefer each of the review methods. These calculations are done in Table 10 · 2.

Table 10 · 3 combines all the information from Tables 10 · 1 and 10 · 2. It illustrates both the actual, or observed, frequency of the employees sampled who prefer each type of job review method and the theoretical, or expected, frequency of sampled employees preferring each type of method.

Remember that the expected frequencies in Table 10 · 3 (those in boldface type) were estimated from our combined proportion estimate.

TABLE 10 · 2 Proportion of sampled employees in each region expected to prefer the two review methods

	Northeast	*Southeast*	*Central*	*West Coast*
Total number sampled	100	120	90	110
Estimated proportion who prefer present method	×.664	×.664	×.664	×.664
Number *expected* to prefer present method	**66**	**80**	**60**	**73**
Total number sampled	100	120	90	110
Estimated proportion who prefer new method	×.336	×.336	×.336	×.336
Number *expected* to prefer new method	**34**	**40**	**30**	**37**

TABLE 10 · 3 Comparison of observed and expected frequencies of sampled employees

	Northeast	*Southeast*	*Central*	*West Coast*
Frequency preferring present method:				
Observed (actual) frequency	68	75	57	79
Expected (theoretical) frequency	**66**	**80**	**60**	**73**
Frequency preferring new method:				
Observed (actual) frequency	32	45	33	31
Expected (theoretical) frequency	**34**	**40**	**30**	**37**

To test the null hypothesis, $p_N = p_S = p_C = p_W$, we must compare the frequencies that were observed (the black ones in Table 10 · 3) with the frequencies we would expect if the null hypothesis is true (those in boldface). If the sets of observed and expected frequencies are nearly alike, we can reason intuitively that we will accept the null hypothesis. If there is a large difference between these frequencies, we may intuitively reject the null hypothesis, and conclude that there are significant differences in the proportions of employees in the four regions preferring the new method.

The chi-square statistic

To go beyond our intuitive feelings about the observed and expected frequencies, we can use the chi-square statistic, which is calculated this way:

an observed frequency   an expected frequency

$$\chi^2 = \sum \frac{(f_0 - f_e)^2}{f_e} \qquad (10 \cdot 1)$$

chi-square (chi is a Greek letter)   symbol meaning "the sum of"

This formula says that chi-square, or χ^2, is the sum we will get if we:

1. Subtract f_e from f_0 for each of the eight boxes, or cells, of Table 10 · 3.
2. Square each of the differences.
3. Divide each squared difference by f_e.
4. Sum all eight of the answers.

Numerically, the calculations are easy to do using a table such as Table 10 · 4, which shows the steps.

TABLE 10 · 4   Calculation of χ^2 (chi-square) statistic from data in Table 10 · 3

f_0	f_e	Step 1: $f_0 - f_e$	Step 2: $(f_0 - f_e)^2$	Step 3: $\dfrac{(f_0 - f_e)^2}{f_e}$
68	66	2	4	.0606
75	80	− 5	25	.3125
57	60	− 3	9	.1500
79	73	6	36	.4932
32	34	− 2	4	.1176
45	40	5	25	.6250
33	30	3	9	.3000
31	37	− 6	36	.9730

Step 4 $\sum \dfrac{(f_0 - f_e)^2}{f_e} = 3.032 \leftarrow \chi^2$ (chi-square)

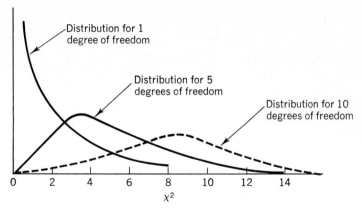

Figure 10·1 Chi-square distributions of 1, 5, and 10 degrees of freedom

*Interpreting
the chi-square
statistic*
The answer of 3.032 is the value for chi-square in our problem comparing preferences for review methods. If this value were as large as say 20, it would indicate a substantial difference between our observed values and our expected values. A chi-square of zero, on the other hand, indicates that the observed frequencies exactly match the expected frequencies. The value of chi-square can never be negative, since the differences between the observed and expected frequencies are always *squared*.

The chi-square distribution

*Describing
a chi-square
distribution*
If the null hypothesis is true, then the sampling distribution of the chi-square statistic, χ^2, can be closely approximated by a continuous curve known as a *chi-square distribution*. As in the case of the t distribution, there is a different chi-square distribution for each different number of degrees of freedom. Figure 10 · 1 indicates the three different chi-square distributions that would correspond to 1, 5, and 10 degrees of freedom. For very small numbers of degrees of freedom, the chi-square distribution is severely skewed to the right. As the number of degrees of freedom increases, the curve rapidly becomes more symmetrical until the number reaches large values, at which point the distribution can be approximated by the normal.

*Finding
probabilities
when using
a chi-square
distribution*
The chi-square distribution is a probability distribution. Therefore, the total area under the curve in each chi-square distribution is 1.0. Like the t distribution, so many different chi-square distributions are possible that it is not practical to construct a table that illustrates the areas under the curve for all possible values of the area. Instead, Appendix Table 5 illustrates only the areas in the tail most commonly used in significance tests using the chi-square distribution.

295   Sec. 2   Chi-square as a test of independence

Determining degrees of freedom

To use the chi-square test, we must calculate the number of degrees of freedom in the contingency table by applying Equation 10 · 2:

$$\begin{matrix} \text{Number of} \\ \text{degrees} \\ \text{of freedom} \end{matrix} = (\text{Number of rows} - 1)(\text{Number of columns} - 1)$$

$$(10 \cdot 2)$$

Let's examine the appropriateness of this equation. Suppose we have a 3 × 4 contingency table like the one in Fig. 10 · 2. We know the row and column totals that are designated RT_1, RT_2, RT_3, and CT_1, CT_2, CT_3, CT_4. As we discussed in Chapter 8, the number of degrees of freedom is equal to the number of values that we can freely specify.

Look now at the first row of the contingency table in Fig. 10 · 2. Once we specify the first three values in that row (denoted by checks in the figure) the fourth value in that row (denoted by a circle) is already determined; we are not free to specify it because we know the row total.

Likewise, in the second row of the contingency table in Fig. 10 · 2, once we specify the first three values (denoted again by checks), the fourth value is determined and cannot be freely specified. We have denoted this fourth value by a circle.

Turning now to the third row, we see that its first entry is determined *because we already know the first two entries in the first column and the column total*; again we have denoted this entry with a circle. We can apply this same reasoning to the second and third entries in the third row, both of which have been denoted by a circle too.

Turning finally to the last entry in the third row (denoted by a star) we see that we cannot freely specify its value because we have already

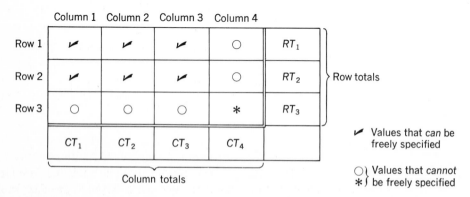

Figure 10 · 2 A 3 × 4 contingency table illustrating determination of the number of degrees of freedom

TABLE 10·5 Determination of degrees of freedom in three contingency tables

Contingency table	Number of rows (r)	Number of columns (c)	(r − 1)	(c − 1)	Degrees of freedom (r − 1)(c − 1)
A	3	4	3 − 1 = 2	4 − 1 = 3	(2)(3) = 6
B	5	7	5 − 1 = 4	7 − 1 = 6	(4)(6) = 24
C	6	9	6 − 1 = 5	9 − 1 = 8	(5)(8) = 40

determined the first two entries in the fourth column. By counting the number of checks in the contingency table in Fig. 10 · 2, you can see that the number of values we are free to specify is 6 (the number of checks). This is equal to 2 × 3, or (the number of row − 1) times (the number of columns − 1).

This is exactly what we have in Equation 10 · 2. Table 10 · 5 illustrates the row-and-column dimensions of three more contingency tables and indicates the appropriate degrees of freedom in each case.

Using the chi-square test

Stating the problem symbolically

Returning to our example of job review preferences of National Health Care hospital employees, we use the chi-square test to determine whether attitude about review is independent of geographical region. If the company wants to test the null hypothesis at the .10 level of significance, our problem can be summarized:

H_0: $p_N = p_S = p_C = p_w$ ← null hypothesis
H_1: $p_N, p_S, p_C,$ and p_W are *not* all equal ← alternative hypothesis
$\alpha = .10$ ← level of significance for testing this hypothesis

---

Calculating degrees of freedom

Since our contingency table (Table 10 · 1) has 2 rows and 4 columns, the appropriate number of degrees of freedom is:

Number of rows   number of columns
↘   ↙

$$\text{Number of degrees of freedom} = (r − 1)(c − 1)$$
$$= (2 − 1)(4 − 1) \qquad (10 · 2)$$
$$= (1)(3)$$
$$= 3 \leftarrow \text{degrees of freedom}$$

Illustrating the hypothesis test

Figure 10 · 3 illustrates a chi-square distribution for 3 degrees of freedom, showing the significance level shaded. In Appendix Table 5, we can look under the .10 column and move down to the 3 degrees of freedom row. There we find the value of the chi-square statistic 6.251. We can

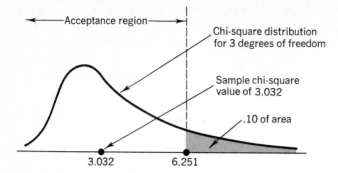

Acceptance region

Chi-square distribution for 3 degrees of freedom

Sample chi-square value of 3.032

.10 of area

3.032   6.251

Figure 10·3 Chi-square hypothesis test at .10 level of significance, showing acceptance region and sample chi-square value of 3.032

interpret this to mean that with 3 degrees of freedom, the region to the right of a chi-square value of 6.251 contains .10 of the area under the curve. Thus, the acceptance region for the null hypothesis in Fig. 10 · 3 goes from the left tail of the curve to the chi-square value of 6.251.

Interpreting the results

As we can see from Fig. 10 · 3, the sample chi-square value of 3.032, which we calculated in Table 10 · 4, falls within the acceptance region. Therefore, we accept the null hypothesis that there is no difference between the attitudes about job reviews in the four geographical regions. In other words, we conclude that attitude about performance reviews is independent of geography.

Contingency tables with more than two rows

Are hospital stay and insurance coverage independent?

Mr. George McMahon, president of National General Health Insurance Company, is opposed to national health insurance. He argues that it would be too costly to implement, particularly since the existence of such a system would, among other effects, tend to encourage people to spend more time in hospitals. George believes that lengths of stays in hospitals are dependent on the types of health insurance that people have. He asked Donna McClish, his staff statistician, to check the matter out. Donna collected data on a random sample of 660 hospital stays and summarized it in Table 10 · 6.

TABLE 10·6 Hospital stay data classified by the type of insurance coverage and length of stay

		Days in hospital			
		< 5	*5 – 10*	*> 10*	*Total*
Fraction of costs	< 25%	40	75	65	**180**
covered by	25–50%	30	45	75	**150**
insurance	> 50%	40	100	190	**330**
	Total	**110**	**220**	**330**	**660**

Table $10 \cdot 6$ gives observed frequencies in the nine different lengths of stay and the types of insurance categories (or "cells") into which we have divided the sample. Donna wishes to test the hypothesis:

H_0: length of stay and type of insurance are independent
H_1: length of stay depends on type of insurance
$\alpha = .01 \leftarrow$ level of significance for testing this hypothesis

---

Finding expected frequencies

We will use a chi-square test, so we first have to find the expected frequencies for each of the nine cells. Let's demonstrate how to find them by looking at the cell that corresponds to stays of less than 5 days and insurance covering less than 25 percent of costs.

Estimating the proportions in the cells

A total of 180 of the 660 stays in the sample had insurance covering less than 25 percent of costs. So we can use the figure 180/660 to *estimate* the proportion in the population having insurance covering less than 25 percent of the costs. Similarly, 110/660 *estimates* the proportion of all hospital stays that last fewer than 5 days. If length of stay and type of insurance really are independent, we can use Equation $5 \cdot 4$ to *estimate* the proportion in the first cell (less than 5 days and less than 25 percent coverage).

We let:

A = the event "a stay corresponds to someone whose insurance covers less than 25 percent of the costs," and

B = the event "a stay lasts less than 5 days."

Then,

$$P(\text{first cell}) = P(A \text{ and } B)$$
$$= P(A) \times P(B)$$
$$= \left(\frac{180}{660}\right)\left(\frac{110}{660}\right) \qquad (5 \cdot 4)$$
$$= 1/22$$

Since 1/22 is the expected *proportion* in the first cell, the expected *frequency* in that cell is:

$$(1/22)(660) = 30 \text{ observations}$$

Calculating the expected frequencies for the cells

In general, we can calculate the expected frequency for any cell with Equation $10 \cdot 3$:

$$f_e = \frac{RT \times CT}{n} \qquad (10 \cdot 3)$$

where:

f_e = expected frequency in a given cell

RT = row total for the row containing that cell

CT = column total for the column containing that cell

n = total number of observations

TABLE 10·7   Calculation of expected frequencies and chi-square from data in Table 10·6

Row	Column	f_0	f_e	$= \dfrac{RT \times CT}{n}$	$f_0 - f_e$	$(f_0 - f_e)^2$	$\dfrac{(f_0 - f_e)^2}{f_e}$
1	1	40	30	$\dfrac{180 \times 110}{660}$	10	100	3.333
1	2	75	60	$\dfrac{180 \times 220}{660}$	15	225	3.750
1	3	65	90	$\dfrac{180 \times 330}{660}$	−25	625	6.944
2	1	30	25	$\dfrac{150 \times 110}{660}$	5	25	1.000
2	2	45	50	$\dfrac{150 \times 220}{660}$	−5	25	0.500
2	3	75	75	$\dfrac{150 \times 330}{660}$	0	0	0.000
3	1	40	55	$\dfrac{330 \times 110}{660}$	−15	225	4.091
3	2	100	110	$\dfrac{330 \times 220}{660}$	−10	100	0.909
3	3	190	165	$\dfrac{330 \times 330}{660}$	25	625	3.788

$$(10 \cdot 1) \quad \Sigma \frac{(f_0 - f_e)^2}{f_e} = 24.315 \leftarrow \chi^2 \text{ chi-square}$$

Now we can use Equations 10 · 3 and 10 · 1 to compute all of the expected frequencies and the value of the chi-square statistic. The computations are done in Table 10 · 7.

Figure 10 · 4 illustrates a chi-square distribution with 4 degrees of freedom (number of rows − 1 = 2) × (number of columns − 1 = 2),

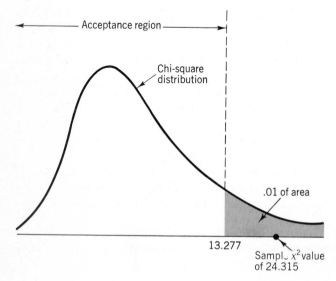

Acceptance region

Chi-square distribution

.01 of area

13.277

Sample χ^2 value of 24.315

Figure 10·4   Chi-square hypothesis test at .01 level of significance, showing acceptance region and sample chi-square value of 24.315

showing the .01 significance level shaded. Appendix Table 5 (in the .01 column and the 4 degrees of freedom row) tells Donna that for her problem, the region to the right of a chi-square value of 13.277 contains .01 of the area under the curve. Thus, the acceptance region for the null hypothesis in Fig. 10 · 4 goes from the left tail of the curve to the chi-square value of 13.277.

Interpreting the results of the test

As Fig. 10 · 4 shows Donna, the sample chi-square value of 24.315 she calculated in Table 10 · 7 is not within the acceptance region. Thus Donna must reject the null hypothesis and inform Mr. McMahon that the evidence supports his belief that length of hospital stay and insurance coverage are dependent on each other.

Precautions about using the chi-square test

Use large sample sizes

To use a chi-square hypothesis test, we must have a sample size large enough to guarantee the similarity between the theoretically correct distribution and our sampling distribution of χ^2, the chi-square statistic. When the expected frequencies are too small, the value of χ^2 will be overestimated and will result in too many rejections of the null hypothesis. To avoid making incorrect inferences from χ^2 hypothesis tests, follow the general rule that an expected frequency of less than 5 in one cell of a contingency table is too small to use.* When the table contains more than one cell with an expected frequency of less than 5, we can combine these in order to get an expected frequency of 5 or more. But in doing this we reduce the number of categories of data and will gain less information from the contingency table.

Use carefully collected data

This rule will enable us to use the chi-square hypothesis test properly, but unfortunately, each test can only reflect (and not improve) the quality of the data we feed into it. So far, we have rejected the null hypothesis if the difference between the observed and expected frequencies, that is, the computed chi-square value, is too large. In the case of the job review preferences (p. 297), we would reject the null hypothesis at a .10 level of significance if our chi-square value was 6.251 or more. But if the chi-square value was zero, we should be careful to question whether *absolutely no difference* exists between observed and expected frequencies. If we have strong feelings that some difference ought to exist, we should examine either the way the data were collected or the manner in which measurements were taken, or both, to be certain that existing differences had not been obscured or missed in collecting sample data.

Mendel's pea data

Experiments with the characteristics of peas led the monk Gregor Mendel to propose the existence of genes. Mendel's experimental results were astoundingly close to those predicted by his theory. Some time

---

*Statisticians have developed correction factors that, in some cases, allow us to use cells with expected frequencies of less than 5. The derivation and use of these correction factors are beyond the scope of this book.

later, statisticians looked at Mendel's "pea data," performed a chi-square test, and concluded that chi-square was too small; that is, Mendel's reported experimental data was so close to what was expected that they could only conclude that he had fudged the data.

EXERCISES

10·4 Given the following dimensions for contingency tables, how many degrees of freedom will the chi-square statistic for each have?
a) 2 rows, 5 columns   **c)** 4 rows, 6 columns   **e)** 3 rows, 6 columns
b) 3 rows, 4 columns   **d)** 5 rows, 5 columns

10·5 A brand manager is concerned that her brand's share may be unevenly distributed throughout the country. In a survey in which the country was divided into 4 geographic regions, a random sampling of 100 consumers in each region was surveyed with the following results:

	Region				
	A	B	C	D	Total
Purchase the brand	47	52	43	49	191
Do not purchase	53	48	57	51	209
Total	100	100	100	100	400

Develop a table of observed and expected frequencies (similar to Table 10 · 3) for this problem.

10·6 For problem 10 · 5:
a) Calculate χ^2, using a frequency table similar to Table 10 · 4.
b) State the null and alternative hypotheses.
c) Using a .05 level of significance, should the null hypothesis be rejected?

10·7 A financial consultant is interested in the differences in capital structure within different firm sizes in a certain industry. The consultant surveys a group of firms with assets of different amounts and divides the firms into three groups. Each firm is classified according to whether its total debt is greater than stockholders' equity or whether its total debt was less than stockholders' equity. The results of the survey are:

	Firm asset size (thousands)			
	< $500	$500 − 2,000	$2,000 +	Total
Debt less than equity	7	10	8	25
Debt greater than equity	10	18	9	37
Total	17	28	17	62

Do the three firm sizes have the same capital structure at the .10 significance level?

10·8 A newspaper publisher, trying to pinpoint his market's characteristics, wondered whether newspaper readership in the community is related to readers' educational achievement. A survey questioned adults in the area on their level of education and their frequency of readership. The results are shown in the following table.

| | Level of educational achievement | | | | |
Frequency of readership	Professional or postgraduate	College graduate	High school graduate	Did not complete high school	Total
Never	6	13	14	17	50
Sometimes	12	16	8	8	44
Morning or evening	38	40	11	6	95
Both editions	21	22	9	13	65
Total	77	91	42	44	254

At the .05 significance level, does the frequency of newspaper readership in the community differ according to the reader's level of education?

---

3 CHI-SQUARE AS A TEST OF GOODNESS OF FIT: TESTING THE APPROPRIATENESS OF A DISTRIBUTION

In the previous section of this chapter, we used the chi-square test to decide whether to accept a null hypothesis that was a hypothesis of independence between two variables. In our example, these two variables were (1) attitude toward job performance reviews and (2) geographical region.

Function of a goodness-of-fit test

The chi-square test can also be used to decide whether a particular probability distribution, such as the binomial, Poisson, or normal, is the *appropriate* distribution. This is an important ability because as decision makers using statistics, we will need to choose a certain probability distribution to approximate the distribution of the data we happen to be considering. We will need the ability to question how far we can go from the assumptions that underlie a particular distribution before we must conclude that this distribution is no longer applicable. The chi-square test enables us to ask this question and to test whether there is a significant difference between an observed frequency distribution and a theoretical frequency distribution. In this manner, we can determine the *goodness of fit* of a theoretical distribution (that is, how well it fits the distribution of data that we have actually observed). Thus we can determine whether we should believe that the observed data constitute a sample drawn from the hypothesized theoretical distribution.

Calculating observed and expected frequencies

Suppose that the Gordon Company requires that college seniors who are seeking positions with them be interviewed by three different executives. This enables the company to obtain a consensus evaluation of each candidate. Each executive gives the candidate either a positive or a negative rating. Table 10 · 8 contains the interview results of the last 100 candidates.

For manpower planning purposes, the director of recruitment for this company thinks that the interview process can be approximated by a binomial distribution with $p = .40$, that is, with a 40 percent chance of any candidate receiving a positive rating on any one interview. If the director wants to test this hypothesis at the .20 level of significance, how should he proceed?

Symbolical statement of the problem

H_0: A binomial distribution with
    $p = .40$ is a good description   ← null hypothesis
    of the interview process
H_1: A binomial distribution with
    $p = .40$ is *not* a good description   ← alternative hypothesis
    of the interview process
$\alpha = .20$ ← level of significance for testing this hypothesis

Calculating the binomial probabilities

To solve this problem, we must determine whether the discrepancies between the observed frequencies and those we would expect (if the binomial distribution is the proper model to use) are actually due to chance. We can begin by determining what the binomial probabilities would be for this interview situation. For three interviews, we would find the probability of success in the Cumulative Binomial Distribution Table (Appendix Table 3) by looking for the column labeled $n = 3$ and $p = .40$. The results are summarized in Table 10 · 9.

Determining the expected frequencies

Now we can use the theoretical binomial probabilities of the outcomes to compute the expected frequencies. By comparing these expected frequencies with our observed frequencies using the χ^2 test, we

TABLE 10 · 8   Interview results of 100 candidates

Possible positive ratings from 3 interviews	*Number of candidates receiving each of these ratings*
0	18
1	47
2	24
3	11
	100

TABLE 10·9 Binomial probabilities for interview problem

Possible positive ratings from 3 interviews	Binomial probabilities of these outcomes
0	1.0000 − .7840 = .2160
1	.7840 − .3520 = .4320
2	.3520 − .0640 = .2880
3	.0640
	1.0000

TABLE 10·10 Observed frequencies, appropriate binomial probabilities, and expected frequencies for interview problem

Possible positive ratings from 3 interviews	Observed frequency of candidates receiving these ratings	Binomial probability of possible outcomes		Number of candidates interviewed		Expected frequency of candidates receiving these ratings
0	18	.2160	×	100	=	22
1	47	.4320	×	100	=	43
2	24	.2880	×	100	=	29
3	11	.0640	×	100	=	6
	100	1.0000				100

can examine the extent of the difference between them. Table 10·10 lists the observed frequencies, the appropriate binomial probabilities from Table 10·9, and the expected frequencies for the sample of 100 interviews.

Calculating the chi-square statistic

To compute the chi-square statistic for this problem, we can use Equation 10·1:

$$\chi^2 = \sum \frac{(f_o - f_e)^2}{f_e} \qquad (10·1)$$

and the format we introduced in Table 10·4. This process is illustrated in Table 10·11.

Determining degrees of freedom in a goodness of-fit test

First count the number of classes

Before we can calculate the appropriate number of degrees of freedom for a chi-square goodness-of-fit test, we must count the number of classes (symbolized k) for which we have compared the observed and expected

TABLE 10·11 Calculation of χ^2 statistic from interview data listed in Table 10 · 10

Observed frequency f_o	Expected frequency f_e	$f_o - f_e$	$(f_o - f_e)^2$	$\dfrac{(f_o - f_e)^2}{f_e}$
18	22	-4	16	.7273
47	43	4	16	.3721
24	29	-5	25	.8621
11	6	5	25	4.1667

$$\sum \frac{(f_o - f_e)^2}{f_e} = 6.1282 \leftarrow \chi^2$$

frequencies. Our interview problem contains 4 such classes: 0, 1, 2, and 3 positive ratings. Thus we begin with 4 degrees of freedom. Yet since the four observed frequencies must sum to 100, the total number of observed frequencies we can freely specify is only $k - 1$ or 3. The fourth is determined, because the total of the four has to be 100.

Then subtract degrees of freedom lost from estimating population parameters

To solve a goodness-of-fit problem, we may be forced to impose additional restrictions on the calculations of the degrees of freedom. Suppose we are using the chi-square test as a goodness-of-fit test to determine whether a normal distribution fits a set of observed frequencies. If we have 6 classes of observed frequencies ($k = 6$), then we would conclude that we have only $k - 1$ or 5 degrees of freedom. If, however, we also have to use the sample mean as an estimate of the population mean, we will have to subtract an additional degree of freedom, which leaves us with only 4. And third, if we have to use the sample standard deviation to estimate the population standard deviation, we will have to subtract *one more* degree of freedom, leaving us with 3. Our general rule in these cases is first employ the $(k - 1)$ rule and then subtract an additional degree of freedom for each population parameter that has to be estimated from the sample data.

In the interview example, we have 4 classes of observed frequencies. As a result, $k = 4$, and the appropriate number of degrees of freedom is $k - 1$ or 3. We are not required to estimate any population parameter, so we need not reduce this number further.

Using the chi-square goodness-of-fit test

Calculating the limit of the acceptance region

In the interview problem, the company desires to test the hypothesis of goodness of fit at the .20 level of significance. In Appendix Table 5, then, we must look under the .20 column and move down to the row labeled 3 degrees of freedom. There we find that the value of the chi-square statistic is 4.642. We can interpret this value as follows: with

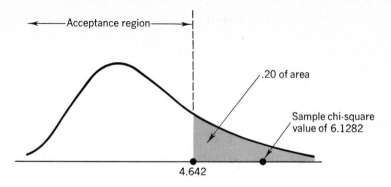

Figure 10·5 Goodness-of-fit test at the .20 level of significance, showing acceptance region and sample chi-square value of 6.1282

Illustrating the problem

Interpreting the results

three degrees of freedom, the region to the right of a chi-square value of 4.642 contains .20 of the area under the curve.

Figure 10 · 5 illustrates a chi-square distribution for 3 degrees of freedom, and shades the .20 level of significance. Notice that the acceptance region for the null hypothesis (the hypothesis that the sample data came from a binomial distribution with $p = .4$) extends from the left tail to the chi-square value of 4.642. Obviously, the sample chi-square value of 6.1282 falls outside of this acceptance region. Therefore, we reject the null hypothesis and conclude that the binomial distribution with $p = .4$ fails to provide a good description of our observed frequencies.

EXERCISES

10·9 Louis Armstrong, salesman for Dillard Paper Company, has 5 accounts to visit per day. It is suggested that the variable, sales by Mr. Armstrong, may be described by the binomial distribution, with the probability of selling each account being .3. Given the following observed frequency distribution of Mr. Armstrong's number of sales per day, can we conclude that the distribution does in fact follow the suggested distribution? Use the .05 significance level.

Number of sales per day	0	1	2	3	4	5
Frequency of the number of sales	20	65	42	14	6	3

10·10 A chemical extraction plant processes seawater to collect sodium chloride and magnesium. From scientific analysis, seawater is known to contain sodium chloride, magnesium, and other elements in the ratio 62 : 42 : 34. A sample of 200 tons of extracted minerals has resulted in 130 tons of sodium chloride and 6 tons of magnesium. Are these data consistent with the scientific model at the .05 level of significance?

10·11 Dennis Barry, a hospital administrator, has examined past records from 300 randomly selected eight-hour shifts to determine the frequency with which the hospital treats fractures. The number of days in which 0, 1, 2, 3, 4, 5, or 6 or more patients with broken bones were treated was 25, 45, 63, 71, 48, 26, and 22, respectively. At the .05 level of significance, can we reasonably believe that the incidence of broken bone cases follows a Poisson distribution with $\lambda = 3$?

10·12 A large city fire department calculates that for any given precinct, during any given 8-hour shift, there is a 30 percent chance of receiving at least one fire alarm. Here is a random sampling of 60 days:

Number of shifts during which alarms were received	1	2	3
Number of days	27	11	6

At the .05 level of significance, do these fire alarms follow a binomial distribution? (*Hint:* Combine the last two groups so that all expected frequencies will be greater than 5.)

10·13 Below is an observed frequency distribution. Using a normal distribution with $\mu = 2.44$ and $\sigma = .4$:

a) Find the probability of falling in each class.
b) From part a, compute the expected frequency of each category.
c) Calculate the chi-square statistic.
d) At the .10 level of significance, does this distribution seem to be well-described by the suggested normal distribution?

Observed value of the variable	less than 1.8	1.8 − 2.19	2.2 − 2.59	2.6 − 2.99	3.0 and above
Observed frequency	3	17	33	22	5

---

4 ANALYSIS OF VARIANCE

Function of analysis of variance

Earlier in this chapter, we used the chi-square test to examine the difference between more than two sample proportions and to make inferences about whether such samples are drawn from populations each having the same proportion. In this section, we will learn a technique known as *analysis of variance* (often abbreviated ANOVA), which will enable us to test for the significance of the difference between more than two sample *means*. Using analysis of variance, we will be able to make inferences about whether our samples are drawn from populations having the same mean.

Analysis of variance will be useful in such situations as comparing the mileage achieved by 5 different brands of gasoline, testing which of 4 different training methods produces the fastest learning record, or comparing the first-year earnings of the graduates of half a dozen different schools of business. In each of these cases, we would compare the means of more than two samples.

Statement of the problem

In the training director's problem that opened this chapter, she wanted to evaluate three different training methods, to determine whether there was

TABLE 10 · 12 Daily production of 16 new employees

Method 1	Method 2	Method 3
		18
15	22	24
18	27	19
19	18	16
22	21	22
11	17	15
85	105	114
÷ 5	÷ 5	÷ 6
$17 = \bar{x}_1$	$21 = \bar{x}_2$	$19 = \bar{x}_3 \leftarrow$ sample means
$n_1 = 5$	$n_2 = 5$	$n_3 = 6 \leftarrow$ sample sizes

any difference in their effectiveness.

Calculating the grand mean

After completion of the training period, the company's statistical staff chose 16 new employees assigned at random to the three training methods.* Counting the production output by these 16 trainees, the staff has summarized the data and calculated the mean production of the trainees (see Table 10 · 12). Now if we wish to determine the *grand mean*, or $\bar{\bar{x}}$ (the mean for the entire group of 16 trainees), we can use one of two methods:

1.
$$\bar{\bar{x}} = \frac{15+18+19+22+11+22+27+18+21+17+18+24+19+16+22+15}{16}$$

$= 19 \leftarrow$ grand mean using all the data

2.
$$\bar{\bar{x}} = (5/16)(17) + (5/16)(21) + (6/16)(19)$$

$= 19 \leftarrow$ grand mean as a weighted average of the sample means, using the relative sample sizes as the weights

Statement of the hypothesis

Stating the problem symbolically

In this case, our reason for using analysis of variance is to decide whether these three samples (a *sample* is the performance of the employees trained by any one method) were drawn from populations (a *population* is the total number of employees trained by any one method) having the same means. Because we are testing the effectiveness of the three training methods, we must determine whether the three samples, represented by the sample means $\bar{x}_1 = 17$, $\bar{x}_2 = 21$, and $\bar{x}_3 = 19$, could have been drawn

*Although in real practice 16 trainees would not constitute an adequate statistical sample, we have limited the number here to be able to demonstrate the basic techniques of analysis of variance and to avoid tedious calculations.

from populations having the same mean, μ. A formal statement of the null hypothesis we wish to test would be:

H_0: $\mu_1 = \mu_2 = \mu_3$ ← null hypothesis
H_1: μ_1, μ_2, and μ_3 are *not* all equal ← alternative hypothesis

---

Interpreting the results

If we can conclude from our test that the sample means do not differ significantly, we can infer that the choice of training method does not influence the productivity of the employee. On the other hand, if we find a difference among the sample means that is too large to attribute to chance sampling error, we can infer that the method used in training *does* influence the productivity of the employee. In that case, we would adjust our training program accordingly.

Analysis of variance: basic concepts

Assumptions made in analysis of variance

In order to use analysis of variance, we must assume that each of the samples is drawn from a normal population and that each of these populations has the same variance σ^2. If, however, the sample sizes are large enough, we do not need the assumption of normality.

In our training methods problem, our null hypothesis states that the three populations have the same means. If this hypothesis is true, classifying the data into three columns in Table 10 · 12 is unnecessary, and the entire set of 16 measurements of productivity can be thought of as a sample from one population. This overall population also has a variance of σ^2.

Analysis of variance is based on a comparison of two different estimates of the variance, σ^2, of our overall population. In this case, we can calculate one of these estimates by examining the variance among the three sample means, which are 17, 21, and 19. The other estimate of the population variance is determined by the variation within the three samples themselves, that is (15, 18, 19, 22, 11), (22, 27, 18, 21, 17), and (18, 24, 19, 16, 22, 15). Then we compare these two estimates of the population variance. Since both are estimates of σ^2, they should be approximately equal in value *when the null hypothesis is true*. If the null hypothesis is *not* true, these two estimates will differ considerably. The three steps in analysis of variance, then, are:

Steps in analysis of variance

1. Determine one estimate of the population variance from the variance *among the sample means*.
2. Determine a second estimate of the population variance from the variance *within the samples*.
3. Compare these two estimates. If they are approximately equal in value, *accept* the null hypothesis.

In the remainder of this section, we shall learn how to calculate these two estimates of the population variance, how to compare these two estimates, and how to make a hypothesis test and interpret the results. As we learn how to do these computations, however, keep in mind that all are based on the concepts we have presented in this section.

Calculating the variance among the sample means

Finding the first estimate of the population variance

Step 1 in analysis of variance indicates that we must obtain one estimate of the population variance from the variance among the three sample means. In statistical language, this estimate is called the *between-column variance*.

In Chapter 4, we used Equation 4 · 10 to calculate the sample variance:

$$\text{sample variance} \searrow s^2 = \frac{\Sigma(x - \bar{x})^2}{n - 1} \qquad (4 \cdot 10)$$

First find the variance among sample means

Now, because we are working with three sample means and a grand mean, let's substitute $\bar{x}$ for x, $\bar{\bar{x}}$ for $\bar{x}$, and k (the number of samples) for n to get a formula for the variance among the sample means:

$$\text{variance among sample means} \searrow s_{\bar{x}^2} = \frac{\Sigma(\bar{x} - \bar{\bar{x}})^2}{k - 1} \qquad (10 \cdot 4)$$

Then find the population variance using this variance among sample means

Next, we can return for a moment to Chapter 7, where we defined the standard error of the mean as the standard deviation of all possible samples of a given size. The formula to derive the standard error of the mean is Equation 7 · 1:

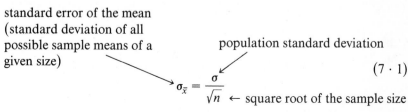

standard error of the mean (standard deviation of all possible sample means of a given size)

population standard deviation

$$\sigma_{\bar{x}} = \frac{\sigma}{\sqrt{n}} \qquad (7 \cdot 1)$$

$\leftarrow$ square root of the sample size

We can simplify this equation by cross multiplying the terms and then squaring both sides in order to change the population standard deviation, σ, into the population variance, σ^2:

$$\text{population variance} \rightarrow \sigma^2 = \sigma_{\bar{x}}^2 \times n \qquad (10 \cdot 5)$$

standard error squared (this is the variance among the sample means)

An acceptable substitution

For our training method problem, we do not have all the information we need to use this equation to find σ^2. Specifically, we do not know $\sigma_{\bar{x}}^2$. We could however, calculate the variance among the 3 sample means $s_{\bar{x}}^2$, using Equation $10 \cdot 4$. So why not substitute $s_{\bar{x}}^2$ for $\sigma_{\bar{x}}^2$ in Equation $10 \cdot 5$ and calculate an estimate of the population variance? This will give us:

$$\hat{\sigma}^2 = s_{\bar{x}}^2 \times n = \frac{\Sigma n (\bar{x} - \bar{\bar{x}})^2}{k - 1}$$

Which sample size to use

There is a slight difficulty in using this equation as it stands. In Equation $7 \cdot 1$, n represents the sample size, but *which* sample size should we use when the different samples have different sizes? We solve this problem with Equation $10 \cdot 6$, where each $(\bar{x}_j - \bar{\bar{x}})^2$ is multiplied by its own appropriate n_j.

first estimate of the population variance $\rightarrow \hat{\sigma}^2 = \dfrac{\Sigma n_j (\bar{x}_j - \bar{\bar{x}})^2}{k - 1}$ $(10 \cdot 6)$

where:

$\hat{\sigma}^2 = $ our first estimate of the population variance based on the variance among the sample means (the *between column* variance)

$n_j = $ size of the jth sample

$\bar{x}_j = $ sample mean of the jth sample

$\bar{\bar{x}} = $ grand mean

$k = $ number of samples

Now we can use Equation $10 \cdot 6$ and the data from Table $10 \cdot 12$ to calculate the between-column variance. Table $10 \cdot 13$ shows how to make these calculations.

TABLE 10·13   Calculation of the between-column variance

n	$\bar{x}$	$\bar{\bar{x}}$	$\bar{x} - \bar{\bar{x}}$	$(\bar{x} - \bar{\bar{x}})^2$	$n(\bar{x} - \bar{\bar{x}})^2$
5	17	19	$17 - 19 = -2$	$(-2)^2 = 4$	$5 \times 4 = 20$
5	21	19	$21 - 19 = 2$	$(2)^2 = 4$	$5 \times 4 = 20$
6	19	19	$19 - 19 = 0$	$(0)^2 = 0$	$6 \times 0 = 0$
					$\Sigma n_j(\bar{x}_j - \bar{\bar{x}})^2 \rightarrow \overline{40}$

$$\hat{\sigma}^2 = \frac{\Sigma n_j (\bar{x}_j - \bar{\bar{x}})^2}{k - 1} = \frac{40}{3 - 1} = 20 \leftarrow \text{between-column variance} \quad (10 \cdot 6)$$

Calculating the variance within the samples

Finding the second estimate of the population variance

Step 2 in ANOVA requires a second estimate of the population variance based on the variance within the samples. In statistical terms, this can be called the *within-column* variance. Our employee training problem has three samples of 5 or 6 items each. We can calculate the variance within each of these three samples using Equation 4 · 10:

$$\text{sample variance} \searrow s^2 = \frac{\Sigma(x - \bar{x})^2}{n - 1} \qquad (4 \cdot 10)$$

Since we have assumed that the variances of our three populations are the same, we could use any one of the three sample variances (s_1^2 or s_2^2 or s_3^2) as the second estimate of the population variance. Statistically, we can get a better estimate of the population variance by using a weighted average of all three sample variances. The general formula for this second estimate of σ^2 is:

$$\begin{array}{c}\text{second estimate of} \\ \text{the population variance}\end{array} \searrow \hat{\sigma}^2 = \Sigma \left(\frac{n_j - 1}{n_T - k} \right) s_j^2 \qquad (10 \cdot 7)$$

where:

$\hat{\sigma}^2$ = our second estimate of the population variance based on the variances within the samples (the *within-column* variance)

n_j = size of the jth sample

s_j^2 = sample variance of the jth sample

k = number of samples

$n_T = \Sigma n_j$ = total sample size

Using all the information at our disposal

This formula uses all the information that we have at our disposal, not just a portion of it. Had there been 7 samples instead of 3 we would have taken a weighted average of all 7. The weights used in Equation 10 · 7 will be explained shortly on page 316. Table 10 · 14 illustrates how to calculate this second estimate of the population variance using the variances within all three of our samples.

The F hypothesis test: computing and interpreting the F statistic

Finding the F ratio

Step 3 in ANOVA compares these two estimates of the population variance by computing their ratio, called *F*, as follows:

$$F = \frac{\begin{array}{c}\text{First estimate of the population variance} \\ \text{based on the variance among the sample means}\end{array}}{\begin{array}{c}\text{Second estimate of the population variance} \\ \text{based on the variances within the samples}\end{array}} \qquad (10 \cdot 8)$$

TABLE 10·14 Calculation of variances within the samples and the within-column variance

Training method 1 Sample mean: $\bar{x} = 17$		Training method 2 Sample mean: $\bar{x} = 21$		Training method 3 Sample mean: $\bar{x} = 19$	
$x - \bar{x}$	$(x - \bar{x})^2$	$x - \bar{x}$	$(x - \bar{x})^2$	$x - \bar{x}$	$(x - \bar{x})^2$
$15 - 17 = -2$	$(-2)^2 = 4$	$22 - 21 = 1$	$(1)^2 = 1$	$18 - 19 = -1$	$(-1)^2 = 1$
$18 - 17 = 1$	$(1)^2 = 1$	$27 - 21 = 6$	$(6)^2 = 36$	$24 - 19 = 5$	$(5)^2 = 25$
$19 - 17 = 2$	$(2)^2 = 4$	$18 - 21 = -3$	$(-3)^2 = 9$	$19 - 19 = 0$	$(0)^2 = 0$
$22 - 17 = 5$	$(5)^2 = 25$	$21 - 21 = 0$	$(0)^2 = 0$	$16 - 19 = -3$	$(3)^2 = 9$
$11 - 17 = -6$	$(-6)^2 = 36$	$17 - 21 = -4$	$(-4)^2 = 16$	$22 - 19 = 3$	$(3)^2 = 9$
				$15 - 19 = -4$	$(-4)^2 = 16$

$$\Sigma(x - \bar{x})^2 = 70 \qquad\qquad \Sigma(x - \bar{x})^2 = 62 \qquad\qquad \Sigma(x - \bar{x})^2 = 60$$

$$\frac{\Sigma(x - \bar{x})^2}{n - 1} = \frac{70}{5 - 1} \qquad \frac{\Sigma(x - \bar{x})^2}{n - 1} = \frac{62}{5 - 1} \qquad \frac{\Sigma(x - \bar{x})^2}{n - 1} = \frac{60}{6 - 1}$$

Sample variance → $s_1^2 = 17.5$ Sample variance → $s_2^2 = 15.5$ Sample variance → $s_3^2 = 12.0$

And:

$$\hat{\sigma}^2 = \Sigma \left(\frac{n_j - 1}{n_T - k} \right) s_j^2 = (4/13)(17.5) + (4/13)(15.5) + (5/13)(12.0) \qquad (10 \cdot 7)$$

second estimate of the population
$= 14.769 \leftarrow$ variance based on the variances within
the samples (the within-column variance)

If we substitute the statistical shorthand for the numerator and denominator of this ratio, Equation 10 · 8 becomes:

$$F = \frac{\text{Between-column variance}}{\text{Within-column variance}} \qquad (10 \cdot 9)$$

Now we can find the F ratio for the training method problem with which we have been working:

$$F = \frac{\text{Between-column variance}}{\text{Within-column variance}}$$

$$= \frac{20}{14.769} \qquad (10 \cdot 9)$$

$$= 1.354 \leftarrow F \text{ ratio}$$

Interpreting the F ratio

Having found this *F ratio* of 1.354, how can we interpret it? First, examine the denominator, which is based on the variance within the samples. The denominator is a good estimate of σ^2 (the population variance) whether the null hypothesis is true or not. What about the numerator? If the null hypothesis that the three methods of training have equal effects is true, then the numerator, or the variation among the sample means of the three methods, is also a good estimate of σ^2 (the population variance). As a result, the denominator and numerator should be about equal if the null hypothesis is true. The nearer the F ratio comes to one, then, the more we are inclined to accept the null hypothesis. Conversely, as the F ratio becomes larger, we will be more inclined to reject the null hypothesis and accept the alternative (that a difference does exist in the effects of the three training methods).

Shortly, we shall learn a more formal way of deciding when to accept or reject the null hypothesis. But even now, you should understand the basic logic behind this F *statistic*. When populations are not the same, the between-column variance (which was derived from the variance among the sample means) will tend to be larger than the within-column variance (which was derived from the variances within the samples), and the value of F will tend to increase. This will lead us to reject the null hypothesis.

The F distribution

Describing an
F distribution

Like other statistics we have studied, if the null hypothesis is true, then the F statistic has a particular sampling distribution. Like the t and chi-square distributions, this F distribution is actually a whole family of distributions, three of which are shown in Fig. $10 \cdot 6$. Notice that each is identified by a *pair* of degrees of freedom, unlike the t and chi-square distributions, which have only one value for the number of degrees of freedom. The first number refers to the number of degrees of freedom in the numerator of the F ratio; the second, to the degrees of freedom in the denominator.

As we can see in Fig. $10 \cdot 6$, the F distribution has a single mode. The specific shape of an F distribution depends upon the number of degrees of freedom in both the numerator and the denominator of the F

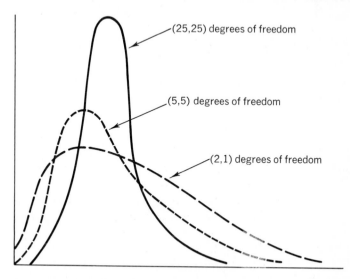

Figure 10·6 Three F distributions (first value in parentheses equals number of degrees of freedom in the numerator of the F ratio; second equals number of degrees of freedom in the denominator)

315 Sec. 4 Analysis of variance

ratio. But in general, the F distribution is skewed to the right and tends to get more symmetrical as the number of degrees of freedom in the numerator and denominator increase.

Using the F distribution: degrees of freedom

Calculating degrees of freedom

As we have mentioned, each F distribution has a pair of degrees of freedom, one for the numerator of the F ratio and the other for the denominator. How can we calculate both of these?

Finding the numerator degrees of freedom

First, think about the numerator, the between-column variance. In Table $10 \cdot 13$, we used three values of $(\bar{x} - \bar{\bar{x}})^2$, one for each sample, to calculate $\Sigma(\bar{x} - \bar{\bar{x}})^2$. Once we knew two of these $(\bar{x} - \bar{\bar{x}})^2$ values, the third was *automatically determined* and could not be freely specified. Thus, one degree of freedom is lost when we calculate the between-column variance, and the number of degrees of freedom for the numerator of the F ratio is always one fewer than the number of samples. The rule, then, is:

$$\text{Number of degrees of freedom in } \textit{numerator} \text{ of the } F \text{ ratio} = (\text{Number of samples} - 1) \quad (10 \cdot 10)$$

Finding the denominator degrees of freedom

Now, what of the denominator? Look at Table $10 \cdot 14$ for a moment. There we calculated the variances within the samples, and we used all three samples. For the jth sample, we used n_j values of $(x - \bar{x})$ to calculate the $(x - \bar{x})^2$ for that sample. Once we knew all but one of these $(x - \bar{x})$ values, the last was *automatically determined* and could not be freely specified. Thus we lost one degree of freedom in the calculations for *each* sample, leaving us with 4, 4, and 5 degrees of freedom in the samples. Since we had three samples, we were left with $4 + 4 + 5 = 13$ degrees of freedom (which could also be calculated as $5 + 5 + 6 - 3 = 13$). We can state the rule like this:

$$\text{Number of degrees of freedom in } \textit{denominator} \text{ of the } F \text{ ratio} = \Sigma(n_j - 1) = n_T - k \quad (10 \cdot 11)$$

where:

$$n_j = \text{size of the } j\text{th sample}$$
$$k = \text{number of samples}$$
$$n_T = \Sigma n_j = \text{total sample size}$$

Now we can see that the weight assigned to s_j^2 in Equation $10 \cdot 7$ was just its fraction of the total number of degrees of freedom in the denominator of the F-ratio.

Using the F table

To do F hypothesis tests, we shall use an F table in which the columns represent the number of degrees of freedom for the numerator and the rows represent the degrees of freedom for the denominator. Separate tables exist for each level of significance.

Suppose we are testing a hypothesis at the .01 level of significance, using the F distribution. Our degrees of freedom are 8 for the numerator and 11 for the denominator. In this instance, we would turn to Appendix Table 6. In the body of that table, the appropriate value for 8 and 11 degrees of freedom is 4.74. If our calculated value of F exceeds this table value of 4.74, we would reject the null hypothesis. If not, we would accept it.

Testing the hypothesis

Finding the F statistic and the degrees of freedom

We can now test our hypothesis that the three different training methods produce identical results, using the material we have developed to this point. Let's begin by reviewing how we calculated the F ratio:

$$F = \frac{\text{First estimate of the population variance based on the variance among the sample means}}{\text{Second estimate of the population variance based on the variances within the samples}} \qquad (10 \cdot 8)$$

$$= \frac{20}{14.769}$$

$$= 1.354 \leftarrow F \text{ statistic}$$

Next, calculate the number of degrees of freedom in the numerator of the F ratio, using Equation 10 · 10 as follows:

$$\text{Number of degrees of freedom in numerator of the } F \text{ ratio} = (\text{Number of samples} - 1)$$

$$= 3 - 1 \qquad (10 \cdot 10)$$

$$= 2 \leftarrow \text{degrees of freedom in the numerator}$$

And we can calculate the number of degrees of freedom in the denominator of the F ratio by use of Equation 10 · 11:

$$\text{Number of degrees of freedom in denominator of the } F \text{ ratio} = \Sigma(n_j - 1) = n_T - k \qquad (10 \cdot 11)$$

$$= (5 - 1) + (5 - 1) + (6 - 1)$$

$$= 16 - 3$$

$$= 13 \leftarrow \text{degrees of freedom in the denominator}$$

Calculating the limit of the acceptance region

Suppose the director of training wants to test at the .05 level the hypothesis that there is no difference between the three training methods. We can look in Appendix Table 6 for 2 degrees of freedom in the

317   Sec. 4   Analysis of variance

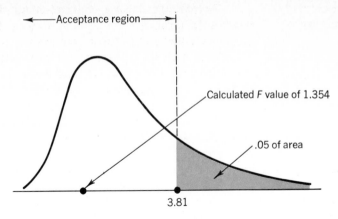

← Acceptance region →

Calculated F value of 1.354

.05 of area

3.81

Figure 10·7 Hypothesis test at the .05 level of significance, using the F distribution and showing the acceptance region and the calculated F value

Interpreting the results

numerator and 13 in the denominator. The value we find there is 3.81. Figure 10 · 7 shows this hypothesis test graphically. The shaded region represents the level of significance. The table value of 3.81 sets the upper limit of the acceptance region. Since the calculated value for F of 1.354 lies within the acceptance region, we would accept the null hypothesis and conclude that, according to the sample information we have, there is no difference in the effects of the three training methods on employee productivity.

Precautions about using the F test

Use large sample sizes

As we stated earlier, our sample sizes in this problem are too small for us to be able to draw valid inferences about the effectiveness of the various training methods. We chose small samples so that we could explain the logic of analysis of variance without tedious calculations. In actual practice, our methodology would be the same, but our samples would be larger.

Control all factors but the one being tested

In our example, we have assumed the absence of many factors that might have affected our conclusions. We accepted as given, for example, the fact that all the new employees we sampled had the same demonstrated aptitude for learning—which may or may not be true. We assumed that all the instructors of the three training methods had the same ability to teach and to manage, which may not be true. And we assumed that the company's statistical staff collected the data on productivity during work periods that were similar in terms of time of day, day of the week, time of the year, and so on. To be able to make significant decisions based on analysis of variance, we need to be certain that all these factors are effectively controlled.

Finally, notice that we have discussed only *one-way*, or one factor, analysis of variance. Our problem examined the effect of the type of training method on employee productivity, nothing else. Had we wished to measure the effect of two factors, such as the training program and the age of the employee, we would need the ability to use two-way analysis of variance, a statistical method best saved for more advanced textbooks.

─────────────────── **EXERCISES** ───────────────────

10·14 A research company has designed four different systems to clean up oil spills. The following table contains the results, measured by how much surface area (in meters^2) is cleared in one hour. The data were found by testing each method in five trials. Are the four systems equally effective at the .05 level of significance?

System A	55	60	58	61	54
System B	47	53	54	49	52
System C	63	59	58	64	63
System D	51	56	54	59	54

10·15 The supervisor of security at a large department store would like to know if the store apprehends relatively more shoplifters during the Christmas holiday season than in the weeks before or after the holiday. He gathered data on the number of shoplifters apprehended in the store during the months of November, December, and January over the past 6 years. The information is shown in the table below.

	Number of shoplifters					
November	42	36	58	54	37	47
December	51	38	45	32	47	46
January	37	29	35	42	31	33

At the .05 level of significance, is the number of apprehended shoplifters the same during these 3 months?

10·16 Three training methods were compared to see if they led to greater productivity after training. Below are productivity measures for individuals trained by each method.

Method 1	36	26	31	20	34	25
Method 2	40	29	38	32	39	34
Method 3	32	18	23	21	33	27

At the .05 level of significance, do the three training methods lead to different levels of productivity?

10·17 The following data show the number of claims processed per day for a group of 5 insurance company employees observed for a number days. Test the hypothesis that the employees' mean claims per day are all the same. Use the .01 level of significance.

Employee 1	15	17	14	11		
Employee 2	12	10	13	17	14	
Employee 3	10	14	13	15	12	
Employee 4	14	9	7	10	8	7
Employee 5	13	12	9	14	10	9

10·18 A study compared the effects of 4 one-month point-of-purchase promotions on sales. Below are the unit sales for 5 stores using all 4 promotions in different months.

Free sample	77	86	80	88	84
On-pack gift	95	92	88	91	89
Cents-off	72	77	68	82	75
Refund by mail	80	84	79	70	82

a) Compute the mean unit sales for each promotion and then determine the grand mean.
b) Calculate the variance among the sample means.
c) Estimate the population variance using the between-column variance (Equation 10 · 6).
d) Estimate the population variance using the within-column variance computed from the variances within the samples.
e) Calculate the F ratio. At the .05 level of significance, do the promotions produce different effects on sales?

10·19 Morristown Shoe Company sets sales quotas every December for each of its 15 salespeople. Unexpected competition, production problems, and an increase in prices prevented Morristown's salespeople from meeting their quotas. The company has divided its salesforce into three regions and compiled the table below to show the percentage of goal that each salesperson reached. At the .05 level of significance, did the three regions meet an equal percentage of their sales goals?

Percent of sales goal met by each salesperson

West Coast	85	84	79	84	88	
East Coast	83	94	96	85	87	90
Midwest	74	76	73	81		

5 TERMS INTRODUCED IN CHAPTER 10

analysis of variance (ANOVA) A statistical technique used to test the equality of 3 or more sample means and thus make inferences as to whether the samples come from populations having the same mean.

between-column variance An estimate of the population variance derived from the variance among the sample means.

chi-square distribution A family of probability distributions, differentiated by their degrees of freedom, used to test a number of different hypotheses about proportions and distributional goodness of fit.

contingency table A table having R rows and C columns. Each row corresponds to a level of one variable; each column, to a level of another variable. Entries in the body of the tables are the frequencies with which each variable combination occurred.

expected frequencies The frequencies we would expect to see in a contingency table or frequency distribution if the null hypothesis is true.

F-distribution A family of distributions differentiated by two parameters (df-numerator, df-denominator), used primarily to test hypotheses in ANOVA.

F-ratio A ratio used in the analysis of variance, among other tests, to compare the magnitude of two estimates of the population variance to determine if the two estimates are approximately equal; in ANOVA, the ratio of between-column variance to within-column variance is used.

goodness-of-fit test A statistical test for determining whether there is a significant difference between an observed frequency distribution and a theoretical probability distribution hypothesized to describe the observed distribution.

grand mean The mean for the entire group of subjects from all the samples in the experiment.

test of independence A statistical test of proportions or frequencies, to determine if membership in categories of one variable is different as a function of membership in the categories of a second variable.

within-column variance An estimate of the population variance based on the variances within the k samples, using a weighted average of the k sample variances.

6 EQUATIONS INTRODUCED IN CHAPTER 10

p. 294
$$\chi^2 = \sum \frac{(f_o - f_e)^2}{f_e}$$
10 · 1

This formula says that the *chi-square statistic* (χ^2) is equal to the sum (Σ) we will get if we

1. Subtract the expected frequencies, f_e, from the observed frequencies, f_o, for each category of our contingency table.
2. Square each of the differences.
3. Divide each squared difference by f_e.
4. Sum all the results of step 3.

Numerically, the calculations are easy to accomplish using a table. A large value for chi-square indicates a great difference between the observed and expected values. A chi-square of zero indicates that the observed frequencies exactly match the expected frequencies. The value of chi-square can never be negative because the differences between observed and expected frequencies are always squared.

p. 295
$$\frac{\text{Number of degrees}}{\text{of freedom}} = (\text{Number of rows} - 1)(\text{Number of columns} - 1)$$
10 · 2

To calculate number of *degrees of freedom for a chi-square test of independence*, multiply the number of rows (less one) times the number of columns (less one).

p. 288
$$f_e = \frac{RT \times CT}{n}$$
10 · 3

With this formula, we can calculate the expected frequency for any cell within a contingency table. RT is the row total for the row containing the cell, CT is the column total for the column containing the cell and n is the total number of observations.

p. 311
$$s_{\bar{x}}^2 = \frac{\sum(\bar{x} - \bar{\bar{x}})^2}{k - 1}$$
10 · 4

To calculate the *variance among the sample means*, use this formula and a format such as Table 10 · 13:

1. Subtract the grand mean, $\bar{\bar{x}}$, from the sample mean, $\bar{x}$, for each sample taken.
2. Square each of the differences.
3. Sum all of the answers.
4. Divide the total by the numer of samples (less one).

$$\sigma^2 = \sigma_{\bar{x}}^2 \times n$$

The *population variance* is equal to the product of the square of the standard error of the mean and the sample size.

$$\hat{\sigma}^2 = \frac{\Sigma n_j \left(\bar{x}_j - \bar{\bar{x}} \right)^2}{k - 1}$$

One estimate of the population variance (the between-column variance) can be obtained by using this equation. We obtain this equation by first substituting $s_{\bar{x}}^2$ for $\sigma_{\bar{x}}^2$ in Equation 10 · 5, and then by weighting each $(\bar{x}_j - \bar{\bar{x}})^2$ by its own appropriate sample size (n_j).

$$\hat{\sigma}^2 = \Sigma \left(\frac{n_j - 1}{n_T - k} \right) s_j^2$$

A second estimate of the population variance (the within-column variance) can be obtained from this equation. This equation uses a weighted average of all the sample variances. In this formulation, $n_T = \Sigma n_j$, the total sample size.

$$F = \frac{\text{First estimate of the population variance based on the variance among the sample means}}{\text{Second estimate of the population variance based on the variances within the samples}}$$

This ratio is the way we can compare the two estimates of the population variance, which we calculated in Equations 10 · 6 and 10 · 7. In a hypothesis test based on an F distribution, we are more likely to accept the null hypothesis if this F *ratio* or F *statistic* is near to the value of one. As the F ratio increases, the more likely it is that we will reject the null hypothesis.

$$F = \frac{\text{Between-column variance}}{\text{Within-column variance}}$$

This restates Equation 10 · 8, using statistical shorthand for the numerator and denominator of the F ratio.

$$\frac{\text{Number of degrees of freedom}}{\text{in numerator of the } F \text{ ratio}} = (\text{Number of samples} - 1)$$

To do an analysis of variance, we calculate the number of *degrees of freedom in the between-column variance* (the numerator of the F ratio) by subtracting one from the number of samples collected.

$$\frac{\text{Number of degrees of freedom in}}{\text{denominator of the } F \text{ ratio}} = \Sigma(n_j - 1) = n_T - k$$

We use this equation to calculate the number of degrees of freedom in the denominator of the F ratio. This turns out to be the total sample size, n_T, minus the number of samples, k.

───────── **7 CHAPTER REVIEW EXERCISES** ─────────

10 · 20 What probability distribution is used in each of these types of statistical tests?
  a) comparing the means of 2 small samples from populations with unknown variances
  b) comparing 3 or more population means

c) value of a single population mean based on large samples

d) comparing 3 or more population proportions

10·21 A production manager experiments with three different processes making the same product, to see if different processes produce different unit manufacturing costs. The table below shows 6 observations of unit manufacturing costs for each process.

Manufacturing cost per unit (in dollars)

Process 1	6.50	7.20	6.80	6.90	6.40	7.30
Process 2	4.90	5.30	4.80	4.60	5.90	5.00
Process 3	6.10	5.90	5.80	6.10	6.00	5.70

At the .01 level of significance, do the three production processes have the same unit manufacturing cost?

10·22 An outdoor advertising company must know whether significantly different traffic volumes pass three billboard locations in Newark, since the company charges different rates for different traffic volumes. The company measures the volume of traffic at the three locations during randomly selected 5-minute intervals. The table below shows the data gathered. At the .05 level of significance, is the volume of traffic passing the three billboards the same?

Volume of traffic

Billboard 1	30	45	26	44	18	38	42	29	
Billboard 2	24	33	31	16	31	13	12	25	27
Billboard 3	35	47	43	46	27	31	21		

10·23 Janet Peterson, media buyer for the Johnston Advertising Agency, is deciding which of three television spots to use. She randomly selects 6 weeks out of the year and looks at the percentage of each program's audience that falls within her defined target market. From the data shown below, can she conclude that the three spots are equal in the percentage of their audiences falling within the target market? Use an F test at the .05 level of significance.

Percent

Program 1	85	71	78	89	74	95
Program 2	65	77	84	75	71	96
Program 3	72	86	77	76	84	85

10·24 For the following contingency table:

a) Construct a table of observed and expected frequencies.

b) Calculate the chi-square statistic.

c) State the null and alternative hypotheses.

d) Using a .05 level of significance, should the null hypothesis be rejected?

	Income level		
Church attendance	*Low*	*Middle*	*High*
Never	28	52	16
Occasional	25	66	14
Regular	18	73	8

10·25 For the contingency table below, calculate the observed and expected frequencies and the chi-square statistic. Test the appropriate hypothesis at the .10 significance level.

	Attitude toward social legislation		
Occupation	Favor	Neutral	Oppose
Blue-collar	18	12	36
White-collar	11	15	42
Professional	24	8	32

10·26 A social psychologist has tested 150 subjects to construct an attitude scale measuring feelings toward the women's movement. She presents a number of statements varying in their favorability toward the movement and the subjects respond either "agree" or "disagree." The final attitude score or measure for each subject is the number of statements agreed with. She thinks that attitudes reflected by her scale should follow a normal distribution. Using the sample mean and sample standard deviation as parameters for the normal distribution, the psychologist constructed the following table. Do the data in this table confirm the conclusion, at the .025 level of significance, that attitudes as measured by this scale follow a normal distribution?

Number of items agreed with	10 or fewer	11–12	13–14	15–16	17–18	19 +
Number of subjects in each group	8	27	53	48	26	4
Number of subjects in normal distribution	14	26	41	36	22	11

10·27 As part of a federal air traffic study at a local airport, a record was made of the number of transient aircraft arrivals during 250 half-hour time intervals. The table below presents the observed number of periods in which there were 0, 1, 2, 3, or 4 or more arrivals, as well as the expected number of such periods if arrivals per half hour have a Poisson distribution with $\lambda = 2$. At the .05 level of significance, does this Poisson distribution describe the observed arrivals?

Number of observed arrivals (per half hour)	0	1	2	3	4 or more
Number of periods observed	47	56	71	44	32
Number of periods expected (Poisson, $\lambda = 2$)	34	68	68	45	36

10·28 A sales manager made a study of the possible relationship between the salespersons' experience before working for the company and their success with the company. Sales representatives were classified by number of years experience in sales before joining the company and their performance during the first year with the company. The results of the study were:

	Prior experience (years)				
Performance	Over 5	2–5	Under 2	None	Total
Poor	24	42	38	29	133
Satisfactory	70	41	45	47	203
Exceptional	36	27	27	29	119
Total	130	110	110	105	455

At the .025 level of significance, is sales experience a significant factor in the performance of salespersons during the first year?

---

8 CHAPTER CONCEPTS TEST

Answers are in the back of the book.

T F 1. Analysis of variance may be used to test whether the means of more than two populations can be considered equal.

T F 2. Analysis of variance is based upon a comparison of two estimates of the variance of the overall population which contains all samples.

T F 3. When using the chi-square distribution as a test of independence, the number of degrees of freedom is related to both the number of rows and the number of columns in the contingency table.

T F 4. Chi-square may be used as a test to decide whether a particular distribution closely approximates a sample from some population. We refer to such tests as goodness-of-fit tests.

T F 5. When using a chi-square test, we must ensure an adequate sample size, so that we can avoid any tendency for the value of the chi-square statistic to be overestimated.

T F 6. The specific shape of an F distribution depends on the number of degrees of freedom in both the numerator and denominator of the F ratio.

T F 7. One convenient aspect of hypothesis testing in ANOVA using the F statistic is that all such tests are upper-tailed tests.

T F 8. Chi-square tests enable us to test whether more than two population proportions can be considered equal.

T F 9. A "3 × 5 contingency table" has 3 columns and 5 rows.

T F 10. The total area under the curve of a chi-square distribution, like that of other distributions, is 1.

T F 11. The expected frequency for any cell in a contingency table can be immediately calculated, once we know only the row and column totals for that cell.

T F 12. If the chi-square value for an observation is zero, we know that there will never be any difference between observed and expected frequencies.

T F 13. Suppose you have observed proportions for three different geographic regions. You wish to test whether the regions have significantly different proportions. Assuming p_1, p_2, and p_3 are the true proportions, which of the following would be your null hypothesis?
a) $p_1 \neq p_2 \neq p_3$ c) $p_1, p_2,$ and p_3 are not all equal.
b) $p_1 = p_2 = p_3$ d) none of these

14. A chi-square value can never be negative because
a) DIfferences between expected and observed frequencies are squared.
b) A negative value would mean that the observed frequencies were negative.
c) The absolute value of the differences is computed.
d) None of the above.
e) a and b but not c.

15. Suppose that there are 8 possible classes under consideration for a goodness-of-fit test. How many degrees of freedom should be used?
    a) 8   c) 6
    b) 7   d) cannot be determined from the information given

16. Which of the following is a step in performing analysis of variance?
    a) Determine an estimate of population variance from within the samples.
    b) Determine an estimate of population variance among the sample means.
    c) Determine the difference between expected and observed frequency for each class.
    d) All of the above.
    e) a and b but not c.

17. Suppose you calculated the following variances for several different groups of samples and all the groups had the same degrees of freedom. For which ratio would you be most likely to accept the null hypothesis of equal means, at a given significance level?
    a) Between-column variance = 8, within-column variance = 3
    b) Between-column variance = 6, within-column variance = 3
    c) Between-column variance = 4, within-column variance = 3
    d) Between-column variance = 30, within-column variance = 20

18. Assume that a chi-square test is to be performed on a contingency table with 4 rows and 4 columns. How many degrees of freedom should be used?
    a) 16   b) 8   c) 9   d) 6

19. When performing a chi-square hypothesis test, what happens when expected frequencies in several cells are too small?
    a) The value of χ^2 will be overestimated.
    b) The null hypothesis will be more likely to be rejected than it should be.
    c) The degrees of freedom are greatly reduced.
    d) None of the above.
    e) a and b but not c.

20. Suppose you are comparing 5 groups exposed to different methods of treatment and have taken a sample of size 10 from each group. You have calculated $\bar{x}$ for each sample. How could you now calculate the grand mean?
    a) Multiply each sample mean by $\frac{1}{5}$ and add these values. Then divide this sum by 50.
    b) Add the five sample means and divide by 50.
    c) Add the five sample means and multiply by $\frac{1}{5}$.
    d) Add the five sample means.
    e) None of the above.

21. The mean for the entire group of subjects from all the samples in an experiment is called the _____ mean.

22. A statistical technique used to test the equality of 3 or more population means is called _____ .

23. A test of _____ is used to determine if membership in categories of one variable is different as a function of membership in the categories of a second variable.

24. A family of distributions differentiated by two parameters and used to test hypotheses in ANOVA is called the _____ distribution.

25. The _____ test determines whether there is a significant difference between the observed and hypothesized distributions for a sample.

Simple Regression and Correlation

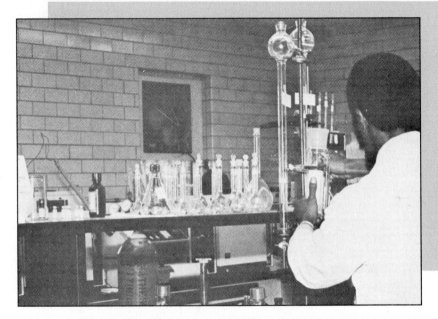

The vice-president for research and development of a large chemical and fiber manufacturing company believes that their annual profits depend on the amount spent on R & D. The new chief executive officer does not agree and has asked for evidence. Here is data for 6 years:

Year	Millions spent on research and development	Annual profit (millions)
1977	2	20
1978	3	25
1979	5	34
1980	4	30
1981	11	40
1982	5	31

The vice-president for R & D wants an equation for predicting annual profits from the amount budgeted for R & D. With methods in this chapter, we can supply such a decision-making tool and tell him something about the accuracy he can expect in using it to make decisions.

327

If your university used your high school grade point average to predict your college grade point average, it may have used the technique of regression analysis, one of the subjects of Chapter 11. And if you have heard the statement that there is a high correlation between smoking and lung cancer, then the word correlation (another topic in Chapter 11) is not strange to you. Correlation analysis is used to measure the degree of association between two variables.

1 INTRODUCTION

Relationship between variables

Every day, managers make personal and professional decisions that are based upon predictions of future events. To make these forecasts, they rely upon the relationship (intuitive and calculated) between what is already known and what is to be estimated. If decision makers can determine how the known is related to the future event, they can aid the decision-making process considerably. That is the subject of this chapter: how to determine the *relationship between variables*.

Difference between chi-square and topics in this chapter

In Chapter 10, we used chi-square tests of independence to determine whether a statistical relationship existed between two variables. The chi-square test tells us *if* there is such a relationship, but it does not tell us *what* that relationship is. Regression and correlation analysis will show us how to determine both the nature and the strength of a relationship between two variables. We will learn to predict, with some accuracy, the value of an unknown variable based on past observations of that variable and others.

Origin of terms regression and multiple regression

The term *regression* was first used as a statistical concept in 1877 by Sir Francis Galton. Galton made a study that showed that the height of children born to tall parents will tend to move back, or "regress," toward the mean height of the population. He designated the word *regression* as the name of the general process of predicting one variable (the height of the children) from another (the height of the parent). Later, statisticians coined the term *multiple regression* to describe the process by which several variables are used to predict another.

Development of an estimating equation

In *regression analysis*, we shall develop an *estimating equation*, that is, a mathematical formula that relates the known variables to the unknown variable. Then, after we have learned the pattern of this relationship, we can apply *correlation analysis* to determine the degree to which the variables are related. Correlation analysis, then, tells us how well the estimating equation actually describes the relationship.

Types of relationships

Independent and dependent variables

Regression and correlation analyses are based on the relationship, or association, between two (or more) variables. The known variable (or variables) is called the *independent* variable(s). The variable we are trying to predict is the *dependent* variable.

Scientists know, for example, that there is a relationship between the annual sales of aerosol spray cans and the quantity of fluorocarbons released into the atmosphere each year. If we studied this relationship, "the number of aerosol cans sold each year" would be the independent variable, and "the quantity of fluorocarbons released annually" would be the dependent variable.

Let's take another example. Economists might base their predictions of the annual gross national product, or GNP, on the final consumption spending within the economy. Thus, "the final consumption spending" is the independent variable, and "the GNP" would be the dependent variable.

In regression, we can have only one dependent variable in our estimating equation. However, we can use more than one independent variable. Often when we add independent variables, we improve the accuracy of our prediction. Economists, for example, frequently add a second independent variable, "the level of investment spending," to improve their estimate of the nation's GNP.

Direct relationship between X and Y

Our two examples of fluorocarbons and GNP are illustrations of direct associations between independent and dependent variables. As the independent variable increases, the dependent variable also increases. In like manner, we expect the sales of a company to increase as the advertising budget increases. We can graph such a *direct relationship*, plotting the independent variable on the X-axis and the dependent variable on the Y-axis. We have done this in Fig. 11 · 1(a). Notice how the line slopes up as X takes on larger and larger values. The slope of this line is said to be *positive* because Y increases as X increases.

Inverse relationship between X and Y

Relationships can also be *inverse* rather than direct. In these cases, the dependent variable decreases as the independent variable increases. The government assumes that such an inverse association exists between a company's increased annual expenditures for pollution abatement

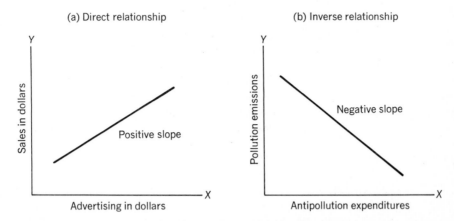

(a) Direct relationship   (b) Inverse relationship

Figure 11 · 1   Direct and inverse relationships between independent variable X and dependent variable Y

329   Sec. 1   Introduction

devices and decreased pollution emissions. This type of relationship is illustrated in Fig. 11 · 1(b) and is characterized by a *negative* slope (the dependent variable Y decreases as the independent variable X increases).

Frequently, we find a *causal* relationship between variables; that is, the independent variable "causes" the dependent variable to change. This is true in the antipollution example above. But in many cases, some other factor causes the change in both the dependent and the independent variables. We might be able to predict the sales of diamond earrings from the sale of new Cadillacs, but we could not say that one is *caused* by the other. Instead, we realize that the sales levels of both Cadillacs and diamond earrings are caused by another factor, such as the level of disposable income.

Relationships of association, not cause and effect

For this reason, it is important that you consider the relationships found by regression to be relationships of association but *not* necessarily of cause and effect. Unless you have specific reasons for believing that the values of the dependent variable are caused by the values of the independent variable(s), do not infer causality from the relationships you find by regression.

Scatter diagrams

Scatter diagram

The first step in determining whether there is a relationship between two variables is to examine the graph of the observed (or known) data. This graph, or chart, is called a *scatter diagram*.

A scatter diagram can give us two types of information. Visually, we can look for patterns that indicate the variables are related. Then, if the variables are related, we can see what kind of line, or estimating equation, describes this relationship.

We are going to develop and use a specific scatter diagram. Suppose a university admissions director asks us to determine whether any relationship exists between a student's scores on an entrance examination and that student's cumulative grade point average (GPA) upon graduation. The administrator has accumulated a random sample of data from the records of the university. This information is recorded in Table 11 · 1.

Transfer tabular information to a graph

To begin, we should transfer the information in Table 11 · 1 to a graph. Since the director wishes to use examination scores to predict success in college, we have placed the cumulative GPA (the dependent

TABLE 11 · 1 Student scores on entrance examinations and cumulative grade point averages at graduation

Student	A	B	C	D	E	F	G	H
Entrance examination scores (100 = maximum possible score)	74	69	85	63	82	60	79	91
Cumulative GPA (4.0 = A)	2.6	2.2	3.4	2.3	3.1	2.1	3.2	3.8

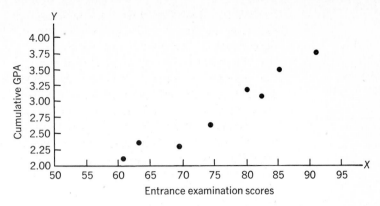

Figure 11·2 Scatter diagram of student scores on entrance examinations plotted against cumulative grade point averages

variable) on the vertical or *Y*-axis and the entrance examination score (the independent variable) on the horizontal or *X*-axis. Figure 11 · 2 shows the completed scatter diagram.

At first glance we can see why we call this a scatter diagram. The pattern of points results from the fact that each pair of data from Table 11 · 1 has been recorded as a single point. When we view all these points together, we can visualize the relationship that exists between the two variables. As a result, we can draw, or "fit," a straight line through our scatter diagram to represent the relationship. We have done this in Fig. 11 · 3. It is common to try to draw these lines so that an equal number of points lie on either side of the line.

In this case, the line drawn through our data points represents a direct relationship because *Y* increases as *X* increases. Because the data points are relatively close to this line, we can say that there is a high

*Drawing
or "fitting,"
a straight line
through a scatter
diagram*

*Interpreting
our straight line*

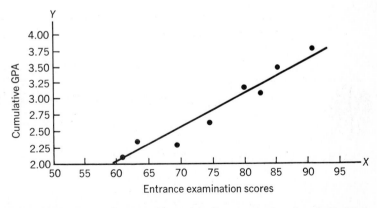

Figure 11·3 Scatter diagram with straight line representing the relationship between *X* and *Y* "fitted" through it

degree of association between the examination scores and the cumulative GPAs. In Fig. 11 · 3, we can see that the relationship described by the data points is well described by a straight line. Thus, we can say that is it a *linear* relationship.

Curvilinear relationships

The relationship between the X and Y variables can also take the form of a curve. Statisticians call such a relationship *curvilinear*. The employees of many industries, for example, experience what is called a "learning curve"; that is, as they produce a new product, the time required to produce one unit is reduced by some fixed proportion as the total number of units doubles. One such industry is aviation. Manufacturing time per unit for a new aircraft tends to decrease by 20 percent each time the total number of completed new planes doubles. Figure 11 · 4 illustrates the curvilinear relationship of this "learning curve" phenomenon.

The direction of the curve can indicate whether the curvilinear relationship is direct or inverse. The curve in Fig. 11 · 4 describes an inverse relationship because Y decreases as X increases.

Review of possible relationships

To review the relationships possible in a scatter diagram, examine the graphs in Fig. 11 · 5. Graphs (a) and (b) show direct and inverse linear relationships. Graphs (c) and (d) are examples of curvilinear relationships that demonstrate direct and inverse associations between variables, respectively. Graph (e) illustrates an inverse linear relationship with a widely scattered pattern of points. This wider scattering indicates that there is a lower degree of association between the independent and dependent variables than there is in graph (b). The pattern of points in graph (f) seems to indicate that there is no relationship between the two variables; therefore, knowledge of the past concerning one variable will not allow us to predict future occurrences of the other.

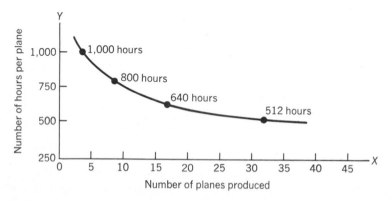

Figure 11·4 Curvilinear relationship between new aircraft construction time and number of units produced

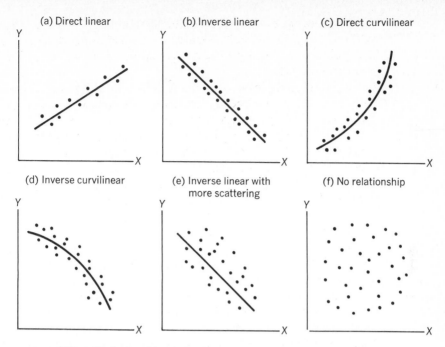

Figure 11·5 Possible relationships between X and Y in scatter diagrams

---
EXERCISES

11·1 What is regression analysis?

11·2 In regression analysis, what is an estimating equation?

11·3 What is the purpose of correlation analysis?

11·4 Define direct and inverse relationships.

11·5 To what does the term *causal relationship* refer?

11·6 Explain the difference between linear and curvilinear relationships.

11·7 Explain why and how we construct a scatter diagram.

11·8 What is multiple regression analysis?

11·9 The president of Decade Real Estate, a large southwestern real estate company, is conducting a study on sales techniques. One relationship of interest is the average length of time an agent spends with each customer and the success of that agent. A group of agents were sampled and the following data were collected. Row X is the average length of time (minutes) a particular agent spends with a prospect, and row Y is the number of houses that agent has sold in the last year. Construct a scatter diagram for this data. Is there a relationship between the variables? If so, is it linear or curvilinear, direct or inverse?

X	40	58	33	65	80	80	56	30	33	90	72
Y	15	14	12	20	26	26	14	12	12	30	22

11·10 For each of the following scatter diagrams, indicate whether a relationship exists and if so, whether it is direct or inverse and linear or curvilinear.

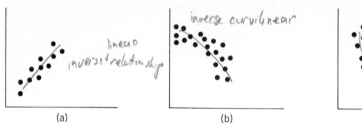

(a)

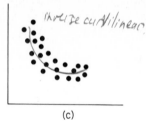

(b)   (c)

---

2 ESTIMATION USING
THE REGRESSION LINE

*Calculating
the regression
line using
an equation*

In the scatter diagrams we have used to this point, the *regression lines* were put in place by fitting the lines visually among the data points. In this section, we shall learn how to calculate the regression line somewhat more precisely using an equation that relates the two variables mathematically. Here, we examine only linear relationships involving two variables. We shall deal with relationships among more than two variables in the next chapter.

*Equation for
a straight line*

The equation for a straight line used to estimate the value of the dependent variable Y corresponding to a given value of the independent variable X is:

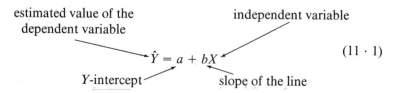

estimated value of the
dependent variable   independent variable

$$\hat{Y} = a + bX$$ (11 · 1)

Y-intercept   slope of the line

*Interpreting
the equation*

Using this equation, we can take a given value of X and compute the estimated value of Y. Notice that we use the symbol $\hat{Y}$ (Y hat) to denote the individual values of the *estimated* points, that is, those points that lie on the estimating line. The a is called the "Y-intercept" because its value is the point at which the regression line crosses the Y-axis, that is, the vertical axis. The b in Equation 11 · 1 is the "slope" of the line. It represents how much each unit change of the independent variable X changes our estimate of the dependent variable Y. Both a and b are numerical *constants* since, for any given straight line, their value does not change.

The method of least squares

Fitting a regression line mathematically

Now that we have seen the appropriate notation for the fitted regression line, let's think about how we can calculate an equation for a line that is drawn through the middle of a set of points in a scatter diagram. How can we "fit" a line mathematically if none of the points lie on the line? To a statistician, the line will have a "good fit" if it *minimizes the error* between the estimated points on the line and the actual observed points that were used to draw it. But how should we measure that error?

For each individual data point, the error in the fit is calculated as:

$$\text{Error in fit} = \hat{Y} - Y \qquad\qquad (11 \cdot 2)$$

where:

$$\hat{Y} = estimated \text{ value of the dependent}$$
$$\text{variable for a given data point}$$

$$Y = observed \text{ value of the dependent}$$
$$\text{variable for a given data point}$$

Using total error to determine best fit

One way we can "measure the error" of our estimating line is to *sum* all the individual differences, or errors, between the estimated points and the observed points. The problem with using this "total error" to measure goodness of fit is illustrated in Fig. 11 · 6, where we look at two possible regression lines for the same three points.

A quick visual examination of the two estimating lines in Fig. 11 · 6 leads most people to conclude that the line in graph (a) fits the three data points better than the line in graph (b). However, our process of summing the individual differences indicates that both lines describe the data equally well (the total error in both cases is zero). Thus, we must conclude that the process of summing individual differences for calculating the error is not a reliable way to judge the goodness of fit of an estimating line.

Using absolute value of error to measure best fit

The problem with adding the individual errors is the canceling effect of the positive and negative values. From this, we might deduce that the proper criterion for judging the goodness of fit would be to add the *absolute values* (the values without their algebraic signs) of each error. For graph (a) in Fig. 11 · 6, the *total absolute error* is 8 (2 + 4 + 2), and for graph (b) it is 12 (6 + 4 + 2). Since the total absolute error in graph (a) is smaller than the total absolute error in graph (b), and since we are looking for the "minimum absolute error," we have confirmed our intuitive impression that the estimating line in graph (a) is the better fit.

On the basis of this success, we might conclude that minimizing the sum of the absolute values of the error is the best criterion for finding a good fit. But before we feel too comfortable with it, we should examine a different situation.

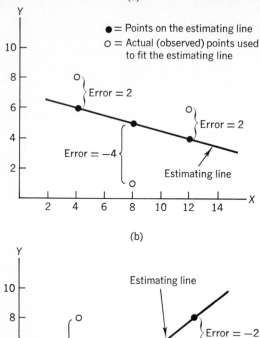

(a)

● = Points on the estimating line
○ = Actual (observed) points used
   to fit the estimating line

Error = 2

Error = 2

Error = −4

Estimating line

(b)

Estimating line

Error = −2

Error = 6

Error = −4

Figure 11·6 Two different estimating lines fitted to the same three observed data points, showing errors in both cases

In Fig. 11 · 7, we again have two identical scatter diagrams with two different estimating lines fitted to three data points. For graph (a) in Fig. 11 · 7, the total absolute error is 4 (0 + 4 + 0), and for graph (b), it is 5 (1 + 3 + 1). Intuitively, however, it appears that the line in graph (b) is the better fit line because it has been moved vertically to take the middle point into consideration. Graph (a), on the other hand, seems to ignore the middle point completely. So we would probably discard this second criterion for finding the best fit. Why? The sum of the absolute values does not stress the *magnitude* of the error.

Giving more weight to farther points; squaring the error

It seems reasonable that the farther away a point is from the estimating line, the more serious is the error. We would rather have several small absolute errors than one large one, as we saw in the last example. In effect, we want to find a way to "penalize" large absolute errors, so that we can avoid them. We can accomplish this if we *square*

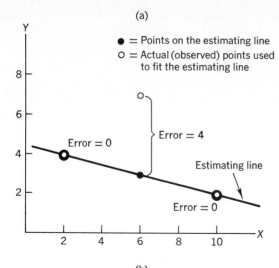

(a)

● = Points on the estimating line
O = Actual (observed) points used
　　to fit the estimating line

Error = 0

Error = 4

Estimating line

Error = 0

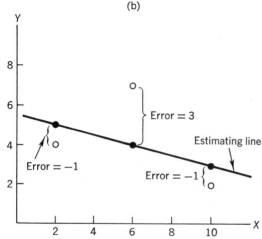

(b)

Error = 3

Estimating line

Error = −1

Error = −1

Figure 11·7 Two different estimating lines fitted to the same three observed data points, showing errors in both cases

the individual errors before we add them. Squaring each term accomplishes two purposes:

1. It magnifies, or penalizes, the larger errors.
2. It cancels the effect of the positive and negative values (a negative error squared is still positive).

Using least squares as a measure of best fit

Since we are looking for the estimating line that minimizes the sum of the squares of the errors, we call this the *least squares method*.

Let's apply the least squares criterion to the problem in Fig. 11 · 7. For graph (a) in Fig. 11 · 7, the sum of the squares of the errors is 16 $(0^2 + 4^2 + 0^2)$, and for graph (b), it is 11 $(1^2 + 3^2 + 1^2)$. By the least squares criterion, we can see that, as we thought, the estimating line in graph (b) is the better fit.

Using the criterion of least squares, we can now determine whether one estimating line is a better fit than another. But for a set of data points through which we could draw an infinite number of estimating lines, how can we tell when we have found *the best-fitting line*?

Statisticians have derived two equations we can use to find the slope and the Y-intercept of the best-fitting regression line. The first formula calculates the slope:

slope of best-fitting
estimating line

$$b = \frac{\Sigma XY - n\overline{X}\,\overline{Y}}{\Sigma X^2 - n\overline{X}^2} \qquad (11 \cdot 3)$$

The second formula calculates the Y-intercept of the line whose slope we calculated using Equation $11 \cdot 3$:

$$Y\text{-intercept} \longrightarrow a = \overline{Y} - b\overline{X} \qquad (11 \cdot 4)$$

In these two formulas:

$a = Y$-intercept of the best-fitting estimating line

$b = $ slope of the best-fitting estimating line

$X = $ values of the independent variable

$Y = $ values of the dependent variable

$\overline{X} = $ mean of the values of the independent variable

$\overline{Y} = $ mean of the values of the dependent variable

$n = $ number of data points (that is, the number of the pairs of values for the independent and dependent variables)

With these two equations, we can find the best-fitting regression line for any two-variable set of data points.

Using the least squares method in two problems

Suppose the director of the Chapel Hill Sanitation Department is interested in the relationship between the age of a garbage truck and the annual repair expense he should expect to incur. In order to determine this relationship, the director has accumulated information concerning 4 of the trucks the city presently owns (Table $11 \cdot 2$).

The first step in calculating the regression line for this problem is to organize the data as outlined in Table $11 \cdot 3$. This allows us to substitute directly into Equations $11 \cdot 3$ and $11 \cdot 4$ in order to find the slope and the Y-intercept of the best-fitting regression line.

TABLE 11 · 2 Annual truck repair expenses

Truck number	Age of truck (X) (years)	Repair expense during last year (Y) (hundreds of dollars)
101	5	7
102	3	7
103	3	6
104	1	4

TABLE 11 · 3 Calculation of inputs for Equations 11 · 3 and 11 · 4

Trucks (n = 4) (1)	Age (X) (2)	Repair expense (Y) (3)	XY (2) × (3)	X^2 (2)²
101	5	7	35	25
102	3	7	21	9
103	3	6	18	9
104	1	4	4	1
	$\Sigma X = \overline{12}$	$\Sigma Y = \overline{24}$	$\Sigma XY = \overline{78}$	$\Sigma X^2 = \overline{44}$

$$\overline{X} = \frac{\Sigma X}{n} = \frac{12}{4} = 3 \qquad \overline{Y} = \frac{\Sigma Y}{n} = \frac{24}{4} = 6 \quad (3 \cdot 2)$$

With the information in Table 11 · 3, we can now use the equations for the slope (Equation 11 · 3) and the Y-intercept (Equation 11 · 4) to find the numerical constants for our regression line. The slope is:

Finding the value of b

$$b = \frac{\Sigma XY - n\overline{X}\,\overline{Y}}{\Sigma X^2 - n\overline{X}^2}$$

$$= \frac{78 - (4)(3)(6)}{44 - (4)(3)^2} \qquad (11 \cdot 3)$$

$$= .75 \leftarrow \text{slope of the line}$$

And the Y-intercept is:

Finding the value of a

$$a = \overline{Y} - b\overline{X}$$

$$= 6 - (.75)(3)$$

$$= 6 - 2.25 \qquad (11 \cdot 4)$$

$$= 3.75 \leftarrow Y\text{-intercept}$$

Determining the estimating equation

To get the estimating equation that describes the relationship between the age of a truck and its annual repair expense, we can substitute the values of *a* and *b* in the general equation for a regression line.

$$\hat{Y} = a + bX$$

$$\hat{Y} = 3.75 + .75X \qquad (11 \cdot 1)$$

Using the estimating equation

Using this estimating equation (which we could plot as a regression line if we wished), the Sanitation Department director can estimate the annual repair expense, given the age of his equipment. If, for example, the city has a truck that is four years old, the director could use the equation to predict the annual repair expense for this truck as follows:

$$\hat{Y} = 3.75 + .75(4)$$

$$= 3.75 + 3$$

$$= 6.75 \leftarrow \text{expected annual repair expense of \$675.00}$$

Thus, the city might expect to spend about $675 annually in repairs on a 4-year-old truck.

Another example

Now we can solve the chapter opening problem concerning the relationship between money spent on research and development and the chemical firm's annual profits. In Table $11 \cdot 4$, we repeat the problem data and calculate the inputs for Equations $11 \cdot 3$ and $11 \cdot 4$.

With this information, we are ready to find the numerical constants a and b for the estimating equation. The value of b is:

Finding b

$$b = \frac{\Sigma XY - n\overline{X}\,\overline{Y}}{\Sigma X^2 - n\overline{X}^2}$$

$$= \frac{1000 - (6)(5)(30)}{200 - (6)(5)^2} \qquad (11 \cdot 3)$$

$$= 2 \leftarrow \text{the slope of the line}$$

TABLE 11·4 Calculation of inputs for Equations $11 \cdot 3$ and $11 \cdot 4$

Year (n = 6)	Expenditures for R & D (X)	Annual profits (Y)	XY	X²
1982	5	31	155	25
1981	11	40	440	121
1980	4	30	120	16
1979	5	34	170	25
1978	3	25	75	9
1977	2	20	40	4
	$\Sigma X = \overline{30}$	$\Sigma Y = \overline{180}$	$\Sigma XY = \overline{1,000}$	$\Sigma X^2 = \overline{200}$

$$\overline{X} = \frac{\Sigma X}{n} = \frac{30}{6} = 5 \qquad \overline{Y} = \frac{\Sigma Y}{n} = \frac{180}{6} = 30 \quad (3 \cdot 2)$$

And the value for *a* is:

$$a = \overline{Y} - b\overline{X}$$

$$= 30 - (2)(5)$$

$$= 30 - 10 \qquad\qquad (11 \cdot 4)$$

$$= 20 \leftarrow \text{the } Y\text{-intercept}$$

Determining the estimating equation

So we can substitute these values for *a* and *b* into Equation 11 · 1 and get:

$$\hat{Y} = a + bX$$

$$\hat{Y} = 20 + 2X \qquad\qquad (11 \cdot 1)$$

Using the estimating equation to predict

Using this estimating equation, the vice-president for research and development can predict what the annual profits will be from the amount budgeted for R & D. If the firm spends $8 million for R & D in 1983, it can expect to earn approximately $36 million in profits during that year:

$$\hat{Y} = 20 + 2(8)$$

$$= 20 + 16$$

$$= 36 \leftarrow \text{expected annual profit (millions)}$$

Shortcoming of the estimating equation

Estimating equations are not perfect predictors. In Fig. 11 · 8, which plots the points found in Table 11 · 4, the $36 million estimate of profit for 1983 is only that—an estimate. Even so, the regression line does give us an idea of what to expect for the coming year.

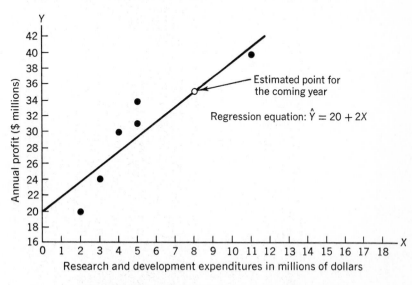

Figure 11·8 Scattering of points around regression line

The standard error of estimate

The next process we need to learn in our study of regression analysis is how to measure the reliability of the estimating equation that we have developed. We alluded to this topic when we introduced scatter diagrams. There, we realized intuitively that a line must be more accurate as an estimator when the data points lie close to the line (as in graph (a) of Fig. 11 · 9) than when the points are farther away from the line (as in graph (b) of Fig. 11 · 9).

*Definition and use
of standard error
of estimate*

To measure the reliability of the estimating equation, statisticians have developed the *standard error of estimate*. This standard error is symbolized s_e and is similar to the standard deviation (which we first examined in Chapter 4) in that both are measures of dispersion. You will recall that the standard deviation is used to measure the dispersion of a set of observations about the mean. The standard error of estimate, on the other hand, measures the variability, or scatter, of the observed values around the regression line. Even so, you will see the similarity between the standard error of estimate and the standard deviation if you compare Equation 11 · 5, which defines the standard error of estimate, with Equation 4 · 11, which defines the standard deviation:

*Equation for
calculation of
standard error
of estimate*

standard error of estimate

$$s_e = \sqrt{\frac{\Sigma(Y - \hat{Y})^2}{n - 2}} \qquad (11 \cdot 5)$$

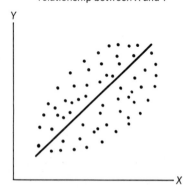

(a) This regression line is a more accurate estimator of the relationship between X and Y

(b) This regression line is a less accurate estimator of the relationship between X and Y

Figure 11·9 Contrasting degrees of scattering of data points and the resulting effect on accuracy of the regression line

where:

Y = values of the dependent variable

$\hat{Y}$ = estimated values from the estimating equation which correspond to each Y value

n = number of data points used to fit the regression line

n − 2 is the divisor in Equation 11 · 5

Notice that in Equation 11 · 5 the sum of the squared deviations is divided by $n − 2$ and not by n. This happens because we have lost two degrees of freedom in estimating the regression line. We can reason that since the values of a and b were obtained from a sample of data points, we lose two degrees of freedom when we use these points to estimate the regression line.

Now let's refer again to our earlier example of the Sanitation Department director who related the age of his trucks to the amount of annual repairs. On page 340 we found the estimating equation in that situation to be:

$$\hat{Y} = 3.75 + .75X$$

where X is the age of the truck and $\hat{Y}$ is the estimated amount of annual repairs (in hundreds of dollars).

Calculating the standard error of estimate

To calculate s_e for this problem, we must first determine the value of $\Sigma(Y − \hat{Y})^2$, that is, the numerator of Equation 11 · 5. We have done this in Table 11 · 5, using $(3.75 + .75X)$ for $\hat{Y}$ wherever it was necessary. Since $\Sigma(Y − \hat{Y})^2$ is equal to 1.50, we can now use Equation 11 · 5 to find the standard error of estimate:

$$s_e = \sqrt{\frac{\Sigma(Y − \hat{Y})^2}{n − 2}}$$

$$(11 \cdot 5)$$

$$= \sqrt{\frac{1.50}{4 − 2}}$$

$$= .866 \leftarrow \text{standard error of estimate of } \$86.60$$

TABLE 11·5   Calculating the numerator of the fraction in Equation 11 · 5

X (1)	Y (2)	$\hat{Y}$(that is, 3.75 + .75X) (3)	Individual error (Y − $\hat{Y}$) (2) − (3)	(Y − $\hat{Y}$)² [(2) − (3)]²
5	7	3.75 + (.75)(5)	7 − 7.5 = −.5	.25
3	7	3.75 + (.75)(3)	7 − 6.0 = 1.0	1.00
3	6	3.75 + (.75)(3)	6 − 6.0 = 0.0	.00
1	4	3.75 + (.75)(1)	4 − 4.5 = −.5	.25

$$\Sigma(Y − \hat{Y})^2 = \overline{1.50} \leftarrow \text{sum of squared errors}$$

Using a shortcut method to calculate the standard error of estimate

To use Equation 11 · 5, we must do the tedious series of calculations outlined in Table 11 · 5. For every value of Y, we must compute the corresponding value of $\hat{Y}$. Then we must substitute these values into the expression $\Sigma(Y - \hat{Y})^2$.

Fortunately, we can eliminate some of the steps in this task by using the shortcut provided by Equation 11 · 6; that is,

$$s_e = \sqrt{\frac{\Sigma Y^2 - a\Sigma Y - b\Sigma XY}{n - 2}} \qquad (11 \cdot 6)$$

where:

X = values of the independent variable

Y = values of the dependent variable

a = Y-intercept from Equation 11 · 4

b = slope of the estimating equation from Equation 11 · 3

n = number of data points

This equation is a shortcut because, when we first organized the data in this problem so that we could calculate the slope and the Y-intercept (Table 11 · 3), we determined every value we will need for Equation 11 · 6 except one—the value of ΣY^2. Referring back to Table 11 · 3, we see that the value of ΣY^2 is 150 ($7^2 + 7^2 + 6^2 + 4^2$).

Now we can refer to our previous calculations of a and b in order to calculate s_e using the shortcut method:

$$s_e = \sqrt{\frac{\Sigma Y^2 - a\Sigma Y - b\Sigma XY}{n - 2}}$$

$$= \sqrt{\frac{150 - (3.75)(24) - (.75)(78)}{4 - 2}} \qquad (11 \cdot 6)$$

$$= .866 \leftarrow \text{standard error of \$86.60}$$

This is the same result as the one we obtained using Equation 11 · 5, but think of how many steps we saved!

Interpreting the standard error of estimate

As was true of the standard deviation, the larger the standard error of estimate, the greater the scattering (or dispersion) of points around the regression line. Conversely, if $s_e = 0$, we expect the estimating equation to be a "perfect" estimator of the dependent variable. In that case, all the data points should lie directly on the regression line, and no points would be scattered around it.

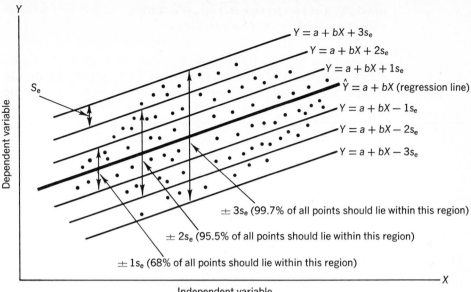

$Y = a + bX + 3s_e$
$Y = a + bX + 2s_e$
$Y = a + bX + 1s_e$
$\hat{Y} = a + bX$ (regression line)
$Y = a + bX - 1s_e$
$Y = a + bX - 2s_e$
$Y = a + bX - 3s_e$

S_e

Dependent variable

$\pm 3s_e$ (99.7% of all points should lie within this region)

$\pm 2s_e$ (95.5% of all points should lie within this region)

$\pm 1s_e$ (68% of all points should lie within this region)

Independent variable

Figure 11·10 $\pm 1s_e$, $\pm 2s_e$, and $\pm 3s_e$ bounds around the regression line

Using s_e to form bounds around the regression line

We shall use the standard error of estimate as a tool in the same way that we can use the standard deviation. That is to say, assuming that the observed points are normally distributed around the regression line, we can expect to find 68 percent of the points within $\pm 1s_e$ (or plus-and-minus one standard error of estimate), 95.5 percent of the points within $\pm 2s_e$, and 99.7 percent of the points within $\pm 3s_e$. Figure 11 · 10 illustrates these "bounds" around the regression line. Another thing to notice in Fig. 11 · 10 is that the standard error of estimate is measured along the Y-axis, rather than perpendicularly from the regression line.

Assumptions we make in use of s_e

At this point, we should state the assumptions we are making, because shortly, we shall make some probability statements based on these assumptions. Specifically, we have assumed that:

1. The observed values for Y are normally distributed around each estimated value of $\hat{Y}$.
2. The variance of the distributions around each possible value of $\hat{Y}$ is the same.

If this second assumption were not true, then the standard error at one point on the regression line could differ from the standard error at another point on the line.

Approximate prediction intervals

One way to view the standard error of estimate is to think of it as the statistical tool we can use to make a probability statement about the

Using s_e
to generate
prediction
intervals

interval around an estimated value of $\hat{Y}$, within which the actual value of Y lies. We can see, for instance, in Fig. 11 · 10 that we can be 95.5 percent certain that the actual value of Y will lie within 2 standard errors of the estimated value of $\hat{Y}$. We call these intervals around the estimated $\hat{Y}$ *approximate prediction intervals*. They serve the same function as the confidence intervals did in Chapter 8.

Now, applying the concept of approximate prediction intervals to the Sanitation Department director's repair expenses, we know that the estimating equation used to predict the annual repair expense is:

$$\hat{Y} = 3.75 + .75X$$

Applying
prediction
intervals

And we know that if the department has a 4-year-old truck, we predict it will have an annual repair expense of $675:

$$\hat{Y} = 3.75 + .75(4)$$

$$= 6.75 \leftarrow \text{expected annual repair expense of \$675}$$

One standard error
prediction
intervals

Finally, you will recall that we calculated the standard error of estimate to be $s_e = .866$, ($86.60). We can now combine these two pieces of information and say that we are roughly 68 percent confident that the actual repair expense will be within ± 1 standard error of estimate from $\hat{Y}$. We can calculate the upper and lower limits of this prediction interval as follows:

$$\hat{Y} \pm 1s_e = \$675 \pm (1)(\$86.60)$$

$$= \$761.60 \leftarrow \text{upper limit of prediction interval}$$

$$\text{and} \quad \$588.40 \leftarrow \text{lower limit of prediction interval}$$

Two standard error
prediction
intervals

If, instead, we say that we are roughly 95.5 percent confident that the actual repair expense will be within plus-and-minus 2 standard errors of estimate from $\hat{Y}$, we would calculate the limits of this new prediction interval like this:

$$\hat{Y} \pm 2s_e = \$675 \pm (2)(\$86.60)$$

$$= \$848.20 \leftarrow \text{upper limit}$$

$$\text{and} \quad \$501.80 \leftarrow \text{lower limit}$$

n is too small
to use the
normal distribution

Keep in mind that statisticians apply prediction intervals based on the normal distribution (68 percent for $1s_e$, 95.5 percent for $2s_e$, and 99.7 percent for $3s_e$) *only* to large samples, that is, where $n > 30$. In this problem, our sample size is too small ($n = 4$). Thus, *our conclusions are inaccurate.* But the method we have used nevertheless demonstrates the principle involved in prediction intervals.

Using the
t distribution
for prediction
intervals

If we wish to avoid the inaccuracies caused by the size of the sample, we need to use the t distribution. Recall that the t distribution is appropriate when n is less than 30 and the population standard deviation is unknown. We meet both these conditions, since $n = 4$ and s_e is an estimate rather than the known population standard deviation.

Now suppose the Sanitation Department director wants to be roughly 90 percent certain that the annual truck repair expense will lie within the prediction interval. How should we calculate this interval? Since the t distribution table focuses on the probability that the parameter we are estimating will lie *outside* the prediction interval, we need to look in Appendix Table 2 under the $100\% - 90\% = 10\%$ value column. Once we locate that column, we look for the row representing two degrees of freedom; since $n = 4$ and since we know we lose two degrees of freedom (in estimating the values of a and b) then $n - 2 = 2$. Here we find the appropriate t value to be 2.920.

Now we can make a more accurate calculation of our prediction interval limits as follows:

$$\hat{Y} + t(s_e) = \$675 + (2.920)(\$86.60)$$
$$= \$675 + \$252.87$$
$$= \$927.87 \leftarrow \text{upper limit}$$
$$\text{and} \quad \$422.13 \leftarrow \text{lower limit}$$

So the director can be 90 percent certain that the annual repair expense on a 4-year-old truck will lie between \$422.13 and \$927.87.

We stress again that the prediction intervals above are only *approximate*. In fact, statisticians can calculate the exact standard error for the prediction, s_p, using this formula:

$$s_p = s_e \sqrt{1 + \frac{1}{n} + \frac{(\overline{X} - X_0)^2}{\Sigma X^2 - n\overline{X}^2}}$$

where:

X_0 = the specific value of X at which we want to predict the value of Y

Notice that if we use this formula, s_p will be different for *each* value of X_0. In particular, if X_0 is *far* from $\overline{X}$, then s_p will be large because $(\overline{X} - X_0)^2$ will be large. If, on the other hand, X_0 is close to X, and n is moderately large (greater than 10), then s_p will be close to s_e. This happens because $1/n$ will be small and $(\overline{X} - X_0)^2$ will be small. Therefore, the value under the square root sign will be close to 1, the square root will be even closer to 1, and s_e will be very close to s_p. This justifies our use of s_e to compute approximate prediction intervals.

───────────────── **EXERCISES** ─────────────────

11·11 Using the data in the table below:
  a) Plot the scatter diagram.
  b) Develop the estimating equation that best describes the data.
  c) Predict Y for $X = 12$, 14, and 18.
  d) Compute the standard error of estimate.

e) Find prediction intervals with a 90 percent confidence level for the predictions made in part c.

X	20	11	15	10	17	19 =
Y	5	15	14	17	8	9 ﹀

11 · 12 For the following set of data:
a) Plot the scatter diagram.
b) Develop the estimating equation that best describes the data.
c) Predict Y for X = 4, 9, and 12.
d) Compute the standard error of estimate.
e) Find prediction intervals with a 95 percent confidence level for the predictions made in part c.

X	7	10	8	5	11	3	7	11	12	6
Y	2.0	3.0	2.4	1.8	3.2	1.5	2.1	3.8	4.0	2.2

11 · 13 A study by the Atlanta, Georgia, Department of Transportation of the effect of bus ticket prices upon the number of passengers produced the following results:

Ticket price (cents)	15	20	25	30	40	50
Passengers per 100 miles	440	430	450	370	340	370

a) Plot these data.
b) Develop the estimating equation that best describes these data.
c) Predict the number of passengers per mile if the ticket price were 35 cents.

11 · 14 The production manager for the Continental Television Company is conducting a study examining the relationship between the absentee rate and the number of defects produced. She sampled production data for 12 weeks and found the following average daily absentee rate (X) and corresponding number of defects produced during that week (Y).

X	7.3	6.4	6.2	5.5	6.4	4.7	5.8	7.9	6.7	9.6	10.3	7.2
Y	22	17	9	8	12	5	7	19	13	29	33	18

a) Develop the estimating equation that best describes these data.
b) Calculate the standard error of estimate for this relationship.
c) Find a prediction interval (with 95 percent confidence level) for the number of defects produced in a week with an average daily absentee rate of 6.0.

11 · 15 William C. Andrews, an organizational behavior consultant for Victory Motorcycles, has designed a test to show the company's foremen the dangers of oversupervising their workers. A worker from the assembly line is given a series of complicated tasks to perform. During the worker's performance, a foreman constantly interrupts the worker to assist him in completing the tasks. The worker, upon completion of the tasks, is then given a psychological test designed to measure the worker's hostility toward authority (a high score equals low hostility). Eight different workers were assigned the tasks and then interrupted for the purpose of instructional assistance varying numbers of times (X). Their corresponding scores on the hostility test are the dependent variable Y.

X (number of times worker interrupted)	5	10	10	15	15	20	20	25
Y (worker's score on hostility test)	58	41	45	27	26	12	16	3

a) Plot these data.

b) Develop the equation that best describes the relationship between number of times interrupted and test score.

c) Predict the expected test score if the worker is interrupted 18 times.

---

3 CORRELATION ANALYSIS

What correlation analysis does

Correlation analysis is the statistical tool that we can use to describe *the degree to which one variable is linearly related to another*. Frequently, correlation analysis is used in conjunction with regression analysis to measure how well the regression line explains the variations of the dependent variable, *Y*. Correlation can also be used by itself, however, to measure the degree of association between two variables.

Two measures that describe correlation

Statisticians have developed two measures for describing the correlation between two variables: the *coefficient of determination* and the *coefficient of correlation*. Introducing these two measures of association is the purpose of this section.

The coefficient of determination

Developing the sample coefficient of determination

The coefficient of determination is the primary way we can measure the extent, or strength, of the association that exists between two variables, *X* and *Y*. Since we have used a sample of points to develop regression lines, we refer to this measure as the *sample coefficient of determination*.

The sample coefficient of determination is developed from the relationship between two kinds of variation: the variation of the *Y* values in a data set around

1. the fitted regression line
2. their own mean

The term *variation* in both these cases is used in its usual statistical sense to mean "the sum of a group of squared deviations." Using this definition, then, it is reasonable to express the variation of the *Y* values around the regression line with this equation:

$$\text{Variation of the } Y \text{ values around the regression line} = \Sigma(Y - \hat{Y})^2 \qquad (11 \cdot 7)$$

And the second variation, that of the *Y* values around their own mean, is determined by:

$$\text{Variation of the } Y \text{ values around their own mean} = \Sigma(Y - \overline{Y})^2 \qquad (11 \cdot 8)$$

One minus the ratio between these two variations is the sample coefficient of determination, which is symbolized r^2:

$$\text{sample coefficient of determination} \rightarrow r^2 = 1 - \frac{\Sigma(Y - \hat{Y})^2}{\Sigma(Y - \overline{Y})^2} \qquad (11 \cdot 9)$$

Now let's see why we say that r^2, as defined by Equation $11 \cdot 9$, is a measure of the degree of linear association between X and Y.

An intuitive interpretation of r^2

Estimating equation appropriate for perfect correlation example

Consider two extreme ways in which the variables X and Y can be related. In Fig. $11 \cdot 11$, every observed value of Y lies on the estimating line. This is *perfect correlation*.

The estimating equation appropriate for this data is easy to determine. Since the regression line passes through the origin, we know that the Y-intercept is zero; and since $\hat{Y}$ increases by 4 every time X increases by 1, the slope must equal 4. Thus, the regression line is:

$$\hat{Y} = 4X$$

Now, to determine the sample coefficient of determination for the regression line in Fig. $11 \cdot 11$, we first note that the numerator of the fraction in Equation $11 \cdot 9$ is 0, since $Y - \hat{Y}$ is 0 for all the data points, since they all lie on the regression line. Since the numerator is 0, the fraction is 0 too. As a result we find that the sample coefficient of

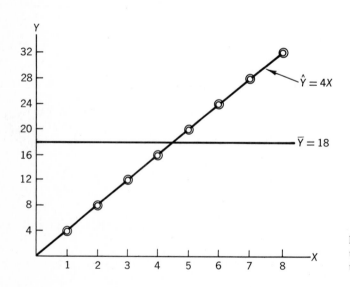

Figure 11·11 Perfect correlation between X and Y: every data point lies on the regression line

determination is equal to $+1$:

$$r^2 = 1 - \frac{\Sigma(Y - \hat{Y})^2}{\Sigma(Y - \overline{Y})^2}$$

$$= 1 - 0 \qquad\qquad (11 \cdot 9)$$

$$= 1 \leftarrow \text{sample coefficient of determination}$$
when there is perfect correlation

The value of r^2 is equal to $+1$, then, whenever the regression line is a perfect estimator.

A second extreme way in which the variables X and Y can be related is that the points could lie at equal distances on both sides of a horizontal regression line, as is pictured in Fig. 11 · 12. The data set here consists of 8 points. Since Y does not depend on X in this example, we say that there is *no correlation*.

Determining sample coefficient of determination for zero correlation

From Fig. 11 · 12, we can see that the least squares regression line appropriate for this data is of the form $\hat{Y} = 9$. The slope of the line is *zero* because the same values of Y appear for all the different values of X. Both the Y-intercept and $\overline{Y}$ the mean of the Y values are equal to 9.

Since $\hat{Y}$ and $\overline{Y}$ both equal 9, the distance of each Y value from the regression line $(Y - \hat{Y})$ is the same as its distance from the mean of the Y values $(Y - \overline{Y})$. Because of this, the numerator of the fraction in Equation 11 · 9 is the same as a denominator of that fraction. (If you work it out, you'll see that they are both equal to 72.) Since any fraction with the same nonzero numerator and denominator is equal to 1, we find

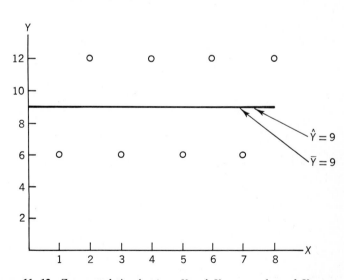

Figure 11·12 Zero correlation between X and Y: same values of Y appear for different values of X

that the sample coefficient of determination is 0:

$$r^2 = 1 - \frac{\Sigma(Y - \hat{Y})^2}{\Sigma(Y - \overline{Y})^2}$$

$$= 1 - 1 \qquad (11 \cdot 9)$$

$= 0 \leftarrow$ sample coefficient of determination
when there is no correlation

Thus, the value of r^2 is zero when there is no correlation.

In the problems most decision makers encounter, r^2 will lie somewhere between these two extremes of 1 and 0. Keep in mind, however, that an r^2 close to 1 indicates a strong correlation between X and Y, while an r^2 near 0 means there is little correlation between these two variables.

One point that we must emphasize strongly is that r^2 measures only the strength of a linear relationship between two variables. For example, if we had a lot of X, Y points that all fell on the circumference of a circle but at randomly scattered places, clearly there would be a relationship among these points (they all lie on the same circle). But in this instance, if we computed r^2 it would turn out in fact to be close to zero, because the points do not have a *linear* relationship with each other.

Interpreting r^2 another way

Statisticians also interpret the sample coefficient of determination by looking at the *amount of the variation in Y that is explained by the regression line.* To understand this meaning of r^2, consider the regression line in Fig. 11 · 13. Here we have singled out one observed value of Y, shown as the upper circle. If we use the mean of the Y values, $\overline{Y}$, to estimate this value of Y, then the *total deviation* of this Y from its mean would be $(Y - \overline{Y})$. Notice that if we used the regression line to estimate this value of Y, we would get a better estimate. However, even though

the regression line accounts for, or explains, $(\hat{Y} - \overline{Y})$ of the total deviation, the remaining portion of the total deviation, $(Y - \hat{Y})$ still is *unexplained*.

But consider a whole set of observed Y values instead of only one value. The total variation, that is, the sum of the squared total deviations, of these points from their mean would be:

$$\Sigma(Y - \overline{Y})^2 \qquad (11 \cdot 8)$$

and the *explained* portion of the total variation, or the sum of the squared explained deviations of these points from their mean, would be:

$$\Sigma(\hat{Y} - \overline{Y})^2$$

The *unexplained* portion of the total variation (the sum of the squared

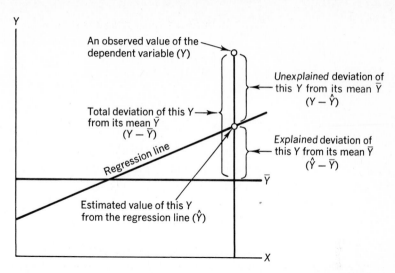

Figure 11 · 13 Total deviation, explained deviation, and unexplained deviation for *one* observed value of *Y*

unexplained deviations) of these points from the regression line would be:

$$\Sigma(Y - \hat{Y})^2 \qquad (11 \cdot 7)$$

If we want to express the fraction of the total variation that remains *unexplained*, we would divide the unexplained variation, $\Sigma(Y - \hat{Y})^2$, by the total variation, $\Sigma(Y - \overline{Y})^2$ as follows:

$$\frac{\Sigma(Y - \hat{Y})^2}{\Sigma(Y - \overline{Y})^2} \leftarrow \text{fraction of the total variation that is unexplained}$$

And finally, if we subtract the fraction of the total variation that remains unexplained from one, we will have the formula for finding that fraction of the total variation of Y which *is* explained by the regression line. That formula is:

$$r^2 = 1 - \frac{\Sigma(Y - \hat{Y})^2}{\Sigma(Y - \overline{Y})^2} \qquad (11 \cdot 9)$$

the same equation that we have previously used to calculate r^2. It is in this sense, then, that r^2 measures how well X explains Y, that is, the degree of association between X and Y.

Shortcut method to calculate r^2

One final word about calculating r^2. To obtain r^2 using Equations 11 · 7, 11 · 8, and 11 · 9 requires a series of tedious calculations. To bypass these calculations, statisticians have developed a shortcut version, using values we would have determined already in the regression analysis.

The formula is:

$$r^2 \text{ calculated by shortcut method} \rightarrow r^2 = \frac{a\Sigma Y + b\Sigma XY - n\overline{Y}^2}{\Sigma Y^2 - n\overline{Y}^2} \qquad (11 \cdot 10)$$

where:

r^2 = sample coefficient of determination

a = Y-intercept of the best-fitting estimating line

b = slope of the best-fitting estimating line

n = number of data points

X = values of the independent variable

Y = values of the dependent variable

$\overline{Y}$ = mean of the observed values of the dependent variable

Applying the shortcut method

To see why this formula is a shortcut, apply it to our earlier regression relating research and development expenditures to profits. Table 11 · 4 gives all the sums needed to compute r^2 with Equation 11 · 11, except ΣY^2. Referring back to that table, we see that the value of ΣY^2 is 5,642 ($31^2 + 40^2 + 30^2 + 34^2 + 25^2 + 20^2$). Recall that when we found the values for a and b on pages 340–41, the regression line for this problem was described by:

$$\hat{Y} = 20 + 2X$$

Using this line, the 5,642 value for ΣY^2 that we just calculated, and the information in Table 11 · 4, we can solve for r^2 as follows:

$$r^2 = \frac{a\Sigma Y + b\Sigma XY - n\overline{Y}^2}{\Sigma Y^2 - n\overline{Y}^2}$$

$$= \frac{(20)(180) + (2)(1{,}000) - (6)(30)^2}{5{,}642 - (6)(30)^2} \qquad (11 \cdot 10)$$

$$= .826 \leftarrow \text{sample coefficient of determination}$$

Interpreting r^2

Thus, we can conclude that the variation in the research and development expenditures (the independent variable X) explains 82.6 percent of the variation in the annual profits (the dependent variable Y).

The coefficient of correlation

Sample coefficient of correlation

The coefficient of correlation is the second measure that we can use to describe how well one variable is explained by another. When we are dealing with samples, the *sample coefficient of correlation* is denoted by r and is the square root of the sample coefficient of determination:

$$r = \sqrt{r^2} \qquad (11 \cdot 11)$$

When the slope of the estimating equation is positive, r is the positive square root, but if b is negative, r is the negative square root. Thus, the sign of r indicates the direction of the relationship between the two variables X and Y. If an inverse relationship exists, that is, if Y decreases as X increases, then r will fall between 0 and -1. Likewise, if there is a direct relationship (if Y increases as X increases), then r will be a value within the range of 0 to 1. Figure $11 \cdot 14$ illustrates these various characteristics of r.

Interpreting r

The coefficient of correlation is more difficult to interpret than r^2. What does $r = .9$ mean? To answer that question, we must remember that $r = .9$ is the same as $r^2 = .81$. The latter tells us that 81 percent of the variation in Y is explained by the regression line. So we see that r is nothing more than the square root of r^2, and we cannot interpret its meaning directly.

Calculating r for the research and development problem

Now let's find the coefficient of correlation for our problem relating research and development expenditures and annual profits. Since, in the previous section, we found that the sample coefficient of determination is $r^2 = .826$, we can substitute this value into Equation $11 \cdot 11$ and find that:

$$r = \sqrt{r^2}$$
$$= \sqrt{.826} \qquad\qquad (11 \cdot 11)$$
$$= .909 \leftarrow \text{sample coefficient of correlation}$$

The relation between the two variables is direct and the slope is positive; therefore, the sign for r is positive.

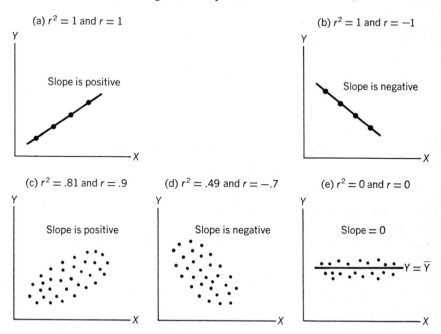

Figure $11 \cdot 14$ Various characteristics of r, the sample coefficient of correlation

11 · 16 What type of correlation (positive, negative, or zero) should we expect from these variables?

  a) ability of supervisors and output of their subordinates
  b) age at first full-time job and number of years of education
  c) weight and blood pressure
  d) college grade point average and student's height

In the following exercises, calculate the sample coefficient of determination and the sample coefficient of correction for the problems specified.

11 · 17 problem 11 · 14, p. 348
11 · 18 problem 11 · 13, p. 348
11 · 19 problem 11 · 15, p. 348

---

4 MAKING INFERENCES ABOUT POPULATION PARAMETERS

Relationship of sample regression line and population regression line

So far, we have used regression and correlation analyses to relate two variables on the basis of sample information. But data from a sample represents only part of the total population. Because of this, we may think of our estimated sample regression line as an estimate of a true, but unknown population regression line of the form:

$$Y = A + BX \qquad (11 \cdot 12)$$

Recall our discussion of the Sanitation Department director who tried to use the age of a truck to explain the annual repair expense on it. That expense will probably consist of two parts:

1. Regular maintenance that does not depend on the age of the truck: tuneups, oil changes, and lubrication. This expense is captured in the intercept term A in Equation 11 · 12.

2. Expenses for repairs due to aging: relining brakes, engine and transmission overhauls, and painting. Such expenses will tend to increase with the age of the truck, and they are captured in the BX term of the population regression line $Y = A + BX$ in Equation 11 · 12.

Why data points do not lie exactly on the regression line

Of course, all the brakes of all the trucks will not wear out at the same time, and some of the trucks will run years without engine overhauls. Because of this, the individual data points will probably not lie exactly on the population regression line. Some will be above it; some will fall below it. So, instead of satisfying Equation 11 · 12, the individual data points will satisfy the formula

$$Y = A + BX + e \qquad (11 \cdot 12a)$$

where e is a random disturbance from the population regression line. On the average, e equals zero because disturbances above the population regression line are canceled out by disturbances below the line. We can denote the standard deviation of these individual disturbances by σ_e. The standard error of estimates s_e, then, is an estimate of σ_e, the standard deviation of the disturbances.

Let us look more carefully at Equations $11 \cdot 12$ and $11 \cdot 12a$. Equation $11 \cdot 12a$ expresses the individual values of Y (in this case, annual repair expense) in terms of (1) the individual values of X (the age of the truck) and (2) the random disturbance (e). Since disturbances above the population regression line are cancelled out by those below the line, we know that the expected value of e is zero, and we see that if we had several trucks of the same age, X, we would expect the average annual repair expense on these trucks to be $Y = A + BX$. This shows us that the population regression line (Equation $11 \cdot 12$) gives the mean value of Y associated with each value of X.

*Making inferences
about B from b*

Since our *sample* regression line, $\hat{Y} = a + bX$ (Equation $11 \cdot 1$), estimates the *population* regression line, $Y = A + BX$ (Equation $11 \cdot 12$), we should be able to use it to make inferences about the population regression line. In this section then, we shall make inferences about the slope B of the "true" regression equation (the one for the entire population) that are based upon the slope b of the regression equation estimated from a sample of values.

Slope of the population regression line

*Difference
between true
regression
equation
and one estimated
from sample
observations*

The regression line is derived from a sample and not from the entire population. As a result, we cannot expect the true regression equation, $Y = A + BX$ (the one for the entire population), to be exactly the same as the equation estimated from the sample observations, or $\hat{Y} = a + bX$. Even so, we can use the value of b, the slope we calculate from a sample, to test hypotheses about the value of the B, the slope of the regression line for the entire population.

*Testing
a hypothesis
about B*

The procedure for testing a hypothesis about B is similar to procedures discussed in Chapter 9, on hypothesis testing. To understand this process, return to the problem that related annual expenditures for research and development to profits. On page 340, we pointed out that $b = 2$. The first step is to find some value for B to compare with $b = 2$.

Suppose that over an extended past period of time the slope of the relationship between X and Y was 2.1. To test if this were still the case, we could define the hypotheses as:

H_0: $B = 2.1$ ← null hypothesis
H_1: B is not equal to 2.1 ← alternative hypothesis

In effect, then, we are testing to learn whether current data indicate that B has changed from its historical value of 2.1.

Standard error of the regression coefficient

To find the test statistic for B, it is necessary first to find the *standard error of the regression coefficient*. Here, the regression coefficient we are working with is b, so the standard error of this coefficient is denoted s_b. Equation 11 · 13 presents the mathematical formula for s_b:

standard error of the
regression coefficient

$$s_b = \frac{s_e}{\sqrt{\Sigma X^2 - n\bar{X}^2}} \qquad (11 \cdot 13)$$

where:

s_b = standard error of the regression coefficient

s_e = standard error of estimate

X = values of the independent variable

$\bar{X}$ = mean of the values of the independent variable

n = number of data points

Finding upper and lower limits of the acceptance region for our hypothesis test

Once we have calculated s_b, we can use the t distribution with $n - 2$ degrees of freedom and the following equation to calculate the upper and lower limits of the acceptance region.

$$\text{Limits of acceptance region} = B \pm t(s_b) \qquad (11 \cdot 14)$$

where:

t = appropriate t value (with $n - 2$ degrees of freedom) for the significance level of the test

B = actual slope hypothesized for the population

s_b = standard error of the regression coefficient

Of course, for a one-tailed test you would calculate only an upper or lower limit as appropriate.

Our computation of r^2 on page 354 gave us all the inputs we need to use the shortcut method to calculate s_e:

Calculating s_e

$$s_e = \sqrt{\frac{\Sigma Y^2 - a\Sigma Y - b\Sigma XY}{n - 2}}$$

$$= \sqrt{\frac{5,642 - (20)(180) - (2)(1,000)}{6 - 2}} \qquad (11 \cdot 6)$$

$$= 3.24 \leftarrow \text{standard error of estimate}$$

Now we can use this value and the values for $\bar{X}$ and ΣX^2 determined in

Table 11 · 4 to find the standard error of the regression coefficient:

Calculating s_b

$$s_b = \frac{s_e}{\sqrt{\Sigma X^2 - n\overline{X}^2}}$$

$$= \frac{3.24}{\sqrt{200 - (6)(5)^2}}$$ (11 · 13)

$= .46 \leftarrow$ standard error of the regression coefficient

Conducting the hypothesis test

Suppose we have reason to test our hypothesis at the 10 percent level of significance. Since we have 6 observations in our sample data, we know that we have $n - 2$ or $6 - 2 = 4$ degrees of freedom. We look in Appendix Table 2 under the 10 percent column and come down until we find the 4 degrees-of-freedom row. There, we see that the appropriate t value is 2.132. Since we are concerned whether b (the slope of the sample regression line) is significantly *different* from B (the hypothesized slope of the population regression line), this is a two-tailed test and the limits of the acceptance region are found using Equation 11 · 14.

$$B \pm t(s_b) = 2.1 \pm 2.132(0.46)$$

$$= 3.081 \leftarrow \text{upper limit of acceptance region} \quad (11 \cdot 14)$$

$$\text{and} \quad 1.119 \leftarrow \text{lower limit of acceptance region}$$

The slope of our regression line (b) is 2.0, which is inside the acceptance region. Therefore, we accept the null hypothesis that B still equals 2.1. In other words, there is not enough difference between b and 2.1 for us to conclude that B has changed from its historical value. Because of this we feel that each additional million dollars spent on research and development still increases annual profits by \$2.1 million as it has in the past.

In addition to hypothesis testing, we can also construct a *confidence interval* for the value of B. In the same way that b is a point estimate of B, such confidence intervals are interval estimates of B. The problem we just completed, and for which we did a hypothesis test, will illustrate the process of constructing a confidence interval. There, we found that:

$b = 2.0$

$s_b = .46$

$t = 2.132 \leftarrow$ 10% level of significance and 4 degrees of freedom

Confidence interval for B

With this information, we can calculate confidence intervals like this:

$$b \pm t(s_b) = 2 \pm (2.132)(.46)$$

$$= 2.981 \leftarrow \text{upper limit}$$

$$\text{and} \quad 1.019 \leftarrow \text{lower limit}$$

Interpreting the confidence interval

In this situation, then, we are 90 percent confident that the true value of B lies between 1.019 and 2.981; that is, each additional million dollars spent on research and development increases annual profits by some amount between $1.02 million and $2.98 million.

11·20 In a regression problem with a sample of size 6, the slope was found to be .75 and the standard error of estimate 30.412. The quantity $(\Sigma X^2 - n\bar{X}^2) = 240{,}083.3$
  a) Find the standard error of the regression coefficient.
  b) Construct a 90 percent confidence interval for the population slope.

11·21 The vice-president of marketing for The Smooth Peanut Butter Company is conducting a study on the success of his company's trade promotions. Over the last 3 years the company's twice-a-year 10 percent discount promotion has been run for varying numbers of days. He is currently examining the relationship between the amount of peanut butter sold during each promotion and the number of days the promotion ran. From the data below, test the hypothesis that the population slope is 1.2 against the alternative that it is not equal to that value.

X	9	17	20	19	20	23	(number of days promotion ran)
Y	23	35	29	33	43	32	(number of carloads of peanut butter sold during promotion)

11·22 For a sample of size 10, the slope was found to be .265 and the standard error of the regression coefficient was .02. Is there reason to believe that the slope has changed from its past value of .30? Use the .01 significance level.

11·23 The Energy Research Administration specifies that the relationship between the number of cars in a train and a diesel engine's consumption of fuel oil has a slope of .046. A particular railroad company has compiled the operation records for 10 different train lengths. From this information, the slope of this relationship (train length versus fuel oil consumption) was calculated to be .061, and the standard error of the regression coefficient was determined to be .005.
  a) Construct a 95 percent confidence interval of estimate of the slope of the true regression line. Does the information from this study indicate that the ERA claim is invalid?
  b) Repeat the analysis from part a at the 99 percent level of confidence.

5 USING REGRESSION AND CORRELATION ANALYSIS: LIMITATIONS, ERRORS, AND CAVEATS

Misuse of regression and correlation

Regression and correlation analysis are statistical tools that, when properly used, can significantly help people make decisions. Unfortunately, they are frequently misused. As a result, decision makers often make inaccurate forecasts and less-than-desirable decisions. We'll mention the most common errors made in the use of regression and correlation in the hopes that you will avoid them.

Extrapolation beyond the range of the observed data

Specific limited range over which regression equation holds

A common mistake is to assume that the estimating line can be applied over any range of values. Hospital administrators can properly use regression analysis to predict the relationship between costs per bed and occupancy levels at various occupancy levels. Some administrators, however, incorrectly use the same regression equation to predict the costs per bed for occupancy levels that are significantly higher than those that were used to estimate the regression line. Although one relationship holds over the range of sample points, an entirely different relationship may exist for a different range. As a result, these people make decisions on one set of costs and find that the costs change drastically as occupancy increases (owing to things such as overtime costs and capacity constraints). Remember that an estimating equation is valid only over the same range as the one from which the sample was taken initially.

Cause and effect

Regression and correlation analyses do not determine cause and effect

Another mistake we can make when we use regression analysis is to assume that a change in one variable is "caused" by a change in the other variable. As we discussed earlier, regression and correlation analyses can in no way determine cause and effect. If we say that there is a correlation between students' grades in college and their annual earnings 5 years after graduation, we are *not* saying that one causes the other. Rather, both may be caused by other factors such as sociological background, parental attitudes, quality of teachers, effectiveness of the job-interviewing process, and economic status of parents—to name only a few potential factors.

We have extensively used the example about research and development expenses and annual profits to illustrate various aspects of regression analysis. But it is really highly unlikely that profits in a given year are *caused* by R & D expenditures in that year. Certainly it would be foolhardy for the VP for R & D to suggest to the chief executive that profits could immediately be increased merely by increasing R & D expenditures. Particularly in high technology industries, the R & D activity can be used to explain profits, but a better way to do so would be to predict current profits in terms of past research and development expenditures as well as in terms of economic conditions, dollars spent on advertising, and other variables. This can be done by using the multiple regression techniques to be discussed in the next chapter.

Using past trends to estimate future trends

Conditions change
and invalidate the
regression
equation

We must take care to reappraise the historical data we use to estimate the regression equation. Conditions can change and violate one or more of the assumptions on which our regression analysis depends. Earlier in this chapter we made the point that we assume that the variance of the disturbance *e* around the mean is constant. In many situations, however, this variance changes from year to year.

Values of variables
change over time

Another error that can arise from the use of historical data concerns the dependence of some variables on time. Suppose a firm uses regression analysis to determine the relationship between the number of employees and the production volume. If the observations used in the analysis extend back for several years, the resulting regression line may be too steep, because it may fail to recognize the effect of changing technology.

Misinterpreting the coefficients of correlation and determination

Misinterpreting
r and r²

The coefficient of correlation is occasionally misinterpreted as a percentage. If $r = .6$, it is incorrect to state that the regression equation "explains" 60 percent of the total variation in Y. Instead, if $r = .6$, then r^2 must be $.6 \times .6 = .36$. Only 36 percent of the total variation is explained by the regression line.

The coefficient of determination is misinterpreted if we use r^2 to describe the percentage of the change in the dependent variable that is *caused* by a change in the independent variable. This is wrong because r^2 is a measure only of how well one variable describes another, *not* of how much of the change in one variable is caused by the other variable.

Finding relationships when they do not exist

Relationships
that have
no common bond

When applying regression analysis, people sometimes find a relationship between two variables that, in fact, have no common bond. Even though one variable does not "cause" a change in the other, they think that there must be some factor common to both variables. It might be possible, for example, to find a statistical relationship between a random sample of the number of miles per gallon consumed by eight different cars and the distance from earth to each of the other eight planets. But since there is absolutely no common bond between gas mileage and the distance to other planets, this "relationship" would be meaningless.

11·24 Explain why an estimating equation is valid over only the range of values used for its development.

11·25 Explain the difference between the coefficient of determination and the coefficient of correlation.

11·26 Why should we be cautious in using past data to predict future trends?

11·27 Why must we not attribute causality in a relationship even when there is strong correlation between the variables or events?

6 TERMS INTRODUCED IN CHAPTER 11

coefficient of correlation The square root of the coefficient of determination. Its sign indicates the direction of the relationship between two variables, direct or inverse.

coefficient of determination A measure of the proportion of variation in Y, the dependent variable, that is explained by the regression line; i.e., by Y's relationship with the independent variable.

correlation analysis A technique to determine the degree to which variables are linearly related.

curvilinear relationship An association between two variables which is described by a curved line.

dependent variable The variable we are trying to predict in regression analysis.

direct relationship A relationship between two variables such that, as the independent variable's value increases, so does the value of the dependent variable.

estimating equation A mathematical formula that relates the unknown variable to the known variables in regression analysis.

independent variables The known variable, or variables, in regression analysis.

inverse relationship A relationship between two variables such that, as the independent variable increases, the dependent variable decreases.

least squares method A technique for fitting a straight line through a set of points in such a way that the sum of the squared vertical distances from the n points to the line is minimized.

linear relationship A particular type of association between two variables that can be described mathematically by a straight line.

multiple regression The statistical process by which several variables are used to predict another variable.

regression The general process of predicting one variable from another by statistical means, using previous data.

regression line A line fitted to a set of data points to estimate the relationship between two variables.

scatter diagram A graph of points on a rectangular grid; the X- and Y-coordinates of each point correspond to the two measurements made on some particular sample element, and the pattern of points illustrates the relationship between the two variables.

slope A constant for any given straight line, the value of which represents how much each unit change of the independent variable changes the dependent variable.

standard error of estimate A measure of the reliability of the estimating equation, indicating the variability of the observed points around the regression line; i.e., the extent to which observed values differ from their predicted values on the regression line.

standard error of the regression coefficient A measure of the variability of sample regression coefficients around the true population regression coefficient.

Y-intercept A constant for any given straight line, whose value represents the predicted value of the Y-variable when the X-variable has a value of 0.

7 EQUATIONS INTRODUCED IN CHAPTER 11

p. 334
$$\hat{Y} = a + bX \qquad \text{11} \cdot \text{1}$$

In regression analysis, $\hat{Y}$ (*Y-hat*) symbolizes the individual Y values of the *estimated* points; that is, those points that lie on the estimating line. Accordingly, Equation $11 \cdot 1$ is the equation for the estimating line.

p. 335
$$\text{Error in fit} = \hat{Y} - Y \qquad \text{11} \cdot \text{2}$$

The difference between the value of the independent variable estimated by the regression line ($\hat{Y}$) and the observed value of the dependent variable (Y) measures the distance of the observed data point from the fitted estimating line; that is called the error in fit.

p. 338
$$b = \frac{\Sigma XY - n\bar{X}\bar{Y}}{\Sigma X^2 - n\bar{X}^2} \qquad \text{11} \cdot \text{3}$$

The equation enables us to calculate the *slope of the best-fitting regression line* for any two-variable set of data points. We introduce two new symbols in this equation, $\bar{X}$ and $\bar{Y}$, which represent the means of the values of the independent variable and the dependent variable, respectively. In addition, this equation contains n, which, in this case, represents the number of data points with which we are fitting the regression line.

p. 338
$$a = \bar{Y} - b\bar{X} \qquad \text{11} \cdot \text{4}$$

Using this formula, we can compute the *Y-intercept of the best-fitting regression line* for any two-variable set of data points.

p. 342
$$s_e = \sqrt{\frac{\Sigma(Y - \hat{Y})^2}{n - 2}} \qquad \text{11} \cdot \text{5}$$

The *standard error of estimate*, s_e, measures the variability or scatter of the observed values around the regression line. In effect, it indicates the reliability of the estimating equation. The denominator is $n - 2$ because we lose two degrees of freedom (for the values a and b) in estimating the regression line.

p. 344
$$s_e = \sqrt{\frac{\Sigma Y^2 - a\Sigma Y - b\Sigma XY}{n - 2}} \qquad \text{11} \cdot \text{6}$$

Since Equation $11 \cdot 5$ requires tedious calculations, statisticians have devised this *shortcut method for finding the standard error of estimate*. In calculating the values for b and a, we already calculated every quantity in Equation $11 \cdot 6$ except ΣY^2, which we can do easily.

p. 349 Variation of the Y values around the regression line $= \Sigma(Y - \hat{Y})^2$ $\qquad \text{11} \cdot \text{7}$

The variation of the Y values in a data set around the fitted regression line is one of two quantities from which the sample coefficient of determination is developed. Equation $11 \cdot 7$ shows how to measure this particular dispersion, which is the *unexplained* portion of the total variation.

p. 349 Variation of the Y values around their own mean $= \Sigma(Y - \overline{Y})^2$ **11·8**

This formula measures the *total variation* of a whole set of Y values; that is, the dispersion of these Y values around their own mean.

p. 350
$$r^2 = 1 - \frac{\Sigma(Y - \hat{Y})^2}{\Sigma(Y - \overline{Y})^2}$$
    11·9

The *sample coefficient of determination*, r^2, gives the fraction of the total variation of Y that is explained by the regression line. It is an important measure of the degree of association between X and Y. If the value of r^2 is $+1$, then the regression line is a perfect estimator. If $r^2 = 0$, there is no correlation between X and Y.

p. 354
$$r^2 = \frac{a\Sigma Y + b\Sigma XY - n\overline{Y}^2}{\Sigma Y^2 - n\overline{Y}^2}$$
    11·10

This is a shortcut equation for calculating r^2.

p. 354
$$r = \sqrt{r^2}$$
    11·11

The *sample coefficient of correlation* is denoted by r and is found by taking the square root of the sample coefficient of determination. It is a second measure (in addition to r^2) we can use to describe how well one variable is explained by another. The sign of r indicates the direction of the relationship between the two variables X and Y.

p. 356
$$Y = A + BX$$
    11·12

Each *population regression line* is of the form in Equation 11·12, where A is the Y-intercept for the population, and B is the slope.

p. 356
$$Y = A + BX + e$$
    11·12a

Because all the individual points in a population do not lie on the population regression line, the *individual* data points will satisfy Formula 11·12a, where e is a random disturbance from the population regression line. On the average, e equals zero because disturbances above the population regression line are canceled out by disturbances below it.

p. 358
$$s_b = \frac{s_e}{\sqrt{\Sigma X^2 - n\overline{X}^2}}$$
    11·13

When we are dealing with a population, we can use this formula to find the *standard error of the regression coefficient, b*.

p. 358   Limits of acceptance region $= B \pm t(s_b)$ **11·14**

Once we have calculated s_b using Equation 11·13, we can determine the upper and lower limits of the acceptance region for a hypothesis test using this pair of equations.

---

8 CHAPTER REVIEW EXERCISES

11·28 Melinda Wilde, an HEW economist, speculates about the relationship between a family's income and its expenditures for food. The following table presents the results of a survey of 8 randomly selected families:

Income ($\times$ $1,000)	8	12	9	24	13	37	19	16
Percent spent for food	36	25	33	15	28	19	20	22

a) Develop an estimating equation that best describes these data.
b) Calculate the standard error of estimate, s_e, for this relationship.
c) Find an approximate 90 percent prediction interval for the percent of income spent on food by a family earning $25,000 annually.
d) Compute the sample coefficient of determination and the sample correlation coefficient.

11·29 The president of Wonx Computers is interested in studying the relationship between the size of the annual raise and the performance of a sales representative over the subsequent year. He sampled 12 sales representatives and determined the sizes of their respective raises (given as a percentage of their individual salaries) and the number of sales made by each one during the 12 months following raises.

Size of raise	7.3	6.4	6.2	5.5	6.4	4.7	5.8	7.9	6.7	9.6	10.3	7.2
Number of sales	64	53	42	29	71	26	32	68	53	64	85	73

a) Develop the best-fitting estimating equation that describes these data.
b) Calculate the standard error of estimate for this relationship.
c) Develop a 90 percent prediction interval for the number of sales made by a salesperson after receiving an 8.6 percent raise.
d) Compute the sample coefficient of determination and the sample correlation coefficient.

11·30 The manager of the Durham, North Carolina, water purification plant has compiled the data shown below to determine whether or not water usage has changed. These pairs of data are the volumes of water consumed and the corresponding number of households serviced for six recent months. Previous studies indicated that the relationship describing these two variables has a slope of 13. At the .10 level of significance, has the slope of this relationship increased?

Number of households (1,000s)	8.1	7.8	8.4	7.6	8.0	8.1
Water consumed (10 million gallons)	94	83	97	85	89	92

11·31 Calculate the sample coefficient of determination and the sample correlation coefficient for problem 11 · 12 on page 348.

11·32 Marc Applestein, president of a consulting firm, is interested in the relationship between environmental work factors and the employee turnover rate. He defined environmental factors as those aspects of a job other than salary and benefits. He visited 10 similar plants and gave each plant a rating from 1 to 25 on its environmental factors. He then obtained each plant's turnover rate and examined the relationship.

Environmental rating	11	19	7	12	13	10	16	22	14	12
Turnover rate (annual %)	6	4	8	3	7	8	3	2	5	6

a) Plot these data.
b) Develop the estimating equation that best describes these data.
c) Predict the turnover rate that might be expected if a plant received a rating of 15.

11·33 For each of the following pairs of plots, state which has a higher value of *r*, the correlation coefficient, and what the sign of *r* is:

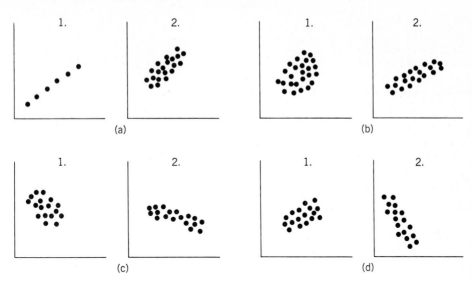

(a)　　　　　　　　　　　　(b)

(c)　　　　　　　　　　　　(d)

11·34 In a CAB study of airline operations, a survey of 12 companies disclosed that the relationship between the number of pilots employed and the number of planes in service has a slope of 3.5. Previous studies indicated that the slope of this relationship was 4.0. If the standard error of the regression coefficient has been calculated to be .20, is there reason to believe that, at the .01 level of significance, the true slope has changed?

11·35 Calculate the sample coefficient of determination and sample correlation coefficient for problem 11 · 11, p. 347.

---
9 CHAPTER CONCEPTS TEST

Answers are in the back of the book.

T F 1. Regression analysis is used to describe how well an estimating equation describes the relationship being studied.

T F 2. Given that the equation for a line is $Y = 26 - 24X$, we may say the relationship of Y to X is direct linear.

T F 3. An r^2 value close to 0 indicates a strong correlation between X and Y.

T F 4. Regression and correlation analysis are used to determine cause and effect relationships.

T F 5. The sample coefficient of correlation, r, is nothing more than $\sqrt{r^2}$, and we cannot interpret its meaning directly as a percentage of some kind.

T F 6. The standard error of estimate measures the variability of the observed values around the regression equation.

T F 7. The regression line is derived from a sample and not the entire population.

T F 8. We may interpret the sample coefficient of determination as the amount of the variation in Y that is explained by the regression line.

T F 9. Lines drawn on either side of the regression line at ± 1, ± 2 and ± 3 times the value of the standard error of estimate are called confidence lines.

T F 10. The estimating equation is valid over only the same range as that given by the original sample data upon which it was developed.

T F 11. In the equation $Y = a + bX$ for dependent variable Y and independent variable X, the Y-intercept is b.

T F 12. If a line is fitted to a set of points by the method of least squares, the individual positive and negative errors from the line sum to zero.

T F 13. If $s_e = 0$ for an estimating equation, it must perfectly estimate the dependent variable at the observed points.

T F 14. Suppose the slope of an estimating equation is positive. Then the value of r must be the positive square root of r^2.

T F 15. If $r = .8$, then the regression equation explains 80 percent of the total variation in the dependent variable.

16. Suppose that we know the height of a student but do not know her weight. We use an estimating equation to determine an estimate of her weight based upon her height. We can therefore surmise that:
   a) Weight is the independent variable.
   b) Height is the dependent variable.
   c) The relationship between weight and height is an inverse one.
   d) None of the above.
   e) b and c but not a.

17. Suppose you are told that there is a direct relationship between the price of artichokes and the amount of rain that fell during the growing season. It can be concluded that:
   a) Prices tend to be high when rainfall is high.
   b) Prices tend to be low when rainfall is high.
   c) A large amount of rain causes prices to rise.
   d) A lack of rain causes prices to rise.

18. Suppose it is calculated that a is 4 and b is 2 for a particular estimating line with one independent variable. If the independent variable has a value of 2, what value should be expected for the dependent variable?
   a) 8   b) 10   c) −1   d) 0

19. Suppose the estimating equation $\hat{Y} = 5 - 2X$ has been calculated for a set of data. Which of the following is true for this situation?
   a) The Y-intercept of the line is 2.
   b) The slope of the line is negative.
   c) The line represents an inverse relationship.
   d) All of the above.
   e) b and c but not a.

20. We know that the standard error is the same at all points on a regression line because we assumed:
   a) Observed values for Y are normally distributed around each estimated value of $\hat{Y}$.

b) The variance of the distributions around each possible value of $\hat{Y}$ is the same.

c) All available data was taken into account when the regression line was calcu-lated.

d) None of the above.

21. The variation of the Y values around the regression line is best expressed as:

a) $\Sigma(Y + \bar{Y})^2$ b) $\Sigma(Y - \bar{Y})^2$ c) $\Sigma(Y - \hat{Y})^2$ d) $\Sigma(Y + \hat{Y})^2$

22. The value of r^2 for a particular situation is .49. What is the coefficient of correlation in this situation?

a) .49   c) .07

b) .7   d) cannot be determined from information given

23. The fraction $\dfrac{\Sigma(Y - \hat{Y})^2}{\Sigma(Y - \bar{Y})^2}$ represents:

a) fraction of total variation in Y that is unexplained

b) fraction of total variation in Y that is explained

c) fraction of total variation in Y that was caused by changes in X

d) none of the above

24. In the equation $Y = A + BX + e$, the e represents:

a) the X-intercept of the observed data

b) the value of Y to which others are compared to determine the "best fit"

c) random disturbances from the population regression line

d) none of the above

25. Suppose you wish to compare the hypothesized value of B to a sample value of b that has been calculated. Which of the following *must* be calculated before the others?

a) s_b c) s_p

b) s_e d) Calculations can be made in any order.

26. If the dependent variable in a relationship decreases as the independent variable increases, the relationship is _____ .

27. An association between two variables which is described by a curved line is a _____ one.

28. Every straight line has a _____ , which represents how much each change of the independent variable changes the dependent variable.

29. The extent to which observed values differ from their predicted values on the regression line is measured by the _____ .

30. _____ is a measure of the proportion of variation in the dependent variable that is explained by the regression line.

Multiple Regression and Modeling Techniques

12

A manufacturer of small office copiers and word-processing machinery pays its salespersons a base salary plus a commission equal to a fixed percent of the person's sales. One of the salespersons charges that this salary structure discriminates against women. Current base salaries for the firm's 9 salespersons are as follows:

Salesmen		Saleswomen	
Months employed	Base salary ($1,000's)	Months employed	Base salary ($1,000's)
6	7.5	5	6.2
10	8.6	13	8.7
12	9.1	15	9.4
18	10.3	21	9.8
30	13.0		

The director of personnel sees that base salary depends on length of service, but she does not know how to use the data to learn if it also depends on sex and if there is discrimination against women. Methods in this chapter will enable her to find out.

Chapter 12 is a continuation of some of the regression ideas introduced in Chapter 11. Here we shall examine how to use regression when we feel that more than one factor is involved in something we are trying to predict. For example, if your university used your high school grade point average as well as your college board scores to predict your college grade point average, chances are they were using multiple regression. Also in Chapter 12, we try a bit of modeling with regression; that is, we'll get a bit deeper into how we can predict some things by looking at others, and what those others ought to be.

1 MULTIPLE REGRESSION AND CORRELATION ANALYSIS

Using more than one independent variable to estimate the dependent variable

As we mentioned in Chapter 11, we may use more than one independent variable to estimate the dependent variable and, in this way, attempt to increase the accuracy of the estimate. This process is called multiple regression and correlation analysis. It is based on the same assumptions and procedures we have encountered using simple regression.

Advantage of multiple regression

The principal advantage of multiple regression is that it allows us to utilize more of the information available to us to estimate the dependent variable. Sometimes the correlation between two variables may be insufficient to determine a reliable estimating equation. Yet, if we add the data from more independent variables, we may be able to determine an estimating equation that describes the relationship with greater accuracy.

Steps in multiple regression and correlation

Multiple regression and correlation analysis is a three-step process such as the one we used in simple regression. In this process, we must:

1. Describe the multiple regression equation.
2. Examine the multiple regression standard error of estimate.
3. Use multiple correlation analysis to determine how well the regression equation describes the observed data.

In addition, in multiple regression, we can look at each of the individual independent variables and test whether it contributes significantly to the way the regression describes the data.

Computer regression packages

In this chapter, we shall see how to find the best fitting regression equation for a given set of data and how to analyze the equation that we get. Although we shall show how to do multiple regression by hand or on a hand-held calculator, it will quickly become obvious to you that you would not want to do even a modest size real-life problem by hand. Fortunately, there are available many computer "packages" for doing multiple regressions and other statistical analyses. We shall also discuss the regression output from a typical package.

Multiple regression will also enable us to fit curves as well as lines. Using the techniques of "dummy variables," we can even include qualitative factors such as sex in our multiple regression. This technique will enable us to analyze the discrimination problem opening this chapter. Dummy variables and fitting curves are only two of the many *modeling techniques* that can be used in multiple regression.

─────────────────── **EXERCISES** ───────────────────

12·1 Why would we use multiple regression instead of simple regression in estimating a dependent variable?

12·2 How will dummy variables be used in our study of multiple regression?

13·3 Will the procedures used in multiple regression differ greatly from those we used in simple regression? Why or why not?

2 FINDING THE MULTIPLE REGRESSION EQUATION

A problem to demonstrate multiple regression

Let's see how we can compute the multiple regression equation. For convenience, we shall use only two independent variables in the problem we work in this section. Keep in mind, however, that the same sort of technique is in principle applicable to any number of independent variables.

The Internal Revenue Service is trying to estimate the monthly amount of unpaid taxes discovered by its auditing division. In the past, the IRS estimated this figure on the basis of the expected number of field audit labor hours. In recent years, however, field audit labor hours have become an erratic predictor of the actual unpaid taxes. As a result, the IRS is looking for another factor with which it can improve the estimating equation.

The auditing division does keep a record of the number of hours their computers are used to detect unpaid taxes. Could we combine this information with the data on field audit labor hours and come up with a more accurate estimating equation for the unpaid taxes discovered each month? Table 12 · 1 presents this data for the last 10 months.

Appropriate symbols

In simple regression, X is the symbol used for the values of the independent variable. In multiple regression, we have more than one independent variable. So we shall continue to use X, but we shall add a subscript (for example, X_1, X_2) to distinguish between the independent variables we are using.

Defining the variables

In this problem X_1 will represent the number of field audit labor hours and X_2 the number of computer hours. The dependent variable, Y, will be the actual unpaid taxes discovered.

TABLE 12·1   Data from IRS auditing records during last 10 months

Month	X_1 Field audit labor hours (00's omitted)	X_2 Computer hours (00's omitted)	Y Actual unpaid taxes discovered (millions of dollars)
January	45	16	$29
February	42	14	24
March	44	15	27
April	45	13	25
May	43	13	26
June	46	14	28
July	44	16	30
August	45	16	28
September	44	15	28
October	43	15	27

Estimating equation for multiple regression

In simple regression, the estimating equation $\hat{Y} = a + bX$ describes the relationship between the two variables X and Y. In multiple regression, we must extend that equation, adding one term for each new variable. In symbolic form, Equation 12 · 1 is the formula we can use when we have two independent variables:

$$\hat{Y} = a + b_1 X_1 + b_2 X_2 \qquad (12 \cdot 1)$$

where:

$\hat{Y}$ = estimated value corresponding to the dependent variable

a = Y-intercept

X_1 and X_2 = values of the two independent variables

b_1 and b_2 = slopes associated with X_1 and X_2, respectively

Visualizing multiple regression

We can visualize the simple estimating equation as a line on a graph; similarly, we can picture a two-variable multiple regression equation as a plane, such as the one shown in Fig. 12 · 1. Here we have a three-dimensional shape that possesses depth, length, and width. To get an intuitive feel for this three-dimensional shape, visualize the intersection of the axes Y, X_1, and X_2 as one corner of a room.

Interpretation of Fig. 12 · 1

Figure 12 · 1 is a graph of the ten sample points from Table 12 · 1 and the plane about which these points seem to cluster. Some points lie above the plane, and some fall below it—just as points lay above and below the simple regression line.

Using the least squares criterion to fit a regression plane

Our problem is to decide which of the possible planes that we could draw will be the best fit. To do this, we shall again use the least squares criterion and locate the plane that minimizes the sum of the squares of the errors; that is, the distances from the points around the plane to the corresponding points *on* the plane. We use our data and the following

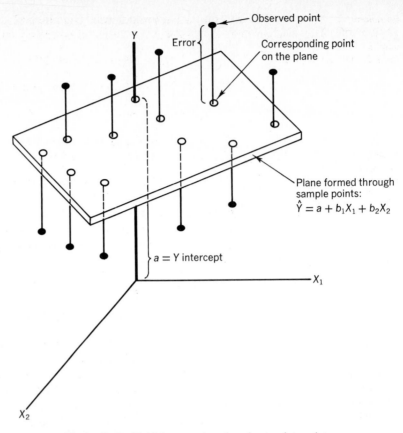

Y

Observed point

Error

Corresponding point
on the plane

Plane formed through
sample points:
$\hat{Y} = a + b_1 X_1 + b_2 X_2$

$a = Y$ intercept

X_1

X_2

Figure 12·1 Multiple regression plane for ten data points

three equations to determine the values of the numerical constants a, b_1, and b_2.

$$\Sigma Y = na + b_1 \Sigma X_1 + b_2 \Sigma X_2 \qquad (12 \cdot 2)$$

$$\Sigma X_1 Y = a\Sigma X_1 + b_1 \Sigma X_1^2 + b_2 \Sigma X_1 X_2 \qquad (12 \cdot 3)$$

$$\Sigma X_2 Y = a\Sigma X_2 + b_1 \Sigma X_1 X_2 + b_2 \Sigma X_2^2 \qquad (12 \cdot 4)$$

Solving Equations 12 · 2, 12 · 3, and 12 · 4 for a, b_1, and b_2 will give us the coefficients for the regression plane. Obviously, the best way to compute all the sums in these three equations by hand is to use a table to collect and organize the necessary information, just as we did in simple regression. If you'll do this, you'll find:

$$n = 10 \qquad \Sigma Y = 272 \qquad \Sigma X_1 = 441$$

$$\Sigma X_2 = 147 \qquad \Sigma X_1 Y = 12{,}005$$

$$\Sigma X_2 Y = 4{,}013 \qquad \Sigma X_1 X_2 = 6{,}485$$

$$\Sigma X_1^2 = 19{,}461 \qquad \Sigma X_2^2 = 2{,}173$$

Equations 12 · 2,
12 · 3, and 12 · 4
used to solve
for a, b_1, and b_2

Now, using this information in Equations 12 · 2, 12 · 3, and 12 · 4, we get three equations in the three unknown constants (a, b_1, and b_2),

$$272 = 10a + 441b_1 + 147b_2$$

$$12{,}005 = 441a + 19{,}461b_1 + 6{,}485b_2$$

$$4{,}013 = 147a + 6{,}485b_1 + 2{,}173b_2$$

Solving
Equations 12 · 2,
12 · 3, and 12 · 4
simultaneously

We can find the values for the three numerical constants by solving these three equations simultaneously.* You can verify that the solution is:

$$a = -13.828 \qquad b_1 = .564 \qquad b_2 = 1.099$$

Substituting the values of a, b_1, and b_2 into Equation 12 · 1 gives us the relationship among the number of field audit labor hours, the number of computer hours, and the unpaid taxes discovered by the auditing division.

$$\hat{Y} = a + b_1 X_1 + b_2 X_2$$

$$\hat{Y} = -13.828 + .564 X_1 + 1.099 X_2$$

$$(12 \cdot 1)$$

The auditing division can use this equation monthly to estimate the amount of unpaid taxes it will discover.

Using the multiple
regression
equation
to estimate

Suppose the IRS wants to increase its discoveries in the coming month. Since trained auditors are scarce, the IRS does not intend to hire additional personnel. The number of field audit labor hours, then, will remain at October's level of about 4,300 hours. But in order to increase its discoveries of unpaid taxes, the IRS expects to increase the number of computer hours to about 1,600. As a result we substitute the values of 43 and 16 for X_1 and X_2 in the regression equation to get:

$$\hat{Y} = -13.828 + .564 X_1 + 1.099 X_2$$

$$= -13.828 + (.564)(43) + (1.099)(16)$$

$$= 28.008 \leftarrow \text{estimated discoveries of } \$28{,}008{,}000$$

Therefore, in the November forecast, the audit division can indicate that it expects about $28 million of discoveries for this combination of factors.

Interpreting
our estimate

So far, we have referred to a as the Y-intercept and to b_1 and b_2 as the slopes of the multiple regression line. But to be more precise, we should say that these numerical constants are the *estimated regression coefficients*. The constant a is the value of $\hat{Y}$ (in this case, the estimated unpaid taxes) *if* both X_1 and X_2 happen to be zero. The coefficients b_1

*If you remember how to solve three equations in three unknowns, great; if you don't remember... or never knew how... don't worry; it's a lot of work and as we'll see shortly, there are computer routines available for doing it.

and b_2 describe how changes in X_1 and X_2 affect the value of $\hat{Y}$. In our regression equation, for example, we can hold the number of field audit labor hours, X_1, constant and change the number of computer hours, X_2. When we do, the value of $\hat{Y}$ will increase \$1,099,000 for every additional 100 hours of computer time. Likewise, we can hold X_2 constant and find that, for every 100-hour increase in the number of field audit labor hours, $\hat{Y}$ increases by \$564,000.

a, b_1, and b_2 are the estimated regression coefficients

EXERCISES

12·4 For the following set of data:
a) Calculate the multiple regression plane.
b) Predict Y for $X_1 = 36$ and $X_2 = 16$.

Y	X_1	X_2
8	10	8
36	37	21
23	18	14
27	29	11
14	14	9
12	21	4

12·5 A developer of food for pigs would like to determine what relationship exists among the age of a pig when it starts receiving a newly developed food supplement, the initial weight of the pig at the same time, and the amount it gains in a one-week period with the food supplement. The following information is the result of a study of eight piglets.

Piglet number	X_1 Initial weight (lb)	X_2 Initial age (weeks)	Y Weight gain
1	39	8	7
2	52	6	6
3	48	7	7
4	46	12	10
5	61	9	9
9	34	6	4
7	25	10	3
8	55	4	4

a) Calculate the least squares equation that best describes the relationship among these three variables.
b) How much might we expect a pig to gain in a week with the food supplement if it was 9 weeks old and weighed 48 pounds?

12·6 Radio station WILD is contemplating a new contest which will require listeners to call the station and guess the identity of a "secret spy." WILD hopes that the contest will capture a larger share of the listening market. Prizes and the number of times per day that calls will be accepted have yet to be determined. The past five contests that WILD has run have yielded the following data:

X_1 Number of calls per day	X_2 Prizes	Y Total percent of listening market during contest
15	$15.00	39
8	3.50	23
19	5.00	28
24	10.00	35
10	1.50	23

a) Calculate the least squares equation that best relates these 3 variables.
b) If WILD takes 13 calls per day and each prize is worth $7.50, what market share should they expect during the contest?

---

3 THE COMPUTER AND MULTIPLE REGRESSION

Impracticality of computing regressions by hand

In Chapter 11, and so far in this chapter, we have presented simplified problems and samples of small sizes. Although we could have given you the details of how to solve the example in the last section, hand solution is so tedious that you would have probably concluded that you were not interested in regression if you had to do the computations by hand. In fact, as sample size gets larger and the number of independent variables in the regression increases, it quickly becomes impractical to do the computations even on a hand-held calculator.

As managers, however, we will have to deal with complex problems requiring larger samples and additional independent variables. To assist us in solving these more detailed problems, we will make use of a computer, which allows us to perform a large number of computations in a very small period of time.

Suppose that we have not one or two independent variables but rather that we have k of them: $X_1, X_2, \ldots, X_k$. As before, we will let n denote the number of data points that we have. The regression equation we are trying to estimate is:

$$\hat{Y} = a + b_1 X_1 + b_2 X_2 + \cdots + b_k X_k \qquad (12 \cdot 5)$$

Now we'll see how we can use a computer to estimate the regression coefficients.

Demonstration of multiple regression using the computer

To demonstrate how a computer handles multiple regression analysis, take our IRS problem from the previous section. Suppose the auditing division adds to their model the information concerning rewards to informants. The IRS wishes to include this third independent variable, X_3, because it feels certain that there is some relationship between these

TABLE 12·2 Factors related to the discovery of unpaid taxes

Months	Field labor hours (00's omitted) X_1	Computer hours (00's omitted) X_2	Rewards to informants (000's omitted) X_3	Actual unpaid taxes discovered (000,000's omitted) Y
January	45	16	71	29
February	42	14	70	24
March	44	15	72	27
April	45	13	71	25
May	43	13	75	26
June	46	14	74	28
July	44	16	76	30
August	45	16	69	28
September	44	15	74	28
October	43	15	73	27

payments and the unpaid taxes discovered. Information for the last ten months is recorded in Table 12 · 2.

Using STATPACK to solve multiple regression problems

To solve this problem, the auditing division has used a computer multiple regression program called STATPACK. This particular program tells the user how to enter (and correct) the data. Actually, typing with one finger is about all the skill you need to use the STATPACK program. Of course, we don't yet know how to interpret the solution provided by STATPACK, but as we shall see, most of the numbers given in the solution correspond fairly closely to things we have already discussed in the context of simple regression.

STATPACK output

Output from the STATPACK program

Once all the data have been entered and the independent and dependent variables chosen, STATPACK computes the regression coefficients and several statistics associated with the regression equation. Let's look at the output for the IRS problem and see what all the numbers mean. The first part of the output is given in Table 12 · 3.

1. *The regression equation.* From the entry opposite "intercept" and the numbers in the "regression coefficient" column, we can read the estimating equation:

$$\hat{Y} = a + b_1 X_1 + b_2 X_2 + b_3 X_3$$
$$\hat{Y} = -45.796 + .597 X_1 + 1.177 X_2 + .405 X_3 \qquad (12 \cdot 5)$$

Finding and interpreting the regression equation

We can interpret this equation in much the same way that we interpreted the two variable regression equation on page 375. If we hold the number of field audit labor hours, X_1, and the number of computer hours, X_2, constant and change the rewards to informants, X_3, then the value of $\hat{Y}$ will increase \$405,000 for each additional \$1,000 paid to informants.

378 Chap. 12 Multiple regression and modeling techniques

TABLE 12·3 STATPACK output

```
VARIABLE     REG.COEF.     STD.ERROR COEF.
   1          0.59697          0.08113
   2          1.17684          0.08 07
   3          0.40511          0.04223

INTERCEPT                    -45.79634
MULTIPLE CORRELATION           0.99167
STD. ERROR OF ESTIMATE         0.28613
```

Similarly, holding X_1 and X_3 constant, we see that each additional 100 hours of computer time used will increase $\hat{Y}$ by \$1,177,000. Finally, if X_2 and X_3 are held constant, we estimate that an additional 100 hours spent in the field audits will uncover an additional \$597,000 in unpaid taxes.

Suppose that in November, the IRS intends to leave field audit labor hours and computer hours at their October levels (4,300 and 1,500) but to increase the rewards paid to informants to \$75,000. How much unpaid taxes do they expect to discover in November? Substituting these values into the estimated regression equation we get:

$$\hat{Y} = -45.796 + .597X_1 + 1.177X_2 + .405X_3$$
$$= -45.796 + .597(43) + 1.177(15) + .405(75)$$
$$= 27.905 \leftarrow \text{estimated discoveries of \$27,905,000}$$

So the audit division expects to discover about \$28 million in unpaid taxes in November.

Measuring dispersion around the multiple regression plane; using the standard error of estimate

2. *A measure of dispersion, the standard error of estimate for multiple regression.* Now that we have determined the equation that relates our three variables, we need some measure of the dispersion around this multiple regression plane. In simple regression, the estimation becomes more accurate as the degree of dispersion around the regression line gets smaller. The same is true of the sample points around the multiple regression plane. To measure this variation, we shall again use the measure called the standard error of estimate:

$$s_e = \sqrt{\frac{\Sigma(Y - \hat{Y})^2}{n - k - 1}} \qquad (12 \cdot 6)$$

where:

Y = sample values of the dependent variable

$\hat{Y}$ = corresponding estimated values from the regression equation

n = number of data points in the sample

k = number of independent variables ($= 3$ in our example)

The denominator of this equation indicates that in multiple regression with k independent variables, the standard error has $n - k - 1$ degrees of freedom. This occurs because the degrees of freedom are reduced by the $k + 1$ numerical constants, $a, b_1, b_2, \ldots, b_k$ that have all been estimated from the sample. From the STATPACK output, we see that the standard error of estimate in our IRS problem is .286; that is to say, $286,000.

Confidence intervals for $\hat{Y}$

As was the case in simple regression, we can use the standard error of estimate and the t distribution to form an *approximate confidence interval* around our estimated value $\hat{Y}$. In the unpaid tax problem, for 4,300 filed audit labor hours, 1,500 computer hours, and $75,000 paid to informants, our $\hat{Y}$ is $27,905,000 estimated unpaid taxes discovered, and our s_e is $286,000. If we want to construct a 95 percent confidence interval around this estimate of $27,905,000, we look in Appendix Table 2 under the 5 percent column until we locate the $n - k - 1 = 10 - 3 - 1 = 6$ degrees of freedom row. The appropriate t value for our interval estimate is 2.447. Therefore, we can calculate the limits of our confidence interval like this:

$$\hat{Y} \pm t(s_e) = 27,905,000 \pm (2.447)(286,000)$$

$$= 28,604,800 \leftarrow \text{upper limit}$$

$$\text{and} \quad 27,205,200 \leftarrow \text{lower limit}$$

Interpreting the confidence interval

With a confidence level as high as 95 percent, the auditing division can feel certain that the actual discoveries will lie in this large interval from $27,205,200 to $28,604,800. If the IRS wishes to use a lower confidence level, such as 90 percent, it can narrow the range of values in estimating the unpaid taxes discovered. As was true with simple regression, we can use the standard normal distribution, Appendix Table 1, to approximate the t distribution whenever our degrees of freedom (n minus the number of estimated regression coefficients) are greater than 30.

Value of additional variables

Did adding the third independent variable (rewards to informants) make our regression better? Since s_e measures the dispersion of the data points around the regression plane, smaller values of s_e should indicate better regressions. For the two variable regression done earlier in this chapter, s_e turns out to be 1.076. Since the addition of the third variable reduced s_e to .286, we see that adding the third variable *did* improve the fit of the regression in this example. It is not true in general, however, that adding variables always reduces s_e.

Meaning of the coefficient of determination

3. *The coefficient of multiple determination.* In our discussion of simple correlation analysis, we measured the strength of the relation between two variables using the sample coefficient of determination, r^2. This coefficient of determination is the fraction of the total variation of the dependent variable Y that is explained by the estimating equation.

Similarly, in multiple correlation we shall measure the strength of the relationship among three variables using the *coefficient of multiple*

Using
the coefficient
of multiple
determination
in multiple
correlation

determination, R^2 or its square root, R (the multiple coefficient of correlation). This coefficient of multiple determination is also the fraction that represents the proportion of the total variation of Y that is "explained" by the regression plane.

Notice that the STATPACK output gives the value of R, not R^2. In our example, $R = .99167$, so $R^2 = (.99167)^2 = .983$. This tells us that 98.3 percent of the total variation in unpaid taxes discovered is explained by the three independent variables. For the two variable regression done earlier, R^2 is only .726, so 72.6 percent of the variation is explained by field audit labor hours and computer hours. Adding in rewards to informants explains another 25.7 percent of the variation.

--- **EXERCISES** ---

12·7 Given the following set of data, use whatever computer package is available to find the best-fitting regression equation and answer the following:
a) What is the regression equation?
b) What is the standard error of estimate?
c) What is R^2 for this regression?
d) Give an approximate 95 percent confidence interval for the value of Y when the values of X_1, X_2, X_3, and X_4 are 15.6, 71.8, 93.4, and 1.7, respectively.

X_1	X_2	X_3	X_4	Y
12.4	92.6	91.2	.8	108.22
15.7	70.4	92.4	1.5	127.39
14.8	81.8	89.6	1.2	119.46
11.8	101.4	90.9	.6	102.91
17.6	62.2	92.1	1.8	138.55
19.9	51.6	90.3	2.0	170.32

12·8 David Mathews is a loan officer for a bank in Richmond, Virginia. He is trying to use past knowledge to determine the value of loans defaulting in given months. David feels that this value will be related to the average size of outstanding loans, the total number of loans outstanding, and the rate of inflation during the previous month. David has compiled this data from past months:

Y Total value of loans defaulting	X_1 Average amount of outstanding loans	X_2 Number of loans outstanding	X_3 Rate of inflation in previous month (%)
$2,033	$1,722	697	1.2
1,908	2,100	528	0.7
1,541	2,694	466	0.9
3,406	1,229	806	1.1
926	3,661	512	0.8
802	2,944	405	1.0

a) Using whatever computer package is available, determine the best-fitting regression equation for this data.

b) What is R^2 for this equation?

c) What is the standard error of the estimate?

d) For October, David estimates that the average dollar amount of loans outstanding is $1,995. There are 516 loans outstanding and the inflation rate in September was 1.2 percent. Give an approximate 95 percent confidence interval for the total value of loans defaulting in October.

12·9 Mary L. Webb owns an investment firm in Boston. Her firm specializes in the sale of bonds, and most of her salespeople are hired after graduation from business school. A little over a year ago, Mary became concerned about the apparent lack of knowledge which many of her salespeople displayed regarding the intricacies of bonds. She contracted with a local college to have a series of 15 courses made available to her sales force. Only one of the courses was required of all sales personnel; it covered basic principles such as the difference between premiums and discounts. The remaining 14 courses were staggered so that any salesperson who wished could take all courses, but few took advantage of more than 10. Mary is now interested in the effects of the courses on sales levels, so she is asking us to prepare an analysis of the data. Because she admits that factors other than training may also influence sales ability, she has added additional information about her sales force, and the data has been fed into STATPACK columns as follows:

> Col. 1 Number of courses taken this year
> Col. 2 Years experience in selling
> Col. 3 Number of clients visited during month
> Col. 4 Sales this month ($1,000's)

The result of a multiple regression run on this data is:

```
VARIABLE      REG.COEF.      STD.ERROR COEF.
    1          4.77515           1.40751
    2         -0.25491           0.52873
    3          0.01561           0.33620


INTERCEPT                       2.54139
MULTIPLE CORRELATION            0.97937
STD. ERROR OF ESTIMATE          4.88820
```

a) What is the best-fitting regression equation, as given by STATPACK?

b) What is the standard error of the estimate for this equation?

c) Calculate R^2 for this regression.

d) What sales level should Mary expect from a salesperson who took 2 courses, has 3 years of selling experience, and visited 61 clients during the month?

---

4 MAKING INFERENCES ABOUT POPULATION PARAMETERS

In Chapter 11 we noted that the *sample regression* line, $\hat{Y} = a + bX$ (Equation 11 · 1), estimates the *population* regression line, $Y = A + BX$

(Equation 11 · 12). The reason we could only estimate the population regression line rather than find it exactly was that the data points didn't fall exactly on the population regression line. Because of random disturbances, the data points satisfied $Y = A + BX + e$ (Equation 11 · 12a) rather than $Y = A + BX$.

Exactly the same sort of thing happens in multiple regression. Our estimated regression plane

$$\hat{Y} = a + b_1 X_1 + b_2 X_2 + \cdots + b_k X_k \qquad (12 \cdot 5)$$

Population regression plane

is an estimate of a true but unknown population regression plane of the form

$$Y = A + B_1 X_1 + B_2 X_2 + \cdots + B_k X_k \qquad (12 \cdot 7)$$

Once again, the individual data points usually won't lie exactly on the population regression plane. Consider our IRS problem to see why this is so. Not all payments to informants will be equally effective. Some of the computer hours may be used for collecting and organizing data; others may be used for analyzing that data to seek errors and fraud. The success of the computer in discovering unpaid taxes may depend on how much time is devoted to each of these activities. For these and other reasons, some of the data points will be above the regression plane and some will be below it. Instead of satisfying

$$Y = A + B_1 X_1 + B_2 X_2 + \cdots + B_k X_k \qquad (12 \cdot 7)$$

Random disturbances move points off the regression plane

the individual data points will satisfy

$$Y = A + B_1 X_1 + B_2 X_2 + \cdots + B_k X_k + e \qquad (12 \cdot 7a)$$

The quantity e in Equation 12 · 7a is a random disturbance, which equals 0 on the average. The standard deviation of the individual disturbances is σ_e, and the standard error of estimate, s_e, which we looked at in the last section, is an estimate of σ_e.

Since our *sample* regression plane, $\hat{Y} = a + b_1 X_1 + b_2 X_2 + \cdots + b_k X_k$ (Equation 12 · 5) estimates the unknown population regression plane $Y = A + B_1 X_1 + B_2 X_2 + \cdots + B_k X_k$ (Equation 12 · 7), we should be able to use it to make inferences about the population regression plane. In this section, we shall make inferences about the slopes $(B_1, B_2, \ldots, B_k)$ of the "true" regression equation (the one for the entire population) that are based on the slopes $(b_1, b_2, \ldots, b_k)$ of the regression equation estimated from the sample of data points.

Inferences about an individual slope B_i

Difference between true regression equation and one estimated from sample observations

The regression plane is derived from a sample and not from the entire population. As a result, we cannot expect the true regression equation, $Y = A + B_1 X_1 + B_2 X_2 + \cdots + B_k X_k$ (the one for the entire population), to be exactly the same as the equation estimated from the sample observations, $\hat{Y} = a + b_1 X_1 + b_2 X_2 + \cdots + b_k X_k$. Even so, we can use the value of b_i, one of the slopes we calculate from a sample, to test hypotheses about the value of the B_i, one of the slopes of the regression plane for the entire population.

Testing
a hypothesis
about B_i

The procedure for testing a hypothesis about B_i is similar to procedures discussed in Chapter 9, on hypothesis testing. To understand this process, return to the problem that related unpaid taxes discovered to field audit labor hours, computer hours, and rewards to informants. On page 378 we pointed out that $b_1 = .597$. The first step is to find some value for B_1 to compare with $b_1 = .597$.

Suppose that over an extended past period of time the slope of the relationship between Y and X_1 was .400. To test if this were still the case, we could define the hypotheses as:

H_0: $B_1 = .400$ ← null hypothesis
H_1: B_1 is not equal to .400 ← alternative hypothesis

In effect, then, we are testing to learn whether current data indicate that B_1 has changed from its historical value of .400.

Standard error
of the
regression
coefficient

To find the test statistic for B_1 it is necessary first to find the *standard error of the regression coefficient.* Here, the regression coefficient we are working with is b_1 so the standard error of this coefficient is denoted s_{b_1}.

It is too difficult to compute s_{b_1} by hand, but fortunately, STAT-PACK computes the standard errors of all the regression coefficients for us. For convenience, Table 12 · 3 is repeated.

Finding upper
and lower limits
of the
acceptance region
for our hypothesis
test

From the output, we see that s_{b_1} is 0.0811. (Similarly, if we want to test a hypothesis about B_2, we see that the appropriate standard error to use is $s_{b_2} = 0.0841$.) Once we have found s_{b_1} we can use the t distribution with $n - k - 1$ degrees of freedom and the following equation to calculate the upper and lower limits of the acceptance region.

$$\text{Limits of acceptance region} = B_i \pm t(s_{b_i}) \qquad (12 \cdot 8)$$

TABLE 12 · 3 STATPACK output

VARIABLE	REG.COEF.	STD.ERROR COEF.
1	0.59697	0.08113
2	1.17684	0.08407
3	0.40511	0.04223
INTERCEPT		-45.79634
MULTIPLE CORRELATION		0.99167

where:

t = appropriate t value (with $n - k - 1$ degrees of freedom) for the significance level of the test

B_i = actual slope hypothesized for the population

s_{b_i} = standard error of the regression coefficient

*Conducting
the hypothesis
test*   Suppose we are interested in testing our hypothesis at the 10 percent level of significance. Since we have 10 observations in our sample data, and 3 independent variables, we know that we have $n - k - 1$ or $10 - 3 - 1 = 6$ degrees of freedom. We look in Appendix Table 2 under the 10 percent column and come down until we find the 6 degrees-of-freedom row. There, we see that the appropriate t value is 1.943. Since we are concerned whether b_1 (the slope of the sample regression plane) is significantly different from B_1 (the hypothesized slope of the population regression plane), this is a two-tailed test and the limits of the acceptance region are found using Equation 12.8, with $i = 1$, since we are testing a hypothesis about B_1.

$$B_1 \pm t(s_{b_1}) = .400 \pm 1.943(0.0811)$$

$$= .558 \leftarrow \text{upper limit of acceptance region} \qquad (12 \cdot 8)$$

$$\text{and} \quad .242 \leftarrow \text{lower limit of acceptance region}$$

The slope of our regression plane (b_1) is .597 which is *not* inside the acceptance region. Therefore, we reject the null hypothesis that B_1 still equals .400. In other words, there *is* enough difference between b_1 and .400 for us to conclude that B_1 has changed from its historical value. Because of this we feel that each additional hundred hours of field audit labor no longer increases unpaid taxes discovered by \$400,000 as it did in the past.

*Confidence
interval for B_i*   In addition to hypothesis testing, we can also construct a *confidence interval* for any one of the values of B_i. In the same way that b_i is a point estimate of B_i, such confidence intervals are interval estimates of B_i. To illustrate the process of constructing a confidence interval, let's find a 95 percent confidence interval for B_3 in our IRS problem. The relevant data are:

$$\left. \begin{array}{l} b_3 = 0.405 \\ s_{b_3} = 0.0422 \end{array} \right\} \text{ from Table } 12 \cdot 3$$

$$t = 2.447 \leftarrow 5 \text{ percent level of significance and} \\ 6 \text{ degrees of freedom}$$

With this information, we can calculate confidence intervals like this:

$$b_3 \pm t(s_{b_3}) = 0.405 \pm 2.447(0.0422)$$

$$= .508 \leftarrow \text{upper limit}$$

$$\text{and} \quad .302 \leftarrow \text{lower limit}$$

We see that we can be 95 percent confident that each additional $1,000 paid to informants increases the unpaid taxes discovered by some amount between $302,000 and $508,000.

Is an explanatory variable significant?

We will often be interested in questions of the form: Does Y really depend on X_i? For example, we could ask whether unpaid taxes discovered really depend on computer hours. Frequently this question is phrased as, "Is X_i a significant explanatory variable for Y?" A bit of thought should convince you that Y depends on X_i (that is, Y varies when X_i varies) if $B_i \neq 0$ and it doesn't depend on X_i if $B_i = 0$.

We see that our question leads to hypotheses of the form:

H_0: $B_i = 0$ ← null hypothesis: X_i is not a significant
                    explanatory variable

H_1: $B_i \neq 0$ ← alternative hypothesis: X_i is a significant
                    explanatory variable

We can test these hypotheses using Equation 12 · 8 just as we did on pp. 383–85 when we tested our hypotheses about whether B_1 still equaled .400. For example, to test whether unpaid taxes discovered really depend on computer hours, the hypotheses are

Testing the significance of computer hours in the IRS problem

---

H_0: $B_2 = 0$ ← null hypothesis: X_2 is not a
                significant explanatory variable

H_1: $B_2 \neq 0$ ← alternative hypothesis: X_2 is a
                significant explanatory variable

Let's test our hypotheses at the .01 significance level. From Appendix Table 2, with $n - k - 1 = 10 - 3 - 1 = 6$ degrees of freedom and $\alpha = .01$, we see that the appropriate t value is 3.707. From Table 12 · 3, we see that $s_{b_2} = 0.0841$, so the limits of the acceptance region are

$$B_2 \pm t(s_{b_2}) = 0 \pm 3.707\,(0.0841)$$

$$= \pm .312 \leftarrow \begin{array}{l} \text{limits of the} \\ \text{acceptance region} \end{array} \tag{12 · 8}$$

Since the observed value of b_2 (1.177) falls outside the acceptance region, we reject H_0 and conclude that X_2 (computer hours) is a significant explanatory variable for Y (unpaid taxes discovered).

Inferences about the regression as a whole

Suppose you put a piece of graph paper over a dart board and randomly tossed a bunch of darts at it. After you took the darts out, you would have something that looked very much like a scatter diagram. Suppose you then fit a simple regression line to this set of "observed data points" and calculated r^2. Since the darts were randomly tossed, you would expect to get a low value of r^2 since in this case X really doesn't explain Y. However, if you did this many times, occasionally you would observe a high value of r^2, just by pure chance.

Significance of the regression as a whole

Well then, given any simple (or multiple) regression, it's natural to ask whether the value of r^2 (or R^2) really indicates that the independent variables explain Y, or might this have happened by chance? This question is often phrased: Is the regression as a whole significant? In the last section we looked at how to tell whether an individual X_i was a significant explanatory variable; now we see how to tell whether all the X_i's taken together significantly explain the variability observed in Y. Our hypotheses are:

$H_0: B_1 = B_2 \ldots = B_k = 0 \leftarrow$ null hypothesis: Y doesn't depend
on the X_i's

$H_1:$ at least one $B_i \neq 0 \leftarrow$ alternative hypothesis: Y depends
on at least one of the X_i's

Analyzing the variation in the Y values

When we discussed r^2 in Chapter 11, we looked at the total variation in Y, $\Sigma(Y - \overline{Y})^2$, the part of that variation which is explained by the regression, $\Sigma(\hat{Y} - \overline{Y})^2$, and the unexplained part of the variation, $\Sigma(Y - \hat{Y})^2$. Figure $12 \cdot 2$ is a duplicate of Fig. $11 \cdot 13$. It reviews the relationship between total deviation, explained deviation, and unexplained deviation for a single data point in a simple regression. Although we can't draw a similar picture for a multiple regression, we are doing the same thing conceptually.

Sums of squares and their degrees of freedom

In discussing the variation in Y, then, we look at three different terms, each of which is a sum of squares. We denote these by:

$$
\left.
\begin{aligned}
\text{SST} &= \text{Total Sum of Squares} & = \Sigma(Y - \overline{Y})^2 \\[1em]
\text{SSR} &= \text{Regression Sum of Squares} & = \Sigma(\hat{Y} - \overline{Y})^2 \\
&\quad \text{(i.e., the explained part of SST)} \\[1em]
\text{SSE} &= \text{Error Sum of Squares} & = \Sigma(Y - \hat{Y})^2 \\
&\quad \text{(i.e., the unexplained part of SST)}
\end{aligned}
\right\} \quad (12 \cdot 9)
$$

These are related by the equation

$$\text{SST} = \text{SSR} + \text{SSE} \qquad (12 \cdot 10)$$

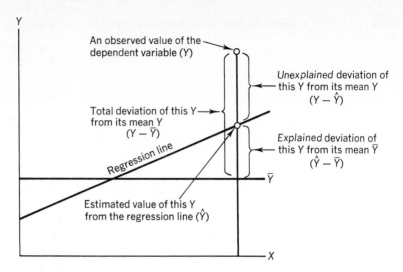

Figure 12·2 Total deviation, explained deviation, and unexplained deviation for *one* observed value of *Y*

which says that the total variation in Y can be broken down into two parts, the explained part and the unexplained part.

Each of these sums of squares has an associated degrees of freedom. SST has $n - 1$ degrees of freedom (n observations, but we lose a degree of freedom because the sample mean is fixed). SSR has k degrees of freedom because there are k independent variables being used to explain Y. Finally, SSE has $n - k - 1$ degrees of freedom (because we used our n observations to estimate $k + 1$ constants, $a, b_1, b_2, \ldots, b_k$). If the null hypothesis is true, the ratio

$$F = \frac{\text{SSR}/k}{\text{SSE}/(n - k - 1)} \qquad (12 \cdot 11)$$

F test of the regression as a whole

has an F distribution with k numerator degrees of freedom and $n - k - 1$ denominator degrees of freedom. If the null hypothesis is false, then the F ratio tends to be larger than it is when the null hypothesis is true. So if the F ratio is too high (as determined by the significance level of the test and the appropriate value from Appendix Table 6), we reject H_0 and conclude that the regression as a whole *is* significant.

Analysis of variance for the regression

Table 12 · 4 gives more of the STATPACK output for the IRS problem. This part of the output includes the computed F ratio for the regression. Notice that the output is headed "analysis of variance for the regression." You probably are wondering whether this has anything to do with the analysis of variance we discussed in Chapter 10. Yes, it does. Although we did not do so, it is possible to show that the analysis of variance in Chapter 10 also looks at the total variation of all of the observations about the grand mean, and breaks it up into two parts: one

TABLE 12·4 More STATPACK output: the analysis of variance

```
                 ANALYSIS OF VARIANCE FOR THE REGRESSION
      SOURCE OF VARIATION        D.F.   SUM OF SQ.    MEAN SQ.    F VALUE
ATTRIBUTABLE TO REGRESSION         3      29.109        9.703     118.515
DEVIATION FROM REGRESSION          6       0.491        0.082
       TOTAL                       9      29.600
```

part explained by the differences among the several groups (corresponding to what we called the "between column variance") and the other part unexplained by those differences (corresponding to what we have called the "within column variance"). This is precisely analogous to what we just did in Equation 12 · 10.

For the IRS problem, we see that SSR = 29.109 (with $k = 3$ degrees of freedom), SSE = 0.491 (with $n - k - 1 = 10 - 3 - 1 = 6$ degrees of freedom) and that

Testing the significance of the IRS regression

$$F = \frac{29.109/3}{0.491/6} = \frac{9.703}{0.082} = 118.515$$

The entries in the "mean square" column are just the sums of squares divided by their degrees of freedom. For 3 numerator degrees of freedom and 6 denominator degrees of freedom, Appendix Table 6 tells us that 9.78 is the upper limit of the acceptance region for a significance level of $\alpha = .01$. Our calculated F value of 118.515 is far above 9.78, so we see that the regression as a whole is highly significant.

Multicollinearity in multiple regression

Definition and effect of multicollinearity

In multiple regression analysis, the regression coefficients often become less reliable as the degree of correlation between the independent variables increases. If there is a high level of correlation between them, we have a problem that statisticians call *multicollinearity*.

Multicollinearity might occur if we wished to estimate a firm's sales revenue, and we used both the number of salespersons employed and their salaries. Since the values associated with these two independent variables are highly correlated, we need to use only one set of them to make our estimate. In fact, adding a second variable that is correlated with the first distorts the values of the regression coefficients. This results in a multiple regression equation which is highly significant as a whole, but in which neither X_1 nor X_2 alone is a significant explanatory variable. This seems very contradictory, and at this point, it is fair to ask, "Which variable is really explaining the variation in total sales in the multiple regression?" The answer is that both are, but we cannot separate out their individual contributions, because they are so highly correlated with each other. As a result of this, their coefficients in the multiple regression have high standard errors, so the coefficients are not significantly different from 0.

Individual contributions can't be separated out

How does this multicollinearity affect us? Since the regression is highly significant as a whole, the standard error of estimate will be relatively small, so we can still make relatively precise predictions of Y even if multicollinearity is present. What we *cannot* do is tell with much precision how much Y will change if we increase X by 1, because b_1 (which is our estimate of this slope) has a high standard error (i.e., a low precision) when multicollinearity is present.

EXERCISES

12·10 Refer to problem 12·9 on page 382. At a significance level of .05, is the number of courses taken this year a significant explanatory variable for monthly sales? (There were 10 salespeople in Mary's sample.)

12·11 Refer to problem 12·9 on page 382. The following additional output was provided by STATPACK when the multiple regression was run:

ANALYSIS OF VARIANCE FOR THE REGRESSION

SOURCE OF VARIATION	D.F.	SUM OF SQ.	MEAN SQ.	F VALUE
ATTRIBUTABLE TO REGRESSION	3	3367.269	1122.423	46.974
DEVIATION FROM REGRESSION	6	143.367	23.894	
TOTAL	9	3510.636		

At a .05 level of significance, is the regression significant as a whole?

12·12 Henry Lander is director of production for the Alecos Corporation of Caracas, Venezuela. Henry has asked you to help him determine a predicting formula for absenteeism in a meat-packing facility. He hypothesizes that percentage absenteeism can be explained by average daily temperature. Data is gathered for several months, you run the simple regression, and you find that temperature explains 66 percent of the variation in absenteeism. But Henry is not convinced that this is a satisfactory predictor. He suggests that daily rainfall may also have something to do with absenteeism. So you gather data, run a regression of absenteeism during rainfall, and get an R^2 of .59. "Eureka!" you cry, "I've got it! With one predictor that explains 66 percent, and another that explains 59 percent, all I have to do is to run a multiple regression using both predictors, and I'll surely have an almost perfect predictor!" To your dismay, however, the multiple regression has an R^2 of only 68 percent, which is just slightly better than the temperature variable alone. How can you account for this apparent discrepancy?

12·13 Suppose that regressions have been run each month for several years on variables 1, 2, and 3. Variable 3 has always been labeled the "dependent variable" and variables 1 and 2 have always been labeled the "independent variables." Historically, the value of B_1 in these regressions has been .150. The regression for this month is based on 8 data points and has just been run on STATPACK. Here are the results:

```
SPECIFY THE DEPENDENT VARIABLE
?* 3

HOW MANY INDEPENDENT VARIABLES
?* 2

SPECIFY THESE VARIABLES
?1,2

VARIABLE     REG.COEF.     STD.ERROR COEF.     COMPUTED T
    1          0.23249          0.08337          2.78863
    2          1.15057          0.09967         11.54347

INTERCEPT                     18.01212
MULTIPLE CORRELATION           0.99568
STD. ERROR OF ESTIMATE         0.94551
```

a) At a significance level of .05, is there significant evidence that the value of B_1 has changed from the historical value?

b) Give an approximate 90 percent confidence interval for the value of B_2 in this regression.

---

5 MODELING TECHNIQUES

Looking at different models

Given a variable we want to explain and a bunch of potential explanatory variables, there may be several different regression equations we can look at, depending on which explanatory variables we include and how we include them. Each such regression equation is called a *model*. *Modeling techniques* are the various different ways in which we can include the explanatory variables and check the appropriateness of our regression models. There are many different modeling techniques, but we shall look at only two of the most commonly used devices.

Qualitative data and dummy variables

In all of the regression examples we have looked at so far, the data have been numerical, or *quantitative*. But occasionally we will be faced with a variable that is categorical, or *qualitative*. In our chapter opening problem, the director of personnel wanted to see if the base salary of a salesperson depended on the individual's sex. Table 12 · 5 repeats the data of that problem.

TABLE 12·5   Data for sex discrimination problem

Salesmen		Saleswomen	
Months employed	Base salary ($1,000's)	Months employed	Base salary ($1,000's)
6	7.5	5	6.2
10	8.6	13	8.7
12	9.1	15	9.4
18	10.3	21	9.8
30	13.0		

Reviewing a previous way to approach the problem

For the moment, ignore the length of employment and use the technique developed in Chapter 9 for testing the difference between means of two populations, to see if men earn more than women. Test this at $\alpha = .01$. You'll find that the observed difference between the means is $\bar{x}_m - \bar{x}_w = 9.7 - 8.525 = 1.175$, and that with 7 (5 + 4 − 2) degrees of freedom, the upper limit of the acceptance region is 3.84. Since 1.175 < 3.84, we cannot reject the hypothesis that the means are the same (i.e., that there is no discrimination). (If you have any trouble checking this result, you should briefly review pp. 266–77.)

The old approach doesn't detect any discrimination

Our analysis therefore concludes that there does not appear to be any sex discrimination in base salaries. But recall that we have ignored the length of employment data thus far in the analysis.

"Eyeballing" the data

Before we go any farther, look at a scatter diagram of the data. In Fig. 12 · 3, the solid points correspond to men and the circles correspond to women. The scatter diagram clearly shows that base salary increases with length of service; but if you try to "eyeball" the regression line,

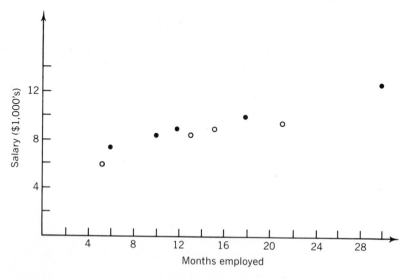

Figure 12·3   Scatter diagram of base salaries plotted against months employed

you'll note that the solid points tend to be above it, and the circles tend to be below it.

Table 12 · 6 gives the output from a regression of base salary on months employed. From that output we see that months employed are a very highly significant explanatory variable. The coefficient b_1 is 9.4 (= .2332/.0249) standard deviations away from 0. This is so high you shouldn't even have to check Appendix Table 2 to do the appropriate test. Also, $r^2 = (.96229)^2 = .9260$, indicating that months employed explains about 93 percent of the variation in base salary. Table 12 · 6 contains part of the output that we haven't seen before, a table of *residuals*. For each data point, the residual is just $Y - \hat{Y}$, which we recognize as the error in the fit of the regression line at that point.

"Squeezing the residuals"

Perhaps the most important part of analyzing a regression output is looking at the residuals. If the regression includes all of the relevant explanatory factors, these residuals ought to be random. Looking at this in another way, if the residuals show any non-random patterns, this indicates that there is something systematic going on that we have failed to take into account. So we look for patterns in the residuals; or to put it somewhat more picturesquely, we "squeeze the residuals until they talk."

TABLE 12 · 6   Regression of base salary on months employed

VARIABLE	REG.COEF.	STD.ERROR COEF.	COMPUTED T
1	0.23320	0.02492	9.35988

INTERCEPT   5.80927
MULTIPLE CORRELATION   0.96229
STD. ERROR OF ESTIMATE   0.54939

ANALYSIS OF VARIANCE FOR THE REGRESSION

SOURCE OF VARIATION	D.F.	SUM OF SQ.	MEAN SQ.	F VALUE
ATTRIBUTABLE TO REGRESSION	1	26.443	26.443	87.607
DEVIATION FROM REGRESSION	7	2.113	0.302	
TOTAL	8	28.556		

DO YOU WISH TO PRINT THE TABLE OF RESIDUALS
?* YES

CASE NO	Y OBSERVED	Y ESTIMATED	RESIDUAL
1	7.500	7.208	0.292
2	8.600	8.141	0.459
3	9.100	8.608	0.492
4	10.300	10.007	0.293
5	13.000	12.805	0.195
6	6.200	6.975	-0.775
7	8.700	8.841	-0.141
8	9.400	9.307	0.093
9	9.800	10.707	-0.907

As we look at the residuals in Table 12 · 6, we note that the first 5 residuals are positive. So for the sales*men*, we have $Y - \hat{Y} > 0$, or $Y > \hat{Y}$; that is to say, the regression line falls below these 5 data points. Three of the last 4 residuals are negative. And thus for the sales*women*, we have $Y - \hat{Y} < 0$, or $Y < \hat{Y}$, so the regression line lies above 3 of the 4 data points. This confirms the observation we made when we looked at the scatter diagram in Fig. 12 · 3. This nonrandom pattern in the residuals suggests that sex *is* a factor in determining base salary.

How can we incorporate the salesperson's sex *into* the regression model? We do this by using a device called a *dummy variable* (or an *indicator variable*). For the points representing salesmen, this variable is given the value 0, and for the points representing saleswomen, it is given the value 1. The input data for our regression using a dummy variable are given in Table 12 · 7.

To the data in Table 12 · 7, we fit a regression of the form

$$\hat{Y} = a + b_1 X_1 + b_2 X_2 \qquad (12 \cdot 5)$$

Let's see what happens if we use this regression to predict the base salary of an individual with X_1 months of service:

Salesman: $\quad \hat{Y} = a + b_1 X_1 + b_2(0) = a + b_1 X_1$

Saleswoman: $\hat{Y} = a + b_1 X_1 + b_2(1) = a + b_1 X_1 + b_2$

For salesmen and saleswomen with the same length of employment, we predict a base salary difference of b_2 thousands of dollars. Now b_2 is just our estimate of B_2 in the population regression

$$Y = A + B_1 X_1 + B_2 X_2 \qquad (12 \cdot 7)$$

If there really is discrimination against women, they should earn less than men with the same length of service. In other words, B_2 should be negative. We can test this at the .01 level of significance.

TABLE 12 · 7 Input data for sex discrimination regression

	X_1 *Months employed*	X_2 *Sex*	Y *Base salary ($1,000's)*
Men	6	0	7.5
	10	0	8.6
	12	0	9.1
	18	0	10.3
	30	0	13.0
Women	5	1	6.2
	13	1	8.7
	15	1	9.4
	21	1	9.8

$H_0: B_2 = 0$ ← null hypothesis: there is no sex discrimination in base salaries

$H_1: B_2 < 0$ ← alternative hypothesis: women are discriminated against

$\alpha = .01$ ← level of significance

In order to test these hypotheses, we run a regression on the data in Table 12 · 7. The results of that regression are given in Table 12 · 8.

Our hypothesis test is based on the t distribution with $n - k - 1 = 9 - 2 - 1 = 6$ degrees of freedom. The appropriate t value from Appendix Table 2 is 3.143. The lower limit of the acceptance region is

$$\text{Lower limit of acceptance region} = B_2 - t(s_{b_2})$$

$$= 0 - 3.143(.238) \quad (12 \cdot 8)$$

$$= -0.748$$

Concluding that discrimination is present

Figure 12 · 4 illustrates this limit of the acceptance region and the observed value of $b_2 = -0.789$. We see that the observed b_2 lies outside the acceptance region, so we reject the null hypothesis and conclude that the firm does discriminate against its saleswomen. Finally, we note that

TABLE 12·8 Output from sex discrimination regression

VARIABLE	REG.COEF.	STD.ERROR COEF.	COMPUTED T
1	0.22707	0.01612	14.08882
2	-0.78897	0.23841	-3.30939

INTERCEPT	6.24848
MULTIPLE CORRELATION	0.98682
STD. ERROR OF ESTIMATE	0.35304

ANALYSIS OF VARIANCE FOR THE REGRESSION

SOURCE OF VARIATION	D.F.	SUM OF SQ.	MEAN SQ.	F VALUE
ATTRIBUTABLE TO REGRESSION	2	27.808	13.904	111.555
DEVIATION FROM REGRESSION	6	0.748	0.125	
TOTAL	8	28.556		

DO YOU WISH TO PRINT THE TABLE OF RESIDUALS
?* YES

CASE NO	Y OBSERVED	Y ESTIMATED	RESIDUAL
1	7.500	7.611	-0.111
2	8.600	8.519	0.081
3	9.100	8.973	0.127
4	10.300	10.336	-0.358E-01
5	13.000	13.061	-0.607E-01
6	6.200	6.595	-0.395
7	8.700	8.411	0.289
8	9.400	8.866	0.534
9	9.800	10.228	-0.428

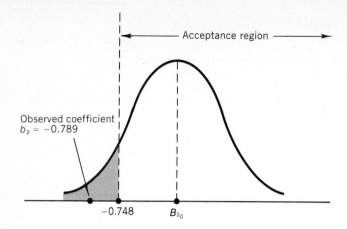

Observed coefficient
$b_2 = -0.789$

-0.748 B_{2_0}

Acceptance region

Figure 12·4 Left-tailed hypothesis test at .01 significance level, showing acceptance region and the observed regression coefficient

the residuals for this regression don't seem to show any nonrandom pattern.

Interpreting the coefficient of the dummy variable

Now to review how we handled the qualitative variable in this problem. We set up a dummy variable, which we gave the value 0 for the men and the value 1 for the women. Then the coefficient of the dummy variable can be interpreted as the difference between a woman's base salary and the base salary for a man. Suppose we had set the dummy variable to 0 for women and 1 for men. Then its coefficient would be the difference between a man's base salary and the base salary for a woman. Can you guess what the regression would have been in this case? It shouldn't surprise you to learn that it would have been

$$\hat{Y} = 5.45951 + 0.22707X_1 + .78897X_2$$

The choice of which category is given the value 0 and which the value 1 is totally arbitrary and affects only the sign, not the numerical value of the coefficient of the dummy variable.

Extensions of dummy variable techniques

Our example had only one qualitative variable (sex), and that variable had only two possible categories (male and female). Although we won't pursue the details here, dummy variable techniques can also be used in problems with several qualitative variables, and those variables can have more than two possible categories.

Transforming variables and fitting curves

A manufacturer of small electric motors uses an automatic milling machine to produce the slots in the shafts of the motors. A batch of shafts is run and then checked. All shafts in the batch that do not meet required dimensional tolerances are discarded. At the beginning of each new batch, the milling machine is readjusted, since its cutter head wears slightly during the production of the batch. The manufacturer is trying to pick an optimal batch size; but in order to do this, he must know how the size of a batch affects the number of defective shafts in the batch.

TABLE 12·9 Number of defective shafts per batch

Batch size	Number defective	Batch size	Number defective
100	5	250	37
125	10	250	41
125	6	250	34
125	7	275	49
150	6	300	53
150	7	300	54
175	17	325	69
175	15	350	82
200	24	350	81
200	21	350	84
200	22	375	92
225	26	375	96
225	29	375	97
225	25	400	109
250	34	400	112

Table 12 · 9 gives data for a sample of 30 batches, arranged by ascending size of batch.

Noticing a pattern in the residuals

Figure 12 · 5 is a scatter diagram for this data. Since there are two batches of size 250 with 34 defective shafts, two of the points in the scatter diagram coincide (this is indicated by a circle in Fig. 12 · 5).

We are going to run a regression of number of defective shafts on the batch size. The output from the regression is in Table 12 · 10. What

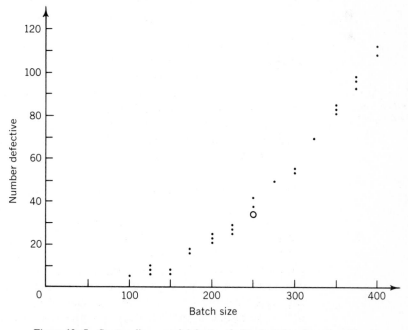

Figure 12·5 Scatter diagram of defective shafts plotted against size of batch

TABLE 12·10 Regression of number of defects on batch size

```
VARIABLE     REG.COEF.    STD.ERROR COEF.    COMPUTED T
    1          0.36713         0.01534         23.93526

INTERCEPT                  -47.90068
MULTIPLE CORRELATION         0.97642
STD. ERROR OF ESTIMATE       7.56016

                 ANALYSIS OF VARIANCE FOR THE REGRESSION
       SOURCE OF VARIATION       D.F.    SUM OF SQ.    MEAN SQ.    F VALUE
ATTRIBUTABLE TO REGRESSION        1      32744.449    32744.449   572.896
DEVIATION FROM REGRESSION        28       1600.367       57.156
           TOTAL                 29      34344.816

DO YOU WISH TO PRINT THE TABLE OF RESIDUALS
?* YES

CASE NO    Y OBSERVED    Y ESTIMATED    RESIDUAL
   1          5.000        -11.188        16.188
   2         10.000         -2.009        12.009
   3          6.000         -2.009         8.009
   4          7.000         -2.009         9.009
   5          6.000          7.169        -1.169
   6          7.000          7.169        -0.169
   7         17.000         16.347         0.653
   8         15.000         16.347        -1.347
   9         24.000         25.526        -1.526
  10         21.000         25.526        -4.526
  11         22.000         25.526        -3.526
  12         26.000         34.704        -8.704
  13         29.000         34.704        -5.704
  14         25.000         34.704        -9.704
  15         34.000         43.882        -9.882
  16         37.000         43.882        -6.882
  17         41.000         43.882        -2.882
  18         34.000         43.882        -9.882
  19         49.000         53.060        -4.060
  20         53.000         62.239        -9.239
  21         54.000         62.239        -8.239
  22         69.000         71.417        -2.417
  23         82.000         80.595         1.405
  24         81.000         80.595         0.405
  25         84.000         80.595         3.405
  26         92.000         89.774         2.226
  27         96.000         89.774         6.226
  28         97.000         89.774         7.226
  29        109.000         98.952        10.048
  30        112.000         98.952        13.048
```

does this output tell us? First of all, we note that batch size does a fantastic job of explaining the number of defective shafts: the computed F value is 573 and $r^2 = (.97642)^2 = .9534$. However, despite the incredibly high F value, and despite the fact that batch size explains 95 percent of the variation in number of defectives, the residuals in this regression are far from random. Notice how they start out as large positive values, become smaller, then go negative, then become more negative, and then turn around again, finishing up with large positive values.

What the pattern suggests

What does this indicate? Look at Fig. $12 \cdot 6$, where we have fit a dashed regression line $(\hat{Y} = -7 + 7X)$ to the 8 points $(X, Y) = (0, 0), (1, 1), (2, 4), (3, 9), \ldots, (7, 49)$, all of which lie on the solid curve $(Y = X^2)$. The figure also shows the residuals and their signs.

The pattern of residuals that we got in our motor shaft problem is quite similar to the pattern seen in Fig. $12 \cdot 6$. Maybe the shaft data are better approximated by a curve than a straight line. Look back at Fig. $12 \cdot 5$; what do you think?

Fitting a curve to the data

But we've only fitted straight lines before. How do we go about fitting a curve? It's simple; all we do is introduce another variable, $X_2 = $ (batch size)^2, and then run a multiple regression.

The results are in Table $12 \cdot 11$.

The curve is much better than the line

Looking at Table $12 \cdot 11$, we see that batch size and (batch size)^2 are *both* significant explanatory variables, since b_1, the coefficient of X_1 (batch size) is 3.81 $(= .120/.0315)$ standard deviations below 0, and b_2, the coefficient of X_2 (batch size squared) is 15.67 $(= .00095/.0000606)$ standard deviations above 0. The multiple coefficient of determination is

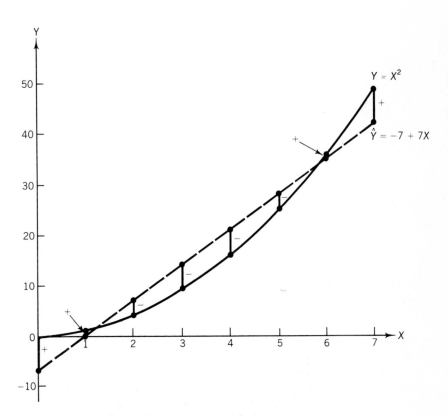

Figure 12·6   Fitting a straight line to points on a curve

TABLE 12 · 11 Regression on batch size and (batch size)^{2*}

VARIABLE	REG.COEF.	STD.ERROR COEF.	COMPUTED T
1	−0.12004	0.03148	−3.81302
2	0.00095	0.60601E−04	15.66680

INTERCEPT   6.89066
MULTIPLE CORRELATION   0.99769
STD. ERROR OF ESTIMATE   2.42363

ANALYSIS OF VARIANCE FOR THE REGRESSION

SOURCE OF VARIATION	D.F.	SUM OF SQ.	MEAN SQ.	F VALUE
ATTRIBUTABLE TO REGRESSION	2	34186.219	17093.109	2909.967
DEVIATION FROM REGRESSION	27	158.598	5.874	
TOTAL	29	34344.816		

*The residuals now appear random and have been omitted from this particular output.

$R^2 = (.99769)^2 = .9954$; so together, our two variables explain 99.5 percent of the variation in the number of defective motor shafts. As a final comparison of our two regressions, notice that the standard error of estimate, which measures the dispersion of the sample points around the fitted model, is 7.560 for the straight-line model but only 2.424 for the curved model. The curved model is far superior to the straight-line model, even though the latter explained 95 percent of the variation! And remember, it was the pattern that we observed in the residuals for the straight-line model that suggested to us that a curved model would be more appropriate.

Transforming variables

In our curved model, we got our second variable (batch size)^2, by doing a *mathematical transformation* of our first variable, batch size. Because we squared a variable, the resulting curved model is known as a *second-degree* (or *quadratic*) regression model. There are many other ways in which we can transform variables to get new variables, and most computer regression packages have these transformations built into them. You do not have to compute the transformed variables by hand.

EXERCISES
---

12 · 14 Suppose that you have a set of data points to which you have fitted a linear regression equation. Even though the R^2 for the line is very high, you wonder whether it would be a good idea to fit a second-degree equation to the data. Describe how you would make your decision based on:

a) a scattergram of the data

b) a table of residuals from the linear regression

12 · 15 Describe three situations in everyday life in which dummy variables could be used in regression models.

12·16 Russ Andrews owns a company that manufactures Whizzos. The failure rate for Whizzos seems to vary from batch to batch, and Russ wants an equation that will help him predict failure rates. Russ feels that one possible explanation for failure rates may be the number of gears in the Whizzo. While the company's models are essentially similar, some contain more gears than others. Also, the material from which the Whizzo is made may affect the failure rate (a Whizzo can be made from either aluminum or wood). Russ has collected data for several days and presented you with a table containing the number of gears, type of material, and failure rate for each of 35 batches of Whizzos. He has asked you to help with his predictions.

a) Describe a model using a dummy variable that the company could use to estimate batch failure rates from number of gears and type of material.

b) Russ also wants to know if the type of material really has any effect on failure rates. Based upon your answer to part a, give the hypotheses you would use for this test.

12·17 Dr. Linda Frazer runs a medical clinic in Philadelphia. She collected data on age, reaction to penicillin, and systolic blood pressure for 13 patients. She established systolic blood pressure as the dependent variable, age as X_1 (independent variable), and reaction to penicillin as X_2 (independent variable). Letting 0 stand for a positive reaction to penicillin, and 1 stand for a negative reaction, she performed a STATPACK multiple regression. The predicting equation was: $\hat{Y} = 13.7 + 3.5X_1 + .206X_2$.

a) After the regression had already been run, Linda discovered that she had meant to code a positive reaction as 1 and a negative reaction as 0. Does she have to rerun the regression? If, so, why? If not, give her the equation she would have gotten if the variable had been coded as she had originally intended.

b) If s_{b_2} has a value of .09, is there evidence at a significance level of .01 that reaction to penicillin is a significant explanatory variable for systolic blood pressure?

---

6 TERMS INTRODUCED IN CHAPTER 12

analysis of variance for regression The procedure for computing the F ratio used to test the significance of the regression as a whole. It is related to the analysis of variance discussed in Chapter 10.

coefficient of multiple correlation, R The positive square root of R^2.

coefficient of multiple determination, R^2 The fraction of the variation of the dependent variable that is explained by the regression. R^2 measures how well the multiple regression fits the data.

computed F ratio A statistic used to test the significance of the regression as a whole.

dummy variable A variable taking the value 0 or 1, enabling us to include in a regression model qualitative factors such as sex, marital status, and education level.

modeling techniques Methods for deciding which variables to include in a regression model and the different ways in which they can be included.

multicollinearity A statistical problem sometimes present in multiple regression analysis in which the reliability of the regression coefficients is reduced, owing to a high level of correlation between the independent variables.

multiple regression The statistical process by which several variables are used to predict another variable.

standard error of a regression coefficient A measure of our uncertainty about the exact value of a regression coefficient.

STATPACK A computer program for doing regression and other statistical analyses. Other commonly available packages include MINITAB, SAS, and SPSS.

transformations Mathematical manipulations for converting one variable into a different form, so we can fit curves as well as lines by regression.

7 EQUATIONS INTRODUCED IN CHAPTER 12

p. 373
$$\hat{Y} = a + b_1 X_1 + b_2 X_2$$
12·1

In multiple regression, this is the formula for the estimating equation that describes the relationship between three variables: Y, X_1, and X_2. Picture a two-variable multiple regression equation as a plane, rather than a line.

$$\Sigma Y = na + b_1 \Sigma X_1 + b_2 \Sigma X_2$$
12·2

p. 374
$$\Sigma X_1 Y = a\Sigma X_1 + b_1 \Sigma X_1^2 + b_2 \Sigma X_1 X_2$$
12·3

$$\Sigma X_2 Y = a\Sigma X_2 + b_1 \Sigma X_1 X_2 + b_2 \Sigma X_2^2$$
12·4

Solving these three equations determines the values of the numerical constants a, b_1, and b_2 and thus the best-fitting multiple regression plane in a two-variable multiple regression.

p. 377
$$\hat{Y} = a + b_1 X_1 + b_2 X_2 + \cdots + b_k X_k$$
12·5

This is the formula for the estimating equation describing the relationship between Y and the k independent variables $X_1, X_2, \ldots, X_k$. Equation 12 · 1 is the special case of this equation for $k = 2$.

p. 379
$$s_e = \sqrt{\frac{\Sigma(Y - \hat{Y})^2}{n - k - 1}}$$
12·6

To measure the variation around a multiple regression equation when there are k independent variables, use this equation to find the *standard error of estimate*. The standard error, in this case, has $n - k - 1$ degrees of freedom, owing to the $k + 1$ numerical constants that must be calculated from the data first $(a, b_1, \ldots, b_k)$.

p. 383
$$Y = A + B_1 X_1 + B_2 X_2 + \cdots + B_k X_k$$
12·7

This is the *population regression equation* for the multiple regression. Its Y intercept is A, and it has k slope coefficients, one for each of the independent variables.

p. 383
$$Y = A + B_1 X_1 + B_2 X_2 + \cdots + B_k X_k + e$$
12·7a

Because all the individual points in a population do not lie on a population regression equation, the *individual* data points will satisfy this equation where e is a random disturbance from the population regression equation. On the average, e equals zero, because disturbances above the population regression equation are canceled out by disturbances below it.

p. 384
$$\text{Limits of acceptance region} = B_i \pm t(s_{b_i})$$
12·8

To test hypotheses about the slopes of multiple regression equations, we use this equation to find the limits of the acceptance region. The standard error of the coefficient (s_{b_i}) is obtained from the computer package we are using, and the t value is taken from the t distribution with $n - k - 1$ degrees of freedom.

$$\left. \begin{array}{ll} \text{SST} = \text{Total Sum of Squares} & = \Sigma (Y - \bar{Y})^2 \\[1em] \text{SSR} = \text{Regression Sum of Squares} & = \Sigma (\hat{Y} - \bar{Y})^2 \\ \quad \text{(i.e., the explained part of SST)} & \\[1em] \text{SSE} = \text{Error Sum of Squares} & = \Sigma (Y - \hat{Y})^2 \\ \quad \text{(i.e., the unexplained part} & \\ \quad \text{of SST)} & \end{array} \right\}$$

12·9

$$\text{SST} = \text{SSR} + \text{SSE}$$ **12·10**

These two equations enable us to break down the variability of the dependent variable into two parts (one explained by the regression and the other unexplained) so we can test for the significance of the regression as a whole.

$$F = \frac{\text{SSR}/k}{\text{SSE}/(n - k - 1)}$$ **2·11**

This F-ratio, which has k numerator degrees of freedom and $n - k - 1$ denominator degrees of freedom is used to test the significance of the regression as a whole. If F is bigger than the critical value, then we conclude that the regression as a whole *is* significant.

––––––––––––––––––––– *8 CHAPTER REVIEW EXERCISES* –––––––––––––––––––––

12·18   David Howell, VP of sales for Landon Clothes, is studying the relationship between a product's wholesale margin, retail margin, and sales level. He sampled 5 items from Landon's product line with the following respective margins (percentage) and annual sales levels (number of units).

Retail margin (%)	Wholesale margin (%)	Number of units sold (× 10,000)
20	11	7
40	16	26
35	19	13
30	12	5
50	26	33

a) Develop an estimating equation best describing these data.
b) If an item had a retail margin of 30 percent and a wholesale margin of 15 percent, what unit sales would be expected?

12·19   Dr. Harden Ricci is a veterinarian in Sacramento, California. Recently, he has been trying to develop a predicting equation for the amount of anesthesia to be used in operations. He feels that the amount used will be affected by weight of the animal, length of the operation, and whether the animal is a cat or a dog. He has entered the following information into a STATPACK run:

X_1 Type of animal (0 = dog, 1 = cat)
X_2 Weight (in pounds)
X_3 Length of operation (hours)
Y Amount of anesthesia (milliliters)

The results of a regression on this data set are:

```
VARIABLE    REG.COEF.    STD.ERROR COEF.    COMPUTED T
   1       -104.82887        44.03326        -2.38067
   2         21.63718         2.77262         7.80386
   3        -28.27536        29.72720        -0.95116

INTERCEPT                 181.98630
MULTIPLE CORRELATION        0.97471
STD. ERROR OF ESTIMATE     59.30493

              ANALYSIS OF VARIANCE FOR THE REGRESSION
      SOURCE OF VARIATION       D.F.   SUM OF SQ.      MEAN SQ.
ATTRIBUTABLE TO REGRESSION       3    602122.313    200707.438
DEVIATION FROM REGRESSION        9     31653.688      3517.076
      TOTAL                     12    633776.000
```

a) What is the predicting equation for amounts of anesthesia, as given by STATPACK?

b) Give a 90 percent confidence interval for the amount of anesthesia to be used in a 2-hour operation on a 20-pound dog.

c) At a significance level of 5 percent, is the amount of anesthesia needed significantly different for dogs and cats?

d) At a significance level of 1 percent, is this regression significant as a whole?

12·20 Gerald Chrisco owns and operates Gerald's Cleaning Service in Winston-Salem, North Carolina. Gerald stocks his own brand of cleaning solvent, and he feels that this gives his service a distinctive edge over the competition. One of the problems with his method, though, is that he has to be careful to give each of his workers the proper amount of solvent before they begin cleaning an establishment. If they are given too little, they cannot properly clean the total area. If they are given too much, they tend to "lose" the excess, and this costs Gerald quite a bit in unnecessary expenses. Gerald has compiled the following data regarding solvent use for 6 recent cleaning projects:

Ounces of solvent used	Total square feet	Days since last cleaning
8.0	1,206	2
10.0	1,771	5
11.0	1,502	4
12.6	1,603	3
13.0	864	9
16.0	1,355	10

a) Use a computer package to calculate the best-fitting regression equation for this data.

b) How much additional solvent should Gerald allow for each additional 100 square feet of area?

c) Suppose that Gerald has a *very* important cleaning job of 1,150 square feet that hasn't been cleaned for 7 days. Because of the importance of the job, he is much more concerned with whether his crew will have sufficient solvent than whether they "lose" any excess. Find the upper limit of a 99 percent confidence interval for the amount of solvent that Gerald should give his crew for this job.

12·21 Homero Martinez is a judge in Barcelona, Spain. He has recently called you in as a statistical consultant to investigate what he purports to be a significant finding. He claims that the number of days a case is in court can be used to estimate the amount of damages which should be awarded. He has gathered data from his court and from the courts of several of his fellow judges. For each of the numbers 1 to 10, he has located a case which took that many days in court, and he has determined the amount of damages awarded in that case. You have entered the information into a STATPACK run as follows:

Col. 1 Number of days in court (1 to 10)
Col. 2 Amount of damages (thousands of pesetas)

The following results have been generated:

```
VARIABLE    REG.COEF.     STD.ERROR COEF.    COMPUTED T
    1      4530.30078        288.03003        15.72857

INTERCEPT              -2516.65234
MULTIPLE CORRELATION       0.98421
STD. ERROR OF ESTIMATE  2616.16504

                ANALYSIS OF VARIANCE FOR THE REGRESSION
    SOURCE OF VARIATION        D.F.   SUM OF SQ.     MEAN SQ.     F VALUE
ATTRIBUTABLE TO REGRESSION      1      0.169E 10     0.169E 10    247.388
DEVIATION FROM REGRESSION       8   54754560.000   6844320.000
        TOTAL                   9      0.175E 10

DO YOU WISH TO PRINT THE TABLE OF RESIDUALS
?* YES

CASE NO    Y OBSERVED    Y ESTIMATED    RESIDUAL
   1        6450.000      2013.648      4436.352
   2        7500.000      6543.949       956.051
   3       10000.000     11074.250     -1074.250
   4       13000.000     15604.551     -2604.551
   5       17500.000     20134.852     -2634.852
   6       22050.000     24665.152     -2615.152
   7       27500.000     29195.453     -1695.453
   8       35000.000     33725.754      1274.246
   9       40000.000     38256.055      1743.945
  10       45000.000     42786.355      2213.645
```

Of course, you are quite pleased with these results, since the value of R^2 is very high. But the judge is not convinced that you are right. He says, "This is the worst job I've ever seen! I don't care if this line *does* fit the data I gave you. I can tell by looking at the output that it won't work for other data! If you can't do any better, just let me know, and I'll hire a *smart* statistician!"

a) Why is the judge upset?
b) Suggest a better model that will calm the judge.

Answers are in the back of the book.

T F 1. The principal advantage of multiple regression over simple regression is that it allows us to use more of the information available to us to estimate the dependent variable.

T F 2. Suppose, in the multiple regression equation $\hat{Y} = 24.4 + 5.6X_1 + 6.8X_2$, $\hat{Y}$ stands for weight (in pounds) and X_2 stands for age (in years). For each additional year of age, then, it can be expected that weight will increase by 24.4 pounds.

T F 3. Although it is theoretically possible to do multiple regression calculations by hand, we seldom do so.

T F 4. Suppose you are attempting to form a confidence interval for a value of Y from a multiple regression equation. If there are 20 elements in the sample and 4 independent variables are used in the regression, you should use 16 degrees of freedom when you get a value from the t table.

T F 5. The standard error of the coefficient b_2 in a multiple regression is denoted s_2.

T F 6. Suppose we wish to test whether the values of Y in a multiple regression really depend upon the values of X_1. The null hypothesis for our test would be: $B_1 = 0$.

T F 7. To determine whether a regression is significant as a whole, an observed value of F is calculated and compared to a value from a table.

T F 8. If one knows the total sum of squares and regression sum of squares for a multiple regression, the error sum of squares can always be quickly calculated.

T F 9. If a multiple regression includes all the relevant explanatory factors for the dependent variable, the residuals are usually nonrandom.

T F 10. Simple regressions of Y on X_1 and Y on X_2 show that X_1 and X_2 are both significant explanatory variables for Y. But a multiple regression of Y on X_1 and X_2 says that neither X_1 nor X_2 is a significant explanatory variable for Y. Clearly, this is a case of multicollinearity.

T F 11. Dummy variables are often used to incorporate qualitative data into multiple regressions.

T F 12. When using a dummy variable with values of 0 and 1, it is very important to make sure that the 0's and 1's are used according to standard practice. Reversing the coding will completely destroy the results of the multiple regression.

T F 13. We can form a second degree regression model by multiplying observed values of an independent variable by 2.

T F 14. Adding additional variables to a multiple regression will always reduce the standard error of the estimate.

T F 15. Suppose a multiple regression yielded this equation: $\hat{Y} = 5.6 + 2.8X_1 - 3.9X_2 + 5.6X_3$. If X_1, X_2, and X_3 all had values of zero, then Y could be expected to have a value of 5.6.

16. Suppose that a multiple regression yielded this equation: $\hat{Y} = 51.21 + 6.88X_1 + 7.06X_2 - 3.71X_3$. The value of b_2 for this equation is:
   a) 51.21   d) −3.71
   b) 6.88   e) cannot be determined from information given
   c) 7.06

17. We have said that the standard error of estimate has $n - k - 1$ degrees of freedom. What does the k stand for in this expression?
   a) number of elements in the sample
   b) number of independent variables in the multiple regression
   c) mean of the sample values of the dependent variable
   d) none of the above

18. Suppose that you have run a multiple regression and have found that the value of b_1 is 1.66. Historical data, however, indicate that the value of B_1 should be 1.34. You wish to test, at a .05 level of significance, the null hypothesis that B_1 is still 1.34. Assuming that you have access to any tables you may need, what other information is required for you to perform your test?
   a) degrees of freedom   d) a and b but not c
   b) s_{b_1} e) a and c but not b
   c) s_e

19. Suppose that a toy manufacturer wishes to determine if his red toys sell better than his blue toys. He gathered data regarding sales levels, color, price, and average age levels for which the toys are intended. He entered these into a computer run. The resulting multiple regression equation was: $\hat{Y} = 70663 - 713X_1 - 59.6X_2 + 66.4X_3$, where $\hat{Y}$ refers to sales levels in units, X_1 refers to color (0 = blue, 1 = red), X_2 refers to retail price (in dollars), and X_3 refers to average age level (in years). Which of the following is true if factors of price and age level are held constant?
   a) Red toys should sell 713 more units than blue toys.
   b) Red toys should sell 713 fewer units than blue toys.
   c) Children will always choose a blue toy over a red one.
   d) b and c but not a.

Questions 20 through 25 deal with a director of personnel who is trying to determine a predicting equation for longevity in his plant. The following data have been entered in a STATPACK run:

Y	Length of employment (months)
X_1	Years of school
X_2	Age when hired
X_3	Score on the company's psychological maturity test
X_4	Number of dependents (including employee)

The result of the multiple regression were:

VARIABLE	REG.COEF.	STD.ERROR COEF.
1	-1.55268	4.36202
2	-1.68538	1.25253
3	0.11022	0.29081
4	6.87546	7.65780

INTERCEPT	82.23830
MULTIPLE CORRELATION	0.94381
STD. ERROR OF ESTIMATE	13.40350

ANALYSIS OF VARIANCE FOR THE REGRESSION

SOURCE OF VARIATION	D.F.	SUM OF SQ.	MEAN SQ.	F VALUE
ATTRIBUTABLE TO REGRESSION	4	7325.332	1831.333	10.194
DEVIATION FROM REGRESSION	5	898.270	179.654	
TOTAL	9	8223.602		

20. The regression equation for these data is:
    a) $\hat{Y} = 82.24 - 1.55X_1 - 1.69X_2 + 0.11X_3 + 6.88X_4$
    b) $\hat{Y} = 13.40 - 1.55X_1 - 1.69X_2 + 0.11X_3 + 6.88X_4$
    c) $\hat{Y} = 82.24 + 4.36X_1 + 1.25X_2 + 0.29X_3 + 7.66X_4$
    d) $\hat{Y} = 82.24 - 0.36X_1 - 1.35X_2 + 0.38X_3 + 0.90X_4$

21. How much of the variation in length of employment is explained by the regression?
    a) 94% b) 82%   c) 89%   d) 13%

22. Suppose you wish to test whether years of school are a significant explanatory variable for longevity. The degrees of freedom you would use would be:
    a) 4   b) 10   c) 6   d) 5

23. What is the value of s_{b_3}?
    a) 13.4   b) .29   c) .38   d) .11

24. How many denominator degrees of freedom would there be for an F test to determine if this regression was significant as a whole?
    a) 5   b) 4   c 9   d) 10

25. How many rows of data did the director enter?
    a) 9   b) 10   c) 18   d) 19

26. _____ are methods for deciding which variables to include in a regression model and the different ways in which they can be included.

27. Mathematical manipulations for converting a variable into a different form so that we can fit regression curves are called _____ .

28. The _____ is a statistic used to test the significance of a regression as a whole.

29. A _____ variable takes on the values 0 and 1 to describe qualitative data.

30. A measure of our uncertainty about the exact value of a multiple regression coefficient is the _____ of the coefficient.

Nonparametric Methods

Although the effect of air pollution on health is a complex problem, an international organization has decided to make a preliminary investigation of (1) average year-round quality of air and (2) the incidence of pulmonary-related diseases. A preliminary study ranked 11 of the world's major cities from 1 (worst) to 11 (best) in these two variables.

City	A	B	C	D	E	F	G	H	I	J	K
Air quality rank	4	7	9	1	2	10	3	5	6	8	11
Pulmonary disease rank	5	4	7	3	1	11	2	10	8	6	9

The health organization's data are different from any we have seen so far in this book: they do not give us the *variable* used to determine these ranks. (We don't know if the rank of pulmonary disease is a result of pneumonia, emphysema, or other illnesses per 100,000 population.) Nor do we know the *values* (whether city D has twice as much pollution as city K or 20 times as much). If we knew the variables and their values, we could use the regression techniques of Chapter 11. Unfortunately, that is not the case; but even without any knowledge of either variables or values, we can use the techniques in this chapter to help the health organization with its problem.

In Chapters 7 to 12, we learned how statisticians take samples from populations and attempt to reach conclusions from those samples. But how can we handle cases in which we do not know what kind of population we are sampling (that is, when we do not know the shape of the population distribution)? In these cases, we can often apply the techniques of nonparametric statistics *discussed in this chapter.*

Parametric statistics

Shortcomings of parametric statistics

The majority of hypothesis tests discussed so far have made inferences about population *parameters*, such as the mean and the proportion. These parametric tests have used the parametric statistics of samples that came from the population being tested. To formulate these tests, we made restrictive assumptions about the populations from which we drew our samples. In each case in Chapter 9, for example, we assumed that our samples either were large or came from *normally distributed* populations. But populations are not always normal. And even if a goodness-of-fit test (Chapter 10) indicates that a population *is* approximately normal, we cannot always be sure we're right, because the test is not 100 percent reliable. Clearly, there are certain situations in which the use of the normal curve is not appropriate. For these cases, we need alternatives to the parametric statistics and the specific hypothesis tests we've been using so far.

1 INTRODUCTION TO NONPARAMETRIC STATISTICS

Nonparametric statistics

Fortunately, in recent times statisticians have developed useful techniques that do not make restrictive assumptions about the shape of population distributions. These are known as *distribution-free* or, more commonly, *nonparametric* tests. The hypothesis of a nonparametric test is concerned with something other than the value of a population parameter. A large number of these tests exist, but this chapter will examine only a few of the better known and more widely used ones:

1. The sign test for paired data, where positive or negative signs are substituted for quantitative values.
2. A rank sum test, often called the Mann-Whitney *U* test, which can be used to determine whether two independent samples have been drawn from the same population. It uses more information than the sign test.
3. The one-sample runs test, a method for determining the randomness with which sampled items have been selected.
4. Rank correlation, a method for doing correlation analysis when the data are not available to use in numerical form, but when information is sufficient to rank the data first, second, third, and so forth.

Advantages of nonparametric methods

Nonparametric methods have a number of clear advantages over parametric methods:

1. *They do not require us to make the assumption that a population is distributed in the shape of a normal curve or another specific shape.*
2. *Generally, they are easier to do and to understand.* Most nonparametric tests do not demand the kind of laborious computations often required, for example, to calculate a standard deviation. A nonparametric test may ask us to replace numerical values with the order in which those values occur in a list, as has been done in Table 13 · 1. Obviously, dealing computationally with 1, 2, 3, 4, and 5 takes less effort than working with 13.33, 76.50, 101.79, 113.45, and 189.42.
3. *Sometimes even formal ordering or ranking is not required.* Often, all we can do is describe one outcome as "better" than another. When this is the case, or when our measurements are not as accurate as is necessary for parametric tests, we can use nonparametric methods.

Disadvantages of nonparametric methods

Two disadvantages accompany the use of nonparametric tests:

1. *They ignore a certain amount of information.* We have demonstrated how the values 1, 2, 3, 4, and 5 can replace the numbers 13.33, 76.50, 101.79, 113.45, and 189.42. Yet if we represent "189.42" by "5," we lose information that is contained in the value 189.42. Notice that in our ordering of the values 13.33, 76.50, 101.79, 113.45, and 189.42, the value 189.42 can become 1,189.42 and still be the fifth, or largest, value in the list. But if this list is a data set, we can learn more knowing that the highest value is 1,189.42 instead of 189.42 than we can by representing both of these numbers by the value 5.

2. *They are often not as efficient or "sharp" as parametric tests.* The estimate of an interval at the 95 percent confidence level using a nonparametric test may be twice as large as the estimate using a parametric test such as those in Chapter 9. When we use nonparametric tests, we make a trade-off: we lose sharpness in estimating intervals, but we gain the ability to use less information and to calculate faster.

TABLE 13 · 1   Converting parametric values to nonparametric ranks

Parametric value	113.45	189.42	76.50	13.33	101.79
Nonparametric rank	4	5	2	1	3

13 · 1 What is the difference between the kinds of questions answered by parametric tests and those answered by nonparametric tests?

13 · 2 What are the primary shortcomings of nonparametric tests?

13 · 3 What are the major advantages of nonparametric methods over parametric methods?

13 · 4 International Communications Corporation is planning to change the benefits package offered to employees. The company is considering different combinations of profit sharing, health care, and retirement benefits. Samples of a broad range of benefit combinations were described in a pamphlet and distributed among employees, whose preferences were then recorded. The results follow:

Rank	1	2	3	4	5	6	7	8	9	10
Profit sharing-health care- retirement combination	15	5	14	4	6	16	7	8	13	3
Number of preferences	52	49	39	38	37	36	32	29	26	25

Rank		11	12	13	14	15	16	17	18	19
Profit sharing-health care- retirement combination		17	18	12	2	9	1	11	19	10
Number of preferences		24	18	15	15	14	10	10	10	9

Will the company sacrifice any real information by using the ranking test as its decision criterion? (Hint: you might graph the data.)

2 THE SIGN TEST FOR PAIRED DATA

One of the easiest nonparametric tests to use is the sign test. Its name comes from the fact that it is based on the direction (or the signs for pluses or minuses) of a pair of observations and not on their numerical magnitude.

Use sign test for paired data

Consider the result of a test panel of 40 college juniors evaluating the effectiveness of two types of classes: large lectures by full professors or small sections by graduate assistants. Table 13 · 2 lists the responses to this request: "Indicate how you rate the effectiveness in transmitting knowledge of these two types of classes by giving them a number from 4 to 1. A rating of 4 is excellent, and 1 is poor." In this case, the sign test lets us test hypotheses about whether students feel there is a difference between the effectiveness of the two types of classes.

Converting values to signs

We can begin, as we have in Table 13 · 2, by converting the evaluations of the two teaching methods into a sign. Here, a plus sign means the student prefers large lectures; a minus sign indicates a preference for small sections; and a zero represents a tie (no preference). If we

TABLE 13 · 2 Evaluation by 40 students of 2 types of classes

Panel member number	1	2	3	4	5	6	7	8	9	10	11	12	13	14	15	16	17	18	19	20
Score for large lectures (1)	2	1	4	4	3	3	4	2	4	1	3	3	4	4	4	1	1	2	2	4
Score for small sections (2)	3	2	2	3	4	2	2	1	3	1	2	3	4	4	3	2	3	2	3	3
Sign of score (1) minus score (2)	−	−	+	+	−	+	+	+	+	0	+	0	0	0	+	−	−	0	−	+

Panel member number	21	22	23	24	25	26	27	28	29	30	31	32	33	34	35	36	37	38	39	40
Score for large lectures (1)	4	4	4	3	3	2	3	4	3	4	3	1	4	3	2	2	2	1	3	3
Score for small sections (2)	1	4	3	3	2	2	1	1	1	3	2	2	4	4	3	3	1	1	4	2
sign of score (1) minus score (2)	+	0	+	0	+	0	+	+	+	+	+	−	0	−	−	−	+	0	−	+

count the bottom row of Table 13 · 2, we get these results:

Number of + signs	19
Number of − signs	11
Number of 0's	10
Total sample size	$\overline{40}$

Stating the hypotheses

Finding the sample size

We are using the sign test to determine whether our panel can discern a real difference between the two types of classes. Since we are testing perceived differences, we shall exclude tie evaluations (0's). We can see that we have 19 plus signs and 11 minus signs, for a total of 30 usable responses. If there is no difference between the two types of classes, p (the probability that the first score exceeds the second score) would be .5, and we would expect to get about 15 plus signs and 15 minus signs. We would set up our hypotheses like this:

H_0: $p = .5$ ← null hypothesis: there is no difference
between the 2 types of classes
H_1: $p \neq .5$ ← alternative hypothesis: there is a
difference between the 2 types of classes

Choosing the distribution

If you look carefully at the hypotheses, you will see that the situation is similar to the fair coin toss that we discussed in Chapter 5. If we tossed a fair coin 30 times, p would be .5, and we would expect about 15 heads and 15 tails. In that case, we would use the binomial distribution as the appropriate sampling distribution. You may also remember that when np and nq are each at least 5, we can use the normal distribution to approximate the binomial. This is just the case with the results from our panel of college juniors. Thus, we can apply the normal distribution to our test of the two teaching methods.

$p_{H_0} = .5$ ← hypothesized proportion of the population
who feel that both types of classes are the same

$q_{H_0} = .5$ ← hypothesized proportion of the population
who feel the 2 types of classes are different
$(q_{H_0} = 1 - p_{H_0})$

$n = 30$ ← sample size

$\bar{p} = .633$ ← proportion of successes in the sample (19/30)

$\bar{q} = .367$ ← proportion of failures in the sample (11/30)

Testing a hypothesis of no difference

*Calculating
the standard error*

Suppose the chancellor's office wants to test the hypothesis that there is no difference between student perception of the two types of classes at the .05 level of significance. We shall conduct this test using the methods we introduced in Chapter 9. The first step is to calculate the standard error of the proportion:

$$\sigma_{\bar{p}} = \sqrt{\frac{pq}{n}}$$

$$= \sqrt{\frac{(.5)(.5)}{30}} \qquad (8 \cdot 4)$$

$$= .091 \leftarrow \text{standard error of the proportion}$$

*Illustrating
the test*

Since we want to know whether the true proportion is larger *or* smaller than the hypothesized proportion, this is a two-tailed test. Figure 13 · 1 illustrates this hypothesis test graphically. The two shaded regions represent the .05 level of significance.

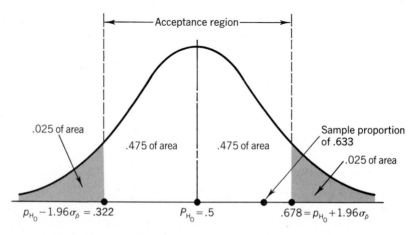

Figure 13 · 1 Two-tailed hypothesis test at the .05 level of significance, illustrating the acceptance region and the sample proportion

Finding the limits of the acceptance region	Because we are using the normal distribution in our test, we can determine from Appendix Table 1 that the z value for .475 of the area under the curve is 1.96. Thus, we can calculate the limits of the acceptance region for the null hypothesis as follows:

$$p_{H_0} \pm 1.96\sigma_{\bar{p}} = .5 \pm (1.96)(.091)$$

$$= .678 \leftarrow \text{upper limit}$$
$$\text{and} \quad .322 \leftarrow \text{lower limit}$$

Interpreting the results	Figure $13 \cdot 1$ illustrates these two limits of the acceptance region, .322 and .678, and the sample proportion, .633. We can see that the sample proportion falls within the acceptance region for this hypothesis test. Therefore, the chancellor should accept the null hypothesis that students perceive no difference between the two types of classes.
A final word about the sign test	A sign test such as this is quite simple to do and applies to both one-tailed and two-tailed tests. It is usually based on the binomial distribution. Remember, however, that we were able to use the normal approximation to the binomial as our sampling distribution because np and nq were both greater than 5. If these conditions are not met, we must use the binomial instead.

EXERCISES

13·5 With the concern over radiation exposure and its relationship to incidence of cancer, city environmental specialists keep a close eye on the types of industry coming into the area and the degree to which they employ radiation in their production. An index of exposure to radioactive contamination has been developed and is used daily to determine if the levels are increasing or are higher under certain atmospheric conditions.

Environmentalists claim that radioactive contamination has increased in the last year because of new industry in the city. City administrators, however, claim that new, more stringent regulations on industry in the area have made levels lower than last year, even with new industry using radiation. To test their claim, records for 10 randomly selected days of the year have been checked, and the index of exposure to radioactive contamination has been noted. The following results were obtained.

Index of radiation exposure

1982	1.402	1.401	1.400	1.404	1.395	1.402	1.406	1.401	1.404	1.406
1983	1.440	1.395	1.398	1.404	1.393	1.400	1.401	1.402	1.400	1.403

Can the administrators be 92 percent sure that the levels of radioactive contamination have changed—or more specifically, that they have been reduced?

13·6 Use the sign test to see if there is a difference between the number of days until the collection of an account receivable before and after a new collection policy. Use the .10 significance level.

Before	32	35	33	36	44	41	32	39	31	47	30	29
After	36	37	34	40	40	42	40	42	33	46	29	35

415 Sec. 2 The sign test for paired data

13·7 As part of the recent interest in population growth and the sizes of families, a population researcher examined a number of hypotheses concerning the family size that various people look upon as ideal. She suspected that variables of race, sex, age, and background might account for some of the different views. In one pilot sample, the researcher tested the hypothesis that women today think of an ideal family as being smaller than the ideal held by their mothers. She asked each of the participants in the pilot study to state the number of children she would choose to have or that she considered ideal. Responses were anonymous, to guard against the possibility that people would feel obligated to give a socially desirable answer. In addition, people of different backgrounds were included in the sample. Below are the responses of the mother-daughter pairs.

							Ideal family size						
Sample pair	*A*	*B*	*C*	*D*	*E*	*F*	*G*	*H*	*I*	*J*	*K*	*L*	*M*
Daughter	3	4	2	1	5	4	2	2	3	3	1	4	2
Mother	4	4	4	3	5	3	3	5	3	2	2	3	1

a) Can the researcher be 97 percent sure that the mothers and daughters do not have essentially the same ideal of family size? Use the binomial distribution.

b) Determine if the researcher could conclude that the mothers do not have essentially the same family size preferences as their daughters by using the normal approximation to the binomial.

c) Assume that for each pair listed there were 10 more pairs who responded in an identical manner. Calculate the range of the proportion for which the researcher would conclude that there is no difference in the mothers and daughters. Is your conclusion changed?

d) Explain any differences in conclusions obtained in parts a, b, and c.

---

3 A RANK SUM TEST:
THE MANN-WHITNEY U TEST

Mann-Whitney U test introduced

Rank sum tests are a whole family of tests. We shall concentrate on one member of this family, the Mann-Whitney U test, which will enable us to determine whether two independent samples have been drawn from the same population (or from two different populations having the same distribution). It uses *ranking* information rather than pluses and minuses and, therefore, is less wasteful of data than the sign test.

Approaching a problem using the Mann-Whitney U test

Suppose that the board of regents of a large eastern state university wants to test the hypothesis that the S.A.T. scores of students at two branches of the state university came from the same distribution. The board keeps statistics on all students at all branches of the system. A random sample of 15 students from each branch has produced the data shown in Table 13 · 3.

TABLE 13 · 3 S.A.T. scores for students at two state university branches

Branch A	1,000	1,100	800	750	1,300	950	1,050	1,250
Branch S	920	1,120	830	1,360	650	725	890	1,600
Branch A		1,400	850	1,150	1,200	1,500	600	775
Branch S		900	1,140	1,550	550	1,240	925	500

Ranking the items to be tested

To apply the Mann-Whitney U test to this problem, we begin by ranking all the scores in order from lowest to highest, indicating beside each the symbol of the branch.

Table 13 · 4 accomplishes this.

Next, let's learn the symbols used in a Mann-Whitney U test in the context of this problem:

Symbols for expressing the problem

n_1 = number of items in sample 1; that is, the number of students at branch A = **15**

n_2 = number of items in sample 2; that is, the number of students at branch S = **15**

R_1 = sum of the ranks of the items in sample 1: the sum from Table 13 · 5 of the ranks of all the branch A scores = **247**

R_2 = sum of the ranks of the items in sample 2: the sum from Table 13 · 5 of the ranks of all the branch S scores = **218**

TABLE 13 · 4 S.A.T. scores ranked from lowest to highest

Rank	Score	Branch	Rank	Score	Branch
1	500	S	16	1,000	A
2	550	S	17	1,050	A
3	600	A	18	1,100	A
4	650	S	19	1,120	S
5	725	S	20	1,140	S
6	750	A	21	1,150	A
7	775	A	22	1,200	A
8	800	A	23	1,240	S
9	830	S	24	1,250	A
10	850	A	25	1,300	A
11	890	S	26	1,360	S
12	900	S	27	1,400	A
13	920	S	28	1,500	A
14	925	S	29	1,550	S
15	950	A	30	1,600	S

TABLE 13·5 Raw data and rank for S.A.T. scores

Branch A	Rank	Branch S	Rank
1,000	16	920	13
1,100	18	1,120	19
800	8	830	9
750	6	1,360	26
1,300	25	650	4
950	15	725	5
1,050	17	890	11
1,250	24	1,600	30
1,400	27	900	12
850	10	1,140	20
1,150	21	1,550	29
1,200	22	550	2
1,500	28	1,240	23
600	3	925	14
775	7	500	1
	$\overline{247}$ ← total ranks		$\overline{218}$ ← total ranks

In this case, both n_1 and n_2 are equal to 15, but it is *not* necessary for both samples to be of the same size. Now in Table 13 · 5, we can reproduce the data from Table 13 · 3, adding the ranks from Table 13 · 4. Then we can total the ranks for each branch. As a result, we have all the values we need to solve this problem.

Calculating the U statistic

Using the values for n_1 and n_2 and the ranked sums of R_1 and R_2, we can determine the *U statistic*, a measurement of the difference between the ranked observations of the two samples of S.A.T. scores:

Defining the U statistic

$$U = n_1 n_2 + \frac{n_1(n_1 + 1)}{2} - R_1$$

$$= (15)(15) + \frac{(15)(16)}{2} - 247 \qquad (13 \cdot 1)$$

$$= 98 \leftarrow U \text{ statistic}$$

If the null hypothesis that the $n_1 + n_2$ observations came from identical populations is true, then this U statistic has a sampling distribution with a mean of:

mean of the *U* statistic →
$$\mu_U = \frac{n_1 n_2}{2}$$

$$= \frac{(15)(15)}{2} = 112.5 \leftarrow \text{mean of the } U \text{ statistic} \qquad (13 \cdot 2)$$

and a standard error of:

Standard error of the U statistic

$$\text{standard error of the } U \text{ statistic} \quad \rightarrow \sigma_U = \sqrt{\frac{n_1 n_2 (n_1 + n_2 + 1)}{12}}$$

$$= \sqrt{\frac{(15)(15)(15 + 15 + 1)}{12}} \qquad (13 \cdot 3)$$

$$= 24.1 \leftarrow \text{standard error of the } U \text{ statistic}$$

Testing the hypothesis

Stating the hypothesis

The sampling distribution of the U statistic can be approximated by the normal distribution when *both* n_1 and n_2 are larger than 10. Because our problem meets this condition, we can use the normal distribution and the z table to make our test. The board of regents wishes to test at the .15 level of significance the hypothesis that these samples were drawn from identical populations.

$H_0: \mu_1 = \mu_2$ ← null hypothesis: there is no difference between the two populations, and so they have the same mean

$H_1: \mu_1 \neq \mu_2$ ← alternative hypothesis: there is a difference between the two populations; in particular, they have different means

$\alpha = .15$ ← level of significance for testing this hypothesis

---

Illustrating the test

The board of regents wants to know whether the mean S.A.T. score for students at either of the two schools is better or worse than the other. Therefore, this is a two-tailed test of the hypothesis. Figure $13 \cdot 2$

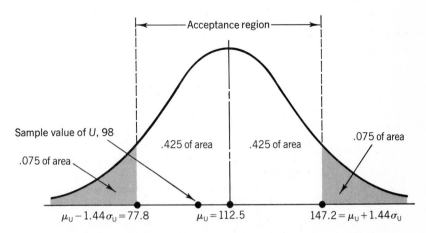

Figure 13·2 Two-tailed hypothesis test at .15 level of significance, showing the acceptance region and the sample U statistic

Finding the limits
of the
acceptance region

illustrates this test graphically. The two shaded areas represent the .15 level of significance. Since we are using the normal distribution as our sampling distribution in this test, we can determine from Appendix Table 1 that the appropriate z value for an area of .425 is 1.44. The two limits of the acceptance region can be calculated like this:

$$\mu_U \pm 1.44\sigma_U = 112.5 \pm (1.44)(24.1)$$

$$= 147.2 \leftarrow \text{upper limit}$$

$$\text{and} \quad 77.8 \leftarrow \text{lower limit}$$

Interpreting
the results

Figure 13 · 2 illustrates the limits of the acceptance region, 77.8 and 147.2, and the U value calculated earlier, 98 We can see that the sample U statistic does lie within the acceptance region. Thus, we would accept the null hypothesis of no difference and conclude that the distributions and hence the mean S.A.T. scores at the two schools, are the same.

Special properties of the U test

Another way
to compute
the U statistic

The U statistic has a feature that enables users to save calculating time when the two samples under observation are of unequal size. We just computed the value of U using Equation 13 · 1:

$$U = n_1 n_2 + \frac{n_1(n_1 + 1)}{2} - R_1 \qquad (13 \cdot 1)$$

But just as easily, we could have computed the U statistic using the R_2 value like this:

$$U = n_1 n_2 + \frac{n_2(n_2 + 1)}{2} - R_2 \qquad (13 \cdot 4)$$

The answer would have been 127 (which is just as far *above* the mean of 112.5 as 98 was *below* it). In this problem we would have spent the same amount of time calculating the value of the U statistic using either Equation 13 · 1 or Equation 13 · 4. In other cases, when the number of items is larger in one sample than in the other, choose the equation that will require less labor. Regardless of whether you calculate U using Equation 13 · 1 or 13 · 4, you will come to the same conclusion. Notice that in this example, the answer 127 falls in the acceptance region just as 98 did.

Handling ties
in the data

What about *ties* that may happen when we rank the items for this test? For example, what if the two scores ranked 13 and 14 in Table 13 · 4 both had the value 920? In this case, we would find the average of their ranks $(13 + 14)/2 = 13.5$, and assign the result to both of them. If there were a three-way tie among the scores ranked 13, 14, and 15, we would average these ranks $(13 + 14 + 15)/3 = 14$, and use that value for all three items.

13·8 Authorities for the Massachusetts Highway Department were considering purchasing a new ferry for the Martha's Vineyard crossing. The existing ferry held, on the average, 32 vehicles. The ferry under consideration was larger, but authorities doubted whether the additional space was really usable. Because of the many differing sizes of vehicles that typically used any ferry, it was impossible to estimate with accuracy whether the new ferry would be able to carry more vehicles. Relative capacities were particularly important because of a Massachusetts law requiring competitive bidding on all public contracts. The highway department had to know whether the ferry it was considering was compatible in size with a duplicate of the original (for which they had received a lower bid).

To aid in the decision, several tests were conducted on the existing ferry. Another state, which already had one of the new ferries in operation, conducted similar tests in response to the request of the Massachusetts Highway Department. The statistic that was recorded was the lengthwise footage for vehicles that were loaded on board. The data are presented below:

Lengthwise footage of vehicles loaded per trip (at capacity)

Existing ferry	453 438 447 449 452 450 439 445 446 454 451 448 442 447
Proposed ferry	458 459 450 448 459 457 462 439 448 454

Use the Mann-Whitney U test to draw a conclusion about the capacity differential of the two ships at the 10 percent significance level.

13·9 To increase sales during heavy shopping days, a chain of stores selling cheese in shopping malls gives away samples at the stores' entrances. The chain's management defines the heavy shopping days and randomly selects the days for sampling. From a sample of days that were considered heavy shopping days, the data below give one store's sales on days when cheese sampling was done and on days when it was not done.

Sales (in hundreds)

Promotion days	18	21	23	15	19	26	17	18	22	20	18	21
Regular days	22	17	15	23	25	22	26	24	16	17	23	21

Use a Mann-Whitney U test and a 9 percent level of significance to decide whether the store-front sampling produced greater sales.

13·10 The following table shows sample retail prices for two brands of manual typewriters. Use the Mann-Whitney U test to determine if there is any difference between the retail prices of the two brands throughout the country. Use the .01 level of significance. (Disregard the fact that we have fewer than 10 observations for n_1 and n_2.)

Typewriter A	$89	90	92	81	76	88	85		
Typewriter B	$78	93	81	87	89	71	90	96	82

13·11 The following data shows sample unit output per day for employees in two age groups. Use the Mann-Whitney U test to determine if there is any difference between the output of older and younger employees. Use the .05 level of significance. (Disregard the fact that we have fewer than 10 observations for n_1 and n_2.)

Over 40	24	28	15	47	23	25	53	20	
Under 40	22	12	30	16	26	14	18	21	16	18

4 ONE-SAMPLE RUNS TESTS

Concept of randomness

So far, we have assumed that the samples in our problems were randomly selected; that is, chosen without preference or bias. What if you were to notice recurrent patterns in a sample chosen by someone else? Suppose that applicants for advanced job training were to be selected without regard to sex from a large population. Using the notation W = woman and M = man, you find that the first group enters in this order:

W, W, W, W, M, M, M, M, W, W, W, W, M, M, M, M

By inspection, you would conclude that although the total number of applicants is equally divided between the sexes, the order is not random. A random process would rarely list two items in alternating groups of four. Suppose now that the applicants begin to arrive in this order:

W, M, W, M, W, M, W, M, W, M, W, M, W, M, W, M

It is just as unreasonable to think that a random selection process would produce such an orderly pattern of men and women. In this case, too, the *proportion* of women to men is right, but you would be suspicious about the *order* in which they are arriving.

The theory of runs

To allow us to test samples for the randomness of their order, statisticians have developed the *theory of runs*. A run is a sequence of identical occurrences preceded and followed by different occurrences or by none at all. If men and women enter as follows, the sequence will contain three runs:

$$\underbrace{W,}_{\text{1st}} \quad \underbrace{M, M, M, M,}_{\text{2nd}} \quad \underbrace{W}_{\text{3rd}}$$

And this sequence contains six runs:

$$\underbrace{W, W, W,}_{\text{1st}} \quad \underbrace{M, M,}_{\text{2nd}} \quad \underbrace{W,}_{\text{3rd}} \quad \underbrace{M, M, M, M,}_{\text{4th}} \quad \underbrace{W, W, W, W,}_{\text{5th}} \quad \underbrace{M}_{\text{6th}}$$

Symbols for expressing the problem

A *test of runs* would use the following symbols if it contained just two kinds of occurrences:

---

n_1 = number of occurrences of type 1
n_2 = number of occurrences of type 2
r = number of runs

Consider a new pattern for the arrival of applicants:

M, W, W, M, M, M, M, W, W, W, M, M, W, M, W, W, M

In this case the values of n_1, n_2, and r would be 8, 9, and 9, respectively.

A problem using a one-sample runs test

A manufacturer of breakfast cereal uses a machine to insert randomly one of two types of toys in each box. The company wants randomness so that every child in the neighborhood does not get the same toy. Testers choose samples of 60 successive boxes to see if the machine is properly mixing the two types of toys. Using the symbols A and B to represent the two types of toys, a tester reported that one such batch looked like this:

B, A, B, B, B, A, A, A, B, B, A, B, B, B, B, A, A, A, A, B,
A, B, A, A, B, B, B, A, A, B, A, A, A, A, B, B, A, B, B, A,
A, A, A, B, B, A, B, B, B, B, A, A, B, B, A, B, A, A, B, B

The values in our test will be:

$n_1 = 29 \leftarrow$ number of boxes containing toy A
$n_2 = 31 \leftarrow$ number of boxes containing toy B
$r = 29 \leftarrow$ number of runs

The sampling distribution of the r statistic

The *number of runs*, or r, is a statistic with its own special sampling distribution and its own test. Obviously, runs may be of differing lengths, and various numbers of runs can occur in one sample. Statisticians can prove that too many or too few runs in a sample indicate that something other than chance was at work when the items were selected. A *one-sample runs test*, then, is based on the idea that *too few* or *too many runs* show that the items were not chosen randomly.

To derive the mean of the sampling distribution of the r statistic, use the following formula:

$$\text{mean of the } r \text{ statistic} \rightarrow \mu_r = \frac{2n_1n_2}{n_1 + n_2} + 1 \qquad (13 \cdot 5)$$

Applying this to the cereal company, the mean of the r statistic would be:

$$\mu_r = \frac{(2)(29)(31)}{29 + 31} + 1 = 30.97 \leftarrow \text{mean of the } r \text{ statistic}$$

The standard error of the r statistic can be calculated with this formidable-looking formula:

$$\text{standard error of the } r \text{ statistic} \rightarrow \sigma_r = \sqrt{\frac{2n_1n_2(2n_1n_2 - n_1 - n_2)}{(n_1 + n_2)^2(n_1 + n_2 - 1)}} \qquad (13 \cdot 6)$$

For our problem, the standard error of the r statistic becomes:

$$\sigma_r = \sqrt{\frac{(2)(29)(31)(2 \times 29 \times 31 - 29 - 31)}{(29 + 31)^2(29 + 31 - 1)}}$$

$$= 3.84 \leftarrow \text{ standard error of the } r \text{ statistic}$$

Testing the hypothesis

In the one-sample runs test, the sampling distribution of r can be closely approximated by the normal distribution if *either* n_1 or n_2 is larger than 20. Since our cereal company has a sample of 60 boxes, we can use the normal approximation. Management is interested in testing at the .20 level the hypothesis that the toys are randomly mixed, so the test becomes:

Stating the hypothesis

H_0: In a one-sample runs test, no symbolic statement of the hypothesis is appropriate.
$\leftarrow$ null hypothesis: the toys are randomly mixed

H_1:
$\leftarrow$ alternative hypothesis: the toys are not randomly mixed

$\alpha = .20$
$\leftarrow$ level of significance for testing this hypothesis

Illustrating the test

Since too many *or* too few runs would indicate that the process by which the toys are inserted is not random, a two tailed test is appropriate. Figure $13 \cdot 3$ illustrates this test graphically.

Finding the limits of the acceptance region

Because we can use the normal distribution, we can turn to Appendix Table 1 to find the appropriate z value for .40 of the area under the curve. We can then use this value, 1.28, to calculate the limits of the

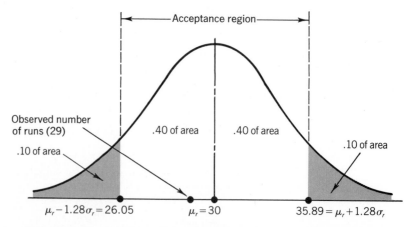

Observed number of runs (29)

.10 of area

.40 of area

.40 of area

.10 of area

$\mu_r - 1.28\sigma_r = 26.05$

$\mu_r = 30$

$35.89 = \mu_r + 1.28\sigma_r$

Figure 13·3 Two-tailed hypothesis test at the .20 level of significance, showing the acceptance region and the observed number of runs

acceptance region:

$$\mu_r \pm 1.28\sigma_r = 30.97 \pm (1.28)(3.84)$$

$$= 35.89 \leftarrow \text{upper limit}$$

$$\text{and} \quad 26.05 \leftarrow \text{lower limit}$$

Interpreting the results

Both these limits to the acceptance region, 26.05 and 35.89, and the number of runs in the sample, 29, are shown in Fig. 13 · 3. There, we can see that the observed number of runs, 29, falls within the acceptance region. Therefore, management should accept the null hypothesis and conclude from this test that the toys are being inserted in the boxes in random order.

EXERCISES

---

13 · 12 The following is the order of male and female resumés received in answer to an advertisement for a commercial artist at an advertising agency. Test this sequence for randomness at the .01 level of significance.

M, F, M, F, M, M, M, F, F, M, F, M, F, M, F, M, M, M, M, F, M, F, M, F, M,
M, F, F, F, M, F, M, F, M, F, M, M, F, M, M, F, M, M, M, M, F, M, F, M, M,

13 · 13 A restaurant owner has noticed over the years that older couples appear to eat earlier than young couples at his quiet, romantic restuarant. He suspects that perhaps it is because of children having to be left with babysitters and also because the older couples may retire earlier at night. One night he decided to keep a record of couples arrivals at the restaurant. He noted whether each couple was over or under 30. His notes are reproduced below. (A = 30 and older; B = younger than 30.)

(5:30 P.M.) A, A, A, A, A, A, B, A, A, A, A, A, A, B, B,
B, A, B, B, B, B, B, B, A, B, B, B, B, B, B, A (10 P.M.)

At a 5 percent level of significance, was the restaurant owner correct in his thought that the age of his customers at different dining hours is less than random?

13 · 14 Kathy Phillips is in charge of production scheduling for a printing company. The company has 6 large presses, which frequently break down, and one of Kathy's biggest problems is meeting deadlines when there are unexpected breakdowns in presses. She suspects that the older presses break down earlier in the week than the newer presses, since all presses are checked and repaired over the weekend. To test her hypothesis, Kathy recorded the number of all the presses as they broke down during the week. Presses numbered 1, 2, and 3 are the older ones.

Number of press in order of breakdown

1, 2, 3, 1, 4, 5, 3, 1, 2, 3, 1, 3, 6, 2, 3, 6, 2, 2, 3, 5, 4,
6, 4, 5, 1, 3, 4, 5, 5, 6, 4, 5, 2, 3, 5, 6, 4, 3, 2, 5, 4, 6

a) At a 2 percent level of significance, does Kathy have a valid hypothesis that the breakdowns of presses are not random?

b) Is her hypothesis appropriate for the decision she wishes to make about rescheduling more work earlier in the week on the newer presses?

13·15 A sequence of small glass sculptures was inspected for shipping damage. The sequence of acceptable and damaged pieces was as follows:

A, A, A, A, D, A, D, D, D, A, A, D, D, A, A, A, A, A, A, A, D, D, D, D, D,

Test for the randomness of the damage to the shipment using the .10 significance level.

---

5 RANK CORRELATION

Function of the rank correlation coefficient

Chapters 11 and 12 introduced us to the notion of correlation and to the correlation coefficient, a measure of the closeness of association between two variables. Often in correlation analysis, information is not available in the form of numerical values like those we used in the problems of that chapter. But if we can assign rankings to the items in each of the two variables we are studying, a *rank correlation coefficient* can be calculated. This is a measure of the correlation that exists between the two sets of ranks, a measure of the degree of association between the variables that we would not have been able to calculate otherwise.

Advantage of using rank correlation

A second reason for learning the method of rank correlation is to be able to simplify the process of computing a correlation coefficient from a very large set of data for each of two variables. To prove how tedious this can be, try expanding one of the correlation problems in Chapter 11 by a factor of 10 and performing the necessary calculations. Instead of having to do these calculations, we can compute a measure of association that is based on the *ranks* of the observations, *not the numerical values* of the data. This measure is called the Spearman rank correlation coefficient, in honor of the statistician who developed it in the early 1900s.

The coefficient of rank correlation

By working an example, we can learn how to calculate and interpret this measure of the association between two ranked variables. Using the information in the chapter-opening problem on air quality and pulmonary-related diseases, all we need is Equation 13 · 7 and a few computations.

coefficient of
rank correlation $\searrow$

$$r_s = 1 - \frac{6\Sigma d^2}{n(n^2 - 1)} \qquad (13 \cdot 7)$$

where:

r_s = coefficient of rank correlation (notice that the subscript s, from Spearman, distinguishes this r from the one we calculated in Chapter 11)

n = number of paired observations

Σ = notation meaning "the sum of"

d = difference between the ranks for each pair of observations

Table 13 · 6 reproduces the data found by the health organization studying the problem. In the same table, we also do some of the calculations needed to find r_s.

Finding the rank correlation coefficient

Using the data in Table 13 · 6 and Equation 13 · 7, we can find the rank correlation coefficient for this problem:

$$r_s = 1 - \frac{6\Sigma d^2}{n(n^2 - 1)}$$

$$= 1 - \frac{6(58)}{11(121 - 1)} \qquad (13 \cdot 7)$$

$$= .736 \leftarrow \text{rank correlation coefficient}$$

Interpreting the results

A correlation coefficient of .736 suggests a substantial positive association between average air quality and the occurrence of pulmonary disease, at least in the eleven cities sampled; that is, high levels of pollution go with high incidence of pulmonary disease.

How can we test this value of .736? We can apply the same methods we used to test hypotheses in Chapter 9. In performing such

TABLE 13 · 6 Ranking of eleven cities

City	Air-quality rank (1)	Pulmonary-disease rank (2)	Difference between the 2 ranks (1) − (2)	Difference squared [(1) − (2)]^2
A	4	5	−1	1
B	7	4	3	9
C	9	7	2	4
D	1	3	−2	4
E	2	1	1	1
F	10	11	−1	1
G	3	2	1	1
H	5	10	−5	25
I	6	8	−2	4
J	8	6	2	4
K	11	9	2	4

Best rank = 11
Worst rank = 1

$\Sigma d^2 = 58 \leftarrow$ sum of the squared differences

tests on r_s we are trying to avoid the error of concluding than an association exists between two variables if, in fact, no such association exists in the population from which these two samples were drawn; that is, if the *population* rank correlation coefficient, ρ_s (*rho sub-s*), is really equal to zero.

For small values of n (n less than or equal to 30), the distribution of r_s is not normal, and unlike other small sample statistics we have encountered, it is not appropriate to use the t distribution for testing hypotheses about the rank correlation coefficient. Instead, we use Appendix Table 7 to determine the acceptance and rejection regions for such hypotheses. In our current problem, suppose that the health organization wants to test, at the .05 level of significance, the null hypothesis that there is zero correlation in the ranked data of *all* cities in the world. Our problem then becomes:

$H_0: \rho_s = 0$ ← null hypothesis: there is no correlation in the ranked data of the population
$H_1: \rho_s \neq 0$ ← alternative hypothesis: there is a correlation in the ranked data of the population
$\alpha = .05$ ← level of significance for testing this hypothesis

A two-tailed test is appropriate; so we look at Appendix Table 7 in the row for $n = 11$ (the number of cities) and the column for a significance level of .05. There we find that the critical values for r_s are $\pm.6091$; that is, the upper limit of the acceptance region is .6091, and the lower limit of the acceptance region is $-.6091$.

Figure $13 \cdot 4$ shows the limits of the acceptance region and the rank correlation coefficient we calculated from the air quality sample. From

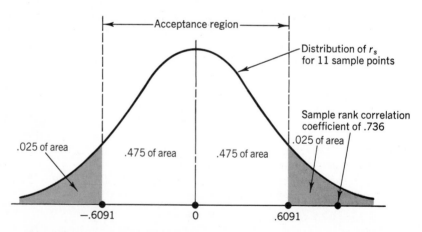

Figure 13·4 Two-tailed hypothesis test, using Appendix Table 7 at the .05 level of significance, showing the acceptance region and the sample rank correlation coefficient

this figure, we can see that the rank correlation coefficient lies outside the acceptance region. Therefore, we would reject the null hypothesis of no correlation and conclude that there is an association between air quality levels and the incidence of pulmonary disease in the world's cities.

The appropriate distribution for values of n greater than 30

If the sample size is greater than 30, we can no longer use Appendix Table 7. However, when n is greater than 30, the sampling distribution of r_s is approximately normal, with a mean of zero and a standard deviation of $1/\sqrt{n-1}$. Thus, the standard error of r_s is:

$$\text{standard error of } r_s \to \sigma_{r_s} = \frac{1}{\sqrt{n-1}} \qquad (13 \cdot 8)$$

and we can use Appendix Table 1 to find the appropriate z values for testing hypotheses about the population rank correlation.

A special property of rank correlation

Advantage of rank correlation

Rank correlation has a useful advantage over the correlation method we discussed in Chapter 11. Suppose we have cases in which one or several very extreme observations exist in the original data. Using numerical values as we did in Chapter 11, the correlation coefficient may not be a good description of the association that exists between two variables. Yet extreme observations in a *rank* correlation test will never produce a large rank difference.

Consider the following data array of two variables X and Y:

X	10	13	16	19	25
Y	34	40	45	51	117

Because of the large value of the fifth Y term, we would get two significantly different answers for r using the conventional and the rank correlation methods. In this case, the rank correlation method would be less sensitive to the extreme value. We would assign a rank order of 5 to the numerical value of 117 and avoid the unduly large effect on the value of the correlation coefficient.

--- **EXERCISES** ---

13·16 Nancy McKenzie, foreman for a lithographic camera assembly process, feels that the longer a group of employees work together, the higher the daily output rate. She has gathered the following data for a group of employees who worked together for 10 days.

Daily output	4.0	6.0	5.0	7.0	2.0	8.0	3.0	0.5	9.0	6.0
Days worked together	1	2	3	4	5	6	7	8	9	10

Can Nancy conclude at a 1 percent significance level that there is no correlation between the number of days worked together and the daily output?

13·17 The Occupational Safety and Health Administration (OSHA) was conducting a study of the relationship of expenditures for plant safety and the accident rate in the plants. OSHA had confined its studies to the synthetic chemical industry. To adjust for the size differential that existed between some of the plants, OSHA had converted its data into expenditures per production employee in relation to accidents per year. The results of the data are listed below.

Company	A	B	C	D	E	F	G	H	I	J	K
Expenditure	$60	$45	$30	$20	$28	$42	$39	$54	$48	$58	$26
Accidents	3	7	6	9	7	4	8	2	4	3	8

Is there a significant correlation between expenditures and accidents in the chemical company plants? Use a rank correlation (with 1 representing highest expenditure and accident rate) to support your conclusion. Test at a 5 percent significance level.

13·18 As part of a standards department's training, time study analysts are tested on their ability to detect differences in work rates. They are not asked to estimate the work rate, only to rank, in order of increasing productivity, the workers who were filmed. Below are the results of one analyst's rankings and the actual ranks as determined by a time study of the film frames.

	Rank									
Analyst's	9	1	10	3	5	2	4	6	7	8
Actual	7	2	6	4	3	5	1	10	8	9

Use the rank correlation test at a 5 percent significance level to decide if the analyst is able to detect different work rates.

13·19 A plant supervisor ranked a sample of 8 workers on the number of hours worked overtime and length of employment. Is the rank correlation between the two measures significant at the .01 level?

Amount of overtime	5.0	8.0	2.0	4.0	3.0	7.0	1.0	6.0
Years employed	1.0	6.0	4.5	2.0	7.0	8.0	4.5	3.0

---

6 TERMS INTRODUCED IN CHAPTER 13

Mann-Whitney U test A nonparametric method used to determine whether two independent samples have been drawn from populations with the same distribution.

nonparametric tests Statistical techniques that do not make restrictive assumptions about the shape of a population distribution when performing a hypothesis test.

one-sample runs test A nonparametric method for determining the randomness with which sampled items have been selected.

rank correlation A method for doing correlation analysis when the data are not available to use in numerical form, but when information is sufficient to rank the data.

rank correlation coefficient A measure of the degree of association between two variables that is based on the ranks of observations, not their numerical values.

rank sum tests A family of nonparametric tests that make use of the order information in a set of data.

run A sequence of identical occurrences preceded and followed by different occurrences or by none at all.

sign test A test for the difference between paired observations where + and − signs are substituted for quantitative values.

theory of runs A theory developed to allow us to test samples for the randomness of their order.

p. 418
$$U = n_1 n_2 + \frac{n_1(n_1 + 1)}{2} - R_1$$
13 · 1

To apply the Mann-Whitney U test, you need this formula to derive the U statistic, a measurement of the difference between the ranked observations of the two variables. R_1 is the sum of the ranked observations of variable 1; n_1 and n_2 the number of items in samples 1 and 2, respectively. Both samples need not be of the same size.

p. 418
$$\mu_U = \frac{n_1 n_2}{2}$$
13 · 2

If the null hypothesis of a Mann-Whitney U test is that $n_1 + n_2$ observations came from identical populations, then the U statistic has a sampling distribution with a mean equal to the product of n_1 and n_2 divided by 2.

p. 419
$$\sigma_U = \sqrt{\frac{n_1 n_2 (n_1 + n_2 + 1)}{12}}$$
13 · 3

This formula enables us to derive the *standard error of the U statistic* of a Mann-Whitney U test.

p. 420
$$U = n_1 n_2 + \frac{n_2(n_2 + 1)}{2} - R_2$$
13 · 4

This formula and Equation 13 · 1 can be used interchangeably to derive the U statistic in a Mann-Whitney U test. Use this formula if the number of observations of variable 2 is significantly smaller than the number of observations of variable 1.

p. 423
$$\mu_r = \frac{2 n_1 n_2}{n_1 + n_2} + 1$$
13 · 5

When doing a one-sample runs test, use this formula to derive the mean of the sampling distribution of the r statistic. This r statistic is equal to the *number of runs* in the sample being tested.

p. 423
$$\sigma_r = \sqrt{\frac{2 n_1 n_2 (2 n_1 n_2 - n_1 - n_2)}{(n_1 + n_2)^2 (n_1 + n_2 - 1)}}$$
13 · 6

This formula enables us to derive the *standard error of the r statistic* in a one-sample runs test.

p. 426
$$r_s = 1 - \frac{6 \Sigma d^2}{n(n^2 - 1)}$$
13 · 7

The *coefficient of rank correlation*, r_s, is a measure of the closeness of association between two ranked variables.

p. 429
$$\sigma_{r_s} = \frac{1}{\sqrt{n - 1}}$$
13 · 8

This formula enables us to calculate the *standard error of r_s* in a hypothesis test on the coefficient of rank correlation.

13·20 Two television weathermen got into a discussion one day about whether years with heavy rainfall tended to occur in spurts. One of them said he thought that there were patterns of annual rainfall amounts, and that several wet years were often followed by a number of drier than average years. The other weatherman was skeptical and said he thought that the amount of rainfall for consecutive years was fairly random. To investigate the question, they decided to look at the annual rainfall for several years back. They found the median amount and classified the rainfall as below (B) or above (A) the median annual rainfall. A summary of their results follows:

A, A, B, B, B, B, A, B, A, A, A, B, A, B, A, B, A, A, B, B, B, A, A, B, A,
B, A, A, B, B, B, A, B, B, B, A, B, A, A, A, B, A, A, A, B, A, B, B, A

If the weathermen test at a 5 percent significance level, will they conclude that the annual rainfall amounts do not occur in patterns?

13·21 The following ratings were made by people who used two detergents for three weeks. Test the hypothesis that the users found no difference in the two products. Use the .05 level of significance.

Product 1	4	4	5	5	3	2	5	3	1	2	5	3	4	2	5	5
Product 2	2	3	3	3	3	3	3	4	3	2	3	2	2	3	3	4

13·22 As part of a survey on restaurant quality, a local magazine asked area residents to rank two steak houses. On a scale of 1 to 10, subjects were to rate characteristics such as food quality, atmosphere, service, and price. After data were collected, one of the restaurant owners proposed that various statistical tests be performed. He specifically mentioned that he would like to see a mean and standard deviation for the responses to each question about each restaurant, in order to see which one had scored better. Several of the magazine workers argued against his suggestion, noting that the quality of input data would not justify a detailed statistical analysis. They argued that what was important was the residents' rankings of the two restaurants. Evaluate the arguments presented by the restaurant owner and the magazine employees.

13·23 Senior business students interviewed by Ohio Insurance Company were asked not to discuss their interviews with others in the school until the recruiter left. The recruiter, however suspected that the later applicants knew more about what the recruiter was looking for. Were her suspicions correct? To find out, rank the interview scores received by subjects. Then test the significance of the rank correlation coefficient between the scores and interview number. Use the .05 significance level.

Interview number	Score	Interview number	Score	Interview number	Score	Interview number	Score
1	25	6	32	11	37	16	43
2	29	7	39	12	41	17	44
3	28	8	34	13	38	18	66
4	33	9	35	14	24	19	47
5	30	10	42	15	45	20	50

13·24 More than three years ago, the Occupational Safety and Health Administration (OSHA) required a number of safety measures to be implemented in the Northbridge Aluminum plant. Now OSHA would like to see whether the changes have resulted in fewer accidents in the plant. They have collected these data:

Accidents at the Northbridge plant

	Jan.	Feb.	Mar.	Apr.	May	June	July	Aug.	Sept.	Oct.	Nov.	Dec.
1979	5	3	4	2	6	4	3	3	2	4	5	3
1980	4	4	3	3	3	4	0	5	4	2	0	1
1981	3	2	1	1	0	2	4	3	2	1	1	2
1982	2	1	0	0	1	2						

a) Determine the median number of accidents per month. If the safety measures have been effective, we should find early months falling above the median and later months below the median. Accordingly, there will be a small number of runs above and below the median. Conduct a test at a .03 level of significance to see if the accidents are randomly distributed.

b) What can you conclude about the effectiveness of the safety measures?

13·25 A small metropolitan airport recently opened a new runway, creating a new flight path over an upper-income residential area. Complaints of excessive noise had deluged the airport authority to the point that the two major airlines servicing the city had installed special engine baffles on the turbines of the jets, to reduce noise and help ease the pressure on the authority. Both airlines wanted to see if the baffles had helped to reduce the number of complaints that had been brought against the airport. If they had not, the baffles would be removed, because they increased fuel consumption. Based on the following data, can it be said at the .045 level of significance that installing the baffles has reduced the number of complaints?

Complaints per day before and after baffles were installed

Before	15	20	24	18	30	46	15	29	17	21	18
After	23	19	12	9	16	12	28	20	16	14	11

13·26 The American Broadcasting System (ABS) had invested a sizeable amount of money into a new program for television, *High Times*. *High Times* was ABS's entry into the situation comedy market and featured the happy-go-lucky life in a college dormitory. Unfortunately, the program had not done as well as expected, and the sponsor was considering canceling. To beef up the ratings, ABS introduced coed dormitories into the series. Presented below are the results of telephone surveys before and after the change in the series. Surveys were conducted in several major metropolitan areas, so the results are a composite from the cities.

a) Using a *U* test, can you infer at the .05 significance level that the change in the series format helped the ratings?

b) Do the results of your test say anything about the effect of sex on TV program ratings?

Share of audience before and after change to coed dormitories

Before	22	18	19	20	27	22	25	19	22	24	18	16	14	28	30	15	16
After	25	28	18	30	33	25	29	29	19	16	30	33	13	25			

13·27 To determine whether small price differences affect sales, a mail-order sportswear company divided its customers into two equal groups in terms of past order amounts. Members of the two groups were sent different catalogs, one with higher priced clothing than the other. Below are the weekly sales (in thousands) for the two groups over the 12-weeks' period after the mailing of the catalog.

High prices	20	22	18	15	17	14	8	10	9	12	19	20
Low prices	16	17	20	15	14	13	10	11	7	10	15	16

Test the hypothesis of no difference between the sales from the two catalogs at the .10 significance level.

---

9 CHAPTER CONCEPTS TEST

Answers are in the back of the book.

T F   1. One advantage of nonparametric methods is that some of the tests do not require us even to rank the observations.

T F   2. The Mann-Whitney U test is one of a family of tests known as rank difference tests.

T F   3. A sign test for paired data is based upon the binomial distribution, but can often be approximated by the normal distribution.

T F   4. One disadvantage of nonparametric methods is that they tend to ignore a certain amount of information.

T F   5. In the Mann-Whitney U test, two samples of size n_1 and n_2 are taken to determine the U statistic. The sampling distribution of the U statistic can be approximated by the normal distribution when either n_1 or n_2 is greater than 10.

T F   6. The Mann-Whitney U test tends to waste less data than the sign test.

T F   7. Assume that in a rank test, two elements are tied for the 10th rank position. We assign each of them a rank of 10.5 and the next element after these two receives a rank of 11.

T F   8. In contrast to regression analysis where one may compute a coefficient of correlation, an equivalent measure may be determined in a ranking of two variables in nonparametric testing. This equivalent measure is called a rank correlation coefficient.

T F   9. In a one-sample runs test, the number of runs is a statistic having its own sampling distribution.

T F 10. One disadvantage in using the rank correlation coefficient is that it is very sensitive to extreme observations in the data set.

T F 11. Nonparametric tests are also known as distribution-free tests.

T F 12. Nonparametric methods are more efficient than parametric methods.

T F 13. The one-sample runs test enables us to determine whether two independent samples have been drawn from populations with the same distributions.

T F 14. The sequence A, A, B, A, B contains four runs.

T F 15. A rank correlation coefficient of -1 represents perfect inverse rank correlation.

16. In a sign test for paired data, 800 students were asked to give ranks (on a scale of 0 to 10) for their attitudes toward true-false and multiple-choice tests. When signs were calculated for the two sets of paired data, 138 of the 800 paired responses received a value of "0." Does this mean that 138 students
   a) did not like either type of test?
   b) did not answer the survey?
   c) ranked the types equally?
   d) thought one of the types was perfect and the other was awful?

17. Suppose that, in question 16, the administration felt that true-false tests were liked 3 times as well as multiple-choice tests. Assuming that a preference for true-false tests is a "success," what is the null hypothesis for the administration's sign test for paired test?
a) $p = .25$ b) $p = .75$ c) $p \neq .25$ d) $p \neq .75$

Questions 18 and 19 refer to the following situation. Five former patients are selected at random from Ward A at Trinity Hospital, and 4 former patients are selected at random from Ward B. The patients stayed the following numbers of days:

Ward A:	13	4	2	10	6
Ward B:	10	9	7	8	

18. A Mann-Whitney U test is to be performed to determine if there is a significant difference between the lengths of the hospital stays for the two wards. If the lengths of stay are ranked from shortest to longest, what is the ranking for the 13-days stay in Ward A.
a) 9   b) 8   c) $9\frac{1}{2}$ d) $7\frac{1}{2}$

19. If the lengths of stay are ranked from shortest to longest, what is the value of $(R_1 - R_2)$?
a) $-\frac{1}{2}$ b) 0   c) $\frac{1}{2}$ d) $2\frac{1}{2}$

20. What is the maximum number of runs possible in a sequence of length 5 using 2 symbols?
a) 6   b) 4   c) 3   d) 5

21. The sequence C, D, C, D, C, D, C, D, C, D would probably be rejected by a test of runs as being truly random because:
a) The pattern "C, D" occurs only 5 times; this is not often enough to guarantee randomness.
b) The sequence contains too many runs.
c) The sequence contains too few runs.
d) The sequence contains only 2 symbols.
e) None of the above.

22. In a Mann-Whitney U test, a particular sampling distribution for U has a mean of 15. One value of U is calculated as $n_1 n_2 + \dfrac{n_1(n_1 + 1)}{2} - R_1$, which equals 22.5. Can we immediately conclude that the value of $n_1 n_2 + \dfrac{n_2(n_2 + 1)}{2} - R_2$ in this situation is
a) 10?   b) 12.5?   c) 7.5?   d) cannot be determined from information given?

Questions 23 to 25 refer to the following situation: Seven businessmen (denoted A – G) were ranked from 1 to 7 on a scale of yearly salary level, with 1 being highest. The results were:

A	B	C	D	E	F	G
2	6	4	1	3	5	7

23. Which of the following is correct?
a) E earned more than 4 others.
b) C and F earned the same amount.
c) C's earnings are less than those of 4 others.

d) All of the above.

e) a and c but not b

24. Suppose that, as the second part of this study, the seven businessmen are ranked according to how happy they seem to be, with 1 being the happiest. If salaries and happiness are perfectly correlated, what must be the happiness ranking for businessman A?

a) 1   b) 2   c) 3   d) 6

25. If, in the happiness ranking of question 24, salaries and happiness were perfectly inversely correlated, what must be the happiness ranking of businessman F?

a) 7   b) 2   c) 5   d) 3

26. A sequence of identical occurrences preceded and followed by different occurrences or none at all is a _____ .

27. A nonparametric method used to determine whether two independent samples have been drawn from populations with the same distribution is the _____ .

28. A nonparametric technique for determining the randomness with which sampled items have been selected is the _____ .

29. A _____ test tests for the difference between paired observations by substituting $+$, $-$, and 0 for quantitative values.

30. A _____ coefficient measures the degree of association between two variables and is based on the ranks of the observations.

Time Series

The management of the New England Resort Hotel has these quarterly occupancy data over a 5-year period:

Year	1st qtr.	2nd qtr.	3rd qtr.	4th qtr.
1977	1,861	2,203	2,415	1,908
1978	1,921	2,343	2,514	1,986
1979	1,834	2,154	2,098	1,799
1980	1,837	2,025	2,304	1,965
1981	2,073	2,414	2,339	1,967

To improve service, management must establish the seasonal pattern of demand for rooms. Using methods covered in this chapter, we shall help the hotel discern such a seasonal pattern, if it exists, and to use it to forecast demand for rooms.

In Chapter 14 we study the behavior of time series, data collected over a period of time. Our purpose will be to see what changes take place over time in the event we are observing. Often we may try to predict what the future behavior of that event will be. If you have ever been asked, "Why isn't your grade point average higher for the last three years?" and you have countered with, "But look what I did last semester," you have invited your questioner to examine the time series of your grades, hoping that the recent behavior of this series will overshadow earlier behavior.

1 INTRODUCTION

Forecasting, or predicting, is an essential tool in any decision-making process. Its uses vary from determining inventory requirements for a local shoe store to estimating the annual sales of General Motors. The quality of the forecasts management can make is strongly related to the information that can be extracted and used from past data. *Time series analysis* is one quantitative method we use to determine patterns in data collected over time. Table 14 · 1 is an example of time series data.

Use of time series analysis

Time series analysis is used to detect patterns of change in statistical information over regular intervals of time. We *project* these patterns to arrive at an estimate for the future. Thus, time series analysis helps us cope with uncertainty about the future.

Four kinds of variation in time series

We use the term *time series* to refer to any group of statistical information accumulated at regular intervals. There are four kinds of change, or variation, involved in time series analysis. They are:

1. secular trend
2. cyclical fluctuation
3. seasonal variation
4. irregular variation

Secular trend

With the first type of change, secular trend, the value of the variable tends to increase or decrease over a long period of time. The steady increase in the cost of living recorded by the Consumer Price Index is an example of secular trend. From year to individual year, the cost of living varies a great deal; but if we examine a long-term period, we see that the trend is toward a steady increase. Figure 14 · 1(a) shows a secular trend in an increasing but fluctuating time series.

Cyclical fluctuation

The second type of variation seen in a time series is cyclical fluctuation. The most common example of cyclical fluctuation is the

TABLE 14 · 1 Time series for the number of ships loaded at Morehead City, N.C.

Year	1974	1975	1976	1977	1978	1979	1980	1981
Number	98	105	116	119	135	156	177	208

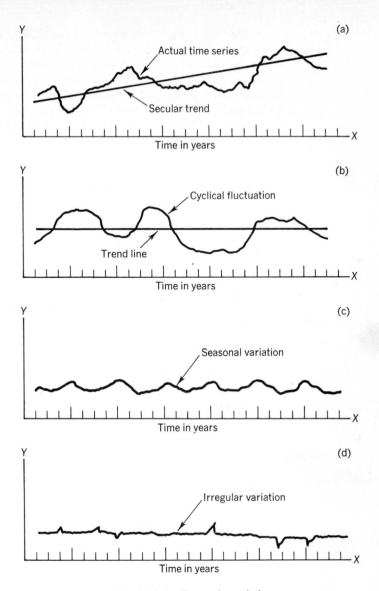

Figure 14 · 1 Time series variations

business cycle. Over time, there are years when the business cycle hits a peak above the trend line. At other times, business activity is likely to slump, hitting a low point below the trend line. The time between hitting peaks or falling to low points is at least one year, and it can be as many as 15 or 20 years. Figure 14 · 1(b) illustrates a typical pattern of cyclical fluctuation above and below a secular trend line. Note that the cyclical movements do not follow any definite trend but move in a somewhat unpredictable manner.

The third kind of change in time series data is seasonal variation. As we might expect from the name, seasonal variation involves patterns of change within a year that tend to be repeated from year to year. For example, a physician can expect a substantial increase in the number of flu cases every winter and of poison ivy every summer. Since these are regular patterns, they are useful in forecasting the future. In Fig. 14 · 1(c) we see a seasonal variation. Notice how it peaks in the fourth quarter of each time period.

Irregular variation is the fourth type of change discussed in time series analysis. In many situations, the value of a variable may be completely unpredictable, changing in a random manner. Irregular variations describe such movements. The effects of the Middle East conflict in 1973 and the Iranian situation in 1979–1981 on gasoline sales in the U.S. are examples of irregular variation. Figure 14 · 1(d) illustrates the characteristics of irregular variation. Typically, irregular variation occurs over short intervals and follows a random pattern.

Thus far we have referred to a time series as exhibiting one or another of these four types of variation. In most instances, however, a time series will contain several of these components. Thus we can describe the overall variation in a single time series in terms of these four different kinds of variation. In the following sections, we will examine the four components and the ways in which we measure each.

Because of the unpredictability of irregular variation, we do not attempt to explain it mathematically. However, we can often isolate its causes. New York City's financial crisis of 1975, for example, was an irregular factor that severely depressed the municipal bond market. Not all causes of irregular variation can be identified so easily, however. One factor that allows managers to cope with irregular variation is that over time these random movements tend to counteract each other.

In the following three sections, we examine the other three components (trend, cyclical variation, and seasonal variation) and the ways in which we measure each.

EXERCISES

14 · 1 Identify the four principal components of a time series and explain the kind of change, over time, to which each applies.

14 · 2 Which of the four components of a time series would we use to describe the effect of Christmas sales upon a retail department store?

14 · 3 What is the advantage of reducing a time series into its four components?

14 · 4 Why don't we project irregular variations into the future?

14 · 5 Which of the following illustrate irregular variations?
   a) an extended drought leading to increasing food prices
   b) the effect of snow upon ski slope business

c) a federal tax rebate provision for the purchase of new houses, leading to an increase in housing sales

14·6 What component of a time series explains the general growth of the steel industry over the last two centuries?

14·7 For what purpose do we apply time series analysis to data collected over a period of time?

14·8 How would errors in forecasts affect a city government?

---

2 TREND ANALYSIS

Two methods of fitting a trend line

Of the four components of a time series, secular trend represents the long-term direction of the series. One way to describe the trend component is to fit a line visually to a set of points on a graph. Any given graph, however, is subject to slightly different interpretations by different individuals. We can also describe a trend by the method of least squares, which we examined in Chapter 11. In our discussion, we will concentrate on the method of least squares, since visually fitting a line to a time series is not a completely dependable process.

Reasons for studying trends

There are three reasons why it is useful to study secular trends.

Three reasons for studying secular trends

1. *The study of secular trends allows us to describe a historical pattern.* There are many instances when we can use a past trend to evaluate the success of a previous policy. For example, a university may evaluate the effectiveness of a recruiting program by examining its past enrollment trends.

2. *Studying secular trends permits us to project past patterns, or trends, into the future.* Knowledge of the past can tell us a great deal about the future. Examining the growth rate of the world's population, for example, can help us estimate the population for some future time.

3. *In many situations, studying the secular trend of a time series allows us to eliminate the trend component from the series.* This makes it easier for us to study the other three components of the time series. If we want to determine the seasonal variation in ski sales, for example, eliminating the trend component gives us a more accurate idea of the seasonal component.

Trend lines take different forms

Trends can be linear, or they can be curvilinear. Before we examine the linear, or straight line, method of describing trends, we should remember that some relationships do not take that form. The increase of pollutants in the environment follows an upward sloping curve similar to that in Fig. 14 · 2(a). Another common example of a curvilinear relationship is the life cycle of a new business product, illustrated in Fig. 14 · 2(b). When a new product is introduced, its sales volume is low (I).

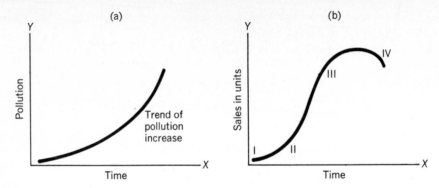

Figure 14·2 Curvilinear trend relationships

As the product gains recognition and success, unit sales grow at an increasingly rapid rate (II). After the product is firmly established, its unit sales grow at a stable rate (III). Finally, as the product reaches the end of its life cycle, unit sales begin to decrease (IV).

Fitting the linear trend by the least squares method

Besides those trends that can be described by a curved line, there are others that are described by a straight line. These are called linear trends. Before developing the equation for a linear trend, we need to review the general equation for estimating a straight line (Equation 11 · 1).

equation for estimating
a straight line $\longrightarrow$ $\hat{Y} = a + bX$ $\qquad$ (11 · 1)

where:

$\hat{Y}$ = estimated value of the dependent variable

X = independent variable (*time* in trend analysis)

a = Y-intercept (the value of Y when $X = 0$)

b = slope of the trend line

Finding the best-fitting trend line

We can describe the general trend of many time series using a straight line. But we are faced with the problem of finding the best-fitting line. As we did in Chapter 11, we can use the least squares method to calculate the best-fitting line, or equation. There we saw that the best-fitting line was determined by Equations 11 · 3 and 11 · 4, which are now renumbered as Equations 14 · 1 and 14 · 2.

$$b = \frac{\Sigma XY - n\overline{X}\,\overline{Y}}{\Sigma X^2 - n\overline{X}^2} \qquad (14 \cdot 1)$$

$$a = \overline{Y} - b\overline{X} \qquad (14 \cdot 2)$$

where:

Y = the values of the dependent variable

X = the values of the independent variable

$\overline{Y}$ = mean of the values of the dependent variable

$\overline{X}$ = mean of the values of the independent variable

n = number of data points in the time series

a = Y-intercept

b = slope

With Equations 14 · 1 and 14 · 2, we can establish the best-fitting line to describe time series data. However, the regularity of time series data allows us to simplify the calculations in Equations 14 · 1 and 14 · 2 through the process we shall now describe.

Translating or coding time

Coding the time variable to simplify computation

Normally we measure the independent variable "time" in terms such as weeks, months, and years. Fortunately, we can convert these traditional measures of time to a form that simplifies the computation. In Chapter 3, we called this process *coding*. To use coding here, we find the mean time and then subtract that value from each of the sample times. Suppose our time series consists of only three points, 1980, 1981, and 1982. If we had to place these numbers in Equations 14 · 1 and 14 · 2, we would find the resultant calculations tedious. Instead we can transform the values 1980, 1981, and 1982 into corresponding values of $-1, 0$, and 1, where 0 represents the mean (1981), -1 represents the first year ($1980 - 1981 = -1$), and 1 represents the last year ($1982 - 1981 = 1$).

Treating odd and even numbers of elements

We need to consider two cases when we translate time values. The first is a time series with an *odd number of elements*, as in the previous example. The second is a series with an *even number of elements*. Consider Table 14 · 2. In part (a) we have an odd number of years. Thus the process is the same as the one we just described, using the years 1980, 1981, and 1982. In part (b) we have an *even* number of elements. In cases like this, when we find the mean and subtract it from each element, the fraction $\frac{1}{2}$ becomes part of the answer. To simplify the coding process and to remove the $\frac{1}{2}$, we multiply each time element by 2. We will denote the "coded," or translated, time with a lowercase x.

Why use coding?

We have two reasons for this translation of time. First, it eliminates the need to square numbers as large as 1976, 1977, 1978, and so on. This method also sets the mean year, $\overline{x}$, equal to zero and allows us to simplify Equations 14 · 1 and 14 · 2.

Simplifying the calculation of a and b

Now we can return to our calculations of the slope (Equation 14 · 1) and the Y-intercept (Equation 14 · 2) to determine the best-fitting line. Since we are using the coded variable x, we replace X and $\overline{X}$ by x

TABLE 14·2 Translating, or coding, time values

(a) When there is an *odd* number of elements in the time series			(b) When there is an *even* number of elements in the time series			
X (1)	$X - \bar{X}$ (2)	*Translated or coded* time (3)	X (1)	$X - \bar{X}$ (2)	$(X - \bar{X}) \times 2$ (3)	*Translated or coded* time (4)
1976	1976 − 1979 =	−3	1976	$1976 - 1978\frac{1}{2} = -2\frac{1}{2} \times 2 =$		−5
1977	1977 − 1979 =	−2	1977	$1977 - 1978\frac{1}{2} = -1\frac{1}{2} \times 2 =$		−3
1978	1978 − 1979 =	−1	1978	$1978 - 1978\frac{1}{2} = -\frac{1}{2} \times 2 =$		−1
1979	1979 − 1979 =	0	1979	$1978 - 1981\frac{1}{2} = \frac{1}{2} \times 2 =$		1
1980	1981 − 1979 =	1	1980	$1980 - 1978\frac{1}{2} = 1\frac{1}{2} \times 2 =$		3
1981	1979 − 1979 =	2	1981	$1981 - 1978\frac{1}{2} = 2\frac{1}{2} \times 2 =$		5
1982	1982 − 1979 =	3				

$\Sigma X = 13{,}853 \quad \bar{x} \text{ (the mean year)} = 0$

$\bar{X} = \dfrac{\Sigma X}{n}$

$= \dfrac{13{,}853}{7} = 1979$

$\Sigma X = 11{,}871 \qquad \bar{x} \text{ (the mean year)} = 0$

$\bar{X} = \dfrac{\Sigma X}{n}$

$= \dfrac{11{,}871}{6} = 1978\frac{1}{2}$

and $\bar{x}$ in Equations 14 · 1 and 14 · 2. Then, since the mean of our coded time variable $\bar{x}$ is zero, we can substitute 0 for $\bar{x}$ in Equations 14 · 1 and 14 · 2 as follows:

$$b = \frac{\Sigma XY - n\bar{X}\bar{Y}}{\Sigma X^2 - n\bar{X}^2} \qquad (14 \cdot 1)$$

$$= \frac{\Sigma xY - n\bar{x}\bar{Y}}{\Sigma x^2 - n\bar{x}^2} \leftarrow \left\{ \begin{array}{l} \bar{x} \text{ (the coded variable) substituted} \\ \text{for } \bar{X} \text{ and } x \text{ substituted for } X \end{array} \right.$$

$$= \frac{\Sigma xY - n0\bar{Y}}{\Sigma x^2 - n0^2} \leftarrow \{\bar{x} \text{ replaced by } 0$$

$$= \frac{\Sigma xY}{\Sigma x^2} \qquad (14 \cdot 3)$$

Equation 14 · 2 changes as follows:

$$a = \bar{Y} - b\bar{X} \qquad (14 \cdot 2)$$

$$= \bar{Y} - b\bar{x} \leftarrow \{\bar{x} \text{ substituted for } \bar{X}$$

$$= \bar{Y} - b0 \leftarrow \{\bar{x} \text{ replaced by } 0$$

$$= \bar{Y} \qquad (14 \cdot 4)$$

Equations 14 · 3 and 14 · 4 represent a substantial improvement over Equations 14 · 1 and 14 · 2.

A problem using the least squares method (even number of elements) in a time series

Using the
least squares
method
Consider the data in Table 14 · 1 where N is the number of ships loaded at Morehead City between 1974 and 1981. In this problem we want to find the equation that will describe the secular trend of loadings. To calculate the necessary values for Equations 14 · 3 and 14 · 4, let us look at Table 14 · 3.

Finding the slope
and Y-intercept
With these values, we can now substitute into Equations 14 · 3 and 14 · 4 to find the slope and the Y-intercept for the line describing the trend in ship loadings.

$$b = \frac{\Sigma xY}{\Sigma x^2} = \frac{1,266}{168} = 7.536 \qquad (14 \cdot 3)$$

and

$$a = \bar{Y} = 139.25 \qquad (14 \cdot 4)$$

Thus, the general linear equation describing the secular trend in ship loadings is:

$$\hat{Y} = a + bx$$
$$= 139.25 + 7.536x \qquad (11 \cdot 1)$$

TABLE 14 · 3 Intermediate calculations for computing the trend

X (1)	Y^* (2)	$X - \bar{X}$ (3)	x (4)	xY (4) × (2)	x^2 (4)^2
1974	98	$1974 - 1977\frac{1}{2}^{\dagger} = -3\frac{1}{2} \times 2 = -7$		-686	49
1975	105	$1975 - 1977\frac{1}{2} = -2\frac{1}{2} \times 2 = -5$		-525	25
1976	116	$1976 - 1977\frac{1}{2} = -1\frac{1}{2} \times 2 = -3$		-348	9
1977	119	$1977 - 1977\frac{1}{2} = -\frac{1}{2} \times 2 = -1$		-119	1
1978	135	$1978 - 1977\frac{1}{2} = \frac{1}{2} \times 2 = 1$		135	1
1979	156	$1979 - 1977\frac{1}{2} = 1\frac{1}{2} \times 2 = 3$		468	9
1980	177	$1980 - 1977\frac{1}{2} = 2\frac{1}{2} \times 2 = 5$		885	25
1981	208	$1981 - 1977\frac{1}{2} = 3\frac{1}{2} \times 2 = 7$		1,456	49
$\Sigma X = \overline{15,820}$	$\Sigma Y = \overline{1,114}$			$\Sigma xY = \overline{1,266}$	$\Sigma x^2 = \overline{168}$

$$\bar{X} = \frac{\Sigma X}{n} = \frac{15,820}{8} = 1977\frac{1}{2}$$

$$\bar{Y} = \frac{\Sigma Y}{n} = \frac{1,114}{8} = 139.25$$

$^*Y$ is in number of ships.
$^{\dagger}1977\frac{1}{2}$ corresponds to $x = 0$.

where:

$\hat{Y}$ = estimated annual number of ships loaded

x = coded time value representing the number of *half-year* intervals. (A minus sign indicates half-year intervals before $1977\frac{1}{2}$; a plus sign indicates half-year intervals after $1977\frac{1}{2}$.)

Projecting with the trend equation

Once we have developed the trend equation, we can project it to forecast the variable in question. In the problem of finding the secular trend in ship loadings, for instance, we determined that the appropriate secular trend equation was:

$$\hat{Y} = 139.25 + 7.536x$$

Using our trend line to predict

Now suppose we want to estimate ship loadings for 1982. First, we must convert 1982 to the value of the coded time (in half-year intervals):

$$x = 1982 - 1977\frac{1}{2}$$
$$= 4.5 \text{ years } (= 9 \text{ half-year intervals})$$

Substituting this value into the equation for the secular trend, we get:

$$\hat{Y} = 139.25 + 7.536(9)$$
$$= 207 \text{ ships loaded}$$

Therefore, we have estimated that 207 ships will be loaded in 1982. If the number of elements in our time series had been odd, not even, our procedure would have been the same, except that we would have dealt with one-year intervals, not half-year intervals.

Use of the second-degree equation in a time series

Handling time series that are described by curves

So far we have described the method of fitting a straight line to a time series. But many time series are best described by curves, not straight lines. In these instances the linear model does not adequately describe the change in the variable as time changes. To overcome this problem we often use a parabolic curve, which is described mathematically by a second degree equation. Such a curve is illustrated in Fig. 14 · 2(a). The general form for an estimated second-degree equation is:

$$\hat{Y} = a + bx + cx^2 \qquad (14 \cdot 5)$$

where:

$\hat{Y}$ = estimate of the dependent variable

a, b, and c = numerical constants

x = coded values of the time variables

Again we use the least squares method to determine the second-degree equation to describe the best fit. The derivation of the second degree equation is beyond the scope of this text. However, we can determine the value of the numerical constants (a, b, and c) from the following three equations:

$$\text{equations to find}\atop a, b, \text{ and } c \text{ to fit} \rightarrow \text{a parabolic curve} \quad \left\{ \begin{array}{ll} \Sigma Y = na + c\Sigma x^2 & (14 \cdot 6) \\ \Sigma x^2 Y = a\Sigma x^2 + c\Sigma x^4 & (14 \cdot 7) \\ b = \dfrac{\Sigma xY}{\Sigma x^2} & (14 \cdot 3) \end{array} \right.$$

When we find the values of a, b, and c by solving Equations 14 · 6, 14 · 7, and 14 · 3, simultaneously, we substitute these values into the second-degree equation, Equation 14 · 5.

As in describing a linear relationship, we transform the independent variable, time (X), into a coded form (x) to simplify the calculation. We'll now work through a problem in which we fit a parabola to a time series.

A problem involving a parabolic trend (odd number of elements in the time series)

In recent years, the sale of electric quartz watches has increased at a significant rate. Table 14 · 4 contains sales information that will help us determine the parabolic trend describing watch sales.

We organize the necessary calculations in Table 14 · 5. The first step in this process is to translate the independent variable X into a

TABLE 14·4 Annual sales of electric quartz watches

X (year)	1976	1977	1978	1979	1980
Y (unit sales in millions)	13	24	39	65	106

TABLE 14·5 Intermediate calculations for computing the trend

Y (1)	X (2)	$X - \bar{X} = x$ (3)	x^2 $(3)^2$	x^4 $(3)^4$	xY $(3) \times (1)$	x^2Y $(3)^2 \times (1)$
13	1976	$1976 - 1978 = -2$	4	16	-26	52
24	1977	$1977 - 1978 = -1$	1	1	-24	24
39	1978	$1978 - 1978 = 0$	0	0	0	0
65	1979	$1979 - 1978 = 1$	1	1	65	65
106	1980	$1980 - 1978 = 2$	4	16	212	424
$\Sigma Y = \overline{247}$	$\Sigma X = \overline{9{,}890}$		$\Sigma x^2 = \overline{10}$	$\Sigma x^4 = \overline{34}$	$\Sigma xY = \overline{227}$	$\Sigma x^2Y = \overline{565}$

$$\bar{X} = \frac{\Sigma X}{n} = \frac{9{,}890}{5} = 1978$$

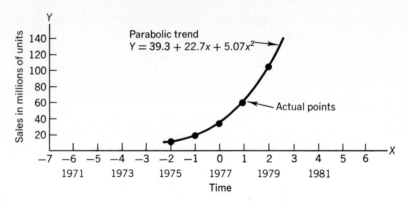

Figure 14·3 Parabolic trend fitted to data in Table 14 · 4

coded time variable x. Note that the coded variable x is listed in one-year intervals because there is an odd number of elements in our time series. Thus, it is not necessary to multiply the variable by 2.

Calculating a, b, and c by substitution

Substituting the values from Table 14 · 5 into equations 14 · 6, 14 · 7, and 14 · 3, we get:

$$247 = 5a + 10c \qquad ① \qquad\qquad (14 \cdot 6)$$

$$565 = 10a + 34c \qquad ② \qquad\qquad (14 \cdot 7)$$

$$b = \frac{227}{10} \qquad ③ \qquad\qquad (14 \cdot 3)$$

From ③ we see that

$$b = 22.7$$

Solving equations ① and ②, we find that $a = 39.3$ and $c = 5.07$. This gives us the appropriate values of a, b, and c to describe the time series presented in Table 14 · 5 by the following equation:

$$\hat{Y} = a + bx + cx^2$$
$$= 39.3 + 22.7x + 5.07x^2 \qquad\qquad (14 \cdot 5)$$

Does our curve fit the data?

In graphing the watch data, our purpose is to see how well the parabola we just derived fits the time series. We've done this in Fig. 14 · 3.

Forecasts based on a second-degree equation

Suppose we want to forecast watch sales for 1985. To make a prediction, we must first translate 1985 into a coded variable x by subtracting the mean year, 1978.

$$X - \bar{X} = x$$
$$1985 - 1978 = 7$$

This value ($x = 7$) is then substituted into the second-degree equation describing watch sales.

$$\hat{Y} = 39.3 + 22.7x + 5.07x^2$$
$$= 39.3 + 22.7(7) + 5.07(7)^2$$
$$= 446.6$$

Making the forecast

We conclude, based on the past secular trend, that watch sales should be approximately 446,600,000 units by 1985. This extraordinarily large forecast suggests, however, that we must be more careful in forecasting with a parabolic curve than we are when using a linear trend. The slope of the second-degree equation in Fig. 14 · 3 is continually increasing. Therefore, the parabolic curve may become a poor estimator as we attempt to predict farther into the future. In using the second-degree equation method, we must also take into consideration factors that may be slowing or reversing the growth rate of the variable.

Being careful in interpreting the forecast

In our watch example, we can assume that during the time period under consideration the product is at a very rapid growth stage in its life cycle. But we must realize that as the cycle approaches a mature stage, sales will probably decelerate and no longer be predicted accurately by our parabolic curve. When we calculate predictions for the future, we need to consider the possibility that the trend line may *change*. Such a situation could cause considerable error. It is therefore necessary to exercise particular care when using a second-degree equation as a forecasting tool.

EXERCISES

14·9 Mike Godfrey, the auditor of a state public school system, has reviewed the inventory records to determine if the current inventory holdings of textbooks are typical. The following inventory amounts are from the previous five years:

Year	1976	1977	1978	1979	1980
Inventory ($\times$ $1,000)	$4,560	$4,850	$5,430	$5,670	$5,930

a) Find the linear equation that describes the trend in the inventory holdings.
b) Estimate for him the value of the inventory amount for the year 1981.

14·10 The owner of Progressive Builders is examining the number of solar homes started in the region in each of the last 7 months.

Month	June	July	Aug.	Sept.	Oct.	Nov.	Dec.
Number of homes	15	15	26	27	33	41	51

a) Plot these data.
b) Develop the linear estimating equation that best describes these data, and plot the line on the graph from part a (let x units equal one month).
c) Develop the second degree estimating equation that best describes these data and plot this curve on the graph from part a.

14·11 The Tasty-Smack hamburger chain has significantly increased its investment in inventory over the last 6 years. The information is printed below.

Year	1974	1975	1976	1977	1978	1979
Inventory ($\times$$100,000)	4	4.5	6	8	8.5	10

a) Plot these data.

b) Develop the linear estimating equation that best describes these data, and plot this line on the graph from part a.

c) Develop the second degree estimating equation that best describes these data, and plot this curve on the graph from part a.

---

3 CYCLICAL VARIATION

Cyclical variation defined

Cyclical variation is the component of a time series that tends to oscillate above and below the secular trend line for periods longer than one year. The procedure used to identify cyclical variation is the residual method.

Residual method

Justification for disregarding seasonal variation

When we look at a time series consisting of annual data, only the secular trend, cyclical, and irregular components are considered. (This is true because seasonal variation makes a complete, regular cycle within each year and thus does not affect one year any more than another.) Since we can describe secular trend using a trend line, we can isolate the remaining cyclical and irregular components from the trend. We will assume that the cyclical component explains most of the variation left unexplained by the trend component. (Many real-life time series do not satisfy this assumption. Methods such as Fourier analysis and spectral analysis can analyze the cyclical component for such time series. These, however, are beyond the scope of this book.)

Expressing cyclical variation as a percent of trend

If we use a time series composed of annual data, we can find the fraction of the trend by dividing the actual value (Y) by the corresponding trend value ($\hat{Y}$) for each value in the time series. We then multiply the result of this calculation by 100. This gives us the measure of cyclical variation as a *percent of trend*. We express this process in Equation 14 · 8:

$$\text{Percent of trend} = \frac{Y}{\hat{Y}} \times 100 \qquad (14 \cdot 8)$$

where:

Y = actual time series value

$\hat{Y}$ = estimated trend value from the same point in the time series

Now let's apply this procedure.

TABLE 14·6 Grain received by farmers' cooperative over 8 years

X Year	Y Actual bushels (× 10,000)	$\hat{Y}$ Estimated bushels (× 10,000)
1974	7.5	7.6
1975	7.8	7.8
1976	8.2	8.0
1977	8.2	8.2
1978	8.4	8.4
1979	8.5	8.6
1980	8.7	8.8
1981	9.1	9.0

A farmers' marketing cooperative wants to measure the variations in its members' wheat harvest over an 8-year period. Table 14 · 6 shows the volume harvested in each of the eight years. Column $\hat{Y}$ contains the values of the linear trend for each time period. The trend line has been generated using the methods illustrated in section 2 of this chapter. Note that when we graph the actual (Y) and the trend ($\hat{Y}$) values for the eight years in Fig. 14 · 4, the actual values move above and below the trend line.

Interpreting cyclical variations

Now we can determine the percent of trend for each of the years in the sample (column 4 in Table 14 · 7). From this column we can see the variation in actual harvests around the estimated trend (98.7 to 102.5). We can attribute these cyclical variations to factors such as rainfall and temperature. However, since these factors are relatively unpredictable,

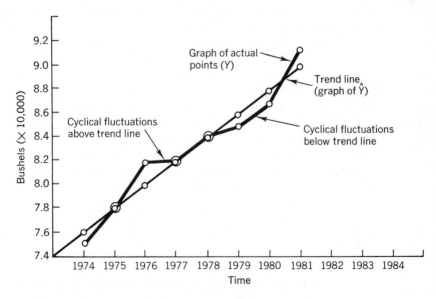

Figure 14·4 Cyclical fluctuations around the trend line

451 Sec. 3 Cyclical variation

TABLE 14·7 Calculation of percent trend

X Year (1)	Y Actual bushels (× 10,000) (2)	$\hat{Y}$ Estimated bushels (× 10,000) (3)	$\dfrac{Y}{\hat{Y}} \times 100$ Percent of trend $(4) = \dfrac{(2)}{(3)} \times 100$
1974	7.5	7.6	98.7
1975	7.8	7.8	100.0
1976	8.2	8.0	102.5
1977	8.2	8.2	100.0
1978	8.4	8.4	100.0
1979	8.5	8.6	98.8
1980	8.7	8.8	98.9
1981	9.1	9.0	101.1

we cannot forecast any specific patterns of variation using the method of residuals.

Expressing cyclical variations in terms of relative cyclical residual

The *relative cyclical residual* is another measure of cyclical variation. In this method the *percentage* deviation from the trend is found for each value. Equation 14 · 9 presents the mathematical formula for determining the relative cyclical residuals. As with percents of trend, this measure is also a percentage.

$$\text{Relative cyclical residual} = \frac{Y - \hat{Y}}{\hat{Y}} \times 100 \qquad (14 \cdot 9)$$

where:

Y = actual time series value

$\hat{Y}$ = estimated trend value from the same point in the time series

We could also just as easily compute the relative cyclical residual by subtracting 100 from the percent of trend (column 4 in Table 14 · 7).

Comparing the two measures of cyclical variation

These two measures of cyclical variation, percent of trend and relative cyclical residual, are percentages of the trend. For example, in 1979 the *percent of trend* indicated that the actual harvest was 98.8 percent of the expected harvest for that year. For the same year, the *relative cyclical residual* indicated that the actual harvest was 1.2 percent short of the expected harvest (a relative cyclical residual of -1.2).

Graphing cyclical variation

Frequently, we graph cyclical variation as the percent of trend. Figure 14 · 5 illustrates how this process eliminates the trend line and isolates the cyclical component of the time series. It must be emphasized that the procedures discussed in this section can be used only for describing past cyclical variations and not for predicting future cyclical variations. Predicting cyclical variation requires the use of techniques beyond the scope of this book.

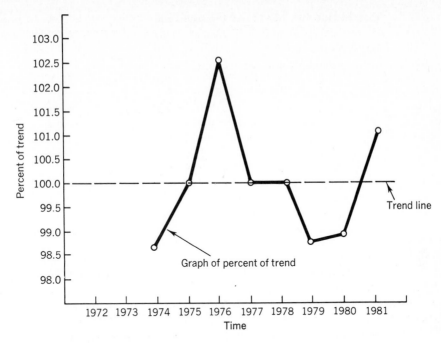

Figure 14·5 Graph of percent of trend around trend line for data in Table 14 · 7

────────────────────── **EXERCISES** ──────────────────────

14·12 The Western Natural Gas Company has supplied 18, 20, 21, 25, and 26 billion cubic feet of gas, respectively, for the years 1977 to 1981.
  a) Find the linear estimating equation that best describes these data.
  b) Calculate the percent of trend for these data.
  c) Calculate the relative cyclical residual for these data.

14·13 Microprocessing, a computer firm specializing in software engineering, has compiled the following revenue record for the years 1974 to 1980:

Year	1974	1975	1976	1977	1978	1979	1980
Revenue (×$100,000)	1.5	1.6	1.6	1.8	1.9	2.2	2.5

The second degree equation that best describes the secular trend for these data is

$$\hat{Y} = 1.75 + .16x + .03x^2, \text{ where } 1977 = 0 \text{ and } x \text{ units} = 1 \text{ year}$$

  a) Calculate the percent of trend for these data.
  b) Calculate the relative cyclical residual for these data.
  c) Plot the percent of trend from part c.

──

4 SEASONAL VARIATION

Seasonal variation defined   Besides secular trend and cyclical variation, time series also include seasonal variation. Seasonal variation is defined as repetitive and predictable movement around the trend line in *one year or less*. In order to detect seasonal variation, time intervals need to be measured in small units, such as days, weeks, months, or quarters.

We have three main reasons for studying seasonal variation.

1. *We can establish the pattern of past changes.* This gives us a way to compare two time intervals that would otherwise be too dissimilar. If a flight training school wants to know if a slump in business during December is normal, it can examine the seasonal pattern in previous years and find the information it needs.

2. *It is useful to project past patterns into the future.* In the case of long-range decisions, secular trend analysis may be adequate. But for short-run decisions, the ability to predict seasonal fluctuations is often essential. Consider a wholesale food chain that wants to maintain a minimum adequate stock of all items. The ability to predict short-range patterns, such as the demand for turkeys at Thanksgiving, candy at Christmas, or peaches in the summer, is useful to the management of the chain.

3. *Once we have established the seasonal pattern that exists, we can eliminate its effects from the time series.* This adjustment allows us to calculate the cyclical variation that takes place each year. When we eliminate the effect of seasonal variation from a time series, we have *deseasonalized* the time series.

Ratio-to-moving average method

In order to measure seasonal variation, we typically use the ratio-to-moving average method. This technique provides an *index* that describes the degree of seasonal variation. The index is based on a mean of 100, with the degree of seasonality measured by variations away from the base. For example, if we examine the seasonality of canoe rentals at a summer resort, we might find that the spring quarter index is 142. The value 142 indicates that 142 percent of the average quarterly rentals occur in the spring. If management recorded 2,000 canoe rentals for all of last year, then the average quarterly rental would be $\frac{2,000}{4} = 500$. Since the spring quarter index is 142, we estimate the number of spring rentals as follows:

$$\text{spring quarter index}$$
$$\downarrow$$
$$\text{average quarterly rental} \rightarrow 500 \times \frac{142}{100} = 710 \leftarrow \begin{array}{l} \textit{seasonalized} \text{ spring} \\ \text{quarter rental} \end{array}$$

Our chapter opening example can illustrate the ratio-to-moving average method. The resort hotel wanted to establish the seasonal pattern of room demand by its clientele. Hotel management wants to improve customer service and is considering several plans to employ enough personnel during peak periods to achieve this goal. Table 14 · 8 contains the quarterly occupancy; that is, the average number of guests during each quarter of the last 5 years.

We will refer to Table 14 · 8 to demonstrate the five steps required to compute a seasonal index.

1. *The first step in computing a seasonal index is to calculate the 4-quarter moving total for the time series.* To do this, we total the values for the quarters during the first year, 1977, in Table 14 · 8: 1,861 + 2,203 + 2,415 + 1,908 = 8,387. Since 8,387 is the total of 4 quarters, it should be placed opposite the midpoint of the 4 quarters in column 4 of Table 14 · 9. However, it is common to "drop it down" one line to avoid the problem of having data "between the lines." Thus, we find the total 8,387 located opposite quarter III instead of between quarters II and III in column 4 of Table 14 · 9.

We find the next moving total by dropping the 1977-I value, 1,861, and adding the 1978-I value, 1,921. By dropping the first value and adding the fifth, we keep 4 quarters in the total. The 4 values added now are 2,203 + 2,415 + 1,908 + 1,921 = 8,447. This total is entered in Table 14 · 9 directly below the first quarterly total of 8,387. We continue the process of "sliding" the 4-quarter total over the time series until we have included the last value in the series. In this example, it is the 1,967 rooms in the fourth quarter of 1981, the last number in column 3 of Table 14 · 9.

2. *In the second step, we compute the 4-quarter moving average by dividing each of the 4-quarter totals by four.* In Table 14 · 9, we divided the values in column 4 by four, to arrive at the values for column 5. Figure 14 · 6 illustrates how the moving average has smoothed the peaks and troughs of the original time series. The seasonal and irregular components have been smoothed, and the resulting dotted line represents the cyclical and trend components.

TABLE 14 · 8   Time series for hotel occupancy

	Number of guests per quarter			
Year	*I*	*II*	*III*	*IV*
1977	1,861	2,203	2,415	1,908
1978	1,921	2,343	2,514	1,986
1979	1,834	2,154	2,098	1,799
1980	1,837	2,025	2,304	1,965
1981	2,073	2,414	2,339	1,967

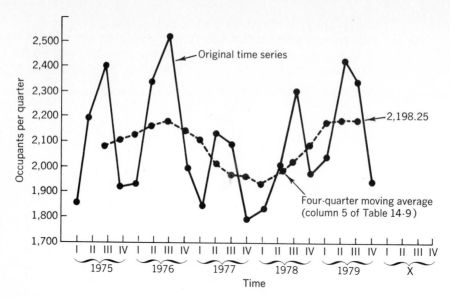

Figure 14·6 Using a moving average to smooth the original time series

Step 3: calculate
percentage
of actual value
to moving average
value

3. *Next, we calculate the percentage of the actual value to the moving average value for each quarter in the time series having a 4-quarter moving average entry.* This step allows us to recover the seasonal component for the quarters. We determine this percentage by dividing each of the actual quarter values in column 3 of Table 14 · 9 by the corresponding 4-quarter moving average values in column 5 and then multiplying the result by 100. For example, we find the percentage for 1977-III as follows:

$$\frac{\text{Actual}}{\text{Moving average}} \times 100 = \frac{2,415}{2,096.75} \times 100 = 115.2$$

Step 4: collect
answers from
step 3
and calculate
modified mean

4. *To collect all the percentage of actual to moving average values in column 6 of Table* 14 · 9, *arrange them by quarter.* Then calculate the "modified mean" for each quarter. The modified mean is calculated by discarding the highest and lowest values for each quarter and averaging the remaining values. In Table 14 · 10, we present the fourth step and show the process for finding the modified mean.

Reducing
extreme cyclical
and irregular
variations

The seasonal values that we recovered for the quarters in column 6 of Table 14 · 9 still contain the cyclical and irregular components of variation in the time series. By eliminating the highest and lowest values from each quarter, we *reduce* the extreme cyclical and irregular variations. When we average the remaining values, we further smooth the cyclical and irregular components. Since cyclical and irregular variations tend to be removed by this process, the modified mean is an index of the seasonality component. (Some statisticians prefer to use the median value instead of computing the modified mean to achieve the same outcome.)

TABLE 14·9 Calculating the 4-quarter moving average

Year (1)	Quarter (2)	Occupancy (3)	Step 1: 4-quarter moving total (4)	Step 2: 4-quarter moving average (5) = (4) ÷ 4	Step 3: Percentage of actual to moving average values (6) = $\frac{(3)}{(5)} \times 100$
1977	I	1,861			
	II	2,203			
	III	2,415	8,387	2,096.75	115.2
	IV	1,908	8,447	2,111.75	90.4
1978	I	1,921	8,587	2,146.75	89.5
	II	2,343	8,686	2,171.50	107.9
	III	2,514	8,764	2,191.00	114.7
	IV	1,986	8,677	2,169.25	91.6
1979	I	1,834	8,488	2,122.00	86.4
	II	2,154	8,072	2,018.00	106.7
	III	2,098	7,885	1,971.25	106.4
	IV	1,799	7,888	1,972.00	91.2
1980	I	1,837	7,759	1,939.75	94.7
	II	2,025	7,965	1,991.25	101.7
	III	2,304	8,131	2,032.75	113.3
	IV	1,965	8,367	2,091.75	93.9
1981	I	2,073	8,756	2,189.00	94.7
	II	2,414	8,791	2,197.75	109.8
	III	2,339	8,793	2,198.25	106.4
	IV	1,967			

TABLE 14·10 Demonstration of step 4 in computing a seasonal index*

Year	Quarter I	Quarter II	Quarter III	Quarter IV
1977	—	—	115.2	90.4
1978	89.5	107.9	114.7	91.6
1979	86.4	106.7	106.4	91.2
1980	94.7	101.7	113.3	93.9
1981	94.7	109.8	106.4	—
	184.2	214.6	334.4	182.8

Modified mean: $\frac{184.2}{2} = 92.1$ $\frac{214.6}{2} = 107.3$ $\frac{334.4}{3} = 111.5$ $\frac{182.8}{2} = 91.4$

Total of indices = 92.1 + 107.3 + 111.5 + 91.4 = 402.3

*Eliminated values are indicated by a slash.

TABLE 14·11 Demonstration of step 5

Quarter	Unadjusted indices	×	Adjusting constant	=	Seasonal index
I	92.1	×	.99428	=	91.6
II	107.3	×	.99428	=	106.7
III	111.5	×	.99428	=	110.9
IV	91.4	×	.99428	=	90.9
			Total of seasonal indices	=	400.1

*Step 5: adjust
the modified mean*

5. *The final step, demonstrated in Table* 14 · 11, *adjusts the modified mean slightly.* Notice that the four indices in Table 14 · 10 total 402.3. However, the base for an index is 100. Thus, the four quarterly indices should total 400, and their mean should be 100. To correct for this error, we multiply each of the quarterly indices in Table 14 · 10 by an adjusting constant. This constant is found by dividing the desired sum of the indices (400) by the actual sum (402.3). In this case, the result is .99428. Table 14 · 11 shows that multiplying the indices by the adjusting constant brings the quarterly indices to a total of 400. (Sometimes even after this adjustment, the mean of the seasonal indices is not exactly 100 because of accumulated rounding errors. In this case it is 100.025.)

Uses of the seasonal index

*Deseasonalizing
the time series*

The ratio-to-moving average method just explained allows us to identify seasonal variation in a time series. The seasonal indices are used to remove the effects of seasonality from a time series. This is called *deseasonalizing* a time series. Before we can identify either the trend or cyclical components of a time series, we must eliminate seasonal variation. To deseasonalize a time series, we divide each of the actual values in the series by the appropriate seasonal index (expressed as a percent). To demonstrate, we shall deseasonalize the value of the first 4 quarters in Table 14 · 8. In Table 14 · 12, we show the deseasonalizing process using the values for the seasonal indices from Table 14 · 11. Once the seasonal effect has been eliminated, the deseasonalized values that remain reflect only the trend, cyclical, and irregular components of the time series.

*Using seasonality
in forecasts*

Once we have removed the seasonal variation, we can compute a deseasonalized trend line, which we can then project into the future. Suppose the hotel management in our example estimates from a deseasonalized trend line that the deseasonalized average occupancy for the fourth quarter of the next year will be 2,158. When this prediction has been obtained, management must then take the seasonality into account. To do this, they multiply the deseasonalized predicted average occupancy of 2,158 by the fourth quarter seasonal index (expressed as a percent) to obtain a seasonalized estimate of 1,962 rooms for the fourth-quarter

TABLE 14·12 Demonstration of deseasonalizing data

Year (1)	Quarter (2)	Actual occupancy (3)		$\left(\dfrac{Seasonal\ index}{100}\right)$ (4)		Deseasonalized occupancy (5) = (3) ÷ (4)
1977	I	1,861	÷	$\left(\dfrac{91.6}{100}\right)$	=	2,032
1977	II	2,203	÷	$\left(\dfrac{106.7}{100}\right)$	=	2,065
1977	III	2,415	÷	$\left(\dfrac{110.9}{100}\right)$	=	2,178
1977	IV	1,908	÷	$\left(\dfrac{90.9}{100}\right)$	=	2,099

average occupancy. Here are the calculations:

seasonal index for fourth
quarter
↓

$$\text{deseasonalized estimated value from trend line} \rightarrow 2{,}158 \times \frac{90.9}{100} = 1{,}962 \leftarrow \text{seasonalized estimate of fourth quarter occupancy}$$

Index numbers

Why use an index number?

Recall that we have used the term *index* and its plural *indices* several times in our discussion of seasonal variation. At some time, everyone faces the question of how much something has changed over time. Typically, we use *index numbers* to measure such differences.

An index number measures how much a variable changes over time. We calculate an index number by finding the ratio of the current value to a base value. Then we multiply the resulting number by 100 to express the index as a percentage. This final value is the *percentage relative*. Note that the index number for the base year is always 100.

Price index

There are three principal types of indices: the price index, the quantity index, and the value index. A *price index* is the one most frequently used. It compares changes in price from one period to another. The familiar Consumer Price Index, tabulated by the Bureau of Labor Statistics, measures overall price changes of a variety of consumer goods and services and is used to define the cost of living.

Quantity index

A *quantity index* measures how much the number or quantity of a variable changes over time.

Value index

The last type of index, the *value index*, measures changes in total monetary worth. That is, it measures changes in the dollar value of a variable. In effect, the value index combines price and quantity changes to present a more informative index. In our room occupancy example, we determined only a quantity index. However, we could have included the dollar effect by computing the total value of rental fees for the years under consideration.

Usually an index measures change in a variable over a period of time, such as in a time series. However, it can also be used to measure differences in a given variable in different locations. This is done by simultaneously collecting data in different locations and then comparing the data. The comparative cost of living index, for example, shows that in terms of the cost of goods and services, it is cheaper to live in Austin, Texas, than in New York City.

Composite index numbers

A single index may reflect a composite, or group, of changing variables. The Consumer Price Index measures the general price level for specific goods and services in the economy. It combines the individual prices of the goods and services to form a composite price index number.

Index numbers can be used in several ways. It is most common to use them by themselves, as an end result. Index numbers such as the Consumer Price Index are often cited in news reports as general indicators of the nation's economic condition.

One use of the Consumer Price Index

Management uses index numbers as part of an intermediate computation to understand other information better. In the room occupancy example, seasonal indices were used to modify and improve estimates of the future. The use of the Consumer Price Index to determine the "real" buying power of money is another example of how index numbers help increase knowledge of other factors.

When managers apply index numbers to everyday problems, they use many sources to obtain the necessary information. The source depends on their information requirements. A firm can use monthly sales reports to determine its seasonal sales pattern. In dealing with broad areas of national economy and the general level of business activity, publications such as the *Federal Reserve Bulletin*, *Moody's*, *Monthly Labor Review*, and the *Consumer Price Index* provide a wealth of data. Many federal and state publications are listed in the U.S. Department of Commerce pamphlet, *Measuring Markets*. Almost all government agencies distribute data about their activities, from which index numbers can be computed. Many financial newspapers and magazines provide information from which index numbers can be computed. When you read these sources, you will find that many of them use index numbers themselves.

Sources of data for index numbers

EXERCISES

14·14 A large manufacturer of automobile springs has determined the following percentages of actual to moving average describing the firm's quarterly cash needs for the last 6 years:

	Spring	Summer	Fall	Winter
1975	108	128	94	70
1976	112	132	88	68
1977	109	134	84	73
1978	110	131	90	69
1979	108	135	89	68
1980	106	129	93	72

Calculate the seasonal index for each quarter.

14 · 15 The owner of The Pleasure-Glide Boat Company has compiled the following quarterly figures regarding the company's investment in accounts receivable over the last 5 years ($\times$ $1,000)

	Spring	Summer	Fall	Winter
1976	101	118	90	79
1977	108	123	94	83
1978	109	125	96	86
1979	113	131	102	91
1980	119	140	108	97

a) Calculate a 4-quarter moving average.
b) Find the percentage of actual-to-moving average for each period.
c) Determine the modified seasonal indices and the seasonal indices.

---

5 A PROBLEM INVOLVING ALL FOUR COMPONENTS OF A TIME SERIES

For a problem that involves all four components of a time series, we turn to a firm that specializes in producing recreational equipment. To forecast future sales based on an analysis of its past pattern of sales, the firm has collected the information in Table 14 · 13. Our procedure for describing this time series will consist of three stages:

1. deseasonalizing the time series
2. developing the trend line
3. finding the cyclical variation around the trend line

TABLE 14 · 13 Quarterly sales

	Sales per quarter ($\times$ $10,000)			
Year	I	II	III	IV
1977	16	21	9	18
1978	15	20	10	18
1979	17	24	13	22
1980	17	25	11	21
1981	18	26	14	25

Since the data are available on a quarterly basis, we must first deseasonalize the time series. The steps to do this are the same as those originally introduced in Section 4 of this chapter. The seasonal indices for quarters I, II, III, and IV turn out to be 94.6, 130.9, 62.7, and 111.8, respectively.

Once we have computed the quarterly seasonal indices, we can find the deseasonalized values of the time series by dividing the actual sales (in Table $14 \cdot 13$) by the seasonal indices. Table $14 \cdot 14$ shows the deseasonalized time series values.

The second step in describing the components of the time series is to develop the trend line. We accomplish this by applying the least squares method to the deseasonalized time series (after we have translated the time variable). When we do this, we find that the trend line is:

$$\hat{Y} = a + bx$$
$$= 18 + .16x$$

$$(11 \cdot 1)$$

We have now identified the seasonal and trend components of the time series. Next we find the cyclical variation around the trend line. This component is identified by measuring deseasonalized variation around the trend line. In this problem, we have calculated the percents of trend. These are shown in Table $14 \cdot 15$.

TABLE 14 · 14 Deseasonalized time series values

	Quarter			
Year	I	II	III	IV
1977	16.9	16.0	14.4	16.1
1978	15.9	15.3	15.9	16.1
1979	18.0	18.3	20.7	19.7
1980	18.0	19.1	17.5	18.8
1981	19.0	19.9	22.3	22.4

TABLE 14 · 15 Percents of trend

	Quarter			
Year	I	II	III	IV
1977	113.0	104.7	92.3	101.1
1978	97.9	92.4	94.2	93.6
1979	102.7	102.6	114.0	106.6
1980	95.7	99.9	90.0	95.1
1981	94.6	97.5	107.6	106.5

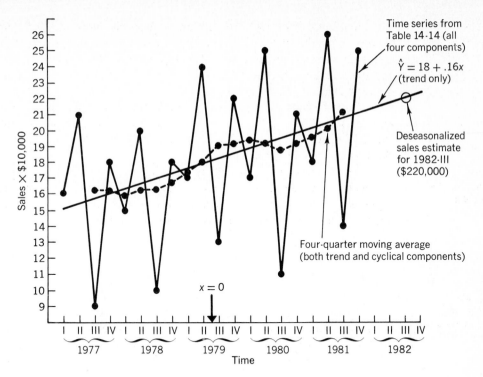

Figure 14·7 Time series, trend line, and 4-quarter moving average for quarterly sales data in Table 14 · 13

Assumptions about irregular variation

If we assume that irregular variation is generally short-term and relatively insignificant, we have completely described the time series in this problem using the trend, cyclical, and seasonal components. Figure 14 · 7 illustrates the original time series, its moving average (containing both the trend and cyclical components), and the trend line.

Predicting using time series

Now suppose that the management of the recreation company we have been using as an example wants to estimate the sales volume for the third quarter of 1982. What should they do?

Step 1: determining the deseasonalized value for sales for the period desired

1. They have to determine the deseasonalized value for sales in the third quarter of 1982 by using the trend equation, $\hat{Y} = 18 + .16x$. This requires them to code the time, 1982-III. That quarter (1982-III) is 12 1/2 quarters after 1979-II 1/2, the time at which $x = 0$. So, for 1982-III, $x = 2(12\ 1/2) = 25$. Substituting this value ($x = 25$) into the trend equation produces the following result:

$$\hat{Y} = a + bx$$
$$= 18 + .16(25) \qquad (11 \cdot 1)$$
$$= 22$$

Thus, the deseasonalized sales estimate for 1982-III is $220,000. This point is shown on the trend line in Fig. 14 · 7.

463   Sec. 5   A problem involving all four components of a time series

2. Now management must seasonalize this estimate by multiplying it by the third quarter seasonal index, expressed as a percent.

$$\text{seasonal index for quarter III}$$
$$\downarrow$$
$$\begin{array}{c}\text{trend estimate from}\\ \text{Equation } 11 \cdot 1\end{array} \rightarrow 22 \times \frac{62.7}{100} = 13.8 \leftarrow \text{seasonal estimate}$$

On the basis of this analysis, the firm estimates that sales for 1982-III will be $138,000. We must stress, however, that this value is only an estimate and does not take into account the cyclical and irregular components. As we noted earlier, the irregular variation cannot be predicted mathematically. Also, remember that our earlier treatment of cyclical variation was descriptive of past behavior and not predictive of future behavior.

EXERCISES

14·16 A state commission designed to monitor energy consumption assembled the following seasonal data regarding natural gas consumption, in millions of cubic feet.

	Winter	Spring	Summer	Fall
1978	291	246	231	280
1979	298	251	228	289
1980	301	258	239	293

a) Determine the seasonal indices and deseasonalize these data (using a 4-quarter moving average).
b) Calculate the least squares line that best describes these data.
c) Identify the cyclical variation in these data by the relative cyclical residual method.
d) Plot the original data, the deseasonalized data, and the trend.

14·17 The following data describe the marketing performance of a regional beer producer:

	Sales by quarter ($\times \$100,000$)			
Year	I	II	III	IV
1977	19	24	38	25
1978	21	28	44	23
1979	23	31	41	23
1980	24	35	48	21

a) Calculate the seasonal indices for these data. (Use a 4-quarter moving average.)
b) Deseasonalize these data using the indices from part a.

14·18 For problem 14 · 17:
a) Find the least squares line that best describes the trend in deseasonalized beer sales.
b) Identify the cyclical component in this time series by computing the percent of trend.

In this chapter, we have examined all four components of a time series. We have described the process of projecting past trend and seasonal variation into the future, while taking into consideration the inherent inaccuracies of this analysis. In addition, we noted that although the irregular and cyclical components do affect the future, they are erratic and difficult to use in forecasting.

Recognizing limitations of time series analysis

We must realize that the mechanical approach of time series analysis is subject to considerable error and change. It is necessary for management to combine these simple procedures with knowledge of other factors in order to develop workable forecasts. Analysts are constantly revising, updating, and discarding their forecasts. If we wish to cope successfully with the future, we must do the same.

When using the procedures described in this chapter, we should pay attention particularly to the following two problems:

1. In forecasting, we project past trend and seasonal variation into the future. We must ask, "How regular and lasting were the past trends? What are the chances that these patterns are changing?"

2. How accurate are the historical data we use in series analysis? If a company has changed from a FIFO (first-in-first-out) to a LIFO (last-in-first-out) inventory accounting system in a period during the time under consideration, the data (such as quarterly profits) before and after the change are not comparable and not very useful for forecasting.

EXERCISES

14·19 List 4 errors that can affect forecasting with time series.

14·20 When using time series to predict the future, what assurances do we need about the historical data on which our forecasts are based?

14·21 What problems would you see developing if we used past college enrollments to predict future college enrollments?

---

7 TERMS INTRODUCED IN CHAPTER 14

coding   A method of converting traditional measures of time to a form that simplifies computation (often called translating).

cyclical fluctuation   A type of variation in time series, in which the value of the variable fluctuates above and below a secular trend line.

deseasonalization   A statistical process used to remove the effects of seasonality from a time series.

irregular variation   A condition in time series when the value of a variable is completely unpredictable.

modified mean A statistical method used in time series. Discards the highest and lowest values when computing a mean.

ratio-to-moving average method A statistical method used to measure seasonal variation. Employs an index describing the degree of that variation.

relative cyclical residual A measure of cyclical variation, it uses the percentage deviation from the trend for each value in the series.

residual method A method of describing the cyclical component of a time series. It assumes that most of the variation in the series not explained by the secular trend is cyclical variation.

seasonal variation Patterns of change in a time series within a year, patterns that tend to be repeated from year to year.

second-degree equation A mathematical form used to describe a parabolic curve that may be used in time series analysis.

secular trend A type of variation in time series, the value of the variable tending to increase or decrease over a long period of time.

time series A statistical method involving information accumulated at regular intervals. Used to determine patterns in data.

8 EQUATIONS INTRODUCED IN CHAPTER 14

p. 442
$$b = \frac{\Sigma XY - n\overline{X}\,\overline{Y}}{\Sigma X^2 - n\overline{X}^2}$$
14 · 1

This formula, originally introduced in Chapter 11 as Equation 11 · 3, enables us to calculate the *slope of the best-fitting regression line* for any two-variable set of data points. The symbols $\overline{X}$ and $\overline{Y}$ represent the means of the value of the independent variable and dependent variable respectively; n represents the number of data points with which we are fitting the line.

p. 442
$$a = \overline{Y} - b\overline{X}$$
14 · 2

We met this formula as Equation 11 · 4. It enables us to compute the *Y-intercept of the best-fitting regression line* for any 2-variable set of data points.

p. 444
$$b = \frac{\Sigma xY}{\Sigma x^2}$$
14 · 3

When the individual years (X) are changed to coded time values (x) by subtracting out the mean $(x = X - \overline{X})$, Equation 14 · 1 for the slope of the trend line is simplified and becomes Equation 14 · 3.

p. 444
$$a = \overline{Y}$$
14 · 4

In a similar fashion, using coded time values also allows us to simplify Equation 14 · 2 for the intercept of the trend line.

p. 446
$$\hat{Y} = a + bx + cx^2$$
14 · 5

Sometimes we wish to fit a trend with a parabolic (or second-degree) curve instead of a straight line $(\hat{Y} = a + bx)$. The general form for a fitted second-degree curve is obtained by including the second-degree term (cx^2) in the equation for $\hat{Y}$.

p. 447
$$\Sigma Y = na + c\Sigma x^2$$
14 · 6

$$\Sigma x^2 Y = a\Sigma x^2 + c\Sigma x^4$$
14 · 7

In order to find the least squares second-degree fitted curve, we must solve Equations 14 · 6 and 14 · 7 simultaneously for the values of a and c. The value for b is obtained from Equation 14 · 3.

$$\text{Percent of trend} = \frac{Y}{\hat{Y}} \times 100$$

We can measure cyclical variation as a *percent of trend* by dividing the actual value (Y) by the trend value ($\hat{Y}$) and then multiplying by 100.

$$\text{Relative cyclical residual} = \frac{Y - \hat{Y}}{\hat{Y}} \times 100$$

Another measure of cyclical variation is the *relative cyclical residual*, obtained by dividing the deviation from the trend ($Y - \hat{Y}$) by the trend value, and multiplying the result by 100. The relative cyclical residual can also be obtained by subtracting 100 from the percent of trend.

---

9 CHAPTER REVIEW EXERCISES

---

14 · 22 Wheeler Airline, a regional carrier, has estimated the number of passengers to be 595,000 (deseasonalized) for the month of December. How many passengers should the company anticipate if the December seasonal index is 128?

14 · 23 An EPA research group has measured the level of mercury contamination in the ocean at a certain point off the East Coast. They found the following percentages of mercury in the water:

	Jan.	*Feb.*	*Mar.*	*Apr.*	*May*	*June*	*July*	*Aug.*	*Sept.*	*Oct.*	*Nov.*	*Dec.*
1978	.4	.6	.9	.7	.8	.6	.7	.5	.5	.6	.3	.4
1979	.5	.8	.8	.9	.6	.7	.8	.6	.5	.5	.4	.3
1980	.3	.5	.7	.8	.8	.6	.9	.7	.6	.5	.4	.4

Construct a 4-month moving average, and plot it on a graph along with the original data.

14 · 24 A production manager for a Canadian paper mill has accumulated the following information describing the number of pounds processed quarterly ($\times 1,000,000$ pounds):

	Winter	*Spring*	*Summer*	*Fall*
1978		4.1	4.8	3.2
1979	2.9	4.5	5.0	3.4
1980	2.8	4.9	5.5	3.3
1981	3.1	5.1	5.6	3.6

a) Calculate the seasonal indices for these data (percentage of actual-to-moving average).
b) Deseasonalize these data, using the seasonal indices from part a.
c) Find the least squares line that best describes these data.
d) Estimate the number of pounds that will be processed during the spring of 1982.

14 · 25 The number of farm loans approved by a small rural bank during the seven years from 1974 to 1980 were 975, 1,364, 1,221, 1,575, 1,776, 1,853, and 2,094, respectively.
a) Develop the linear estimating equation that best describes these data.
b) How many farm loans can the bank expect to make in 1981?

14·26 An assistant undersecretary in the U.S. Commerce Department has the following data describing the value of grain exported during the last 15 quarters (in billions):

	I	II	III	IV
1978		3	6	4
1979	2	2	7	5
1980	2	4	8	5
1981	1	3	8	6

a) Determine the seasonal indices and deseasonalize these data (using a 4-quarter moving average).

b) Calculate the least squares line that best describes these data.

c) Identify the cyclical variation in these data by the relative cyclical residual method.

d) Plot the original data, the deseasonalized data, and the trend.

14·27 Richie Bell's College Bicycle Shop has determined from a previous trend analysis that spring sales should be 156 bicycles (deseasonalized). If the spring seasonal index is 140, how many bicycles should the shop sell this spring?

14·28 An Ohio manufacturer of heavy earth-moving equipment has recorded the following sales records over the past twenty years (in millions of dollars): 25, 28, 27, 29, 31, 29, 32, 34, 30, 32, 29, 26, 28, 33, 32, 36, 35, 37, 39, and 35. Construct a 4-year moving average of sales and plot it on a graph along with the original data.

---

10 CHAPTER CONCEPTS TEST

Answers are in the back of the book.

T   F   1. Time series analysis is used to detect patterns of change in statistical information over regular intervals of time.

T   F   2. Secular trends represent the long-term direction of a time series.

T   F   3. When coding time values, we subtract from each value the smallest time value in the series; hence, the code of the smallest value is zero.

T   F   4. When using the least squares method to determine a second-degree equation of best fit, the values of 4 numerical constants must be determined.

T   F   5. Time series analysis helps us to analyze past trends, but it cannot aid us in coping with future uncertainties.

T   F   6. When predicting far into the future, a second-degree equation usually gives more accurate predictions than a linear equation.

T   F   7. When using the residual method, we assume that the cyclical component explains most of the variation left unexplained by the trend component.

T   F   8. The relative cyclical residual can be computed for an entry in a time series by subtracting 10 from the percent of trend for that entry.

T   F   9. The repetitive movement around a trend line in a 2-year period is best described as seasonal.

T F 10. Once seasonal indices are computed for a time series, the series can be deseasonalized so that only the trend component remains.

T F 11. The percent of trend should not be used for predicting future cyclical variations.

T F 12. Over time, random movements tend to counteract one another in irregular variation in a time series.

T F 13. Before percent of trend can be calculated, a trend line (graph of $\hat{Y}$) must first be calculated.

T F 14. If a time series contains an odd number of elements, then the coding for some of the entries will be in half-units.

T F 15. To be considered a time series, a group of statistical information must have been accumulated at *regular* intervals.

16. A time series of annual data can contain which of the following components?
    a) secular trend
    b) cyclical fluctuation
    c) seasonal variation
    d) all of the preceding
    e) a and b but not c

17. Suppose you were considering a time series of data for the quarters of 1978 and 1979. The third quarter of 1979 would be coded as:
    a) 2   b) 3   c) 5   d) 6

18. Suppose that a particular time series should be fitted with a parabolic curve. The general form for this second-degree equation is $\hat{Y} = a + bx + cx^2$. What do the x's represent in this formula?
    a) coded values of the time variables
    b) a numerical constant which is determined by a formula
    c) estimates of the dependent variable
    d) none of the above

19. Assume that a time series with annual data for the years 1969 – 1977 is described well by the second-degree equation $\hat{Y} = 5 + 3x + 9x^2$. Based only upon this secular trend, what is the forecast value for 1978?
    a) 161   b) 245   c) 347   d) 293.75   e) 200.75

20. Suppose that the linear equation $\hat{Y} = 10 + 3x$ describes well an annual time series for 1975 – 1981. If the actual value of Y for 1978 is 8, what is the percent of trend for 1978?
    a) 125%   b) 112.5%   c) 90%   d) 80%

21. A time series for the years 1970 – 1981 had the following relative cyclical residuals, in chronological order: -1%, -2%, 1%, 2%, -1%, -2%, 1%, 2%, -1%, -2%, 1%, 2%. The relative cyclical residual for 1982 should be:
    a) 3%   c) -2%
    b) -1% d) cannot be determined from information given

22. Assume that you have been given quarterly sales data for a 5-year period. To use the ratio-to-moving average method of computing a seasonal index, your first step would be:
    a) Compute the 4-quarter moving average.
    b) Discard highest and lowest values for each quarter.
    c) Calculate the 4-quarter moving total.
    d) None of the above.

Questions 23 through 25 deal with a seasonal index being computed, using the ratio-to-moving average method for quarterly data from 1976 – 1980. The percentages of actual to moving average for the third quarter of each year are:

1976: 109.0; 1977: 112.8; 1978: 110.0; 1979: 108.0; 1980: 104.6

23. What is the *unadjusted* index for the third quarter?
    a) 108.88   b) 109.0   c) 110.23   d) 110.96   e) None of these.

24. Assume that the total of the unadjusted indices for the four quarters is 404.04. If the unadjusted index for the first quarter is 97.0, what is the adjusted seasonal index for the first quarter?
    a) 96.03   d) 99.00
    b) 97.98   e) cannot be determined from information given
    c) 24.01

25. The adjusted seasonal index for the fourth quarter is 95.0. If the deseasonalized trend line that was calculated to estimate quarterly sales is $\hat{Y} = 400 + 9x$, what would be the seasonalized sales estimate for the fourth quarter of 1981?
    a) 499.7   b) 643.0   c) 610.85   d) 676.8

26. Dividing each actual value in a time series by the corresponding trend value, and multiplying by 100, gives the _____ .

27. Repetitive and predictable movement around the trend line in one year or less is _____ variation.

28. _____ variation in time series is characterized by unpredictable, random movement and usually occurs over short intervals.

29. _____ variation is the time series component that oscillates above and below the trend line for periods longer than one year.

30. Using seasonal indices to remove effects of seasonality from a time series is known as _____ the time series.

Appendix Tables

Areas under the Standard Normal Probability Distribution
between the Mean and Successive Values of z.*

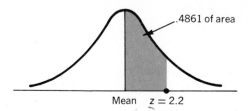

.4861 of area

Mean $z = 2.2$

EXAMPLE To find the area under the curve between the mean and a point
2.2 standard deviations to the right of the mean, look up the value opposite 2.2
in the table; .4861 of the area under the curve lies between the mean and a z
value of 2.2. $0,0^c$

z	.00	.01	.02	.03	.04	.05	.06	.07	.08	.09
0.0	.0000	.0040	.0080	.0120	.0160	.0199	.0239	.0279	.0319	.0359
0.1	.0398	.0438	.0478	.0517	.0557	.0596	.0636	.0675	.0714	.0753
0.2	.0793	.0832	.0871	.0910	.0948	.0987	.1026	.1064	.1103	.1141
0.3	.1179	.1217	.1255	.1293	.1331	.1368	.1406	.1443	.1480	.1517
0.4	.1554	.1591	.1628	.1664	.1700	.1736	.1772	.1808	.1844	.1879
0.5	.1915	.1950	.1985	.2019	.2054	.2088	.2123	.2157	.2190	.2224
0.6	.2257	.2291	.2324	.2357	.2389	.2422	.2454	.2486	.2517	.2549
0.7	.2580	.2611	.2642	.2673	.2704	.2734	.2764	.2794	.2823	.2852
0.8	.2881	.2910	.2939	.2967	.2995	.3023	.3051	.3078	.3106	.3133
0.9	.3159	.3186	.3212	.3238	.3264	.3289	.3315	.3340	.3365	.3389
1.0	.3413	.3438	.3461	.3485	.3508	.3531	.3554	.3577	.3599	.3621
1.1	.3643	.3665	.3686	.3708	.3729	.3749	.3770	.3790	.3810	.3830
1.2	.3849	.3869	.3888	.3907	.3925	.3944	.3962	.3980	.3997	.4015
1.3	.4032	.4049	.4066	.4082	.4099	.4115	.4131	.4147	.4162	.4177
1.4	.4192	.4207	.4222	.4236	.4251	.4265	.4279	.4292	.4306	.4319
1.5	.4332	.4345	.4357	.4370	.4382	.4394	.4406	.4418	.4429	.4441
1.6	.4452	.4463	.4474	.4484	.4495	.4505	.4515	.4525	.4535	.4545
1.7	.4554	.4564	.4573	.4582	.4591	.4599	.4608	.4616	.4625	.4633
1.8	.4641	.4649	.4656	.4664	.4671	.4678	.4686	.4693	.4699	.4706
1.9	.4713	.4719	.4726	.4732	.4738	.4744	.4750	.4756	.4761	.4767
2.0	.4772	.4778	.4783	.4788	.4793	.4798	.4803	.4808	.4812	.4817
2.1	.4821	.4826	.4830	.4834	.4838	.4842	.4846	.4850	.4854	.4857
2.2	.4861	.4864	.4868	.4871	.4875	.4878	.4881	.4884	.4887	.4890
2.3	.4893	.4896	.4898	.4901	.4904	.4906	.4909	.4911	.4913	.4916
2.4	.4918	.4920	.4922	.4925	.4927	.4929	.4931	.4932	.4934	.4936
2.5	.4938	.4940	.4941	.4943	.4945	.4946	.4948	.4949	.4951	.4952
2.6	.4953	.4955	.4956	.4957	.4959	.4960	.4961	.4962	.4963	.4946
2.7	.4965	.4966	.4967	.4968	.4969	.4970	.4971	.4972	.4973	.4974
2.8	.4974	.4975	.4976	.4977	.4977	.4978	.4979	.4979	.4980	.4981
2.9	.4981	.4982	.4982	.4983	.4984	.4984	.4985	.4985	.4986	.4986
3.0	.4987	.4987	.4987	.4988	.4988	.4989	.4989	.4989	.4990	.4990

*From Robert D. Mason, *Essentials of Statistics*, Prentice-Hall, Inc., 1976.

471

APPENDIX TABLE 2

Areas in Both Tails Combined for Student's t Distribution.*

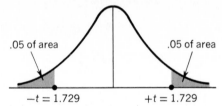

.05 of area

.05 of area

$-t = 1.729$

$+t = 1.729$

EXAMPLE To find the value of t which corresponds to an area of .10 in both tails of the distribution combined, when there are 19 degrees of freedom, look under the .10 column, and proceed down to the 19 degrees of freedom row; the appropriate t value there is 1.729.

Degrees of freedom	Area in both tails combined			
	.10	.05	.02	.01
1	6.314	12.706	31.821	63.657
2	2.920	4.303	6.965	9.925
3	2.353	3.182	4.541	5.841
4	2.132	2.776	3.747	4.604
5	2.015	2.571	3.365	4.032
6	1.943	2.447	3.143	3.707
7	1.895	2.365	2.998	3.499
8	1.860	2.306	2.896	3.355
9	1.833	2.262	2.821	3.250
10	1.812	2.228	2.764	3.169
11	1.796	2.201	2.718	3.106
12	1.782	2.179	2.681	3.055
13	1.771	2.160	2.650	3.012
14	1.761	2.145	2.624	2.977
15	1.753	2.131	2.602	2.947
16	1.746	2.120	2.583	2.921
17	1.740	2.110	2.567	2.898
18	1.734	2.101	2.552	2.878
19	1.729	2.093	2.539	2.861
20	1.725	2.086	2.528	2.845
21	1.721	2.080	2.518	2.831
22	1.717	2.074	2.508	2.819
23	1.714	2.069	2.500	2.807
24	1.711	2.064	2.492	2.797
25	1.708	2.060	2.485	2.787
26	1.706	2.056	2.479	2.779
27	1.703	2.052	2.473	2.771
28	1.701	2.048	2.467	2.763
29	1.699	2.045	2.462	2.756
30	1.697	2.042	2.457	2.750
40	1.684	2.021	2.423	2.704
60	1.671	2.000	2.390	2.660
120	1.658	1.980	2.358	2.617
Normal Distribution	1.645	1.960	2.326	2.576

*Taken from Table III of Fisher and Yates, *Statistical Tables for Biological, Agricultural and Medical Research*, published by Longman Group Ltd., London (previously published by Oliver & Boyd, Edinburgh) and by permission of the authors and publishers.

The Cumulative Binomial Distribution*

EXAMPLE   These tables describe the cumulative binomial distribution; a sample problem will illustrate how they are used. Suppose that we are grading bar examinations and wish to find the probability of finding 7 or more failures in a batch of 15, when the probability that any one exam is a failure is .20.

In binomial notation, the elements in this example can be represented:

$n = 15$ (number of exams to be graded)

$p = .20$ (probability that any one exam will be a failure)

$r = 7$ (number of failures in question)

Steps for solution:

1. Since the problem involves 15 trials or inspections, first find the table for $n = 15$.
2. The probability of a failing examination is .20; therefore, we look through the $n = 15$ table until we find the column where $p = 20$.
3. We then move down the $p = 20$ column until we are opposite the $r = 7$ row.
4. The answer there is found to be 0181; this is interpreted to be a probability of .0181.

This problem asked for the probability of 7 *or more* failures. Had it asked for the probability of *more than* 7 failures, we would have looked up the probability of 8 or more.

Note that this table only goes up to $p = .50$. When p is *larger* than .50, q ($1 - p$) is *less* than .50. Therefore the problem is worked in terms of q and the number of passing exams ($n - r$) rather than in terms of p and r (the number of failures). For example, suppose $p = .60$ and $n = 15$. What is the probability of more than 12 failures? More than 12 failures (13, 14, or 15 failures) is the same as 2 or fewer successes. The probability of 2 or fewer successes is 1 – the probability of 3 or more successes. We look in the $n = 15$ table for the $p = 40$ column and the $r = 3$ row. There we see the number 9729, which we interpret as a probability of .9729; so the answer is $1 - .9729$, or .0271.

*Reproduced from Robert Schlaifer, *Introduction to Statistics for Business Decisions*, published by McGraw-Hill Book Company, 1961, by specific permission from the copyright holder, the President and Fellows of Harvard College.

$$n = 1$$

P	01	02	03	04	05	06	07	08	09	10
R										
1	0100	0200	0300	0400	0500	0600	0700	0800	0900	1000

P	11	12	13	14	15	16	17	18	19	20
R										
1	1100	1200	1300	1400	1500	1600	1700	1800	1900	2000

P	21	22	23	24	25	26	27	28	29	30
R										
1	2100	2200	2300	2400	2500	2600	2700	2800	2900	3000

P	31	32	33	34	35	36	37	38	39	40
R										
1	3100	3200	3300	3400	3500	3600	3700	3800	3900	4000

P	41	42	43	44	45	46	47	48	49	50
R										
1	4100	4200	4300	4400	4500	4600	4700	4800	4900	5000

$$n = 2$$

P	01	02	03	04	05	06	07	08	09	10
R										
1	0199	0396	0591	0784	0975	1164	1351	1536	1719	1900
2	0001	0004	0009	0016	0025	0036	0049	0064	0081	0100

P	11	12	13	14	15	16	17	18	19	20
R										
1	2079	2256	2431	2604	2775	2944	3111	3276	3439	3600
2	0121	0144	0169	0196	0225	0256	0289	0324	0361	0400

P	21	22	23	24	25	26	27	28	29	30
R										
1	3759	3916	4071	4224	4375	4524	4671	4816	4959	5100
2	0441	0484	0529	0576	0625	0676	0729	0784	0841	0900

P	31	32	33	34	35	36	37	38	39	40
R										
1	5239	5376	5511	5644	5775	5904	6031	6156	6279	6400
2	0961	1024	1089	1156	1225	1296	1369	1444	1521	1600

P	41	42	43	44	45	46	47	48	49	50
R										
1	6519	6636	6751	6864	6975	7084	7191	7296	7399	7500
2	1681	1764	1849	1936	2025	2116	2209	2304	2401	2500

$$n = 3$$

P	01	02	03	04	05	06	07	08	09	10
R										
1	0297	0588	0873	1153	1426	1694	1956	2213	2464	2710
2	0003	0012	0026	0047	0073	0104	0140	0182	0228	0280
3				0001	0001	0002	0003	0005	0007	0010

P	11	12	13	14	15	16	17	18	19	20
R										
1	2950	3185	3415	3639	3859	4073	4282	4486	4686	4880
2	0336	0397	0463	0533	0608	0686	0769	0855	0946	1040
3	0013	0017	0022	0027	0034	0041	0049	0058	0069	0080

$$n = 3$$

P	21	22	23	24	25	26	27	28	29	30
R										
1	5070	5254	5435	5610	5781	5948	6110	6268	6421	6570
2	1138	1239	1344	1452	1563	1676	1793	1913	2035	2160
3	0093	0106	0122	0138	0156	0176	0197	0220	0244	0270

P	31	32	33	34	35	36	37	38	39	40
R										
1	6715	6856	6992	7125	7254	7379	7500	7617	7730	7840
2	2287	2417	2548	2682	2818	2955	3094	3235	3377	3520
3	0298	0328	0359	0393	0429	0467	0507	0549	0593	0640

P	41	42	43	44	45	46	47	48	49	50
R										
1	7946	8049	8148	8244	8336	8425	8511	8594	8673	8750
2	3665	3810	3957	4104	4253	4401	4551	4700	4850	5000
3	0689	0741	0795	0852	0911	0973	1038	1106	1176	1250

$$n = 4$$

P	01	02	03	04	05	06	07	08	09	10
R										
1	0394	0776	1147	1507	1855	2193	2519	2836	3143	3439
2	0006	0023	0052	0091	0140	0199	0267	0344	0430	0523
3			0001	0002	0005	0008	0013	0019	0027	0037
4									0001	0001

P	11	12	13	14	15	16	17	18	19	20
R										
1	3726	4003	4271	4530	4780	5021	5254	5479	5695	5904
2	0624	0732	0847	0968	1095	1228	1366	1509	1656	1808
3	0049	0063	0079	0098	0120	0144	0171	0202	0235	0272
4	0001	0002	0003	0004	0005	0007	0008	0010	0013	0016

P	21	22	23	24	25	26	27	28	29	30
R										
1	6105	6298	6485	6664	6836	7001	7160	7313	7459	7599
2	1963	2122	2285	2450	2617	2787	2959	3132	3307	3483
3	0312	0356	0403	0453	0508	0566	0628	0694	0763	0837
4	0019	0023	0028	0033	0039	0046	0053	0061	0071	0081

P	31	32	33	34	35	36	37	38	39	40
R										
1	7733	7862	7985	8103	8215	8322	8425	8522	8615	8704
2	3660	3837	4015	4193	4370	4547	4724	4900	5075	5248
3	0915	0996	1082	1171	1265	1362	1464	1569	1679	1792
4	0092	0105	0119	0134	0150	0168	0187	0209	0231	0256

P	41	42	43	44	45	46	47	48	49	50
R										
1	8788	8868	8944	9017	9085	9150	9211	9269	9323	9375
2	5420	5590	5759	5926	6090	6252	6412	6569	6724	6875
3	1909	2030	2155	2283	2415	2550	2689	2834	2977	3125
4	0283	0311	0342	0375	0410	0448	0488	0531	0576	0625

$$n = 5$$

P	01	02	03	04	05	06	07	08	09	10
R										
1	0490	0961	1413	1846	2262	2661	3043	3409	3760	4095
2	0010	0038	0085	0148	0226	0319	0425	0544	0674	0815
3		0001	0003	0006	0012	0020	0031	0045	0063	0086
4						0001	0001	0002	0003	0005

P	11	12	13	14	15	16	17	18	19	20
R										
1	4416	4723	5016	5296	5563	5818	6061	6293	6513	6723
2	0965	1125	1292	1467	1648	1835	2027	2224	2424	2627
3	0112	0143	0179	0220	0266	0318	0375	0437	0505	0579
4	0007	0009	0013	0017	0022	0029	0036	0045	0055	0067
5				0001	0001	0001	0001	0002	0002	0003

P	21	22	23	24	25	26	27	28	29	30
R										
1	6923	7113	7293	7464	7627	7781	7927	8065	8196	8319
2	2833	3041	3251	3461	3672	3883	4093	4303	4511	4718
3	0659	0744	0836	0933	1035	1143	1257	1376	1501	1631
4	0081	0097	0114	0134	0156	0181	0208	0238	0272	0308
5	0004	0005	0006	0008	0010	0012	0014	0017	0021	0024

P	31	32	33	34	35	36	37	38	39	40
R										
1	8436	8546	8650	8748	8840	8926	9008	9084	9155	9222
2	4923	5125	5325	5522	5716	5906	6093	6276	6455	6630
3	1766	1905	2050	2199	2352	2509	2670	2835	3003	3174
4	0347	0390	0436	0486	0540	0598	0660	0726	0796	0870
5	0029	0034	0039	0045	0053	0060	0069	0079	0090	0102

P	41	42	43	44	45	46	47	48	49	50
R										
1	9285	9344	9398	9449	9497	9541	9582	9620	9655	9688
2	6801	6967	7129	7286	7438	7585	7728	7865	7998	8125
3	3349	3525	3705	3886	4069	4253	4439	4625	4813	5000
4	0949	1033	1121	1214	1312	1415	1522	1635	1753	1875
5	0116	0131	0147	0165	0185	0206	0229	0255	0282	0313

$$n = 6$$

P	01	02	03	04	05	06	07	08	09	10
R										
1	0585	1142	1670	2172	2649	3101	3530	3936	4321	4686
2	0015	0057	0125	0216	0328	0459	0608	0773	0952	1143
3		0002	0005	0012	0022	0038	0058	0085	0118	0159
4					0001	0002	0003	0005	0008	0013
5										0001

P	11	12	13	14	15	16	17	18	19	20
R										
1	5030	5356	5664	5954	6229	6487	6731	6960	7176	7379
2	1345	1556	1776	2003	2235	2472	2713	2956	3201	3446
3	0206	0261	0324	0395	0473	0560	0655	0759	0870	0989
4	0018	0025	0034	0045	0059	0075	0094	0116	0141	0170
5	0001	0001	0002	0003	0004	0005	0007	0010	0013	0016
6										0001

$$n = 6$$

P	21	22	23	24	25	26	27	28	29	30
R										
1	7569	7748	7916	8073	8220	8358	8487	8607	8719	8824
2	3692	3937	4180	4422	4661	4896	5128	5356	5580	5798
3	1115	1250	1391	1539	1694	1856	2023	2196	2374	2557
4	0202	0239	0280	0326	0376	0431	0492	0557	0628	0705
5	0020	0025	0031	0038	0046	0056	0067	0079	0093	0109
6	0001	0001	0001	0002	0002	0003	0004	0005	0006	0007

P	31	32	33	34	35	36	37	38	39	40
R										
1	8921	9011	9095	9173	9246	9313	9375	9432	9485	9533
2	6012	6220	6422	6619	6809	6994	7172	7343	7508	7667
3	2744	2936	3130	3328	3529	3732	3937	4143	4350	4557
4	0787	0875	0969	1069	1174	1286	1404	1527	1657	1792
5	0127	0148	0170	0195	0223	0254	0288	0325	0365	0410
6	0009	0011	0013	0015	0018	0022	0026	0030	0035	0041

P	41	42	43	44	45	46	47	48	49	50
R										
1	9578	9619	9657	9692	9723	9752	9778	9802	9824	9844
2	7819	7965	8105	8238	8364	8485	8599	8707	8810	8906
3	4764	4971	5177	5382	5585	5786	5985	6180	6373	6563
4	1933	2080	2232	2390	2553	2721	2893	3070	3252	3438
5	0458	0510	0566	0627	0692	0762	0837	0917	1003	1094
6	0048	0055	0063	0073	0083	0095	0108	0122	0138	0156

$$n = 7$$

P	01	02	03	04	05	06	07	08	09	10
R										
1	0679	1319	1920	2486	3017	3515	3983	4422	4832	5217
2	0020	0079	0171	0294	0444	0618	0813	1026	1255	1497
3		0003	0009	0020	0038	0063	0097	0140	0193	0257
4				0001	0002	0004	0007	0012	0018	0027
5								0001	0001	0002

P	11	12	13	14	15	16	17	18	19	20
R										
1	5577	5913	6227	6521	6794	7049	7286	7507	7712	7903
2	1750	2012	2281	2556	2834	3115	3396	3677	3956	4233
3	0331	0416	0513	0620	0738	0866	1005	1154	1313	1480
4	0039	0054	0072	0094	0121	0153	0189	0231	0279	0333
5	0003	0004	0006	0009	0012	0017	0022	0029	0037	0047
6					0001	0001	0001	0002	0003	0004

P	21	22	23	24	25	26	27	28	29	30
R										
1	8080	8243	8395	8535	8665	8785	8895	8997	9090	9176
2	4506	4775	5040	5298	5551	5796	6035	6266	6490	6706
3	1657	1841	2033	2231	2436	2646	2861	3081	3304	3529
4	0394	0461	0536	0617	0706	0802	0905	1016	1134	1260
5	0058	0072	0088	0107	0129	0153	0181	0213	0248	0288
6	0005	0006	0008	0011	0013	0017	0021	0026	0031	0038
7					0001	0001	0001	0001	0002	0002

$$n = 7$$

P	31	32	33	34	35	36	37	38	39	40
R										
1	9255	9328	9394	9454	9510	9560	9606	9648	9686	9720
2	6914	7113	7304	7487	7662	7828	7987	8137	8279	8414
3	3757	3987	4217	4447	4677	4906	5134	5359	5581	5801
4	1394	1534	1682	1837	1998	2167	2341	2521	2707	2898
5	0332	0380	0434	0492	0556	0625	0701	0782	0869	0963
6	0046	0055	0065	0077	0090	0105	0123	0142	0164	0188
7	0003	0003	0004	0005	0006	0008	0009	0011	0014	0016

P	41	42	43	44	45	46	47	48	49	50
R										
1	9751	9779	9805	9827	9848	9866	9883	9897	9910	9922
2	8541	8660	8772	8877	8976	9068	9153	9233	9307	9375
3	6017	6229	6436	6638	6836	7027	7213	7393	7567	7734
4	3094	3294	3498	3706	3917	4131	4346	4563	4781	5000
5	1063	1169	1282	1402	1529	1663	1803	1951	2105	2266
6	0216	0246	0279	0316	0357	0402	0451	0504	0562	0625
7	0019	0023	0027	0032	0037	0044	0051	0059	0068	0078

$$n = 8$$

P	01	02	03	04	05	06	07	08	09	10
R										
1	0773	1492	2163	2786	3366	3904	4404	4868	5297	5695
2	0027	0103	0223	0381	0572	0792	1035	1298	1577	1869
3	0001	0004	0013	0031	0058	0096	0147	0211	0289	0381
4			0001	0002	0004	0007	0013	0022	0034	0050
5							0001	0001	0003	0004

P	11	12	13	14	15	16	17	18	19	20
R										
1	6063	6404	6718	7008	7275	7521	7748	7956	8147	8322
2	2171	2480	2794	3111	3428	3744	4057	4366	4670	4967
3	0487	0608	0743	0891	1052	1226	1412	1608	1815	2031
4	0071	0097	0129	0168	0214	0267	0328	0397	0476	0563
5	0007	0010	0015	0021	0029	0038	0050	0065	0083	0104
6		0001	0001	0002	0002	0003	0005	0007	0009	0012
7									0001	0001

P	21	22	23	24	25	26	27	28	29	30
R										
1	8483	8630	8764	8887	8999	9101	9194	9278	9354	9424
2	5257	5538	5811	6075	6329	6573	6807	7031	7244	7447
3	2255	2486	2724	2967	3215	3465	3718	3973	4228	4482
4	0659	0765	0880	1004	1138	1281	1433	1594	1763	1941
5	0129	0158	0191	0230	0273	0322	0377	0438	0505	0580
6	0016	0021	0027	0034	0042	0052	0064	0078	0094	0113
7	0001	0002	0002	0003	0004	0005	0006	0008	0010	0013
8									0001	0001

$n = 8$

P	31	32	33	34	35	36	37	38	39	40
R										
1	9486	9543	9594	9640	9681	9719	9752	9782	9808	9832
2	7640	7822	7994	8156	8309	8452	8586	8711	8828	8936
3	4736	4987	5236	5481	5722	5958	6189	6415	6634	6846
4	2126	2319	2519	2724	2936	3153	3374	3599	3828	4059
5	0661	0750	0846	0949	1061	1180	1307	1443	1586	1737
6	0134	0159	0187	0218	0253	0293	0336	0385	0439	0498
7	0016	0020	0024	0030	0036	0043	0051	0061	0072	0085
8	0001	0001	0001	0002	0002	0003	0004	0004	0005	0007

P	41	42	43	44	45	46	47	48	49	50
R										
1	9853	9872	9889	9903	9916	9928	9938	9947	9954	9961
2	9037	9130	9216	9295	9368	9435	9496	9552	9602	9648
3	7052	7250	7440	7624	7799	7966	8125	8276	8419	8555
4	4292	4527	4762	4996	5230	5463	5694	5922	6146	6367
5	1895	2062	2235	2416	2604	2798	2999	3205	3416	3633
6	0563	0634	0711	0794	0885	0982	1086	1198	1318	1445
7	0100	0117	0136	0157	0181	0208	0239	0272	0310	0352
8	0008	0010	0012	0014	0017	0020	0024	0028	0033	0039

$n = 9$

P	01	02	03	04	05	06	07	08	09	10
R										
1	0865	1663	2398	3075	3698	4270	4796	5278	5721	6126
2	0034	0131	0282	0478	0712	0978	1271	1583	1912	2252
3	0001	0006	0020	0045	0084	0138	0209	0298	0405	0530
4			0001	0003	0006	0013	0023	0037	0057	0083
5						0001	0002	0003	0005	0009
6										0001

P	11	12	13	14	15	16	17	18	19	20
R										
1	6496	6835	7145	7427	7684	7918	8131	8324	8499	8658
2	2599	2951	3304	3657	4005	4348	4685	5012	5330	5638
3	0672	0833	1009	1202	1409	1629	1861	2105	2357	2618
4	0117	0158	0209	0269	0339	0420	0512	0615	0730	0856
5	0014	0021	0030	0041	0056	0075	0098	0125	0158	0196
6	0001	0002	0003	0004	0006	0009	0013	0017	0023	0031
7						0001	0001	0002	0002	0003

P	21	22	23	24	25	26	27	28	29	30
R										
1	8801	8931	9048	9154	9249	9335	9411	9480	9542	9596
2	5934	6218	6491	6750	6997	7230	7452	7660	7856	8040
3	2885	3158	3434	3713	3993	4273	4552	4829	5102	5372
4	0994	1144	1304	1475	1657	1849	2050	2260	2478	2703
5	0240	0291	0350	0416	0489	0571	0662	0762	0870	0988
6	0040	0051	0065	0081	0100	0122	0149	0179	0213	0253
7	0004	0006	0008	0010	0013	0017	0022	0028	0035	0043
8			0001	0001	0001	0001	0002	0003	0003	0004

$$n = 9$$

P	31	32	33	34	35	36	37	38	39	40
R										
1	9645	9689	9728	9762	9793	9820	9844	9865	9883	9899
2	8212	8372	8522	8661	8789	8908	9017	9118	9210	9295
3	5636	5894	6146	6390	6627	6856	7076	7287	7489	7682
4	2935	3173	3415	3662	3911	4163	4416	4669	4922	5174
5	1115	1252	1398	1553	1717	1890	2072	2262	2460	2666
6	0298	0348	0404	0467	0536	0612	0696	0787	0886	0994
7	0053	0064	0078	0094	0112	0133	0157	0184	0215	0250
8	0006	0007	0009	0011	0014	0017	0021	0026	0031	0038
9				0001	0001	0001	0001	0002	0002	0003

P	41	42	43	44	45	46	47	48	49	50
R										
1	9913	9926	9936	9946	9954	9961	9967	9972	9977	9980
2	9372	9442	9505	9563	9615	9662	9704	9741	9775	9805
3	7866	8039	8204	8359	8505	8642	8769	8889	8999	9102
4	5424	5670	5913	6152	6386	6614	6836	7052	7260	7461
5	2878	3097	3322	3551	3786	4024	4265	4509	4754	5000
6	1109	1233	1366	1508	1658	1817	1985	2161	2346	2539
7	0290	0334	0383	0437	0498	0564	0637	0717	0804	0898
8	0046	0055	0065	0077	0091	0107	0125	0145	0169	0195
9	0003	0004	0005	0006	0008	0009	0011	0014	0016	0020

$$n = 10$$

P	01	02	03	04	05	06	07	08	09	10
R										
1	0956	1829	2626	3352	4013	4614	5160	5656	6106	6513
2	0043	0162	0345	0582	0861	1176	1517	1879	2254	2639
3	0001	0009	0028	0062	0115	0188	0283	0401	0540	0702
4			0001	0004	0010	0020	0036	0058	0088	0128
5					0001	0002	0003	0006	0010	0016
6									0001	0001

P	11	12	13	14	15	16	17	18	19	20
R										
1	6882	7215	7516	7787	8031	8251	8448	8626	8784	8926
2	3028	3417	3804	4184	4557	4920	5270	5608	5932	6242
3	0884	1087	1308	1545	1798	2064	2341	2628	2922	3222
4	0178	0239	0313	0400	0500	0614	0741	0883	1039	1209
5	0025	0037	0053	0073	0099	0130	0168	0213	0266	0328
6	0003	0004	0006	0010	0014	0020	0027	0037	0049	0064
7			0001	0001	0001	0002	0003	0004	0006	0009
8									0001	0001

$$n = 10$$

P R	21	22	23	24	25	26	27	28	29	30
1	9053	9166	9267	9357	9437	9508	9570	9626	9674	9718
2	6536	6815	7079	7327	7560	7778	7981	8170	8345	8507
3	3526	3831	4137	4442	4744	5042	5335	5622	5901	6172
4	1391	1587	1794	2012	2241	2479	2726	2979	3239	3504
5	0399	0479	0569	0670	0781	0904	1037	1181	1337	1503
6	0082	0104	0130	0161	0197	0239	0287	0342	0404	0473
7	0012	0016	0021	0027	0035	0045	0056	0070	0087	0106
8	0001	0002	0002	0003	0004	0006	0007	0010	0012	0016
9							0001	0001	0001	0001

P R	31	32	33	34	35	36	37	38	39	40
1	9755	9789	9818	9843	9865	9885	9902	9916	9929	9940
2	8656	8794	8920	9035	9140	9236	9323	9402	9473	9536
3	6434	6687	6930	7162	7384	7595	7794	7983	8160	8327
4	3772	4044	4316	4589	4862	5132	5400	5664	5923	6177
5	1679	1867	2064	2270	2485	2708	2939	3177	3420	3669
6	0551	0637	0732	0836	0949	1072	1205	1348	1500	1662
7	0129	0155	0185	0220	0260	0305	0356	0413	0477	0548
8	0020	0025	0032	0039	0048	0059	0071	0086	0103	0123
9	0002	0003	0003	0004	0005	0007	0009	0011	0014	0017
10								0001	0001	0001

P R	41	42	43	44	45	46	47	48	49	50
1	9949	9957	9964	9970	9975	9979	9983	9986	9988	9990
2	9594	9645	9691	9731	9767	9799	9827	9852	9874	9893
3	8483	8628	8764	8889	9004	9111	9209	9298	9379	9453
4	6425	6665	6898	7123	7340	7547	7745	7933	8112	8281
5	3922	4178	4436	4696	4956	5216	5474	5730	5982	6230
6	1834	2016	2207	2407	2616	2832	3057	3288	3526	3770
7	0626	0712	0806	0908	1020	1141	1271	1410	1560	1719
8	0146	0172	0202	0236	0274	0317	0366	0420	0480	0547
9	0021	0025	0031	0037	0045	0054	0065	0077	0091	0107
10	0001	0002	0002	0003	0003	0004	0005	0006	0008	0010

$$n = 11$$

P R	01	02	03	04	05	06	07	08	09	10
1	1047	1993	2847	3618	4312	4937	5499	6004	6456	6862
2	0052	0195	0413	0692	1019	1382	1772	2181	2601	3026
3	0002	0012	0037	0083	0152	0248	0370	0519	0695	0896
4			0002	0007	0016	0030	0053	0085	0129	0185
5					0001	0003	0005	0010	0017	0028
6								0001	0002	0003

$n = 11$

P	11	12	13	14	15	16	17	18	19	20
R										
1	7225	7549	7839	8097	8327	8531	8712	8873	9015	9141
2	3452	3873	4286	4689	5078	5453	5811	6151	6474	6779
3	1120	1366	1632	1915	2212	2521	2839	3164	3494	3826
4	0256	0341	0442	0560	0694	0846	1013	1197	1397	1611
5	0042	0061	0087	0119	0159	0207	0266	0334	0413	0504
6	0005	0008	0012	0018	0027	0037	0051	0068	0090	0117
7		0001	0001	0002	0003	0005	0007	0010	0014	0020
8							0001	0001	0002	0002

P	21	22	23	24	25	26	27	28	29	30
R										
1	9252	9350	9436	9511	9578	9636	9686	9730	9769	9802
2	7065	7333	7582	7814	8029	8227	8410	8577	8730	8870
3	4158	4488	4814	5134	5448	5753	6049	6335	6610	6873
4	1840	2081	2333	2596	2867	3146	3430	3719	4011	4304
5	0607	0723	0851	0992	1146	1313	1493	1685	1888	2103
6	0148	0186	0231	0283	0343	0412	0490	0577	0674	0782
7	0027	0035	0046	0059	0076	0095	0119	0146	0179	0216
8	0003	0005	0007	0009	0012	0016	0021	0027	0034	0043
9			0001	0001	0001	0002	0002	0003	0004	0006

P	31	32	33	34	35	36	37	38	39	40
R										
1	9831	9856	9878	9896	9912	9926	9938	9948	9956	9964
2	8997	9112	9216	9310	9394	9470	9537	9597	9650	9698
3	7123	7361	7587	7799	7999	8186	8360	8522	8672	8811
4	4598	4890	5179	5464	5744	6019	6286	6545	6796	7037
5	2328	2563	2807	3059	3317	3581	3850	4122	4397	4672
6	0901	1031	1171	1324	1487	1661	1847	2043	2249	2465
7	0260	0309	0366	0430	0501	0581	0670	0768	0876	0994
8	0054	0067	0082	0101	0122	0148	0177	0210	0249	0293
9	0008	0010	0013	0016	0020	0026	0032	0039	0048	0059
10	0001	0001	0001	0002	0002	0003	0004	0005	0006	0007

P	41	42	43	44	45	46	47	48	49	50
R										
1	9970	9975	9979	9983	9986	9989	9991	9992	9994	9995
2	9739	9776	9808	9836	9861	9882	9900	9916	9930	9941
3	8938	9055	9162	9260	9348	9428	9499	9564	9622	9673
4	7269	7490	7700	7900	8089	8266	8433	8588	8733	8867
5	4948	5223	5495	5764	6029	6288	6541	6787	7026	7256
6	2690	2924	3166	3414	3669	3929	4193	4460	4729	5000
7	1121	1260	1408	1568	1738	1919	2110	2312	2523	2744
8	0343	0399	0461	0532	0610	0696	0791	0895	1009	1133
9	0072	0087	0104	0125	0148	0175	0206	0241	0282	0327
10	0009	0012	0014	0018	0022	0027	0033	0040	0049	0059
11	0001	0001	0001	0001	0002	0002	0002	0003	0004	0005

$$n = 12$$

P	01	02	03	04	05	06	07	08	09	10
R										
1	1136	2153	3062	3873	4596	5241	5814	6323	6775	7176
2	0062	0231	0486	0809	1184	1595	2033	2487	2948	3410
3	0002	0015	0048	0107	0196	0316	0468	0652	0866	1109
4		0001	0003	0010	0022	0043	0075	0120	0180	0256
5				0001	0002	0004	0009	0016	0027	0043
6							0001	0002	0003	0005
7										0001

P	11	12	13	14	15	16	17	18	19	20
R										
1	7530	7843	8120	8363	8578	8766	8931	9076	9202	9313
2	3867	4314	4748	5166	5565	5945	6304	6641	6957	7251
3	1377	1667	1977	2303	2642	2990	3344	3702	4060	4417
4	0351	0464	0597	0750	0922	1114	1324	1552	1795	2054
5	0065	0095	0133	0181	0239	0310	0393	0489	0600	0726
6	0009	0014	0022	0033	0046	0065	0088	0116	0151	0194
7	0001	0002	0003	0004	0007	0010	0015	0021	0029	0039
8					0001	0001	0002	0003	0004	0006
9										0001

P	21	22	23	24	25	26	27	28	29	30
R										
1	9409	9493	9566	9629	9683	9730	9771	9806	9836	9862
2	7524	7776	8009	8222	8416	8594	8755	8900	9032	9150
3	4768	5114	5450	5778	6093	6397	6687	6963	7225	7472
4	2326	2610	2904	3205	3512	3824	4137	4452	4765	5075
5	0866	1021	1192	1377	1576	1790	2016	2254	2504	2763
6	0245	0304	0374	0453	0544	0646	0760	0887	1026	1178
7	0052	0068	0089	0113	0143	0178	0219	0267	0322	0386
8	0008	0011	0016	0021	0028	0036	0047	0060	0076	0095
9	0001	0001	0002	0003	0004	0005	0007	0010	0013	0017
10						0001	0001	0001	0002	0002

P	31	32	33	34	35	36	37	38	39	40
R										
1	9884	9902	9918	9932	9943	9953	9961	9968	9973	9978
2	9256	9350	9435	9509	9576	9634	9685	9730	9770	9804
3	7704	7922	8124	8313	8487	8648	8795	8931	9054	9166
4	5381	5681	5973	6258	6533	6799	7053	7296	7528	7747
5	3032	3308	3590	3876	4167	4459	4751	5043	5332	5618
6	1343	1521	1711	1913	2127	2352	2588	2833	3087	3348
7	0458	0540	0632	0734	0846	0970	1106	1253	1411	1582
8	0118	0144	0176	0213	0255	0304	0359	0422	0493	0573
9	0022	0028	0036	0045	0056	0070	0086	0104	0127	0153
10	0003	0004	0005	0007	0008	0011	0014	0018	0022	0028
11				0001	0001	0001	0001	0002	0002	0003

$$n = 12$$

P	41	42	43	44	45	46	47	48	49	50
R
1	9982	9986	9988	9990	9992	9994	9995	9996	9997	9998
2	9834	9860	9882	9901	9917	9931	9943	9953	9961	9968
3	9267	9358	9440	9513	9579	9637	9688	9733	9773	9807
4	7953	8147	8329	8498	8655	8801	8934	9057	9168	9270
5	5899	6175	6443	6704	6956	7198	7430	7652	7862	8062
6	3616	3889	4167	4448	4731	5014	5297	5577	5855	6128
7	1765	1959	2164	2380	2607	2843	3089	3343	3604	3872
8	0662	0760	0869	0988	1117	1258	1411	1575	1751	1938
9	0183	0218	0258	0304	0356	0415	0481	0555	0638	0730
10	0035	0043	0053	0065	0079	0095	0114	0137	0163	0193
11	0004	0005	0007	0009	0011	0014	0017	0021	0026	0032
12				0001	0001	0001	0001	0001	0002	0002

$$n = 13$$

P	01	02	03	04	05	06	07	08	09	10
R
1	1225	2310	3270	4118	4867	5526	6107	6617	7065	7458
2	0072	0270	0564	0932	1354	1814	2298	2794	3293	3787
3	0003	0020	0062	0135	0245	0392	0578	0799	1054	1339
4		0001	0005	0014	0031	0060	0103	0163	0242	0342
5				0001	0003	0007	0013	0024	0041	0065
6						0001	0001	0003	0005	0009
7									0001	0001

P	11	12	13	14	15	16	17	18	19	20
R
1	7802	8102	8364	8592	8791	8963	9113	9242	9354	9450
2	4270	4738	5186	5614	6017	6396	6751	7080	7384	7664
3	1651	1985	2337	2704	3080	3463	3848	4231	4611	4983
4	0464	0609	0776	0967	1180	1414	1667	1939	2226	2527
5	0097	0139	0193	0260	0342	0438	0551	0681	0827	0991
6	0015	0024	0036	0053	0075	0104	0139	0183	0237	0300
7	0002	0003	0005	0008	0013	0019	0027	0038	0052	0070
8			0001	0001	0002	0003	0004	0006	0009	0012
9								0001	0001	0002

P	21	22	23	24	25	26	27	28	29	30
R
1	9533	9604	9666	9718	9762	9800	9833	9860	9883	9903
2	7920	8154	8367	8559	8733	8889	9029	9154	9265	9363
3	5347	5699	6039	6364	6674	6968	7245	7505	7749	7975
4	2839	3161	3489	3822	4157	4493	4826	5155	5478	5794
5	1173	1371	1585	1816	2060	2319	2589	2870	3160	3457
6	0375	0462	0562	0675	0802	0944	1099	1270	1455	1654
7	0093	0120	0154	0195	0243	0299	0365	0440	0527	0624
8	0017	0024	0032	0043	0056	0073	0093	0118	0147	0182
9	0002	0004	0005	0007	0010	0013	0018	0024	0031	0040
10			0001	0001	0001	0002	0003	0004	0005	0007
11									0001	0001

n = 13

P	31	32	33	34	35	36	37	38	39	40
R										
1	9920	9934	9945	9955	9963	9970	9975	9980	9984	9987
2	9450	9527	9594	9653	9704	9749	9787	9821	9849	9874
3	8185	8379	8557	8720	8868	9003	9125	9235	9333	9421
4	6101	6398	6683	6957	7217	7464	7698	7917	8123	8314
5	3760	4067	4376	4686	4995	5301	5603	5899	6188	6470
6	1867	2093	2331	2581	2841	3111	3388	3673	3962	4256
7	0733	0854	0988	1135	1295	1468	1654	1853	2065	2288
8	0223	0271	0326	0390	0462	0544	0635	0738	0851	0977
9	0052	0065	0082	0102	0126	0154	0187	0225	0270	0321
10	0009	0012	0015	0020	0025	0032	0040	0051	0063	0078
11	0001	0001	0002	0003	0003	0005	0006	0008	0010	0013
12							0001	0001	0001	0001

P	41	42	43	44	45	46	47	48	49	50
R										
1	9990	9992	9993	9995	9996	9997	9997	9998	9998	9999
2	9895	9912	9928	9940	9951	9960	9967	9974	9979	9983
3	9499	9569	9630	9684	9731	9772	9808	9838	9865	9888
4	8492	8656	8807	8945	9071	9185	9288	9381	9464	9539
5	6742	7003	7254	7493	7721	7935	8137	8326	8502	8666
6	4552	4849	5146	5441	5732	6019	6299	6573	6838	7095
7	2524	2770	3025	3290	3563	3842	4127	4415	4707	5000
8	1114	1264	1426	1600	1788	1988	2200	2424	2659	2905
9	0379	0446	0520	0605	0698	0803	0918	1045	1183	1334
10	0096	0117	0141	0170	0203	0242	0287	0338	0396	0461
11	0017	0021	0027	0033	0041	0051	0063	0077	0093	0112
12	0002	0002	0003	0004	0005	0007	0009	0011	0014	0017
13							0001	0001	0001	0001

n = 14

P	01	02	03	04	05	06	07	08	09	10
R										
1	1313	2464	3472	4353	5123	5795	6380	6888	7330	7712
2	0084	0310	0645	1059	1530	2037	2564	3100	3632	4154
3	0003	0025	0077	0167	0301	0478	0698	0958	1255	1584
4		0001	0006	0019	0042	0080	0136	0214	0315	0441
5				0002	0004	0010	0020	0035	0059	0092
6						0001	0002	0004	0008	0015
7									0001	0002

P	11	12	13	14	15	16	17	18	19	20
R										
1	8044	8330	8577	8789	8972	9129	9264	9379	9477	9560
2	4658	5141	5599	6031	6433	6807	7152	7469	7758	8021
3	1939	2315	2708	3111	3521	3932	4341	4744	5138	5519
4	0594	0774	0979	1210	1465	1742	2038	2351	2679	3018
5	0137	0196	0269	0359	0467	0594	0741	0907	1093	1298
6	0024	0038	0057	0082	0115	0157	0209	0273	0349	0439
7	0003	0006	0009	0015	0022	0032	0046	0064	0087	0116
8		0001	0001	0002	0003	0005	0008	0012	0017	0024
9						0001	0001	0002	0003	0004

$$n = 14$$

P	21	22	23	24	25	26	27	28	29	30
R										
1	9631	9691	9742	9786	9822	9852	9878	9899	9917	9932
2	8259	8473	8665	8837	8990	9126	9246	9352	9444	9525
3	5887	6239	6574	6891	7189	7467	7727	7967	8188	8392
4	3366	3719	4076	4432	4787	5136	5479	5813	6137	6448
5	1523	1765	2023	2297	2585	2884	3193	3509	3832	4158
6	0543	0662	0797	0949	1117	1301	1502	1718	1949	2195
7	0152	0196	0248	0310	0383	0467	0563	0673	0796	0933
8	0033	0045	0060	0079	0103	0132	0167	0208	0257	0315
9	0006	0008	0011	0016	0022	0029	0038	0050	0065	0083
10	0001	0001	0002	0002	0003	0005	0007	0009	0012	0017
11						0001	0001	0001	0002	0002

P	31	32	33	34	35	36	37	38	39	40
R										
1	9945	9955	9963	9970	9976	9981	9984	9988	9990	9992
2	9596	9657	9710	9756	9795	9828	9857	9881	9902	9919
3	8577	8746	8899	9037	9161	9271	9370	9457	9534	9602
4	6747	7032	7301	7556	7795	8018	8226	8418	8595	8757
5	4486	4813	5138	5458	5773	6080	6378	6666	6943	7207
6	2454	2724	3006	3297	3595	3899	4208	4519	4831	5141
7	1084	1250	1431	1626	1836	2059	2296	2545	2805	3075
8	0381	0458	0545	0643	0753	0876	1012	1162	1325	1501
9	0105	0131	0163	0200	0243	0294	0353	0420	0497	0583
10	0022	0029	0037	0048	0060	0076	0095	0117	0144	0175
11	0003	0005	0006	0008	0011	0014	0019	0024	0031	0039
12		0001	0001	0001	0001	0002	0003	0003	0005	0006
13										0001

P	41	42	43	44	45	46	47	48	49	50
R										
1	9994	9995	9996	9997	9998	9998	9999	9999	9999	9999
2	9934	9946	9956	9964	9971	9977	9981	9985	9988	9991
3	9661	9713	9758	9797	9830	9858	9883	9903	9921	9935
4	8905	9039	9161	9270	9368	9455	9532	9601	9661	9713
5	7459	7697	7922	8132	8328	8510	8678	8833	8974	9102
6	5450	5754	6052	6344	6627	6900	7163	7415	7654	7880
7	3355	3643	3937	4236	4539	4843	5148	5451	5751	6047
8	1692	1896	2113	2344	2586	2840	3105	3380	3663	3953
9	0680	0789	0910	1043	1189	1348	1520	1707	1906	2120
10	0212	0255	0304	0361	0426	0500	0583	0677	0782	0898
11	0049	0061	0076	0093	0114	0139	0168	0202	0241	0287
12	0008	0010	0013	0017	0022	0027	0034	0042	0053	0065
13	0001	0001	0001	0002	0003	0003	0004	0006	0007	0009
14										0001

$$n = 15$$

P	01	02	03	04	05	06	07	08	09	10
R										
1	1399	2614	3667	4579	5367	6047	6633	7137	7570	7941
2	0096	0353	0730	1191	1710	2262	2832	3403	3965	4510
3	0004	0030	0094	0203	0362	0571	0829	1130	1469	1841
4		0002	0008	0024	0055	0104	0175	0273	0399	0556
5			0001	0002	0006	0014	0028	0050	0082	0127
6					0001	0001	0003	0007	0013	0022
7								0001	0002	0003

P	11	12	13	14	15	16	17	18	19	20
R										
1	8259	8530	8762	8959	9126	9269	9389	9490	9576	9648
2	5031	5524	5987	6417	6814	7179	7511	7813	8085	8329
3	2238	2654	3084	3520	3958	4392	4819	5234	5635	6020
4	0742	0959	1204	1476	1773	2092	2429	2782	3146	3518
5	0187	0265	0361	0478	0617	0778	0961	1167	1394	1642
6	0037	0057	0084	0121	0168	0227	0300	0387	0490	0611
7	0006	0010	0015	0024	0036	0052	0074	0102	0137	0181
8	0001	0001	0002	0004	0006	0010	0014	0021	0030	0042
9					0001	0001	0002	0003	0005	0008
10									0001	0001

P	21	22	23	24	25	26	27	28	29	30
R										
1	9709	9759	9802	9837	9866	9891	9911	9928	9941	9953
2	8547	8741	8913	9065	9198	9315	9417	9505	9581	9647
3	6385	6731	7055	7358	7639	7899	8137	8355	8553	8732
4	3895	4274	4650	5022	5387	5742	6086	6416	6732	7031
5	1910	2195	2495	2810	3135	3469	3810	4154	4500	4845
6	0748	0905	1079	1272	1484	1713	1958	2220	2495	2784
7	0234	0298	0374	0463	0566	0684	0817	0965	1130	1311
8	0058	0078	0104	0135	0173	0219	0274	0338	0413	0500
9	0011	0016	0023	0031	0042	0056	0073	0094	0121	0152
10	0002	0003	0004	0006	0008	0011	0015	0021	0028	0037
11			0001	0001	0001	0002	0002	0003	0005	0007
12									0001	0001

P	31	32	33	34	35	36	37	38	39	40
R										
1	9962	9969	9975	9980	9984	9988	9990	9992	9994	9995
2	9704	9752	9794	9829	9858	9883	9904	9922	9936	9948
3	8893	9038	9167	9281	9383	9472	9550	9618	9678	9729
4	7314	7580	7829	8060	8273	8469	8649	8813	8961	9095
5	5187	5523	5852	6171	6481	6778	7062	7332	7587	7827
6	3084	3393	3709	4032	4357	4684	5011	5335	5654	5968
7	1509	1722	1951	2194	2452	2722	3003	3295	3595	3902
8	0599	0711	0837	0977	1132	1302	1487	1687	1902	2131
9	0190	0236	0289	0351	0422	0504	0597	0702	0820	0950
10	0048	0062	0079	0099	0124	0154	0190	0232	0281	0338
11	0009	0012	0016	0022	0028	0037	0047	0059	0075	0093
12	0001	0002	0003	0004	0005	0006	0009	0011	0015	0019
13					0001	0001	0001	0002	0002	0003

P	41	42	43	44	45	46	47	48	49	50
R										
1	9996	9997	9998	9998	9999	9999	9999	9999	10000	10000
2	9958	9966	9973	9979	9983	9987	9990	9992	9994	9995
3	9773	9811	9843	9870	9893	9913	9929	9943	9954	9963
4	9215	9322	9417	9502	9576	9641	9697	9746	9788	9824
5	8052	8261	8454	8633	8796	8945	9080	9201	9310	9408
6	6274	6570	6856	7131	7392	7641	7875	8095	8301	8491
7	4214	4530	4847	5164	5478	5789	6095	6394	6684	6964
8	2374	2630	2898	3176	3465	3762	4065	4374	4686	5000
9	1095	1254	1427	1615	1818	2034	2265	2510	2767	3036
10	0404	0479	0565	0661	0769	0890	1024	1171	1333	1509
11	0116	0143	0174	0211	0255	0305	0363	0430	0506	0592
12	0025	0032	0040	0051	0063	0079	0097	0119	0145	0176
13	0004	0005	0007	0009	0011	0014	0018	0023	0029	0037
14			0001	0001	0001	0002	0002	0003	0004	0005

APPENDIX TABLE 4

Values of $e^{-\lambda}$ (for computing Poisson probabilities)

λ	$e^{-\lambda}$	λ	$e^{-\lambda}$	λ	$e^{-\lambda}$	λ	$e^{-\lambda}$
0.1	0.90484	2.6	0.07427	5.1	0.00610	7.6	0.00050
0.2	0.81873	2.7	0.06721	5.2	0.00552	7.7	0.00045
0.3	0.74082	2.8	0.06081	5.3	0.00499	7.8	0.00041
0.4	0.67032	2.9	0.05502	5.4	0.00452	7.9	0.00037
0.5	0.60653	3.0	0.04979	5.5	0.00409	8.0	0.00034
0.6	0.54881	3.1	0.04505	5.6	0.00370	8.1	0.00030
0.7	0.49659	3.2	0.04076	5.7	0.00335	8.2	0.00027
0.8	0.44933	3.3	0.03688	5.8	0.00303	8.3	0.00025
0.9	0.40657	3.4	0.03337	5.9	0.00274	8.4	0.00022
1.0	0.36788	3.5	0.03020	6.0	0.00248	8.5	0.00020
1.1	0.33287	3.6	0.02732	6.1	0.00224	8.6	0.00018
1.2	0.30119	3.7	0.02472	6.2	0.00203	8.7	0.00017
1.3	0.27253	3.8	0.02237	6.3	0.00184	8.8	0.00015
1.4	0.24660	3.9	0.02024	6.4	0.00166	8.9	0.00014
1.5	0.22313	4.0	0.01832	6.5	0.00150	9.0	0.00012
1.6	0.20190	4.1	0.01657	6.6	0.00136	9.1	0.00011
1.7	0.18268	4.2	0.01500	6.7	0.00123	9.2	0.00010
1.8	0.16530	4.3	0.01357	6.8	0.00111	9.3	0.00009
1.9	0.14957	4.4	0.01228	6.9	0.00101	9.4	0.00008
2.0	0.13534	4.5	0.01111	7.0	0.00091	9.5	0.00007
2.1	0.12246	4.6	0.01005	7.1	0.00083	9.6	0.00007
2.2	0.11080	4.7	0.00910	7.2	0.00075	9.7	0.00006
2.3	0.10026	4.8	0.00823	7.3	0.00068	9.8	0.00006
2.4	0.09072	4.9	0.00745	7.4	0.00061	9.9	0.00005
2.5	0.08208	5.0	0.00674	7.5	0.00055	10.0	0.00005

APPENDIX TABLE 5

Area in the Right Tail of a Chi-square (χ^2) Distribution.*

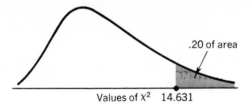

Values of χ^2 14.631

EXAMPLE In a chi-square distribution with 11 degrees of freedom, if we want to find the appropriate chi-square value for .20 of the area under the curve (the shaded area in the right tail) we look under the .20 column in the table and proceed down to the 11 degrees of freedom row; the appropriate chi-square value there is 14.631.

Degrees of freedom	Area in right tail				
	.20	.10	.05	.025	.01
1	1.642	2.706	3.841	5.024	6.635
2	3.219	4.605	5.991	7.378	9.210
3	4.642	6.251	7.815	9.348	11.345
4	5.989	7.779	9.488	11.143	13.277
5	7.289	9.236	11.070	12.833	15.086
6	8.558	10.645	12.592	14.449	16.812
7	9.803	12.017	14.067	16.013	18.475
8	11.030	13.362	15.507	17.535	20.090
9	12.242	14.684	16.919	19.023	21.666
10	13.442	15.987	18.307	20.483	23.209
11	14.631	17.275	19.675	21.920	24.725
12	15.812	18.549	21.026	23.337	26.217
13	16.985	19.812	22.362	24.736	27.688
14	18.151	21.064	23.685	26.119	29.141
15	19.311	22.307	24.996	27.488	30.578
16	20.465	23.542	26.296	28.845	32.000
17	21.615	24.769	27.587	30.191	33.409
18	22.760	25.989	28.869	31.526	34.805
19	23.900	27.204	30.144	32.852	36.191
20	25.038	28.412	31.410	34.170	37.566
21	26.171	29.615	32.671	35.479	38.932
22	27.301	30.813	33.924	36.781	40.289
23	28.429	32.007	35.172	38.076	41.638
24	29.553	33.196	36.415	39.364	42.980
25	30.675	34.382	37.652	40.647	44.314
26	31.795	35.563	38.885	41.923	45.642
27	32.912	36.741	40.113	43.194	46.963
28	34.027	37.916	41.337	44.461	48.278
29	35.139	39.087	42.557	45.722	49.588
30	36.250	40.256	43.773	46.979	50.892

*Taken from Table IV of Fisher and Yates, *Statistical Tables for Biological, Agricultural and Medical Research*, published by Longman Group Ltd., London (previously published by Oliver & Boyd, Edinburgh) and by permission of the authors and publishers.

APPENDIX TABLE 6
Values of F for F Distributions with .05 of the Area in the Right Tail.*

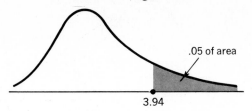

.05 of area

3.94

EXAMPLE For a test at a significance level of .05 where we have 15 degrees of freedom for the numerator and 6 degrees of freedom for the denominator, the appropriate F value is found by looking under the 15 degrees of freedom column and proceeding down to the 6 degrees of freedom row; there we find the appropriate F value to be 3.94.

Degrees of freedom for numerator

	1	2	3	4	5	6	7	8	9	10	12	15	20	24	30	40	60	120	∞
1	161	200	216	225	230	234	237	239	241	242	244	246	248	249	250	251	252	253	254
2	18.5	19.0	19.2	19.2	19.3	19.3	19.4	19.4	19.4	19.4	19.4	19.4	19.4	19.5	19.5	19.5	19.5	19.5	19.5
3	10.1	9.55	9.28	9.12	9.01	8.94	8.89	8.85	8.81	8.79	8.74	8.70	8.66	8.64	8.62	8.59	8.57	8.55	8.53
4	7.71	6.94	6.59	6.39	6.26	6.16	6.09	6.04	6.00	5.96	5.91	5.86	5.80	5.77	5.75	5.72	5.69	5.66	5.63
5	6.61	5.79	5.41	5.19	5.05	4.95	4.88	4.82	4.77	4.74	4.68	4.62	4.56	4.53	4.50	4.46	4.43	4.40	4.37
6	5.99	5.14	4.76	4.53	4.39	4.28	4.21	4.15	4.10	4.06	4.00	3.94	3.87	3.84	3.81	3.77	3.74	3.70	3.67
7	5.59	4.74	4.35	4.12	3.97	3.87	3.79	3.73	3.68	3.64	3.57	3.51	3.44	3.41	3.38	3.34	3.30	3.27	3.23
8	5.32	4.46	4.07	3.84	3.69	3.58	3.50	3.44	3.39	3.35	3.28	3.22	3.15	3.12	3.08	3.04	3.01	2.97	2.93
9	5.12	4.26	3.86	3.63	3.48	3.37	3.29	3.23	3.18	3.14	3.07	3.01	2.94	2.90	2.86	2.83	2.79	2.75	2.71
10	4.96	4.10	3.71	3.48	3.33	3.22	3.14	3.07	3.02	2.98	2.91	2.85	2.77	2.74	2.70	2.66	2.62	2.58	2.54
11	4.84	3.98	3.59	3.36	3.20	3.09	3.01	2.95	2.90	2.85	2.79	2.72	2.65	2.61	2.57	2.53	2.49	2.45	2.40
12	4.75	3.89	3.49	3.26	3.11	3.00	2.91	2.85	2.80	2.75	2.69	2.62	2.54	2.51	2.47	2.43	2.38	2.34	2.30
13	4.67	3.81	3.41	3.18	3.03	2.92	2.83	2.77	2.71	2.67	2.60	2.53	2.46	2.42	2.38	2.34	2.30	2.25	2.21
14	4.60	3.74	3.34	3.11	2.96	2.85	2.76	2.70	2.65	2.60	2.53	2.46	2.39	2.35	2.31	2.27	2.22	2.18	2.13
15	4.54	3.68	3.29	3.06	2.90	2.79	2.71	2.64	2.59	2.54	2.48	2.40	2.33	2.29	2.25	2.20	2.16	2.11	2.07
16	4.49	3.63	3.24	3.01	2.85	2.74	2.66	2.59	2.54	2.49	2.42	2.35	2.28	2.24	2.19	2.15	2.11	2.06	2.01
17	4.45	3.59	3.20	2.96	2.81	2.70	2.61	2.55	2.49	2.45	2.38	2.31	2.23	2.19	2.15	2.10	2.06	2.01	1.96
18	4.41	3.55	3.16	2.93	2.77	2.66	2.58	2.51	2.46	2.41	2.34	2.27	2.19	2.15	2.11	2.06	2.02	1.97	1.92
19	4.38	3.52	3.13	2.90	2.74	2.63	2.54	2.48	2.42	2.38	2.31	2.23	2.16	2.11	2.07	2.03	1.98	1.93	1.88
20	4.35	3.49	3.10	2.87	2.71	2.60	2.51	2.45	2.39	2.35	2.28	2.20	2.12	2.08	2.04	1.99	1.95	1.90	1.84
21	4.32	3.47	3.07	2.84	2.68	2.57	2.49	2.42	2.37	2.32	2.25	2.18	2.10	2.05	2.01	1.96	1.92	1.87	1.81
22	4.30	3.44	3.05	2.82	2.66	2.55	2.46	2.40	2.34	2.30	2.23	2.15	2.07	2.03	1.98	1.94	1.89	1.84	1.78
23	4.28	3.42	3.03	2.80	2.64	2.53	2.44	2.37	2.32	2.27	2.20	2.13	2.05	2.01	1.96	1.91	1.86	1.81	1.76
24	4.26	3.40	3.01	2.78	2.62	2.51	2.42	2.36	2.30	2.25	2.18	2.11	2.03	1.98	1.94	1.89	1.84	1.79	1.73
25	4.24	3.39	2.99	2.76	2.60	2.49	2.40	2.34	2.28	2.24	2.16	2.09	2.01	1.96	1.92	1.87	1.82	1.77	1.71
30	4.17	3.32	2.92	2.69	2.53	2.42	2.33	2.27	2.21	2.16	2.09	2.01	1.93	1.89	1.84	1.79	1.74	1.68	1.62
40	4.08	3.23	2.84	2.61	2.45	2.34	2.25	2.18	2.12	2.08	2.00	1.92	1.84	1.79	1.74	1.69	1.64	1.58	1.51
60	4.00	3.15	2.76	2.53	2.37	2.25	2.17	2.10	2.04	1.99	1.92	1.84	1.75	1.70	1.65	1.59	1.53	1.47	1.39
120	3.92	3.07	2.68	2.45	2.29	2.18	2.09	2.02	1.96	1.91	1.83	1.75	1.66	1.61	1.55	1.50	1.43	1.35	1.25
∞	3.84	3.00	2.60	2.37	2.21	2.10	2.01	1.94	1.88	1.83	1.75	1.67	1.57	1.52	1.46	1.39	1.32	1.22	1.00

Degrees of freedom for denominator

*Source: M. Merrington and C. M. Thompson, *Biometrika*, vol. 33 (1943).

Values of F for F Distributions with .01 of the Area in the Right Tail.

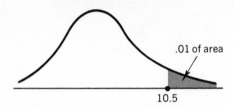

.01 of area

10.5

EXAMPLE For a test at a significance level of .01 where we have 7 degrees of freedom for the numerator and 5 degrees of freedom for the denominator, the appropriate F value is found by looking under the 7 degrees of freedom column and proceeding down to the 5 degrees of freedom row; there we find the appropriate F value to be 10.5.

Degrees of freedom for numerator

	1	2	3	4	5	6	7	8	9	10	12	15	20	24	30	40	60	120	∞
1	4,052	5,000	5,403	5,625	5,764	5,859	5,928	5,982	6,023	6,056	6,106	6,157	6,209	6,235	6,261	6,287	6,313	6,339	6,366
2	98.5	99.0	99.2	99.2	99.3	99.3	99.4	99.4	99.4	99.4	99.4	99.4	99.4	99.5	99.5	99.5	99.5	99.5	99.5
3	34.1	30.8	29.5	28.7	28.2	27.9	27.7	27.5	27.3	27.2	27.1	26.9	26.7	26.6	26.5	26.4	26.3	26.2	26.1
4	21.2	18.0	16.7	16.0	15.5	15.2	15.0	14.8	14.7	14.5	14.4	14.2	14.0	13.9	13.8	13.7	13.7	13.6	13.5
5	16.3	13.3	12.1	11.4	11.0	10.7	10.5	10.3	10.2	10.1	9.89	9.72	9.55	9.47	9.38	9.29	9.20	9.11	9.02
6	13.7	10.9	9.78	9.15	8.75	8.47	8.26	8.10	7.98	7.87	7.72	7.56	7.40	7.31	7.23	7.14	7.06	6.97	6.88
7	12.2	9.55	8.45	7.85	7.46	7.19	6.99	6.84	6.72	6.62	6.47	6.31	6.16	6.07	5.99	5.91	5.82	5.74	5.65
8	11.3	8.65	7.59	7.01	6.63	6.37	6.18	6.03	5.91	5.81	5.67	5.52	5.36	5.28	5.20	5.12	5.03	4.95	4.86
9	10.6	8.02	6.99	6.42	6.06	5.80	5.61	5.47	5.35	5.26	5.11	4.96	4.81	4.73	4.65	4.57	4.48	4.40	4.31
10	10.0	7.56	6.55	5.99	5.64	5.39	5.20	5.06	4.94	4.85	4.71	4.56	4.41	4.33	4.25	4.17	4.08	4.00	3.91
11	9.65	7.21	6.22	5.67	5.32	5.07	4.89	4.74	4.63	4.54	4.40	4.25	4.10	4.02	3.94	3.86	3.78	3.69	3.60
12	9.33	6.93	5.95	5.41	5.06	4.82	4.64	4.50	4.39	4.30	4.16	4.01	3.86	3.78	3.70	3.62	3.54	3.45	3.36
13	9.07	6.70	5.74	5.21	4.86	4.62	4.44	4.30	4.19	4.10	3.96	3.82	3.66	3.59	3.51	3.43	3.34	3.25	3.17
14	8.86	6.51	5.56	5.04	4.70	4.46	4.28	4.14	4.03	3.94	3.80	3.66	3.51	3.43	3.35	3.27	3.18	3.09	3.00
15	8.68	6.36	5.42	4.89	4.56	4.32	4.14	4.00	3.89	3.80	3.67	3.52	3.37	3.29	3.21	3.13	3.05	2.96	2.87
16	8.53	6.23	5.29	4.77	4.44	4.20	4.03	3.89	3.78	3.69	3.55	3.41	3.26	3.18	3.10	3.02	2.93	2.84	2.75
17	8.40	6.11	5.19	4.67	4.34	4.10	3.93	3.79	3.68	3.59	3.46	3.31	3.16	3.08	3.00	2.92	2.83	2.75	2.65
18	8.29	6.01	5.09	4.58	4.25	4.01	3.84	3.71	3.60	3.51	3.37	3.23	3.08	3.00	2.92	2.84	2.75	2.66	2.57
19	8.19	5.93	5.01	4.50	4.17	3.94	3.77	3.63	3.52	3.43	3.30	3.15	3.00	2.92	2.84	2.76	2.67	2.58	2.49
20	8.10	5.85	4.94	4.43	4.10	3.87	3.70	3.56	3.46	3.37	3.23	3.09	2.94	2.86	2.78	2.69	2.61	2.52	2.42
21	8.02	5.78	4.87	4.37	4.04	3.81	3.64	3.51	3.40	3.31	3.17	3.03	2.88	2.80	2.72	2.64	2.55	2.46	2.36
22	7.95	5.72	4.82	4.31	3.99	3.76	3.59	3.45	3.35	3.26	3.12	2.98	2.83	2.75	2.67	2.58	2.50	2.40	2.31
23	7.88	5.66	4.76	4.26	3.94	3.71	3.54	3.41	3.30	3.21	3.07	2.93	2.78	2.70	2.62	2.54	2.45	2.35	2.26
24	7.82	5.61	4.72	4.22	3.90	3.67	3.50	3.36	3.26	3.17	3.03	2.89	2.74	2.66	2.58	2.49	2.40	2.31	2.21
25	7.77	5.57	4.68	4.18	3.86	3.63	3.46	3.32	3.22	3.13	2.99	2.85	2.70	2.62	2.53	2.45	2.36	2.27	2.17
30	7.56	5.39	4.51	4.02	3.70	3.47	3.30	3.17	3.07	2.98	2.84	2.70	2.55	2.47	2.39	2.30	2.21	2.11	2.01
40	7.31	5.18	4.31	3.83	3.51	3.29	3.12	2.99	2.89	2.80	2.66	2.52	2.37	2.29	2.20	2.11	2.02	1.92	1.80
60	7.08	4.98	4.13	3.65	3.34	3.12	2.95	2.82	2.72	2.63	2.50	2.35	2.20	2.12	2.03	1.94	1.84	1.73	1.60
120	6.85	4.79	3.95	3.48	3.17	2.96	2.79	2.66	2.56	2.47	2.34	2.19	2.03	1.95	1.86	1.76	1.66	1.53	1.38
∞	6.63	4.61	3.78	3.32	3.02	2.80	2.64	2.51	2.41	2.32	2.18	2.04	1.88	1.79	1.70	1.59	1.47	1.32	1.00

Degrees of freedom for denominator

APPENDIX TABLE 7

Values for Spearman's Rank Correlation (r_s) for Combined Areas in Both Tails.*

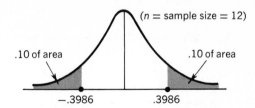

(n = sample size = 12)

.10 of area   .10 of area

−.3986   .3986

EXAMPLE For a two-tailed test of significance at the .20 level, with $n = 12$, the appropriate value for r_s can be found by looking under the .20 column and proceeding down to the 12 row; there we find the appropriate r_s value to be .3986.

n	.20	.10	.05	.02	.01	.002
4	.8000	.8000				
5	.7000	.8000	.9000	.9000		
6	.6000	.7714	.8286	.8857	.9429	
7	.5357	.6786	.7450	.8571	.8929	.9643
8	.5000	.6190	.7143	.8095	.8571	.9286
9	.4667	.5833	.6833	.7667	.8167	.9000
10	.4424	.5515	.6364	.7333	.7818	.8667
11	.4182	.5273	.6091	.7000	.7455	.8364
12	.3986	.4965	.5804	.6713	.7273	.8182
13	.3791	.4780	.5549	.6429	.6978	.7912
14	.3626	.4593	.5341	.6220	.6747	.7670
15	.3500	.4429	.5179	.6000	.6536	.7464
16	.3382	.4265	.5000	.5824	.6324	.7265
17	.3260	.4118	.4853	.5637	.6152	.7083
18	.3148	.3994	.4716	.5480	.5975	.6904
19	.3070	.3895	.4579	.5333	.5825	.6737
20	.2977	.3789	.4451	.5203	.5684	.6586
21	.2909	.3688	.4351	.5078	.5545	.6455
22	.2829	.3597	.4241	.4963	.5426	.6318
23	.2767	.3518	.4150	.4852	.5306	.6186
24	.2704	.3435	.4061	.4748	.5200	.6070
25	.2646	.3362	.3977	.4654	.5100	.5962
26	.2588	.3299	.3894	.4564	.5002	.5856
27	.2540	.3236	.3822	.4481	.4915	.5757
28	.2490	.3175	.3749	.4401	.4828	.5660
29	.2443	.3113	.3685	.4320	.4744	.5567
30	.2400	.3059	.3620	.4251	.4665	.5479

*Source: W. J. Conover, *Practical Nonparametric Statistics*, John Wiley & Sons, Inc., New York, 1971.

Answers to Even-Numbered Exercises and Concepts Tests

Some answers or parts of answers have been omitted. When an exercise calls for simple rearrangement or display of data with no computation or interpretation, the resulting answer may not appear.

Chapter 2

2·2 The franchises that make up the average are chosen as being representative of the entire collection of franchises from 5 states. They form a *sample* of the larger *population* of franchises. From the sample, an inference is drawn about the population as a whole; when the average goes down, all sales as a whole are considered to have gone down.

2·4 The sample may have contained a greater percentage of conservatives (or liberals) than the actual voting population, a greater percentage of Republicans (or Democrats) than the actual voting population, or maybe a greater percentage of farm persons (or city dwellers) than the actual voting population. The sample could also have been biased. Maybe the questions were slanted toward one candidate, or perhaps the pollsters did not ask the right questions. The sample could also have been too small. (*Note*: Experts have attributed the real cause of the turnabout to the fact that Dewey supporters became so confident of victory that they did not bother to vote, whereas Truman supporters did.)

2·6

450–499.9	1	550–599.9	9	650–699.9	4
500–549.9	10	600–649.9	15	700–749.9	1

2·8 a) 7 equal intervals   b) 13 equal intervals

Class	Frequency	Class	Frequency
30–39	.02	35–39	.02
40–49	.08	40–44	.04
50–59	.20	45–49	.04
60–69	.28	50–54	.08
70–79	.22	55–59	.12
80–89	.12	60–64	.12
90–99	.08	65–69	.16
	1.00	70–74	.12
		75–79	.10
		80–84	.06
		85–89	.06
		90–94	.04
		95–99	.04
			1.00

2·10

Class marks	Stated limits	Real limits
8.50	7.0– 9.99	6.995– 9.995
11.50	10.0–12.99	9.995–12.995
14.50	13.0–15.99	12.995–15.995
17.50	16.0–18.99	15.995–18.995
20.50	19.0–21.99	18.995–21.995
23.50	22.0–24.99	21.995–24.995
26.50	25.0–27.99	24.995–27.995
29.50	28.0–30.99	27.995–30.995

2·12

Closed	Open
Single	Single
Married	Married
Divorced	Other
Separated	
Widowed	

2·14

Class marks	Real limits	Stated limits
102.45	99.95–104.95	100.0–104.9
107.45	104.95–109.95	105.0–109.9
112.45	109.95–114.95	110.0–114.9
117.45	114.95–119.95	115.0–119.9
122.45	119.95–124.95	120.0–124.9
127.45	124.95–129.95	125.0–129.9
132.45	129.95–134.95	130.0–134.9
137.45	134.95–139.95	135.0–139.9

2·16

2·18 a)

Class	Cumulative frequency
Less than 3.0	0
Less than 3.2	1
Less than 3.4	5
Less than 3.6	16
Less than 3.8	31
Less than 4.0	43
Less than 4.2	54
Less than 4.4	62
Less than 4.6	69
Less than 4.8	75

c)

Class	Cumulative frequency
More than 2.99	75
More than 3.19	74
More than 3.39	70
More than 3.59	59
More than 3.79	44
More than 3.99	32
More than 4.19	21
More than 4.39	13
More than 4.59	6
More than 4.80	0

(b)

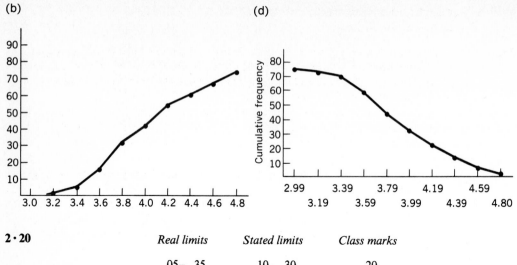

(d)

2·20

Real limits	Stated limits	Class marks
.05– .35	.10– .30	.20
.35– .65	.40– .60	.50
.65– .95	.70– .90	.80
.95–1.25	1.00–1.20	1.10
1.25–1.55	1.30–1.50	1.40
1.55–1.85	1.60–1.80	1.70
1.85–2.15	1.90–2.10	2.00
2.15–2.45	2.20–2.40	2.30
2.45–2.75	2.50–2.70	2.60
2.75–3.05	2.80–3.00	2.90
3.05–	3.10–	none

2·22 To calculate the answer, construct a "less than" cumulative distribution.

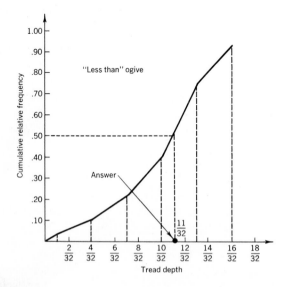

Tread depth (inches) "less than"	0/32	1/32	4/32	7/32	10/32	13/32	16/32	17/32
Cumulative relative frequency	0	.03	.10	.22	.42	.75	.92	1.00

2·24 ① Age—This distribution would be quantitative and discrete. The distribution would be discrete because people report age at their last birthday. The distribution would also be most likely to be open on both ends, because the company would not be interested in very young or very old age classifications for marketing purposes.

② Income—This is again a quantitative, continuous distribution because of the numerical data. Here the company would most certainly use group, rather than individual, categories. Also, the distribution would most likely be open-ended for the same reasons as the age distribution.

③ Marital Status—Here we have a qualitative, discrete distribution because the categories of marital status would not be numerical. Depending on the choice of categories, the list might or might not be open-ended. The possible answers to the question are sufficiently limited that the company might wish to break down the data into all possible categories. However, the company might also choose to limit the categories and use "other" to make the distribution open-ended.

④ and ⑤ Where and Why—Both of these distributions would be qualitative and discrete. However, in contrast to "Marital Status," the answers could be so varied that it is unlikely that the company would choose to list all possibilities. Instead, the most frequent responses would be used and "other" included to cover all other possibilities. Therefore, these distributions would most likely be open-ended.

2·26 No, because it has been analyzed to some extent to get averages for each week's attendance and to get percentages of full attendance. Raw data would be the actual number of absences for each day or week of the time period.

2·28 a)

1st ten		Largest ten	
226	198	267	264
210	233	259	258
222	175	257	252
215	191	248	245
201	175	244	243

b) No. The sample of the first ten elements is more representative because the items in it more adequately represent the distribution of items in the whole population in terms of their values.

2·30

Classes	Frequency	Relative frequency
0–10	1	.05
11–20	0	.00
21–30	1	.05
31–40	6	.30
41–50	3	.15
51–60	4	.20
61–70	2	.10
71–80	0	.00
81–90	3	.15
91–100	0	.00
	20	1.00

2·32 The distributions must all contain the amounts between $0 and $20,000 as a minimum.

a) The distribution meeting all the requirements is given below:

$ 0–$ 1,999	You may	$ 0–$ 2,000
2,000– 3,999	have elected to	2,001– 4,000
4,000– 5,999	start with $0–	4,001– 6,000
6,000– 7,999	$2,000 as your first	6,001– 8,000
8,000– 9,999	interval. For this	8,001– 10,000
10,000– 11,999	case, the correct	10,001– 12,000
12,000– 13,999	distribution is given	12,001– 14,000
14,000– 15,999	on the right.	14,001– 16,000
16,000– 17,999		16,001– 18,000
18,000– 19,999		18,001– 20,000
20,000– 21,999		

b) The distribution which meets all requirements is given below:

$ 0–$ 1,999	Again, if you	$ 0–$ 2,000
2,000– 3,999	were to	2,000– 4,000
4,000– 5,999	use $2,000 as the	4,001– 6,000
6,000– 7,999	end point of the	6,001– 8,000
8,000– 9,999	first interval,	8,001– 10,000
10,000– 11,999	the distribution	10,001– 12,000
12,000– 13,999	would be as on the	12,001– 14,000
14,000– 15,999	right.	14,001– 16,000
16,000– 17,999		16,001– 18,000
18,000 and above		above $18,000

Chapter 3

3·2

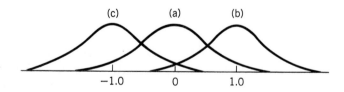

3·4 **a)**

Interval	5–44	45–54	55–64	65–74	75–84	85–94	95–104
Class mark	40	50	60	70	80	90	100
Frequency	1	6	4	10	9	7	3

b) 72.225   **c)** 73.25   **d)** Very close to each other

3·6 $43,096

3·8 88.4   86.2   90.4   85.75   89.7

3·10 1.976

3·12 **a)** 330–349.5   **b)** ave. of 150th and 151st   **c)** .694   **d)** 326.73

3·14 29.5 min   **3·16** 65.85

3·18 **a)** negatively skewed   **b)** positively skewed   **c)** negatively skewed

3·20 7,110 tons   **3·22** 20.35 mpg   **3·24** 440 people

3·26 14.6 lbs   **3·28** 7.47 minutes

Chapter 4

4·2 *a*, because the values tend to cluster more around the mean.

4·4 There are many ways that the concept may be involved. Certainly, the FTC would examine the price variability for the industry and compare the result to that of the suspect companies. The agency might examine price distributions for similar products, for the same products in a city, or for the same products in different cities. If the variability was significantly different in any of these cases, this result might constitute evidence of a conspiracy to set prices at the same levels.

4·6 **a)** 1260   **b)** 407   **c)** 281   **d)** 140.5   **e)** 169
    f) 140.5 measures the average range of 1/4 of the data, whereas 169 measures the range of a particular 1/4 of the data.

4·8

Percentile	20		40		60		80
Interfractile range		4		2		2	

4·10 **a)** 3.5
    b) 22.456
    c) 4.74

4·12 **a)** $\mu = 7.1$ days; $\sigma = 3.87$ days
    b) 195 should be; 249 are
    c) 247

4·14 The second machine

4·16 The first program

4·18 Ohio

4·20 **a)** Day 1 = 1.9
    Day 2 = 1.0
    b) In this case it is not an accurate measure, since the Day 1 range is distorted by one large value.

4·22 Number 2   **4·24** Var. 37778.57 Std. Dev. 194.367

4·26 A person making this statement has missed the point of variability. By definition, you *always* have an equal chance of falling above or below the median, regardless of the variability. We are not considering the average result when we consider variability, however. Instead, we are looking at what a single outcome might be. Even though the outcome might be the same on average, you wouldn't want to be the "one guy in a thousand" who happens to get the lowest possible result. The variability of a distribution describes this risk of having an outcome other than the mean value. You might say that variability tells us how bad or how good the outcome might be and gives us a relative measure of how likely these extreme values are.

Chapter 5

5·2 The Surgeon General's office undoubted studied the incidence of sickness and death among smokers and nonsmokers. (These studies are examples of sampling from a larger population.) Evidence indicated that smokers were more likely to have poor health (or earlier deaths).

5·4 This decision involves estimates of demand, costs, physical plant additions required, and new employees necessary. Each of these estimates involves a degree of uncertainty and therefore a probability estimate.

5·6 a) 0   b) $\frac{1}{36}$ c) $\frac{5}{36}$ d) $\frac{6}{36}$ e) $\frac{4}{36}$ f) $\frac{3}{36}$ g) $\frac{2}{36}$

5·8 a) Only two events would apply to this decision:
 1) Royal wins
 2) Royal losses
 b) The list in part (a) is collectively exhaustive and the events are mutually exclusive.
 c) Knowing nothing about the decision, you would be forced to assign a probability of 1/2 (or .50) to each event [i.e. equally likely].

5·10 a) $\frac{1}{13}$ b) $\frac{1}{4}$ c) $\frac{1}{26}$ d) $\frac{1}{2}$ e) $\frac{3}{13}$ (These are classical probabilities.)

5·12 a) subjective   d) relative frequency
 b) relative frequency   e) classical
 c) subjective

5·14 .30, .40, .62   **5·16** .145

5·20 a) $\frac{1}{2}$ b) $\frac{1}{2}$ **5·18** a) $\frac{1}{4}$ b) $\frac{1}{2}$ c) $\frac{1}{13}$

5·22 a) .57   b) .15   c) .60   d) .45   **5·24** a) .60   b) .30

5·26 a) .48   b) .39   c) .13

5·28 Indianapolis

5·30 a) .36   b) .64

5·32 c)   **5·34** a) .60   b) .50

5·36 a) .0031   b) .475   c) .03

5·38 e)   **5·40** The increase is purely a subjective estimate and cannot be answered from the data given.

Chapter 6

6·2

Total	Probability of total
2	1/36
3	2/36
4	3/36
5	4/36
6	5/36
7	6/36
8	5/36
9	4/36
10	3/36
11	2/36
12	1/36
	1.0

6·4

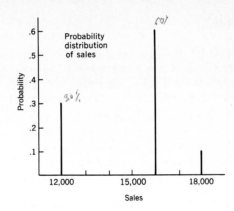

6·6 a)

Outcome	Probability
0	.03
1	.08
2	.30
3	.42
4	.12
5	.05
	1.00

b) $2.67

6·8 a) 4100 pounds   **b)** $3900 loss

6·10 a) .0102   **b)** .0109   **c)** .4202   **d)** .2557

6·12 a) $\mu = 3; \sigma = 1.5$ **b)** $\mu = 15; \sigma = 2.45$ **c)** $\mu = 50; \sigma = 6.71$ **d)** $\mu = 2; \sigma = 1.38$
e) $\mu = 2137.5; \sigma = 10.34$

6·14 .5859; move the employee

6·16 a) .1913   **b)** .9985   **c)** .4493

6·18 a) .3209   **b)** .4633   **c)** .0771

6·20 $112.800   **6·22 a)** 23.76   **b)** 18.64   **6·24** .8585

6·26 about 12

6·28 45,000 pairs   **6·30** Introduce the product with the comprehensive promotion scheme.

6·32 It is probably not Bernoulli. We don't know if the production of these machines is independent.

6·34 a) .2708   **b)** .4206   **6·36 a)** .8491   **b)** .5000   **c)** .0592

6·38 a) .2676   **b)** .8238

6·40 Expected profit without the analysis is $4500; expected profit if the analysis is used is $4900. Since the cost of the analysis is $2000, it should *not* be used.

6·42 b) expected sales 30   **c)** stockout of 6   **6·44 a)** .8485   **b)** .5000
c) .0606 The worst error is only about 2 percent off.

6·46 a) $55,000   **b)** 50,000 lbs.   **c)** $2250

Chapter 7

7·2 If we are only generalizing to the same group of observations in making our conclusions, then the set of elements is the population under study. If, however, we wish to draw conclusions about some larger group of which these elements are only a part, then the set of observations would be considered a sample.

7·4 Probability samples involve more statistical analysis and planning at the beginning of a study and usually take more time and money than judgment samples.

7·6 Situation *b*. The distributions have greater between-group variance and less within-group variance than in *a*.

7·8 Yes.

7·10 Yes. The accident times during the year are probably randomly distributed, making that a good candidate for systematic sampling.

7·12 The older buyer is correct. It is strictly chance that the number served averaged 120. The probability of its not averaging 120 is greater than the probability that it will.

7·14 No. The mean of a sample does not exactly equal the mean of the population, because of sampling error. If it differed greatly, there might be doubts, but that is not the case here.

7·16 No. This is not a sampling distribution of the mean because a sampling distribution refers to a theoretical distribution based on all samples of a given size from a population. These samples by region are of varying size.

7·18 No; the statement can be made only with a .9648 probability.

7·20 a) .8480   b) .9689

7·22 about 16   **7·24** .7242   **7·26** a) .483   b) .268   c) .166

7·28 No, cluster sampling will not give representative results. Problems in one department may be quite different from those in another.

7·30 In this case the company is not constrained by cost, time, or destruction of the population; but given the effort it would require to poll all contractors, sampling is probably a better alternative.

7·32 .0475   **7·34** .0640

Chapter 8

8·2 Measuring an entire population may not be feasible because of time and cost considerations. A sample yields only an estimate and is subject to sampling errors.

8·4 An estimator is a sample statistic used to estimate a population parameter. An estimate is a specific numerical value for an estimator.

8·6 It assures us that the estimator becomes more reliable with larger samples.

8·8 .568   **8·10** $6.0 \pm .16$ inches

8·12 The confidence interval is the range of an estimate; i.e., the interval between and including the upper confidence limit and the lower confidence limit.

8·14 a) High confidence levels produce large confidence intervals; thus the more confident we are, the less we can be confident of.

b) Narrow confidence intervals produce low confidence levels; thus the more definite our estimate, the less confidence we can have in it.

8·16 **a)** 1.8   **b)** .2   **c)** $26 \pm .33$ **8·18** **a)** 67.428, 69.372   **b)** 67.12, 69.68
8·20 **a)** .0215   **b)** .3247–.3953   **8·22** $80\% \pm 11.1\%$ **8·24** 34.6 ± 2.939
8·26 **a)** 90%   **b)** 95%   **c)** 99%   **8·28** 78
8·30 1068   **8·32** 93   **8·34** **a)** $\$28,640 \pm 166.6$ **b)** $\$28,640 \pm 198.05$
8·36 $\$10.50 \pm \$2.09$
8·38 To indicate the statistic's reliability as an estimator of a population parameter. The smaller the standard error, the more likely it is that the statistic falls close to the true value of the population parameter.
8·40 **a)** 95.5%   **b)** 98.76%   **c)** 59.9%
8·42 **a)** 2.120 and .415   **b)** .415   **c)** $2.120 \pm .695$ **8·44** $.4 \pm .065$

Chapter 9

9·2 Theoretically, one could toss a coin a large number of times to see if the proportion of heads was very different from .5. Similarly, by recording the outcomes of many dice rolls, one could see if the proportion of any side was very different from $\frac{1}{6}$. A large number of trials would be needed for each of these examples.
9·4 **a)** Assume a hypothesis about a population.   **b)** Collect sample data.   **c)** Calculate a sample statistic.   **d)** Use the sample statistic to evaluate the hypothesis.
9·6 We mean that we would not have reasonably expected to find that particular sample if in fact the hypothesis had been true.
9·8 There is a 31.74 percent probability of mistakenly rejecting the hypothesis.
9·10 We should accept the claim.
9·12 A null hypothesis represents the hypothesis you are trying to reject; the alternative hypothesis represents all other possibilities.
9·14 Type I: the probability that we will reject the null hypothesis when in fact it is true.
Type II: the probability that we will accept the null hypothesis when in fact it is false
9·16 **a)** normal   **b)** normal   **c)** t with 15 d.f.   **d)** normal   **e)** t with 24 d.f.
9·18 $H_0 : \mu = 10$ tons $H_1 : \mu > 10$ tons   **9·20** Accept H_0 **9·22** Accept H_0
9·24 $9.5 : 1 - \beta = .0099; 10.0 : 1 - \beta = .0582; 10.5 : -\beta = .2061$ **9·28** Accept H_0
9·30 Accept H_0
9·26 Accept H_0
9·32 Accept H_0 **9·34** Accept H_0 **9·36** Reject H_0 **9·38** Reject H_0
9·40 Reject H_0 **9·42** Accept H_0 **9·44** Accept H_0
9·46 A Type I error would not be serious for the patient. A Type II error would be serious because the battery might run down before the next scheduled operation.
9·48 **a)** .2611   **b)** .6406   **c)** .9131   **9·50** Accept H_0 **9·52** Reject H_0
9·54 Reject H_0

Chapter 10

10·2 To determine whether or not three or more populations means can be considered equal.
10·4 **a)** 4   **b)** 6   **c)** 15   **d)** 16   **e)** 10

10·6 a) 1.723 **b)** $H_0: p_A = p_B = p_C = p_D$ **c)** Accept H_0
$H_1: p_A, p_B, p_C, p_D$ are not equal

10·8 Reject H_0 **10·10** Accept H_0 **10·12** Accept H_0
10·14 Reject H_0 **10·16** Reject H_0
10·18 Reject H_0
10·20 a) t test **b)** F distribution **c)** normal **d)** chi-square **10·22** Reject H_0
10·24 b) 8.4398 **c)** H_0: attendance is independent of income level
H_1: attendance and income level are not independent
d) Accept H_0
10·26 Reject H_0 **10·28** Accept H_0

Chapter 11

11·2 An estimating equation is the mathematical relationship describing the association between a dependent variable and one or more independent variables.

11·4 The term *direct relationship* applies to the situation in which the dependent variable increases as the independent variable(s) increases. The term *indirect relationship* describes the situation in which the dependent variable decreases as the independent variable(s) increases.

11·6 A linear relationship describes the situation in which the dependent variable changes a constant amount for equal incremental changes in the independent variable(s). A curvilinear relationship describes the situation in which the dependent variable changes at an increasing (or decreasing) rate with equal incremental changes in the independent variable(s).

11·8 It is the process that determines the relationship between a dependent variable and more than one independent variable.

11·10 a) Yes, direct and linear **b)** Yes, inverse and curvilinear. **c)** Yes, inverse and curvilinear.

11·12 b) $\hat{Y} = .384 + .277X$ **c)** $X = 4: \hat{Y} = 1.492$ **d)** $S_e = .2731$
$X = 9: \hat{Y} = 2.877$ **e)** $\hat{Y} = .630$
$X = 12: \hat{Y} = 3.708$

11·14 b) $\hat{Y} = 99.5 - 10X$ **c)** 27

11·16 a) positive **b)** positive **c)** positive **d)** zero **11·18** $r^2 = .6244;$
$r = -.7902$

11·20 a) .062 **b)** .6178 − .8822 **11·22** Accept H_0

11·24 Because it is *determined* by the relationship of the values over a certain range and therefore may be different for other values.

11·26 The relationship may no longer be the same as it was in earlier studies made under different conditions. New variables may be present, which will affect the relationship between variables studied earlier.

11·28 a) $\hat{Y} = 34.76 - .58X$ **b)** 4.95 **c)** 10.64 − 29.88 **d)** $r^2 = .5955$
$r = -.7717$

11·30 Accept H_0
11·32 b) $\hat{Y} = 10.5 - .39X$ **c)** 4.65 **11·34** Accept H_0

Chapter 12

12·2 To include qualitative factors in our regression.

12·4 **a)** $\hat{Y} = -2.9961 + .5996\,X_1 + .9049\,X_2$
   b) $\hat{Y} = 33.0679$

12·6 **a)** $\hat{Y} = 18.01 + .23\,X_1 + 1.15\,X_2$
   b) $\hat{Y} = 29.625\%$

12·8 **a)** $\hat{Y} = 2275.88 - 0.61\,X_1 + 3.61\,X_2 - 1168.64\,X_3$
   b) 93.99%
   c) 366.197
   d) $177.30 - 3328.80$

12·10 The number of courses *is* a significant explanatory variable.

12·12 Temperature and rainfall must be highly correlated variables. Adding both to the equation as independent variables had led to a multicollinearity situation.

12·14 **a)** If a 2nd degree equation is needed, a straight line through the data points will show a group of points at one end lying above/below the line, followed by a group below/above the line, and another group above/below. In other words, deviations from the line will *not* be random.
   b) The residuals will exhibit the same nonrandom patterns as in part a. They will be positive/negative, then negative/positive, then positive/negative.

12·16 **a)** Aluminum and wood should be coded as 0 and 1, respectively (or vice versa). This data, along with number of gears, should be used to predict failure rates. The equation would be:

$$\hat{Y} = b_0 + b_1 X_1 + b_2 X_2$$

where $\hat{Y}$ is failure rate, X_1 is a dummy variable for material, and X_2 is the number of gears.
   b) $\text{H}_0 : B_1 = 0$
   $\text{H}_1 : B_1 \neq 0$

12·18 **a)** $\hat{Y} = -17.7930 + .9121\,X_1 + .1589\,X_2$
   b) $11.9535(\times 10{,}000)$

12·20 **a)** $\hat{Y} = 4.76 + .002\,X_1 + .767\,X_2$
   b) Allow .002 per square foot (.2 ounce for each 100 square feet)
   c) 23.82 ounces

Chapter 13

13·2 They do not use all the information contained in the data since they rely on counts or ranks.

13·4 Yes, a great deal of information is sacrificed by using a ranking test. If the data were examined, it could be seen that there is a very distinct bi-modal distribution. In this instance, choice of two packages might well be the better alternative.

13·8 Reject H_0 **13·10** Accept H_0 **13·12** Reject the hypothesis of randomness.

13·14 **a)** Accept Kathy's hypothesis   **b)** No.

13·16 There is no significant positive correlation. In fact, r_s is negative.

13·18 Yes, the subject does significantly well in detecting differences in work rates.

13·20 Yes, they will conclude the annual rainfall does not occur in patterns.

13·22 Two reasons that might be advanced for favoring the restaurant owner's proposal are (1) statistical tests on real data are sharper than nonparametric tests, and (2) no information is lost as it perhaps would be with ranking.

Although there is some validity in the first reason, the second one falls short. The quality of information received must first be evaluated before determining what will be lost by using "distribution-free" tests.

In this instance, given a scale of such a broad range and without established norms as to how the form will be filled out, the actual numbers supplied take on little significance. What is really important is the ranking of the data.

13·24 **a)** The number of accidents is not randomly distributed.   **b)** Whereas the number of accidents seems to have declined since the safety measures were installed, we can only infer *relationship* not *causality*. We don't know what other factors may also be involved. The runs test does not permit us to conclude that accidents have declined, only that the number is not random. A linear regression of number of accidents on time would give a better test.

13·26 **a)** The ratings have improved.   **b)** Possibly, but before a definitive answer can be given, we would have to analyze the other variables that might have had an effect on the ratings: quality of acting, competitive shows, weather, and others. A change in any one of these could have caused the ratings to change.

Chapter 14

14·2 Seasonal.

14·4 Since there is no mathematical model for irregular variations, we have no way of predicting future irregular variations.

14·6 Secular trend.

14·8 Demands for services such as water and sewer would perhaps not be met; adjustment of tax rate to provide for municipal services might lag behind the actual demand for those services. Extra resources would probably be needed to allow a smooth municipal operation in a situation in which forecasting is poor.

14·10 **a)** $\hat{Y} = 29.71 + 13.18x$ **b)** $\hat{Y} = 27.57 + 13.18x + .5357x^2$

14·12 **a)** $\hat{Y} = 22 + 2.1x$

b) 101.1, 100.5, 95.5, 103.7, 99.2

c) 1.1, .5, −4.5, 3.7, −.8

14·14

Spring	108.75
Summer	131.50
Fall	90.00
Winter	69.75
	400.00

14·16 **a)** 74.9; 103.6; 144.6; 76.9

b) 1977: 25.4; 23.2; 26.3; 32.5   1979: 30.7; 29.9; 28.4; 29.9
1978: 28.0; 27.0; 30.4; 29.9   1980: 32.0; 33.8; 33.2; 27.3

14·18 **a)** $\hat{Y} = 29.24 + .19X$ ($X = \frac{1}{8}$ yr.)

b) 96.2, 86.7, 96.9, 118.1, 100.3, 95.4, 106.0, 102.9, 104.3, 100.3, 94.1, 97.8, 103.4, 107.9, 104.7, 85.1

14·20 Since we cannot expect the future to be exactly like the past, perhaps the only assurance we need about historical data is that they be accurate, reflective of what actually happened, and represent the best data available.

14·22 761,600 passengers

14·24 **a)** 72.0; 116.6; 127.1; 84.2

b) 1978: 3.5; 3.8; 3.8   1980: 3.9; 4.2; 4.3; 3.9
1979: 4.0; 3.9; 3.9; 4.0   1981: 4.3; 4.4; 4.4; 4.3

c) $\hat{Y} = 4.04 + .05x$ (where 1980 winter = 0 and x units = $\frac{1}{4}$ year).

d) 4,490,000 pounds

14·26 **a)** 44.3, 70.4, 174.5, 110.8   **b)** $\hat{Y} = 4.2 + .061x$ (1980 I = 0)

c) 14.1, -11.2, -7.5, 13.6, -30.3, -2.0, 8.7, 7.1, 33.8, 6.5, 2.7, -48.2, -4.7, 0.7, 16.6

14·28 27.25; 28.75; 29.00; 30.25; 31.50; 31.25; 32.00; 31.25; 29.25; 28.75; 29.00; 29.75; 32.25; 34.00; 35.00; 36.75; 36.50

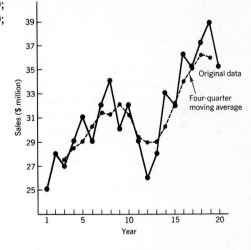

Chap. 2

1. T	23. b
2. T	24. e
3. F	25. d
4. F	26. population,
5. T	sample
6. T	27. frequency
7. T	28. discrete,
8. T	continuous
9. F	29. mark
10. F	30. ogive
11. F	
12. F	
13. T	
14. T	
15. F	
16. d	
17. b	
18. a	
19. c	
20. c	
21. a	
22. d	

Chap. 3

1. F	23. b
2. T	24. c
3. F	25. e
4. F	26. symmetrical,
5. F	skewed
6. T	27. sample,
7. T	population
8. F	28. coding
9. T	29. disadvantage,
10. F	extreme
11. T	30. bimodal
12. F	
13. T	
14. F	
15. F	
16. c	
17. a	
18. b	
19. a	
20. b	
21. c	
22. d	

Chap. 4

1. T	23. d
2. T	24. d
3. F	25. e
4. T	26. fractile
5. T	27. interquartile
6. F	28. variance
7. T	standard deviation
8. F	29. coefficient
9. T	of variation
10. F	30. standard score
11. T	
12. T	
13. F	
14. T	
15. T	
16. d	
17. b	
18. b	
19. c	
20. a	
21. a	
22. c	

Chap. 5

1. F	23. c
2. F	24. c
3. T	25. e
4. T	26. event
5. T	experiment
6. F	27. sample space
7. F	28. Venn diagram
8. T	29. mutually
9. T	exclusive
10. T	30. conditional
11. F	
12. F	
13. F	
14. T	
15. T	
16. b	
17. c	
18. b	
19. e	
20. a	
21. d	
22. d	

Chap. 6

1. F	23. e
2. F	24. e
3. T	25. c
4. F	26. expected
5. T	value
6. T	27. binomial
7. F	Bernoulli
8. F	28. right, left
9. T	29. decision
10. T	points
11. T	chance
12. F	events
13. T	30. a decision
14. F	process
15. F	
16. e	
17. b	
18. a	
19. d	
20. d	
21. c	
22. c	

Chap. 7

1. T	23. c
2. F	24. b
3. F	25. d
4. F	26. sample
5. T	27. sampling fraction
6. T	28. systematic
7. T	29. Precision
8. F	30. clusters
9. T	
10. F	
11. T	
12. F	
13. T	
14. F	
15. F	
16. d	
17. e	
18. e	
19. e	
20. d	
21. b	
22. a	

Chap. 8

1. F	17. b		
2. F	18. a		
3. T	19. c		
4. T	20. e		
5. F	21. d		
6. F	22. a		
7. T	23. a		
8. T	24. d		
9. T	25. e		
10. T	26. point		
11. T	27. interval		
12. F	28. degrees		
13. T	of freedom		
14. T	29. Students' t		
15. F	distribution		
16. e	30. Confidence		

Chap. 9

1. F	17. b
2. T	28. a
3. F	29. c
4. T	20. c
5. T	21. b
6. F	22. b
7. T	23. c
8. T	24. a
9. T	25. a
10. F	26. hypothesis
11. F	27. II
12. F	β (beta)
13. F	28. null
14. F	alternative
15. T	29. paired
16. d	30. tailed

Chap. 10

1. T	17. a
2. T	18. d
3. F	19. e
4. T	20. c
5. T	21. b
6. F	22. d
7. T	23. c
8. T	24. e
9. T	25. c
10. F	26. grand
11. T	27. analysis of
12. F	variance (ANOVA)
13. T	28. independence
14. F	29. F
15. F	30. goodness-of-fit
16. b	

Chap. 11

1. F	16. d
2. F	17. a
3. F	18. a
4. F	19. e
5. T	20. b
6. T	21. c
7. T	22. d
8. T	23. a
9. F	24. c
10. T	25. b
11. F	26. inverse
12. T	27. curvilinear
13. T	28. slope
14. T	29. standard error of estimate
15. F	30. coefficient of determination

Chap. 12

1. T	16. c
2. F	17. b
3. T	18. d
4. F	19. b
5. F	20. a
6. T	21. c
7. T	22. d
8. T	23. b
9. F	24. a
10. T	25. b
11. T	26. modeling techniques
12. F	27. transformations
13. F	28. computed F-ratio
14. F	29. dummy
15. T	30. standard error

Chap. 13

1. T	16. c
2. F	17. b
3. T	18. a
4. T	19. b
5. F	20. d
6. T	21. b
7. F	22. c
8. T	23. a
9. T	24. b
10. F	25. d
12. T	26. run
11. F	27. Mann-Whitney U test
13. F	28. one-sample runs test

Chap. 14

1. T	16. e
2. T	17. c
3. F	18. a
4. F	19. b
5. F	20. d
6. F	21. d
7. T	22. c
8. F	23. b
9. F	24. a
10. F	25. c
11. T	26. percent of trend
12. T	27. seasonal
13. T	28. irregular

Index